T0230250

Lecture Notes in Computer Science 1103
Edited by G. Goos, J. Hartmanis and J. van Leeuwen

Advisory Board: W. Brauer D. Gries J. Stoer

Springer
Berlin
Heidelberg
New York
Barcelona
Budapest
Hong Kong
London
Milan
Paris
Santa Clara
Singapore
Tokyo

Harald Ganzinger (Ed.)

Rewriting Techniques and Applications

7th International Conference, RTA-96
New Brunswick, NJ, USA, July 27-30, 1996
Proceedings

Springer

Series Editors

Gerhard Goos, Karlsruhe University, Germany

Juris Hartmanis, Cornell University, NY, USA

Jan van Leeuwen, Utrecht University, The Netherlands

Volume Editor

Harald Ganzinger
Max-Planck-Institut für Informatik
Im Stadtwald, D-66123 Saarbrücken, Germany

Cataloging-in-Publication data applied for

Die Deutsche Bibliothek - CIP-Einheitsaufnahme

Rewriting techniques and applications : 7th international conference ; proceedings / RTA-96, New Brunswick, NJ, USA, July 27 - 30, 1996. Harald Ganzinger (ed.). - Berlin ; Heidelberg ; New York ; Barcelona ; Budapest ; Hong Kong ; London ; Milan ; Paris ; Santa Clara ; Singapore ; Tokyo : Springer, 1996
(Lecture notes in computer science ; Vol. 1103)
ISBN 3-540-61464-8
NE: Ganzinger, Harald [Hrsg.]; RTA <7, 1996, New Brunswick, NJ>; GT

CR Subject Classification (1991): D.3, F.3.2, F.4, I.1, I.2.2-3

ISSN 0302-9743
ISBN 3-540-61464-8 Springer-Verlag Berlin Heidelberg New York

This work is subject to copyright. All rights are reserved, whether the whole or part of the material is concerned, specifically the rights of translation, reprinting, re-use of illustrations, recitation, broadcasting, reproduction on microfilms or in any other way, and storage in data banks. Duplication of this publication or parts thereof is permitted only under the provisions of the German Copyright Law of September 9, 1965, in its current version, and permission for use must always be obtained from Springer-Verlag. Violations are liable for prosecution under the German Copyright Law.

© Springer-Verlag Berlin Heidelberg 1996
Printed in Germany

Typesetting: Camera-ready by author
SPIN 10513356 06/3142 – 5 4 3 2 1 0 Printed on acid-free paper

Preface

This volume contains the papers presented at the Seventh International Conference on Rewriting Techniques and Applications (RTA-96) held in New Brunswick, NJ, July 27–July 30, 1996, at Rutgers University, hosted by the Center for Discrete Mathematics and Computer Science (DIMACS). RTA-96 was one of the conferences participating in the 1996 Federated Logic Conference (FLoC). FLoC was modeled after the successful Federated Computer Research Conference (FCRC); the intention was to bring together as a synergetic group several conferences that apply logic to computer science. The other participating conferences were the Thirteenth Conference on Automated Deduction (CADE-13), the Eighth International Conference on Computer Aided Verification (CAV 96), and the Eleventh IEEE Symposium on Logic in Computer Science (LICS'96).

Term rewriting is one of the major logical concepts we use for modelling computation by deduction. The themes of the RTA-96 programme include the analysis of term rewriting systems, string and graph rewriting, rewrite-based theorem proving, conditional term rewriting, higher-order rewriting, unification, symbolic and algebraic computation, and efficient implementation of rewriting on sequential and parallel machines. Some of the highlights of the 1996 programme and hence of this volume are the answers to two longstanding open problems. Manfred Schmidt-Schauß has proved the decidability of distributive unification, while Ralf Treinen has shown that the elementary theory of one-step rewriting is undecidable.

Eighty-four papers were submitted to RTA-96: 78 regular papers and 6 system descriptions. Of these 84 papers, 28 regular papers and all 6 system descriptions were accepted. One of the accepted papers was withdrawn by its author, hence this volume contains 27 regular papers in addition to the system descriptions and abstracts of three invited talks. Gérard Huet's talk was given in a plenary session with LICS.

RTA-96 has received support from the ESPRIT Basic Research Working Groups CCL and COMPASS and from the Max Planck Institute for Computer Science. I would also like to thank the many people who have made RTA-96 possible. I am grateful: to the Programme Committee and the additional referees for reviewing the papers in a very short time, and maintaining the high standard of RTA conferences; to the Local Arrangements Chair, Leo Bachmair, and to the other members of the FLoC Organizing Committee, Rajeev Alur, Amy Felty, Douglas J. Howe, Stephen Mahaney, Jon G. Riecke (chair), and Moshe Vardi (Chair of Steering Committee), for organising an excellent and outstanding conference; and last but not least, to Ellen Fries, Manfred Jaeger, Uwe Waldmann, and the other members of my research group at MPI who helped with the many tasks of the programme chair, and with his lack of technical expertise in certain text processing tools.

Saarbrücken, May 1996

Harald Ganzinger
RTA-96 Programme Chair

Conference Organization

RTA-96 Program Chair: Harald Ganzinger

RTA-96 Local Arrangements Chair: Leo Bachmair

RTA-96 Program Committee:

Jürgen Avenhaus (Kaiserslautern)
Hubert Comon (Orsay)
Nachum Dershowitz (Urbana)
Harald Ganzinger (Saarbrücken)
Pierre Lescanne (Nancy)
Ursula Martin (St. Andrews)
Aart Middledorp (Tsukuba)
Paliath Narendran (Albany)
Robert Nieuwenhuis (Barcelona)
Tobias Nipkow (München)
Friedrich Otto (Kassel)
Frank Pfenning (Pittsburgh)
David Plaisted (Chapel Hill)
Wayne Snyder (Boston)
Hantao Zhang (Iowa City)

RTA Organizing Committee:

Ronald Book (Santa Barbara)
Jieh Hsiang (Taipei)
Claude Kirchner (Nancy, Chair)
Klaus Madlener (Kaiserslautern)
David Plaisted (Chapel Hill)
Mitsuhiro Okada (Tokio)

List of Referees

The program committee gratefully acknowledges the help of the following referees:

Andrew Adams
Yohji Akama
Gilles Amiot
Andrea Asperti
David Basin
Kalyan S. Basu
Denis Bechet
Maria Paola Bonacina
Alexandre Boudet
I. Cervesato
Shangching Chou
Evelyne Contejean
Robert Cremanns
Nick Cropper
Vincent Danos
Max Dauchet
Jörg Denzinger
Dan Dougherty
Gilles Dowek
Irène Durand
Rachid Echahed
Maribel Fernández
Roland Fettig
A.C. Fleck
Philippa Gardner
Rémi Gilleron
Bernhard Gramlich
Philippe de Groote
Kevin Hammond
Michael Hanus
Xiaorong Huang
M. Huber
Felix Joachimski
Stefan Kahrs
Deepak Kapur
Zurab Khasidashvili
Richard Kennaway
Delia Kesner
J.W. Klop
M.R.K. Krishna Rao
Masahito Kurihara
Carolina Lavatelli
Jordi Levy
Francisco Lopez-Fraguas
Christopher Lynch
Olav Lysne
Klaus Madlener
Claude Marché
Robert McNaughton
Xumin Nie
Vincent van Oostrom
Fernando Orejas
Michio Oyamaguchi
Nicolas Peltier
Detlef Plump
Andreas Podelski
Christian Prehofer
Femke van Raamsdonk
I.V. Ramakrishnan
Christian Rétoré
Albert Rubio
Andrea Sattler-Klein
Géraud Sénizergues
Duncan Shand
Marianne Simonot
Joachim Steinbach
John Stell
Georg Struth
Jürgen Stuber
M. Subramaniam
Ralf Treinen
Marc Tommasi
Yoshihito Toyama
Patrick Viry
Sergei Vorobyov
Fer-Jan de Vries
Roel de Vrijer
Uwe Waldmann
Christoph Weidenbach
Claus-Peter Wirth

Table of Contents

Regular Papers

System Descriptions

Rewrite-Based Automated Reasoning: Challenges Ahead

Deepak Kapur

Institute for Programming and Logics
State University of New York
Albany, NY 12222.
kapur@cs.albany.edu

Abstract

Since the seminal paper of Knuth and Bendix, a number of automated reasoning systems based on rewrite techniques have been developed for equational logic over the past 25 years or so. We have been building a theorem prover *RRL*, *Rewrite Rule Laboratory*, and using it for many problems for nearly a decade.

I will discuss how the development of *RRL* has benefited from working on challenges at every stage – starting from checking equivalence of single axiom characterizations of free groups to their conventional axiomatizations, leading to attacking ring commutative problems, and now to mechanizing proofs by induction in applications of both hardware and software design, specification and analysis.

In the early stage, we focussed on developing a fast implementation of completion in *RRL*, emphasizing the role of normalization strategies, efficient implementation of basic primitive operations including matching, unification and termination orderings, and identification of redundant computations.

Over the last few years, we have focussed on mechanizing proofs by induction since such problems arise in reasoning about systems and computations, be they hardware, software or mixed. We have been investigating contextual rewriting, integration of semantics of commonly used data structures in rewriting as well as in the generation of induction schemes using decision procedures. Recently, we have been developing heuristics that aid in finding inductive proofs with minimal user guidance and interaction. This has led to work on identifying structural conditions on definitions and lemmas using which it is possible to predict a priori whether a proof attempt based on an induction scheme will fail. On the positive side, techniques have been explored to generate, using knowledge about the application domain, relevant intermediate lemmas needed in proofs.

Researchers interested in developing rewrite-rule based provers should identify challenges over the next several years from different fronts. This would lead not only in rejuvenating theoretical investigations, but also in producing powerful reasoning systems which would be in demand. Below, I list a few such challenges, hoping others would join in identifying more.

The first challenge is obvious: developing and implementing a uniform strategy for efficiently solving routine problems in first-order reasoning. TPTP library is an example of such a collection of problems.

The second challenge is the development of a reasoning system that can aid in working on difficult and open problems in mathematics, algebra and logic. An exciting open problem is that of Robbins algebras – to prove or disprove that algebraic structures satisfying Robbins' axioms are boolean structures.

The third challenge is in developing heuristics and techniques to make reasoning systems based on induction, more of proof finders than proof checkers. Two important technical problems are identification of application-specific lemma speculation strategies and induction schemes. A fruitful approach is likely to be the integration of efficient decision procedures and heuristics in rewrite-based provers for special domains and data structures – from numbers, lists, arrays, sequences, sets and matrices to time, finite state machines, traces, and homomorphism constructions.

The reasoning capabilities of rewrite-based systems will be greatly enhanced if they can call upon algorithms of computer algebra systems as specialized decision procedures. On the other side, there would be more faith in the soundness of computer algebra systems if reasoning systems can be used to keep track of assumptions under which algorithms in computer algebra systems are executed. Intellectual challenge in combining/interfacing reasoning systems and computer algebra systems is enormous. The rewriting approach, I conjecture, can provide a unifying framework.

Fine-Grained Concurrent Completion

Claude Kirchner Christopher Lynch Christelle Scharff

INRIA Lorraine & CRIN,
615, rue du Jardin Botanique, BP 101,
54602 Villers-lès-Nancy Cedex, France.

E-mail: {Claude.Kirchner, Christopher.Lynch, Christelle.Scharff}@loria.fr
http://www.loria.fr/equipe/protheo.html

Abstract. We present a concurrent Completion procedure based on the use of a SOUR graph as data structure. The procedure has the following characteristics. It is asynchronous, there is no need for a global memory or global control, equations are stored in a SOUR graph with maximal structure sharing, and each vertex is a process, representing a term. Therefore, the parallelism is at the term level. Each edge is a communication link, representing a (subterm, ordering, unification or rewrite) relation between terms. Completion is performed on the graph as local graph transformations by cooperation between processes. We show that this concurrent Completion procedure is sound and complete with respect to the sequential one, provided that the information is locally time stamped in order to detect out of date information.

1 Introduction

Parallelization is an attractive way for improving efficiency of automated deduction, and the main approaches are surveyed in [BH94] and [SS93]. We present in this paper a new approach to term rewriting completion which is based on fine grain concurrency, and which relies on a novel approach to completion.

The resolution (and paramodulation) inference systems are theorem proving procedures for first-order logic (with equality) that can run exponentially long for subclasses which have polynomial time decision procedures, as in the case of the Knuth-Bendix ground completion procedure. Wayne Snyder proved that completion of ground equations can be done in $nlog(n)$ [Sny93]. Recently C. Lynch has shown [Lyn95] that a special form of paramodulation which does not need to copy terms or literals runs in polynomial time in ground cases that include ground completion. This can be implemented in an elegant way using the notion of SOUR graph [LS95]. These graphs represent in a very convenient way a state of the completion, where all the basic ingredients (i.e. orientation, unification and rewriting) are made explicit at the object level. This makes explicit the fundamental operations of completion. A SOUR graph has its edges labelled by S when representing a subterm relation, by O when representing an orientation, by U when representing a unification problem and by R when representing a rewrite rule. The nodes of the graph are labelled by function symbols, and edges are labelled by constraints and renamings.

The properties of SOUR graphs are useful to study the parallelization and implementation of automated deduction on parallel distributed memory machines. There is no duplication of work since there is no copying. There is also no need of a consistency check. The explicit representation of basic operations allows a direct implementation of the inference rules as transition rules and thus to get completion as the result of independent (and asynchronous) operations as well as an easier way to describe and prove soundness and completeness of the graph transformations. This property is always desirable, but the increased complexity of concurrent processes makes it even more important.

Thus this paper presents a new fine-grained concurrent completion procedure based on the notion of distributed SOUR graphs and it is proved to be sound and complete, for simplicity in the case of ground completion, although everything can be extended to non-ground completion.

We consider each node of the SOUR graph as a process and the edges as communication links between processes. Each process is in charge of detecting particular configurations corresponding to critical pairs, unification problems or ordering of terms. A node acts only in response to a message, independently of the other nodes. The processes are thus completely asynchronous. When a successful configuration is found, the corresponding operation is performed, typically directing a subterm or a rewrite edge from one node to another. In the first design of the approach we were thought that this was enough to ensure correctness of the process. But after investigations, we discovered that since all these detections and actions are performed asynchronously, we need to keep account of only the newest information arriving from a given node, in order to ensure the global consistency of the SOUR graph. This is performed via the use of local time stamps, so that the system still works asynchronously, but old information is ignored.

The paper describes the principles of this approach and its current implementation on a network of processors. We show that this implements ground completion using fine-grain concurrency. This relies in particular on an original parallelization of the detection of the satisfiability of unification and LPO orientation constraints, detection that runs concurrently with the standard completion process. Because it is fine-grained and completely asynchronous, our approach is quite different from the PaReDuX work [BGK95] and the clause diffusion method [BH95] but it also allows backward contraction. It is also quite different from the discount approach [ADF95] or the work on Partheo [LS90]. Let us finally emphasise that we think our approach quite promising since as opposed to the unsuccessful attempts to parallelize prolog on fine-grained architectures, it is backed by a very simple concept, SOUR graphs, no synchronization is needed, and each process gets enough work because of the internalization of unification and ordering constraint satisfiability.

The paper is structured as follows. Assuming the reader familiar with term rewriting (see [DJ90]), we summarize in section 2 the notion of SOUR graph. In section 3, we present the principle of concurrent completion on SOUR graphs. We show how critical pairs are detected, how unification and LPO ordering constraints are checked satisfiable, why time stamps are needed and how they are used. We also show how to detect the termination of the completion process and we prove that this model of completion is sound and complete.

The full version of this paper that includes full proofs and a complete description of the transitions at the node level is available in [KLS96].

2 Preliminaries

To simplify our presentation of inference rules, we will present them for ground terms. We refer the reader to [LS95] to see how the definitions and the inference rules are lifted to non-ground terms.

The symbol $\approx$ is a binary symbol, written in infix notation, representing semantic equality. Let EQ be a set of equations. We define a function Sub so that $Sub(EQ)$ is the set of subterms of EQ. If $t = f(t_1, \cdots, t_k)$ with $k \geq 0$, then $Sub(t) = \{t\} \cup \bigcup_{1 \leq i \leq k} Sub(t_i)$. We define $Sub(s \approx t) = Sub(s) \cup Sub(t)$ and $Sub(EQ) = \bigcup_{eq \in EQ} Sub(eq)$.

In this paper $\preceq$ will refer to the *lexicographic path ordering* ($\prec$ in its strict version). If $u[s]$ is a ground term, and EQ is a set of ground equations, we write $u[s] \Rightarrow u[t]$ and say that $u[s]$ *rewrites in one step* to $u[t]$ if there is an equation $s \approx t \in EQ$ such that $s \succ t$. We write $u_0 \overset{*}{\Rightarrow} u_n$ and say that u_0 *rewrites* to u_n if there is a a set of terms $\{u_1, \cdots, u_{n-1}\}$ such that for all i, $1 \leq i \leq n$, $u_{i-1} \Rightarrow u_i$. A ground set of equations is *convergent* if it is terminating and confluent.

A $SOUR$ graph is a compact dag representation of a set of equations. Let EQ be a set of equations. The SOUR graph of EQ is the graph which has one node associated with each element of $t \in Sub(EQ)$, labelled with the root symbol of t. For each element $f(t_1 \cdots, t_k) \in Sub(EQ)$, with $k > 0$, for each i, $1 \leq i \leq k$, there is a directed edge called a *subterm edge* in the SOUR Graph from the node associated with $f(t_1, \cdots, t_k)$ to the node associated with t_i labelled with i, its index. For each equation $s \approx t \in EQ$ with $s \succ t$, there is a directed edge called a *rewrite edge* from the node associated with s to the node associated with t.

We define a semantic function $Term$ from the nodes of the graph to the set of terms. If v is a node in the graph labelled with f such that $arity(f) = k$, then there are k subterms edges from v labelled $1, \cdots, k$ to terms $v_1 \cdots, v_k$ respectively. Then $Term(v) = f(Term(v_1), \cdots, Term(v_k))$. We define a function $Rule$ from the rewrite edges in the graph to the set of equations. If e is a rewrite edge from v_1 to v_2, then $Rule(e)$ is $Term(v_1) \approx Term(v_2)$. Graph G represents $\{Rule(e) \mid e \text{ is a rewrite edge in } G\}$.

We also add other kinds of edges to the SOUR graph. Some terms have an undirected edge called a *unification edge* between them, including between a node and itself. For now, we assume these edges are placed between every pair of nodes v_1 and v_2 such that $Term(v_1) = Term(v_2)$. There is a directed edge called an *orientation edge* between some pairs of nodes v_1 and v_2 such that $Term(v_1) \succ Term(v_2)$. These edges are used to perform inferences. The graph is called a *SOUR graph* because of **S**ubterm, **O**rientation, **U**nification and **R**ewrite edges.

The inference rule that we are coding with SOUR Graphs in the ground case is the *critical pair* inference rule.

$$\text{Critical Pair} \qquad \frac{s \approx t \qquad u[s] \approx v}{u[t] \approx v} \quad \text{if } s \succ t \text{ and } u[s] \succ v$$

We simulate the completion inference rules by searching for patterns (or configurations) in the graph and performing a transformation of the graph whenever we find one. A transformation consists of removing a subterm or rewrite edge and adding a new subterm or rewrite edge. Afterwards, unification and orientation edges are re-calculated. There are three graph transformations.

The first transformation is called an *SUR transformation*. It consists of finding a set of edges v_1, v_2, v_3 and v_4 such that there is a subterm edge e_S from v_1 to v_2, a unification edge e_U between v_2 and v_3, and a rewrite edge v_R from v_3 to v_4. Then e_S is removed, and a new subterm edge e is added from v_1 to v_4, labelled with the same index as e_S (see Figure 1). This simulates the critical pair rule, because it unifies a subterm of a term with the larger side of an equation and replaces it with the smaller side of the equation. Figure 1 shows a critical pair between $f(a) \approx c$ and $a \approx b$.

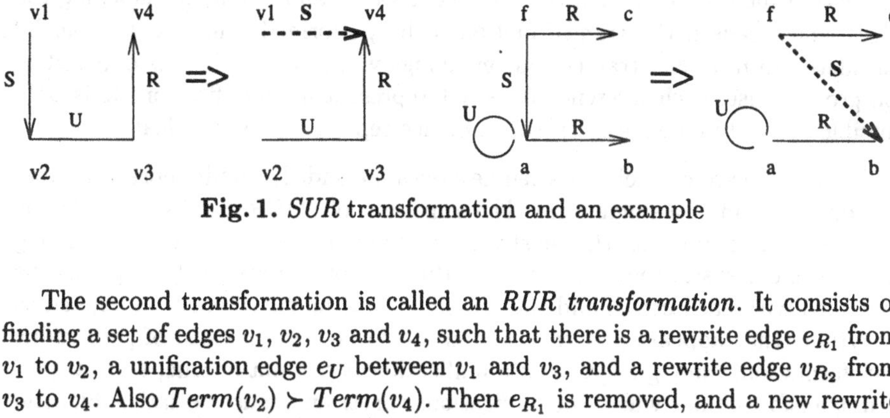

Fig. 1. *SUR* transformation and an example

The second transformation is called an *RUR transformation*. It consists of finding a set of edges v_1, v_2, v_3 and v_4, such that there is a rewrite edge e_{R_1} from v_1 to v_2, a unification edge e_U between v_1 and v_3, and a rewrite edge v_{R_2} from v_3 to v_4. Also $Term(v_2) \succ Term(v_4)$. Then e_{R_1} is removed, and a new rewrite edge e is added from v_2 to v_4 (see Figure 2). This simulates the critical pair rule, because it unifies the larger side of two equations and adds a new equation between the two smaller sides.

The third transformation is called an *RUR − rhs transformation*. It consists of finding a set of edges v_1, v_2, v_3 and v_4, such that there is a rewrite edge e_{R_1} from v_1 to v_2, a unification edge e_U between v_2 and v_3, and a rewrite edge v_{R_2} from v_3 to v_4. Then e_{R_1} is removed, and a new rewrite edge e is added from v_1 to v_4 (see Figure 2). This simulates a simplification of the smaller side of an equation, because is unifies the smaller side with the larger side of another equation and replaces it with the smaller side of the other equation.

The completeness result from [LS95] says that if a SOUR graph is created from a set of equations EQ and the above transformations are performed in

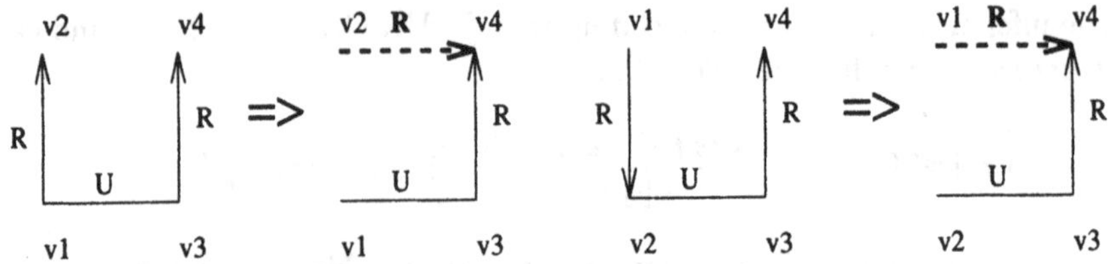

Fig. 2. *RUR* and *RUR-rhs* transformation

any order, until no longer possible, then the resulting SOUR graph represents a convergent system, logically equivalent to EQ.

We describe briefly how this is lifted to the non-ground case, and refer the reader to [LS95] for more details. For the non-ground case, the initial SOUR graph is constructed in exactly the same way. However, the transformations are handled differently. We simulate Basic Completion. Therefore, each inference is performed by renaming the variables in one of the premises, and by applying a constraint to the conclusion of the inference, representing the unification problem. In the SOUR graph, the new edge that is added to the graph in a transformation is labelled with the constraint and renaming associated with the inference, which is a combination of the constraints and renamings labelling the edges which caused the transformation to be performed. Initial edges can be considered to have constraints and renamings which are trivial. As opposed to the ground case, each inference does not represent a simplification. It is only possible to delete an edge when the inference represents a simplification.

Since edges are not deleted when new ones are added, a node represents a set of terms, instead of a single term. The semantics of SOUR graphs must also be modified to accommodate the constraints and renamings on the edges. Each dag of subterm edges still represents a term. But the constraints on the dag must be conjoined with each other, and the renamings on the edges must be applied to everything that appears underneath it in the term. Also, instead of performing transformations among edges with a unification constraint of true, we now perform transformations where the unifications constraints must be satisfiable, and the constraint representing the orientation is satisfiable. These constraints are passed along to to the new edge in a transformation, along with the constraints on the old edges.

In summary, the algorithm for completion of SOUR graphs is the same in the non-ground case as in the ground case, except for the fact that an old edge might not be deleted in a transformation, and the new edge is labelled by a renaming inherited from the old edges, and a constraint inherited from the old edges and the unification constraint determined by the unification problem. For simplicity, we present the completion procedure in the ground case, but the algorithm for the non-ground case is the same, except that messages will contain constraints and nodes will try to satisfy these constraints.

3 Concurrent Completion using SOUR Graphs

We now present our concurrent method for performing completion using SOUR graphs. At the beginning of the concurrent completion process, the *root process* has knowledge of the whole SOUR graph. For each node, it launches a process. To each process is associated its identification number called its *tid*. The preliminary information that is initially loaded by each process, is the symbol of the node and a dictionary containing for each symbol its arity and its place in the precedence. Then, for each node, unification edges, subterm edges, and rewrite edges are sent in this order to the associated process using messages called *INITU*, *INITS* and *INITR* respectively. The root process creates a unification edge between every pair of nodes with the same symbol, with an initial value of false. One node adjacent to each unification edge is designated as being the node in charge of calculating the unification constraint. An *INITU* message is sent to the nodes on both ends of each unification edge. The INITU message contains the *tid* of the process at the other end of the edge, the initial false unification constraint, and a notification whether that node is in charge of calculating the unification problem. *INITS* is sent to each node adjacent to a subterm edge. It contains the *tid* and the symbol of the process at the other end of the edge, a boolean indicating if the edge is incoming or outgoing, and the index of the subterm edge. *INITR* is sent to each node adjacent to a rewrite edge. It contains the *tid*, the symbol of the process at the other end of the edge and a boolean indicating if the rewrite edge is incoming or outgoing. We call this phase the *Initialization phase.*

The set of information stored in a node is called its *state*. It is composed of its symbol *symb*, its dictionary *dico_order_arity* and its unification edges, its outgoing and incoming subterm edges and its outgoing and incoming rewrite edges, which are saved in data structures : *U_list*, *S_out_list*, *S_in_list*, *R_out_list*, *R_in_list*. Initially, the U_list of a process contains the unary cycle between the node and itself, which forms a unification edge with a true unification constraint.

Completion, including the following different phases: configuration creation, configuration processing and Unification and Orientation computation, concerns all but the *root process*. A process works only by *reaction to messages*, which allows the whole process to be fully asynchronous.

Actions of a process implied by a received message are formalized using the *transition rules*. An *α-transition* describes the transformation of a *state* of a process, when it receives a message. It is denoted by: $(\{Mesg\}, State) \xrightarrow{\alpha} (Mesgset, State')$, where α is a phase of completion, $Mesg$ is the received message, $State$ is the state or a part of the state of the process before receiving the message, $Mesgset$ is the set of all messages that must be sent as computed consequences of the message $Mesg$, and $State'$ is the new *state* of the process after processing the message $Mesg$. In the set $Mesgset$, each message $mesg$ is characterized by its destination $dest$, and is denoted $mesg[dest]$. We have *D-transitions* for the creation of configurations, *P-transitions* for the processing of configurations, *U-transitions* and *O-transitions* for the calculation of Unification and Orientation respectively. We now give more details on these transitions.

3.1 Implementation of Inference Rules for Completion

Completion, i.e. local graph transformation, is performed by cooperation between processes by message passing. Each process has a local view of the graph.

Creation of configurations: For the creation of a configuration, we use the fact that a process can detect a sequence of two adjacent edges forming a configuration: *SUR* , *RUR-rhs*, *RUR* with a unification edge between a node and itself, or two adjacent edges forming a semi-configuration *UR*, (a unification edge and an outgoing rewrite edge). These patterns of two adjacent edges are detected when a subterm or rewrite edge is added or when the unification constraint of a unification edge becomes true.

When a semi-configuration *UR* is detected, a message called *SEMICONF* is sent to the process at the other end of the unification edge. When a configuration of type *SUR*, *RUR-rhs* or *RUR* is detected, a message called *CONFIG* containing this configuration is sent to only one process, since we want to avoid redundant work. *SUR* and *RUR-rhs* configurations are sent to the process at the top left with respect to figures 1 and 2. An *RUR* configuration is sent to the process of the outgoing end of the rewrite edge with the maximal *tid*.

Processing of configurations: When a *CONFIG* message is received, it releases a sequence of actions depending on the type of the received configuration. The process receiving the message processes the configuration. i.e. performs the associated transformation, and sends messages which will be used to update information of other processes. The two main steps of the processing of a configuration are the addition and the deletion of an edge. Both these actions can be expressed using *P-transitions*. However, the processing of configurations of type *RUR-rhs* or *RUR* is linked to the calculation of Orientation, which is calculated by *O-transitions* (see section 3.2).

Messages used for the processing of configurations are *INITS*, *INITR*, *UPDATES*, *UPDATER* and *UPDATESEMICONF*. These three last messages are used to delete respectively a subterm edge, a rewrite edge or a semi-configuration.

For example, the following *P-transition* processes an SUR configuration:

$$(\{CONFIG\},\ \{St.S\_out\_list\})$$
$$\xrightarrow{P}$$
$$(\{INITS(e')[tid1],\ UPDATES(e)[tid2]\},\ \{St.S\_out\_list + e' - e\})$$

where *St* is the *state* of the process receiving *CONFIG*, e is the subterm edge contained in the *SUR* configuration, *tid*2 is the *tid* at the outgoing end of e, e' is the new outgoing subterm edge and *tid*1 is the *tid* of the process at the outgoing end of the rewrite edge contained in the *SUR* configuration.

The transformations for the full completion process are described in the full version of the paper.

3.2 Concurrent Unification and Orientation

Although concurrency cannot improve the worst-case behavior of unification [DKM84], we give an algorithm that reduces the amount of processing by a single node. Unification is evaluated by a request-answer method A process sends a request to each child to ask if there is a unification edge with a true constraint between itself and another process. The child responds only if the constraint is true.

Consider the problem represented by figure 3. U_0 is the unification edge between the process representing term $f(s_1, \ldots, s_n)$ and the process representing term $f(t_1, \ldots, t_n)$. Computation of the unification constraint c_0 of unification edge U_0 depends on the calculation of unification constraints $c_1,\ldots,c_n$ of unification edges $U_1,\ldots,U_n$. We have $c_0 = c_1 \wedge \ldots \wedge c_n$. Each constraint c_i represents the unification problem $s_i \stackrel{?}{=} t_i$.

Unification must be re-calculated when subterm edges are added or deleted.

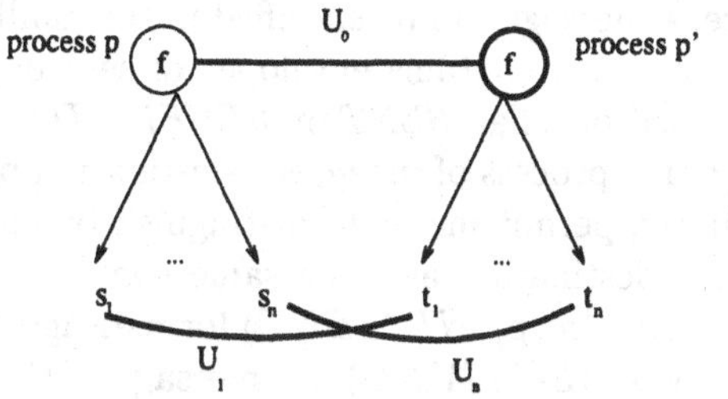

Fig. 3. Calculation of the unification constraint c_0 of the unification edge U_0

Using figure 3, we will explain the principles of the calculation of the unification constraint c_0 concurrently:

— Suppose process p represents $f(s_1, \ldots, s_n)$ and p' represents $f(t_1, \ldots, t_n)$, such that p' in charge of computing c_0. Process p sends to p' the *tids* of processes representing terms $s_1, \ldots, s_n$, so that p' knows on which children's unification constraints c_0 depends.

— When p' receives this information, it asks the processes representing terms t_1, ..., t_n, if their unification constraints c_1, ..., c_n respectively are true. This calculation is top-down.

— If a unification constraint c_i ($i > 0$) becomes true and has a saved request concerning the computation of c_0, then the process representing term t_i informs process p' that c_i became true. This calculation is bottom-up.

— If process p' detects that the unification constraint c_0 becomes true i.e. the number of answer messages received for the calculation of c_0 is equal to the arity of the symbol of p', then it must tell the node at the other end of the unification edge that the unification constraint became true.

Soundness and completeness results for this concurrent Unification algorithm are given in section 3.5.

An Orientation problem is to determine if a term s is bigger than a term t with respect to a given LPO. If it is, we create an outgoing orientation edge from the process representing term s to the process representing term t. We use a request-answer method as we did for Unification.

3.3 Detection of the termination of the program

It is difficult to detect termination of an asynchronous concurrent program, because a process cannot detect that it will not receive any more messages. We give a termination detection algorithm different from the classical one [DFvG83].

Definition 1. The program terminates when all processes are *idle* and all sent messages have been received.

Our termination detection algorithm uses a mailbox, which can be handled by the *root process*. It is based on the following principles.

Sent and received messages are notified to the mailbox using a message called *NOTIFY*. In practice, a message can be specified in the mailbox as received and not yet as sent. The mailbox contains envelopes of sent or received messages. An envelope is composed of a flag *SENT* or *RECEIVED* for a sent or received message *mesg*, the source process of *mesg*, the destination process of *mesg* and an identification number, permitting us to distinguish two messages having the same origin, the same destination and the same contents. So, an envelope is one of the following forms: $(p_i, p_j, NB, SENT)$ for message NB sent by process p_i to p_j, and $(p_j, p_i, NB, RECEIVED)$ for message NB received by process p_i from p_j. A mailbox consists of two lists: *list_sent*, which contains envelopes of messages specified as sent but not received and *list_received*, which contains envelopes of messages specified as received but not sent.

Processes cycle from idle to busy to idle. The busy state is entered when a message is received. Other messages are sent as a result of this message. In the busy state, other messages may be received and messages are sent as a result of them. When the process re-enters the idle state, it sends the mailbox one NOTIFY message for each message received in that cycle. The NOTIFY message contains one envelope for the received message, and an envelope for each message sent as a result of this received message. This fact is crucial for the correctness of our termination detection algorithm.

When the mailbox receives a message *NOTIFY* containing an envelope $(p_i, p_j, NB, SENT)$, the mate of this envelope $(p_j, p_i, NB, RECEIVED)$ is searched for in the list *list_received*. If the envelope $(p_j, p_i, NB, RECEIVED)$ does not belong to this list, $(p_i, p_j, NB, SENT)$ is added to the list *list_sent*, otherwise $(p_j, p_i, NB, RECEIVED)$ is deleted from *list_received*. RECEIVED messages are processed similarly.

Initially, *list_sent* contains all the envelopes of SENT messages of the *Initialization phase*. This ensures the correctness of the algorithm.

Theorem 2. *The program is terminated iff* list_sent *and* list_received *are empty.*

3.4 Time Stamps

Why are time stamps needed? Let $E = \{g(f(a)) \approx b, f(a) \approx f(b), a \approx c\}$. be the set of equations to complete. Consider the precedence $g \prec f \prec c \prec b \prec a$. The set of equations E can be represented by the *SOUR graph* of figure 4.

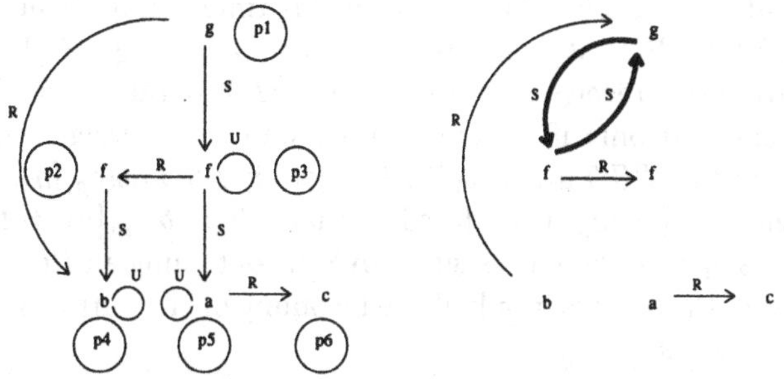

Fig. 4. The SOUR Graph representing E and the result of the execution plan

Consider the following execution plan. Process p_3 detects an SUR configuration $conf1$ and sends it to process p_1. Process p_5 detects an SUR configuration $conf2$ and sends it to process p_3. Process p_3 receives the SUR configuration $conf2$ and processes it. Process p_3 changes the direction of its rewrite edge because $f(b) \succ f(c)$. Process p_1 processes a message from p_3 to tell it to change the direction of its rewrite edge because $b \succ g(f(c))$. Process p_4 detects an SUR configuration $conf3$ and sends it to p_2. Process p_1 receives and processes the SUR configuration $conf1$. Process p_2 receives and processes the SUR configuration $conf3$. On the graph, we notice a cycle of subterm edges. To prevent this critical case, we use *Time Stamps.* They are not used for synchronization, but to avoid using old information.

Time stamp definition and usage

Definition 3. The time stamp of a process is a counter initialized to 0. We denote the current time stamp of a process p by TS_p.

Each process p contains a time stamp TS_p and a table of time stamps that we denote TS_Table_p. The table has n entries, where n is the arity of the symbol of p. For process p', $TS\_Table_p[p']$ is the last time stamp $TS_{p'}$ of process p' known by p, initially 0. When p sends a message to one of its parent processes, it sends its current time stamp TS_p in the message.

A unification edge between processes p and p' has two time stamps associated with it: the time stamps of the processes at the ends of the edge. These time stamps are stored in p and p'. The same thing is done for orientation edges.

Use of time stamps for the creation of configurations: Consider a semi-configuration containing a rewrite edge r from process p_3 to process p_4 and a unification edge between processes p_2 and p_3. This semi configuration is sent to p_2 only if the calculation of the direction of the rewrite edge r gives that r is from p_3 to p_4 and the calculation of Unification for the unification edge u between p_2 and p_3 gives a true unification constraint and the time stamp of p_3 used for calculating Unification is the same as the time stamp of p_3 used for calculating Orientation. The message *SEMICONF* is sent to p_2 containing the time stamp of p_2 used to calculate Unification. Let t be this time stamp. When p_2 receives the message *SEMICONF*, it sends to process p_1 a message *CONFIG* only if $TS_{p_2} = t$. If process p_1 receives a message *CONFIG* containing an SUR configuration, it processes it only if the subterm edge in the message still exists and $TS\_Table_{p_1}[p_2] = t$ or $TS\_Table_{p_1}[p_2] < t$. Then, if $TS\_Table_{p_1}[p_2] < t$, TS_{p_1} is incremented and $TS\_Table_{p_1}$ is updated so that $TS\_Table_{p_1}[p_2] = t$.

When process p_1 receives a message *CONFIG* containing an RUR or an RUR-*rhs* configuration, it processes it only if the incoming or the outgoing rewrite edge respectively still exists.

Use of time stamps for Unification (It is similar for Orientation): Suppose that we want to calculate the Unification constraint of unification edge u between process p_0 and process p_1, such that p_1 decides the calculation.

Suppose that process p_2 (k^{th} child process of p_1) receives a request asking if there is a unification edge with constraint true between processes p_2 and p_3 (k^{th} child process of p_0). Answers will be sent to p_1 (for conditions of this sending see section 3.2). Answer messages contain t_2 and t_3 the last time stamps of p_2 and p_3 used in the calculation of the unification constraint between p_2 and p_3.

When p_1 receives an answer from p_2 containing time stamps t_2 and t_3, the answer message is processed only if the following conditions are respected:

— There is a subterm edge going from p_1 to p_2 with index k.

— $TS\_Table_{p_1}[p_2] = t_2$ or $TS\_Table_{p_1}[p_2] < t_2$. For this second case, $TS\_Table_{p_1}$ is updated, such that $TS\_Table_{p_1}[p_2] = t_2$ and the current time stamp of p_1 is incremented.

If an answer message permits us to determine that the unification constraint of the unification edge u between p_0 and p_1 is true i.e. n answer messages have been received by p_1 where n is the arity of the symbol of p_1, then the message *INITU* corresponding to the fact that the unification constraint of u is true, is sent to p_0 containing t_3.

When p_0 receives from p_1 a message *INITU* containing the time stamp t_3, this message is processed only if the following conditions are respected:

— There is a subterm edge going from p_0 to p_3 with index k.

— $TS\_Table_{p_0}[p_3] = t_3$ or $TS\_Table_{p_0}[p_3] < t_3$. For this second case, $TS\_Table_{p_0}$ is updated, such that $TS\_Table_{p_0}[p_3] = t_3$ and the current time stamp of p_0 is incremented.

Semantics of a time stamped ground SOUR Graph

Definition 4. We define the semantics of the term representing process p by $T(p, TS_p)$, where TS_p is the current time stamp of process p. We have:

$T(p, TS_p) = f(T(p_1, t_1), \ldots, T(p_n, t_n))$ where:
— f is the symbol of process p.
— p_i are processes such that there exists a subterm edge going out from p to p_i with index i, when the time stamp of p is TS_p.
— t_i is the last time stamp of p_i known by p, $\forall i \in \{1, \ldots, n\}, TS\_Table_p[p_i] = t_i$.

Using time stamps, we have the following results.

Lemma 5. *For all time stamps t and t' such that $t' < t$, and for all processes p, we have: $T(p, t') \succeq T(p, t)$.*

Definition 6. The term of a process is persisting, if the time stamp of the process is persisting.

Corollary 7. *For each process, its term becomes persisting.*

Theorem 8. *Concurrent ground completion using SOUR graphs terminates.*

3.5 Soundness and Completeness Results

In this section, we give results for the soundness and completeness of our concurrent calculation of Unification and Orientation.

We call *CWD* the concurrent implementation of completion using SOUR Graphs and all the concurrent operations that we describe. We give results for the soundness and the completeness of *CWD*. Let E be the equational theory the graph represents.

Concurrent unification is *sound* if whenever message INITU is sent saying the unification constraint between terms s and t is true, then $E \models s \approx t$ is true and remains true.

Concurrent unification is *complete* if whenever s and t are persisting terms and s and t are unifiable, then at some time the unification edge between the processes representing terms s and t will have a true unification constraint. The concurrent computation of orientation is *complete* if whenever s and t are persisting terms and $s \succ_{lpo} t$ then, at some time, the orientation edge between processes representing terms s and t goes from s to t and does not change.

Theorem 9. *The concurrent computation of Unification is sound and complete, and the concurrent computation of Orientation is complete.*

CWD is *sound* if (i) after a rewrite edge is added between two processes with terms s and t, then $E \models s \approx t$ is true and remains true, and (ii) no subterm edge is added so that a cycle of subterm edges is created.

CWD is complete, if there are no configuration between persisting nodes.

Theorem 10. CWD *is sound and complete.*

4 Implementation and Experimental Results

Implementation : *CWD* is currently implemented in *C++* using *LEDA* (Library of Efficient Data types) and *PVM* (Parallel Virtual Machine). It is tested on a network of Unix and Solaris Sun4SparcStations, and Sgi workstations and on a Power Challenge Array (PCA) with 8 R8000 processors.

Experimental Results : Measurements have been made with many benchmark examples. *Table 1* shows a selection of results of measurements obtained on different platforms for two particular problems. *Table 1* summarizes, for each problem, the platform we use, the total number of messages sent between processes, the total number of *NOTIFY* messages (used for detecting termination) , and the real time of execution given in seconds.

Counter5 Example [GNP+93]: Precedence : $f \succ g \succ c$. Set of equations : $E = \{f(c) = g(c)\ ,\ f(g(c)) = g(f(c)),\ f(g(g(c)) = g(f(f(c))),\ f(g(g(g(c))) = g(f(f(f(c)))),\ f(g(g(g(g(c))))) = g(f(f(f(f(c)))))\}$

Number of child processes (the number of vertices of the initial graph representing the set of equations to complete) : 17

Expf6 Example: Precedence : $aa \succ ab \succ ac \succ ad \succ ae \succ af \succ ag \succ f \succ b$.

Set of equations : $E = \{aa = f(ab,ab,ab,ab,ab,ab), ab = f(ac,ac,ac,ac,ac,ac), ac = f(ad,ad,ad,ad,ad,ad), ad = f(ae,ae,ae,ae,ae,ae), ae = f(af,af,af,af,af,af), af = f(ag,ag,ag,ag,ag,ag), f(aa,aa,aa,aa,aa,aa) = b\}$.

On this example, *OTTER-3.0* runs out of memory after 20 minutes on a Digital server.

Number of child processes: 15

Problem	Platform	Completion Messages	Termination Messages	Real time
Counter5	1 Sun4	582	627	13.00 s
Counter5	5 Sun4	470	514	4.00 s
Counter5	10 Sun4	648	696	3.62 s
Counter5	15 Sun4	616	663	3.23 s
Counter5	5 Sgi	500	545	4.77 s
Counter5	PCA	594	639	1.88 s
Expf6	1 Sun4	724	822	11.00 s
Expf6	5 Sun4	737	835	5.52 s
Expf6	10 Sun4	734	832	3.00 s
Expf6	15 Sun4	729	827	3.00 s
Expf6	5 Sgi	715	813	4.56 s
Expf6	PCA	722	820	2.32 s

Table 1

5 Conclusion

We have presented a concurrent algorithm for completion using SOUR graphs. The initial set of equations is divided up into small pieces, stored in a graph. Initially each vertex represents one of the subterms in the initial set of equations.

Edges represent relations between those pieces. Inferences are local graph transformations, which remove existing edges and create new edges constrained by constraints and renamings. In the concurrent implementation, vertices represent processes and edges represent communication links between processes.

For simplicity, the algorithm we have given in this paper is for ground completion. However, we have summarized in the preliminaries how the theory of SOUR graphs is lifted to the non-ground case. The modification of our algorithm to the non-ground case is simple. Unification messages now contain a satisfiable equational constraint instead of just an assertion that a unification problem is true. Orientation messages contain a satisfiable ordering constraint. Configuration messages pass around these constraints, plus renamings. And new edges that are added are labelled with the combination constraint and renaming. This gives the processes more work to do. Whenever a node receives constraints, it must combine them, determine the satisfiability of the combination, and pass along the solved form.

Our presentation and algorithm has several desirable properties. As far as we know, it is the first fine-grained completion or theorem proving procedure, in the sense that each process represents a subterm of the equational system.

Another feature of most concurrent completion and theorem proving techniques is that they either require a global memory which all processes need to read and write to, or else a master process which controls all the other processes. In contrast, our algorithm works in a completely local fashion. All processes operate independently, because the algorithm is based on the local transformations of the SOUR graph algorithm. The work of a process is based on receiving a message from another process. However, a process does not need to wait, because there are lots of different things that are done by one process, and the message passing is asynchronous. Our algorithm has no need for any consistency checks, and two processes never do the same thing.

We feel that the property of having no global memory or global control is important. As mentioned in [BH94], contraction-based strategies are the most efficient strategies, but they are the most difficult to parallelize. Their parallelization almost always requires a global control or global memory, because anything can be a simplifier, and it is not known which simplifiers will simplify which equations. Our approach allows a contraction based strategy with all local operations.

Acknowledgements This work is partially supported by the Esprit Basic Research working group 6028, CCL. We would like to thank Polina Strogova, Ilies Alouini, Dominique Fortin and the anonymous referees for their comments.

References

[ADF95] J. Avenhaus, J. Denzinger, and M. Fuchs. DISCOUNT: A system for distributed equational deduction. In Hsiang [Hsi95], pages 397–402.

[BGK95] R. Bündgen, M. Göbel, and W. Küchlin. Parallel ReDuX → PaReDuX. In Hsiang [Hsi95], pages 408–413.

[BH94] M. P. Bonacina and J. Hsiang. Parallelization of deduction strategies: an analytical study. *Journal of Automated Reasoning*, 13:1–33, 1994.

[BH95] M. P. Bonacina and J. Hsiang. Distributed deduction by clause-diffusion: Distributed contraction and the aquarius prover. *Journal of Symbolic Computation*, 19:245–267, March 1995.

[DFvG83] E. Dijkstra, W. Feijen, and A. van Gasteren. Derivation of a termination detection algorithm for distributed computation. *Information Processing Letters*, 16:217–219, 1983.

[DJ90] N. Dershowitz and J.-P. Jouannaud. *Handbook of Theoretical Computer Science*, volume B, chapter 6: Rewrite Systems, pages 244–320. Elsevier Science Publishers B. V. (North-Holland), 1990. Also as: Research report 478, LRI.

[DKM84] C. Dwork, P. Kanellakis, and J. C. Mitchell. On the sequential nature of unification. *Journal of Logic Programming*, 1(1):35–50, 1984.

[GNP+93] J. Gallier, P. Narandran, D. Plaisted, S. Raatz, and W. Snyder. Finding canonical rewriting systems equivalent to a finite set of ground equations in polynomial time. *Journal of Association for Computing Machinery*, 40(1):1–16, 1993.

[Hsi95] J. Hsiang, editor. *Rewriting Techniques and Applications, 6th International Conference, RTA-95*, LNCS 914, Kaiserslautern, Germany, April 5–7, 1995. Springer-Verlag.

[KLS96] C. Kirchner, C. Lynch, and C. Scharff. Fine-grained concurrent completion. Technical Report 96-R-058, CRIN, 1996.

[LS90] R. Letz and J. Schumann. Partheo: A high-performance parallel theorem prover. In *Proceedings 10th International Conference on Automated Deduction, Kaiserslautern (Germany)*, volume 446 of *Lecture Notes in Artificial Intelligence*, pages 40–56. Springer-Verlag, 1990.

[LS95] C. Lynch and P. Strogova. Sour graphs for efficient completion. Technical Report 95-R-343, CRIN, 1995.

[Lyn95] C. Lynch. Paramodulation without duplication. In D. Kozen, editor, *Proceedings 10th IEEE Symposium on Logic in Computer Science, San Diego (Ca., USA)*, pages 167–177, San Diego, June 1995. IEEE.

[Sny93] W. Snyder. A fast algorithm for generating reduced ground rewriting systems from a set of ground equations. *Journal of Symbolic Computation*, 15:415–450, 1993.

[SS93] C. Suttner and J. Schumann. Parallel automated theorem proving. *Parallel Processing for Artificial Intelligence*, 1993.

AC-Complete Unification and its Application to Theorem Proving *

Alexandre Boudet, Evelyne Contejean and Claude Marché

LRI, CNRS URA 410
Bât. 490, Université Paris-Sud, Centre d'Orsay
91405 Orsay Cedex, France
Email: {boudet,contejea,marche}@lri.fr

Abstract. The inefficiency of AC-completion is mainly due to the doubly exponential number of AC-unifiers and thereby of critical pairs generated. We present AC-complete E-unification, a new technique whose goal is to reduce the number of AC-critical pairs inferred by performing unification in a extension E of AC (*e.g.* ACU, Abelian groups, Boolean rings, ...) in the process of normalized completion [24, 25]. The idea is to represent complete sets of AC-unifiers by (smaller) sets of E-unifiers. Not only do the theories E used for unification have exponentially fewer most general unifiers than AC, but one can remove from a complete set of E-unifiers those solutions which have no E-instance which is an AC-unifier.

First, we define AC-complete E-unification and describe its fundamental properties. We show how AC-complete E-unification can be done in the elementary case, and how the known combination techniques for unification algorithms can be reused for our purposes. Finally, we give some evidence of the kind of speedup that can be obtained by presenting some experiments with the C*i*ME theorem prover.

Introduction

The completion of rewriting systems modulo an equational theory T was introduced by Jouannaud and Kirchner [16, 3]. This allows to cope with permutative theories (the most popular being associativity and commutativity, denoted hereafter as AC), avoiding the non-termination of rules like $x+y \longrightarrow y+x$. In the case of AC-completion, one will make no distinction between the terms $a+b$ and $b+a$. The price to pay for identifying the terms that are equal modulo an equational theory T, is that T has to be taken into account in the deduction mechanism: standard unification is replaced by T-unification. Unfortunately, AC-unification may compute doubly exponentially many most general unifiers. A solution to this problem is to consider rewrite rules *constrained* by AC-unification problems, such a constrained rule representing the set of its instances by the *AC*-unifiers of the constraint. This is the *basic strategy* [26, 4, 27, 31]. Another possibility

* This research was supported in part by the EWG CCL, the HCM Network CONSOLE, and the "GDR de programmation du CNRS".

is to represent complete sets of AC-unifiers by ACU-unifiers [14, 11, 12]. In this paper, we show how to extend this latter idea to an extension E of AC, other than ACU, in the context of T-normalized completion.

Marché has introduced T-normalized completion [24, 25] where the equations are normalized eagerly with a convergent term rewriting system equivalent to T. The theory T may range from AC to Boolean rings. T-normalized completion originated in the solution to the problem of AC-completion with unit [5, 17] (denoted hereafter as ACU). It also gave an elegant solution to the problem raised by Loos and Buchberger [23, 10] of designing a uniform procedure which can specialize to Knuth-Bendix completion [21], AC-completion [28, 22] and to Gröbner basis computation [9]. Unfortunately, T-normalized completion is by essence incompatible with the basic strategy since one needs to apply the unifiers in order to perform T-normalization.

Let us go into details about the motivation of this paper: during the AC-completion process, new equations are computed using AC-unification, in order to reduce the so-called *AC critical peaks*:

$$s \xleftarrow[l_1 \to r_1]{\sigma, p} t \xleftrightarrow[\mathrm{AC}]{pq} t' \xrightarrow[l_2 \to r_2]{\sigma, pq} u$$

Indeed, with such a peak we have $l_1|_p\sigma =_{\mathrm{AC}} l_2\sigma$ hence there is a θ in the complete set of AC-unifiers of $l_1|_p$ and l_2 such that $\sigma =_{\mathrm{AC}} \theta\sigma'$. The peak is then transformed into the equational proof:

$$s \xleftrightarrow[AC]{p} s' \xleftrightarrow[l_1|_p\theta = l_2\theta]{\sigma', p} u' \xleftrightarrow[AC]{p} u$$

where the AC steps come from $\sigma =_{\mathrm{AC}} \theta\sigma'$. In T-normalized completion, it has been shown correct to use E-unification instead of AC-unification, for any E ranging from AC to T, since E is valid in the theory to be completed. One can then pick a θ' in the complete set of E-unifiers of $l_1|_p$ and l_2 such that $\sigma =_E \theta'\sigma'$, and transform the peak into:

$$s \xleftrightarrow[E]{p} s' \xleftrightarrow[l_1|_p\theta' = l_2\theta']{\sigma', p} u' \xleftrightarrow[E]{p} u$$

The choice of E between AC and T is very important because one can choose E such that E-unification behaves better than AC-unification:

- E must be a sub-theory of T so as to ensure the soundness of the deductions;
- E must be rich enough to avoid the complexity of AC unification: for instance ACU is preferable to AC;
- E must have decidable and finitary unification.

In practice, we are interested in ACU-unification which is simply exponential whereas AC-unification is doubly exponential, and in Abelian Group and Boolean Ring unification which are unitary (in the elementary case) [20].

In this article, the first idea is to pursue this idea more deeply: complete sets of E-unifiers are in fact used as a compact representation of complete sets of

AC-unifiers, hence for completion it is still complete to compute only E-unifiers *which have at least one AC-unifier as an instance*: this is what we call *AC-complete* unification. The second idea is that AC-complete E-unification should compute less unifiers than E-unification, since those E-unifiers which have no instance which is an E-unifier can be discarded. For example, when computing AC-complete set of unifiers modulo ACU(+, 0) of the equation $x + a = a$, we find immediately no solution, whereas there is in fact an ACU-unifier ($\{x \mapsto 0\}$) which does not have any AC-solution as instance (there is no AC-solution!). Unfortunately, this idea is not true in general, as shown by example 4. In fact, the *Clash* and *Occur-check* rules are correct only in a first step of the algorithm, that's why we will present an algorithm in two steps.

We show that the size of minimal AC-complete sets of E-unifiers can never be greater than the size of minimal complete sets of AC-unifiers nor of minimal complete sets of E-unifiers of the same unification problem. The main result is Theorem 9 where we show the soundness and completeness of our algorithm. The last important result is the validation in practice of our approach, shown by some benchmarks in Section 4.

This paper is organized as follows: we first study some general properties of AC-complete E-unification. Then we consider the elementary case (*i.e.* when there is only one AC operator in the signature), then we show how the known combination techniques for unification algorithms can be used to solve the general problem. Finally, we give some benchmarks obtained with our implementation[2] of normalized completion called C*i*ME, in which we implemented AC-complete unification modulo ACU and Abelian Groups.

1 Basic concepts

1.1 Definitions

As we mentioned above, we intend to represent all AC-unifiers by a set of E-unifiers for a theory E which extends AC. The main theories E we are interested in are the following:

Definition 1.

$$\begin{aligned}
\mathrm{AC}(+) &= \{x + y = y + x; x + (y + z) = (x + y) + z\} \\
\mathrm{ACU}(+,0) &= \mathrm{AC}(+) \cup \{x + 0 = x\} \\
\mathrm{AG}(+,0,-) &= \mathrm{ACU}(+,0) \cup \{x + (-x) = 0\} \\
\mathrm{BR}(+,*,0,1) &= \mathrm{ACU}(+,0) \cup \mathrm{ACU}(*,1) \cup \\
&\quad \{x + x = 0; x * x = x; x * (y + z) = (x * y) + (x * z)\}
\end{aligned}$$

Whenever a theory E contains several AC-symbols $+_1, \ldots, +_n$, for short, we use AC instead of $\bigcup_{i=1}^{n} \mathrm{AC}(+_i)$.

[2] available as `http://www.lri.fr/~marche/cime.html`.

Definition 2. Let E be an equational theory on $\mathcal{T}(F,X)$ containing AC. Let P be a unification problem. An E-solution θ of P is *AC-compatible* if there exist σ and ρ such that $\sigma =_E \theta\rho$ and $\sigma \in \mathrm{Sol}_{\mathrm{AC}}(P)$. $\mathrm{Sol}_{E/\mathrm{AC}}(P)$ denotes the set of AC-compatible E-unifiers of P.

A set Θ of substitutions is an *AC-complete* set of E-solutions of P if

(i) $\forall\theta \in \Theta \;\; \theta \in \mathrm{Sol}_E(P)$. (Soundness)
(ii) $\forall\sigma \in \mathrm{Sol}_{\mathrm{AC}}(P) \;\; \exists\theta,\rho \;\; \theta \in \Theta \;\wedge\; \theta\rho =_E \sigma$. (Completeness)

An AC-complete set of E-solutions of P is said to be *minimal* if it has no proper subset that is still AC-complete.

Example 1. Consider the equation

$$f(x+y,z+t) = f(a+b,u+v)$$

where $+$ is associative-commutative, f is a free function symbol, a,b are free constants and x,y,z,t,u,v are variables. This problem has 14 most general *AC* unifiers corresponding to the conjunctions of one of the two solutions

$$\{x \mapsto a, y \mapsto b\} \quad \{x \mapsto b, y \mapsto a\}$$

of the equation $x+y = a+b$, and one of the seven solutions

$$\begin{array}{l}\{z \mapsto w_1+w_2, t \mapsto w_3+w_4, u \mapsto w_1+w_3, v \mapsto w_2+w_4\}\\ \{z \mapsto w_1, t \mapsto w_3+w_4, u \mapsto w_1+w_3, v \mapsto w_4\}\\ \{z \mapsto w_2, t \mapsto w_3+w_4, u \mapsto w_3, v \mapsto w_2+w_4\}\\ \{z \mapsto w_1+w_2, t \mapsto w_4, u \mapsto w_1, v \mapsto w_2+w_4\}\\ \{z \mapsto w_1+w_2, t \mapsto w_3, u \mapsto w_1+w_3, v \mapsto w_2\}\\ \{z \mapsto w_2, t \mapsto w_3, u \mapsto w_3, v \mapsto w_2\}\\ \{z \mapsto w_1, t \mapsto w_4, u \mapsto w_1, v \mapsto w_4\}\end{array}$$

of the equation $z+t = u+v$.

Now, the same equation has 4 most general ACU$(+,0)$-unifiers, corresponding to the conjunctions of one of the four solutions

$$\{x \mapsto a+b, y \mapsto 0\} \;\; \{x \mapsto a, y \mapsto b\} \;\; \{x \mapsto b, y \mapsto a\} \;\; \{x \mapsto 0, y \mapsto a+b\}$$

of the equation $x+y = a+b$ and the unique most general ACU-unifier

$$\{z \mapsto w_1+w_2, t \mapsto w_3+w_4, u \mapsto w_1+w_3, v \mapsto w_2+w_4\}$$

of the equation $z+y = u+v$.

But the two ACU solutions which respectively map x and y onto 0 are not AC-compatible. In this case, a minimal, AC-complete set of ACU-unifiers is reduced to the two substitutions

$$\begin{array}{l}\{x \mapsto a, y \mapsto b, z \mapsto w_1+w_2, t \mapsto w_3+w_4, u \mapsto w_1+w_3, v \mapsto w_2+w_4\}\\ \{x \mapsto b, y \mapsto a, z \mapsto w_1+w_2, t \mapsto w_3+w_4, u \mapsto w_1+w_3, v \mapsto w_2+w_4\}\end{array}$$

The reader can check that the 14 AC-unifiers of the original equation can be obtained by mapping some of the variables introduced by these two substitutions onto 0.

Remark. In no way, AC-compatible E-unification can be seen as unification in a quotient algebra. Indeed two terms s and t can be equal modulo E while the first unifies with a term u and the second doesn't. For instance $x+y$ is equal to $1*(x+y)$ in Boolean rings but the first term has two most general AC-compatible BR-unifiers with $a+b$, and the second has none.

1.2 General Properties

As in the case of standard E-unification, a minimal, AC-complete set of E-unifiers is unique in a certain way:

Lemma 3. *If Σ_1 and Σ_2 are two minimal AC-complete sets of E-solutions of a problem P, then they are equivalent up to E-similarity. In particular they have the same cardinality.*

The proof is the same as in the standard E-unification case. As a consequence, every AC-complete set of E-solutions of P has a larger cardinality. The following property shows that AC-complete E-unification cannot be worse than AC-unification or E-unification, provided one can compute a *minimal* AC-complete set of E-unifiers.

Proposition 4. *For an arbitrary unification problem P, if Σ is a minimal AC-complete set of E-unifiers of P, then $|\mathrm{CSU}_{\mathrm{AC}}(P)| \geq |\Sigma|$ and $|\mathrm{CSU}_E(P)| \geq |\Sigma|$.*

Proof. We simply remark that $\mathrm{CSU}_{\mathrm{AC}}(P)$ is itself an AC-complete set of E-solutions of P, hence the first inequality is true by minimality of Σ (Lemma 3). The set $\mathrm{CSU}_E(P) \cap \mathrm{Sol}_{E/\mathrm{AC}}$ is also an AC-complete set of E-solutions of P hence the second inequality.

Removing from a minimal complete set of E-unifiers those solutions which are not AC-compatible always yields an AC-complete set of E-unifiers, but unfortunately, this does not guarantee minimality.

Example 2. Let E be the Boolean ring theory $\mathrm{BR}(+,*,0,1)$ on the term algebra $\mathcal{T}(\{+,,0,1\} \cup \{f\}, \mathcal{X})$. Consider the equation

$$f(x) + f(y) = f(u) + f(v),$$

where x, y, u and v are variables. This equation has only two most general AC-unifiers:

$$\sigma_1 \equiv \{x \mapsto z, y \mapsto w, u \mapsto z, v \mapsto w\} \quad \sigma_2 \equiv \{x \mapsto z, y \mapsto w, u \mapsto w, v \mapsto z\}$$

but it has three minimal E-unifiers which are AC-compatible: σ_1, σ_2 and

$$\sigma_3 \equiv \{x \mapsto z, y \mapsto z, u \mapsto w, v \mapsto w\}$$

But σ_3 is useless since its E-instances which are AC-solutions are not minimal, hence $\{\sigma_1, \sigma_2\}$ is an AC-complete set of E-unifiers.

2 The elementary case

As we already said, it is sound and complete to just replace AC-unification by E-unification, provided $AC \subseteq E \subseteq T$. In this section we show how one can further reduce the number of unifiers in the elementary *AC* case (*i.e.* when the signature is reduced to one AC-operator and free constants), by discarding those E-unifiers which are not AC-compatible. We can even obtain a minimal AC-complete set of E-unifiers in two particular cases: ACU and unitary theories. This turns out to be sufficient for our purpose since besides ACU, the theories that we have in mind are those of Abelian groups and Boolean rings which happen to be unitary for unification.

2.1 AC-complete ACU-unification

It is easy to see if an ACU-unifier σ is AC-compatible. Indeed, if σ maps some variable x onto the unit, then no further instantiation will turn σ into an AC-unifier. On the other hand, if no variable is mapped onto the unit, then σ *is* an AC-unifier. Example 2 showed that discarding the useless E-unifiers from a minimal complete set of E-unifiers does not yield a minimal AC-complete set of E-unifiers in general. But in the case of ACU, the remaining substitutions are all incomparable AC-unifiers, hence the minimality of the obtained set.

2.2 Unitary theories

The case of unitary theories is even easier since if there exists a most general E-unifier σ and at least an AC-unifier, then necessarily $\{\sigma\}$ is a minimal AC-complete set of E-unifiers.

Lemma 5. *Assume that a unification problem has a most general E-unifier σ and is AC-unifiable. Then $\{\sigma\}$ is a minimal AC-complete set of E-unifiers.*

This holds because AC being a sub-theory of E, all the AC-solutions are E-solutions, and σ being a most general E-unifier represents all of them.

This particular case is relevant for us since two theories of interest (BR and AG) are unitary, and in addition meet the additional requirements that we describe below.

2.3 Further useful assumptions

We describe some useful properties that a theory E must have in order to use AC-compatible E-unification in the general case (*i.e.* in presence of several AC-operators and free function symbols). These are essentially the same assumptions that are made on equational theories for the combination of unification algorithms [29, 6, 1, 7].

Definition 6. A theory E defined on a signature $\mathcal{F}$ is *combinable* if

- E has a complete unification algorithm for terms in $\mathcal{T}(\mathcal{F} \cup \mathcal{C}, \mathcal{X})$, where $\mathcal{C}$ is a set of free constants.
- E has a *constant elimination algorithm.*

It is well-known that ACU, BR and AG are combinable theories [29].

Before addressing the general case, let us give an example of the kind of speedup that can be obtained with our technique:

Example 3. Assume that $+$ is an AC-operator and that E is the theory of Boolean rings over $\{+, *, 0, 1\}$. All the equations of the form

$$x + s = t$$

for arbitrary terms s and t in which x has no occurrence have the most general E-unifier $\sigma = \{x \mapsto s + t\}$. Now, as soon as such an equation is AC-unifiable, $\{\sigma\}$ is an AC-complete set of E-unifiers.

3 The general case

One of the major difficulties with AC-unification is the combination of the elementary AC-unification algorithms for each AC-operator [30, 19, 13, 8]. Indeed, it took almost a decade before the termination of Stickel's combination algorithm [30] was proved by Fages[3] [13]. Yet AC theories, being *simple theories* (*i.e.* theories in which there is no equality between a term and one of its proper subterms), are in the easiest class for the combination problem.

What we intend to do here is not to re-design a combination procedure for our specific purpose, but to reuse the standard combination techniques. A first difficulty is that the combination methods for simple theories are not complete for AC-compatible E-unification.

3.1 Purification

Let us see why we need more than the known combination techniques for AC-unification. The two rules of Figure 1 are well-known to be complete for AC-unification [8, 15]. A naïve attempt would be to use these rules since we can discard the input problems that are not AC-unifiable. This is not complete as examplified below:

Example 4. Assume that $+$ and $*$ are AC symbols, and that we want to use $\mathrm{ACU}(+, 0) \cup \mathrm{ACU}(*, 1)$ as theory E for solving the problem

$$x + y = u + v \wedge x * y' = u * v'$$

[3] Stickel's algorithm goes back to '75 and Fages' proof to '84.

Clash
$x = f(s_1, \ldots, s_n) \wedge x = g(t_1, \ldots, t_m) \quad \rightarrow \bot$
if $f \neq g$.

Check*
$x_1 = s_1[x_2] \wedge x_2 = s_2[x_3] \wedge \cdots \wedge x_n = s_n[x_1] \quad \rightarrow \bot$
if some s_i is not a variable.

Fig. 1. rules **Clash** and **Check***

Replacing each equation by an ACU-solved form results in the problem:

$$\begin{array}{c} x = z_1 + z_2 \ \wedge \ y = z_3 + z_4 \ \wedge \ u = z_1 + z_3 \ \wedge \ v = z_2 + z_4 \\ \bigwedge \\ x = w_1 * w_2 \ \wedge \ y' = w_3 * w_4 \ \wedge \ u = w_1 * w_3 \ \wedge \ v' = w_2 * w_4 \end{array}$$

Clash applies to x and u but the theory conflicts can be solved by applying the substitution $\{z_2 \mapsto 0, w_3 \mapsto 1\}$. This produces the problem

$$\begin{array}{c} x = z_1 \ \wedge \ y = z_3 + z_4 \ \wedge \ u = z_1 + z_3 \ \wedge \ v = z_4 \\ \bigwedge \\ x = w_1 * w_2 \ \wedge \ y' = w_4 \ \wedge \ u = w_1 \ \wedge \ v' = w_2 * w_4 \end{array}$$

to which **Check*** now applies since there is a cycle

$$x = w_1 * w_2 \ \wedge \ w_1 = u \ \wedge \ u = z_1 + z_3 \ \wedge \ z_1 = x$$

Yet, the original problem is surely AC-unifiable since it unifies in the free theory.

What we want to point out is that the combination rules of AC-unification are not correct *after* solving a subproblem in E. This is because E-unification of a subproblem does not yield an AC-equivalent one. Conversely these rules are obviously correct *before* E-unification since they just transform an AC-unification problem into an equivalent one.

Hence the set of rules **Purify** of Figure 2 can be applied as a first step of an AC-complete E-unification algorithm. These rules terminate as a strict subset of the rules of [8, 6] for AC-unification.

What example 4 shows is that we need all the power of the combination techniques for arbitrary equational theories. We now show how to use these techniques for solving our problem.

3.2 The disjunction lemma

After applying the rules of **Purify** as long as possible, we obtain a problem which is either $\bot$, or a DAG-solved form [15], or a unification problem that we will write under the form

Decompose
$f(s_1, \ldots, s_n) = f(t_1, \ldots, t_n) \quad \rightarrow \quad s_1 = t_1 \ \wedge \ \cdots \ \wedge \ s_n = t_n$
if f is not an AC operator.

Clash
$f(s_1, \ldots, s_n) = g(t_1, \ldots, t_m) \quad \rightarrow \ \bot$
if $f \neq g$.

Coalesce
$x = y \ \wedge \ P \quad \rightarrow \ x = y \ \wedge \ P\{x \mapsto y\}$
if $x, y \in \mathcal{V}(P)$ and x is existentially quantified or y is free.

Variable Abstraction
$s[u]_p = t \quad \rightarrow \ (\exists x) \ s[x]_p = t \ \wedge \ x = u$
if u is an alien subterm of s at position p with respect to the disjoint signatures $\{+_1\}, \ldots, \{+_n\}, (\mathcal{F} \setminus \{+_1, \ldots, +_n\})$.

Merge
$x = s \ \wedge \ x = t \quad \rightarrow \ x = s \ \wedge \ s = t$
If $s, t \notin \mathcal{X}$ and $|s| \leq |t|$.

Check*
$x_1 = s_1[x_2] \ \wedge \ x_2 = s_2[x_3] \ \wedge \ \cdots \ \wedge \ x_n = s_n[x_1] \quad \rightarrow \ \bot$
if some s_i is not a variable.

Fig. 2. the set of rules **Purify** for AC-complete E-unification

$$P \equiv (\exists y_1, \ldots, y_m) P_V \ \wedge \ P_\emptyset \ \wedge \ P_{+_1} \ \wedge \ \cdots \ \wedge \ P_{+_n}$$

where

- P_V contains only equations of the form $x = y$ with $x, y \in \mathcal{X}$ and x or y has no other occurrence in P.
- $P_\emptyset \equiv x_1 = s_1 \ \wedge \ \cdots \ \wedge \ x_n = s_n$ where s_i is a non-variable term with no occurrence of an AC-operator.
- P_{+_i} is a conjunction of pure equations in $AC(+_i)$.
- **Clash**, **Merge** and **Check*** do not apply.

Now, we wish to use a theory E, extending $\bigcup_i \mathrm{AC}(+_i)$ instead of AC-unification for solving the pure AC-subproblems P_{+_i}. But this is no longer unification in a combination of disjoint equational theories: if the AC-symbols are $+$ and $*$, and the theory E is a Boolean ring over $\{+, *, 0, 1\}$, AC(+)-complete BR-unification and AC($*$)-complete BR-unification will not be performed with disjoint alphabets. We show that we can simulate the disjoint case by a technical trick which reflects the fact that AC(+) and AC($*$) *are* disjoint theories. We shall use different *copies* of E for each AC-operator.

Definition 7. Let E be an equational theory defined on $\mathcal{T}(\mathcal{F},\mathcal{X})$ and containing $\mathrm{AC} = \bigcup_{i=1}^{n} \mathrm{AC}(+_i)$. A *copy* of $\mathcal{F}$ with respect to $+_i$ is a one-to-one mapping κ_i from $\mathcal{F}$ onto a set $\mathcal{F}_i$ such that

- $\kappa_i(+_i) = +_i$,
- $\kappa_i(f) = f$ if f is a free function symbol,
- $\kappa_i(f) = f^i$ $(\neq f)$ otherwise.

κ_i can be uniquely extended to $\mathcal{T}(\mathcal{F},\mathcal{X})$. $\kappa_i(E)$ is the equational theory defined on $\mathcal{T}(\mathcal{F}_i,\mathcal{X})$ by replacing the symbols f in the equations of E by $\kappa_i(f)$. $\kappa(E)$ is the equational theory $\bigcup_{i=1}^{n} \kappa_i(E)$ defined on $\mathcal{T}(\mathcal{F} \cup \bigcup_{i=1}^{n} \mathcal{F}_i),\mathcal{X})$. κ^{-1} retrieves the original function symbols:

- $\kappa^{-1}(f) = f$ if f is in $\mathcal{F}$,
- $\kappa^{-1}(f^i) = \kappa_i^{-1}(f^i)$ otherwise (f^i is in $\mathcal{F}_i$).

Lemma 8 Disjunction lemma. *Let Θ be an AC-complete set of $\kappa(E)$-unifiers for the unification problem*

$$P \equiv (\exists y_1,\ldots,y_m)\ P_V \ \wedge\ P_\emptyset \ \wedge\ P_{+_1} \ \wedge\ \cdots\ \wedge\ P_{+_n}$$

obtained from the original problem by applying as long as possible the rules of ***Purify****. Then $\kappa^{-1}(\Theta)$ is an AC-complete set of E-unifiers for P.*

Proof. First, it is obvious that if θ is a $\kappa(E)$-unifier for P, $\kappa^{-1}(\theta)$ is an E-unifier: any proof modulo $\kappa(E)$ can still be performed modulo E with the "original" function symbols.

Now let σ be an AC-unifier of P. We can assume without loss of generality that σ is minimal, hence σ contains only functions symbols occuring in $\mathcal{F}$: this implies that $\kappa^{-1}(\sigma) = \sigma$. Since Θ is AC-complete, there exist θ and ρ such that $\theta \in \Theta$ and $\sigma =_{\kappa(E)} \theta\rho$. Hence $\sigma = \kappa^{-1}(\sigma) =_E \kappa^{-1}(\theta)\kappa^{-1}(\rho)$.

This simple result allows us to reuse the machinery of unification in combination of disjoint equational theories. Elementary AC-unification will be replaced by E-unification in the associated copy. For this, recall that we must be able to compute AC-complete sets of E-unifiers with the traditional additional restrictions on E.

Theorem 9. *Let* $\mathrm{AC} = \bigcup_{i=1}^{n} \mathrm{AC}(+_i)$. *Let* $E \supseteq \mathrm{AC}$ *be a combinable equational theory. The following algorithm*

1. *apply as long as possible the rules of* ***Purify****,*
2. *run a combination algorithm for arbitrary combinable equational theories replacing elementary* $\mathrm{AC}(+_i)$*-unification by AC-complete* $\kappa_i(E)$*-unification,*
3. *apply* κ^{-1} *to the solutions computed at step 2,*

is an AC-complete E-unification algorithm.

4 Some experiments

In this section we present some experiments with our prototype C*i*ME. We have used Boudet's technique [7] for combining the elementary AC-complete unification algorithms. In the tables below, T is the normalization theory used for rewriting, and E is the unification theory. For each case we give the number of calls to unification, the number of solutions generated, the number of rules generated during completion, the number of rules persisting at the end of completion, the total computation time of completion, and the time spent in unification (computation times are in seconds, on a PC Pentium 90 running Linux 1.2.13, C*i*ME compiled with the Caml Special Light optimizing compiler).

4.1 Abelian Group theory

T	E	# calls to unif.	# of sol.	# rules gener.	# pers. rules	total time	unif. time
AC(+)	AC(+)	37	227	6	5	1.49	0.51
ACU(+,0)	AC(+)	30	206	5	4	1.57	0.50
	ACU(+,0)	37	47	7	4	0.54	0.21

In this case, times get better with ACU unification. One surprising point is the number of rules generated during completion with ACU unification : we discuss in detail this point on the next example.

4.2 Ring theory

The Ring theory is presented by

$$x + 0 = x \qquad (x * y) * z = x * (y * z) \qquad (x + y) * z = (x * z) + (y * z)$$
$$x * 1 = x \quad 1 * x = x \qquad x + (-x) = 0 \qquad x * (y + z) = (x * y) + (x * z)$$

where + is AC.

T	E	# calls to unif.	# of sol.	# rules gener.	# pers. rules	total time	unif. time
AC(+)	AC(+)	143	407	23	14	3.90	0.96
ACU(+,0)	AC(+)	128	372	23	13	4.03	0.76
	ACU(+,0)	269	325	26	13	7.72	0.98
ACU(+,0) AU(∗,1)	AC(+)	99	423	22	10	5.82	0.90
	ACU(+,0)	337	372	25	10	10.97	1.13
AG(+,0,−)	AC(+)	75	100	10	9	1.42	0.08
	ACU(+,0)	75	56	10	9	1.02	0.07
	AG(+,0,−)	75	52	10	9	0.85	0.09
AG(+,0,−) AU(∗,1)	AC(+)	25	67	6	6	1.21	0.09
	ACU(+,0)	25	23	6	6	0.78	0.02
	AG(+,0,−)	25	19	6	6	0.61	0.05

In this case, it's getting worse when using ACU-normalized completion with ACU-unification : in fact, there are problems with C*i*ME's completion strategy, useless rules (like $0.0 \to 0$ or $x.-(1) \to -(x)$) are considered (on lines 3 and 5, one can see that the number of rules generated is larger). An evidence of this strategy problem is obtained if we try to complete the already known convergent set of rules for commutative rings, that is if we simply want to prove the confluence. The results are then as follows:

T	E	# calls to unif.	# of sol.	# rules gener.	# pers. rules	total time	unif. time
ACU(+,0)	AC(+)	81	169	13	13	2.33	0.18
	ACU(+,0)	81	71	13	13	1.19	0.13

In fact, it is obvious that when completion is simply used for proving confluence, ACU unification is always better, since the strategy is irrelevant in this case.

4.3 Commutative Ring theory

The Commutative Ring theory is presented by the equations

$$x + 0 = x \qquad x * 1 = x$$
$$x + (-x) = 0 \qquad x * (y + z) = (x * y) + (x * z)$$

where $+$ and $*$ are AC.

T	E	# calls to unif.	# of sol.	# rules gener.	# pers. rules	total time	unif. time
AC(+) AC(*)	AC(+) AC(*)	69	324	14	9	2.42	0.72
ACU(+,0) ACU(*,1)	AC(+) AC(*)	66	340	13	7	3.11	0.77
	ACU(+,0) ACU(*,1)	131	178	17	7	2.92	0.73
AG(+,0,−) AC(*)	AC(+) AC(*)	12	46	4	4	0.46	0.04
	ACU(+,0) AC(*)	12	24	4	4	0.33	0.05
	AG(+,0,−) AC(*)	12	25	4	4	0.25	0.04
AG(+,0,−) ACU(*,1)	AC(+) AC(*)	8	39	3	3	0.42	0.06
	ACU(+,0) ACU(*,1)	8	12	3	3	0.23	0.03
	AG(+,0,−) ACU(*,1)	8	12	3	3	0.22	0.04

Again, there are some problems with the completion strategy in the case of ACU-normalized completion with ACU unification, but in the other cases ACU-unification and AG-unification are better.

4.4 A finitely generated Abelian group

Let us complete the presentation of the Abelian group generated by a, b, c and the relations

$$2a - 3b + c = 0 \qquad -3a + 2b + 3c = 0 \qquad 2a + 2b - 2c = 0$$

T	E	# calls to unif.	# of sol.	# rules gener.	# pers. rules	total time	unif. time
AC(+)	AC(+)	369	1531	33	9	40.84	3.10
ACU(+,0)	AC(+)	334	1466	32	8	42.46	2.84
	ACU(+,0)	184	427	23	8	43.34	1.23
AG(+,0,−)	AC(+)	17	13	9	4	0.88	0.02
	ACU(+,0)	17	13	9	4	0.82	0.02
	AG(+,0,−)	17	13	9	4	0.93	0.02

Here, ACU unification is clearly an enhancement for ACU-normalized completion. AG-normalized completion is much more efficient, so there is no relevant difference between the different unification theories.

4.5 A Gröbner basis of a polynomial ideal

It has been noticed that CR-normalized completion (where CR is commutative rings theory) can be used for computing polynomial ideals over $\mathbb{Z}$. Here is an example:

$$2X^2Y - Y = 0 \quad 3XY^2 - X = 0$$

which we complete modulo CR$(+,0,-,*,1)$.

T	E	# calls to unif.	# of sol.	# rules gener.	# pers. rules	total time	unif. time
AC	AC(+) AC(*)	1241	1942	46	22	61.24	6.50
CR	AC(+) AC(*)	176	108	16	13	4.93	0.48
	ACU(+,0) ACU(*,1)	201	89	17	13	4.26	0.54
	AG(+,0,−) ACU(*,1)	201	90	17	13	4.35	0.49

In this case, ACU unification is slightly better. Note that the problem with the completion strategy arises here also (there is one intermediary rule more, and consequently more calls to unification), hence we expect better results with a clever strategy.

We have obtained similar results with polynomial ideals over finite fields.

As a conclusion of this section, we remark that the cases where the improvement due to the use of ACU or AG unification is the best are when the initial set of rules is already confluent, or is almost confluent, like in AG-normalized completion of (commutative or non-commutative) ring theory.

5 Conclusion

Thanks to the use of AC-complete E-unification, we succeeded to reduce significantly the number of critical pairs generated during normalized completion. AC-complete E-unification computes less critical pairs than AC unification or E-unification. The implementation, though, highlightened some lacks in the completion strategy of our prover C*i*ME. From an algebraic point of view, it is not clear what minimal AC-complete sets of E-unifiers are. We saw that they are *not* complete sets of unifiers modulo an equational theory. From the practical point of view, we do not know how to compute minimal sets, although our experiments on the prototype implementation shows that we do compute small sets of unifiers in practice. Note however that the standard combination techniques for AC-unification do not compute minimal sets either in general. One important thing that remains to do is to study how to combine this new method with other known methods for reducing the number of critical pairs : critical pair criteria [2, 18]. Another future work is to extend our results to Horn clauses, that is to study the use of AC-complete unification with paramodulation inference rules.

References

1. F. Baader and K. Schulz. Unification in the union of disjoint equational theories: Combining decision procedures. In D. Kapur, editor, *Proc. 11th Int. Conf. on Automated Deduction, Saratoga Springs, NY, LNAI 607*, 1992.
2. L. Bachmair and N. Dershowitz. Critical pair criteria for completion. *Journal of Symbolic Computation*, 6(1):1–18, 1988.
3. L. Bachmair and N. Dershowitz. Completion for rewriting modulo a congruence. *Theoretical Comput. Sci.*, 67(2&3):173–201, Oct. 1989.
4. L. Bachmair, H. Ganzinger, C. Lynch, and W. Snyder. Basic paramodulation and superposition. In D. Kapur, editor, *Proc. 11th Int. Conf. on Automated Deduction, Saratoga Springs, NY, LNAI 607*. Springer-Verlag, June 1992.
5. T. Baird, G. Peterson, and R. Wilkerson. Complete sets of reductions modulo Associativity, Commutativity and Identity. In *Proc. 3rd Rewriting Techniques and Applications, Chapel Hill, LNCS 355*, pages 29–44. Springer-Verlag, Apr. 1989.
6. A. Boudet. *Unification dans les Mélanges de Théories équationnelles.* Thèse de doctorat, Université Paris-Sud, Orsay, France, Feb. 1990.
7. A. Boudet. Combining unification algorithms. *Journal of Symbolic Computation*, 16:597–626, 1993.
8. A. Boudet, E. Contejean, and H. Devie. A new AC-unification algorithm with a new algorithm for solving diophantine equations. In *Proc. 5th IEEE Symp. Logic in Computer Science, Philadelphia*, pages 289–299. IEEE Computer Society Press, June 1990.
9. B. Buchberger. *An Algorithm for Finding a Basis for the Residue Class Ring of a Zero-Dimensional Ideal.* PhD thesis, University of Innsbruck, Austria, 1965. (in German).
10. B. Buchberger and R. Loos. Algebraic simplification. In *Computer Algebra, Symbolic and Algebraic Computation. Computing Supplementum 4*. Springer-Verlag, 1982.
11. H. J. Bürckert. Solving disequations in equational theories. In *Proc. 9th Int. Conf. on Automated Deduction, Argonne, IL, LNCS 310*. Springer-Verlag, May 1988.
12. E. Domenjoud. AC unification through order-sorted AC1 unification. *Journal of Symbolic Computation*, 14(6):537–556, Dec. 1992.
13. F. Fages. Associative-commutative unification. *Journal of Symbolic Computation*, 3(3), June 1987.

14. A. Herold and J. H. Siekmann. Unification in abelian semi-groups. *Journal of Automated Reasoning*, 3(3):247–283, 1987.
15. J.-P. Jouannaud and C. Kirchner. Solving equations in abstract algebras: A rule-based survey of unification. In J.-L. Lassez and G. Plotkin, editors, *Computational Logic: Essays in Honor of Alan Robinson*. MIT-Press, 1991.
16. J.-P. Jouannaud and H. Kirchner. Completion of a set of rules modulo a set of equations. *SIAM J. Comput.*, 15(4):1155–1194, 1986.
17. J.-P. Jouannaud and C. Marché. Termination and completion modulo associativity, commutativity and identity. *Theoretical Comput. Sci.*, 104:29–51, 1992.
18. D. Kapur, D. Musser, and P. Narendran. Only prime superpositions need be considered for the Knuth-Bendix procedure. *Journal of Symbolic Computation*, 4:19–36, 1988.
19. C. Kirchner. Méthodes et outils de conception systématique d'algorithmes d'unification dans les théories equationnelles. Thèse d'Etat, Univ. Nancy, France, 1985.
20. C. Kirchner, editor. *Unification*. Academic Press, 1990.
21. D. E. Knuth and P. B. Bendix. Simple word problems in universal algebras. In J. Leech, editor, *Computational Problems in Abstract Algebra*, pages 263–297. Pergamon Press, 1970.
22. D. S. Lankford and A. M. Ballantyne. Decision procedures for simple equational theories with permutative axioms: Complete sets of permutative reductions. Research Report Memo ATP-37, Department of Mathematics and Computer Science, University of Texas, Austin, Texas, USA, Aug. 1977.
23. R. Loos. Term reduction systems and algebraic algorithms. In *Proceedings of the Fifth GI Workshop on Artificial Intelligence*, pages 214–234, Bad Honnef, West Germany, 1981. Available as *Informatik Fachberichte*, Vol. 47.
24. C. Marché. Normalised rewriting and normalised completion. In *Proceedings of the Ninth Annual IEEE Symposium on Logic in Computer Science*, pages 394–403, Paris, France, July 1994. IEEE Comp. Soc. Press.
25. C. Marché. Normalized rewriting: an alternative to rewriting modulo a set of equations. *Journal of Symbolic Computation*, 1996. to appear.
26. R. Nieuwenhuis and A. Rubio. Basic superposition is complete. In B. Krieg-Bruckner, editor, *Proc. European Symp. on Programming, LNCS 582*, pages 371–389, Rennes, 1992. Springer-Verlag.
27. R. Nieuwenhuis and A. Rubio. AC-superposition with constraints: no AC unifier needed. In *Proc. 12th Int. Conf. on Automated Deduction*, LNAI, Nancy, June 1994. Springer-Verlag.
28. G. E. Peterson and M. E. Stickel. Complete sets of reductions for some equational theories. *J. ACM*, 28(2):233–264, Apr. 1981.
29. M. Schmidt-Schauß. Unification in a combination of arbitrary disjoint equational theories. *Journal of Symbolic Computation*, 1990. Special issue on Unification.
30. M. Stickel. A unification algorithm for associative-commutative functions. *J. ACM*, 28(3):423–434, 1981.
31. L. Vigneron. Associative commutative deduction with constraints. In *Proc. 12th Int. Conf. on Automated Deduction*, LNAI, Nancy, June 1994. Springer-Verlag.

Superposition Theorem Proving for Abelian Groups Represented as Integer Modules*

Jürgen Stuber†

Abstract

We define a superposition calculus specialized for abelian groups represented as integer modules, and show its refutational completeness. This allows to substantially reduce the number of inferences compared to a standard superposition prover which applies the axioms directly. Specifically, equational literals are simplified, so that only the maximal term of the sums is on the left-hand side. Only certain minimal superpositions need to be considered; other superpositions which a standard prover would consider become redundant. This not only reduces the number of inferences, but also reduces the size of the AC-unification problems which are generated. That is, AC-unification is not necessary at the top of a term, only below some non-AC-symbol. Further, we consider situations where the axioms give rise to variable overlaps and develop techniques to avoid these explosive cases where possible.

1 Introduction

Historically, starting from plain resolution, more and more problematic axioms have been built into theorem provers. This ranges from paramodulation and superposition, where the axioms of equality are built-in, to equational theorem proving modulo AC. We develop a superposition calculus for first-order theories containing integer modules or equivalently abelian groups. There the inverse law is problematic, since it allows to move the terms of a sum from one side of an equation to the other in an uncontrolled way. We represent the built-in theory by a ground convergent term rewriting system. Ground equations are reduced with respect to this system and simplified such that the maximal monomial of the two terms is on the left-hand side and all other terms are on the right-hand side. This allows to derive a mapping from such a simplified equation to a *symmetrized* set of rules, that is, a set of rules such that critical peaks and cliffs with the built-in theory converge. These symmetrizations are not actually computed, but used in the model construction for the completeness proof. Another innovation of our calculus is that integer coefficients represent multiple occurrences of the same term in the sum. Note that we are not interested in proving theorems about integers; for our purposes it suffices that integers are handled by some kind of constraint solver.

*Proofs are available at `http://www.mpi-sb.mpg.de/~juergen/publications/RTA96/`.

†Max-Planck-Institut für Informatik, Im Stadtwald, D-66123 Saarbrücken.
Tel: +49-681-9325-228, fax: +49-681-9325-299, email: `juergen@mpi-sb.mpg.de`
WWW: `http://www.mpi-sb.mpg.de/~juergen/`

Syntactically this means that we do not allow equations between integers. Apart from that we have no restrictions on the problem; our calculus is refutationally complete for any set of first-order clauses. In particular, we allow arbitrary *uninterpreted function symbols*. These are symbols which do not occur in the built-in axioms.[1]

We now compare our approach to a more general prover, which represents at least part of the theory of abelian groups explicitly by some subset T of its clause set $T \cup N$, where our prover would operate on N only. We consider superposition inferences which the general prover would perform, and distinguish three cases, based on how many premises of the inference are from T.

Both premises are from T. Since we use a convergent term rewriting system to represent the built-in theory, we need not perform these inferences at all.

One premise is from T and the other from N. We carefully control these inferences. On the ground level, we reduce an equation until it is *sufficiently simplified*. That is, we reduce the maximal terms of both sides, and as a specialty we can also reduce the whole equation, so that the maximal term is isolated on the left-hand side and the other terms are on the right-hand side. Note that we do not arrive at a normal form, since we avoid reductions in non-maximal terms. When lifted to the non-ground level, each reduction step leads to an inference. The restriction to maximal terms allows to strengthen the ordering restrictions, so that they not only select a literal or a term in an equation, but reach inside a sum and select terms of the sum for superposition.

Both premises are from N. We may restrict inferences to those where both premises are sufficiently simplified. The selected term of these clauses doesn't have the AC-symbol $+$ at the root, hence AC-extensions are not needed. Moreover, AC-unification problems are smaller than they would be for a standard AC-prover, since only maximal terms are unified. On the other hand, we additionally need to superpose with the extensions from the symmetrization into unextended clauses. For groups it is however not necessary to superpose into extensions or to consider superpositions between two extensions.

Let us demonstrate the method by a simple example.

$$\neg(5 \cdot f(a+0) + a \approx f(a) + 3 \cdot a) \tag{1}$$
$$2 \cdot f(x) \approx x \tag{2}$$

where $f(a) \succ a \succ b \succ c$ in the reduction ordering. The clause (1) needs to be simplified. We first reduce $a+0$ to a and then we isolate all occurrences of $f(a)$ on the left-hand side.

$$\neg(4 \cdot f(a) \approx (-1) \cdot a + 3 \cdot a) \tag{3}$$

Superposition with the extension $4 \cdot f(x) \approx 2 \cdot x$ of (2) into (3) yields

$$\neg(2 \cdot a \approx (-1) \cdot a + 3 \cdot a) \tag{4}$$

which is simplified to $\neg(0 \approx 0)$ and in turn to the empty clause.

A particularly problematic case is that of variables in *top positions*, that is not below an uninterpreted function symbol. In this case the axioms give rise to variable overlaps. We develop techniques to avoid these explosive cases where possible.

[1] Our inference system specializes to the corresponding Gröbner base algorithm for the case of unconditional ground equations with a finite set of constants as the uninterpreted function symbols. Note that these constants represent the unknowns of the polynomials.

2 Preliminaries

We assume the reader is familiar with term rewriting (see Dershowitz and Jouannaud 1990) and first-order logic (see Fitting 1990). For constraints consult (Kirchner, Kirchner and Rusinowitch 1990).

Logic We use $\approx$ for syntactical equality and $=$ for equality on the meta level ($=$). Equations are multisets of two terms. In this way symmetry is built into the notation. The set of function symbols is denoted by F. For $f \in F$ we denote the arity of f by $\alpha(f)$. Let AC be the set consisting of the associativity axiom $(x+y)+z \approx x+(y+z)$ and the commutativity axiom $x + y \approx y + x$. We say s and t are *AC-equivalent*, written $s =_{AC} t$, if $AC \models s \approx t$. We let *Eq* be the set of equality axioms, consisting of reflexivity, symmetry, transitivity and the congruence axioms.

Termination orderings A strict partial ordering $\succ$ is called *monotonic* if $s \succ t$ implies $u[s] \succ u[t]$ for all contexts u and *stable under substitutions* if $s \succ t$ implies $s\sigma \succ t\sigma$ for all substitutions σ. We say that $\succ$ has the *subterm property* if $u[t] \succ t$ for any nonempty context u. A *reduction ordering* is a strict partial ordering that is well-founded, monotonic and stable under substitutions. If in addition it has the subterm property, it is called a *simplification ordering*.

An ordering is called *AC-compatible* if $s' =_{AC} s \succ t =_{AC} t'$ implies $s' \succ t'$ for all terms s, t, s' and t'. An ordering is called *total up to AC* if $s \succ t$, $t \succ s$ or $s =_{AC} t$ for all s and t.

Term rewriting modulo AC Let R be a set of rewrite rules. Then $t[l']$ *rewrites to* $t[r\sigma]$ with AC-matching, written $t[l'] \rightarrow_{AC\backslash R} t[r\sigma]$, if there exists a rule $l \rightarrow r$ in R and a substitution σ such that $l' =_{AC} l\sigma$. $\downarrow_{AC\backslash R}$ is defined as $\overset{*}{\rightarrow}_{AC\backslash R} \cdot \overset{*}{\leftrightarrow}_{AC} \cdot \overset{*}{\leftarrow}_{AC\backslash R}$. The system R is *Church-Rosser modulo AC* if $s \overset{*}{\leftrightarrow}_{AC\cup R} t$ implies $s \downarrow_{AC\backslash R} t$, and *terminating modulo AC* if there exists an AC-compatible reduction ordering that contains R. If R is both Church-Rosser and terminating modulo AC it is called *convergent modulo AC*. Given termination, it suffices to test convergence of all peaks of the forms $\leftarrow_R \cdot \rightarrow_{AC\backslash R}$ and cliffs $\leftrightarrow_{AC} \cdot \rightarrow_{AC\backslash R}$, to obtain convergence modulo AC (Jouannaud and Kirchner 1986). Convergence of cliffs is ensured by adding AC-extensions: For a rule $l \rightarrow r$ in R with $l = s + t$ its AC-extension is $x + l \rightarrow x + r$, where x is a new variable.

3 Integer Modules

To separate coefficients from ordinary terms we introduce a new sort Coef; the other terms will be of sort Term. We partition the set of function symbols F into a set F_I of *interpreted function symbols* and a set F_U of *uninterpreted function symbols*. Specifically, F_I contains the following function symbols:

$$\begin{array}{lll} 0 : \ \rightarrow \mathsf{Term} & i : \ \rightarrow \mathsf{Coef} & \text{for all } i \in \mathbb{Z} \\ + : \mathsf{Term} \times \mathsf{Term} \rightarrow \mathsf{Term} & +, \cdot : \mathsf{Coef} \times \mathsf{Coef} \rightarrow \mathsf{Coef} & \\ - : \mathsf{Term} \rightarrow \mathsf{Term} & - : \mathsf{Coef} \rightarrow \mathsf{Coef} & \end{array}$$

$$\cdot : \mathsf{Coef} \times \mathsf{Term} \rightarrow \mathsf{Term}$$

For overloaded symbols it will always be clear from the context which is meant. For Coef-multiplication we will omit the dot. Neither the rewrite system nor the clauses contain equations between Coef-terms. On the ground level only integers will occur as Coef-terms. On the non-ground level, rules and literals may contain only Coef-variables, and constraints may contain arbitrary Coef-terms. F_U contains all other function symbols

$$f_i : \mathsf{Term}^{\alpha(f_i)} \to \mathsf{Term}.$$

Since we do not want to bother about computation in $\mathbb{Z}$, we formalize it by using constrained rules $l \to r\ [\Gamma]$. On the ground level this denotes all ground instances $l\sigma \to r\sigma$ such that σ satisfies Γ. On the non-ground level the constraint will be added to the constraint on a clause when an inference is made. We will use the following term rewriting system *ZMod*:

$$-x \to v \cdot x \quad [v = -1] \tag{5}$$
$$x + 0 \to x \tag{6}$$
$$v \cdot 0 \to 0 \tag{7}$$
$$v \cdot x \to 0 \quad [v = 0] \tag{8}$$
$$v \cdot x \to x \quad [v = 1] \tag{9}$$
$$v \cdot (x + y) \to v \cdot x + v \cdot y \tag{10}$$
$$v_1 \cdot (v_2 \cdot x) \to v \cdot x \quad [v = v_1 v_2] \tag{11}$$
$$x + x \to v \cdot x \quad [v = 2] \tag{12}$$
$$y + x + x \to y + v \cdot x \quad [v = 2] \tag{12^e}$$
$$x + v_1 \cdot x \to v \cdot x \quad [v = v_1 + 1] \tag{13}$$
$$y + x + v_1 \cdot x \to y + v \cdot x \quad [v = v_1 + 1] \tag{13^e}$$
$$v_1 \cdot x + v_2 \cdot x \to v \cdot x \quad [v = v_1 + v_2] \tag{14}$$
$$y + v_1 \cdot x + v_2 \cdot x \to y + v \cdot x \quad [v = v_1 + v_2] \tag{14^e}$$

Note that *ZMod* already contains the necessary AC-extensions. The rule (5) allows to completely eliminate subtraction by negating the coefficient. Henceforth we assume that terms do not contain $-$.

We will use the following notational conventions: ϕ and ψ denote terms with an uninterpreted function symbol at the root, p, q, r, s, t and u are used for arbitrary terms, x, y and z denote variables of sort Term, and v is used for variables of sort Coef. To avoid several equivalent versions, our meta-level notation for inference rules will be modulo ACU for $+$. That is, when we write $p = c \cdot \phi + p'$ then $c \cdot \phi$ occurs somewhere in the sum, not necessarily at the front. Moreover, p' need not be present, which is to say that $p' = 0$. p may also be of the form $\phi + p'$, in this case we assume $c = 1$, or just p', where we assume $c = 0$.

4 The Termination Ordering

AC-superposition uses a total AC-compatible reduction ordering on ground terms. We additionally require that the ordering orients the rules of the built-in theory and the symmetrizations left-to-right.

Let the ordering $\succ$ on integers be defined such that $c \succ d$ if either $c > d \geq 0$ or $c < 0$ and $c < d$. We say that an ordering $\succ$ on ground terms has the *multiset property* if $\phi \succ \phi_1, \ldots, \phi_k$ implies $\phi \succ c_1 \cdot \phi_1 + \cdots + c_k \cdot \phi_k$ for all terms $\phi, \phi_1, \ldots, \phi_k$ and integers

$c_1, \ldots, c_k$. A term s is called *maximal* with respect to a term $t = c_1 \cdot t_1 + \cdots + c_k \cdot t_k$ if $s \succeq t_i$ for $i = 1, \ldots, k$. It is called *strictly maximal* if $s \succ t_i$ for $i = 1, \ldots, k$. The latter is equivalent to $s \succ t$ by the multiset property of the ordering and the subterm property. Thus the multiset property allows to isolate the maximal term of a ground equation on the left-hand side, and to use it as a rewrite rule.

Proposition 1 *There exists a simplification ordering $\succ$ that is AC-compatible, total up to AC on ground terms, that orients all ground instances of the rules in ZMod left-to-right, that orients ground equations of the form $c \cdot \phi \approx d' \cdot \phi + d \cdot r$, where $\phi \succ r$ and $c \succ d'$, left-to-right, and that has the multiset property.*

Proposition 2 *ZMod is ground convergent modulo AC.*

We extend the ordering to clauses in the usual manner: Equations (atoms) are considered as two-element multisets, a positive literal $s \approx t$ is the two-level multiset $\{\{s\}, \{t\}\}$ and a negative literal is $\{\{s, t\}\}$. A clause is the multiset of its literals. The ordering is extended accordingly.

5 Redundancy and Saturation

Since we do theorem proving with constraints we need slightly more complicated notions of redundancy for clauses and inferences, which consider only reduced instances of clauses. An instance $C\sigma$ of a clause C is called *reduced* with respect to a rewrite system R if σ is irreducible with respect to R (Nieuwenhuis and Rubio 1992, Bachmair, Ganzinger, Lynch and Snyder 1993).

The ground instance $C\sigma$ with maximal term t is called *redundant* in N (with respect to *ZMod*) if for any rewriting system R such that σ is reduced with respect to $ZMod \cup R$ there exist ground instances $C_1\sigma_1, \ldots, C_k\sigma_k$ of clauses $C_1, \ldots, C_k$ in N which are reduced with respect to $ZMod \cup R$ such that $C\sigma \succ C_i\sigma_i$ for $i = 1, \ldots, k$, and $\{C_1\sigma_1, \ldots, C_k\sigma_k\} \cup Eq \cup ZMod \models C\sigma$.

A ground inference with premises $C_1\sigma, \ldots, C_n\sigma$ and conclusion $C\sigma$ where $C_n\sigma$ is the maximal premise is called *redundant* in N (with respect to *ZMod*) if for any rewriting system R such that $C\sigma$ is reduced with respect to $ZMod \cup R$ either one of the premises $C_1\sigma, \ldots, C_n\sigma$ is redundant, or if there exist ground instances $D_1\sigma_1, \ldots, D_k\sigma_k$ of N which are reduced with respect to $ZMod \cup R$ such that $C_n\sigma \succ D_i\sigma_i$ for $i = 1, \ldots, k$ and $\{D_1\sigma_1, \ldots, D_k\sigma_k\} \cup Eq \cup ZMod \models C\sigma$. A non-ground clause or inference is redundant if all its ground instances are redundant. A set of clauses is called *saturated* with respect to an inference system C if all inferences in C from premises in N are redundant. Saturated sets are obtained by computing inferences in a fair way (see for instance Bachmair and Ganzinger 1994b).

From redundancy we derive the notion of *simplification*. A clause $C \in N$ may be simplified to a clause D if D is a logical consequence of $\{C\} \cup N$ and C is redundant with respect to *ZMod* in $\{D\} \cup N$. Here we will be mainly concerned with *simplification rules*

$$\frac{C}{D}\rightarrow$$

which express that C may be simplified to D independently of N. Their main purpose will be to simplify any ground equation to a standard form. These rules use only the theory of **Z**-modules for simplification. Standard simplification techniques can be found in the literature (e.g. Bachmair and Ganzinger 1994b) and appropriately extended.

Ground Theory Reduction $\frac{[\neg](u[l'] \approx p) \vee C}{[\neg](u[r] \approx p) \vee C}$

if $l \to r$ is a ground instance of a rule in *ZMod* and $l' =_{AC} l$.

Ground Isolation $\frac{[\neg](c \cdot \phi + p \approx d \cdot \phi + q) \vee C}{[\neg]((c-d) \cdot \phi \approx q + (-1) \cdot p) \vee C}$

if (i) $c \geq d$, and (ii) $\phi \succ p, q$.[2]

While Theory Reduction uses *ZMod* for term rewriting, Isolation may be seen as an extension of rewriting from terms to atoms.

Proposition 3 *Ground Theory Reduction and Ground Isolation are simplification rules.*

An equation $l \approx r$ is *sufficiently simplified* if either (i) $l = r = 0$, or (ii) $l \succ r$, l is irreducible with respect to *ZMod* and $l \approx r$ has one of the forms (a) $c \cdot \phi \approx r$, where $c \geq 2$, or (b) $\phi \approx r$. A literal $l \approx r$ or $l \not\approx r$ is *sufficiently simplified* if the equation $l \approx r$ is sufficiently simplified. Any ground equation or ground literal can be brought into sufficiently simplified form using Ground Theory Reduction and Ground Isolation.

6 Symmetrization

Historically, symmetrization arose first in non-abelian group theory. Le Chenadec (1984) used it also for theories like abelian groups, rings and modules. He didn't formally define the notion, but from his examples it becomes clear that the symmetrization causes critical pairs between the built-in theory and user rules to converge.

We call a rewrite system R *symmetrized* (with respect to *ZMod*) if for all peaks $p \leftarrow_{ZMod} \cdot \rightarrow_{AC\backslash R} q$ and $p \leftarrow_R \cdot \rightarrow_{AC\backslash ZMod} q$, and cliffs $p \leftrightarrow_{AC} \cdot \rightarrow_{AC\backslash R} q$ we have $p \downarrow_{AC\backslash(ZMod \cup R)} q$.

Lemma 4 *Let R be a rewrite system which is symmetrized, and let $R \subseteq (\succ)$. If for all peaks $p \leftarrow_R \cdot \rightarrow_{AC\backslash R} q$ we have $p \downarrow_{AC\backslash(ZMod \cup R)} q$ then $AC\backslash(ZMod \cup R)$ is Church-Rosser modulo AC.*

A *symmetrization function* $\mathcal{S}$ (for *ZMod*) maps each sufficiently simplified equation $l \approx r$ to a symmetrized set of rewrite rules $\mathcal{S}(l \approx r)$ such that $ZMod \cup AC \cup \{l \approx r\} \models \mathcal{S}(l \approx r)$ and $l \downarrow_{AC\backslash(ZMod \cup \mathcal{S}(l \approx r))} r$. We extend $\mathcal{S}$ to a mapping from sets of equations (or rules) to sets of rules in the standard way by $\mathcal{S}(R) = \bigcup_{l \approx r \in R} \mathcal{S}(l \approx r)$. The set of rules $\mathcal{S}(R)$ is symmetrized for any set of sufficiently simplified ground equations R. We call a rule $l' \to r'$ in $\mathcal{S}(l \to r) \setminus \{l \to r\}$ an *extension* (of $l \to r$).

[2]On the non-ground level these simplifications have more complicated side conditions, for instance one needs to check implications between constraints.

One can derive a symmetrization function by considering critical pairs between a sufficiently simplified equation and the rules in *ZMod*. Here we choose the following as our symmetrization function:

$$\mathcal{S}(c \cdot \phi \approx r) = \{d \cdot \phi \to d'' \cdot \phi + d' \cdot r \mid d = cd' + d'' \text{ and } d \succ d''\} \quad (15)$$

$$\mathcal{S}(\phi \approx r) = \{\phi \to r\} \quad (16)$$

$$\mathcal{S}(0 \approx 0) = \emptyset \quad (17)$$

Lemma 5 *$\mathcal{S}$ is a symmetrization function for ZMod.*

Intuitively, the rules replace a multiple of $c \cdot \phi$ by the corresponding multiple of r, leaving a remainder $d'' \cdot \phi$. One would like to restrict this further, so that the reduction goes in one step to the minimal remainder; that is, one would do an integer division. This is indeed possible once convergence is obtained. However, for the proofs the less restricted version is more suitable. The symmetrization is infinite in case (15), but this does not pose a problem since it is only a theoretical device. Provers don't need to explicitly construct it.

7 Constraints

Our main motivation for using constraints is to handle the coefficients. But constraints also become especially useful in our context, since they can preserve ordering constraints for terms of sums, which is particularly important if these are variables.

On the non-ground level we consider constrained clauses $C\,[\Gamma][\Delta]$ where Γ is a constraint necessary for soundness, while Δ serves only as a restriction on the inference. That distinction allows to arbitrarily weaken Δ, for instance because constraint solving may be too costly to be practical. This subsumes a wide spectrum of possible theorem proving strategies. One extreme is using no constraints at all, in that case we propagate Γ into C and discard Δ immediately after an inference. The disadvantage of this approach is that valuable information is lost, for instance which term in a sum is maximal. Also, AC-unification will in general generate many instances of C. The other extreme is to use a complete constraint solver to determine satisfiability of $\Gamma \cup \Delta$ before an inference is made. This becomes infeasible when constraints grow, since constraint solving is usually of exponential complexity in this context. An intermediate approach would be to keep the constraints, but to apply only computationally cheap operations on them, for instance by avoiding case splits. The constraint will still cut down the number of possible inferences that have to be made.

Γ cannot simply be discarded, since it is necessary for soundness of the calculus. However, we may strengthen it by moving parts of the constraint from Δ to Γ, which may result in a simpler problem. Also, solving Γ can be delayed until the empty clause is derived. At that point at least a semi-decision procedure is needed, which may be interleaved in a fair way with the computation of more inferences. Thus if Γ is satisfiable, this will eventually be discovered. Similar observations have already been made by Nieuwenhuis and Rubio (1994).

We do not discuss constraint solving in detail. For Γ one can of course enumerate substitutions and test the constraint, thereby obtaining a semi-decision procedure.[3]

[3]In practice one will try to apply better methods, for instance from nonlinear integer programming.

We have complete freedom on how to treat Δ, which allows us to take a very liberal approach to that part of the constraint language. Restrictions that were previously expressed as a side condition on the inference may become constraints, which allows to concisely express them. We have the following constraints in our language:

$s =_{AC} t$: s and t of sort Term are equal modulo AC.[4]

$c = d$: c and d of sort Coef are equal when interpreted in $\mathbb{Z}$.

$c \leq d$: c is less or equal to d, and similarly for $<$, $\geq$ and $>$.

$s \succ t$: s is greater than t in the reduction ordering $\succ$.

$\mathsf{simplified}(l, r)$: $l \approx r$ is sufficiently simplified.

$\mathsf{maximal}(u, p)$: u is the maximal term in the sum p.

$\mathsf{uninterpreted}(t)$: t has a function symbol from F_U at the root position.

Constraints are first-order formulas $\exists\phi$ where ϕ is a quantifier-free formula over this language.

8 The Inference System

As usual we assume that variables in premises are renamed. Also, no inference takes place at or below a variable position, except where explicitly noted. We assume that there exists a function on non-empty ground clauses which selects one of the literals in the clause, such that this literal is either some negative literal, or a positive literal that is maximal in the entire clause. For each inference rule we have the additional implicit restriction that the literal upon which the inference operates is selected. Other ordering restrictions, which select terms inside the literal, are made explicit.

We begin with the inference rules that result from lifting the simplification. We assume that on the non-ground level the clause is reduced, such that equations have the form $c_1 \cdot \phi_1 + \cdots + c_m \cdot \phi_m \approx c_{m+1} \cdot \phi_{m+1} + \cdots + c_n \cdot \phi_n$ where ϕ_i is either a term with an uninterpreted function symbol at the root or a variable. Theory Superposition operates only on single maximal terms, while Sum Contraction is used for those cases where the maximal term occurs more than once. We cannot avoid certain simplifications below variables in top positions; this is reflected in the Sum Contraction 2/3 and Isolation 2–4 inferences. They are necessary for those ground instances where a variable, say x, is instantiated to some irreducible term $c \cdot \phi + r$ such that ϕ is maximal.

Sum Contraction 1 $$\frac{[\neg](v_1 \cdot \phi_1 + v_2 \cdot \phi_2 + p \approx q) \vee C\,[\Gamma][\Delta]}{[\neg](v \cdot \phi_1 + p \approx q) \vee C\,[\Gamma'][\Delta']}$$

where $\Gamma' = \; v = v_1 + v_2 \wedge \phi_1 =_{AC} \phi_2 \wedge \Gamma$

and $\Delta' = \; v_1 \cdot \phi_1 + v_2 \cdot \phi_2 + p \succ q \wedge \mathsf{maximal}(\phi_1, p) \wedge \Delta$.

As said, we have analogous inference rules where v_1 or v_2 are missing. In these cases we assume $v_1 = 1$ or $v_2 = 1$, respectively, and modify the inference accordingly. The

[4] One could introduce another constraint $s =_T t$ for some theory T between AC and $ZMod$, using $s =_T t$ in Γ and $s =_{AC} t$ in Δ. This clearly is sound, since $ZMod \models T$, and complete, since it suffices to consider AC-unifiers. Thus we may use AC-complete sets of T-unifiers in our inference rules (Boudet, Contejean and Marché 1996).

inferences below are also be understood in this way.

Sum Contraction 2
$$\frac{[\neg](v_1 \cdot \phi + x + p \approx q) \vee C\,[\Gamma][\Delta]}{[\neg](v \cdot \phi + y + p \approx q) \vee C\,[\Gamma'][\Delta']}$$

where $\Gamma' = \; x =_{AC} v_2 \cdot \phi + y \wedge v = v_1 + v_2 \wedge \Gamma$
and $\Delta' = \; \phi \succ y \wedge c_1 \cdot \phi + x + p \succ q \wedge \mathsf{maximal}(\phi, p) \wedge \Delta$.

Sum Contraction 3
$$\frac{[\neg](x_1 + x_2 + p \approx q) \vee C\,[\Gamma][\Delta]}{[\neg](v \cdot z + y_1 + y_2 + p \approx q) \vee C\,[\Gamma'][\Delta']}$$

where $\Gamma' = \; x_1 =_{AC} v_1 \cdot z + y_1 \wedge x_2 =_{AC} v_2 \cdot z + y_2 \wedge v = v_1 + v_2 \wedge \Gamma$
and $\Delta' = \; z \succ y_1 \wedge z \succ y_2 \wedge x_1 + x_2 + p \succ q$
$\wedge\ \mathsf{maximal}(z, p) \wedge \mathsf{uninterpreted}(z) \wedge \Delta$.

Theory Superposition
$$\frac{[\neg](u[l] + p \approx q) \vee C\,[\Gamma][\Delta]}{[\neg](u[r] + p \approx q) \vee C\,[\Gamma'][\Delta']}$$

where $\Gamma' = \; l =_{AC} l' \wedge \Gamma'' \wedge \Gamma$, $\Delta' = \; u[l] \succ p \wedge u[l] \succ q \wedge \Delta$,
$l' \to r\ [\Gamma'']$ is a rule in *ZMod*, and u doesn't have $+$ at the root.

Isolation 1
$$\frac{[\neg](v_1 \cdot \phi_1 + p \approx v_2 \cdot \phi_2 + q) \vee C\,[\Gamma][\Delta]}{[\neg](v \cdot \phi_1 \approx q + (-1) \cdot p) \vee C\,[\Gamma'][\Delta']}$$

where $\Gamma' = \; v = v_1 - v_2 \wedge \phi_1 =_{AC} \phi_2 \wedge \Gamma$
and $\Delta' = \; v_1 \geq v_2 \wedge \phi_1 \succ p \wedge \phi_1 \succ q \wedge \mathsf{uninterpreted}(\phi_1) \wedge \Delta$.

Isolation 2
$$\frac{[\neg](v_1 \cdot \phi + p \approx x + q) \vee C\,[\Gamma][\Delta]}{[\neg](v \cdot \phi \approx y + q + (-1) \cdot p) \vee C\,[\Gamma'][\Delta']}$$

where $\Gamma' = \; x =_{AC} v_2 \cdot \phi + y \wedge v = v_1 - v_2 \wedge \Gamma$
and $\Delta' = \; v_1 \geq v_2 \wedge \phi \succ p \wedge \phi \succ y + q \wedge \mathsf{uninterpreted}(\phi) \wedge \Delta$.

Isolation 3
$$\frac{[\neg](x + p \approx v_2 \cdot \phi + q) \vee C\,[\Gamma][\Delta]}{[\neg](v \cdot \phi \approx q + (-1) \cdot (y + p)) \vee C\,[\Gamma'][\Delta']}$$

where $\Gamma' = \; x =_{AC} v_1 \cdot \phi + y \wedge v = v_1 - v_2 \wedge \Gamma$
and $\Delta' = \; v_1 \geq v_2 \wedge \phi \succ y + p \wedge \phi \succ q \wedge \mathsf{uninterpreted}(\phi) \wedge \Delta$.

Isolation 4
$$\frac{[\neg](x_1 + p \approx x_2 + q) \vee C\,[\Gamma][\Delta]}{[\neg](v \cdot z \approx y_2 + q + (-1) \cdot (y_1 + p)) \vee C\,[\Gamma'][\Delta']}$$

where $\Gamma' = \; x_1 =_{AC} v_1 \cdot z + y_1 \wedge x_2 =_{AC} v_2 \cdot z + y_2 \wedge v = v_1 - v_2 \wedge \Gamma$
and $\Delta' = \; v_1 \geq v_2 \wedge z \succ y_1 + p \wedge z \succ y_2 + q \wedge \mathsf{uninterpreted}(z) \wedge \Delta$.

The following inferences are well known from the standard superposition calculus.

Superposition
$$\frac{v_1 \cdot \phi_1 \approx r \vee D\,[\Gamma_1][\Delta_1] \qquad [\neg](p[v_2 \cdot \phi_2] \approx q) \vee C\,[\Gamma_2][\Delta_2]}{[\neg](p[v' \cdot \phi_1 + v \cdot r] \approx q) \vee C \vee D\,[\Gamma][\Delta]}$$

where $\Gamma = \; v_2 = v_1 v + v' \wedge \phi_1 =_{AC} \phi_2 \wedge \Gamma_1 \wedge \Gamma_2$
and $\Delta = \; 0 \leq v' \wedge v' < v_1 \wedge \mathsf{simplified}(v_1 \cdot \phi_1, r) \wedge \mathsf{simplified}(p, q)$
$\wedge\ \Delta_1 \wedge \Delta_2$.

Note that a constraint $\mathsf{simplified}(s, t)$ implies $s \succ t$.

On the ground level, Superposition corresponds to the reduction of a subterm by a rule in the symmetrization. We may choose the reduction so that $v\sigma$ and $v'\sigma$ are the quotient and remainder obtained by integer division of $v_1\sigma$ by $v_2\sigma$. This is reflected in the constraint $0 \leq v' \wedge v' < v_1$.

If we compare this to AC-superposition calculi we see that we have the additional restriction that both literals must be sufficiently simplified, and that we have to use extended rules only to superpose into non-extended rules. Consider two ground rules $c_1 \cdot \phi \to r_1$ and $c_2 \cdot \phi \to r_2$ which have overlapping extensions $d \cdot \phi \to d_1' \cdot \phi + d_1 \cdot r_1$ and $d \cdot \phi \to d_2' \cdot \phi + d_2 \cdot r_2$, respectively. If we assume without loss of generality that $c_1 \succeq c_2$ then already $c_1 \cdot \phi$ is reducible by some extension of $c_2 \cdot \phi \to r_2$. This overlap corresponds to an ordinary superposition inference and makes the bigger overlap redundant.[5]

Reflexivity Resolution $$\frac{p \not\approx q \vee C\,[\Gamma][\Delta]}{C'\,[p =_{AC} q \wedge \Gamma][\mathsf{simplified}(p,q) \wedge \Delta]}$$

Factoring can be restricted to sufficiently simplified clauses. Note that the constraint $\mathsf{simplified}(s, r_1)$ includes the ordering constraint $s \succ r_1$. Here $s \approx r_1$ is supposed to be the selected literal, which implies that it is maximal. Hence we have the ordering restriction $r_1 \succeq r_2$.

Factoring $$\frac{s \approx r_1 \vee t \approx r_2 \vee C''\,[\Gamma][\Delta]}{r_1 \not\approx r_2 \vee t \approx r_2 \vee C''\,[\Gamma'][\Delta']}$$

where $\Gamma' = s =_{AC} t \wedge \Gamma$
and $\Delta' = \mathsf{simplified}(s, r_1) \wedge r_1 \succeq r_2 \wedge \Delta$.

Let ZMod be the set of these inferences, let Simp be the subset of ZMod consisting of Sum Contraction, Theory Superposition and Isolation, and let Sup be the subset of ZMod consisting of Superposition.

9 Refutational Completeness

To show refutational completeness we use the model construction method of Bachmair and Ganzinger (1994b). The model construction differs in several respects from the standard one. Firstly, the built-in rewrite system *ZMod* is included to obtain the interpretation. This ensures that all interpretations are integer modules. Secondly, we have the additional restriction that a clause can be productive only if the equation it is reductive for is sufficiently simplified. Thirdly, the rewrite systems are not built from single rules but from symmetrizations of rules, which ensures that the rewrite systems themselves are symmetrized. Hence critical pairs with the built-in system converge.

A ground clause $C \vee s \approx t$ is called *reductive* for $s \approx t$ if $s \approx t \succ C$ and $s \succ t$. By $R^{\downarrow}$ we denote the set of equations provable by a rewrite proof, that is, $\{s \approx t \mid s \downarrow_{AC\backslash R} t\}$. Let N be a set of clauses. We define an interpretation I_N inductively, based on the total well-founded ordering $\succ$ on ground clauses. For any ground clause C we define the set E_C of rules produced by C, rewrite systems

[5] This restriction was motivated by the observation that Gröbner base algorithms compute only one superposition for any pair of polynomials.

R_C and R^C, and corresponding interpretations I_C and I^C, assuming that for all ground clauses $D \prec C$ the sets E_D, R_D, R^D, I_D and I^D are already defined.

$$R_C = \bigcup_{D \prec C} E_D \qquad I_C = (ZMod \cup R_C)^{\downarrow}$$

$$E_C = \begin{cases} S(l \approx r) & \text{if (i) } C = \hat{C}\sigma \text{ where } \hat{C} \in N, \text{ (ii) } \sigma \text{ is irreducible with respect to } ZMod \cup R_C, \text{ (iii) } \hat{C} = \hat{l} \approx \hat{r} \vee \hat{C}', \text{ (iv) } C = l \approx r \vee C', \text{ where } l = \hat{l}\sigma, \ r = \hat{r}\sigma \text{ and } C' = \hat{C}'\sigma, \text{ (v) } C \text{ is false in } I_C, \text{ (vi) } C \text{ is reductive for } l \approx r, \text{ (vii) } l \approx r \text{ is sufficiently simplified, (viii) } l \text{ is irreducible by } R_C,^{6} \text{ and (ix) } C' \text{ is false in } (ZMod \cup R_C \cup S(l \approx r))^{\downarrow}; \text{ or} \\ \emptyset & \text{otherwise.} \end{cases}$$

$$R^C = R_C \cup E_C \qquad I^C = (ZMod \cup R^C)^{\downarrow}$$

$$R_N = \bigcup_C E_C \qquad I_N = (ZMod \cup R_N)^{\downarrow}$$

If $E_C \neq 0$ we say C *produces* E_C, or C is *productive*.

Given the model construction, the completeness proof is obtained in a straightforward manner. Its structure is similar to other proofs obtained by this method, with the main difference that literals need to be sufficiently simplified before other inferences are applied. Since we use constraints, we show that all reduced ground instances of clauses in N are true in I_N.

Theorem 6 *Let N be a set of clauses that is saturated with respect to* ZMod *up to redundancy and that does not contain the empty clause. Then I_N is a model of $Eq \cup ZMod \cup N$.*

Proof: Since for any non-reduced ground instance $C\sigma$ we can reduce σ to some τ such that τ is reduced, and since $C\tau$ is true in $I_{C\tau}$ and hence also in I_N, we conclude that $C\sigma$ is true in I_N. □

10 Improving Superpositions at the Root Position

Consider two positive ground literals $c_1 \cdot \phi \approx r_1$ and $c_2 \cdot \phi \approx r_2$ where $c_1 \geq c_2 \geq 2$. By superposition we get the following sequence, which corresponds to the computation of the greatest common divisor by Euclid's algorithm:

$$\begin{aligned} c_1 \cdot \phi &\approx r_1 \\ c_2 \cdot \phi &\approx r_2 \\ c_3 \cdot \phi &\approx r_3 \text{ where } r_3 = r_1 + (-c_3') \cdot r_2 \\ &\vdots \\ c_n \cdot \phi &\approx r_n \text{ where } r_n = d_1 \cdot r_1 + d_2 \cdot r_2 \\ 0 &\approx r_{n+1} \end{aligned}$$

Equation number $i+2$ is obtained by superposing with equation $i+1$ into i, hence c_{i+2} is the remainder of the integer division of c_i by c_{i+1}. Finally, c_n is the greatest common

[6] Irreducibility with respect to *ZMod* is implied by (vii).

divisor of c_1 and c_2, and for d_1 and d_2 we have the property that $c = c_1d_1 + c_2d_2$. In the presence of the last two equations the other equations become redundant. Their left-hand side can be reduced by equation n such that it no longer contains the maximal term ϕ, and the resulting equation is a consequence of equation $n+1$. Note that those two equations are smaller than the equations to be shown redundant. This argument extends to clauses, since after the first superposition no new literals and unification constraints for ϕ are added. Hence we may introduce specialized superposition inferences for this case, thereby avoiding the computation of intermediate results. To formalize the notion of greatest common divisor we use an additional predicate in the constraint language:

$\mathsf{gcd}(c_1, c_2, c)$: c is the greatest common divisor of c_1 and c_2.

Then we may replace Superpositions at the top by the following inferences:

GCD Superposition 1 $$\frac{v_1 \cdot \phi_1 \approx r_1 \,\vee\, C\,[\Gamma_1][\Delta_1] \qquad v_2 \cdot \phi_2 \approx r_2 \,\vee\, D\,[\Gamma_2][\Delta_2]}{v \cdot \phi_1 \approx v_1' \cdot r_1 + v_2' \cdot r_2 \,\vee\, C \,\vee\, D\,[\Gamma][\Delta]}$$

where $\Gamma = \; v \approx v_1v_1' + v_2v_2' \wedge \phi_1 =_{AC} \phi_2 \wedge \Gamma_1 \wedge \Gamma_2$
and $\Delta = \; \mathsf{gcd}(v_1, v_2, v) \wedge \mathsf{simplified}(v_1 \cdot \phi_1, r_1) \wedge \mathsf{simplified}(v_2 \cdot \phi_2, r_2) \wedge \Delta_1 \wedge \Delta_2$.

GCD Superposition 2 $$\frac{v_1 \cdot \phi_1 \approx r_1 \,\vee\, C\,[\Gamma_1][\Delta_1] \qquad v_2 \cdot \phi_2 \approx r_2 \,\vee\, D\,[\Gamma_2][\Delta_2]}{v_1'' \cdot r_1 + v_2'' \cdot r_2 \approx r_1 \,\vee\, C \,\vee\, D\,[\Gamma][\Delta]}$$

where $\Gamma = \; v \approx v_1v_1' + v_2v_2' \wedge vv' \approx v_1 \wedge v_1'' \approx v'v_1' \wedge v_2'' \approx v'v_2' \wedge \phi_1 =_{AC} \phi_2 \wedge \Gamma_1 \wedge \Gamma_2$
and $\Delta = \; \mathsf{gcd}(v_1, v_2, v) \wedge \mathsf{simplified}(v_1 \cdot \phi_1, r_1) \wedge \mathsf{simplified}(v_2 \cdot \phi_2, r_2) \wedge \Delta_1 \wedge \Delta_2$.

Analogous inferences were used by Kandri-Rody and Kapur (1988) for the computation of Gröbner bases over a Euclidean domain and by Wang (1988) for integer module reasoning.

11 Avoiding Variable Superpositions

Variables occurring in certain contexts give rise to a particularly huge number of inferences. The most problematic case is that of variables in top positions, like x in $x + p \approx q$, where x can contain the maximal term. This happens only if the variable is not *shielded*, that is it doesn't occur below an uninterpreted function symbol somewhere else in C. In this case inferences below x are necessary, namely Sum Contraction 2/3 and Isolation 2–4. Also, variables immediately below $\cdot$ are problematic, as x in some subterm $v \cdot x$. Any productive equation $d \cdot \phi \approx r$ where $2 \leq d \leq c$ gives rise to a superposition inference with such a subterm. In this case there are also many inferences with *ZMod*, in particular with distributivity, which replaces $v \cdot x$ by $v \cdot y + v \cdot z$, and with (11), which replaces $v \cdot x$ by $v' \cdot x$ and adds a constraint $v' = vv''$.

We now investigate situations where these problems can be avoided or at least alleviated somewhat. Let us first consider the general case for unshielded variables at the top. We try to eliminate these variables by simplification. As an example consider the clause

$$4 \cdot x \not\approx a \,\vee\, 6 \cdot x \not\approx b \,\vee\, 3 \cdot x \approx c.$$

Under the assumption that x is the maximal term, it can be simplified to

$$2 \cdot x \not\approx b + (-1) \cdot a \lor 3 \cdot a \not\approx 2 \cdot b \lor x \approx a + (-1) \cdot b + c.$$

In general there remains at most one negative literal where the coefficient c on x is the greatest common divisor of the coefficients of the negative literals in the original clause. It has been used to reduce all coefficients on x in positive literals, which thus are smaller than c. If the GCD is 1, x can be eliminated completely.[7] Since x need not be maximal, one has to do a case split with respect to x being maximal or not, which can be represented by suitable constraints. Note that we cannot simplify clauses where x occurs only in positive literals in this way; take for instance $2 \cdot x \approx a \lor 3 \cdot x \approx b$.

One can carry this further if each equation $c \cdot \phi \approx r$ can be simplified to an equation $\phi \approx r'$. For instance, for fields this is possible, provided one finds a suitable r' that is smaller than ϕ. Let us for the moment consider rational coefficients. A suitable ordering would be the lexicographic combination of $>$ on the denominator and $\succ$ on the numerator, where denominators are natural numbers ≥ 1 and fractions are assumed to be reduced. The ordering obtained in this way still has all the necessary properties, and $\frac{1}{c} \cdot r$ is smaller than ϕ since r is smaller than ϕ. Since $c \neq 0$ there is no problem with zero division. So, we are allowed to divide equations by coefficients. Hence any negative literal $c \cdot x \not\approx r$ allows to eliminate x from a clause.

If additionally we know that all models are infinite, we can eliminate the positive part as well. Suppose we are given the clause $C = x \approx r_1 \lor \ldots \lor x \approx r_n \lor C'$, where x occurs neither in C' nor in any r_i, which is true in an infinite model I. Then any assignment of values in I to variables in C satisfies C. Given any assignment, since the model is infinite there exists some value in the model which is distinct from all the r_i under that assignment. If we assign this to x, leaving other variables unchanged, C' must be true under that assignment. Since x doesn't occur in C', all assignments satisfy C' and we may simplify C to C'.

Also, if all left-hand sides of rules in R_C have the form ϕ instead of $c \cdot \phi$, no overlaps with subterms of form $c \cdot x$ need to be considered.

Theorem 7 *Let T be a theory such that all models of T are infinite and for each equation $c \cdot \phi \approx r$ there exists a T-equivalent equation $\phi \approx r'$ such that $\phi \succ r'$. Then all variables in top positions can be eliminated.*

12 Relation to Previous Work

Boyer and Moore (1988) discuss a hierarchical approach, where black-box decision methods are used whenever a problem falls entirely into the domain of the built-in theory. They argue that this is too rarely the case to achieve a substantial speed-up. They propose a tighter integration of the theorem prover and the built-in theory, which is what we try to achieve with our approach.

Bachmair, Ganzinger and Stuber (1995) develop a calculus for commutative rings with a unit element. They build the calculus on top of the AC-superposition calculus (Bachmair and Ganzinger 1994a), showing that AC-superposition inferences with axioms become redundant if instead some inferences tailored to rings are made. The

[7] Actually this result can be obtained by applying ground completion to the negated clause – an instance of a standard technique.

proof technique was not strong enough to avoid certain shortcomings, namely the explicit representation of the symmetrization and the weaker notion of redundancy.

Ganzinger and Waldmann (1996) consider cancellative abelian monoids, which have a slightly weaker theory than abelian groups. Since additive inverses are in general not available in that theory, they use a notion of rewriting on equations instead of terms.

Marché (1994) builds a range of theories from AC to commutative rings into equational completion. For abelian groups what he calls symmetrization is our notion of sufficient simplification, while the first component of his normalizing pair corresponds to our notion of symmetrization. Symmetrizations are added to the set of rules explicitly. In contrast to our approach redundancy of certain inferences between symmetrizations is not proved beforehand and hence not built into the inference system. Marché doesn't compute inferences below variables; in that case the equation would not be orientable and the completion would fail. In contrast, our inference system is refutationally complete, and hence unfailing. Also, we are not restricted to equations but allow first-order clauses.

Wang (1988) uses a different approach to integer modules. The problems are restricted to Horn clauses, that is deducing one equation from a set of equations. Completeness is shown only for the case without uninterpreted function symbols.

Wertz (1992), Bachmair and Ganzinger (1994a), Nieuwenhuis and Rubio (1994), and Vigneron (1994) consider superposition calculi modulo AC, and the last three also use constraints.

13 Conclusion and Further Work

We have presented a refutationally complete superposition calculus for first-order theories that contain abelian groups or integer modules. We have also shown that certain variables in top positions can be eliminated, which limits the applicability of some particularly prolific inferences with built-in axioms.

We plan to implement the calculus as the next step. This will enable us to compare it to a standard superposition calculus as well as to an AC-calculus. It would also be interesting to try a plain abelian group calculus that uses no coefficients. At the moment it is not clear how useful the representation as an integer module is in practice for the general case of abelian groups. Part of our motivation for this approach is that we plan to develop calculi for rings and fields, where coefficients should be more useful. For instance one would want to use rational coefficients for fields.

The extension of this calculus to commutative rings with 1 reintroduces superpositions of extensions, since multiplication occurs at the root of left-hand-sides of rules. This in turn causes transitivity to hold only below certain bounds, as in the AC-case, which complicates the completeness proof. Especially in the case of isolation it is difficult to find proofs that respect that bound.

Other theories which we plan to treat in the long run are ordered structures, since most interesting examples in practice involve inequalities. This will need a combination of ideas from this work and the work on transitive relations by Bachmair and Ganzinger (1994c).

References

BACHMAIR, L. AND GANZINGER, H. (1994a). Associative-commutative superposition. In *Proc. 4th Int. Workshop on Conditional and Typed Rewriting*, Jerusalem, LNCS 968, pp. 1–14. Springer.

BACHMAIR, L. AND GANZINGER, H. (1994b). Rewrite-based equational theorem proving with selection and simplification. *Journal of Logic and Computation* **4**(3): 217–247.

BACHMAIR, L. AND GANZINGER, H. (1994c). Rewrite techniques for transitive relations. In *Proc. 9th Ann. IEEE Symp. on Logic in Computer Science*, Paris, pp. 384–393.

BACHMAIR, L., GANZINGER, H. AND STUBER, J. (1995). Combining algebra and universal algebra in first-order theorem proving: The case of commutative rings. In *Proc. 10th Workshop on Specification of Abstract Data Types*, Santa Margherita, Italy, LNCS 906.

BACHMAIR, L., GANZINGER, H., LYNCH, C. AND SNYDER, W. (1993). Basic paramodulation. Technical Report MPI-I-93-236, Max-Planck-Institut für Informatik, Saarbrücken.

BOUDET, A., CONTEJEAN, E. AND MARCHÉ, C. (1996). AC-complete unification and its application to theorem proving. This volume.

BOYER, R. S. AND MOORE, J. S. (1988). Integrating decision procedures into heuristic theorem provers: A case study of linear arithmetic. In J. E. Hayes, D. Michie and J. Richards (eds), *Machine Intelligence 11*, pp. 83–124. Clarendon Press, Oxford.

DERSHOWITZ, N. AND JOUANNAUD, J.-P. (1990). Rewrite systems. In J. van Leeuwen (ed.), *Handbook of Theoretical Computer Science: Formal Models and Semantics*, Vol. B, chapter 6, pp. 243–320. Elsevier/MIT Press.

FITTING, M. (1990). *First-Order Logic and Automated Theorem Proving*. Springer.

GANZINGER, H. AND WALDMANN, U. (1996). Theorem proving in cancellative abelian monoids. Technical Report MPI-I-96-2-001, Max-Planck-Institut für Informatik, Saarbrücken, Germany.

JOUANNAUD, J.-P. AND KIRCHNER, H. (1986). Completion of a set of rules modulo a set of equations. *SIAM Journal on Computing* **15**(4): 1155–1194.

KANDRI-RODY, A. AND KAPUR, D. (1988). Computing a Gröbner basis of a polynomial ideal over a euclidean domain. *Journal of Symbolic Computation* **6**: 19–36.

KIRCHNER, C., KIRCHNER, H. AND RUSINOWITCH, M. (1990). Deduction with symbolic constraints. *Revue Française d'Intelligence Artificielle* **4**(3): 9–52.

LE CHENADEC, P. (1984). Canonical forms in finitely presented algebras. In *Proc. 7th Int. Conf. on Automated Deduction*, Napa, CA, LNCS 170, pp. 142–165. Springer. Book version published by Pitman, London, 1986.

MARCHÉ, C. (1994). Normalised rewriting and normalised completion. In *Proc. 9th Symp. on Logic in Computer Science*, Paris, pp. 394–403. IEEE Computer Society Press.

NIEUWENHUIS, R. AND RUBIO, A. (1992). Theorem proving with ordering constrained clauses. In *11th International Conference on Automated Deduction*, Saratoga Springs, NY, LNCS 607, pp. 477–491. Springer.

NIEUWENHUIS, R. AND RUBIO, A. (1994). AC-superposition with constraints: no AC-unifiers needed. In *Proc. 12th Int. Conf. on Automated Deduction*, Nancy, France, LNCS 814, pp. 545–559. Springer.

VIGNERON, L. (1994). Associative-commutative deduction with constraints. In *Proc. 12th Int. Conf. on Automated Deduction*, Nancy, France, LNCS 814, pp. 530–544. Springer.

WANG, T. C. (1988). Elements of Z-module reasoning. In *Proc. 9th Int. Conf. on Automated Deduction*, Argonne, LNCS 310, pp. 21–40. Springer.

WERTZ, U. (1992). First-order theorem proving modulo equations. Technical Report MPI-I-92-216, Max-Planck-Institut für Informatik, Saarbrücken.

Symideal Gröbner Bases

Manfred Göbel

Wilhelm-Schickard-Institut für Informatik
Sand 13, 72076 Tübingen, Germany
E-mail: goebel@informatik.uni-tuebingen.de

Abstract. This paper presents a completion technique for a set of polynomials in $K[X_1, \ldots, X_n]$ which is closed under addition and under multiplication with symmetric polynomials as well as a solution for the corresponding membership problem. Our algorithmic approach is based on a generalization of a novel rewriting technique for the computation of bases for rings of permutation-invariant polynomials.

1 Introduction

In [3, 4], the author presents a generalization of the classical algorithm for symmetric polynomials (see [1], section 10.7, or [8], section 1.1) to the class of permutation groups. By a novel rewriting technique, any G-invariant polynomial f of the ring of G-invariant polynomials $R[X_1, \ldots, X_n]^G$ can be represented as a finite linear combination of the elements of a basis B with symmetric polynomials as coefficients. The algorithm works independently of the given ground ring R and the basis B contains only G-invariant polynomials of maximal variable degree $\leq \max\{1, n-1\}$ and total degree $\leq \max\{n, n(n-1)/2\}$, independent of the size of the given permutation group $G \subseteq S_n$, where S_n denotes the symmetric group. We refer to [3], which we adopt here as a starting point.

The integration and generalization of the rewriting technique within a completion algorithm is the subject of this paper. A symideal $S \subseteq R[X_1, \ldots, X_n]$ is a set of polynomials which is closed under addition and under multiplication with symmetric polynomials, or in other words, a $R[X_1, \ldots, X_n]^{S_n}$-submodule of $R[X_1, \ldots, X_n]$. Special cases of symideals are ideals, and rings of permutation-invariant polynomials. We present an algorithmic solution for the symideal membership problem in $K[X_1, \ldots, X_n]$ based on the reduction approach in [3] and obtain – as a by-product – a characterization of unique reduced bases of $K[X_1, \ldots, X_n]^G$. Our algorithm is strongly related to the classical and well-known completion techniques of Buchberger [2] for systems of polynomials and of Knuth-Bendix [5] for term rewriting systems [7]. The algorithms have been implemented in the computer algebra system MAS [6].

The plan of our work is as follows: Section 2 presents the basic definitions and presents a traditional solution for the symideal membership problem. Section 3 deals with divisors and least common multiples and Section 4 describes how polynomials are reduced. Section 5 proves existence and uniqueness for symideal Gröbner bases and Section 6 deals with the construction of symideal Gröbner bases and presents a list of examples.

2 Basics

Let $\mathbb{N}$ and $\mathbb{Q}$ be the set of the natural and rational numbers, respectively. Let R (K) be an arbitrary commutative ring (field) with 1, let $R[X_1,\ldots,X_n]$ be the commutative polynomial ring over R in the indeterminates X_i, let T be the set of terms (= power-products of the X_i) in $R[X_1,\ldots,X_n]$, let $M = \{at \mid a \in R, t \in T\}$ be the set of monomials in $R[X_1,\ldots,X_n]$, and let $T(f)$, $M(f)$ be the set of terms and monomials occurring in $f \in R[X_1,\ldots,X_n]$ with non-zero coefficients, respectively. $AO(T)$ denote the set of all admissible orders on T. In the following, we fix $<_{lex}$ as the lexicographical order on T.

G denotes any permutation group operating on the n indeterminates $X_1,\ldots,X_n$. Any $\pi \in G$ extends in a unique way to an endomorphism of the R-algebra $R[X_1,\ldots,X_n]$ defined by $\pi(f) := f(\pi(X_1),\pi(X_2),\ldots,\pi(X_n))$. $f \in R[X_1,\ldots,X_n]$ is G-invariant, if $f = \pi(f)$ for all $\pi \in G$. $R[X_1,\ldots,X_n]^G$ denotes the R-algebra of G-invariant polynomials in $R[X_1,\ldots,X_n]$, $orbit_G(t) = \sum_{s\in\{\pi(t)|\pi\in G\}} s$ the G-invariant orbit of $t \in T$, and $\sigma_1, \ldots, \sigma_n$ the elementary symmetric polynomials.

$Sy(F) = \{\sum_{f\in F} p_f(\sigma_1,\ldots,\sigma_n)\cdot f \mid p_f \in R[X_1,\ldots,X_n]\}$ denote the (finitely generated) symideal from $F \subseteq R[X_1,\ldots,X_n]$ (finite). In the rest of this section, we present a traditional solution for the membership problem $f \in Sy(f_1,\ldots,f_l)$ with f, f_1, $\ldots f_l \in K[X_1,\ldots,X_n]$ by the computation of Gröbner bases for modules.

The set $\mathcal{M} = \{X_1^{e_1}\ldots X_n^{e_n} \mid 0 \le e_i < i\}$ generate $R[X_1,\ldots,X_n]$ as a free $R[X_1,\ldots,X_n]^{S_n}$-module of finite rank $n!$ (see [8], proposition 2.7.8 and theorem 2.7.9). Let $s_1,\ldots s_{n!}$ be an enumeration of the elements of $\mathcal{M}$, and let $(K[X_1,\ldots,X_n])^m$ be the m-fold Cartesian product, which consists of all m-tuples of elements of $K[X_1,\ldots,X_n]$. To solve the membership problem, we proceed as follows: First, we compute $(p_{i1},\ldots,p_{in!}) \in (K[X_1,\ldots,X_n])^{n!}$ such that $f_i = \sum_{j=1}^{n!} p_{ij}(\sigma_1,\ldots,\sigma_n)\cdot s_j$ for $1 \le i \le l$, and $(q_1,\ldots,q_{n!}) \in (K[X_1,\ldots,X_n])^{n!}$ such that $f = \sum_{j=1}^{n!} q_j(\sigma_1,\ldots,\sigma_n)\cdot s_j$ (see [8], theorem 1.2.7 and proof of theorem 2.7.9). And second, we calculate a reduced Gröbner basis G for the set $\{(p_{i1},\ldots,p_{in!}) \mid 1 \le i \le l\}$ (see [1], section 10.4). Then we obtain $f \in Sy(f_1,\ldots,f_l)$ iff the normal form of $(q_1,\ldots,q_{n!})$ modulo G is $(0,\ldots,0)$.

Note that to save storage, the components $p_{ij} = 0$ for all $1 \le i \le l$ can be ignored during the computation of the Gröbner basis G. If $p_{ij} = 0$ for all $1 \le i \le l$ and $q_j \ne 0$ for a $1 \le j \le n!$, then $f \notin Sy(f_1,\ldots,f_l)$.

3 Divisors and Least Common Multiples

This section introduces a divisibility relation and least common multiples.

Definition 1. Let $t \in T$ and let $\pi \in S_n$ such that $\pi(t) = X_1^{e_1}\ldots X_n^{e_n}$ and $e_1 \ge e_2 \ge \ldots \ge e_n$. Then $desc(t) = \pi(t)$ is the descending term of t and the polynomial $\Omega(t) = \sigma_1^{e_1-e_2}\ldots\sigma_{n-1}^{e_{n-1}-e_n}\sigma_n^{e_n}$ is the elementary symmetric product of t. π is not necessarily unique, but $desc(t)$ is uniquely determined by t.

Lemma 2. *Let $t \in T$. Then $a \cdot t \in M(\Omega(t))$ with $a = 1$, i.e. t occurs always with coefficient 1 in the polynomial $\Omega(t)$.* *Proof: See [3], lemma 3.3.*

Lemma 3. *Let $t_1, t_2 \in T$ and $\pi \in S_n$ with $X_1^{d_1} \ldots X_n^{d_n} = \pi(t_1) = desc(t_1)$ and $X_1^{e_1} \ldots X_n^{e_n} = \pi(t_2) = desc(t_2)$. Then $\Omega(t_1 t_2) = \Omega(t_1) \cdot \Omega(t_2)$.*

Proof. We have $\Omega(t_1 t_2) = \Omega(desc(t_1 t_2))$ and so

$$\begin{aligned}\Omega(t_1t_2) &= \Omega(\pi(t_1t_2)) = \Omega(\pi(t_1)\pi(t_2)) = \Omega(X_1^{d_1+e_1} \ldots X_n^{e_n+d_n}) \\ &= \sigma_1^{d_1+e_1-(d_2+e_2)} \ldots \sigma_n^{d_n+e_n} = \sigma_1^{d_1-d_2} \ldots \sigma_n^{d_n} \cdot \sigma_1^{e_1-e_2} \ldots \sigma_n^{e_n} \\ &= \Omega(\pi(t_1)) \cdot \Omega(\pi(t_2)) = \Omega(desc(t_1)) \cdot \Omega(desc(t_2)) = \Omega(t_1) \cdot \Omega(t_2).\end{aligned}$$

Definition 4. Let $t = X_1^{e_1} \ldots X_n^{e_n}$ be non-special and maximal $(k_1, \ldots, k_n)$-connected w.r.t. the multiset $\mathcal{I} = \{I_0, \ldots, I_r\}$ (cf. [3], definition 3.8) and let $\mathcal{J} \subseteq \mathcal{I}$. Then the $\mathcal{J}$-reduced term of t is defined as $Red^{\mathcal{J}}(t) = X_1^{d_1} \ldots X_n^{d_n}$ with $d_i = e_i - k$, if k different elements of $\mathcal{J}$ contain i.

Lemma 5. *Let t be maximal $(k_1, \ldots, k_n)$-connected w.r.t. $\mathcal{I}_t$ and let $s = Red^{\mathcal{J}}(t)$ be maximal $(l_1, \ldots, l_n)$-connected w.r.t. $\mathcal{I}_s$. Then $l_i \leq k_i$ for $1 \leq i \leq n$.*

Proof. We have $\mathcal{I}_s = \mathcal{I}_t \setminus \mathcal{J}$ and so $l_i \leq k_i$ for $1 \leq i \leq n$.

Lemma 6. *Let $t = X_1^{e_1} \ldots X_n^{e_n}$ be non-special and maximal $(k_1, \ldots, k_n)$-connected w.r.t. $\mathcal{I}$, let $\mathcal{J} \subseteq \mathcal{I}$ and let $u \in T$ such that $t = u \cdot Red^{\mathcal{J}}(t)$. Then for all $s \in T(\Omega(u)Red^{\mathcal{J}}(t) - t)$ the following holds: $desc(t) >_{lex} desc(s)$*

Proof. This is a consequence of Definition 4 (see also [3], lemma 3.7 and lemma 3.10). Only the term $u \in T(\Omega(u))$ is equal to the power product of the variables belonging to the indices in the index sets of $\mathcal{J}$. And so $desc(t) >_{lex} desc(s)$ holds for all other terms $s \in T(\Omega(u)Red^{\mathcal{J}}(t) - t)$.

Definition 7. Let t be maximal $(k_1, \ldots, k_n)$-connected w.r.t. $\mathcal{I}$. Then $v \in T$ is a special divisor of t, if there exists a $\mathcal{J} \subseteq \mathcal{I}$ such that $v = Red^{\mathcal{J}}(t)$.

Example 1. Let $t = X_1^5 X_2^6 X_4^3$ be maximal $(0, 1, 2, 0)$-connected w.r.t. $\mathcal{I} = \{\{1, 2\}, \{1, 2, 4\}, \{1, 2, 4\}\}$ and let $\mathcal{J} = \{\{1, 2\}, \{1, 2, 4\}\}$. Then $X_1^3 X_2^4 X_4^2 = Red^{\mathcal{J}}(t)$ is a special divisor of t.

Lemma 8. *Let $v, t \in T$ such that v is a special divisor of t and let $t = u \cdot v$. Then for all $s \in T(\Omega(u)v - t)$ the following holds: $desc(t) >_{lex} desc(s)$*

Proof. This is a consequence of Lemma 6 and Definition 7.

Dickson's lemma (cf. [1], corollary 4.48 and theorem 5.2) states that the natural partial order on $\mathbb{N}^n$ has the Dickson property (cf. [1], definition 4.39). The following is a variant of Dickson's lemma which is suitable for our rewriting technique.

Lemma 9. *Let $\emptyset \neq S \subseteq T$. Then there exists a finite divisibility basis $B \subset S$ such that for all $s \in S$, there exists a $t \in B$ with t is a special divisor of s.*

Proof. Let U be the finite set of special terms, let $u \in U$ and let V_u be the set of all $s \in S$ maximal $(k_{s1}, \ldots, k_{sn})$-connected w.r.t. $\mathcal{I}_s$ such that $u = Red^{\mathcal{I}_s}(s)$. Furthermore, let $W_u = \{(k_{s1}, \ldots, k_{sn}) \mid s \in V_u\}$. W_u has a Dickson basis $(k_{u_1 1}, \ldots, k_{u_1 n}), \ldots, (k_{u_r 1}, \ldots, k_{u_r n})$ (see [1], corollary 4.48). And so V_u has the finite divisibility basis $\{t_{u1}, \ldots, t_{ur}\}$ by Lemma 5. Hence the finite union of the Dickson bases for all V_u, $u \in U$ is a Dickson basis of S.

Definition 10. Let $t_1, t_2 \in T$. Then $t_1 \prec t_2$, if $desc(t_1) <_{lex} desc(t_2)$, or $(desc(t_1) = desc(t_2)$ and $t_1 <_{lex} t_2)$.

There exists no infinite chain $t_1, t_2, \ldots \in T$ with $t_i \succ t_{i+1}$ for all $i \in \mathbb{N}$. The relation $\prec$ induces a total order on T and – in a natural way – a linear quasi-order $\prec$ on $R[X_1, \ldots, X_n]$: $f \prec g$ iff there exists $t \in T(g) \setminus T(f)$ such that for all $\hat{t} \succ t$, $\hat{t} \in T(f)$ iff $\hat{t} \in T(g)$. The induced quasi-order on $R[X_1, \ldots, X_n]$ is well-founded.

Lemma 11. *Let $t_1 \neq t_2 \in T$ such that t_2 is a special divisor of t_1. Then $t_2 \prec t_1$.*

Proof. This is a consequence of Definition 7.

Definition 12. Let $f \in R[X_1, \ldots, X_n]$. Then $HT_\prec(f)$, $HC_\prec(f)$ and $HM_\prec(f)$ denotes the highest term, coefficient and monomial of f w.r.t. $\prec$.

Lemma 13. *Let $1 \neq t \in T$ and let $t_1, t_2, u \in T$. Then (1) $1 \prec t$ and (2) $t_1 \prec t_2$ implies $HT_\prec(\Omega(u)t_1) \prec HT_\prec(\Omega(u)t_2)$.*

Proof. (1) $desc(1) <_{lex} desc(t)$ and so $1 \prec t$. (2) Choose $s_2 \in T(\Omega(u))$ such that $s_2 t_2$ is maximal w.r.t. $\prec$. If $desc(t_1) <_{lex} desc(t_2)$, then $desc(s_1 t_1) <_{lex} desc(s_2 t_2)$ for all $s_1 \in T(\Omega(u))$. If $desc(t_1) = desc(t_2)$ and $t_1 <_{lex} t_2$, then either $desc(s_1 t_1) <_{lex} desc(s_2 t_2)$, or $desc(s_1 t_1) = desc(s_2 t_2)$ and $s_1 t_1 <_{lex} s_2 t_2$ for all $s_1 \in T(\Omega(u))$. And so $HT_\prec(\Omega(u)t_1) \prec HT_\prec(\Omega(u)t_2)$.

In order to generalize our special divisor relation, we have to understand the relation between t and $HT_\prec(\Omega(u)t)$ for any $t, u \in T$. The following lemma and definition will prepare us for a theorem clarifying this context.

Lemma 14. *Let $t \in T$ and let $\Pi = \{\phi \in S_n \mid \phi^{-1}(t) = desc(t)\}$. Then there exists a unique $\pi \in \Pi$ such that for all $\phi \in \Pi$ and $1 \leq i \leq n$ the following holds: $\pi(X_1 \ldots X_i) \geq_{lex} \phi(X_1 \ldots X_i)$*

Proof. Let $t = X_1^{d_1} \ldots X_n^{d_n}$, let $X_1^{e_1} \ldots X_n^{e_n} = desc(t)$, let $I = \{1, \ldots, n\}$, let $k_j = \min\{k \mid k \in I \setminus \bigcup_{l<j}\{k_l\}, e_j = d_k\}$ for $1 \leq j \leq n$ and let $\pi = \begin{pmatrix} 1 & 2 & \ldots & n \\ k_1 & k_2 & \ldots & k_n \end{pmatrix}$. Then by construction $\pi(X_1 \ldots X_i) \geq_{lex} \phi(X_1 \ldots X_i)$ for all $\phi \in \Pi$ and $1 \leq i \leq n$. The uniqueness of π is obvious.

Definition 15. Let $t \in T$, let $\Pi = \{\phi \in S_n \mid X_1^{e_1} \dots X_n^{e_n} = \phi^{-1}(t) = desc(t)\}$ and let $\pi \in \Pi$ such that $\pi(X_1 \dots X_i) \geq_{lex} \phi(X_1 \dots X_i)$ for all $\phi \in \Pi$ and $1 \leq i \leq n$. Then t is $(e_1 - e_2, \dots, e_{n-1} - e_n, e_n)$-multilinear w.r.t. ($\pi(X_1)$, $\pi(X_1X_2)$, ..., $\pi(X_1 \dots X_n)$).

Example 2. Let $t = X_1X_2^3X_5^6$. Then t is $(3,2,1,0,0)$-multilinear w.r.t. (X_5, X_2X_5, $X_1X_2X_5$, $X_1X_2X_3X_5$, $X_1X_2X_3X_4X_5$).

Lemma 16. *Let t be $(k_{i1}, \dots, k_{in})$-multilinear w.r.t. $(s_{i1}, \dots, s_{in})$, $i \in \{1,2\}$. Then $s_{1j} = s_{2j}$ and $k_{1j} = k_{2j}$ for all $1 \leq j \leq n$. Furthermore, the maximal variable (total) degree of t is $\sum_{j=1}^n k_{1j}$ $(\sum_{j=1}^n jk_{1j})$ and $t = s_{11}^{k_{11}} \dots s_{1n}^{k_{1n}}$.*

Proof. This is a consequence of Lemma 14 and Definition 15.

Theorem 17. *Let t be $(k_1, \dots, k_n)$-multilinear w.r.t. S and let $u \in T$ with $X_1^{e_1} \dots X_n^{e_n} = desc(u)$. Then $HT_\prec(\Omega(u)t)$ is $(k_1 + e_1 - e_2, \dots, k_{n-1} + e_{n-1} - e_n, k_n + e_n)$-multilinear w.r.t. S.*

Proof. Let $S = (s_1, \dots, s_n)$. By Definition 15, $s_i \in T(\sigma_i)$ for $1 \leq i \leq n$ and

$$\begin{aligned} HT_\prec(\Omega(u)t) &= HT_\prec(\sigma_1^{e_1-e_2} \dots \sigma_n^{e_n} \cdot s_1^{k_1} \dots s_n^{k_n}) \\ &= s_1^{e_1-e_2} \dots s_{n-1}^{e_{n-1}-e_n} s_n^{e_n} \cdot s_1^{k_1} \dots s_n^{k_n} \\ &= s_1^{k_1+e_1-e_2} \dots s_{n-1}^{k_{n-1}+e_{n-1}-e_n} s_n^{k_n+e_n}. \end{aligned}$$

Furthermore, $e_i - e_{i+1} \geq 0$ for all $1 \leq i < n$. And so $HT_\prec(\Omega(u)t)$ must be $(k_1 + e_1 - e_2, \dots, k_{n-1} + e_{n-1} - e_n, k_n + e_n)$-multilinear w.r.t. S.

Example 3. X_3^2 is $(2,0,0)$-multilinear w.r.t. $S = (X_3, X_1X_3, X_1X_2X_3)$ and so $X_1X_3^4 = HT_\prec(\Omega(X_1^2X_2)X_3^2)$ is $(3,1,0)$-multilinear w.r.t. S.

Corollary 18. *Let t_i be $(k_1, \dots, k_n)$-multilinear w.r.t. S_i, $i \in \{1,2\}$ with $S_1 \neq S_2$. Then there exists no $u \in T$ such that $t_1 = HT_\prec(\Omega(u)t_2)$. (This is a consequence of Theorem 17.)*

Lemma 19. *Let t_i be $(k_{i1}, \dots, k_{in})$-multilinear w.r.t. $S = (s_1, \dots, s_n)$, $i \in \{1,2\}$ with $k_{1j} \geq k_{2j}$ for all $1 \leq j \leq n$ and let $u = s_1^{k_{11}-k_{21}} \dots s_n^{k_{1n}-k_{2n}}$. Then $t_1 = ut_2$ and $t_1 = HT_\prec(\Omega(u)t_2)$.*

Proof. By Lemma 16, we have $s_1^{k_{11}} \dots s_n^{k_{1n}} = s_1^{k_{11}-k_{21}} \dots s_n^{k_{1n}-k_{2n}} \cdot s_1^{k_{21}} \dots s_n^{k_{2n}}$. and so $t_1 = ut_2$. Furthermore, $desc(u) = X_1^{\sum_{j=1}^n k_{1j}-k_{2j}} \dots X_n^{\sum_{j=n}^n k_{1j}-k_{2j}}$ and so $t_1 = HT_\prec(\Omega(u)t_2)$ by Theorem 17.

Definition 20. Let t_i be $(k_{i1}, \dots, k_{in})$-multilinear w.r.t. $S = (s_1, \dots, s_n)$, $i \in \{1,2\}$. Then t_2 is a divisor of t_1 w.r.t. symmetry, if $t_1 = s_1^{k_{11}-k_{21}} \dots s_n^{k_{1n}-k_{2n}} t_2$. (Notation: $t_2 \mid_{S_n} t_1$)

Example 4. 1. $t_1 = X_1^5X_2^6X_4^3$ is $(1,2,3,0)$-multilinear w.r.t. $S = (X_2, X_1X_2, X_1X_2X_4, X_1X_2X_3X_4)$ and $t_2 = X_1^3X_2^4X_4^2$ is $(1,1,2,0)$-multilinear w.r.t. S. Then $t_1 = (X_1X_2)(X_1X_2X_4)t_2$ and so $t_2 \mid_{S_n} t_1$.

2. $t_1 = X_1^2X_2$ is $(1,1,0)$-multilinear w.r.t. $S = (X_1,\ X_1X_2,\ X_1X_2X_3)$ and $t_2 = X_1$ is $(1,0,0)$-multilinear w.r.t. S. Then $t_1 = (X_1X_2)t_2$ and so $t_2 \mid_{S_n} t_1$. (t_2 is not a special divisor of t_1.)
3. $t_1 = X_1^2X_2^3$ is $(1,2)$-multilinear w.r.t. $S = (X_2, X_1X_2)$ and $t_2 = X_1X_2^3$ is $(2,1)$-multilinear w.r.t. S. Then $t_1 \neq (X_2)^{l_1}(X_1X_2)^{l_2}t_2$ for all $l_1, l_2 \in \mathbb{N}$ and so $t_2 \not\mid_{S_n} t_1$.

Definition 20 is also justified by the following observation.

Lemma 21. *Let $u \in T$ and let t_i be $(k_{i1},\ldots,k_{in})$-multilinear w.r.t. S, $i \in \{1,2\}$ such that $t_2 \mid_{S_n} t_1$ and $t_1 = ut_2$. Then for all $s \in T(\Omega(u)t_2 - t_1)$ the following holds: $t_1 \succ s$*

Proof. By Lemma 19, we have $t_1 = HT_{\prec}(\Omega(u)t_2)$ and so $t_1 \succ s$ holds for all $s \in T(\Omega(u)t_2 - t_1)$.

Lemma 22. *Let $t_1, t_2 \in T$ such that t_2 is a special divisor of t_1. Then $t_2 \mid_{S_n} t_1$, i.e. Definition 20 subsumes Definition 7.*

Proof. Let t_1 be $(k_{11},\ldots,k_{1n})$-multilinear w.r.t. $S = (s_1,\ldots,s_n)$. As a consequence of Definition 7, t_2 must be $(k_{21},\ldots,k_{2n})$-multilinear w.r.t. S and $t_1 = s_1^{k_{11}-k_{21}} \ldots s_n^{k_{1n}-k_{2n}} t_2$ and so $t_2 \mid_{S_n} t_1$.

Remark. The relation $\mid_{S_n}$ induces a partial order on T.

Lemma 23. *Let $u, t_1 \in T$, let t_2 be $(k_1,\ldots,k_n)$-multilinear w.r.t. $S = (s_1,\ldots,s_n)$ such that $t_1 = HT_{\prec}(\Omega(u)t_2)$ and let $X_1^{e_1}\ldots X_n^{e_n} = desc(u)$. Then $t_2 \mid_{S_n} t_1$ and $\Omega(u) = \Omega(s_1^{e_1-e_2}\ldots s_{n-1}^{e_{n-1}-e_n} s_n^{e_n})$.*

Proof. By Theorem 17, t_1 is $(k_1+e_1-e_2,\ldots,k_{n-1}+e_{n-1}-e_n, k_n+e_n)$ -multilinear w.r.t. S and $t_1 = s_1^{e_1-e_2}\ldots s_{n-1}^{e_{n-1}-e_n} s_n^{e_n} t_2$ and so $t_2 \mid_{S_n} t_1$. Furthermore, $desc(s_1^{e_1-e_2}\ldots s_n^{e_n}) = X_1^{e_1}\ldots X_n^{e_n}$ and so $\Omega(u) = \Omega(s_1^{e_1-e_2}\ldots s_{n-1}^{e_{n-1}-e_n} s_n^{e_n})$.

Definition 24. Let $t, t_1, t_2 \in T$. Then t is the least common multiple of t_1 and t_2 w.r.t. symmetry, if $t_1 \mid_{S_n} t$ and $t_2 \mid_{S_n} t$, and $t \mid_{S_n} u$ whenever $t_1 \mid_{S_n} u$ and $t_2 \mid_{S_n} u$ for $u \in T$. (Notation: $lcm_{S_n}(t_1,t_2)$)

Remark. There exists no least common multiple for t_i $(k_{i1},\ldots,k_{in})$-multilinear w.r.t. S_i, $i \in \{1,2\}$ with $S_1 \neq S_2$.

Lemma 25. *Let t_i be $(k_{i1},\ldots,k_{in})$-multilinear w.r.t. $S = (s_1,\ldots,s_n)$, $i \in \{1,2\}$ and let $k_j = max\{k_{1j}, k_{2j}\}$ for $1 \leq j \leq n$. Then $lcm_{S_n}(t_1,t_2) = s_1^{k_1}\ldots s_n^{k_n}$.*

Proof. Let $t = s_1^{k_1}\ldots s_n^{k_n}$. Assume for a contradiction that $t \neq \hat{t} = lcm_{S_n}(t_1,t_2)$ is $(\hat{k}_1,\ldots,\hat{k}_n)$-multilinear w.r.t. S. By Definition 24, we must have $\hat{t} \mid_{S_n} t$ and so $\hat{k}_j < k_j$ for a $1 \leq j \leq n$. Hence $\hat{k}_j < k_{1j}$ or $\hat{k}_j < k_{2j}$, i.e. $t_1 \not\mid_{S_n} \hat{t}$ or $t_2 \not\mid_{S_n} \hat{t}$ (contradiction).

Corollary 26. *Let $t_1, t_2 \in T$. Then the least common multiple of t_1 and t_2 exists, if $HT_{\prec}(\Omega(u_1)t_1) = HT_{\prec}(\Omega(u_2)t_2)$ for some $u_1, u_2 \in T$. (This is a consequence of Theorem 17 and Lemma 23.)*

4 Polynomial Reductions for Symideals

This section presents a normal form algorithm for symideals and proves some properties of the reduction relation.

Definition 27. Let $f, g, p \in K[X_1, \ldots, X_n]$ with $f, p \neq 0$ and let P be a subset of $K[X_1, \ldots, X_n]$. Then we say "f reduces to g modulo p by eliminating t" (Notation: $f \xrightarrow[p]{} g\,[t]$), if for a $t \in T(f)$, there exists $s \in T$ with $t = s \cdot HT_{\prec}(p)$, $HT_{\prec}(p) \mid_{S_n} t$, and $g = f - \frac{a}{HC_{\prec}(p)} \cdot \Omega(s) \cdot p$ where a is the coefficient of t in f, and "f reduces to g modulo p" (Notation: $f \xrightarrow[p]{} g$), if $f \xrightarrow[p]{} g\,[t]$ for some $t \in T(f)$. "f reduces to g modulo P" (Notation: $f \xrightarrow[P]{} g$), if $f \xrightarrow[p]{} g$ for some $p \in P$, and "f is reducible modulo P", if f reduces to g modulo P for some $g \in K[X_1, \ldots, X_n]$.

If f is not reducible modulo P then we say f is in normal form modulo P. A normal form of f modulo P is a polynomial g that is in normal form modulo P and satisfies $f \xrightarrow[P]{*} g$ where $\xrightarrow[P]{*}$ is the reflexive-transitive closure of $\xrightarrow[P]{}$. We call $f \xrightarrow[p]{} g\,[t]$ a top-reduction of f, if $t = HT_{\prec}(f)$; whenever a top-reduction of f exists (with $p \in P$), we say that f is top-reducible modulo p (modulo P). $\xleftrightarrow[P]{}$ denotes the symmetric closure of $\xrightarrow[P]{}$, i.e. $f \xleftrightarrow[P]{} g$ iff $f \xrightarrow[P]{} g$ or $g \xrightarrow[P]{} f$, and $\xleftrightarrow[P]{*}$ denotes the reflexive-transitive closure of $\xleftrightarrow[P]{}$. $f \downarrow_P g$ iff $f \xrightarrow[P]{*} h$ and $g \xrightarrow[P]{*} h$ for some $h \in K[X_1, \ldots, X_n]$.

Theorem 28. *Let $P \subseteq K[X_1, \ldots, X_n]$. Then the relation $\xrightarrow[P]{}$ is a noetherian reduction relation on $K[X_1, \ldots, X_n]$.*

Proof. $\prec$ is well-founded. It suffices to show that $f \xrightarrow[P]{} g$ implies $f \succ g$ for $f, g \in K[X_1, \ldots, X_n]$. This is a consequence of Definition 20, Lemma 21 and Definition 27.

Lemma 29. *Let $P \subset K[X_1, \ldots, X_n]$ finite and let $f \in K[X_1, \ldots, X_n]$. Then there exists an algorithm to compute a normal form $g \in K[X_1, \ldots, X_n]$ of f modulo P. (Notation: $normalform_{S_n}(f, P)$)* *Proof: See [4], lemma 5.36.*

The reduction relation for symideals corresponds in a natural way to the reduction relation for ideals. This will be shown in the rest of this section.

Lemma 30. *Let $h \in K[X_1, \ldots, X_n]^{S_n}$ and let $f \in K[X_1, \ldots, X_n]$. Then $HT_{\prec}(hf) = HT_{\prec}(\Omega(u)f)$ for some $u \in T(h)$.*

Proof. We have $HT_{\prec}(hf) = u \cdot HT_{\prec}(f)$ for some $u \in T(h)$. Let $HT_{\prec}(f)$ be $(k_1, \ldots, k_n)$-multilinear w.r.t. $(s_1, \ldots, s_n)$ and let $X_1^{e_1} \ldots X_n^{e_n} = desc(u)$. Then $u = s_1^{e_1 - e_2} \ldots s_{n-1}^{e_{n-1} - e_n} s_n^{e_n}$ and

$$\begin{aligned} HT_{\prec}(\Omega(u)f) &\overset{L.13}{=} HT_{\prec}(\Omega(u) HT_{\prec}(f)) \\ &= HT_{\prec}(\sigma_1^{e_1 - e_2} \ldots \sigma_n^{e_n} \cdot s_1^{k_1} \ldots s_n^{k_n}) \\ &= s_1^{e_1 - e_2} \ldots s_n^{e_n} \cdot s_1^{k_1} \ldots s_n^{k_n} = u \cdot HT_{\prec}(f) = HT_{\prec}(hf). \end{aligned}$$

Lemma 31. *Let $f \in P \subseteq K[X_1, \ldots, X_n]$ and let $h \in K[X_1, \ldots, X_n]^{S_n}$. Then $hf \xrightarrow[P]{*} 0$.*

Proof. Assume that $H = \{h \in K[X_1, \ldots, X_n]^{S_n} \mid \text{not}\, hf \xrightarrow[P]{*} 0\}$ is non-empty. Then H contains a minimal element $h \neq 0$ w.r.t. $\prec$. We obtain $HT_{\prec}(hf) = HT_{\prec}(\Omega(s)f)$ for some $s \in T(h)$ by Lemma 30 and so $hf \xrightarrow[f]{} hf - c\Omega(s)f = \hat{h}f$ for some $c \in K$. We have $\hat{h} \notin H$ since $\hat{h} \prec h$ and so $\hat{h}f \xrightarrow[P]{} 0$. It follows that $hf \xrightarrow[P]{*} 0$ (contradiction).

Lemma 32. *Let $P \subseteq K[X_1, \ldots, X_n] \ni f$ such that $f \xrightarrow[P]{*} 0$ and let $a \in K$ and $u \in T$. Then $a\Omega(u)f \xrightarrow[P]{*} 0$.*

Proof. Let $F = \{f \in K[X_1, \ldots, X_n] \mid f \xrightarrow[P]{*} 0\}$ and fix w.l.o.g. a descending $u \in T$. Assume for a contradiction that $F_u = \{f \in F \mid \text{not}\, a\Omega(u)f \xrightarrow[P]{*} 0\}$ is non-empty. Then F_u contains a minimal element $f_u \neq 0$ w.r.t. $\prec$. f_u is top-reducible modulo P, say $f_u \xrightarrow[P]{} f_u - b\Omega(s)p = \hat{f}_u$ for some $b \in K$, $s \in T$ descending and $p \in P$, such that $F \ni \hat{f}_u \prec f_u$. We obtain $HT_{\prec}(a\Omega(u)b\Omega(s)p) = HT_{\prec}(a\Omega(u)f_u)$ and

$$a\Omega(u)f_u \xrightarrow[P]{} \underbrace{a\Omega(u)f_u - \overbrace{a\Omega(u)b\Omega(s)}^{ab\Omega(us)}p}_{a\Omega(u)\hat{f}_u}.$$

Furthermore, $\hat{f}_u \notin F_u$ since $\hat{f}_u \prec f_u$ and so $a\Omega(u)\hat{f}_u \xrightarrow[P]{*} 0$. It follows that $a\Omega(u)f_u \xrightarrow[P]{*} 0$, contradicting the assumption $f_u \in F_u$.

Lemma 33. *(Translation lemma) Let $P \subseteq K[X_1, \ldots, X_n]$ and let $f, g, h, h_1 \in K[X_1, \ldots, X_n]$.*

1. *If $f - g = h$ and $h \xrightarrow[P]{*} h_1$, then there exist $f_1, g_1 \in K[X_1, \ldots, X_n]$ such that $f_1 - g_1 = h_1$, $f \xrightarrow[P]{*} f_1$, and $g \xrightarrow[P]{*} g_1$.*
2. *If $f - g \xrightarrow[P]{*} 0$, then $f \downarrow_P g$.*

Proof. (1) We show by induction that $f - g = h$ and $h \xrightarrow[P]{k} h_1$, $k \in \mathbb{N}$ implies the existence of $f_1, g_1 \in K[X_1, \ldots, X_n]$ with the indicated properties. For $k = 0$, we take $f_1 = f$ and $g_1 = g$. Let now $h \xrightarrow[P]{k+1} h_1$, say $h \xrightarrow[P]{k} h_2 \xrightarrow[P]{} h_1$. By the induction hypothesis, there exist $f_2, g_2 \in K[X_1, \ldots, X_n]$ with $f_2 - g_2 = h_2$, $f \xrightarrow[P]{*} f_2$, and $g \xrightarrow[P]{*} g_2$. It now suffices to find $f_1, g_1 \in K[X_1, \ldots, X_n]$ with $f_1 - g_1 = h_1$, $f_2 \xrightarrow[P]{*} f_1$, and $g_2 \xrightarrow[P]{*} g_1$, as indicated in the diagram below:

$$\begin{array}{ccccc} f & - & g & = & h \\ P\downarrow * & & P\downarrow * & & P\downarrow k \\ f_2 & - & g_2 & = & h_2 \\ P\downarrow * & & P\downarrow * & & P\downarrow \\ f_1 & - & g_1 & = & h_1 \end{array}$$

Suppose $h_1 = h_2 - \frac{c}{b}\Omega(s)p$, where $p \in P$, $b = HT_{\prec}(p)$, $s \in T$, and $0 \neq c$ is the coefficient of the monomial in $M(h_2)$ whose term is $s \cdot HT_{\prec}(p)$. Let c_1 be the coefficient of the monomial in $M(f_2)$ with term $s \cdot HT_{\prec}(p)$, if $s \cdot HT_{\prec}(p) \in T(f_2)$, let c_1 be zero otherwise. Define c_2 in the same way w.r.t. g_2. Set $f_1 = f_2 - \frac{c_1}{b}\Omega(s)p$ and $g_1 = g_2 - \frac{c_2}{b}\Omega(s)p$. Then $c_1 - c_2 = c$ because $h_2 = f_2 - g_2$, and we see that $f_1 - g_1 = h_1$. Furthermore, we have defined f_1 and g_1 in such a way that $f_2 \xrightarrow[P]{*} f_1$ and $g_2 \xrightarrow[P]{*} g_2$. (2) This is the special case $h_1 = 0$ of (1).

Lemma 34. *Let $P \subseteq K[X_1, \ldots, X_n] \ni f, g$. Then $f \xleftrightarrow[P]{*} g \iff f - g \in Sy(P)$, and $f \xrightarrow[P]{*} 0 \implies f \in Sy(P)$.*

Proof. "$\Longrightarrow$" We show by induction on $k \in \mathbb{N}$ that $f \xleftrightarrow[P]{k} g$ implies $f - g \in Sy(P)$. If $k = 0$, then $f = g$ and so $f - g \in Sy(P)$. If $f \xleftrightarrow[P]{k+1} g$, say $f \xleftrightarrow[P]{k} h \xleftrightarrow[P]{} g$, then $f - h \in Sy(P)$ by the induction hypothesis, and $h - g = c\Omega(u)p$ for some $c \in K$, $u \in T$ and $p \in P$ by the definition of $\xrightarrow[P]{}$. Consequently, $f - g = (f - h) + (h - g) \in Sy(P)$.
"$\Longleftarrow$" Let $f - g \in Sy(P)$. Then there exists $p_i \in P$, $c_i u_i \in M$, $1 \leq i \leq k$ such that $f = g + \sum_{i=1}^{k} c_i \Omega(u_i) p_i$. We show by induction on $k \in \mathbb{N}$ that $f \xleftrightarrow[P]{*} g$. If $k = 0$, then $f = g$. If $f = g + \sum_{i=1}^{k} c_i \Omega(u_i) p_i + c_{k+1}\Omega(u_{k+1})p_{k+1}$, then $f \xleftrightarrow[P]{*} g + c_{k+1}\Omega(u_{k+1})p_{k+1}$ by the induction hypothesis. It now suffices to show that $g + c_{k+1}\Omega(u_{k+1})p_{k+1} \xleftrightarrow[P]{*} g$. This follows from Lemma 33 and the fact that $c_{k+1}\Omega(u_{k+1})p_{k+1} \xrightarrow[P]{} 0$ by Lemma 31.

5 Symideal Gröbner Bases – Existence and Uniqueness

This section introduces symideal Gröbner bases and presents proofs for existence and uniqueness of such bases.

Lemma 35. *Let $0 \neq p \in K[X_1, \ldots, X_n]$. Then $\xrightarrow[p]{}$ is locally confluent.*

Proof. Suppose $f \xrightarrow[p]{} f_i\,[t_i]$ for $i = 1, 2$. In order to show that $f_1 \,{}_p\!\downarrow f_2$, it suffices by Lemma 33 to verify that $f_2 - f_1 \xrightarrow[p]{*} 0$. Let $f_i = f - c_i \Omega(t_i)p$ with $t_i \in T$ and $c_i \in K$. Then $f_2 - f_1 = (c_1\Omega(t_1) - c_2\Omega(t_2))p \xrightarrow[p]{*} 0$ by Lemma 31.

Lemma 36. *Let $P \subseteq K[X_1, \ldots, X_n]$ such that $Sy(P) = Sy(p)$ for some $0 \neq p \in P$. Then $\xrightarrow[P]{}$ is locally confluent.*

Proof. Let $f \xrightarrow[P]{} f_i$ for $i = 1, 2$. Then $f_1 \xleftrightarrow[P]{*} f_2$ and so by Lemma 34, $f_1 - f_2 \in Sy(P) = Sy(p)$. It follows that $f_1 \xleftrightarrow[p]{*} f_2$, so $f_1 \,{}_p\!\downarrow f_2$ by Newman's lemma and the fact that $\xrightarrow[p]{}$ is locally confluent and so $f_1 \,{}_P\!\downarrow f_2$.

Theorem 37. *Let $G \subseteq K[X_1, \ldots, X_n]$. Then the following are equivalent:*

1. *$\xrightarrow[G]{}$ is locally confluent, i.e. $\xrightarrow[G]{}$ has the Church-Rosser property.*
2. *$f \xrightarrow[G]{*} 0$ for all $f \in Sy(G)$.*
3. *Every $0 \neq f \in Sy(G)$ is reducible modulo G.*
4. *Every $0 \neq f \in Sy(G)$ is top-reducible modulo G.*
5. *For every $s \in HT_{\prec}(Sy(G))$ there exists $t \in HT_{\prec}(G)$ with $t \mid_{S_n} s$.*

6. *The polynomials $h \in K[X_1,\dots,X_n]$ that are in normal form w.r.t. $\underset{G}{\longrightarrow}$ form a system of unique representatives for the partition $\{f + Sy(G) \mid f \in K[X_1,\dots,X_n]\}$ of $K[X_1,\dots,X_n]$.*

Proof. (1) $\Longrightarrow$ (2): Let $f \in Sy(G)$. Then $f - 0 \in Sy(G)$ and thus $f \overset{*}{\underset{G}{\longrightarrow}} 0$ by Lemma 34. Since $\underset{G}{\longrightarrow}$ has the Church-Rosser property, there exists $h \in K[X_1,\dots,X_n]$ with $f \overset{*}{\underset{G}{\longrightarrow}} h$ and $0 \overset{*}{\underset{G}{\longrightarrow}} h$. Since 0 is always in normal form, we get $h = 0$.
(2) $\Longrightarrow$ (3): Let $0 \neq f \in Sy(G)$. By (2), there exists $h \in K[X_1,\dots,X_n]$ with $f \underset{G}{\longrightarrow} h \overset{*}{\underset{G}{\longrightarrow}} 0$.
(3) $\Longrightarrow$ (4): Assume for contradiction that $0 \neq f \in Sy(G)$ is minimal (w.r.t. $\prec$) such that it is not top-reducible w.r.t. $\underset{G}{\longrightarrow}$. Then by (3), there exists $h \in K[X_1,\dots,X_n]$ with $f \underset{G}{\longrightarrow} h$. It follows that $h \in Sy(G)$ and $h \prec f$. Moreover, $HT_\prec(h) = H_\prec(f)$ since f was not top-reducible. By the minimal choice of f, h is top-reducible w.r.t. $\underset{G}{\longrightarrow}$, say $h \underset{g}{\longrightarrow} h_1$ for some $g \in G$. But then $HT_\prec(g) \mid_{S_n} HT_\prec(h)$ and so f is top-reducible modulo g (contradiction).
(4) $\Longrightarrow$ (5): (5) is a simple reformulation of (4).
(5) $\Longrightarrow$ (6): Assume for a contradiction that there exist $f_1, f_2 \in K[X_1,\dots,X_n]$ both in normal form w.r.t. $\underset{G}{\longrightarrow}$ with $f_1 \neq f_2$ and $f_1 + Sy(G) = f_2 + Sy(G)$. Then $f_1 - f_2 \in Sy(G)$, and so there exists $g \in G$ with $HT_\prec(g) \mid_{S_n} HT_\prec(f_1 - f_2)$. But $HT_\prec(f_1 - f_2) \in T(f_1) \cup T(f_2)$ and so f_1 or f_2 is reducible modulo G.
(6) $\Longrightarrow$ (1): Let $f_1, f_2 \in K[X_1,\dots,X_n]$ with $f_1 \overset{*}{\underset{G}{\longleftrightarrow}} f_2$. Then $f_1 - f_2 \in Sy(G)$ by Lemma 34, and so $f_1 + Sy(G) = f_2 + Sy(G)$. Let h_1 and h_2 be normal forms of f_1 and f_2, respectively. Then $h_1, h_2 \in f_1 + Sy(G)$ again by Lemma 34 and so $h_1 = h_2$ by (6).

Definition 38. A subset G of $K[X_1,\dots,X_n]$ is called a symideal Gröbner basis (w.r.t. $\prec$) if it is finite, $0 \notin G$ and G satisfies the equivalent conditions of Theorem 37. If S is a symideal in $K[X_1,\dots,X_n]$, then a symideal Gröbner basis of S is a symideal Gröbner basis G such that $Sy(G) = S$.

Theorem 39. *Let S be a symideal in $K[X_1,\dots,X_n]$ and $0 \notin G \subset S$ finite. Then each of the following is equivalent to G being a symideal Gröbner basis of S (w.r.t. $\prec$).*

1. *$f \overset{*}{\underset{G}{\longrightarrow}} 0$ for all $f \in S$.*
2. *Every $0 \neq f \in S$ is reducible modulo G.*
3. *Every $0 \neq f \in S$ is top-reducible modulo G.*
4. *For every $s \in HT_\prec(S)$ there exists $t \in HT_\prec(G)$ with $t \mid_{S_n} s$.*
5. *The polynomials $h \in K[X_1,\dots,X_n]$ that are in normal form w.r.t. $\underset{G}{\longrightarrow}$ form a system of unique representatives for the partition $\{f + S \mid f \in K[X_1,\dots,X_n]\}$ of $K[X_1,\dots,X_n]$.*

Proof. We have just explained how G being a symideal Gröbner basis if S implies each of the listed conditions. Now assume that (1) holds. We have $Sy(G) \subseteq S$ by assumption, and so the condition trivially implies that G is a symideal Gröbner basis. It remains to be shown that $S \subseteq Sy(G)$. If $f \in S$, then $f \overset{*}{\underset{G}{\longrightarrow}} 0$ and thus

$f \in Sy(G)$ by Lemma 34. The proof can now be finished by showing that (1)–(5) are equivalent, which can easily be achieved using exactly the same arguments as in the proof of Theorem 37.

Theorem 40. *Let S be a symideal in $K[X_1, \ldots, X_n]$. Then there exists a symideal Gröbner basis G of S w.r.t. $\prec$.*

Proof. The divisibility relation $|_{S_n}$ is a Dickson partial order on T (see Lemma 9, Lemma 22 and [1], theorem 5.2). The set $H = \{HT_{\prec}(f) \mid f \in S\}$ has a finite basis B w.r.t. $|_{S_n}$. For each $t \in B$, there exists $f_t \in S$ such that $HT_{\prec}(f_t) = t$. And so $\{f_t \mid t \in B\}$ is a finite basis of S.

Corollary 41. *Every symideal in $K[X_1, \ldots, X_n]$ is finitely generated. (This is a consequence of Theorem 40.)*

Lemma 42. *Suppose S is a symideal in $K[X_1, \ldots, X_n]$, m is a monomial, and f and g are minimal polynomials in S such that $HM_{\prec}(f) = HM_{\prec}(g) = m$. Then $f = g$.*

Proof. We must have $T(f) = T(g)$ since otherwise $f \prec g$ or $g \prec f$. Furthermore, $f - g \in S$, and $f - g = 0$ or $s = HT_{\prec}(f - g) \prec m$. In the latter case, $s \in T(f) = T(g)$. It follows that there exists $0 \neq c \in K$ such that $s \notin T(h)$, where $h = f - c(f - g) \in S$. So $HM_{\prec}(h) = m$ and $h \prec f$, contradicting the minimality of f.

Definition 43. Let $P \subseteq K[X_1, \ldots, X_n]$. Then P is monic if every $p \in P$ is monic. P is called reduced if every $p \in P$ is in normal form modulo $P \setminus \{p\}$ and $HC_{\prec}(p) = 1$.

Theorem 44. *Let S be a symideal in $K[X_1, \ldots, X_n]$. Then there exists a unique reduced symideal Gröbner basis G of S w.r.t. $\prec$. Proof: See [4], theorem 5.52.*

6 Symideal Gröbner Bases – Construction

This section presents an algorithm for the construction of (unique reduced) symideal Gröbner bases.

Lemma 45. *Let G be a finite subset of $K[X_1, \ldots, X_n]$ with $0 \notin G$. Assume that whenever $g_1, g_2 \in G$ with $g_1 \neq g_2$ and $a_1, a_2 \in K$, $u_1, u_2 \in T$ such that*

$$HM_{\prec}(a_1 \Omega(u_1) g_1) = HM_{\prec}(a_2 \Omega(u_2) g_2),$$

it follows that $a_1 \Omega(u_1) g_1 - a_2 \Omega(u_2) g_2 \xrightarrow[G]{*} 0$. Then G is a symideal Gröbner basis.

Proof. We show that $\xrightarrow[G]{}$ is locally confluent. Let $f, f_1, f_2 \in K[X_1, \ldots, X_n]$ with $f \xrightarrow[G]{} f_i$, where $f_i = f - a_i \Omega(u_i) g_i$ for some $a_i \in K$, $u_i \in T$ and $g_i \in G$, $i \in \{1,2\}$. Then by Lemma 33, $f_1 \downarrow_G f_2$ provided that $a_1 \Omega(u_1) g_1 - a_2 \Omega(u_2) g_2 = f_2 - f_1 \xrightarrow[G]{*} 0$.
Case 1: $HM_{\prec}(a_1 \Omega(u_1) g_1) \neq HM_{\prec}(a_2 \Omega(u_2) g_2)$, say

$$HM_{\prec}(a_1 \Omega(u_1) g_1) \succ HM_{\prec}(a_2 \Omega(u_2) g_2).$$

Then we may reduce $a_1 \Omega(u_1) g_1 - a_2 \Omega(u_2) g_2$ to 0 modulo G by means of two top-reductions: $a_1 \Omega(u_1) g_1 - a_2 \Omega(u_2) g_2 \xrightarrow[g_1]{} -a_2 \Omega(u_2) g_2 \xrightarrow[g_2]{} 0$
Case 2: $HM_{\prec}(a_1 \Omega(u_1) g_1) = HM_{\prec}(a_2 \Omega(u_2) g_2) = t$. Then $HM_{\prec}(a_1 \Omega(u_1) g_1) = HM_{\prec}(a_2 \Omega(u_2) g_2)$ since both eliminate the same term t from f. It follows that $a_1 \Omega(u_1) g_1 - a_2 \Omega(u_2) g_2 \xrightarrow[G]{*} 0$ by the hypothesis of the lemma.

Definition 46. Let $g_i \in K[X_1, \ldots, X_n]$, let $a_i = HC_{\prec}(g_i)$, let $t_i = HT_{\prec}(g_i)$ be $(k_{i1}, \ldots, k_{in})$-multilinear w.r.t. S, $i \in \{1,2\}$ and let $u_1, u_2 \in T$ with $lcm_{S_n}(t_1, t_2) = u_1 t_1 = u_2 t_2$. Then $spol_{S_n}(g_1, g_2) = a_2 \Omega(u_1) g_1 - a_1 \Omega(u_2) g_2$ is the S-polynomial of g_1 and g_2 w.r.t. symmetry.

Example 5. $t_1 = X_1^5 X_2^6 X_4^3$ is $(1,2,3,0)$-multilinear w.r.t. $S = (X_2,\ X_1X_2,\ X_1X_2X_4,\ X_1X_2X_3X_4)$ and $t_2 = X_1^3 X_2^8 X_4^2$ is $(5,1,2,0)$-multilinear w.r.t. S. Hence $lcm_{S_n}(t_1, t_2) = X_1^5 X_2^{10} X_4^3 = X_2^4 \cdot t_1 = X_1^2 X_2^2 X_4 \cdot t_2$ is $(5,2,3,0)$-multilinear w.r.t. S and $spol_{S_n}(t_1, t_2) = \Omega(X_2^4) t_1 - \Omega(X_1^2 X_2^2 X_4) t_2$.

Remark. Let $g_i \in K[X_1, \ldots, X_n]$ and let $t_i = HT_{\prec}(g_i)$ be $(k_{i1}, \ldots, k_{in})$-multilinear w.r.t. S_i, $i \in \{1,2\}$.

1. Let $S_1 \neq S_2$. Then there exists no least common multiple of t_1 and t_2 and therefore $spol_{S_n}(g_1, g_2)$ is not defined. Here $a_1 \Omega(u_1) g_1 - a_2 \Omega(u_2) g_2 \xrightarrow[\{g_1, g_2\}]{*} 0$ holds for all $a_1, a_2 \in K$ and $u_1, u_2 \in T$ by the proof of Lemma 45, case 1.
2. Let $S_1 = S_2$. Then either $spol_{S_n}(g_1, g_2) = 0$, or else $HT_{\prec}(spol_{S_n}(g_1, g_2)) \prec lcm_{S_n}(HT_{\prec}(g_1), HT_{\prec}(g_2))$ by Definition 46.

Theorem 47. *Let G be a finite subset of $K[X_1, \ldots, X_n]$ with $0 \notin G$. Then the following are equivalent:*

1. *G is a symideal Gröbner basis.*
2. *Whenever $g_1,\ g_2 \in G$ and $h \in K[X_1, \ldots, X_n]$ is a normal form of $spol_{S_n}(g_1, g_2)$ modulo G, then $h = 0$.*
3. *$spol_{S_n}(g_1, g_2) \xrightarrow[G]{*} 0$ for all $g_1,\ g_2 \in G$.*

Proof. (1) $\Longrightarrow$ (2): $spol_{S_n}(g_1, g_2)$ is obviously in $Sy(G)$ for all $g_1, g_2 \in G$. So by Theorem 37 $spol_{S_n}(g_1, g_2)$ has 0 as a normal form modulo G. Since moreover normal forms are unique, it follows $h = 0$.
(2) $\Longrightarrow$ (3): trivial.
(3) $\Longrightarrow$ (1): By Lemma 45, it suffices to show that polynomials of the form $b_1 \Omega(u_1) g_1 - b_2 \Omega(u_2) g_2$ with $g_1 \neq g_2 \in G$, $b_i \in K$, $u_i \in T$, $i \in \{1,2\}$, and

$$HM_{\prec}(b_1 \Omega(u_1) g_1) = HM_{\prec}(b_2 \Omega(u_2) g_2), \tag{1}$$

reduce to 0 modulo G. Let $t_i = HT_\prec(g_i)$ and $a_i = HC_\prec(g_i)$. Then equation 1 becomes

$$HM_\prec(b_1\Omega(u_1)a_1t_1) = HM_\prec(b_2\Omega(u_2)a_2t_2) \qquad (2)$$

and we can assume w.l.o.g. that $HT_\prec(\Omega(u_1)t_1) = u_1t_1$ and $HT_\prec(\Omega(u_2)t_2) = u_2t_2$ by Theorem 17 and Lemma 23. By Corollary 26, there exists a least common multiple of t_1 and t_2. Let $s_1, s_2 \in T$ such that $s_1t_1 = lcm_{S_n}(t_1, t_2) = s_2t_2$. Then $u_1t_1 = vs_1t_1 = v \cdot lcm_{S_n}(t_1, t_2) = vs_2t_2 = u_2t_2$, where t_1 and t_2 are multilinear w.r.t. the same S and u_1, u_2, s_1, s_2 and v are power products of the components of S. Hence $HM_\prec(b_1a_1\Omega(vs_1)t_1) = HM_\prec(b_2a_2\Omega(vs_2)t_2)$ and $HM_\prec(b_1a_1\Omega(v)\Omega(s_1)t_1) = HM_\prec(b_2a_2\Omega(v)\Omega(s_2)t_2)$.
Furthermore, equation 2 implies $\frac{b_1}{a_2} = \frac{b_2}{a_1}$ and so

$$\begin{aligned} b_1\Omega(u_1)g_1 - b_2\Omega(u_2)g_2 &= b_1\Omega(vs_1)g_1 - b_2\Omega(vs_2)g_2 \\ &\overset{L.\,3}{=} b_1\Omega(v)\Omega(s_1)g_1 - b_2\Omega(v)\Omega(s_2)g_2 \\ &= \tfrac{b_1}{a_2}\Omega(v)(a_2\Omega(s_1)g_1 - a_1\Omega(s_2)g_2) \\ &= \tfrac{b_1}{a_2}\Omega(v)spol_{S_n}(g_1, g_2). \end{aligned}$$

By Lemma 32, we conclude $\frac{b_1}{a_2}\Omega(v)spol_{S_n}(g_1, g_2) \xrightarrow[G]{*} 0$.

Corollary 48. *Let $G \subseteq K[X_1, \ldots, X_n]$ be a finite set of elementary symmetric products. Then G is a symideal Gröbner basis. (This follows immediately from the fact that the S-polynomial of two elementary symmetric products equals zero.)*

Theorem 49. *Let $F \subset K[X_1, \ldots, X_n]$ finite. Then there exists an algorithm to compute a symideal Gröbner basis G such that $F \subseteq G$ and $Sy(G) = Sy(F)$.*

Proof. We present such an algorithm:

Algorithm 50.

INPUT $F \subset K[X_1, \ldots, X_n]$ *finite;*
$G := F$;
$B := \{\{g_1, g_2\} \mid g_1 \neq g_2 \in G\}$;
WHILE $B \neq \emptyset$ *DO*
    select $\{g_1, g_2\}$ *from* B; $B := B \setminus \{g_1, g_2\}$;
    $h := spol_{S_n}(g_1, g_2)$;   /* *Definition 46* */
    $h_0 := normalform_{S_n}(h, G)$;   /* *cf. [4], algorithm 5.37* */
    IF $h_0 \neq 0$ *THEN*
        $B := B \cup \{\{g, h_0\} \mid g \in G\}$; $G := G \cup \{h_0\}$;
    ENDIF;
    ENDWHILE;
OUTPUT symideal Gröbner basis G *such that* $F \subseteq G$ *and* $Sy(G) = Sy(F)$;

Termination: Assume for a contradiction that the while-loop does not terminate. Let $F = G_0 \subset G_1 \subset G_2 \subset \ldots$ be the successive values of G. Considering those runs through the while-loop that actually enlarge G, we see that there exists an ascending sequence $\{n_i\}_{i \in \mathbb{N}}$ of natural numbers such that for all $1 \leq i \in$

$\mathbb{N}$, there exists $h_i \in G_{n_i} \setminus G_{n_{i-1}}$ which is in normal form modulo $G_{n_{i-1}}$. Let $t_k = HT_{\prec}(h_k)$ for all $k \in \mathbb{N}$; then $i < j$ implies $t_i \not|_{S_n} t_j$, otherwise h_j would be top-reducible modulo $\{h_i\}$ and hence modulo $G_{n_{j-1}}$. Since divisibility of terms is a Dickson partial order, this contradicts Lemma 9.

Correctness: We claim that the following are loop invariants of the while-loop: G is a finite subset of $K[X_1,\ldots,X_n]$ such that $F \subseteq G \subseteq Sy(F)$, and $spol_{S_n}(g_1,g_2) \xrightarrow[G]{*} 0$ for all $g_1, g_2 \in G$ such that $\{g_1,g_2\} \notin B$. The first claim follows easily from the fact that a normal form of an S-polynomial of two elements of G is in $Sy(G)$. For the second one, it suffices to note that $spol_{S_n}(g_1,g_2) \xrightarrow[G]{*} h_0$ implies $spol_{S_n}(g_1,g_2) \xrightarrow[G\cup h_0]{*} 0$. Upon termination, we have $B = \emptyset$ and so $spol_{S_n}(g_1,g_2) \xrightarrow[G]{*} 0$ for all $g_1, g_2 \in G$. It now follows from Theorem 47 that G is a symideal Gröbner basis.

Lemma 51. *Let $G \subset K[X_1,\ldots,X_n]$ be a symideal Gröbner basis. Then there exists an algorithm to compute a unique reduced symideal Gröbner basis H such that $Sy(G) = Sy(H)$.* *Proof: See [4], lemma 5.62 and algorithm 5.63.*

Example 6. A_n, D_n and Z_n denotes the alternating, dihedral and cyclic permutation group operating on n variables, respectively.

1. Let $F = \{X_1^i + X_2^i + X_3^i + X_4^i + X_5^i \mid 1 \le i \le 5\} \subset \mathbb{Q}[X_1,\ldots,X_5]$. The unique reduced symideal Gröbner basis of F is $\{\sigma_1,\ldots,\sigma_5\}$.
2. Let $F = \{X_i + 1 \mid 1 \le i \le 3\} \subset \mathbb{Q}[X_1,X_2,X_3]$ and $\hat{F} = \{t \cdot f \mid t \in T \text{ special}, f \in F\}$. Then $Id(F) = Sy(\hat{F})$ and the unique reduced symideal Gröbner basis of $\hat{F}$ is $\{X_3+1,\ X_2+1,\ X_1+1,\ X_2X_3-1,\ X_1X_3-1,\ X_1X_2-1,\ X_1X_2X_3+1,\ X_2X_3^2+1\}$.
3. Let $F = \{orbit_{S_4}(t) \mid t \in T \text{ special}\}$, i.e. $Sy(F) = \mathbb{Q}[X_1,X_2,X_3,X_4]^{S_4}$. The unique reduced symideal Gröbner basis of F is $\{1\}$.
4. Let $F = \{orbit_{A_4}(t) \mid t \in T \text{ special}\}$, i.e. $Sy(F) = \mathbb{Q}[X_1,X_2,X_3,X_4]^{A_4}$. The unique reduced symideal Gröbner basis of F is $\{1, orbit_{A_4}(X_1^3X_2^2X_4)\}$ and so every $f \in \mathbb{Q}[X_1,X_2,X_3,X_4]^{A_4}$ has a representation as $f = p_1(\sigma_1,\ldots,\sigma_4) + p_2(\sigma_1,\ldots,\sigma_4) \cdot orbit_{A_4}(X_1^3X_2^2X_4)$.
5. Let $F = \{orbit_{D_4}(t) \mid t \in T \text{ special}\}$, i.e. $Sy(F) = \mathbb{Q}[X_1,X_2,X_3,X_4]^{D_4}$. The unique reduced symideal Gröbner basis of F is $\{1,\ orbit_{D_4}(X_1X_3),\ orbit_{D_4}(X_1^2X_2X_4)\}$.
6. Let $F = \{orbit_{Z_4}(t) \mid t \in T \text{ special}\}$, i.e. $Sy(F) = \mathbb{Q}[X_1,X_2,X_3,X_4]^{Z_4}$. The unique reduced symideal Gröbner basis of F is $\{1,\ orbit_{Z_4}(X_1X_3),\ orbit_{Z_4}(X_1^2X_4),\ orbit_{Z_4}(X_1^2X_3X_4),\ orbit_{Z_4}(X_1^2X_2X_4),\ orbit_{Z_4}(X_1^2X_2^2X_4),\ orbit_{Z_4}(X_1^3X_3X_4^2)\}$.
7. Let $F = \{t \mid t \in T \text{ special}\}$, i.e. $Sy(F) = \mathbb{Q}[X_1,X_2,X_3]$. The unique reduced symideal Gröbner basis of F is $\{1,\ X_3,\ X_2,\ X_2X_3,\ X_1X_3,\ X_2X_3^2\}$.

It is to suppose that many more results from Gröbner bases theory can be taken over and integrated in the computation of symideal Gröbner bases, for example Buchberger's first and second criterion (see [1], lemma 5.66 and proposition 5.70) to avoid S-polynomials which need not to be considered, the extended Gröbner basis algorithm (see [1], section 5.6), or a general concept for admissible orders [9] w.r.t. symmetry satisfying the constraints in Lemma 13.

Corollary 52. *A unique reduced symideal Gröbner basis of all special G-invariant orbits in* $K[X_1, \ldots, X_n]$ *is a unique reduced basis B for the invariant ring* $K[X_1, \ldots, X_n]^G$*. B is a subset of all special G-invariant orbits; we have* $f \xrightarrow[B]{*} 0$ *and* $f = \sum_{g \in B} p(\sigma_1, \ldots, \sigma_n) \cdot g$ *for all* $f \in K[X_1, \ldots, X_n]^G$*. (This is a consequence of [3], theorem 3.11.)*

We have shown, how the reduction approach presented in [3] can be embedded in a completion algorithm. The possibilities of this completion technique are a straightforward computation of unique reduced bases for symideals and an algorithmic solution of the symideal membership problem.

7 Acknowledgements

The results of this note are part of the author's Ph.D. thesis written under the supervision of Prof. Dr. Loos (Tübingen) and Prof. Dr. Weispfenning (Passau). The author would like to thank Prof. Dr. Sturmfels (Berkeley) and the anonymous referees for their comments, and Prof. Dr. Küchlin (Tübingen) for his support.

References

1. Becker, T., Weispfenning, V., in Cooperation with Kredel, H. (1993). Gröbner Bases: A Computational Approach to Commutative Algebra. Springer, New York
2. Buchberger, B. (1985). Gröbner Bases: An Algorithmic Method in Polynomial Ideal Theory. In: Bose, N. K. (ed.), Multidimensional Systems Theory. Reidel, Dordrecht, 184-232
3. Göbel, M. (1995). Computing Bases for Permutation-Invariant Polynomials. Journal of Symbolic Computation 19, 285-291
4. Göbel, M. (1996). Computing Bases for Permutation-Invariant Polynomials. Dissertation, Universität Tübingen. Shaker, Aachen
5. Knuth, D. E., Bendix, P. B. (1970). Simple Word Problems in Universal Algebras. In: Leech, J. (ed.), Computational Problems in Abstract Algebra. Pergamon Press, 263-297
6. Kredel, H. (1990). MAS: Modula-2 Algebra System. In: Gerdt, V. P., Rostovtsev, V. A., and Shirkov, D. V. (eds.), IV International Conference on Computer Algebra in Physical Research. World Scientific Publishing Co., Singapore, 31-34
7. Loos, R. (1981). Term Reduction Systems and Algebraic Algorithms. In: Siekmann, J. H. (ed.), GWAI-81, German Workshop on Artificial Intelligence, Bad Honnef. Informatik-Fachberichte, Herausgegeben von W. Brauer im Auftrag der Gesellschaft für Informatik (GI), 47. Springer, Berlin, 214-234
8. Sturmfels, B. (1993). Algorithms in Invariant Theory. Springer, Vienna
9. Weispfenning, V. (1987). Admissible Orders and Linear Forms. ACM SIGSAM Bulletin 21/2, 16-18

Termination of Constructor Systems*

Thomas Arts[1] and Jürgen Giesl[2]

[1] Dept. of Computer Science, Utrecht University, P.O. Box 80.089, 3508 TB Utrecht, The Netherlands, E-mail: thomas@cs.ruu.nl

[2] FB Informatik, TH Darmstadt, Alexanderstr. 10, 64283 Darmstadt, Germany, E-mail: giesl@inferenzsysteme.informatik.th-darmstadt.de

Abstract. We present a method to prove termination of constructor systems automatically. Our approach takes advantage of the special form of these rewrite systems because for constructor systems instead of left- and right-hand sides of rules it is sufficient to compare so-called *dependency pairs* [Art96]. Unfortunately, standard techniques for the generation of well-founded orderings cannot be directly used for the automation of the dependency pair approach. To solve this problem we have developed a transformation technique which enables the application of known synthesis methods for well-founded orderings to prove that dependency pairs are decreasing. In this way termination of many (also non-simply terminating) constructor systems can be proved fully automatically.

1 Introduction

One of the most interesting properties of a term rewriting system is termination, cf. e.g. [DJ90]. While in general this problem is undecidable [HL78], several methods for proving termination have been developed (e.g. path orderings [Pla78, Der82, Ges94, DH95, Ste95b], Knuth-Bendix orderings [KB70, Mar87], semantic interpretations [MN70, Lan79, BCL87, BL93, Ste94, Zan94, Gie95a], transformation orderings [BD86, BL90, Ste95a], semantic labelling [Zan95] etc. — for surveys see e.g. [Der87, Ste95b]).

In this paper we are concerned with the *automation* of termination proofs for *constructor systems* (CS for short). Due to the special form of these rewrite systems it is possible to use a different approach for CSs than is necessary for termination of general rewrite systems. Therefore, in this paper we focus on a technique specially tailored for CSs, viz. the so-called *dependency pair* approach [Art96]. With this approach it is also possible to prove termination of systems where all simplification orderings fail. In Sect. 2 we describe which steps have to be performed (automatically) to verify termination of CSs using this approach. Although the dependency pair approach may be used for arbitrary CSs, in this paper we focus on special hierarchical combinations of CSs ensuring that all steps can be performed automatically.

The main task in this approach is to prove that all dependency pairs are decreasing w.r.t. a well-founded ordering. Up to now only some heuristics existed to perform this step automatically. On the other hand, several techniques have

* This work was supported by the Deutsche Forschungsgemeinschaft under grant no. Wa 652/7-1 as part of the focus program "Deduktion".

been developed to synthesize suitable well-founded orderings for termination proofs of term rewriting systems. Hence, one would like to apply these techniques for the automation of the dependency pair approach. Unfortunately, as we will show in Sect. 3, this is not directly possible.

Therefore in Sect. 4 we suggest a new technique to enable the application of standard methods for the generation of well-founded orderings to prove that dependency pairs are decreasing. For that purpose we transfer a variant of the *estimation* method [Wal94, Gie95b, Gie95c], which was originally developed for termination proofs of functional programs, to rewrite systems.

By the combination of the dependency pair approach and the estimation method we obtain a very powerful technique for automated termination proofs of CSs which can prove termination of numerous CSs whose termination could not be proved automatically before, cf. [AG96].

2 Dependency Pairs

A *constructor system* $(\mathcal{D}, \mathcal{C}, \mathcal{R})$ is a term rewriting system with a set of rules $\mathcal{R}$ and with a signature that can be partitioned into two disjoint sets $\mathcal{D}$ and $\mathcal{C}$ such that for every left-hand side $f(t_1, \ldots, t_n)$ of a rewrite rule of $\mathcal{R}$ the root symbol f is from $\mathcal{D}$ and the terms $t_1, \ldots, t_n$ only contain function symbols from $\mathcal{C}$. Function symbols from $\mathcal{D}$ are called *defined symbols* and function symbols from $\mathcal{C}$ are called *constructors*. As an example consider the following CS:

$$\begin{aligned} \mathsf{minus}(x, \mathsf{0}) &\to x, \\ \mathsf{minus}(\mathsf{succ}(x), \mathsf{succ}(y)) &\to \mathsf{minus}(x, y), \\ \mathsf{quot}(\mathsf{0}, \mathsf{succ}(y)) &\to \mathsf{0}, \\ \mathsf{quot}(\mathsf{succ}(x), \mathsf{succ}(y)) &\to \mathsf{succ}(\mathsf{quot}(\mathsf{minus}(x, y), \mathsf{succ}(y))). \end{aligned}$$

Most methods for automated termination proofs of term rewriting systems are restricted to *simplification orderings* [Der79, Ste95b]. These methods cannot prove termination of the above CS, because no simplification ordering can orient the fourth rule if y is instantiated to $\mathsf{succ}(x)$. The reason is that simplification orderings $\succ$ are monotonic and satisfy the subterm property and this implies $\mathsf{succ}(\mathsf{quot}(\mathsf{minus}(x, \mathsf{succ}(x)), \mathsf{succ}(\mathsf{succ}(x)))) \succ \mathsf{quot}(\mathsf{succ}(x), \mathsf{succ}(\mathsf{succ}(x)))$. All other known techniques for automated termination proofs of non-simply terminating systems [Zan94, Ste95a, Ken95, FZ95] fail with this example, too.

However, with the *dependency pair* approach an automated termination proof of the above CS is possible. The idea of this approach is to use an interpretation on terms which assigns for every rewrite rule of the CS the same value to the left-hand side as to the right-hand side. Then for termination of the CS it is sufficient if there exists a well-founded ordering such that the interpretations of the arguments of all defined symbols are decreasing in each recursive occurrence.

To represent the interpretation another CS $\mathcal{E}$ is used which is *ground-convergent* (i.e. ground-confluent and terminating) and in which the CS $\mathcal{R}$ is *contained*, i.e. $(l\sigma)\downarrow_{\mathcal{E}} = (r\sigma)\downarrow_{\mathcal{E}}$ holds for all rewrite rules $l \to r$ of $\mathcal{R}$ and all ground substitutions σ (where we always assume that there exist ground terms, i.e. there must be a constant in the signature $\mathcal{D} \cup \mathcal{C}$). Then for any ground term t the interpretation is $t{\downarrow_{\mathcal{E}}}$.

If a term $f(t_1, \ldots, t_n)$ rewrites to another term $C[g(s_1, \ldots, s_m)]$ (where f and g are defined symbols and C denotes some context), then we will try to show that the interpretation of the tuple $t_1, \ldots, t_n$ is greater than the interpretation of the tuple $s_1, \ldots, s_m$. In order to avoid the comparison of *tuples* we extend our signature by a tuple function symbol F for each $f \in \mathcal{D}$ and compare the *terms* $F(t_1, \ldots, t_n)$ and $G(s_1, \ldots, s_m)$ instead. To ease readability we assume that $\mathcal{D} \cup \mathcal{C}$ consists of lower case function symbols only and denote the tuple functions by the corresponding upper case symbols. Pairs of terms that have to be compared are called *dependency pairs*.

Definition 1. Let $(\mathcal{D}, \mathcal{C}, \mathcal{R})$ be a CS. If $f(t_1, \ldots, t_n) \to C[g(s_1, \ldots, s_m)]$ is a rewrite rule of $\mathcal{R}$ and $f, g \in \mathcal{D}$, then $\langle F(t_1, \ldots, t_n), G(s_1, \ldots, s_m)\rangle$ is called a *dependency pair* (of $\mathcal{R}$).

In our example we obtain the following set of dependency pairs (where M and Q denote the tuple function symbols for minus and quot):

$$\langle \mathsf{M}(\mathsf{succ}(x), \mathsf{succ}(y)), \mathsf{M}(x, y)\rangle, \tag{1}$$

$$\langle \mathsf{Q}(\mathsf{succ}(x), \mathsf{succ}(y)), \mathsf{M}(x, y)\rangle, \tag{2}$$

$$\langle \mathsf{Q}(\mathsf{succ}(x), \mathsf{succ}(y)), \mathsf{Q}(\mathsf{minus}(x, y), \mathsf{succ}(y))\rangle\ . \tag{3}$$

The following theorem states that if the interpretations of the dependency pairs are decreasing, then the CS is terminating.

Theorem 2. *Let $(\mathcal{D}, \mathcal{C}, \mathcal{R})$ be a CS and let $(\mathcal{D}, \mathcal{C}, \mathcal{E})$ be a ground-convergent CS such that $\mathcal{R}$ is contained in $\mathcal{E}$. If there exists a well-founded ordering $\succ$ on ground terms such that $(s\sigma){\downarrow_{\mathcal{E}}} \succ (t\sigma){\downarrow_{\mathcal{E}}}$ holds for all[1] dependency pairs $\langle s, t\rangle$ and all ground substitutions σ, then $\mathcal{R}$ is terminating.*

The proofs of all theorems of this section are based on semantic labelling [Zan95] and can be found in [Art96].

Hence, to prove termination of a CS $\mathcal{R}$ with the dependency pair technique two tasks have to be performed: first, one has to find a ground-convergent CS $\mathcal{E}$ such that $\mathcal{R}$ is contained in $\mathcal{E}$ and second, one has to prove that the $\mathcal{E}$-interpretations of the dependency pairs are decreasing w.r.t. a well-founded ordering.

For the first task, in [Art96] a method is presented to generate suitable CSs $\mathcal{E}$ for a subclass of CSs $\mathcal{R}$ automatically. This subclass consists of non-overlapping[2] hierarchical combinations [KR95] (a CS is a hierarchical combination of two CSs if defined symbols of the first CS occur as constructors in the second CS, but not vice versa) without nested defined symbols in the second CS (i.e. the rules

[1] In many examples it is sufficient if only certain dependency pairs are decreasing and several methods to determine those dependency pairs have been suggested in [Art96].

[2] This requirement can even be weakened to overlay systems with joinable critical pairs.

do not contain subterms of the form $f(\ldots g \ldots)$, where f, g are defined symbols of $\mathcal{R}_1$). We remark that the hierarchical combinations that we focus on, differ from the ***proper-extensions*** defined by Krishna Rao [KR95].

If $\mathcal{R}$ is such a hierarchical combination of $\mathcal{R}_0$ with $\mathcal{R}_1$ and $\mathcal{R}_0$ is terminating, then it suffices if just the ***subsystem*** $\mathcal{R}_0$ is contained in $\mathcal{E}$ and hence, one can simply define $\mathcal{E}$ to be $\mathcal{R}_0$. Moreover, one does not have to consider all dependency pairs of $\mathcal{R}$, but it is sufficient to examine only those dependency pairs $\langle F(\ldots), G(\ldots)\rangle$ where f and g are defined symbols of $\mathcal{R}_1$. In this way it is possible to prove termination of hierarchical combinations by successively proving termination of each subsystem and by defining $\mathcal{E}$ to consist of those subsystems whose termination has already been proved before. Thus, we recursively apply the following theorem.

Theorem 3. *Let $(\mathcal{D}, \mathcal{C}, \mathcal{R})$ be a non-overlapping hierarchical combination of $(\mathcal{D}_0, \mathcal{C}, \mathcal{R}_0)$ with $(\mathcal{D}_1, \mathcal{C} \cup \mathcal{D}_0, \mathcal{R}_1)$ such that $\mathcal{R}_0$ is terminating and such that symbols from $\mathcal{D}_1$ do not occur nested in the rules. If there exists a well-founded ordering $\succ$ on ground terms such that $(s\sigma)\downarrow_{\mathcal{R}_0} \succ (t\sigma)\downarrow_{\mathcal{R}_0}$ holds for all dependency pairs $\langle s, t\rangle$ of $\mathcal{R}_1$ and all ground substitutions σ, then $\mathcal{R}$ is terminating.*

For instance, our example is a hierarchical combination of the minus-subsystem with the quot-subsystem. Hence, if we already proved termination of the first two minus-rules[3], then we now only have to prove termination of the quot-rules and let $\mathcal{E}$ consist of the two minus-rules. Now the only dependency pair we have to consider is (3).

Hence, the main problem with automated termination proofs using dependency pairs is the second task, i.e. to find a well-founded ordering such that the interpretations of dependency pairs are decreasing.

3 Using Well-Founded Orderings

Numerous methods for the automated generation of suitable well-founded orderings have been developed to prove termination of term rewriting systems. Hence, for the automation of the dependency pair approach we would like to use these standard methods to prove that dependency pairs are decreasing.

However, we will illustrate in Sect. 3.1 that, unfortunately, the direct application of standard methods for this purpose is unsound. The reason is that arbitrary orderings do not respect the equalities induced by $\mathcal{E}$.

In Sect. 3.2 we show that the straightforward solution of restricting ourselves to orderings that respect the equalities induced by $\mathcal{E}$ results in a method which is not powerful enough.

[3] This can for instance be done with standard techniques like e.g. the recursive path ordering [Der82] or again by the dependency pair approach. Then, $\mathcal{E}$ can be chosen to be any ground-convergent CS (even the empty one), because in the CS consisting of the two minus-rules defined symbols do not occur nested and this CS may be regarded as a hierarchical combination where $\mathcal{R}_0$ is empty.

But in Sect. 3.3 we prove that as long as the dependency pairs do not contain *defined* symbols, the direct approach of Sect. 3.1 is sound. Therefore our aim will be to eliminate all defined symbols in the dependency pairs. A transformation procedure for the elimination of defined symbols will be presented in Sect. 4.

3.1 Direct Application of Well-Founded Orderings

Let $\mathcal{DP}$ be a set of inequalities which represent the constraints that left-hand sides of dependency pairs have to be greater than right-hand sides, i.e. $\mathcal{DP} = \{s \succ t | \langle s, t\rangle \text{ dependency pair}\}$. Now one could use standard methods to generate a well-founded ordering $\succ$ satisfying the constraints $\mathcal{DP}$. But unfortunately, this approach is *unsound*, i.e. it is not sufficient for the termination of the CS $\mathcal{R}$ under consideration. As an example let $\mathcal{R}$ be the CS

$$\begin{aligned} \mathsf{double}(0) &\to 0, \\ \mathsf{double}(\mathsf{succ}(x)) &\to \mathsf{succ}(\mathsf{succ}(\mathsf{double}(x))), \\ \mathsf{f}(\mathsf{succ}(x)) &\to \mathsf{f}(\mathsf{double}(x)). \end{aligned}$$

Assume that we have already proved termination of the double-subsystem. Hence by Thm. 3, we can define $\mathcal{E}$ to consist of the first two rules of $\mathcal{R}$ and we only have to examine the dependency pair $\langle \mathsf{F}(\mathsf{succ}(x)), \mathsf{F}(\mathsf{double}(x))\rangle$. The constraint

$$\mathcal{DP} = \{\mathsf{F}(\mathsf{succ}(x)) \succ \mathsf{F}(\mathsf{double}(x))\}$$

is for instance satisfied by the recursive path ordering $\succ_{rpo}$, cf. [Der82]. Nevertheless, $\mathcal{R}$ is not terminating (e.g. $\mathsf{f}(\mathsf{succ}(\mathsf{succ}(0)))$ starts an infinite reduction).

This direct application of orderings is not possible because the constraints in $\mathcal{DP}$ only compare the terms s and t but not their $\mathcal{E}$-interpretations. However, $s \succ_{rpo} t$ is not sufficient for $(s\sigma)\downarrow_{\mathcal{E}} \succ_{rpo} (t\sigma)\downarrow_{\mathcal{E}}$, because $\succ_{rpo}$ does not respect the equalities induced by $\mathcal{E}$. For instance, $\mathsf{F}(\mathsf{succ}(\mathsf{succ}(0))) \succ_{rpo} \mathsf{F}(\mathsf{double}(\mathsf{succ}(0)))$, but $\mathsf{F}(\mathsf{succ}(\mathsf{succ}(0)))\downarrow_{\mathcal{E}} \not\succ_{rpo} \mathsf{F}(\mathsf{double}(\mathsf{succ}(0)))\downarrow_{\mathcal{E}} = \mathsf{F}(\mathsf{succ}(\mathsf{succ}(0)))$.

So we have to ensure that whenever $s\downarrow_{\mathcal{E}} = t\downarrow_{\mathcal{E}}$ holds for two ground terms s and t, these terms must also be "equivalent" w.r.t. the used ordering. To formalize the notion of "equivalence" we will now regard *quasi*-orderings.

3.2 Quasi-Orderings Respecting $\mathcal{E}$

A *quasi-ordering* $\succsim$ is a reflexive and transitive relation. For every quasi-ordering $\succsim$, let $\sim$ denote the associated equivalence relation (i.e. $s \sim t$ iff $s \succsim t$ and $t \succsim s$) and let $\succ$ denote the strict part of the quasi-ordering (i.e. $s \succ t$ iff $s \succsim t$, but not $t \succsim s$). We say $\succsim$ is well-founded iff the strict part $\succ$ is well-founded. In this paper we restrict ourselves to relations on ground terms and (for notational convenience) we extend every quasi-ordering $\succsim$ to arbitrary terms by defining $s \succsim t$ iff $s\sigma \succsim t\sigma$ holds for all ground substitutions σ. Analogously, $s \succ t$ (resp. $s \sim t$) is defined as $s\sigma \succ t\sigma$ (resp. $s\sigma \sim t\sigma$) for all ground substitutions σ.

A straightforward solution for the problem discussed in the preceding section would be to try to find a well-founded quasi-ordering which satisfies both $\mathcal{DP}$

and $\mathcal{EQ}$, where $\mathcal{EQ} = \{s \sim t \mid s, t$ ground terms with $s{\downarrow_\mathcal{E}} = t{\downarrow_\mathcal{E}}\}$. Obviously the existence of such a quasi-ordering is sufficient for the termination of the CS $\mathcal{R}$.

Lemma 4. *If there exists a well-founded quasi-ordering satisfying the constraints $\mathcal{DP} \cup \mathcal{EQ}$, then $\mathcal{R}$ is terminating.*

Proof. If $\succsim$ satisfies $\mathcal{DP}$, then we have $s\sigma \succ t\sigma$ for each dependency pair $\langle s, t\rangle$ and each ground substitution σ. If $\succsim$ also satisfies $\mathcal{EQ}$, then $(s\sigma){\downarrow_\mathcal{E}} \sim s\sigma \succ t\sigma \sim (t\sigma){\downarrow_\mathcal{E}}$. Hence, the lemma follows from Thm. 2 (resp. Thm. 3). □

But unfortunately, standard techniques usually cannot be used to find a well-founded quasi-ordering $\succsim$ satisfying the constraints $\mathcal{DP} \cup \mathcal{EQ}$. As an example regard the CS for minus and quot again. Assume that we have already proved termination of the minus-subsystem and let us now prove termination of the quot-rules. According to Thm. 3, we can define $\mathcal{E}$ to consist of the two minus-rules and we obtain the constraint

$$\mathcal{DP} = \{\mathsf{Q}(\mathsf{succ}(x), \mathsf{succ}(y)) \succ \mathsf{Q}(\mathsf{minus}(x, y), \mathsf{succ}(y))\}. \tag{4}$$

None of the well-founded quasi-orderings that can be generated automatically by the usual techniques satisfies $\mathcal{DP} \cup \mathcal{EQ}$: Virtually all of those quasi-orderings are quasi-*simplification*-orderings[4] [Der82]. Hence, if $\succsim$ is a quasi-simplification-ordering satisfying $\mathcal{EQ}$, then we have

$$\mathsf{Q}(\mathsf{minus}(x, y), \mathsf{succ}(y)) \sim \mathsf{Q}(\mathsf{minus}(\mathsf{succ}(x), \mathsf{succ}(y)), \mathsf{succ}(y))$$

(as $\mathsf{minus}(x, y) \sim \mathsf{minus}(\mathsf{succ}(x), \mathsf{succ}(y))$ holds and as quasi-simplification-orderings are (weakly) monotonic). Moreover, we have

$$\mathsf{Q}(\mathsf{minus}(\mathsf{succ}(x), \mathsf{succ}(y)), \mathsf{succ}(y)) \succsim \mathsf{Q}(\mathsf{succ}(x), \mathsf{succ}(y))$$

(as quasi-simplification-orderings satisfy the (weak) subterm property). Hence, $\mathsf{Q}(\mathsf{minus}(x, y), \mathsf{succ}(y)) \succsim \mathsf{Q}(\mathsf{succ}(x), \mathsf{succ}(y))$ which is a contradiction to (4).

So the standard techniques for the automated generation of well-founded quasi-orderings fail here (and the same problem appears with most other examples). Hence, demanding $\mathcal{DP} \cup \mathcal{EQ}$ is ***too strong***, i.e. in this way most termination proofs will not succeed.

3.3 Constraints Without Defined Symbols

In Sect. 3.1 we showed that the existence of a well-founded quasi-ordering $\succsim$ satisfying $\mathcal{DP}$ is in general not sufficient for the termination of $\mathcal{R}$, because $\succsim$ does not necessarily respect the equalities induced by $\mathcal{E}$ (i.e. the equalities $\mathcal{EQ}$).

Nevertheless, if $\mathcal{DP}$ contains no defined symbols (from $\mathcal{D}$) then it is sufficient to find a well-founded quasi-ordering satisfying $\mathcal{DP}$. The reason is that any such quasi-ordering can be transformed into a well-founded quasi-ordering satisfying both $\mathcal{DP}$ and $\mathcal{EQ}$:

[4] $\mathcal{DP} \cup \mathcal{EQ}$ is not satisfied by polynomial orderings [Lan79] either (which do not have to be quasi-*simplification*-orderings).

Lemma 5. *Let $(\mathcal{D}, \mathcal{C}, \mathcal{E})$ be a ground-convergent CS, let $\mathcal{DP}$ be a set of inequalities containing no defined symbols. If there exists a well-founded quasi-ordering $\succsim$ satisfying $\mathcal{DP}$, then there also exists a well-founded quasi-ordering $\succsim'$ satisfying both $\mathcal{DP}$ and $\mathcal{EQ}$.*

Proof. For two ground terms s, t let $s \succsim' t$ iff $s{\downarrow_\mathcal{E}} \succsim t{\downarrow_\mathcal{E}}$. Since $\succsim$ is a well-founded quasi-ordering, $\succsim'$ is a well-founded quasi-ordering and obviously, $\succsim'$ satisfies $\mathcal{EQ}$.

We will now show that $\succsim'$ satisfies $\mathcal{DP}$: Let s and t be terms without defined symbols. As $\succsim$ satisfies $\mathcal{DP}$, it is sufficient to prove that $s \succsim t$ implies $s \succsim' t$. Note that for terms without defined symbols we have $(s\sigma){\downarrow_\mathcal{E}} = s(\sigma{\downarrow_\mathcal{E}})$ for each ground substitution σ (where $\sigma{\downarrow_\mathcal{E}}$ denotes the substitution of x by $(\sigma(x)){\downarrow_\mathcal{E}}$ for each $x \in DOM(\sigma)$). Now $s \succsim t$ implies $s(\sigma{\downarrow_\mathcal{E}}) \succsim t(\sigma{\downarrow_\mathcal{E}})$ for all ground substitutions σ or, respectively, $(s\sigma){\downarrow_\mathcal{E}} \succsim (t\sigma){\downarrow_\mathcal{E}}$. Hence, $s\sigma \succsim' t\sigma$ holds for all σ and therefore $s \succsim t$ implies $s \succsim' t$. Similarly it can be proved that $s \succ t$ implies $s \succ' t$. □

As an example consider the CS which only consists of the two rules for minus. Here, $\mathcal{DP}$ contains only the inequality $\mathsf{M}(\mathsf{succ}(x), \mathsf{succ}(y)) \succ \mathsf{M}(x, y)$ in which no defined symbol occurs. Of course there exist well-founded quasi-orderings satisfying this constraint (e.g. $\succsim_{rpo}$). For any ground-convergent $\mathcal{E}$ (cf. Footnote 3), $\succsim_{rpo}$ can be transformed into a well-founded quasi-ordering $\succsim'$ (as in the proof of Lemma 5) where $s \succsim' t$ holds iff $s{\downarrow_\mathcal{E}} \succsim_{rpo} t{\downarrow_\mathcal{E}}$. This quasi-ordering satisfies both $\mathcal{DP}$ and $\mathcal{EQ}$. Hence, termination of this CS is proved.

So if $\mathcal{DP}$ does not contain defined symbols we can just use standard techniques to generate a well-founded quasi-ordering satisfying $\mathcal{DP}$. By the two Lemmata 4 and 5 this is sufficient for the termination of $\mathcal{R}$.

To conclude, we have shown that the direct use of well-founded quasi-orderings is unsound (except if $\mathcal{DP}$ does not contain defined symbols) and we have illustrated that the straightforward solution (i.e. the restriction to quasi-orderings which also satisfy $\mathcal{EQ}$) imposes too strong requirements such that termination proofs often fail. In the next section we present a different, powerful approach to deal with CSs where $\mathcal{DP}$ *does* contain defined symbols. (This always happens if defined symbols occur within the arguments of a recursive call in $\mathcal{R}$.)

4 Elimination of Defined Symbols

If we want to prove termination of the quot-subsystem then we have to show that there exists a well-founded quasi-ordering satisfying both $\mathcal{EQ}$ (where $\mathcal{E}$ consists of the first two minus-rules) and the constraint

$$\mathcal{DP} = \{\mathsf{Q}(\mathsf{succ}(x), \mathsf{succ}(y)) \succ \mathsf{Q}(\mathsf{minus}(x, y), \mathsf{succ}(y))\}. \tag{4}$$

As demonstrated in Sect. 3 the application of methods for the synthesis of well-founded quasi-orderings is only possible if the constraints in $\mathcal{DP}$ do not contain defined symbols (like minus). Therefore our aim is to transform the constraint (4) into new constraints $\mathcal{DP}'$ *without defined symbols*. The invariant of this transformation will be that every quasi-ordering satisfying $\mathcal{EQ}$ and the resulting constraints $\mathcal{DP}'$ also satisfies the original constraints $\mathcal{DP}$. (In fact, this soundness result for our transformation only holds for a certain (slightly restricted) class of quasi-orderings, cf. Sect. 4.2.)

The constraints $\mathcal{DP}'$ resulting from the transformation contain no defined symbols any more. Hence, if we find a well-founded quasi-ordering which satisfies just $\mathcal{DP}'$ (by application of standard methods for the automated generation of such quasi-orderings), then by Lemma 5 there exists a well-founded quasi-ordering satisfying $\mathcal{DP}' \cup \mathcal{EQ}$. Hence, this quasi-ordering also satisfies $\mathcal{DP}$. Thus by Lemma 4, termination is proved. So, existence of a well-founded quasi-ordering satisfying the constraints $\mathcal{DP}'$ suffices for the termination of the CS.

In Sect. 4.1 we introduce the central idea of our transformation, viz. the *estimation technique*. To apply the estimation technique we need so-called *estimation inequalities* and Sect. 4.2 shows how they are computed. This section also contains the soundness theorem for our transformation. For the transformation we have to make a slight restriction on the used quasi-orderings. We present a generalized version of Lemma 5 in Sect. 4.3 which shows how to use methods for the automated generation of well-founded quasi-orderings to synthesize the quasi-orderings we need.

4.1 Estimation

The constraint (4) contains the defined symbol minus. The central idea of our transformation procedure is the *estimation* of defined symbols by new *non-defined* function symbols. For that purpose we extend our signature by a new estimation function $\overline{f}$ for each $f \in \mathcal{D}$. Now minus is replaced by the new non-defined symbol $\overline{\mathsf{minus}}$ and we demand that the result of $\overline{\mathsf{minus}}$ is always greater or equal than the result of minus, i.e. we demand

$$\overline{\mathsf{minus}}(x,y) \succsim \mathsf{minus}(x,y). \tag{5}$$

In contrast to minus the semantics of the non-defined symbol $\overline{\mathsf{minus}}$ are not determined by the equalities in $\mathcal{EQ}$. Our method transforms constraints like (4) into inequalities which contain non-defined symbols like $\overline{\mathsf{minus}}$, but no defined symbols like minus. If these resulting inequalities are satisfied by a well-founded quasi-ordering, then termination of the CS is proved.

Assume for the moment that we know a set of so-called *estimation inequalities* $\mathcal{IN}_{\overline{\mathsf{minus}} \succsim \mathsf{minus}}$ (without defined symbols) such that every quasi-ordering satisfying $\mathcal{IN}_{\overline{\mathsf{minus}} \succsim \mathsf{minus}}$ and $\mathcal{EQ}$ also satisfies (5). Moreover, let us restrict ourselves to quasi-orderings that are weakly monotonic on non-defined symbols (i.e. $s \succsim t$ implies $f(\ldots s \ldots) \succsim f(\ldots t \ldots)$ for all $f \notin \mathcal{D}$). Then $\mathcal{IN}_{\overline{\mathsf{minus}} \succsim \mathsf{minus}}$ and $\mathcal{EQ}$ do not only imply $\overline{\mathsf{minus}}(x,y) \succsim \mathsf{minus}(x,y)$, but they also ensure

$$\mathsf{Q}(\overline{\mathsf{minus}}(x,y), \mathsf{succ}(y)) \succsim \mathsf{Q}(\mathsf{minus}(x,y), \mathsf{succ}(y)).$$

Now

$$\mathsf{Q}(\mathsf{succ}(x), \mathsf{succ}(y)) \succ \mathsf{Q}(\overline{\mathsf{minus}}(x,y), \mathsf{succ}(y)) \tag{6}$$

and $\mathcal{IN}_{\overline{\mathsf{minus}} \succsim \mathsf{minus}}$ are sufficient for the original constraint (4), i.e. every quasi-ordering which satisfies (6), $\mathcal{IN}_{\overline{\mathsf{minus}} \succsim \mathsf{minus}}$ and $\mathcal{EQ}$ (and is weakly monotonic on non-defined symbols) also satisfies (4).

The restriction to quasi-orderings that are weakly monotonic on non-defined symbols allows to estimate function symbols *within* a term (i.e. function symbols that are not the root symbol of the term). If such a quasi-ordering satisfies $\mathcal{IN}_{\bar{f} \succsim f}$, then it also satisfies $C[\bar{f}(\ldots)] \succsim C[f(\ldots)]$ for all contexts C with no defined symbols above f.

In this way every inequality can be transformed into inequalities without defined symbols: we replace every defined symbol f by the new non-defined symbol $\bar{f}$ and add the estimation inequalities $\mathcal{IN}_{\bar{f} \succsim f}$ to the constraints.

Definition 6. For every term t we define its *estimation* by

$$\mathrm{est}(f(t_1,\ldots,t_n)) = \begin{cases} \bar{f}(\mathrm{est}(t_1),\ldots,\mathrm{est}(t_n)) & \text{if } f \in \mathcal{D} \\ f(\mathrm{est}(t_1),\ldots,\mathrm{est}(t_n)) & \text{if } f \notin \mathcal{D}. \end{cases}$$

Let $\mathcal{DP}$ be a set of inequalities. Then we define

$$\mathcal{DP}' = \{s \succ \mathrm{est}(t) | s \succ t \in \mathcal{DP}\} \cup \bigcup_{f \in \mathcal{D} \text{ occurs in } \mathcal{DP}} \mathcal{IN}_{\bar{f} \succsim f}.$$

In our example, minus is estimated by $\overline{\mathsf{minus}}$ and hence, the resulting set of constraints $\mathcal{DP}'$ consists of (6) and $\mathcal{IN}_{\overline{\mathsf{minus}} \succsim \mathsf{minus}}$.

4.2 Estimation Inequalities

In this section we show how to compute *estimation inequalities* $\mathcal{IN}_{\bar{f} \succsim f}$ which are needed for the estimation technique of Sect. 4.1 and we prove the soundness of our transformation. The estimation inequalities $\mathcal{IN}_{\overline{\mathsf{minus}} \succsim \mathsf{minus}}$ have to guarantee that $\overline{\mathsf{minus}}$ really is an upper bound for minus. To compute $\mathcal{IN}_{\overline{\mathsf{minus}} \succsim \mathsf{minus}}$ we consider each minus-rule of $\mathcal{E}$ separately. Instead of $\overline{\mathsf{minus}}(x,y) \succsim \mathsf{minus}(x,y)$ we therefore demand

$$\overline{\mathsf{minus}}(x,\mathsf{0}) \succsim x, \tag{7}$$

$$\overline{\mathsf{minus}}(\mathsf{succ}(x),\mathsf{succ}(y)) \succsim \mathsf{minus}(x,y). \tag{8}$$

We cannot define $\mathcal{IN}_{\overline{\mathsf{minus}} \succsim \mathsf{minus}} = \{(7),(8)\}$ because inequality (8) still contains the defined symbol minus. Defined symbols occurring in such formulas have to be eliminated by *estimation* again.

But the problem here is that minus *itself* appears in inequality (8). We cannot use the transformation of Definition 6 for the estimation of minus, because we do not know the estimation inequalities $\mathcal{IN}_{\overline{\mathsf{minus}} \succsim \mathsf{minus}}$ yet.

We solve this problem by constructing $\mathcal{IN}_{\overline{\mathsf{minus}} \succsim \mathsf{minus}}$ *inductively* with respect to the *computation ordering* of $\mathcal{E}$. The *computation ordering* $>_{\mathcal{E}}$ of a rewrite system $\mathcal{E}$ is a relation on ground terms where $s >_{\mathcal{E}} t$ iff $s \to_{\mathcal{E}}^{+} C[t]$ holds for some (possibly empty) context C. Obviously (as $\mathcal{E}$ is ground-convergent) its computation ordering is well-founded, i.e. inductions w.r.t. such orderings are sound.

The first case of our inductive construction of $\mathcal{IN}_{\overline{\mathsf{minus}} \succsim \mathsf{minus}}$ corresponds to the non-recursive first minus-rule. Inequality (7) ensures that for pairs of terms of the form $(t, 0)$, $\overline{\mathsf{minus}}$ is an upper bound for minus.

For the second minus-rule we have to ensure that inequality (8) holds, i.e. for terms of the form $(\mathsf{succ}(t_1), \mathsf{succ}(t_2))$, the result of $\overline{\mathsf{minus}}$ must be greater or equal than the result of minus. As *induction hypothesis* we can now use that this estimation is already correct for (t_1, t_2), because $\mathsf{minus}(\mathsf{succ}(t_1), \mathsf{succ}(t_2)) >_{\mathcal{E}} \mathsf{minus}(t_1, t_2)$. Hence when regarding $\overline{\mathsf{minus}}(\mathsf{succ}(x), \mathsf{succ}(y))$, we can use the induction hypothesis $\overline{\mathsf{minus}}(x, y) \succsim \mathsf{minus}(x, y)$. Then it is sufficient for (8) if

$$\overline{\mathsf{minus}}(\mathsf{succ}(x), \mathsf{succ}(y)) \succsim \overline{\mathsf{minus}}(x, y) \tag{9}$$

is true. Therefore we can replace (8) by inequality (9) which does not contain defined symbols.

Note that to eliminate the defined symbol minus from (8) due to an inductive argument we could again use the estimation technique. Now we have finished our inductive construction of $\mathcal{IN}_{\overline{\mathsf{minus}} \succsim \mathsf{minus}}$ and obtain

$$\begin{aligned} \mathcal{IN}_{\overline{\mathsf{minus}} \succsim \mathsf{minus}} = \{&\overline{\mathsf{minus}}(x, 0) \succsim x, & (7)\\ &\overline{\mathsf{minus}}(\mathsf{succ}(x), \mathsf{succ}(y)) \succsim \overline{\mathsf{minus}}(x, y)\}. & (9) \end{aligned}$$

Definition 7. Let $(\mathcal{D}, \mathcal{C}, \mathcal{E})$ be a ground-convergent CS. For each $f \in \mathcal{D}$ we define the set of *estimation inequalities* $\mathcal{IN}_{\bar{f} \succsim f}$ as follows (here, s^* abbreviates a tuple of terms $s_1, \ldots, s_n$):

$$\mathcal{IN}_{\bar{f} \succsim f} = \{\bar{f}(s^*) \succsim \mathsf{est}(t) \mid s^*, t \text{ are terms}, f(s^*) \to t \in \mathcal{E}\} \cup \bigcup_{\substack{g \in \mathcal{D} \text{ occurs in the} \\ f\text{-rules of } \mathcal{E} \text{ and } g \neq f}} \mathcal{IN}_{\bar{g} \succsim g}.$$

But $\mathcal{IN}_{\overline{\mathsf{minus}} \succsim \mathsf{minus}}$ is not yet sufficient for $\overline{\mathsf{minus}}(x, y) \succsim \mathsf{minus}(x, y)$. The reason is that for the construction of $\mathcal{IN}_{\overline{\mathsf{minus}} \succsim \mathsf{minus}}$ we only considered $\overline{\mathsf{minus}}(s_1, s_2)$ for terms s_1, s_2 of the form $(t, 0)$ or $(\mathsf{succ}(t_1), \mathsf{succ}(t_2))$ (i.e. we only considered terms where $\mathsf{minus}(s_1, s_2)$ is $\mathcal{E}$-reducible[5]). But for instance, $\mathcal{IN}_{\overline{\mathsf{minus}} \succsim \mathsf{minus}}$ does not guarantee $\overline{\mathsf{minus}}(0, \mathsf{succ}(0)) \succsim \mathsf{minus}(0, \mathsf{succ}(0))$.

Therefore we additionally have to demand that irreducible ground terms with a defined root symbol are minimal, i.e. we also demand the constraints

$$\mathcal{MIN} = \{t \succsim f(r^*) \mid f \in \mathcal{D}, t, r^* \text{ are ground terms}, f(r^*) \text{ is } \mathcal{E}\text{-normal form}\}.$$

If $\mathcal{MIN}$ is also satisfied, then irreducible terms like $\mathsf{minus}(0, \mathsf{succ}(0))$ are minimal, and hence $\overline{\mathsf{minus}}(0, \mathsf{succ}(0)) \succsim \mathsf{minus}(0, \mathsf{succ}(0))$ obviously holds. Now we can prove the soundness of our transformation:

[5] While in the original estimation method for functional programs [Gie95c] functions had to be completely defined, here we have to extend the estimation method to incompletely defined functions. This allows to prove termination of CSs that are not sufficiently complete [Pla85], too.

Theorem 8. *Let $(\mathcal{D}, \mathcal{C}, \mathcal{E})$ be a ground-convergent CS, let $\mathcal{DP}$ be a set of inequalities. Then every quasi-ordering $\succsim$ which is weakly monotonic on non-defined symbols and which satisfies $\mathcal{DP}' \cup \mathcal{EQ} \cup \mathcal{MIN}$ also satisfies $\mathcal{DP}$.*

Proof.

(a) We first prove that all $\mathcal{IN}_{\bar{f} \succsim f}$ for $f \in \mathcal{D}$ are sound. More precisely, if $\succsim$ satisfies $\mathcal{IN}_{\bar{f} \succsim f}$, then $\bar{f}(r^*) \succsim f(r^*)$ holds for all ground terms r^*. The proof is done by induction w.r.t. the computation ordering $>_{\mathcal{E}}$ of $\mathcal{E}$.
If $f(r^*)$ is irreducible then the statement follows from the fact that $\succsim$ satisfies $\mathcal{MIN}$. Otherwise there must be a rule $f(s^*) \to t$ where $r^* = s^*\sigma$ for some σ. Hence, $\mathcal{IN}_{\bar{f} \succsim f}$ contains $\bar{f}(s^*) \succsim \mathrm{est}(t)$ and the inequalities $\mathcal{IN}_{\bar{g} \succsim g}$ for all $g \in \mathcal{D}$ occurring in t.
Note that $\mathrm{est}(t)$ is obtained from t by successively replacing each subterm $g(u^*)$ of t with a defined root symbol $g \in \mathcal{D}$ by $\bar{g}(u^*)$. As the estimation starts with the outermost defined symbol, only such subterms $g(u^*)$ are estimated which have no defined symbol above them any more. Therefore, if $\bar{g}(u^*) \succsim g(u^*)$ holds for all these subterms, then $\mathrm{est}(t) \succsim t$ must obviously be true. Analogously, the instantiation $\mathrm{est}(t)\sigma$ is obtained from $t\sigma$ by replacing subterms $g(u^*)\sigma$ by $\bar{g}(u^*)\sigma$. Hence, if $\bar{g}(u^*)\sigma \succsim g(u^*)\sigma$ holds for all these subterms, then this implies $\mathrm{est}(t)\sigma \succsim t\sigma$.
All subterms $g(u^*)\sigma$ in $t\sigma$ are $>_{\mathcal{E}}$-smaller than $f(r^*)$. If g is a defined symbol ($g = f$ is possible) then $\mathcal{IN}_{\bar{f} \succsim f}$ must contain $\mathcal{IN}_{\bar{g} \succsim g}$ and by the induction hypothesis $\mathcal{IN}_{\bar{g} \succsim g}$ implies $\bar{g}(u^*)\sigma \succsim g(u^*)\sigma$. Hence, we have $\mathrm{est}(t)\sigma \succsim t\sigma$ and (as $\bar{f}(s^*) \succsim \mathrm{est}(t)$ is in $\mathcal{IN}_{\bar{f} \succsim f}$ and as $\succsim$ is closed under substitutions), $\bar{f}(r^*) \succsim \mathrm{est}(t)\sigma \succsim t\sigma$. As $t\sigma \sim f(r^*) \in \mathcal{EQ}$, this implies $\bar{f}(r^*) \succsim f(r^*)$.

(b) Now we can show that $\succsim$ satisfies $\mathcal{DP}$. Let $\mathcal{IN}_{\bar{f} \succsim f}$ hold for all defined symbols f occurring in a term t. Due to (a), this implies $\bar{f}(r^*) \succsim f(r^*)$ for all subterms $f(r^*)$ of t which have a defined root symbol. As illustrated in (a), we therefore can conclude $\mathrm{est}(t) \succsim t$. Hence, $s \succ \mathrm{est}(t)$ implies $s \succ t$. As $\succsim$ satisfies $\mathcal{DP}'$, it must also satisfy $\mathcal{DP}$. □

4.3 Automated Generation of Suitable Quasi-Orderings

Thm. 8 states that if we restrict ourselves to quasi-orderings that are weakly monotonic on non-defined symbols and that satisfy $\mathcal{EQ}$ and $\mathcal{MIN}$, then our transformation is sound, i.e. by application of the estimation technique to $\mathcal{DP}$ we obtain a set of inequalities $\mathcal{DP}'$ without defined symbols, such that every quasi-ordering (as above) satisfying $\mathcal{DP}'$ also satisfies $\mathcal{DP}$.

Recall that the reason for eliminating defined symbols was that we wanted to apply standard techniques to generate well-founded quasi-orderings that satisfy a given set of constraints. If these constraints contain no defined symbols, then by Lemma 5 every such quasi-ordering can be extended to a well-founded quasi-ordering satisfying also the equalities $\mathcal{EQ}$.

To use our transformation procedure we had to restrict ourselves to quasi-orderings which have a certain monotonicity property and which satisfy $\mathcal{MIN}$.

Therefore we now have to prove a stronger version of Lemma 5. It must state that if we have a well-founded quasi-ordering of this restricted form which satisfies some constraints $\mathcal{DP}'$ without defined symbols, then we can transform it into one of the same restricted form which additionally satisfies $\mathcal{EQ}$. (Then, by Thm. 8 this quasi-ordering also satisfies $\mathcal{DP}$ and therefore (by Lemma 4) termination of the CS under consideration is proved.)

So with this lemma it would be sufficient to synthesize a well-founded quasi-ordering which is weakly monotonic on non-defined symbols and which satisfies $\mathcal{MIN}$ and $\mathcal{DP}'$. Standard techniques can easily be used to generate suitable quasi-orderings that satisfy the required monotonicity condition, but an automated generation of quasi-orderings satisfying the (infinitely many) constraints in $\mathcal{MIN}$ seems to be hard at first sight.

Here, instead of demanding the constraints $\mathcal{MIN}$ the solution will be to restrict ourselves to quasi-orderings which have a minimal element, i.e. there must be a term m such that $t \succsim m$ holds for all ground terms t. Such quasi-orderings can easily be generated automatically (e.g. one could add a constraint of the form $x \succsim m$).

We will now prove a variant of Lemma 5 which states that if there is a well-founded quasi-ordering which is weakly monotonic on non-defined symbols, has a minimal element, and satisfies $\mathcal{DP}'$, then there also exists a well-founded quasi-ordering which is weakly monotonic on non-defined symbols and satisfies all $\mathcal{DP}'$, $\mathcal{EQ}$ and $\mathcal{MIN}$. Hence, for termination it is sufficient to find a well-founded quasi-ordering which is weakly monotonic on non-defined symbols, has a minimal element and satisfies $\mathcal{DP}'$. Such quasi-orderings can be generated automatically by standard techniques.

Lemma 9. *Let $(\mathcal{D}, \mathcal{C}, \mathcal{E})$ be a ground-convergent CS, let $\mathcal{DP}'$ be a set of inequalities containing no defined symbols. If there exists a well-founded quasi-ordering $\succsim$ which is weakly monotonic on non-defined symbols, has a minimal element, and satisfies $\mathcal{DP}'$, then there also exists a well-founded quasi-ordering $\succsim'$ which is weakly monotonic on non-defined symbols and satisfies $\mathcal{DP}' \cup \mathcal{EQ} \cup \mathcal{MIN}$.*

Proof. Let m be the minimal element of $\succsim$. For each ground term we define

$$[\![f(t_1,\ldots,t_n)]\!] = \begin{cases} f([\![t_1]\!],\ldots,[\![t_n]\!]) & \text{if } f \notin \mathcal{D} \\ m & \text{if } f \in \mathcal{D}, f(t_1,\ldots,t_n) \text{ is } \mathcal{E}\text{-normal form} \\ [\![f(t_1,\ldots,t_n)\downarrow_{\mathcal{E}}]\!] & \text{otherwise.} \end{cases}$$

For two ground terms s, t let $s \succsim' t$ iff $[\![s]\!] \succsim [\![t]\!]$. Since $\succsim$ is a well-founded quasi-ordering, $\succsim'$ is also a well-founded quasi-ordering and obviously, $\succsim'$ satisfies $\mathcal{MIN}$ and $\mathcal{EQ}$ (as $[\![t]\!] = [\![t\downarrow_{\mathcal{E}}]\!]$ holds for all ground terms t).

The quasi-ordering $\succsim'$ is weakly monotonic on every non-defined symbol f, because $s \succsim' t$ implies $[\![s\sigma]\!] \succsim [\![t\sigma]\!]$ for all ground substitutions σ, which in turn implies $f([\![\ldots]\!][\![s\sigma]\!][\![\ldots]\!]) \succsim f([\![\ldots]\!][\![t\sigma]\!][\![\ldots]\!])$ as $\succsim$ is weakly monotonic. Note that for $f \notin \mathcal{D}$ we have $f([\![\ldots]\!][\![s\sigma]\!][\![\ldots]\!]) = [\![f(\ldots(s\sigma)\ldots)]\!]$. Hence, $[\![f(\ldots(s\sigma)\ldots)]\!] \succsim [\![f(\ldots(t\sigma)\ldots)]\!]$, resp. $[\![f(\ldots s \ldots)\sigma]\!] \succsim [\![f(\ldots t \ldots)\sigma]\!]$ holds for all ground substitutions σ and therefore $f(\ldots s \ldots) \succsim' f(\ldots t \ldots)$.

That $\succsim'$ also satisfies $\mathcal{DP}'$ can be shown like in the proof of Lemma 5. □

The following final theorem summarizes our approach for termination proofs of constructor systems.

Theorem 10. *If there exists a well-founded quasi-ordering which is weakly monotonic on non-defined symbols, has a minimal element, and satisfies $\mathcal{DP}'$, then $\mathcal{R}$ is terminating.*

Proof. By Lemma 9 every such quasi-ordering can be extended to a well-founded weakly monotonic quasi-ordering which also satisfies $\mathcal{EQ}$ and $\mathcal{MIN}$ and by Thm. 8 this quasi-ordering must also satisfy the original constraints $\mathcal{DP}$. Hence, by Lemma 4 the CS $\mathcal{R}$ is terminating. □

So in our example, it is sufficient to find a well-founded weakly monotonic quasi-ordering which has a minimal element and satisfies the computed constraints (6) and $\mathcal{IN}_{\overline{\mathsf{minus}} \succsim \mathsf{minus}} = \{(7), (9)\}$. For instance, we can use a polynomial ordering [Lan79] where the function symbol $\mathsf{0}$ is mapped to the number 0, $\mathsf{succ}(x)$ is mapped to $x + 1$ and $\mathsf{Q}(x, y)$ and $\overline{\mathsf{minus}}(x, y)$ are both mapped to the polynomial x. Methods for the automated generation of such polynomial orderings have for instance been developed in [Ste94, Gie95a]. In this way termination of the CS for minus and quot can be proved fully automatically.

5 Conclusion and Further Work

We have developed a method for automated termination proofs of constructor systems which uses an estimation technique to automate the analysis of dependency pairs. Our method works as follows:

- For a CS $\mathcal{R}$ a ground-convergent CS $\mathcal{E}$ is synthesized in which $\mathcal{R}$ is contained. (For CSs that are hierarchical combinations of a certain type, a suitable $\mathcal{E}$ can be immediately obtained automatically, cf. [Art96].)
- Let $\mathcal{DP}$ be the set of inequalities which ensure that all dependency pairs are decreasing. Then by application of the estimation technique $\mathcal{DP}$ is transformed into a new set of inequalities $\mathcal{DP}'$ without defined symbols.
- Standard methods are used to generate a well-founded weakly monotonic quasi-ordering which has a minimal element and satisfies $\mathcal{DP}'$. If there exists such a quasi-ordering, then the CS $\mathcal{R}$ is terminating.

The presented method utilizes the special structure of hierarchical combinations of constructor systems. Therefore in this way termination of many CSs can be proved automatically where all other known techniques fail. Apart from that, with our approach one can still prove termination of all CSs satisfying the requirements of Thm. 3 that, by any other method, can be oriented by a simplification ordering with a minimal element. Our method has been tested on numerous practically relevant CSs from different areas of computer science (using a system for the automated generation of polynomial orderings [Gie95a]) and proved successful. A collection of examples which demonstrate the power of our method (including arithmetical operations such as gcd and logarithm, several sorting algorithms such as quicksort or selection_sort as well as functions on trees and graphs (e.g. a reachability algorithm)) can be found in [AG96].

Our approach fails if a well-founded quasi-ordering satisfying the generated constraints $\mathcal{DP}'$ cannot be found automatically. Therefore apart from the estimation technique we plan to examine alternative possibilities to derive suitable constraints $\mathcal{DP}'$, which may be advantageous for further sophisticated termination proofs (cf. [BM79, BL93, Wal94, Gie95c]). For that purpose, future work will include an investigation on possible combinations of our method with induction theorem proving systems (e.g. [BM79, BHHW86, KZ89, BHHS90, BKR92]).

Acknowledgements

Thanks are due to Hans Zantema and Thomas Kolbe for the discussions we have had on the subjects described in this paper and for their very helpful criticism.

References

[Art96] T. Arts. Termination by absence of infinite chains of dependency pairs. In *Proc. Coll. Trees in Algebra and Programming*, Linköping, Sweden, 1996.

[AG96] T. Arts & J. Giesl. Termination of constructor systems. Technical Report UU-CS-1996-07, Utrecht University, The Netherlands, 1996. Available from `http://www.cs.ruu.nl`.

[BD86] L. Bachmair & N. Dershowitz. Commutation, transformation and termination. In *Proc. 8th CADE, LNCS 230*, Oxford, England, 1986.

[BL90] F. Bellegarde & P. Lescanne. Termination by completion. *Applicable Algebra in Engineering, Communication and Computing*, 1:79-96, 1990.

[BL93] E. Bevers & J. Lewi. Proving termination of (conditional) rewrite systems. *Acta Informatica*, 30:537-568, 1993.

[BCL87] A. Ben Cherifa & P. Lescanne. Termination of rewriting systems by polynomial interpretations and its implementation. *Science of Computer Programming*, 9(2):137-159, 1987.

[BHHW86] S. Biundo, B. Hummel, D. Hutter & C. Walther. The Karlsruhe induction theorem proving system. *8th CADE, LNCS 230*, Oxford, England, 1986.

[BKR92] A. Bouhoula, E. Kounalis & M. Rusinowitch. SPIKE: an automatic theorem prover. In *Proceedings of the Conference on Logic Programming and Automated Reasoning, LNAI 624*, St. Petersburg, Russia, 1992.

[BM79] R. S. Boyer & J S. Moore. *A computational logic.* Academic Press, 1979.

[BHHS90] A. Bundy, F. van Harmelen, C. Horn & A. Smaill. The OYSTER-CLAM system. In *Proc. 10th CADE, LNAI 449*, Kaiserslautern, Germany, 1990.

[Der79] N. Dershowitz. A note on simplification orderings. *Information Processing Letters*, 9(5):212-215, 1979.

[Der82] N. Dershowitz. Orderings for term-rewriting systems. *Theoretical Computer Science*, 17:279-301, 1982.

[Der87] N. Dershowitz. Termination of rewriting. *Journal of Symbolic Computation*, 3(1, 2):69-115, 1987.

[DJ90] N. Dershowitz & J.-P. Jouannaud. Rewrite systems. *Handbook of Theoret. Comp. Sc.*, J. van Leeuwen, ed., vol. B, ch. 6, pp. 243-320, Elsevier, 1990.

[DH95] N. Dershowitz & C. Hoot. Natural Termination. *Theoretical Computer Science*, 142(2):179-207, 1995.

[FZ95] M. C. F. Ferreira & H. Zantema. Dummy elimination: making termination easier. In *Proceedings of the 10th International Conference on Fundamentals of Computation Theory, LNCS 965*, Dresden, Germany, 1995

[Ges94] A. Geser. An improved general path order. Technical Report MIP-9407, Universität Passau, Germany. To appear in *Applicable Algebra in Engineering, Communication, and Computation.*

[Gie95a] J. Giesl. Generating polynomial orderings for termination proofs. In *Proc. 6th RTA, LNCS 914*, Kaiserslautern, Germany, 1995.

[Gie95b] J. Giesl. Automated termination proofs with measure functions. In *Proc. 19th Annual German Conf. on AI, LNAI 981*, Bielefeld, Germany, 1995.

[Gie95c] J. Giesl. Termination analysis for functional programs using term orderings. In *Proceedings of the Second International Static Analysis Symposium, LNCS 983*, Glasgow, Scotland, 1995.

[HL78] G. Huet & D. S. Lankford. On the uniform halting problem for term rewriting systems. Rapport Laboria 283, Institut de Recherche d'Informatique et d'Automatique, Le Chesnay, France, 1978.

[KZ89] D. Kapur & H. Zhang. An overview of Rewrite Rule Laboratory (RRL). In *Proc. 3rd RTA, LNCS 355*, Chapel Hill, NC, 1989.

[Ken95] R. Kennaway. Complete term rewrite systems for decimal arithmetic and other total recursive functions. Presented at the *Second International Workshop on Termination*, La Bresse, France, 1995.

[KB70] D. E. Knuth & P. B. Bendix. Simple word problems in universal algebras. *Computational Problems in Abstract Algebra*, J. Leech, ed., Pergamon Press, pp. 263-297, 1970.

[KR95] M. R. K. Krishna Rao. Modular proofs for completeness of hierarchical term rewriting systems. *Theoretical Computer Science*, 151:487-512, 1995.

[Lan79] D. S. Lankford. On proving term rewriting systems are noetherian. Tech. Report Memo MTP-3, Louisiana Tech. University, Ruston, LA, 1979.

[MN70] Z. Manna & S. Ness. On the termination of Markov algorithms. In *Proc. of the 3rd Hawaii Int. Conf. on System Science*, Honolulu, HI, 1970.

[Mar87] U. Martin. How to choose weights in the Knuth-Bendix ordering. In *Proc. 2nd RTA, LNCS 256*, Bordeaux, France, 1987.

[Pla78] D. A. Plaisted. A recursively defined ordering for proving termination of term rewriting systems. Report R-78-943, Dept. of Computer Science, University of Illinois, Urbana, IL, 1978.

[Pla85] D. A. Plaisted. Semantic confluence tests and completion methods. *Inform. and Control*, 65(2/3):182-215, 1985.

[Ste94] J. Steinbach. Generating polynomial orderings. *Information Processing Letters*, 49:85-93, 1994.

[Ste95a] J. Steinbach. Automatic termination proofs with transformation orderings. In *Proc. 6th RTA, LNCS 914*, Kaiserslautern, Germany, 1995.

[Ste95b] J. Steinbach. Simplification orderings: history of results. *Fundamenta Informaticae*, 24:47-87, 1995.

[Wal94] C. Walther. On proving the termination of algorithms by machine. *Artificial Intelligence*, 71(1):101-157, 1994.

[Zan94] H. Zantema. Termination of term rewriting: interpretation and type elimination. *Journal of Symbolic Computation* 17:23-50, 1994.

[Zan95] H. Zantema. Termination of term rewriting by semantic labelling. *Fundamenta Informaticae*, 24:89-105, 1995.

Dummy Elimination in Equational Rewriting

M. C. F. Ferreira*

Utrecht University, Dep. of Computer Science, P.O. box 80.089, 3508 TB Utrecht, The Netherlands; Dep. de Informática, Fac. Ciências e Tecnologia, Univ. Nova de Lisboa - Quinta da Torre - 2825 Monte da Caparica, Portugal, tel: +351-1-294 85 36, fax: +351-1- 294 85 41, e-mail: cf@fct.unl.pt

Abstract. In [5] we introduced the concept of dummy elimination in term rewriting: a transformation on terms which eliminates function symbols simplifying the rewrite rules and making, in general, the task of proving termination easier. Here we consider the more general setting of rewriting modulo an equational theory; we show that, in contrast with most techniques developed for proving termination of rewrite systems, dummy elimination remains valid in the presence of equational theories. Furthermore using the same proof technique, the soundness of a family of transformations (containing dummy elimination) can be shown. This work was motivated by an application in the area of Process Algebra.

1 Introduction

We are interested in simplifying the process of proving termination of (equational) term rewriting systems (TRS's). A possibility is to devise sound transformations such that the transformed systems are somehow easier to deal with, wrt termination proofs, than the original ones. Examples of this approach are *transformation orderings* [1, 7], *semantic labelling* [13] and *distribution elimination* [12] (see also [14]); all these transformations are meant for standard term rewriting (the equational theory considered coincides with syntactic equality).

While trying to solve a conjecture about distribution elimination, we arrived at a different transformation both simpler and seemingly more powerful namely *dummy elimination* [5]. Later, combining ideas of *distribution* and *dummy elimination*, a family of transformations was devised [4]. *Dummy elimination* seemed to be particularly useful for proving termination of TRS's arising from the description of Process Algebra systems [6]; however process terms are considered modulo associativity and commutativity of some operators so this raised the pertinent question of validity of the transformations in an equational setting. In this paper we show that the transformations remain indeed valid for rewriting modulo a set of equations, provided the equations have a certain shape. This is a point that should be stressed since most techniques developed for proving termination of TRS's do not carry over to rewriting modulo equational theories.

* Partially supported by NWO, the Dutch Organization for Scientific Research, under grant 612-316-041.

Suppose we want to prove termination of the following system

$$x * (y + z) \rightarrow (a(x, y) * y) + (x * a(z, x))$$

modulo associativity and commutativity of "+". Intuitively, the function symbol a is created but seems not to have any influence on the reductions. Taking that into account, we can eliminate it and transform the given rule into

$$x * (y + z) \rightarrow (\diamond * y) + (x * \diamond) \qquad x * (y + z) \rightarrow x$$
$$x * (y + z) \rightarrow y \qquad x * (y + z) \rightarrow z$$

where $\diamond$ is a fresh constant. Termination of the first system is not easy to prove; termination of the second system can be proven by defining a polynomial interpretation in the set of positive integers $\mathbb{N}_1$, with the usual order, as follows: $\diamond_{\mathbb{N}_1} = 1$, $x +_{\mathbb{N}_1} y = x + y + 2$ and $x *_{\mathbb{N}_1} y = x + 2y$ (note also that if we do not consider "+" as being associative and commutative, the first system cannot be handled by orders as recursive path order, while the transformed version can). If the transformation is sound wrt to termination, our task is done. Proving that this transformation is sound in the equational setting constitutes the main result of this paper. We will concentrate on the transformation exemplified and sketch how the other transformations in the family can be obtained; we do so to simplify the presentation and because when comparing the transformations dummy elimination seemed to be the one with better properties [4].

The paper is organized as follows: in sec. 2 we introduce some notions on orders and rewriting needed, in sec. 3 we introduce dummy elimination for equational rewriting and in sec. 4 we prove the soundness of this transformation. In sec. 5 we show how to obtain the other transformations and make some remarks on the relationship between them. Concluding remarks are found in sec. 6.

2 Preliminaries

We introduce some notation and give some basic notions over orders, TRS's and equational rewriting. For more information the reader is referred to [2, 9, 10].

A *poset* $(S, >)$ is a set S together with a partial order, $>$; we say that $>$ is well-founded if there are no infinite sequences of the form $s_0 > s_1 > \cdots$. Given a poset $(S, >)$, $M(S)$ denotes the finite multisets over S and $>_{mul}$ denotes the multiset extension of $>$ to $M(S)$, defined as usual. The multiset extension of a partial order is a partial order; it is also well-foundedness preserving and monotone wrt the order extended [3]. We use the parentheses $\{\!\{ \ \}\!\}$ to denote multisets. Also, whenever possible multiset operations will be denoted by squared symbols (eg. $\sqcup$) and set operations by rounded symbols (eg. $\cup$).

Quasi-orders over a set S are denoted, in general, by $\succeq$. Any quasi-order defines an equivalence relation, namely $\succeq \cap \preceq$ (denoted by $\sim$ or $\mathtt{eq}(\succeq)$ when confusion may arise), and a partial order, which we consider to be $\succeq \setminus \preceq$ (the reverse is another possibility), denoted by $\succ$ or $\mathtt{ord}(\succeq)$. Conversely, the union of a given partial order $\succ$ and equivalence $\sim$ is a quasi-order only if they satisfy

$$(\sim \circ \succ \circ \sim) \subseteq \succ \qquad (1)$$

where $\circ$ represents relation composition; in this case we say that $\succ$ and $\sim$ are *compatible*. From now on if we characterize a quasi-order via $\succ \cup \sim$, we assume compatibility. A quasi-order $\succeq$ is well-founded if $\succ$ is.

If $\succeq$ and $\succeq'$ are quasi-orders over the same set, we say that $\succeq'$ extends $\succeq$ iff $\succ \subseteq \succ'$ and $\sim \subseteq \sim'$. Given a quasi-order $\succeq$ over S, the quotient $S/\sim$ consists of the equivalence classes of $\sim$; classes are denoted by $\langle\ \rangle$. We can extend $\succ$ to $S/\sim$ in a natural way, namely $\langle s\rangle \sqsupset \langle t\rangle$ iff $s \succ t$. Since $\succ$ and $\sim$ satisfy condition (1), the relation $\sqsupset$ is well-defined. Furthermore $\sqsupset$ is a partial order over $S/\sim$. When this extension is well-defined we abusively write $\succ$ instead of $\sqsupset$.

For any quasi-order $\succeq$, $\succeq_{mul}$ denotes its multiset extension, defined as follows: X $\mathbf{eq}(\succeq_{mul})$ $Y \iff \langle X\rangle = \langle Y\rangle$ and X $\mathbf{ord}(\succeq_{mul})$ $Y \iff \langle X\rangle \succ_{mul} \langle Y\rangle$, where for any multiset $A = \{\!\{a_1, \cdots, a_m\}\!\}$, $\langle A\rangle$ is given by $\{\!\{\langle a_1\rangle, \cdots, \langle a_m\rangle\}\!\}$. As for partial orders, this extension preserves well-foundedness.

Given a non-empty set S, we consider non-empty trees over S, defined by the following data type: $Tr(S) \cong S \times M(Tr(S))$, i. e., $Tr(S)$ is the least fixed point of $f(X) = S \times M(X)$. We give the definition of $\geq_{rpo}$, modified to be applied on trees, and an equivalent characterization of it.

Definition 1. Let $(S, \geq)$ be a quasi-ordered set. For any trees $s, t \in Tr(S)$, $s = (a, M) \geq_{rpo} t$ if and only if either

- $t = (b, M')$ and $\forall u \in M' : s >_{rpo} u$, and either
  - $a > b$, or
  - $a \sim b$ and $M \geq_{rpo,mul} M'$; or
- $\exists v \in M : v \geq_{rpo} t$.

where $\geq_{rpo,mul}$ is the multiset extension of $\geq_{rpo}$.

Lemma 2. *For any trees $A, B \in Tr(S)$, we have that:*

1. *$A \sim_{rpo} B$ if and only if $A = (a, \{\!\{u_1, \ldots, u_k\}\!\})$, $B = (b, \{\!\{v_1, \ldots, v_m\}\!\})$, with $k, m \geq 0$, and $a \sim b$, $k = m$, and there is a permutation π of $\{1, \ldots, k\}$ such that $u_i \sim_{rpo} v_{\pi(i)}$, for all $1 \leq i \leq k$; we abbreviate this last condition to $\{\!\{u_1, \ldots, u_k\}\!\} \sim_{rpo}^{mul} \{\!\{v_1, \ldots, v_m\}\!\}$.*
2. *$A >_{rpo} B$ if and only if $A = (a, M)$, $B = (b, M')$ and either*
   - *$a > b$ and $\forall U \in M' : A >_{rpo} U$; or*
   - *$a \sim b$ and M $\mathbf{ord}(\geq_{rpo,mul})$ M'; or*
   - *$\exists U \in M : U >_{rpo} B$ or $U \sim_{rpo} B$.*

It is well-known that $\geq$ is well-founded on S if and only if $\geq_{rpo}$ is well-founded on $Tr(S)$. Furthermore $\geq_{rpo}$ has the "subtree property" (trees are greater than proper subtrees) and is monotone wrt the (quasi-)order used.

$\mathcal{T}(\mathcal{F}, \mathcal{X})$ denotes the set of terms over $\mathcal{F}$, a non-empty set of fixed arity function symbols, possibly infinite, and $\mathcal{X}$, a denumerable set of variables such that $\mathcal{F} \cap \mathcal{X} = \emptyset$. For $t \in \mathcal{T}(\mathcal{F}, \mathcal{X})$, the set $var(t)$ contains the variables occurring in t and $mvar(t)$ denotes the multiset of variables of t. We denote by $|t|$ the number of symbols occurring in a term t.

A *TRS* is a tuple $(\mathcal{F}, \mathcal{X}, R)$, with $R \subseteq \mathcal{T}(\mathcal{F}, \mathcal{X}) \times \mathcal{T}(\mathcal{F}, \mathcal{X})$. The elements (l, r) of R are the rules of the TRS and are usually denoted by $l \to r$; we require that they satisfy $l \notin \mathcal{X}$ and $var(r) \subseteq var(l)$, for every rule $l \to r$. In the following, unless otherwise specified, we identify the TRS with R, being $\mathcal{F}$ the set of function symbols occurring in R. The *reduction relation* on $\mathcal{T}(\mathcal{F}, \mathcal{X})$ induced by a TRS R is denoted by $\to_R$; its transitive closure is denoted by $\to_R^+$ and its reflexive-transitive closure by $\to_R^*$. By $\to_R^n$, with $n \in \mathbb{N}$, we denote the composition of $\to_R$ with itself n times (if $n = 0$ then $\to_R^n$ is the identity). A *rewrite sequence* is a sequence of reduction steps $t_0 \to_R t_1 \to_R \cdots$.

A binary relation Θ over $\mathcal{T}(\mathcal{F}, \mathcal{X})$ is said to be: *closed under substitutions* if $s\Theta t \Rightarrow s\sigma\Theta t\sigma$, for any substitution $\sigma : \mathcal{X} \to \mathcal{T}(\mathcal{F}, \mathcal{X})$, *closed under contexts* if $s\Theta t \Rightarrow C[s]\Theta C[t]$, for any linear context C (equivalently, $s\Theta t \Rightarrow f(\ldots, s, \ldots)\Theta f(\ldots, t, \ldots)$, for all non-constant $f \in \mathcal{F}$), and a *congruence* if it is an equivalence relation closed under contexts.

A partial order $>$ (resp. quasi-order $\geq$) on $\mathcal{T}(\mathcal{F}, \mathcal{X})$ is a *rewrite order* (resp. *rewrite quasi-order*) if it is closed under contexts and substitutions (resp. both $>$ and $\sim$ are closed under contexts and substitutions); a *reduction (quasi-)order* is a well-founded rewrite (quasi-)order.

An *equation* (or *axiom*) over $\mathcal{T}(\mathcal{F}, \mathcal{X})$ is a pair of terms (s, t); an *equational system* over $\mathcal{T}(\mathcal{F}, \mathcal{X})$ is a set of equations. Any equational system EQ generates a congruence on the set of terms; we denote by $=_{EQ}$ the least congruence closed under substitutions containing EQ. Without loss of generality, we assume that any equational system is symmetric, i. e., if $(s, t) \in EQ$ then also $(t, s) \in EQ$; however for the sake of simplicity, when expressing EQ extensively we omit symmetric equations. With this assumption, the equational theory generated by a set of equations becomes:

Definition 3. The equational theory generated by an equational system EQ is denoted by $=_{EQ}$ and is the least congruence on $\mathcal{T}(\mathcal{F}, \mathcal{X})$ containing EQ and closed under substitutions, i. e., $s =_{EQ} t$ iff either

- $s = t$,
- $s = C[e_1\sigma]$ and $t = C[e_2\sigma]$, for some equation $(e_1, e_2) \in EQ$, linear context C and substitution σ,
- $s =_{EQ} u$ and $u =_{EQ} t$, for some term u.

Definition 4. An equational rewrite system R/EQ consists of a TRS R and an equational system EQ, both defined over the same set of terms. Its associated equational rewrite relation $\to_{R/EQ}$ is given by: $s \to_{R/EQ} t$ iff there are terms u, v such that $s =_{EQ} u \to_R v =_{EQ} t$. We speak of *equational rewriting* or *rewriting modulo a set of equations*.

A TRS is *terminating* if it admits no infinite rewrite sequence. If EQ is an equational system and R a TRS, we say that R is E-terminating (or that R/EQ is terminating) if the relation $\to_{R/EQ}$ is terminating, i. e., if there are no infinite sequences of the form: $s_0 =_{EQ} s'_0 \to_R s_1 =_{EQ} s'_1 \to_R s_2 =_{EQ} s'_2 \to_R s_3 \ldots$

An equational rewrite system R/EQ is compatible with a quasi-order $\succeq = \succ \cup \sim$ (on $\mathcal{T}(\mathcal{F}, \mathcal{X})$) if $=_{EQ} \subseteq \sim$ and $\to_R \subseteq \succ$. We have that:

Theorem 5. *An equational rewrite system R/EQ is terminating if and only if it is compatible with a reduction quasi-order.*

The following result can easily be proven using the definitions and properties of equational rewriting.

Theorem 6. *Let R/EQ be an equational rewrite system over $\mathcal{T}(\mathcal{F},\mathcal{X})$. Then*

1. $=_{EQ} \circ \rightarrow^{+}_{R/EQ} \circ =_{EQ} \subseteq \rightarrow^{+}_{R/EQ}$,
2. *If R/EQ is terminating then $\rightarrow^{+}_{R/EQ}$ is a reduction order on $\mathcal{T}(\mathcal{F},\mathcal{X})$. Furthermore $\rightarrow^{+}_{R/EQ} \cup =_{EQ}$ is a reduction quasi-order on $\mathcal{T}(\mathcal{F},\mathcal{X})$.*

Proving E-termination is in general more complicated than proving termination (see [8]) and most methods developed for TRS's (eg. recursive path order) cannot be applied in the presence of equations. Recently a lot of effort has been put into extending existing path orders to rewriting modulo AC-theories (see [11] for a description of such orders); for more general theories still little is known.

3 Transforming the equational system

We will consider fixed-arity signatures and elimination of only one function symbol. The theory can also be presented for varyadic signatures and/or simultaneous elimination of several function symbols, but the presentation becomes messier and the results obtained are actually weaker, as we will show later. Let a be a function symbol with arity $N > 0$, and not occurring in signature $\mathcal{F}$; a is the function symbol to be eliminated. Let $\diamond$ be a constant also not occurring in $\mathcal{F}$. We denote by $\mathcal{F}_a$, $\mathcal{F}_\diamond$ and $\mathcal{F}_{a,\diamond}$ resp. the sets $\mathcal{F}\cup\{a\}$, $\mathcal{F}\cup\{\diamond\}$ and $\mathcal{F}\cup\{a,\diamond\}$. We name *alien terms* those terms of $T(\mathcal{F}_a, X)$ whose root symbol is a.

Since we are concerned with E-termination, we want to exclude equations that will force non-termination (independently of the form of the TRS). In [8], two essential restrictions equations have to satisfy are identified, namely:

1. (non-erasing) $var(e_1) = var(e_2)$, for any equation (e_1, e_2);
2. (e_1, e_2) can not be a collapsing equation, i. e., have the form $e_1 = x$ while e_2 contains more than one occurrence of the variable x (or vice-versa).

Condition (2) above can be generalized: equations of the form $(D[C[x]], C[x])$ where x is a variable also occurring in context D, also prevent termination. Due to a technicality in our proof, we need to sharpen condition (1) above, we require that the equations are variable-preserving, i. e., that $mvar(e_1) = mvar(e_2)$ for any equation (e_1, e_2).

In $T(\mathcal{F}_a,\mathcal{X})$, we consider the relation $\rightarrow_{R/EQ}$, where EQ is a set of (variable-preserving) equations not containing the function symbol a. We define a set of transformations on terms that induce transformations on the TRS's, and then show that termination of $\rightarrow_{R/EQ}$ can be inferred from termination of $\rightarrow_{\mathcal{E}(R)/EQ}$, where $\mathcal{E}$ is the transformation used. We will concentrate in one transformation, later we define the full family and justify our choice. As can be seen in [4], the soundness proof for all transformations is practically the same (the proof is parameterized by the transformation used).

The main idea behind the transformation is to recursively break a term into pieces (also terms) that do not contain the function symbol to be eliminated. One of these blocks, namely the one above all occurrences of the function symbol "a", is denoted by **cap**(t) and treated especially. The other blocks are collected in a set denoted by **dec**(t).

Example 1. The following term t

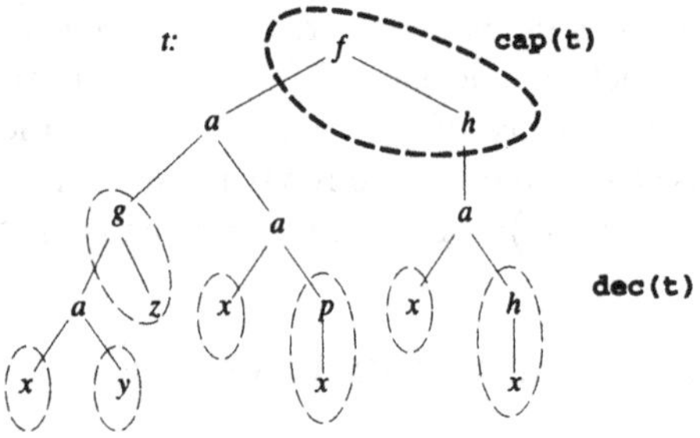

has $\mathbf{cap}(t) = f(\diamond, h(\diamond))$ and $\mathbf{dec}(t) = \{g(\diamond, z), x, y, \diamond, p(x), h(x)\}$.

Both **cap**(t) and **dec**(t) have very simple inductive definitions. Strictly speaking their domain need only be $T(\mathcal{F}_a, \mathcal{X})$, however to simplify the treatment later (basicly avoid defining extensions only to include $\diamond$ in its domain), we use the extended signature $\mathcal{F}_{a,\diamond}$. This same observation applies to other definitions.

Definition 7. Functions **cap**: $T(\mathcal{F}_{a,\diamond}, \mathcal{X}) \to T(\mathcal{F}_\diamond, \mathcal{X})$ and **dec**: $T(\mathcal{F}_{a,\diamond}, \mathcal{X}) \to \mathcal{P}(T(\mathcal{F}_\diamond, \mathcal{X}))$ are defined inductively as follows:

t	**cap**(t)	**dec**(t)
x	x	$\emptyset$
$f(t_1, \ldots, t_m)$	$f(\mathbf{cap}(t_1), \ldots, \mathbf{cap}(t_m))$	$\bigcup_{i=1}^{m} \mathbf{dec}(t_i)$
$a(t_1, \ldots, t_N)$	$\diamond$	$\bigcup_{i=1}^{N} (\{\mathbf{cap}(t_i)\} \cup \mathbf{dec}(t_i))$

We can extend the function **cap** to substitutions as follows.

Definition 8. Let $\sigma : \mathcal{X} \to T(\mathcal{F}_a, \mathcal{X})$ be an arbitrary substitution. The substitution $\mathbf{cap}(\sigma) : \mathcal{X} \to T(\mathcal{F}_\diamond, \mathcal{X})$ is defined by $\mathbf{cap}(\sigma)(x) = \mathbf{cap}(\sigma(x))$, for all $x \in \mathcal{X}$.

Next lemmas (easily proven by induction on terms) state that **cap** distributes over substitution application and is idempotent.

Lemma 9. *Let* $t \in T(\mathcal{F}_a, \mathcal{X})$ *and let* $\sigma : \mathcal{X} \to T(\mathcal{F}_a, \mathcal{X})$ *be an arbitrary substitution; then* $\mathtt{cap}(t\sigma) = \mathtt{cap}(t)\mathtt{cap}(\sigma)$.

Lemma 10. *Let* $t \in T(\mathcal{F}_a, \mathcal{X})$ *be any term. Then* $\mathtt{cap}(\mathtt{cap}(t)) = \mathtt{cap}(t)$.

We can now define the transformation on TRS's. As can be expected we will transform the left and righthand-sides of the rules in R and create new rules. Since the transformation of a term gives, in general, a set containing more than one term, we have to specify which element will be chosen for the lefthand-side of the new rules; our choice is the cap of the lefthand-side of the original rule.

Definition 11. Given an equational rewrite system R/EQ over $T(\mathcal{F}_a, \mathcal{X})$ such that the function symbol a does not occur in the equations of EQ, $\mathcal{E}(R)/EQ$ is an equational rewrite system over $T(\mathcal{F}_\diamond, \mathcal{X})$ where $\mathcal{E}(R)$ is given by

$$\mathcal{E}(R) = \{\mathtt{cap}(l) \to u \mid l \to r \in R \text{ and } u \in \{\mathtt{cap}(r)\} \cup \mathtt{dec}(r)\}$$

We make some remarks about the transformation defined.

- In some cases $\mathcal{E}(R)$ may not be a TRS in the usual sense, since $\mathtt{cap}(l)$ may either be a variable or eliminate variables needed in the righthand-sides of the transformed rules.
- Allowing the function symbol to be eliminated to occur in the lefthand-sides of rules of the TRS is a possibility that was first remarked by Middeldorp and Ohsaki (personal communication).
- When the function symbol a does not occur in a term t, we have that $\mathtt{dec}(t) = \emptyset$ and $\mathtt{cap}(t) = t$. Since the equations in EQ satisfy this restriction, it is not necessary to apply the transformation to them.

Example 2. The following example (which motivated this work) was taken from [6]. It is part of an equational system representing a finite axiomatization of Basic Process Algebra with prefix iteration, deadlock and empty process. In order to prove the completeness of this axiomatization with respect to strong bisimulation equivalence, E-termination of the rules below is required.

Let $\mathcal{F} = \{+, *, \centerdot, c, d\}$, with $+, \centerdot, *$ having arity 2 and c, d being constants. Let EQ consist of the associative and commutative equations for the function symbol "+", and let R be given by the rules (in infix notation):

$$(c * y) + z \to (c \centerdot (c * y)) + (y + z); \qquad c * (d * z) \to c * ((d \centerdot (d * z)) + z)$$

By eliminating "$\centerdot$" we get the TRS

$$\begin{array}{ll} (c * y) + z \to \diamond + (y + z); & c * (d * z) \to c * (\diamond + z) \\ (c * y) + z \to c; & c * (d * z) \to d \\ (c * y) + z \to c * y; & c * (d * z) \to d * z \end{array}$$

E-termination of the original TRS is quite difficult to prove while E-termination of the transformed system is easy; just use the weight function w on the positive naturals, given by $w(x+y) = w(x*y) = w(x)+w(y)$, $w(\diamond) = 1$, $w(c) = w(d) = 2$.

From the definition of $\mathcal{E}$, we see that in general the TRS $\mathcal{E}(R)$ has more rules but is syntactically simpler than the original one, so the transformation can be useful if we are able to infer termination of R/EQ from termination of $\mathcal{E}(R)/EQ$. Termination however is not preserved. The system with $EQ = \emptyset$ and rule $f(x,x) \to f(a(x),x)$, is terminating. The transformed TRS $\mathcal{E}(R)$ is given by: $f(x,x) \to f(\diamond,x), f(x,x) \to x$, and is obviously not terminating (note also that it is not essential that $EQ = \emptyset$). In general different transformations can lead to systems with different termination properties.

4 Soundness of the transformation

We now show that termination of $\mathcal{E}(R)/EQ$ implies termination of R/EQ. Before going into the technical details we give a general idea of the proof. If $\mathcal{E}(R)/EQ$ is terminating, there is a well-founded quasi-order $\geq$ on $T(\mathcal{F}_\diamond,\mathcal{X})$ compatible with $\mathcal{E}(R)/EQ$. If we consider the quasi-ordered set $(Tr(T(\mathcal{F}_\diamond,\mathcal{X})), \geq_{rpo})$ (where $\geq_{rpo}$ is the recursive path order associated with $\geq$) then $\geq_{rpo}$ is also well-founded. We now use the trees over $T(\mathcal{F}_\diamond,\mathcal{X})$ to interpret the terms of $T(\mathcal{F}_a,\mathcal{X})$ in such a way that rewrite chains in R/EQ translate to descending chains of trees. Preservation of well-foundedness by $\geq_{rpo}$ gives then termination of $\to_{R/EQ}$.

Definition 12. A term $t \in T(\mathcal{F}_a,\mathcal{X})$ is mapped to tree $\mathtt{tree}(t) \in Tr(T(\mathcal{F}_\diamond,\mathcal{X}))$, by the function $\mathtt{tree} : T(\mathcal{F}_{a,\diamond},\mathcal{X}) \to Tr(T(\mathcal{F}_\diamond,\mathcal{X}))$, defined inductively as:

- $\mathtt{tree}(x) = (x,\emptyset)$, for any $x \in \mathcal{X}$,
- $\mathtt{tree}(f(s_1,\ldots,s_m)) = (\mathtt{cap}(f(s_1,\ldots,s_m)), \bigsqcup_{j=1}^{m} M_j)$, where for all $1 \leq j \leq m$, $\mathtt{tree}(s_j) = (\mathtt{cap}(s_j), M_j)$,
- $\mathtt{tree}(a(s_1,\ldots,s_N)) = (\mathtt{cap}(a(s_1,\ldots,s_N)), \bigsqcup_{j=1}^{N} \{\!\{\mathtt{tree}(s_j)\}\!\})$.

Example 3. The following picture shows the same term as in example 1 together with its corresponding tree.

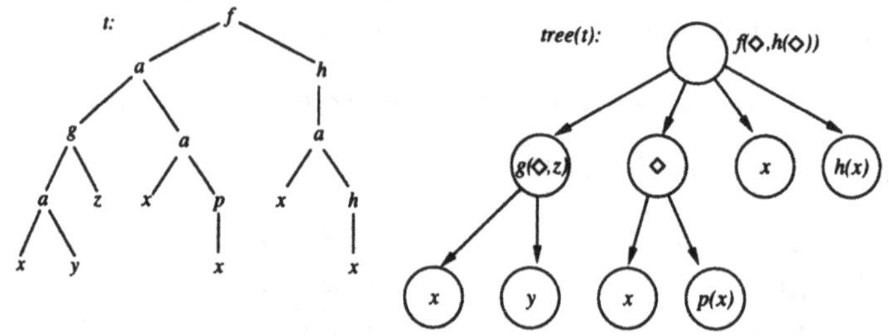

Note 13. From now on we assume we have an equational rewriting system R/EQ, such that the equations in EQ are variable-preserving, and do not contain the function symbol a. We consider the equational theory generated by EQ over

the set of terms $T(\mathcal{F}_\diamond, \mathcal{X})$, so $\mathcal{E}(R)/EQ$ is an equational rewrite system over $T(\mathcal{F}_\diamond, \mathcal{X})$. Furthermore we assume that $\mathcal{E}(R)$ is well-defined and that $\mathcal{E}(R)/EQ$ is terminating.

Since $\mathcal{E}(R)/EQ$ is terminating, by theorem 6, we have that $\rightarrow^+_{\mathcal{E}(R)/EQ}$ is a well-founded partial order on $T(\mathcal{F}_\diamond, \mathcal{X})$, closed under contexts and substitutions, compatible with $\mathcal{E}(R)$ and compatible with $=_{EQ}$. We will interpret terms in $T(\mathcal{F}_a, \mathcal{X})$ as trees in $Tr(T(\mathcal{F}_\diamond, \mathcal{X}))$ and it seems natural to use $\geq_{rpo}$ over the quasi-order $\rightarrow^+_{\mathcal{E}(R)/EQ} \cup =_{EQ}$. However in order to prove that $s \rightarrow_R t \Rightarrow \mathtt{tree}(s) >_{rpo} \mathtt{tree}(t)$ (by induction on the definition of reduction), at some point we need the order $\rightarrow^+_{\mathcal{E}(R)/EQ}$ to satisfy a weakened form of subterm property (modulo EQ). In general this will not be the case, but we can extend $\rightarrow^+_{\mathcal{E}(R)/EQ}$ to another order on $T(\mathcal{F}_\diamond, \mathcal{X})$, that while loosing closedness under contexts, maintains all the other nice properties enjoyed by $\rightarrow^+_{\mathcal{E}(R)/EQ}$ and also has the property required. So before proceeding further, we introduce this order.

Definition 14. We define a relation $\gg$ on $T(\mathcal{F}_\diamond, \mathcal{X})$ as follows:

$$s \gg t \text{ iff } s\ (\trianglerighteq \circ \rightarrow_{\mathcal{E}(R)/EQ})^+\ t,$$

where $p \trianglerighteq q$ iff $\exists C: s =_{EQ} C[t]$.

The following result is not difficult to prove.

Lemma 15. *In the conditions of definition 14, if $\mathcal{E}(R)/EQ$ is terminating then $\gg$ is a well-founded partial order on $T(\mathcal{F}_\diamond, \mathcal{X})$ extending $\rightarrow_{\mathcal{E}(R)/EQ}$, compatible with $=_{EQ}$, closed under substitutions and satisfying $(\trianglerighteq \circ \gg) \subseteq \gg$. Furthermore we have $(\trianglerighteq \circ \rightarrow_{\mathcal{E}(R)/EQ}) \subseteq (\rightarrow_{\mathcal{E}(R)/EQ} \circ \trianglerighteq)$.*

Note 16. From now on we use the quasi-order $\gg \cup =_{EQ}$ and the trees over $T(\mathcal{F}_\diamond, \mathcal{X})$ with a rpo associated with $\gg \cup =_{EQ}$, denoted by $\sqsupset_{rpo} \cup \sim_{rpo}$.

We will show that $u =_{EQ} v \Rightarrow \mathtt{tree}(u) \sim_{rpo} \mathtt{tree}(v)$ and $u \rightarrow_R v \Rightarrow \mathtt{tree}(u) \sqsupset_{rpo} \mathtt{tree}(v)$. The following two lemmas are not difficult to prove (by induction on the definition of $=_{EQ}$, and induction on terms, resp.).

Lemma 17. *Let s, t be terms in $T(\mathcal{F}_a, \mathcal{X})$. If $s =_{EQ} t$ then $\mathtt{cap}(s) =_{EQ} \mathtt{cap}(t)$.*

Lemma 18. *Let $t \in T(\mathcal{F}, \mathcal{X})$ be an arbitrary term and $\sigma : \mathcal{X} \rightarrow T(\mathcal{F}_a, \mathcal{X})$ an arbitrary substitution. Then $\mathtt{tree}(t\sigma) = (\mathtt{cap}(t\sigma), \bigsqcup_{x \in mvar(t)} M_x)$, where $\mathtt{tree}(\sigma(x)) = (\mathtt{cap}(\sigma(x)), M_x)$, for all $x \in mvar(t)$.*

Lemma 19. *Let $s, t \in T(\mathcal{F}_a, \mathcal{X})$; then $s =_{EQ} t \Rightarrow \mathtt{tree}(s) \sim_{rpo} \mathtt{tree}(t)$.*

Proof. (Sketch) By induction on the definition of $=_{EQ}$. The first and last cases of the definition of $=_{EQ}$ pose no problem. Suppose $s = C[e_1\sigma]$ and $t = C[e_2\sigma]$, for some context C, equation $(e_1, e_2) \in EQ$ and substitution $\sigma : \mathcal{X} \rightarrow T(\mathcal{F}_a, \mathcal{X})$.

We proceed by induction on the context. If C is the trivial context, the result follows using lemma 18, the fact that $mvar(e_1) = mvar(e_2)$, for all equations (e_1, e_2), and lemma 17. Suppose now that $C = f(v_1, \ldots, D, \ldots, v_m)$, where D occurs at position $1 \leq j \leq m$, and that the result holds for context D. If $f \neq a$

$$\mathtt{tree}(s) = (f(\mathtt{cap}(v_1), \ldots, \mathtt{cap}(D[e_1\sigma]), \ldots, \mathtt{cap}(v_m)), \bigsqcup_{k=1}^{m} M_k)$$

with $\mathtt{tree}(v_k) = (\mathtt{cap}(v_k), M_k)$, if $k \neq j$, $\mathtt{tree}(D[e_1\sigma]) = (\mathtt{cap}(D[e_1\sigma]), M_j)$. Similarly, $\mathtt{tree}(t) = (f(\mathtt{cap}(v_1), \ldots, \mathtt{cap}(D[e_2\sigma]), \ldots, \mathtt{cap}(v_m)), \bigsqcup_{k=1}^{m} M'_k)$, where, for $k \neq j$, $M'_k = M_k$ and $\mathtt{tree}(D[e_2\sigma]) = (\mathtt{cap}(D[e_2\sigma]), M'_j)$. By induction hypothesis, $\mathtt{tree}(D[e_1\sigma]) \sim_{rpo} \mathtt{tree}(D[e_2\sigma])$ and this means that $M_j \sim_{rpo}^{mul} M'_j$. But then also $\bigsqcup_{k=1}^{m} M_k \sim_{rpo}^{mul} \bigsqcup_{k=1}^{m} M'_k$. Since $D[e_1\sigma] =_{EQ} D[e_2\sigma]$ and $=_{EQ}$ is closed under contexts, we can apply lemma 17 to conclude

$$f(\ldots, \mathtt{cap}(D[e_1\sigma]), \ldots) =_{EQ} f(\ldots, \mathtt{cap}(D[e_2\sigma]), \ldots)$$

implying $\mathtt{cap}(f(v_1, \ldots, D[e_1\sigma], \ldots, v_m)) =_{EQ} \mathtt{cap}(f(v_1, \ldots, D[e_2\sigma], \ldots, v_m))$; consequently $\mathtt{tree}(s) \sim_{rpo} \mathtt{tree}(t)$. If $f = a$ then $C = a(v_1, \ldots, D, \ldots, v_N)$ and

$$\mathtt{tree}(s) = (\diamond, \bigsqcup_{k=1, k\neq j}^{N} \{\!\{\mathtt{tree}(v_k)\}\!\} \sqcup \{\!\{\mathtt{tree}(D[e_1\sigma])\}\!\})$$

In a similar way we obtain $\mathtt{tree}(t) = (\diamond, \bigsqcup_{k=1, k\neq j}^{N} \{\!\{\mathtt{tree}(v_k)\}\!\} \sqcup \{\!\{\mathtt{tree}(D[e_2\sigma])\}\!\})$. Since by induction hypothesis $\mathtt{tree}(D[e_1\sigma]) \sim_{rpo} \mathtt{tree}(D[e_2\sigma])$, we also have

$$\bigsqcup_{k=1, k\neq j}^{N} \{\!\{\mathtt{tree}(v_k)\}\!\} \sqcup \{\!\{\mathtt{tree}(D[e_1\sigma])\}\!\} \sim_{rpo}^{mul} \bigsqcup_{k=1, k\neq j}^{N} \{\!\{\mathtt{tree}(v_k)\}\!\} \sqcup \{\!\{\mathtt{tree}(D[e_2\sigma])\}\!\}$$

and consequently $\mathtt{tree}(s) \sim_{rpo} \mathtt{tree}(t)$ (recall that their roots are equal).

We turn now to the case of inequality, and first see that $\mathtt{tree}(\mathtt{cap}(l)\sigma) \sqsupset_{rpo} \mathtt{tree}(r\sigma)$. Next lemma can be proven by induction on t.

Lemma 20. *Let $s \in T(\mathcal{F}, \mathcal{X}) \setminus \mathcal{X}$, $t \in T(\mathcal{F}_a, \mathcal{X})$ such that $var(t) \subseteq var(s)$ and $s \gg v$ for all $v \in \mathtt{dec}(t)$. Let $\sigma : \mathcal{X} \to T(\mathcal{F}_a, \mathcal{X})$ be any substitution and suppose that $\mathtt{tree}(s\sigma) = (\mathtt{cap}(s\sigma), M_s)$, $\mathtt{tree}(t\sigma) = (\mathtt{cap}(t\sigma), M_t)$; then*

1. *for all $U \in M_t$, $\mathtt{tree}(s\sigma) \sqsupset_{rpo} U$.*
2. *for all $U \in M_t$, either $(\exists V \in M_s : V \sqsupseteq_{rpo} U)$ or $\mathtt{cap}(s\sigma) \gg \mathtt{root}(U)$ (where $\mathtt{root}(T)$ represents the root of tree T).*

Lemma 21. *Let $s \in \mathcal{T}(\mathcal{F},\mathcal{X})\setminus\mathcal{X}$ and $t \in \mathcal{T}(\mathcal{F}_a,\mathcal{X})$ be terms such that $var(t) \subseteq var(s)$ and $s \gg v$ for all $v \in \mathtt{dec}(t) \cup \{\mathtt{cap}(t)\}$. Let $\sigma : \mathcal{X} \to \mathcal{T}(\mathcal{F}_a,\mathcal{X})$ be any substitution. Then $\mathtt{tree}(s\sigma) \sqsupset_{rpo} \mathtt{tree}(t\sigma)$.*

Proof. $\mathtt{tree}(s\sigma) = (\mathtt{cap}(s\sigma), M_s) = (\mathtt{cap}(s)\mathtt{cap}(\sigma), M_s) = (s\ \mathtt{cap}(\sigma), M_s)$ (by def. 12, lemma 9). Similarly $\mathtt{tree}(t\sigma) = (\mathtt{cap}(t)\mathtt{cap}(\sigma), M_t)$. By lemma 20, for any $U \in M_t$, $\mathtt{tree}(s\sigma) \sqsupset_{rpo} U$. Since $s \gg \mathtt{cap}(t)$, $\gg$ is closed under substitutions, we have $s\ \mathtt{cap}(\sigma) \gg \mathtt{cap}(t)\mathtt{cap}(\sigma)$; lemma 2 gives $\mathtt{tree}(s\sigma) \sqsupset_{rpo} \mathtt{tree}(t\sigma)$.

Lemma 22. *Let $l \to r$ be a rule in R and $\sigma : \mathcal{X} \to \mathcal{T}(\mathcal{F}_a,\mathcal{X})$ an arbitrary substitution. Then $\mathtt{tree}(\mathtt{cap}(l)\sigma) \sqsupset_{rpo} \mathtt{tree}(r\sigma)$.*

Proof. From the definition of $\mathcal{E}(R)$ (def. 11), we know that $\mathtt{cap}(l) \to u$, with $u \in \{\mathtt{cap}(r)\} \cup \mathtt{dec}(r)$, is a rule in $\mathcal{E}(R)$ and therefore $\mathtt{cap}(l) \gg u$ for any $u \in \{\mathtt{cap}(r)\} \cup \mathtt{dec}(r)$. Since we are under the assumption that $\mathcal{E}(R)/EQ$ is terminating, we can state that $\mathtt{cap}(l) \notin \mathcal{X}$ and that $var(r) \subseteq var(\mathtt{cap}(l))$; also a does not occur in $\mathtt{cap}(l)$, therefore all the hypothesis of lemma 21 are satisfied, so we can apply it to conclude that $\mathtt{tree}(\mathtt{cap}(l)\sigma) \sqsupset_{rpo} \mathtt{tree}(r\sigma)$.

In order to obtain $\mathtt{tree}(l\sigma) \sqsupset_{rpo} \mathtt{tree}(r\sigma)$, we need to be able to compare the tree of a term with the tree of its cap. The following result (which can be proven by induction on t) provides this comparison.

Lemma 23. *Let $t \in \mathcal{T}(\mathcal{F}_a,\mathcal{X})$ be any term and $\sigma : \mathcal{X} \to \mathcal{T}(\mathcal{F}_a,\mathcal{X})$ be any substitution. Then $\mathtt{tree}(t\sigma) \sqsupseteq_{rpo} \mathtt{tree}(\mathtt{cap}(t)\sigma)$. Furthermore if $\mathtt{tree}(t\sigma) = (\mathtt{cap}(t\sigma), M)$ and $\mathtt{tree}(\mathtt{cap}(t)\sigma) = (\mathtt{cap}(\mathtt{cap}(t\sigma)), M')$, then $M' \sqsubseteq M$.*

Theorem 24. *Let $l \to r$ be any rule in R and let $\sigma : \mathcal{X} \to \mathcal{T}(\mathcal{F}_a,\mathcal{X})$ be any substitution. Then $\mathtt{tree}(l\sigma) \sqsupset_{rpo} \mathtt{tree}(r\sigma)$.*

Proof. Combining lemmas 22, 23 we have

$$\mathtt{tree}(l\sigma) \sqsupseteq_{rpo} \mathtt{tree}(\mathtt{cap}(l)\sigma) \sqsupset_{rpo} \mathtt{tree}(r\sigma).$$

We have seen that $l\sigma \to_R r\sigma$ implies that $\mathtt{tree}(l\sigma) \sqsupset_{rpo} \mathtt{tree}(r\sigma)$. We still have to check that if a reduction occurs within a non-trivial context, the same results holds, i. e., $C[l\sigma] \to_R C[r\sigma]$ implies $\mathtt{tree}(C[l\sigma]) \sqsupset_{rpo} \mathtt{tree}(C[r\sigma])$. For that we need some more auxiliary results.

Lemma 25. *Let $S = (s, M_s), T = (t, M_t)$ be trees satisfying $S \sqsupset_{rpo} T$ and satisfying $\forall U \in M_t : (\exists V \in M_s : V \sqsupseteq_{rpo} U)$ or $s \gg \mathtt{root}(U)$. If M is such that $M_s \sqsubseteq M$ then $\forall U \in M_t : (f(\ldots, s, \ldots), M) \sqsupset_{rpo} U$, for any $f \in \mathcal{F}$.*

Proof. By induction on the depth of T.

Lemma 26. *[5] Let $s,t \in \mathcal{T}(\mathcal{F}_a,\mathcal{X})$. If $s \to_R t$ then $\mathtt{cap}(s) \to^{0,1}_{\mathcal{E}(R)} \mathtt{cap}(t)$.*

Lemma 27. *Let $s, t \in T(\mathcal{F}_a, \mathcal{X})$ such that $s \to_R t$. Suppose that* $\mathtt{tree}(s) = (\mathtt{cap}(s), M_s)$, $\mathtt{tree}(t) = (\mathtt{cap}(t), M_t)$. *Then*

1. $\mathtt{tree}(s) \sqsupset_{rpo} \mathtt{tree}(t)$, *and*
2. $\forall U \in M_t : (\exists V \in M_s : V \sqsupseteq_{rpo} U)$ *or* $\mathtt{cap}(s) \gg \mathtt{root}(U)$.

Proof. We show (1) and (2) simultaneously by induction on the definition of reduction. Suppose that $s = l\sigma$, $t = r\sigma$ for some rule $l \to r$ in R and substitution $\sigma : \mathcal{X} \to T(\mathcal{F}_a, \mathcal{X})$. (1) has already been proven in theorem 24; as for (2), applying lemma 20 to $\mathtt{cap}(l)$ and r, we conclude that, if $\mathtt{tree}(r\sigma) = (\mathtt{cap}(r\sigma), M_r)$ and $\mathtt{tree}(\mathtt{cap}(l)\sigma) = (\mathtt{cap}(\mathtt{cap}(l)\sigma), M)$, then $\forall U \in M_r : (\exists V \in M : V \sqsupseteq_{rpo} U)$ or $\mathtt{cap}(\mathtt{cap}(l)\sigma) \gg \mathtt{root}(U)$. The result now follows using lemmas 23, 9, 10.
Suppose that $s \to t$, (1) and (2) hold for s and t, and $f(s_1, \ldots, s, \ldots, s_k) \to f(s_1, \ldots, t, \ldots, s_k)$ (where s and t occur at position $1 \leq j \leq k$). First we consider the case $f \neq a$. Then

$$\mathtt{tree}(f(s_1, \ldots, s, \ldots, s_k)) = (f(\mathtt{cap}(s_1), \ldots, \mathtt{cap}(s), \ldots, \mathtt{cap}(s_k)), \bigsqcup_{i=1}^{k} M_i),$$

with $\mathtt{tree}(s_i) = (\mathtt{cap}(s_i), M_i)$, if $1 \leq i \leq k$, $i \neq j$, and $\mathtt{tree}(s) = (\mathtt{cap}(s), M_j)$. Similarly $\mathtt{tree}(f(s_1, \ldots, t, \ldots, s_k)) = (f(\ldots, \mathtt{cap}(t), \ldots), \sqcup_{i=1}^{k} M_i')$, with $M_i = M_i'$, for $1 \leq i \leq k$, $i \neq j$, $\mathtt{tree}(t) = (\mathtt{cap}(t), M_j')$. We show (2). Fix $U \in \sqcup_{i=1}^{k} M_i'$. If $U \in M_i'$ for $i \neq j$, (2) holds trivially. If $U \in M_j'$, by induction hypothesis either $V \sqsupseteq_{rpo} U$, for some $V \in M_j$, and so (2) holds; or $\mathtt{cap}(s) \gg \mathtt{root}(U)$, and since $f(\ldots, \mathtt{cap}(s), \ldots) \trianglerighteq \mathtt{cap}(s)$ and $(\trianglerighteq \circ \gg) \subseteq \gg$, (2) also holds. As for (1), since $s \to t$, we have that $\mathtt{cap}(s) \to_{\mathcal{E}(R)}^{0,1} \mathtt{cap}(t)$. If they are equal, since $\mathtt{tree}(s) \sqsupset_{rpo} \mathtt{tree}(t)$, we must have $M_j \; \mathtt{ord}(\sqsupseteq_{rpo,mul}) \; M_j'$; consequently $\sqcup_{i=1}^{k} M_i \; \mathtt{ord}(\sqsupseteq_{rpo,mul}) \; \sqcup_{i=1}^{k} M_i'$. Since $\mathtt{cap}(f(\ldots, s, \ldots)) = f(\ldots, \mathtt{cap}(s), \ldots) = f(\ldots, \mathtt{cap}(t), \ldots) = \mathtt{cap}(f(\ldots, t, \ldots))$, by lemma 2, $\mathtt{tree}(f(\ldots, s, \ldots)) \sqsupset_{rpo} \mathtt{tree}(f(\ldots, t, \ldots))$.
If $\mathtt{cap}(s) \to_{\mathcal{E}(R)} \mathtt{cap}(t)$, then $f(\ldots, \mathtt{cap}(s), \ldots) \to_{\mathcal{E}(R)} f(\ldots, \mathtt{cap}(t), \ldots)$, and we only need to see that $\forall U \in M_j' : \mathtt{tree}(f(\ldots, s, \ldots)) \sqsupset_{rpo} U$; fix such U. From lemma 25, we conclude $(f(\mathtt{cap}(s_1), \ldots, \mathtt{cap}(s), \ldots, \mathtt{cap}(s_k)), \sqcup_{i=1}^{k} M_i) \sqsupset_{rpo} U$, i. e., $\mathtt{tree}(f(s_1, \ldots, s, \ldots, s_k)) \sqsupset_{rpo} U$.

If $f = a$, then $\mathtt{tree}(a(s_1, \ldots, s, \ldots, s_N)) = (\diamond, \bigsqcup_{i=1, i \neq j}^{N} \{\!\{\mathtt{tree}(s_i)\}\!\} \sqcup \{\!\{\mathtt{tree}(s)\}\!\})$, and $\mathtt{tree}(a(s_1, \ldots, t, \ldots, s_N)) = (\diamond, \sqcup_{i=1, i \neq j}^{N} \{\!\{\mathtt{tree}(s_i)\}\!\} \sqcup \{\!\{\mathtt{tree}(t)\}\!\})$. Using the fact $\mathtt{tree}(s) \sqsupset_{rpo} \mathtt{tree}(t)$, it is not difficult to see that $\mathtt{tree}(a(\ldots, s, \ldots)) \sqsupset_{rpo} \mathtt{tree}(a(\ldots, t, \ldots))$, so (1) holds. For (2), if $U \in \bigsqcup_{i=1, i \neq j}^{N} \{\!\{\mathtt{tree}(s_i)\}\!\} \sqcup \{\!\{\mathtt{tree}(t)\}\!\}$, either $U = \mathtt{tree}(s_i)$, for some $i \neq j$, in which case (2) holds; or $U = \mathtt{tree}(t)$ and since $\mathtt{tree}(s) \sqsupset_{rpo} \mathtt{tree}(t)$, (2) also holds.

We can now prove our main result.

Theorem 28. *Provided that EQ is variable-preserving, if $\mathcal{E}(R)/EQ$ is terminating then R/EQ is terminating.*

Proof. Suppose that R/EQ does not terminate. Then we have an infinite sequence of the form $s_0 =_{EQ} s'_0 \rightarrow_R s_1 =_{EQ} s'_1 \rightarrow_R s_2 =_{EQ} s'_2 \ldots$ Using lemmas 19, 27, theorem 24 and the definition of reduction relation (modulo an equational theory) this translates to the following sequence on trees:

$$\texttt{tree}(s_0) \sim_{rpo} \texttt{tree}(s'_0) \sqsupset_{rpo} \texttt{tree}(s_1) \sim_{rpo} \texttt{tree}(s'_1) \sqsupset_{rpo} \texttt{tree}(s_2) \ldots$$

since $\sim_{rpo}$ and $\sqsupset_{rpo}$ are compatible, this contradicts well-foundedness of $\sqsupset_{rpo}$.

5 The family of transformations

In dummy elimination, alien terms $a(t_1, \ldots, t_N)$ are replaced by a fresh constant $\diamond$ and the subterms $t_1, \ldots, t_N$ originate loose terms; but there are other possibilities for the replacement of alien terms. We illustrate the idea with an example. Suppose we have the term $f(a(s(0), x), s(y))$; we may want to replace the alien term $a(s(0), x)$ by either $s(0)$, or x or both arguments. The associated transformations on terms would yield, resp.: $\{f(s(0), s(y)), x\}$, $\{f(x, s(y)), s(0)\}$ and $\{f(s(0), s(y)), f(x, s(y))\}$. We associate a choice function τ to the function symbol a indicating how its arguments are to be treated, and coding which element in the transformation of a term is to be chosen as lefthand-side of transformed rules; therefore $\tau(a)$ has the form (X, i) where X is a subset of $\{1, \ldots, N\}$ and i is either an element of X or 0 (if $X = \emptyset$). The transformation we were concerned with in previous sections corresponds to the choice $\tau(a) = (\emptyset, 0)$, the decompositions shown above correspond to the choices resp. $(\{1\}, 1)$, $(\{2\}, 2)$ and $(\{1, 2\}, i)$, where in the last case i can be either 1 or 2.

The functions **cap** and **dec** become parameterized by the choice function and a new similar decomposition function E has to be defined. For the functions **cap** (now denoted by $\mathbf{cap}_i$) and **dec**, the only change wrt definition 7 is in the last clause, namely $\mathbf{cap}_i(a(t_1, \ldots, t_N))$ becomes $\mathbf{cap}_i(t_i)$ if $i \neq 0$, and $\diamond$, otherwise, and $\texttt{dec}(a(t_1, \ldots, t_N))$ becomes $(\bigcup_{i=1}^{N} \texttt{dec}(t_i)) \cup (\bigcup_{j \in \{1,\ldots,N\} \setminus X} E(t_j))$ (note that if $X = \emptyset$, this will coincide with the clause in definition 7).

Definition 29. The functions $E, E_i : T(\mathcal{F}_{a,\diamond}, \mathcal{X}) \rightarrow \mathcal{P}(T(\mathcal{F}_\diamond, \mathcal{X}))$, wrt a choice $\tau(a) = (X, i)$, are defined inductively as follows:

t	$E_i(t)$ $(i \neq 0)$	$E(t)$
x	$\{x\}$	$\{x\}$
$f(t_1, \ldots, t_m)$	$\{f(\ldots, u_j, \ldots) \mid \forall 1 \leq j \leq m : u_j \in E_i(t_j)\}$	$\begin{cases} \bigcup_{j \in X} E_j(t)) & \text{if } X \neq \emptyset \\ \{\mathbf{cap}_0(t)\} & \text{if } X = \emptyset \end{cases}$
$a(t_1, \ldots, t_N)$	$E(t_i)$	$\begin{cases} \bigcup_{j \in X} E(t_j) & \text{if } X \neq \emptyset \\ \{\mathbf{cap}_0(t)\} & \text{if } X = \emptyset \end{cases}$

The transformed version of R/EQ, wrt a choice $\tau(a) = (X, i)$, is the equational system $\mathcal{E}(R)/EQ$, with $\mathcal{E}(R)$ now given by:

$$\mathcal{E}(R) = \{\mathtt{cap}_i(l) \rightarrow u \mid l \rightarrow r \in R \text{ and } u \in E(r) \cup \mathtt{dec}(r)\}$$

Using this definition, the main result (theorem 28) remains valid.

In general transformations associated with different choice functions are unrelated wrt to termination properties, (see [4]). However when we restrict ourselves to simple termination, and if $EQ = \emptyset$, "a" does not occur in the lefthand-sides of the rules of R and R is left-linear, then simple termination of $\mathcal{E}^{\tau}(R)$ implies simple termination of $\mathcal{E}(R)$, where $\mathcal{E}(R)$ is the transformation we concentrated on $\mathcal{E}^{\tau}(R)$ is any other transformation; while the reverse is not true. So in this particular case, the choice $\tau'(a) = (\emptyset, 0)$ seems to be the best.

6 Final Remarks

With an example, we see why eliminating more than one function symbol simultaneously or considering varyadic symbols does not constitute an enrichment of the theory. Fix the choice function as $(\emptyset, 0)$ and $EQ = \emptyset$.

Example 4. Consider the terminating one-rule TRS: $f(x, x) \rightarrow f(a(x), b(x))$. If we eliminate both a and b at the same time we get the system: $f(x, x) \rightarrow f(\diamond, \diamond)$; $f(x, x) \rightarrow x$, which is not terminating. If we eliminate first a and then b (or vice-versa) we get the terminating system: $f(x, x) \rightarrow f(\diamond_1, \diamond_2)$; $f(x, x) \rightarrow x$.

For the varyadic case, suppose the symbol a admits arities 1 and 2 and consider the one-rule terminating TRS: $f(x, x) \rightarrow f(a(x), a(x, x))$. As far as termination is concerned, this rule is equivalent to: $f(x, x) \rightarrow f(a_1(x), a_2(x, x))$. If we now eliminate first a_1 and then a_2, the result is the TRS: $f(x, x) \rightarrow f(\diamond_1, \diamond_2)$; $f(x, x) \rightarrow x$, which is still a terminating system. Eliminating a_1 and a_2 simultaneously (which amounts to the same as eliminating the varyadic function symbol a in the original system) results in the following non-terminating TRS: $f(x, x) \rightarrow f(\diamond, \diamond)$; $f(x, x) \rightarrow x$.

We presented a new technique for proving termination of equational rewrite systems based on elimination of function symbols. Provided the symbol eliminated does not occur in the equational system, and that the system is variable-preserving, we can show that termination of R/EQ can be inferred from termination of $\mathcal{E}(R)/EQ$, where $\mathcal{E}(R)$ is a transformation associated to a given choice function. These transformations are interesting from a practical point of view since they can substantially simplify the systems considered and they can easily be automatized. It is still open whether the restriction on the equational system is indeed necessary; since it arises from technicalities in the proof it seems that it can be weakened.

Another interesting point consists in imposing more restrictions on the equations considered but allow for the possibility of eliminating function symbols occurring in the equations; following this approach, elimination of AC symbols is currently under investigation.

References

1. F. Bellegarde and P. Lescanne. Termination by completion. *Applicable Algebra in Engineering, Communication and Computing*, 1(2):79–96, 1990.
2. N. Dershowitz and J.-P. Jouannaud. Rewrite systems. In J. van Leeuwen, editor, *Handbook of Theoretical Computer Science*, volume B, chapter 6, pages 243–320. Elsevier, 1990.
3. N. Dershowitz and Z. Manna. Proving termination with multiset orderings. *Communications ACM*, 22(8):465–476, 1979.
4. M. C. F. Ferreira. *Termination of Term Rewriting - Wellfoundedness, totality and transformations*. PhD thesis, Universiteit Utrecht, November 1995.
5. M. C. F. Ferreira and H. Zantema. Dummy elimination: making termination easier. In H. Reichel, editor, *Fundamentals of Computation Theory, 10th International Conference FCT'95*, volume 965 of *Lecture Notes in Computer Science*, pages 243–252. Springer, 1995. Appeared also as technical report UU-CS-1994-47, University of Utrecht, October 1994.
6. W. J. Fokkink and H. Zantema. Prefix iteration in basic process algebra: applying termination techniques. In C. V. A. Ponse and S. F. M. van Vlijmen, editors, *Proceedings of the second workshop on Algebra of Communicating Processes, ACP 95*, volume 95-14 of *Computing Science Reports*, pages 139–156. Department of Mathematics and Computing Science, Eindhoven University of Technology, 1995.
7. A. Geser. *Relative termination*. PhD thesis, Universität Passau, 1990. Also available as: Report 91-03, Ulmer Informatik-Berichte, Universität Ulm, 1991.
8. J.-P. Jouannaud and M. Muñoz. Termination of a set of rules modulo a set of equations. In *Proceedings of the seventh International Conference onAutomated Deduction*, volume 170 of *Lecture Notes in Computer Science*, pages 175 – 193. Springer, Napa, CA, 1984.
9. J. W. Klop. Term rewriting systems. In S. Abramsky, D. M. Gabbay, and T. S. E. Maibaum, editors, *Handbook of Logic in Computer Science*, volume II, pages 1–116. Oxford University Press, 1992.
10. D. A. Plaisted. Equational reasoning and term rewriting systems. In D. Gabbay, C. J. Hogger, and J. A. Robinson, editors, *Handbook of Logic in Artificial Intelligence and Logic Programming*, volume 1 - Logical Foundations, pages 273–364. Oxford Science Publications, Clarendon Press - Oxford, 1993.
11. J. Steinbach. *Termination of Rewriting - Extension, Comparison and Automatic Generation of Simplification Orderings*. PhD thesis, University of Kaiserslautern, 1994.
12. H. Zantema. Termination of term rewriting: interpretation and type elimination. *Journal of Symbolic Computation*, 17:23–50, 1994.
13. H. Zantema. Termination of term rewriting by semantic labelling. *Fundamenta Informaticae*, 24:89–105, 1995. Appeared also as technical report RUU-CS-93-24, Utrecht University, July 1993.
14. H. Zantema and A. Geser. A complete characterization of termination of $0^p1^q \to 1^r0^s$. In J. Hsiang, editor, *Proceedings of the 6th Conference on Rewriting Techniques and Applications*, volume 914 of *Lecture Notes in Computer Science*, pages 41–55. Springer, 1995. Appeared as report UU-CS-1994-44, Utrecht University.

On Proving Termination by Innermost Termination

Bernhard Gramlich*

INRIA Lorraine, 615, rue du Jardin Botanique, BP 101
54602 Villers-lès-Nancy, France
gramlich@loria.fr

Abstract. We present a new approach for proving termination of rewrite systems by innermost termination. From the resulting abstract criterion we derive concrete conditions, based on critical peak properties, under which innermost termination implies termination (and confluence). Finally, we show how to apply the main results for providing new sufficient conditions for the modularity of termination.

1 Introduction and Overview

Properties of rewriting under strategies are generally not well explored, despite the fact that such restricted versions of rewriting are of great importance, for instance as model for describing semantics of computation formalisms. *Innermost* rewriting, i.e., rewriting where always minimal redexes are chosen for replacement, corresponds to a call-by-value semantics (via innermost evaluation), and *outermost* rewriting, where always maximal redexes are chosen, may be used to model call-by-name semantics ([17]). Hence, the study of basic properties, in particular the fundamental ones of termination and confluence, of such restricted versions of rewriting is of independent interest. Moreover, from a conceptual point of view it is perfectly natural to ask: How do basic properties of rewriting under some strategy relate to the corresponding properties of arbitrary rewriting. Results in this direction may be useful in order to facilitate the verification of proof tasks for arbitrary rewriting.

Here we shall mainly be concerned with the termination property of innermost and arbitrary rewriting. In certain cases, verifying innermost termination may be much easier than proving general termination, i.e., termination of unrestricted rewriting. Another perhaps even more important aspect is that innermost rewriting has a much better modularity behaviour than arbitrary rewriting w.r.t. to (various syntactically restricted, e.g., disjoint types of) combinations of systems ([6]).

* This research was supported in part by 'DFG, SFB 314 D4' while the author was still employed by *Fachbereich Informatik, Universität Kaiserslautern, Postfach 3049, D-67653 Kaiserslautern, Germany*.

Clearly, termination of arbitrary rewriting implies *innermost termination*, i.e., termination of innermost rewriting, but not vice versa. A very simple example illustrating this gap is the system $\mathcal{R} = \{f(a) \to f(a), a \to b\}$ which is obviously non-terminating, but innermost terminating.

Thus, developing criteria which guarantee the equivalence of termination and innermost termination is very useful. In [6] we have shown that for non-overlapping systems as well as for the more general case of locally confluent overlay systems innermost termination is indeed equivalent to termination.[2] The proof crucially relies both on the overlay property and on a transformation construction (for a non-terminating derivation) where all (parallel) maximal terminating (and thus also confluent) subterms are normalized. In this paper, starting from the result for non-overlapping systems, we shall develop another approach for obtaining new results. Actually, one basic idea has already been used in the technical report version of [6], however, without further exploiting its potential. The point is that under certain conditions, instead of performing a parallel normalization of the maximal terminating subterms one may proceed more 'economically' in the transformation construction, namely, by a parallel one-step reduction of all terminating innermost redexes. In order to make this construction well-defined and work, two syntactical properties will turn out to be crucial. From the obtained abstract result we shall derive a couple of more concrete critical peak based criteria which suffice for the equivalence of termination and innermost termination. Finally, we show how the presented equivalence criteria for termination and innermost termination easily yield new modularity results for termination.

The rest of the paper is structured as follows. In Section 2 we review some needed basic terminology and known results. Then, in the main Section 3 we develop the above sketched new approach. And finally, in Section 4, we show how to obtain corresponding new modularity results for termination.

2 Basics and Known Results

We assume familiarity with the basic no(ta)tions, terminology and theory of term rewriting (cf. e.g. [3], [9], [17]). The set of terms over some given signature $\mathcal{F}$ and some (disjoint) denumerable set $\mathcal{V}$ of variables is denoted by $\mathcal{T}(\mathcal{F}, \mathcal{V})$. Positions (in terms) are ordered by the prefix ordering $\leq$ as usual. The 'empty' root position is denoted by λ. If $p \leq q$ we say that p is *above* q (or q is *below* p). For *subtracting* positions we use $\backslash$, i.e., we write $p\backslash q = q'$ if $p = qq'$. Two positions p and q are said to be *parallel* (or *independent, disjoint*), denoted by $p \parallel q$, if neither $p \leq q$ nor $q \leq p$. The set of positions of a term s is denoted by $Pos(s)$. The sets of variable positions and of non-variable, i.e., function symbol, positions of s are denoted by $\mathcal{V}Pos(s)$ and $\mathcal{F}Pos(s)$, respectively. The subterm

[2] Implicitly, for non-overlapping systems this result also follows from [4] where termination conditions in terms of *forward* and *overlap* closures are investigated (cf. also [2]).

of s at some position $p \in Pos(s)$ is denoted by s/p. The result of replacing in s the subterm at position $p \in Pos(s)$ by t is denoted by $s[p \leftarrow t]$.

For rewrite rules $\to r$ of a term rewriting system (TRS) $\mathcal{R}^{\mathcal{F}} = \mathcal{R}$ (over $\mathcal{T}(\mathcal{F}, \mathcal{V})$) we require that l is not a variable, and that all variables of r occur in l (this excludes only degenerate cases). For reduction steps with the rewrite relation $\to_{\mathcal{R}} = \to$ induced by $\mathcal{R}$ we sometimes add additional information as in $s \to_{p,\sigma,l\to r} t$ with the obvious meaning. Furthermore, we make free use of context notations like $s = C[\sigma(l)] \to_{l\to r} C[\sigma(r) = t$. The innermost reduction relation $\underset{i}{\to}$ (induced by $\mathcal{R}$) is given by: $s \underset{i}{\to} t$ if $s = C[\sigma(l)] \to_{l\to r} C[\sigma(r)] = t$ for some $l \to r \in \mathcal{R}$, some context $C[.]$ and some substitution σ such that no proper subterm of $\sigma(l)$ is reducible. The parallel reduction relation (induced by $\mathcal{R}$) is denoted by $\twoheadrightarrow\!\!\!\!\!\!\!\parallel\;$. If s reduces to t by a parallel contraction of redexes in s at some set P of mutually disjoint positions, we also write $s \twoheadrightarrow\!\!\!\!\!\!\!\parallel_P\; t$.

A TRS is non-overlapping (NO) if it has no critical pairs. It is an overlay system (OS) if critical overlaps between rules of $\mathcal{R}$ occur only at the root position. For the properties termination (equivalently: strong normalization), weak termination (equivalently: weak normalization), confluence and uniform confluence (i.e., $\leftarrow \circ \to \subseteq (\mathrm{id} \cup \to \circ \leftarrow)$, with id being the identity relation) we also use the abbreviations SN, WN, CR and WCR[1], respectively. Innermost termination, i.e., termination (or strong normalization) of the innermost reduction relation $\underset{i}{\to}$, is abbreviated by SIN. Furthermore, we also use local versions ('below' some term) of these properties like SN(s) (meaning that there is no infinite derivation issuing form s). Completeness (or, equivalently, convergence) means termination plus confluence.

The following sufficient conditions for the (local and global) equivalence of termination and innermost termination are known.

Theorem 1. ([6])

(1) Any innermost terminating (term in a) non-overlapping TRS is terminating (and hence complete).

(2) Any innermost terminating (term in a) locally confluent overlay TRS is terminating (and hence complete).

3 New Conditions for the Equivalence of Termination and Innermost Termination

3.1 The Basic Approach

As already mentioned, the basic idea pursued in this paper for deriving (SIN $\Longrightarrow$ SN) is to use as transformation construction a parallel one-step reduction of all terminating innermost redexes in the terms considered (instead of a parallel normalization of all maximal terminating redexes). Two properties are essential for this intended construction to work, namely, that contracting some (terminating) innermost redex in a term (at some fixed position) yields a unique result, and that certain 'innermost-critical' steps in infinite derivations can be avoided.

Definition 2. Let $\mathcal{R}$ be a TRS. We say that *innermost reduction (in $\mathcal{R}$) is unique* (at some fixed position), (denoted by UIR($\mathcal{R}$) or simply UIR), if

$$\forall s, t_1, t_2, p \in Pos(s) : s \xrightarrow[i]{}_p t_1 \wedge s \xrightarrow[i]{}_p t_2 \implies t_1 = t_2 .$$

To state the second property, we first introduce a new definition and some compact notations.

Definition 3. Let $\mathcal{R}$ be a TRS. A reduction step $s \to t$ is called *innermost-uncritical*, denoted by $s \xrightarrow[iu]{} t$, if $s \to_{p,\sigma,l\to r} t$ (for some p, σ, $l \to r \in \mathcal{R}$) such that either s/p is an innermost redex (of s), or else all innermost redexes of s strictly below p correspond to variable overlaps w.r.t. l, i.e., for every innermost redex s/pp' of s, $p' > \lambda$, we have: $p' \geq q$ for some $q \in \mathcal{V}Pos(l)$ (if $s \xrightarrow[iu]{} t$ with some p, σ, $l \to r$ as above, we also write $s \xrightarrow[iu]{}_{p,\sigma,l\to r} t$). Otherwise, i.e., if $s \to t$ but not $s \xrightarrow[iu]{} t$, the step $s \to t$ is called *innermost-critical* and denoted by $s \xrightarrow[ic]{} t$.

Remark. By definition, $s \xrightarrow[ic]{} t$ means $s \to_{p,\sigma,l\to r} t$ (for some p, σ, $l \to r \in \mathcal{R}$) such that there exists an innermost redex $s/pp' = \tau l'$ (for some τ and $l' \to r' \in \mathcal{R}$) of s with $p' > \lambda$ and $p' \in \mathcal{F}Pos(l)$. Obviously, this entails the existence of a corresponding critical pair by overlapping $l' \to r'$ into $l \to r$. Moreover note that an innermost reduction step is by definition innermost-uncritical, and an innermost-critical step must be non-innermost, due to $\to = \xrightarrow[iu]{} \uplus \xrightarrow[ic]{}$.

Now the second property required subsequently reads as follows.

Definition 4. Let $\mathcal{R}$ be a TRS. We say that *innermost-critical reduction steps can be avoided* (denoted by AICR($\mathcal{R}$) or simply AICR), if

$$\forall s, t : [s \to t \implies [s \xrightarrow[iu]{} t \vee \exists s' : s \xrightarrow[i]{} s' \to^* t]] .$$

This property guarantees that innermost-critical steps in infinite reductions can be avoided.

Lemma 5. *Let $\mathcal{R}$ be a TRS satisfying property AICR, and let t be a term. If t is non-terminating, then there exists an infinite derivation $t =: t_0 \to t_1 \to t_2 \ldots$ initiating from t which does only contain innermost-uncritical steps, i.e., for all $n \geq 0$ we have $t_n \xrightarrow[iu]{} t_{n+1}$.*

Proof. Let t be non-terminating. We give a construction for obtaining an infinite derivation issuing from t with the desired property. Assume that we have already constructed an initial segment

$$t =: t_0 \to t_1 \to \ldots \to t_n$$

of length n of an infinite derivation, i.e. with t_n non-terminating such that every step $t_k \to t_{k+1}$, $0 \leq k < n$ is innermost-uncritical. Now, if there exists a non-terminating t_{n+1} such that $t_n \xrightarrow[iu]{} t_{n+1}$, we can simply extend the initial segment by one step of the desired form. Otherwise, any step $t_n \to t'_{n+1}$ with t'_{n+1} non-terminating must be innermost-critical (note that at least one such t'_{n+1} must exist, due to non-termination of t_n). By AICR we conclude that there exists some term t_{n+1} with $t_n \xrightarrow[i]{} t_{n+1} \to^* t'_{n+1}$. This means that we can properly extend the initial segment to

$$t =: t_0 \to t_1 \to \ldots \to t_n \to t_{n+1}$$

with t_{n+1} still non-terminating where all steps have the desired form (note that $\xrightarrow[i]{} \subseteq \xrightarrow[iu]{}$). By induction we finally conclude that there exists an infinite derivation issuing from t which contains only innermost-uncritical steps. □

Next we introduce some notions for reduction steps contracting terminating and non-terminating redexes, respectively. If $s \to t$ by contracting a terminating redex in s (i.e., $s \to_p t$ for some $p \in Pos(s)$, with $\mathrm{SN}(s/p)$), we write $s \to_{\mathrm{sn}} t$. If $s \to t$ by contracting a non-terminating redex in s (i.e., $s \to_p t$ for some $p \in Pos(s)$, with $\neg\mathrm{SN}(s/p)$), we write $s \to_{\neg\mathrm{sn}} t$. Obviously, every reduction step can be written as $s \to_{\mathrm{sn}} t$ or $s \to_{\neg\mathrm{sn}} t$. In other words, we have $\to = \to_{\mathrm{sn}} \cup \to_{\neg\mathrm{sn}}$.[3]

Lemma 6. *Let $\mathcal{R}$ be a TRS. The relation $\to_{\mathrm{sn}}$ is terminating (on all terms). Moreover, any infinite $\to$-derivation must contain infinitely many $\to_{\neg\mathrm{sn}}$-steps which are not $\to_{\mathrm{sn}}$-steps.*

Proof. Straightforward by structural induction. □

Now we formally introduce the mentioned transformation function.

Definition 7. Let $\mathcal{R}$ be a TRS satisfying property UIR. Then the transformation function Ψ on terms is defined by a parallel one-step reduction of all terminating innermost redexes, i.e.:

$$\Psi(t) := C[t'_1, \ldots, t'_n], \text{ if } t = C[t_1, \ldots, t_n],\ t_k \xrightarrow[i]{}_\lambda t'_k\ (1 \le k \le n),$$

where the t_k, $1 \le k \le n$, are all the terminating innermost redexes of t (equivalently: $s \dashv\!\vdash\!\!\to_P \Psi(s)$ where P consists of the positions of all terminating innermost redexes of s).

Reduction steps in a given derivation D can be transformed into reduction steps of the transformed derivation $\Psi(D)$ as follows.

Lemma 8. *Let $\mathcal{R}$ be a TRS satisfying property UIR, and let s, t be terms with $s \xrightarrow[iu]{}_{p,\sigma,l\to r} t$. Then we have:*

(1) $SN(s/p) \Longrightarrow \Psi(s) \to^* \Psi(t)$.

[3] Note, however, that it is possible that s reduces to t both by contracting a terminating or a non-terminating redex in s. For $\mathcal{R} = \{a \to b, f(a) \to f(b), f(b) \to f(a)\}$, we have both $f(a) \to_{\mathrm{sn}} f(b)$ and $f(a) \to_{\neg\mathrm{sn}} f(b)$. Hence, in general we do not have $\to_{\mathrm{sn}} \cap \to_{\neg\mathrm{sn}} = \emptyset$. Nevertheless this could be enforced by slightly modifying the definition of $\to_{\neg\mathrm{sn}}$ as follows: $\to_{\neg\mathrm{sn}} = \to \setminus \to_{\mathrm{sn}}$.

(2) $\neg SN(s/p) \Longrightarrow \Psi(s) \to^+ \Psi(t)$.

Proof. Due to property UIR, the transformation Ψ is well-defined. Let P be defined by $s \mathrel{+\!\!\!\!+\!\!\!\!\to}_P \Psi(s)$ as in Definition 7.

(1) We distinguish two cases. First assume that s/p is an innermost redex of s. Then we know by definition of Ψ, SN(s/p) and property UIR that $\Psi(s)/p = t/p$, and moreover, that $\Psi(s)$ is obtained from t via $t \mathrel{+\!\!\!\!+\!\!\!\!\to}_{P\setminus\{p\}} \Psi(s)$. Now, in order to obtain $\Psi(t)$ from $\Psi(s)$ one may have to contract additionally some newly introduced terminating innermost redexes in t. If $\sigma(r)$ is irreducible, new (terminating) innermost redexes can only be introduced above p in t, and only at positions disjoint from those of $P \setminus \{p\}$. If $\sigma(r)$ is reducible, all new innermost redexes in t must be below p (and all of these are indeed terminating, since the contracted redex s/p of s was terminating). Hence, in both cases, we obtain $\Psi(t)$ from $\Psi(s)$ by an additional parallel innermost reduction (at positions disjoint from those of P). Thus, we get $\Psi(s) \to^* \Psi(t)$ as desired. In the other case s/p is a terminating non-innermost redex. Since the step $s \to_{p,\sigma,l\to r} t$ is non-innermost innermost-uncritical, every innermost redex of s (there exists at least one!) strictly below p, s/pq ($q > \lambda$), must correspond to a variable overlap, i.e., $q \geq u$, for some $u \in \mathcal{V}Pos(l)$. This implies (together with UIR) that $\Psi(s)/p$ is still an instance of l, let's say $\Psi(s)/p = \sigma'(l)$, with $\sigma \mathrel{+\!\!\!\!+\!\!\!\!\to} \sigma'$. Hence we get $s \underset{i}{\longrightarrow}^+ \Psi(s) \to_{p,\sigma',l\to r} \Psi(s)[p \leftarrow \sigma'(r)] =: t'$ and $s \to_{p,\sigma,l\to r} t \mathrel{+\!\!\!\!+\!\!\!\!\to}_Q t'$, where $Q = P \setminus \{q \in P \mid q \geq p\} \cup P'$ with P' consisting of the positions of those (terminating) innermost redexes of t which are descendents of the terminating innermost redexes of s below p w.r.t. the step $s \to_{p,l\to r} t$. Again, in order to obtain $\Psi(t)$ from t', additionally some newly introduced terminating innermost redexes (above or below p) may have to be reduced. Thus we obtain $\Psi(s) \to t' \to^* \Psi(t)$, hence $\Psi(s) \to^+ \Psi(t)$ as desired.

(2) Again we distinguish two cases. First assume that s/p is an innermost redex of s. Since s/p is non-terminating we have $p \notin P$ and $p \parallel P$. Hence the two steps commute: $s \underset{i}{\mathrel{+\!\!\!\!+\!\!\!\!\to}}_P \Psi(s) \underset{i}{\longrightarrow}_p t'$, $s \underset{i}{\longrightarrow}_p t \underset{i}{\mathrel{+\!\!\!\!+\!\!\!\!\to}}_P t'$. Moreover, $\Psi(t)$ is obtained from t' by additionally contracting those terminating innermost redexes which are introduced (in t and also in t') by the step $s \underset{i}{\longrightarrow}_p t$ (and $\Psi(s) \underset{i}{\longrightarrow}_p t'$, respectively) above or below p. Again the positions of the latter introduced (terminating) innermost redexes are disjoint from those of $P \setminus \{p\}$. Hence we have $s \underset{i}{\mathrel{+\!\!\!\!+\!\!\!\!\to}}_P \Psi(s) \underset{i}{\longrightarrow}_p t' \mathrel{+\!\!\!\!+\!\!\!\!\to} \Psi(t)$ and thus $\Psi(s) \to^+ \Psi(t)$. In the other case s/p is a non-terminating, non-innermost redex. Hence, every innermost redex of s (there exists at least one!) strictly below p, s/pq ($q > \lambda$), must correspond to a variable overlap, i.e., $q \geq u$, for some $u \in \mathcal{V}Pos(l)$. This implies (together with UIR) that $\Psi(s)/p$ is still an instance of l, let's say $\Psi(s)/p = \sigma'(l)$, with $\sigma \mathrel{+\!\!\!\!+\!\!\!\!\to} \sigma'$. Hence, as in the corresponding second subcase of **(1)**, we then obtain $\Psi(s) \to t' \to^* \Psi(t)$ and thus $\Psi(s) \to^+ \Psi(t)$ as desired. □

Next we prove that under certain conditions the transformation Ψ preserves the possibility of infinite reductions.

Lemma 9. *Let $\mathcal{R}$ be a TRS satisfying properties UIR and AICR. Then, for any term t we have: $SN(\Psi(t)) \Longrightarrow SN(t)$.*

Proof. Assume $\neg\mathrm{SN}(t)$, i.e., there exists an infinite derivation D issuing from t. Due to property AICR and Lemma 5 we may assume that in

$$D : t =: t_0 \to t_1 \to t_2 \to \ldots$$

every step is innermost-uncritical. If $t_k \xrightarrow[iu]{}_{p,\sigma,l\to r} t_{k+1}$ with $\mathrm{SN}(t_k/p)$ (for some $p, \sigma, l \to r$), then, by Lemma 8(1), we know $\Psi(t_k) \to^* \Psi(t_{k+1})$. If $t_k \xrightarrow[iu]{}_{p,\sigma,l\to r} t_{k+1}$ with $\neg\mathrm{SN}(t_k/p)$ (for some $p, \sigma, l \to r$), we conclude by Lemma 8(2), that $\Psi(t_k) \to^+ \Psi(t_{k+1})$. Clearly, steps of the form are $t_k \to_p t_{k+1}$ with $\mathrm{SN}(t_k/p)$ are $\to_{\mathrm{sn}}$-steps, and steps of the form are $t_k \to_p t_{k+1}$ with $\neg\mathrm{SN}(t_k/p)$ are $\to_{\neg\mathrm{sn}}$-steps. Hence, by Lemma 6, D contains infinitely many $\to_{\neg\mathrm{sn}}$-steps of the latter form $t_k \xrightarrow[iu]{}_{p,\sigma,l\to r} t_{k+1}$ with $\neg\mathrm{SN}(t_k/p)$. We conclude that the transformed derivation

$$\Psi(D) : \Psi(t) = \Psi(t_0) \to^* \Psi(t_1) \to^* \Psi(t_2) \to^* \ldots$$

is infinite, too. Hence we are done. □

Now we are in a position to establish the main abstract result of this section.

Theorem 10. *Let $\mathcal{R}$ be a TRS satisfying properties UIR and AICR. Then, for any term t we have: $SIN(t) \iff SN(t)$.*

Proof. For a proof by contradiction (of SIN $\implies$ SN, the other direction is trivial), suppose that t admits an infinite derivation. Every infinite derivation starting from t must contain a non-innermost step, due to $\mathrm{SIN}(t)$. Now consider an infinite derivation D starting from t with the property that the first non-innermost step is essential: Contracting any innermost redex at that point would result in a term with the property SN. Let

$$D : t =: t_0 \to t_1 \to \ldots \to t_n \to t_{n+1} \to \ldots$$

where $t_n \to t_{n+1}$ is the first non-innermost step. Note that this step must be innermost-uncritical (i.e., $t_n \xrightarrow[iu]{} t_{n+1}$) because, otherwise, it could not be essential in the above sense, due to property AICR. By assumption, contracting an innermost redex in t_n yields a terminating term. This implies in particular that $\Psi(t_n)$, which is obtained from t_n by a (non-empty) parallel reduction step contracting all innermost redexes of t_n (all of which must be terminating), is terminating. But then, by Lemma 9 we conclude that t_n is terminating, too. Hence, we have a contradiction (to the infinity of D). □

3.2 Concrete Equivalence Criteria

The above criterion for the implication (SIN $\implies$ SN) is still rather abstract in nature. Subsequently we shall investigate more concrete syntactic conditions satisfying the properties UIR, uniqueness of innermost reduction (at some fixed position), and AICR, the possibility to avoid (non-innermost) innermost-critical steps in infinite reductions. This will result in concrete critical peak conditions for the considered TRS $\mathcal{R}$.

First we introduce some more useful terminology for reasoning about critical peaks (and pairs).

Definition 11. Let $\mathcal{R}$ be a TRS. A critical peak $s\ {}_p\!\leftarrow u \rightarrow_\lambda t$ (and its corresponding critical pair $\langle s = t\rangle$) is *joinable* if $s \downarrow t$. It is *trivial* if $s = t$. It is said to be *left-to-right joinable* if $s \rightarrow^* t$. It is *overlay joinable* or *outside joinable* if $p = \lambda$ and $s \downarrow t$. If $p > \lambda$ it is an *inside* critical peak, if $p = \lambda$ it is an *outside* critical peak or *critical overlay*. If $p = \lambda$ and $s/p = s$ is an innermost redex, we speak of an *innermost critical overlay*. $\mathcal{R}$ *has joinable critical peaks (pairs)* (JCP) if all its critical peaks (pairs) are joinable. $\mathcal{R}$ is *weakly non-overlapping* (WNO) if it has only trivial critical peaks. $\mathcal{R}$ *has left-to-right joinable critical peaks* (LRJCP) if all its critical peaks are left-to-right joinable. $\mathcal{R}$ *has strongly left-to-right joinable critical peaks* (SLRJCP) if all its critical peaks are left-to-right joinable and, moreover, all its outside critical peaks are even trivial. $\mathcal{R}$ *has weakly left-to-right joinable critical peaks* (WLRJCP) if all its inside critical peaks are left-to-right joinable and all its outside critical peaks are joinable. $\mathcal{R}$ *has overlay joinable critical peaks* (OJCP) if every critical peak of $\mathcal{R}$ is overlay joinable (note: OJCP $\iff$ OS $\wedge$ JCP). $\mathcal{R}$ *has weakly overlay joinable critical peaks* (WOJCP) if all its inside critical peaks are trivial, and all its outside critical peaks are joinable.

Next we give a critical peak condition which is sufficient for the crucial properties UIR and AICR needed above.

Definition 12. Let $\mathcal{R}$ be a TRS. We say that $\mathcal{R}$ *satisfies CPC* (CPC($\mathcal{R}$) or CPC for short) if the following holds: For every every critical peak $t_1\ {}_p\!\leftarrow s \rightarrow_\lambda t_2$ of $\mathcal{R}$ we have:[4]

(1) if $p = \lambda$ and both steps are innermost (i.e., s is an innermost redex), then $t_1 = t_2$, and
(2) if $p > \lambda$ and the inside step is innermost (i.e., $s \xrightarrow[i]{} {}_p t_1$), then $t_1 \rightarrow^* t_2$.

Lemma 13. *For any TRS, CPC implies both UIR and AICR.*

Proof. Assume CPC. Then, UIR follows easily by definition and CPC (1). Proving AICR, the possibility of avoiding innermost-critical steps, amounts to showing

$$\forall s,t : [s \rightarrow t \implies [s \xrightarrow[iu]{} t \vee \exists s' : s \xrightarrow[i]{} s' \rightarrow^* t]\,].$$

Now, w.l.o.g. we may assume $s \rightarrow t$, but not $s \xrightarrow[iu]{} t$, hence $s \xrightarrow[ic]{} t$. This means (cf. Remark 3.1) $s \rightarrow_{p,\sigma,l\rightarrow r} t$ (for some p, σ, $l \rightarrow r$) such that there exists an innermost redex in $s/p = \sigma(l)$ at some position $q \in \mathcal{F}Pos(l)$, $q > \lambda$, with $s/pq = \sigma(l)/q = \tau(l')$ for some rule $l' \rightarrow r' \in \mathcal{R}$. But this implies that the divergence

$$s/p[q \leftarrow \tau(r')]\ {}_q\!\leftarrow s/p = \sigma(l) \rightarrow_\lambda \sigma(r) = t/p$$

[4] In other words, these requirements mean: every innermost critical overlay must be trivial, and every inside critical peak where the inside step is innermost must be left-to-right joinable.

is an instance of a critical peak of the form in (2) above. Therefore we get $s/p[q \leftarrow \tau(r')] \to^* \sigma(r)$ and hence

$$s \xrightarrow[i]{}_{pq} s[pq \leftarrow \tau(r')] \to^* s[p \leftarrow \sigma(r)] = t$$

as desired. □

Remark. Note that the reverse implication in Lemma 13 does not hold. For example, the TRS

$$\mathcal{R} = \begin{cases} f(a,a) \to f(a,a) \\ a \to b \\ f(b,x) \to f(x,x) \end{cases}$$

satisfies both UIR and AICR, but not CPC. The point is that for the inside critical peak $f(a,b) \underset{i}{\not\leftarrow} f(a,a) \to_\lambda f(a,a)$ we do not have $f(a,b) \to^* f(a,a)$. However, the step $f(a,a) \to f(a,a)$ which is innermost-critical has two innermost-critical redexes. And, indeed, choosing the left innermost-critical redex a corresponds to the other critical peak $f(b,a) \underset{i}{\leftarrow} f(a,a) \to_\lambda f(a,a)$ which is left-to-right-joinable, yielding $f(a,a) \xrightarrow[i]{} f(b,a) \to f(a,a)$.

Combining Theorem 10 and Lemma 13 we obtain the following (local and global) results.

Theorem 14. *Any innermost terminating (term in a) TRS $\mathcal{R}$ satisfying the critical pair condition CPC is terminating.*

In particular, we get the following concrete critical pair criteria, which extend the equivalence result (SIN $\iff$ SN) for non-overlapping systems (cf. Theorem 1(1)) to more general classes of TRSs.

Theorem 15. *An innermost terminating (term in a) TRS $\mathcal{R}$ is terminating if $\mathcal{R}$*

(1) is weakly non-overlapping (WNO), or
(2) has strongly left-to-right joinable critical peaks (SLRJCP), or
(3) has left-to-right joinable critical peaks (LRJCP).

Proof. (1) is a special case of (2). And (2) holds by Theorem 14 and the fact that according to the definition of SLRJCP any violation of the critical pair condition CPC (in Lemma 13) is impossible. (3) is not a direct consequence of Theorem 14 and Lemma 13, but holds for similar reasons. Namely, LRJCP still implies AICR as is easily seen. However, UIR need not hold any more. Nevertheless, a careful inspection of Definitions 3, 4, 7, Lemmas 8, 9 and Theorem 10 reveals that UIR is only needed in the slightly weakened version

$$\forall s, t_1, t_2, p \in Pos(s) : s \xrightarrow[i]{}_p t_1 \wedge s \xrightarrow[i]{}_p t_2 \wedge \mathrm{SN}(s/p) \implies t_1 = t_2 .$$

And indeed, an innermost divergence $t_1 \;{}_\lambda\!\!\leftarrow s \to_\lambda t_2$ with SN(s) which is non-trivial, i.e., with $t_1 \neq t_2$, cannot be an instance of a non-trivial innermost critical overlay. Because then, by left-to-right-joinability of all innermost critical overlays (according to LRJCP), we could conclude both $t_1 \to^* t_2$ and $t_2 \to^* t_1$, thus contradicting SN(s).[5] □

Interestingly, and in contrast to the situation for non-overlapping and for locally confluent overlay systems, TRSs satisfying the critical pair condition CPC need not be (locally) confluent.

Example 1. The TRS

$$\mathcal{R} = \begin{cases} f(x) \to x \\ f(a) \to b \\ f(a) \to c \\ \quad a \to f(a) \end{cases}$$

is easily verified to satisfy CPC (in particular, we note that CPC ignores the critical overlays between the first three rules since they comprise non-innermost divergences). However, $\mathcal{R}$ is not locally confluent, as shown by the non-joinable critical overlay $b \ {}_{\lambda}\!\leftarrow f(a) \to_{\lambda} c$.

We observe that in this example $\mathcal{R}$ is obviously not innermost terminating. And, fortunately, it turns out that SIN combined with CPC does indeed imply not only termination, but also confluence, hence completeness.

Theorem 16. *Any innermost terminating TRS satisfying the critical peak condition CPC is complete, i.e., terminating and confluent.*

Proof. Let $\mathcal{R}$ be a TRS with SIN($\mathcal{R}$) and CPC($\mathcal{R}$). By Theorem 14 we know that $\mathcal{R}$ must be terminating. Thus, it remains to show confluence. This can be done directly by induction (for the stronger local version of the result): Using $\to^+$ as well-founded ordering, one proves

$$\forall s : [\,[\forall t : s \to^+ t \Longrightarrow \mathrm{CR}(t)] \implies \mathrm{CR}(s)\,]$$

by induction via a (not too difficult, but tedious) case analysis concerning the shape of the initial one-step divergence issuing from s in an arbitrary divergence $t_1 \ {}^+\!\leftarrow s \to^+ t_2$, and exploiting CPC($\mathcal{R}$). However, we shall not present this proof in detail but simply reduce it to a special case of some known result. More precisely, we apply the following ***critical pair criterion*** for confluence of terminating TRSs due to [8]:

> If $\mathcal{R}$ is a terminating TRS such every critical pair which corresponds to a ***prime*** critical peak is joinable, then $\mathcal{R}$ is confluent.

Here, a critical peak $t_1 \ {}_p\!\leftarrow s \to_{\lambda} t_2$ of $\mathcal{R}$ is ***prime*** if it is not *composite*. And it is ***composite*** if the inner redex s/p has a proper reducible subterm. Indeed, it is straightforward to verify that CPC ignores only composite critical peaks, and the ones considered are clearly joinable according to CPC. Hence, applying this result we get confluence of $\mathcal{R}$ for free. □

[5] In fact, any TRS $\mathcal{R}$ which has a non-trivial, left-to-right joinable critical overlay is necessarily non-terminating. For this reason, such systems are not so interesting from a termination point of view.

Remark. Interestingly, it seems difficult to prove the implication (CPC $\wedge$ SIN $\Longrightarrow$ CR) directly, without making use of SN (which is allowed according to Theorem 14).

Example 1 above showed that, given CPC, we cannot simply drop innermost termination when trying to infer confluence or termination (or both of them). In view of (the proof of) Theorem 16 one might be tempted to conjecture that the combination of innermost termination and the critical pair criterion of [8], i.e., joinability of all prime critical peaks, suffices for guaranteeing confluence and termination or at least one of them. However, this is also not the case.

Example 2. The TRS

$$\mathcal{R} = \begin{cases} f(b) \to f(c) \\ f(c) \to f(b) \\ \quad b \to a \\ \quad c \to d \end{cases}$$

is clearly innermost terminating and locally confluent, but non-terminating and non-confluent, and both critical peaks to be considered are obviously prime.

Let us mention that Theorem 15 captures only some special cases of Theorem 14. According to the latter result, for inferring termination from innermost termination it suffices to show that every innermost critical overlay is trivial, and every inside critical pair where the inside step is innermost is left-to-right joinable. In particular, non-trivial critical overlays may exist provided they comprise a non-innermost divergence.

Example 3. The TRS

$$\mathcal{R} = \begin{cases} f(a) \to b \\ f(a) \to f(c) \\ \quad a \to d \\ f(d) \to b \\ f(c) \to b \\ \quad d \to c \end{cases}$$

innermost terminating and satisfies CPC, hence must be complete by Theorem 14. But note that there exists a non-trivial critical overlay (between the first two rules) which is ignored by CPC since it is not a divergence by innermost reduction.

As exhibited above, under uniqueness of innermost reduction (UIR, cf. Definition 2), left-to-right joinability of all critical pairs (LRJCP, cf. Definition 11) has turned out to be sufficient for the implication (SIN $\Longrightarrow$ SN) to hold (Theorem 15 (3)). Hence, in view of the fact that overlay joinability of all critical pairs (OJCP) also suffices for (SIN $\Longrightarrow$ SN) (Theorem 1(2)), it is quite natural to ask whether these two criteria can be combined. In other words, we have the following

Open Problem. Does termination follow from innermost termination if all critical overlays are joinable and all inside critical peaks are even left-to-right joinable? (or, more concisely: WLRJCP $\wedge$ SIN $\Longrightarrow$ SN?)

Unfortunately, we have neither been able to prove this criterion nor to find a counterexample. The careful reader may recognize that the problem lies with allowing both non-trivial innermost critical overlays and inside critical peaks. In fact, even for the special case that we require any inside critical peaks to be trivial, i.e., for the conjecture (WOJCP $\wedge$ SIN $\Longrightarrow$ SN), we could not provide a solution. Intuitively, the reason for our failure is due to the problem, that the two different proof techniques we applied somehow seem to be incompatible. More precisely, the latter proof technique presented here crucially relies on uniqueness of innermost reduction, which is destroyed by allowing non-trivial innermost critical overlays. And the other proof technique of [6] (for Theorem 1(2)) makes essential use of the (pure) overlay property which conflicts with allowing inside critical peaks.

Finally, we present some further results, relying on the properties UIR and AICR, which generalize the corresponding results of [6] for non-overlapping TRSs.

Theorem 17. *For any TRS $\mathcal{R}$ the following properties hold:*

(1) $UIR \Longrightarrow WCR^1(\xrightarrow[i]{}) \Longrightarrow CR(\xrightarrow[i]{})$.
(2) $UIR \Longrightarrow [\, WIN(s) \Longleftrightarrow SIN(s)\,]$.
(3) $UIR \wedge AICR \Longrightarrow [\, WIN(s) \Longleftrightarrow SIN(s) \Longleftrightarrow SN(s)\,]$.
(4) $UIR \wedge AICR \Longrightarrow [\, s \xrightarrow[i]{} t \wedge SN(t) \Longrightarrow SN(s)\,]$.

Proof. (1) is straightforward by definition of UIR and using the well-known fact that uniform confluence (WCR^1) implies confluence (CR). (2) follows from (1), observing the equivalences (WIN $\Longleftrightarrow$ WN($\xrightarrow[i]{}$)) and (SIN $\Longleftrightarrow$ SN($\xrightarrow[i]{}$)) (which also hold 'below' some term s), and applying the following old result from Newmman ([14]): $WCR^1 \wedge WN \Longrightarrow SN$. Finally, (3) is a consequence of (2) and Theorem 10, and (4) is a corollary of (3). □

4 Applications in Modularity

The study of the modularity behaviour of rewrite systems (w.r.t. to the preservation of important properties) under various types of combinations has become a very active and fruitful area of research (cf. [12], [15], [7] for surveys). A property P of rewrite systems is said to be *modular* (for disjoint systems) if, for all (disjoint) systems $\mathcal{R}_1^{\mathcal{F}_1}$, $\mathcal{R}_2^{\mathcal{F}_2}$ and $\mathcal{R}^{\mathcal{F}}$ with $\mathcal{R}^{\mathcal{F}} = (\mathcal{R}_1 \uplus \mathcal{R}_2)^{\mathcal{F}_1 \uplus \mathcal{F}_2}$: $P(\mathcal{R}_1^{\mathcal{F}_1}) \wedge P(\mathcal{R}_2^{\mathcal{F}_2}) \Longleftrightarrow P(\mathcal{R}^{\mathcal{F}})$. The 'if'-part here is most often trivial, so, the interesting question is whether the combination inherits the property from the constituent systems. Under disjoint unions, confluence is well-known to be modular, whereas termination is not modular ([19]).

The known positive results for modularity of termination are, roughly speaking, based on three different approaches concerning the essential ideas and proof structures (cf. [7]):

- the **general approach via an abstract structure theorem** where the basic idea is to reduce non-termination in the union to non-termination of a slightly modified generic version of one of the systems ([5] [16]),
- the **modular approach via modularity of innermost termination** where sufficient criteria for the equivalence of innermost termination (SIN) and general termination (SN) are combined with the (not so difficult to establish) modularity of SIN ([6][6]), and
- the **syntactic approach via left-linearity** which in essence is based on commutation and uniqueness properties for rewriting in left-linear systems ([20], [18]).

Due to lack of space we cannot give a more detailed account of the (numerous) papers on the subject and the above classification, but shall only concentrate on the **modular approach via modularity of innermost termination** (for the case of disjoint unions). The 'modular' idea here is quite simple: Since innermost termination is modular (which is easily proved by structural induction, cf. [6]), it suffices to ensure that, for the disjoint union, innermost termination implies termination. According to Theorem 1, this is the case, if both constituent systems are (besides terminating) non-overlapping, or locally confluent overlay systems.[7] Alternately, one can also use Theorems 14-16 to derive corresponding modularity results.

Lemma 18. *The properties UIR, CPC, WNO and SLRJCP are modular for disjoint unions of TRSs.*[8]

Proof. Straightforward by the respective definitions and the facts that in the disjoint union of two TRSs the set of critical peaks is the disjoint[9] union of the sets of critical peaks in the disjoint component TRSs, and that joinability of a critical peak belonging to one system does not depend on the other system. □

Theorem 19. *Termination and completeness are modular for disjoint unions of TRSs satisfying CPC.*

---

[6] Cf. also [13] where (*composable*) combinations of *constructor systems*, which are in particular overlay systems, are considered.

[7] Observe that the the properties NO (being non-overlapping), OS (being an overlay system) and local confluence (which is eqivalent to JCP, joinability of all critical pairs) are obviously modular!

[8] In fact, a couple of further related syntactical (e.g., critical peak) properties are also easily seen to be modular.

[9] This does not hold necessarily for critical pairs, due to degenerate cases where a critical pair consists of two variables. However, such critical pairs do not constitute a substantial problem either, since they are either trivial or not joinable (due to our assumption of excluding variables as left hand sides).

Proof. Straightforward by combining Theorem 16, Lemma 18 (i.e., the modularity of CPC) and the modularity of innermost termination. □

In view of the implications (WNO $\Longrightarrow$ CPC) and (SLRJCP $\Longrightarrow$ CPC), and Lemma 18 this entails the following.

Corollary 20. *Termination and completeness are modular for disjoint unions of weakly non-overlapping TRSs (WNO) and of TRSs with strongly left-to-right-joinable critical peaks (SLRJCP).*

Let us give an example for illustrating the applicability of Theorem 19 (and of Corollary 20).

Example 4. The disjoint TRSs

$$\mathcal{R}_1 = \begin{cases} f(a,b,x) \to f(x,x,x) \\ a \to c \\ f(c,b,x) \to f(x,x,x) \end{cases}$$

and

$$\mathcal{R}_2 = \begin{cases} K(x,y,y) \to x \\ K(y,y,x) \to x \end{cases}$$

are both terminating and confluent, and moreover have strongly left-to-right joinable critical peaks (SLRJCP) as is easily verified. Hence, Corollary 20 yields completeness of their disjoint union. We note that none of the previous modularity results is applicable here. In particular, $\mathcal{R}_1$ is not an overlay system, and $\mathcal{R}_2$ is not left-linear.

We remark that the same approach as above also yields corresponding modularity results for the more general cases of *constructor-sharing* TRSs ([11]) and of *composable* TRSs ([13], [15]). This is straightforward, since innermost termination (SIN) as well the other syntactical properties involved (CPC, WNO, SLRJCP) are modular for such combinations, too. Moreover, it seems plausible that the new criteria for the equivalence (SIN $\Longleftrightarrow$ SN) can also be used for deriving new inheritence results for termination of *hierarchical* combinations of TRSs (as in [10], [1]).

References

1. N. Dershowitz. Hierarchical termination. In N. Dershowitz and N. Lindenstrauss, editors, *Proc. of 4th Int. Workshop on Conditional and Typed Rewriting Systems, Jerusalem, Israel (1994)*, *Lecture Notes in Computer Science* 968, pages 89–105. Springer-Verlag, 1995.
2. N. Dershowitz and C. Hoot. Natural termination. *Theoretical Computer Science*, 142(2):179–207, May 1995.
3. N. Dershowitz and J.-P. Jouannaud. Rewrite systems. In J. van Leeuwen, editor, *Formal models and semantics, Handbook of Theoretical Computer Science*, volume B, chapter 6, pages 243–320. Elsevier - The MIT Press, 1990.

4. O. Geupel. Overlap closures and termination of term rewriting systems. Technical Report MIP-8922, Fakultät für Informatik, Universität Passau, July 1989.
5. B. Gramlich. Generalized sufficient conditions for modular termination of rewriting. *Applicable Algebra in Engineering, Communication and Computing*, 5:131–158, 1994.
6. B. Gramlich. Abstract relations between restricted termination and confluence properties of rewrite systems. *Fundamenta Informaticae*, 24:3–23, 1995. Special issue on term rewriting systems, ed. D. A. Plaisted. (A preliminary version of this paper appeared as 'Relating innermost, weak, uniform and modular termination of term rewriting systems' in Proc. *LPAR'92*, *LNAI* 624, pages 285–296, see also SEKI-Report SR-93-09, FB Informatik, Univ. Kaiserslautern).
7. B. Gramlich. *Termination and Confluence Properties of Structured Rewrite Systems*. PhD thesis, Fachbereich Informatik, Universität Kaiserslautern, Jan. 1996.
8. D. Kapur, D. Musser, and P. Narendran. Only prime superpositions need be considered in the Knuth-Bendix completion procedure. *Journal of Symbolic Computation*, 1988(6):19–36, 1988.
9. J. W. Klop. Term rewriting systems. In S. Abramsky, D. Gabbay, and T. Maibaum, editors, *Handbook of Logic in Computer Science*, volume 2, chapter 1, pages 2–117. Clarendon Press, Oxford, 1992.
10. M. Krishna Rao. Modular proofs for completeness of hierarchical term rewriting systems. *Theoretical Computer Science*, 151(2):487–512, Nov. 1995.
11. M. Kurihara and A. Ohuchi. Modularity of simple termination of term rewriting systems with shared constructors. *Theoretical Computer Science*, 103:273–282, 1992.
12. A. Middeldorp. *Modular Properties of Term Rewriting Systems*. PhD thesis, Free University, Amsterdam, 1990.
13. A. Middeldorp and Y. Toyama. Completeness of combinations of constructor systems. *Journal of Symbolic Computation*, 15:331–348, Sept. 1993.
14. M. Newman. On theories with a combinatorial definition of equivalence. *Annals of Mathematics*, 43(2):223–242, 1942.
15. E. Ohlebusch. *Modular Properties of Composable Term Rewriting Systems*. PhD thesis, Universität Bielefeld, 1994. Report 94-01.
16. E. Ohlebusch. On the modularity of termination of term rewriting systems. *Theoretical Computer Science*, 136:333–360, 1994.
17. D. A. Plaisted. Equational reasoning and term rewriting systems. In D. Gabbay, C. Hogger, and J. Robinson, editors, *Handbook of Logic in Artificial Intelligence and Logic Programming - Logical Foundations*, volume 1 of *Handbooks of Logic in Computer Science and of Logic in Artificial Intelligence and Logic Programming*, pages 273–364. Clarendon Press, Oxford, 1994.
18. M. Schmidt-Schauß, M. Marchiori, and S. Panitz. Modular termination of r-consistent and left-linear, term rewriting systems. *Theoretical Computer Science*, 149(2):361–374, Oct. 1995.
19. Y. Toyama. On the Church-Rosser property for the direct sum of term rewriting systems. *Journal of the ACM*, 34(1):128–143, 1987.
20. Y. Toyama, J. Klop, and H. Barendregt. Termination for the direct sum of left-linear term rewriting systems. In N. Dershowitz, editor, *Proc. 3rd Int. Conf. on Rewriting Techniques and Applications*, *Lecture Notes in Computer Science* 355, pages 477–491. Springer-Verlag, 1989.

A Recursive Path Ordering for Higher-Order Terms in η-Long β-Normal Form*

Jean-Pierre Jouannaud†** and **Albert Rubio**‡

† LRI, Bat. 490, CNRS/Université de Paris Sud, 91405 Orsay, FRANCE
Email: Jean-Pierre.Jouannaud@lri.fr
‡ Technical University of Catalonia, Pau Gargallo 5, 08028 Barcelona, SPAIN
Email: rubio@lsi.upc.es

Abstract: This paper extends the termination proof techniques based on rewrite orderings to a higher-order setting, by defining a recursive path ordering for simply typed higher-order terms in η-long β-normal form. This ordering is powerful enough to show termination of several complex examples.

1 Introduction

Higher-order rewrite rules are used in various programming languages and logical systems. In functional languages like Elf, or theorem provers like Isabelle, higher-order rewrite rules define functions by higher-order pattern matching. Higher-order rewriting in this sense enjoys a theory which parallels the usual theory of first-order rewriting. In particular, the main property of first-order rewriting, the critical pair lemma, still holds for some restricted cases [12].

Computer systems like RRL [7], *Saturate* [13] or CiME [11] make available semi-automated techniques for proving termination of first-order rewrite rules by comparing their left and right hand sides in some reduction ordering, of which the most popular one is the recursive path ordering [4]. Its principle is to generate recursively an ordering on terms from a user-defined ordering on function symbols called a precedence.

Our goal is to develop similar techniques for the higher-order case, thus further closing the gap between the practical needs and the existing results [9, 10, 3]. These orderings will of course need to be compatible with the underlying typed λ-calculus. Since higher-order pattern matching is used, compatibility with $\beta\eta$-conversion implies that the ordering operates on $\beta\eta$-equivalence classes of terms. This can be achieved by defining an ordering on canonical representatives, like terms in β-normal η-long form.

Our contribution is precisely the definition of a recursive path ordering for higher-order terms operating on terms in β-normal η-long form. This ordering extends, on one hand a precedence on the function symbols, on the other hand a

* This work was partly supported by the ESPRIT Basic Research Action CCL and the EU Human Capital and Mobility Network *Console*.

** This work results from a stay of the author at the Technical University of Catalonia.

well-founded ordering on the type structure compatible with the signature, that is, such that the output type of any function symbol should be bigger than or equal to its arguments type. Terms are compared by type first, then by head function symbol, before the comparison can proceed recursively. In practice, the ordering on types can itself be a recursive path ordering generated by an arbitrary precedence between the basic types and the arrow, or by interpreting a type expression by its maximal basic type. Several examples are carried out.

This idea of extending a recursive path ordering to higher-order terms in η-long β-normal form was first explored in [9]. The authors restricted their study to patterns in the sense of Miller, and this restriction survived in subsequent work [8, 10]. We were able to get rid of this superflous assumption by proving the properties of our ordering for ground terms. For instance, we prove that (a first approximation of) our ordering enjoys the subterm property for ground terms. This does not contradict the fact that a term $X(a)$ is not greater than a under our ordering on terms in η-long β-normal form. The point is that the term $X(a)$ has ground instances whose η-long β-normal form is not a superterm of a. A similar phenomenon occurs regarding the monotonicity property. Finally these properties on ground terms together with stability under ground substitutions and well-foundedness for ground terms ensure the correctness of the ordering as a termination proof method.

Our ordering is no panacea, unfortunately. There are many important examples such as the apply function or Gödels recursors that cannot be oriented with our current definition. A careful analysis points at a potential remedy, an original, powerful notion of higher-order subterm discussed in [8]. We believe that its use in our definition would overcome the limitations of our current proposal.

Our framework is described in section 2 and the ordering in section 3. Section 4 is devoted to compatible orderings on types and examples of application. A comparison with previous work is given in section 5 and conclusions and future work in section 6.

We expect the reader to be familiar with the basic concepts and notations of term rewriting systems [5] and typed lambda calculi [1, 2].

2 Algebraic λ-Terms

To introduce the language we are going to investigate, we define successively types, terms, typing rules, and computation rules. For simplicity, we consider only one type operator, namely $\rightarrow$, although our results accommodate other type operators as well, e.g., product types and sum types.

2.1 Types

We are first given a set $\mathcal{S}$ of *sorts*. The set $\mathcal{T}_\mathcal{S}$ of types is generated from the set of sorts (or *basic types*) by the constructor $\rightarrow$ for *functional types*:

$$\mathcal{T}_\mathcal{S} := \mathcal{S} \mid (\mathcal{T}_\mathcal{S} \rightarrow \mathcal{T}_\mathcal{S})$$

In the following, we use σ, τ and ρ to denote types. *Type declarations* are expressions of the form $\sigma_1 \times \ldots \times \sigma_n \to \sigma$, where $\sigma_1, \ldots, \sigma_n, \sigma$ are types. Types occurring before the arrow are called input types, while the type occurring after the arrow is called the output type. The latter is assumed to be a sort. Type declarations are not types, although they are used for typing purposes.

2.2 Signature

We are given a set of function symbols which are meant to be algebraic operators, equipped with a fixed number n of arguments (called the *arity*) of respective types $\sigma_1, \ldots, \sigma_n$, and an output type (thereafter assumed to be a sort) σ:

$$\mathcal{F} = \bigcup_{\sigma_1,\ldots,\sigma_n,\sigma} \mathcal{F}_{\sigma_1 \times \ldots \times \sigma_n \to \sigma}$$

We will assume that there are finitely many symbols of a given output type σ.

2.3 Terms

The set of *untyped terms* is generated from a denumerable set $\mathcal{X}$ of variables according to the grammar:

$$\mathcal{T} := \mathcal{X} \mid (\lambda\mathcal{X}.\mathcal{T}) \mid \mathcal{T}(\mathcal{T}) \mid \mathcal{F}(\mathcal{T}, \ldots, \mathcal{T})$$

$u(v)$ denotes the application of u to v. We write $u(v_1, \ldots, v_n)$ for $u(v_1) \ldots (v_n)$, and may sometimes identify the first order variable x with $x()$. We use $\mathcal{V}ar(t)$ for the set of free variables of t. We may assume for convenience that bound variables are all different, and are different from the free ones.

Terms are identified with finite labelled trees by considering $\lambda x.$, for each variable x, as a unary function symbol λx. *Positions* are strings of positive integers. Λ denotes the empty string (root position). The *subterm* of t at position p is denoted by $t|_p$, and we write $t \trianglerighteq t|_p$. The result of replacing $t|_p$ at position p in t by u is denoted by $t[u]_p$. We use $t[u]$ to indicate that u is a subterm of t.

Substitutions are written as in $\{x_1 \mapsto t_1, \ldots, x_n \mapsto t_n\}$ where t_i is assumed different from x_i. We use the letter γ for substitutions and postfix notation for their application. Remember that substitutions behave as endomorphisms defined on free variables (avoiding captures).

2.4 Typing Rules

Typing rules restrict the set of terms by constraining them to follow a precise discipline. Environments are sets of pairs of the form $x : \sigma$, where x is a variable and σ is a type. Our typing judgements are written as $\Gamma \vdash M : \sigma$ if the term M can be proved to have the type σ in the environment Γ:

$$Variables : \frac{X{:}\sigma \in \Gamma}{\Gamma \vdash X{:}\sigma} \;\Bigg|\; \frac{F{:}\sigma_1 \times \ldots \times \sigma_n \to \sigma \in \mathcal{F} \quad \Gamma \vdash t_1{:}\sigma_1 \;\ldots\; \Gamma \vdash t_n{:}\sigma_n}{\Gamma \vdash F(t_1, \ldots, t_n){:}\sigma} : Functions$$

$$Abstraction : \frac{\Gamma \cup \{x{:}\sigma\} \vdash M{:}\tau}{\Gamma \vdash (\lambda x{:}\sigma.M){:}\sigma \rightarrow \tau} \Bigg| \frac{\Gamma \cup \{x{:}\sigma\} \vdash M{:}\sigma \rightarrow \tau \quad \Gamma \vdash N{:}\sigma}{\Gamma \vdash M(N){:}\tau} : Application$$

A term M has type σ in the environment Γ if $\Gamma \vdash M : \sigma$ is provable in the above inference system. A term M is typable in the environment Γ if there exists a (necessarily unique) type σ such that M has type σ in the environment Γ. A term M is typable if it is typable in some environment Γ.

2.5 η-Long β-Normal Forms

Two particular rules originate from the λ-calculus, β-reduction and η-expansion:

$$(\lambda x.v)(u) \longrightarrow_\beta u\{x \mapsto v\}$$

$$u \longrightarrow_\eta (\lambda x.u(x)) \text{ } if\ u : \sigma \rightarrow \tau\ and\ x : \sigma \notin \mathcal{V}ar(u)\ and\ u \text{ is not an abstraction}$$

Given a term s, we will denote by $s\!\downarrow$ its η-long β-normal form, defined as the β-normal form of its η-expansion. We will say that s is normalized when $s = s\!\downarrow$, and use $\underset{\beta\eta}{\overset{*}{\longleftrightarrow}}$ for the congruence generated by these two rules.

The use of the extensionality rule as an expansion, and the assumption that the output type of each algebraic symbol is a sort allows us to hide applications:

Lemma 1. *Normalized terms are of either one of the two forms:*
$(\lambda x.u)$, *for some normalized term* u, *or*
$F(u_1, \ldots, u_n)$, *for some* $F \in \mathcal{F} \cup \mathcal{X}$ *and normalized terms* $u_1, \ldots, u_n$.
Moreover, terms with an arrow type are headed by an abstraction.

Note that application is implicitely present in terms headed by a higher-order variable. Abstraction-free normalized terms will be called *algebraic*.

2.6 Higher-Order Rewrite Rules

A (possibly higher-order) *term rewriting system* is a set of rewrite rules $R = \{\Gamma_i : l_i \rightarrow r_i\}_i$, where l_i and r_i are normalized terms such that l_i and r_i have the same type σ_i in the environment Γ_i. Given a term rewriting system R, a normalized term s rewrites to a term t at position p with the rule $l \rightarrow r$ and the substitution γ, written $s \underset{l \rightarrow r}{\overset{p}{\longrightarrow}} t$, or simply $s \rightarrow_R t$, if $s|_p \longleftrightarrow^*_{\beta\eta} l\gamma$ and $t = s[r\gamma\!\downarrow]_p$. Note that t is normalized since s is. Such a term s is called *reducible*. $l\gamma$ is a *redex* in s, and t is the *reduct* of s. Irreducible terms are said to be in *normal form*. A substitution γ is in normal form if $x\gamma$ is in normal form for all x. We denote by $\rightarrow^*_R$ the reflexive, transitive closure of the rewrite relation $\rightarrow_R$, and by $\longleftrightarrow^*_R$ its reflexive, symmetric, transitive closure.

A rewrite relation $\rightarrow$ is *terminating* (or *strongly normalizing*) if all terms are strongly normalizable, in which case it is called a *reduction*. It is confluent if $s \longrightarrow^* u$ and $s \longrightarrow^* v$ implies that $u \longrightarrow^* t$ and $v \longrightarrow^* t$ for some t.

2.7 Example 1 : Sorting

The following example presents a set of rewrite rules defining the insertion algorithm for the (ascending or descending) sort of a list of natural numbers. Note that the left and right hand sides of each rule are normalized terms.

$\mathcal{S} = \{Nat, List\}$,
$\mathcal{F}_{List} = \{nil\}, \mathcal{F}_{Nat \times Nat \to Nat} = \{max, min\}, \mathcal{F}_{Nat \times List \to List} = \{cons\}$,
$\mathcal{F}_{Nat \times List \times (Nat \times Nat \to Nat) \times (Nat \times Nat \to Nat) \to List} = \{insert\}$,
$\mathcal{F}_{List \times (Nat \times Nat \to Nat) \times (Nat \times Nat \to Nat) \to List} = \{sort\}$,
$\mathcal{F}_{List \to List} = \{ascending\_sort, descending\_sort\}, \mathcal{X}_{Nat \times Nat \to Nat} = \{X, Y\}$.

$$\begin{array}{rlrl} max(0,x) & \to x & min(0,x) & \to 0 \\ max(x,0) & \to x & min(x,0) & \to 0 \\ max(s(x),s(y)) & \to s(max(x,y)) & min(s(x),s(y)) & \to s(min(x,y)) \end{array}$$

$$\begin{array}{l} insert(n, nil, \lambda xy.X(x,y), \lambda xy.Y(x,y)) \to cons(x, nil) \\ insert(n, cons(m,l), \lambda xy.X(x,y), \lambda xy.Y(x,y)) \to \\ \quad cons(X(n,m), insert(Y(n,m), l, \lambda xy.X(x,y), \lambda xy.Y(x,y))) \end{array}$$

$$\begin{array}{l} sort(nil, \lambda xy.X(x,y), \lambda xy.Y(x,y)) \to nil \\ sort(cons(n,l), \lambda xy.X(x,y), \lambda xy.Y(x,y)) \to \\ \quad insert(n, sort(l, \lambda xy.X(x,y), \lambda xy.Y(x,y)), \lambda xy.X(x,y), \lambda xy.Y(x,y)) \end{array}$$

$$\begin{array}{l} ascending\_sort(l) \to sort(l, \lambda xy.min(x,y), \lambda xy.max(x,y)) \\ descending\_sort(l) \to sort(l, \lambda xy.max(x,y), \lambda xy.min(x,y)) \end{array}$$

2.8 Rewrite Orderings

We will make intensive use of well-founded monotonic orderings for proving strong normalization properties. We will use the vocabulary of rewrite systems for orderings: *rewrite orderings* are *monotonic* orderings, and *reduction orderings* are in addition well-founded. Monotonicity of $>$ is defined as $u > v$ implies $s[u\gamma]_p > s[v\gamma]_p$ for all terms s, positions p and substitutions γ for which this makes sense. A *quasi reduction ordering* is made of a reduction ordering for its strict part, and a congruence for its equivalence. (Quasi-) reduction orderings are used to prove termination of rewrite systems by simply comparing the left and right hand sides of rules. The following results will play a key role, see [5]:

Assume $\to_1$ and $\to_2$ are well-founded orderings on sets S_1, S_2. Then $(\to_1, \to_2)_{lex}$ is a well-founded ordering on $S_1 \times S_2$.

Assume $>$ is a well-founded ordering on a set S. Then $>_{mul}$ is a well-founded ordering on the set of multisets of elements of S. It is defined as the transitive closure of the following relation on multisets (using $\cup$ for multiset union):

$$M \cup \{s\} >> M \cup \{t_1, \ldots, t_n\} \quad if\ s > t_i\ \forall i \in [1..n]$$

Finally, we will also make use of simplification orderings, that is rewrite orderings that have the so-called *subterm property*: any term is strictly bigger than any of its proper subterms. Simplification orderings contain the *embedding relation* defined as the rewrite ordering generated by subterm, that is by the projection rules $f(\vec{x}) \to x_i$ for all $f \in \mathcal{F}$ and $i \in [1..arity(f)]$. Kruskal proved that embedding is a well-order of the set of terms, see [5]. This property is the key to prove that simplification orderings are well-founded.

3 Recursive Path Ordering for Algebraic λ-Terms

Our path ordering is defined in two steps. First, we define an original extension of the recursive path ordering for algebraic terms. This extension makes an essential use of the type structure. The obtained ordering is shown to be well-founded via a simple extension of Kruskal's theorem to typed structures. Then, we define an interpretation of normalized terms into the set of purely algebraic terms, before applying the previous technique. The difficulty here is in proving that the induced ordering is closed under appropriate substitutions.

3.1 Typed Recursive Path Ordering

Our typed recursive path ordering operates on algebraic terms. It uses three basic ingredients: a quasi-ordering on types, a precedence, and a status.

The *quasi-ordering on types* $\geq_{\mathcal{T}_S}$ satisfies the following properties:

1. its strict part $>_{\mathcal{T}_S}$ is well-founded
2. $\geq_{\mathcal{T}_S}$ is *compatible with the term structure*:
   for all ground normalized terms s, $s : \sigma \trianglerighteq t : \tau$ implies $\sigma \geq_{\mathcal{T}_S} \tau$.

Note that the compatibility property of the type ordering with the term structure is actually equivalent to its *compatibility with the signature* defined as:

$$\forall F : \sigma_1 \times \ldots \times \sigma_n \to \sigma \in \mathcal{F},\ \forall i \in [1..n]\ \sigma \geq_{\mathcal{T}_S} \sigma_i$$

There are many compatible orderings, including the recursive path ordering generated by a precedence on the set of sorts and the arrow operator. Compatibility is discussed in length in section 4.

The quasi-ordering on function symbols $\geq_{\mathcal{F}}$ compares symbols of the same output type only. Its strict part $>_{\mathcal{F}}$ must be well-founded. As usual, a free variable $x : \sigma$ is considered as a function symbol comparable only to itself.

The function symbols enjoy a multiset or lexicographic status. We allow for more complex statuses like right-to-left lexicographic status for our examples. See [6] for a general notion of status.

We can now define the typed recursive path ordering:
$s : \sigma = F(\vec{s}) \succ t : \tau = G(\vec{t})$ iff

1. $\sigma >_{\mathcal{T}_S} \tau$, or
2. $\sigma =_{\mathcal{T}_S} \tau$, and

(a) $F \notin \mathcal{X}$ and $s_i \succeq t$ for some s_i, or
(b) $F >_{\mathcal{F}} G$ and $s \succ t_i$ for all i, or
(c) $F = G \in Mul$ and $\vec{s} \succ_{mul} \vec{t}$, or
(d) $F = G \in Lex$ and $\vec{s} \succ_{lex} \vec{t}$ and $s \succ t_i$ for all i

The condition $F \notin \mathcal{X}$ prevents us to prove that $X(c) \succ c$. While it is not at all necessary in the context of algebraic terms, it becomes crucial in the next subsection, in which higher-order variables can be instantiated by abstractions.

Lemma 2. *$\succeq$ is transitive, and $\succ$ is irreflexive.*

Proof. The proof is by induction on the sum of the sizes of the terms involved. Comparisons involving case 1 are straightforward. Others use the same arguments as in the corresponding proofs for rpo. □

Lemma 3. *$\succ$ has the subterm property for ground terms.*

Proof. Let $s : \sigma$ be an arbitrary ground term, and $t : \tau$ be one of its strict subterms. We proceed by induction on the size of s. If $\sigma >_{\mathcal{T}_S} \tau$, we are done. Otherwise, by the compatibility property of the type ordering with the term structure, we have $\sigma =_{\mathcal{T}_S} \tau$. Since $s = F(\vec{s})$ and t is a subterm of some s_i we can conclude by induction. □

Lemma 4. *$\succ$ is stable under ground context for equal type terms.*

Proof. Similar as for rpo. □

Lemma 5. *$\succ$ is stable under ground substitutions.*

Proof. We prove that $s \succ t$ implies $s\gamma \succ t\gamma$, for all ground substitution γ by induction on $|s|+|t|$. Assume $s : \sigma = F(s_1, \ldots, s_n)$ and $t : \tau = G(t_1, \ldots, t_m)$. We are done if $\sigma >_{\mathcal{T}_S} \tau$, since types are preserved under substitution. Otherwise, we distinguish four cases:

1. $s_i \succeq t$ for some i. By induction hypothesis, $s_i\gamma \succeq t\gamma$, and hence $s\gamma \succ t\gamma$.
2. $F >_{\mathcal{F}} G$ and $s \succ t_i$ for all i. By induction, $s\gamma \succ t_i\gamma$, and therefore $s\gamma \succ t\gamma$.
3. $F = G \in Mul$ and $\vec{s} \succ_{mul} \vec{t}$. By induction, $\vec{s\gamma} \succ_{mul} \vec{t\gamma}$.
4. $F = G \in Lex$, $\vec{s} \succ_{lex} \vec{t}$ and $s \succ t_i$ for all i. By induction, $\vec{s\gamma} \succ_{lex} \vec{t\gamma}$ and $s\gamma \succ t_i\gamma$. □

We are left with the proof of well-foundedness, which follows the usual pattern. To overcome the difficulty that the signature may be infinite, we will use our hypothesis that there are finitely many symbols for a given output type σ.

Lemma 6. *Let $\{s_i\}_{i \in \mathcal{N}}$ be an infinite sequence of ground terms of the same type σ. Then, there exist two indices $i < j$ such that s_i is embedded in s_j.*

Proof. The proof is by contradiction. If there is a counterexample sequence $\{s^i : \sigma\}_i$, there must be one of minimal type. Among such sequences of minimal type σ, we choose a minimal one (in the usual sense, by comparing the size of the corresponding terms in the sequence). Since the sequence is of type σ, terms are all headed by function symbols of output type σ, and since there are finitely many of them, we can extract an infinite subsequence of terms of the form $F(\vec{u})$, all headed by some function symbol $F \in \mathcal{F}_{\sigma_1 \times \ldots \times \sigma_n \to \sigma}$ such that $\sigma \geq_{\mathcal{T}_S} \sigma_k$ for all $k \in [1..n]$ by compatibility property of the type ordering with the term structure. We now proceed to show that infinite sequences of type σ_k built up from the terms u_k satisfy the lemma. If $\sigma >_{\mathcal{T}_S} \sigma_k$, this results from our assumption that σ is minimal. Otherwise $\sigma_k =_{\mathcal{T}_S} \sigma$, and this results from the usual minimality argument. We can therefore find indices $i < j$ such that the term u_k^i is embedded in the term u_k^j for all $k \in [1..n]$. Then $F(\vec{u^i})$ is embedded in $F(\vec{u^j})$ contradicting our assumption that there was a counterexample sequence. □

Theorem 7. *$\succeq$ is a simplification ordering on ground terms whose strict part is well-founded.*

Proof. We are left to show that $\succ$ is well-founded. Assuming an infinite decreasing sequence, all terms must have the same type from some point on in the sequence, since the ordering on types is well-founded by assumption. We use then as usual the previous lemma together with the fact that simplification orderings contain the embedding relation. □

Although we have assumed that there are finitely many symbols of the same output type σ, this is not necessary. We know that Kruskal's theorem holds for any embedding relation generated by a well-order on the set of function symbols. Since rpo generated by a given precedence contains the associated embedding relation, we can then conclude by an easy modification of our argument.

3.2 Recursive Path Ordering for Normalized Terms

The ordering for normalized terms works by comparing interpretations of normalized terms. Because bound variables cannot be substituted, they will be considered as new (non-variable) symbols c_σ of their respective type σ. Abstractions are considered as operators of some input type τ (the type of the body) and output type $\sigma \to \tau$ (σ is the type of the abstracted variable). Finally, we will index all symbols by their output type, thus making the type of a term easily readable on its head. This results in the following extended signature:

$$\begin{aligned}
\mathcal{X}_{\mathcal{T}} &= \{x_\sigma \mid x : \sigma \in \mathcal{X}\} \\
\mathcal{F}_{\mathcal{T}} &= \{F_\sigma \mid F \in \mathcal{F}_{\sigma_1 \times \ldots \times \sigma_n \to \sigma}\} \\
\lambda\mathcal{F} &= \mathcal{X}_{\mathcal{T}} \cup \mathcal{F} \cup \bigcup_{\sigma \in \mathcal{T}_S} \{c_\sigma\} \cup \bigcup_{\sigma, \tau \in \mathcal{T}_S} \{\lambda_{\sigma \to \tau}\}
\end{aligned}$$

Note that we have a single symbol c_σ for each type σ and a single λ operator for each arrow type. Therefore if $\mathcal{F}$ has a finite set of function symbols for each output type then $\lambda\mathcal{F}$ has a finite set of function symbols for each type.

The interpretation function maps normalized terms to typed algebraic terms over the new signature:

$$\begin{aligned} \|x:\sigma\| &= x_\sigma \\ \|(\lambda x.u):\sigma\rightarrow\tau\| &= \lambda_{\sigma\rightarrow\tau}(\|u\|\{x_\sigma\mapsto c_\sigma\}) \\ \|F(\ldots,u_i,\ldots):\sigma\| &= F_\sigma(\ldots,\|u_i\|,\ldots) \end{aligned}$$

Before we can introduce our ordering, we need to define the precedence on the new signature. It will simply extend the precedence over the former signature, by adding new pairs for taking care of the c_σ and $\lambda_{\sigma\rightarrow\tau}$ operators. Being unary operators, abstractions may have any status. Finally, the compatibility property for the abstraction operators requires that $\sigma\rightarrow\tau \geq_{\mathcal{T}_S} \tau$. Compatibility is investigated thoroughly in section 4.

Assuming that s and t are two normalized terms such that no variable is both free and bound nor bound twice in the pair (s,t), we define:

$$s \succ_{horpo} t \text{ iff } \|s\| \succ \|t\|$$

Lemma 8. *$\succ_{horpo}$ is well-founded on ground normalized terms.*

Proof. The property is inherited from the previous ordering. □

Lemma 9. *If $s \succ_{horpo} t$ then $u[s] \succ_{horpo} u[t]$ for all contexts u and terms $s:\tau$ and $t:\tau$ such that $u[s]$ and $u[t]$ are ground normalized terms.*

Proof. Since s and t have the same type τ, $u[s]$ and $u[t]$ have the same type. We prove that $F(\ldots,s,\ldots) \succ_{horpo} F(\ldots,t,\ldots)$ for all possible F. Since the context must be ground, F cannot be a variable, resulting in two cases:

1. If F is an algebraic function symbol, then $F(\ldots,s,\ldots) \succ_{horpo} F(\ldots,t,\ldots)$ iff $\|F(\ldots,s,\ldots)\| \succ \|F(\ldots,t,\ldots)\|$, that is $F_\tau(\ldots,\|s\|,\ldots) \succ F_\tau(\ldots,\|t\|,\ldots)$, where τ is the output type of F. Since $\|s\| \succ \|t\|$ holds by assumption that $s \succ_{horpo} t$ and definition of $\succ_{horpo}$, the result holds by monotonicity of $\succ$ with respect to ground contexts.
2. Otherwise, let F be λx, for some x of type σ. Since $s \succ_{horpo} t$ iff $\|s\| \succ \|t\|$, then $\|s\|\{x_\sigma\mapsto c_\sigma\} \succ \|t\|\{x_\sigma\mapsto c_\sigma\}$ by lemma 5.
   By definition, $\lambda x.s \succ_{horpo} \lambda x.t$ iff $\|\lambda x.s\| \succ \|\lambda x.t\|$ iff $\lambda_{\sigma\rightarrow\tau}(\|s\|\{x\mapsto c_\sigma\}) \succ \lambda_{\sigma\rightarrow\tau}(\|t\|\{x\mapsto c_\sigma\})$. We therefore conclude by stability of $\succ$ under ground contexts.

□

Lemma 10. *$\succ_{horpo}$ is stable under ground normalized substitutions.*

Proof. Assuming that $s:\sigma$ and $t:\tau$ are normalized, we need to show that $s \succ_{horpo} t$ implies $s\gamma\!\downarrow \succ_{horpo} t\gamma\!\downarrow$ for all ground normalized substitutions γ. This amounts to show that $s' = \|s\| \succ \|t\| = t'$ implies $\|s\gamma\!\downarrow\| \succ \|t\gamma\!\downarrow\|$. This cannot be proved directly due to the replacement of bound variables by new function symbols (the c_σ) in the interpretation. We will therefore prove a more general statement, namely $\|s\|\psi_1 \succ \|t\|\psi_2$ implies $\|s\gamma\!\downarrow\|\psi_1 \succ \|t\gamma\!\downarrow\|\psi_2$, where ψ_1 and

ψ_2 are (well-typed) substitutions taking their value in $\bigcup_{\sigma\in\mathcal{T}_S}\{c_\sigma\}$, and such that if $X_{\sigma'}\in\mathcal{D}om(\psi_1)\cup\mathcal{D}om(\psi_2)$ (for some type σ') then $X\notin\mathcal{D}om(\gamma)$. We proceed by induction on $|s'|+|t'|$.

The statement holds if $\sigma >_{\mathcal{T}_S} \tau$, since types are preserved under substitution, normalization and interpretation.

Otherwise, let $s' = F_\sigma(s'_1,\ldots,s'_n)$ and $t' = G_\sigma(t'_1,\ldots,t'_m)$. We distinguish five cases:

1. $s'\psi_1 \succ t'\psi_2$ by case 2a, that is $s'_i\psi_1 \succeq t'\psi_2$ for some subterm s'_i of s'. Since the head symbol of $s'\psi_1$ cannot be a variable by definition of the ordering, there are two possibilities: (i) $s = F(s_1,\ldots,s_n)$, where $F\in\mathcal{F}$ or $F\in\mathcal{X}$ and $F_\sigma\psi_1 = c_\sigma$; or else (ii) s is an abstraction $\lambda x.s_1$, with $x:\sigma'$.
   i. In the first case, we have $s'\psi_1 = F_\sigma\psi_1(s'_1\psi_1,\ldots,s'_n\psi_1)$, where $s'_i = \|s_i\|$. By induction hypothesis, $s'_i\psi_1 \succ t'$ implies $\|s_i\gamma\!\downarrow\|\psi_1 \succ \|t\gamma\!\downarrow\|\psi_2$. Since $\|F(s_1,\ldots,s_n)\gamma\!\downarrow\|\psi_1 = F_\sigma\psi_1(\|s_1\gamma\!\downarrow\|\psi_1,\ldots,\|s_n\gamma\!\downarrow\|\psi_1)$, the result holds.
   ii. In the second case, $s'\psi_1 = \lambda_\sigma(s'_1\psi_1)$, where $s'_1 = \|s_1\|\{x_{\sigma'}\mapsto c_{\sigma'}\}$. Then $s'_1\psi_1$ can be written as $\|s_1\|\psi'_1$, with $\psi'_1 = \{x_{\sigma'}\mapsto c_{\sigma'}\}\cup\psi_1$. Note that x cannot appear in the domain of γ since it is bound in s. Likewise, $x_{\sigma'}$ cannot appear in the domain of ψ_1. Therefore, by induction hypothesis, $s'_1\psi_1 = \|s_1\|\psi'_1 \succ t'\psi_2$ implies $\|s_1\gamma\!\downarrow\|\psi'_1 \succ \|t\gamma\!\downarrow\|\psi_2$. The expected result follows, since $\|(\lambda x.s_1)\gamma\!\downarrow\|\psi_1 = \lambda_\sigma((\|s_1\gamma\!\downarrow\|\{x_{\sigma'}\mapsto c_{\sigma'}\})\psi_1) = \lambda_\sigma(\|s_1\gamma\!\downarrow\|\psi'_1)$.
2. $F_\sigma\psi_1 >_{\lambda\mathcal{F}} G_\sigma\psi_2$ and $s'\psi_1 \succ t'_i\psi_2$ for all i. There are again two cases.
   i. If $G_\sigma \neq \lambda_\sigma$, then, by induction, $\|s\gamma\downarrow\|\psi_1 \succ \|t_i\gamma\downarrow\|\psi_2$. Since $\|G(t_1,\ldots,t_m)\gamma\!\downarrow\|\psi_2 = G_\sigma\psi_2(\|t_1\gamma\!\downarrow\|\psi_2,\ldots,\|t_m\gamma\!\downarrow\|\psi_2)$, the result follows.
   ii. If $G_\sigma = \lambda_\sigma$ then, $t'\psi_2 = \lambda_\sigma(t'_1\psi_2)$, where $t'_1 = \|t_1\|\{x_{\sigma'}\mapsto c_{\sigma'}\}$ for some $x:\sigma'$. Since $t'_1\psi_2$ can be written as $\|t_1\|\psi'_2$ (with $\psi'_2 = \{x_{\sigma'}\mapsto c_{\sigma'}\}\cup\psi_2$), by induction hypothesis, $\|s\gamma\!\downarrow\|\psi_1 \succ \|t_1\gamma\!\downarrow\|\psi'_2$, and since $\|(\lambda x.t_1)\gamma\!\downarrow\|\psi_2 = \lambda_\sigma(\|t_1\gamma\!\downarrow\|\psi'_2)$, the result holds.
3. $F_\sigma = G_\sigma = \lambda_\sigma$ and $s'_1\psi_1 \succ t'_1\psi_2$. Then $s'\psi_1 = \lambda_\sigma(s'_1\psi_1)$, where $s'_1 = \|s_1\|\{x_{\sigma'}\mapsto c_{\sigma'}\}$ for some $x:\sigma'$, and $t'\psi_2 = \lambda_\sigma(t'_1\psi_2)$, where $t'_1 = \|t_1\|\{y_{\sigma'}\mapsto c_{\sigma'}\}$ for some $y:\sigma'$. Since $s'_1\psi_1$ can be written as $\|s_1\|\psi'_1$ (with $\psi'_1 = \{x_{\sigma'}\mapsto c_{\sigma'}\}\cup\psi_1$) and $t'_1\psi_2$ can be written as $\|t_1\|\psi'_2$ (with $\psi'_2 = \{y_{\sigma'}\mapsto c_{\sigma'}\}\cup\psi_2$), by induction hypothesis, $\|s_1\gamma\!\downarrow\|\psi'_1 \succ \|t_1\gamma\!\downarrow\|\psi'_2$. Since $\|(\lambda x.s_1)\gamma\!\downarrow\|\psi_1 = \lambda_\sigma(\|s_1\gamma\!\downarrow\|\psi'_1)$ and $\|(\lambda y.t_1)\gamma\!\downarrow\|\psi_2 = \lambda_\sigma(\|t_1\gamma\!\downarrow\|\psi'_2)$, the result holds.
4. $F_\sigma\psi_1 = G_\tau\psi_2 \in Mul$ and $\overrightarrow{s'\psi_1}\succ_{mul}\overrightarrow{t'\psi_2}$. By induction, the result holds.
5. $F_\sigma\psi_1 = G_\tau\psi_2 \in Lex$ and $\overrightarrow{s'\psi_1}\succ_{lex}\overrightarrow{t'\psi_2}$ and $s'\psi_1 \succ t'_i\psi_2$ for all i. By induction, the result follows similarly.

Note that the cases in which the head symbol may change, namely when the head symbol is a higher-order variable, are always solved by type, therefore avoiding potential problems. □

Theorem 11. *If $l \succ r$ for all rules $l \to r$ in R then R is terminating.*

Proof. First, terms in a derivation can always be considered as ground, therefore allowing us to use the previous properties. Assume now that $s \xrightarrow[l\to r]{p} t$, where s and t are ground normalized terms. Then, $s|_p =_{\beta\eta} l\gamma$, and $t = s[r\gamma\downarrow]_p$. Since $\longrightarrow_{\beta\eta}$ is confluent, and s is normalized, then $s|_p = l\gamma\downarrow$. By assumption, $l \succ_{horpo} r$, hence $l\gamma\downarrow \succ_{horpo} r\gamma\downarrow$ by lemma 10, and $s = s[l\gamma\downarrow]_p \succ_{horpo} s[r\gamma\downarrow]_p = t$ by lemma 9. Since $\succ_{horpo}$ is well-founded, R is therefore terminating. □

The above theorem is aimed at proving termination of higher-order rewrite rules operating on normalized terms via higher-order pattern matching. The use of first-order pattern matching does not change the situation very much, as long as rewriting operates on normalized terms.

4 Compatible Type Orderings

The goal of this section is to provide a sufficient condition ensuring the compatibility property of the type ordering with the term structure, that is $s : \sigma \trianglerighteq t : \tau$ implies $\sigma \geq_{\mathcal{T}_S} \tau$ for all ground normalized terms s and t. We will then exhibit two actual orderings which satisfy these conditions and hence can be used as a component of our ordering on higher-order terms.

Definition 12. The quasi-ordering on types $\geq_{\mathcal{T}_S}$ is *compatible with the type structure* if
(i) $\forall f : \sigma_1 \times \ldots \times \sigma_n \to \sigma \in \mathcal{F}$, $\forall i \in [1..n]$, $\sigma \geq_{\mathcal{T}_S} \sigma_i$,
(ii) $\sigma \to \tau \geq_{\mathcal{T}_S} \sigma$ and $\sigma \to \tau \geq_{\mathcal{T}_S} \tau$.

Note that conditions (i) and (ii) are indeed necessary. For the first part of (ii), consider the example $\lambda x.x(a)$, in which a is a constant of type $\tau >_{\mathcal{T}_S} \sigma$, and $x : \tau \to \sigma$.

Lemma 13. *Let $\geq_{\mathcal{T}_S}$ be a quasi-ordering on types compatible with the type structure. Then, for every ground normalized term $s : \sigma$ and for every ground normalized subterm $t : \tau$, we have $\sigma \geq_{\mathcal{T}_S} \tau$.*

Proof. We prove the more general property that $\sigma \geq_{\mathcal{T}_S} \tau$ for every normalized term $s : \sigma$ and every subterm $t : \tau$ not below a free variable (free variables may not satisfy the compatibility property). We proceed by induction on the size of the term. The property trivially holds if t is a constant or is headed by a free variable. Otherwise, there are two possible cases:

1. $s = F(s_1, \ldots, s_n)$, with $s_i : \sigma_i$. By compatibility of the type ordering with the type structure, $\sigma \geq_{\mathcal{T}_S} \sigma_i$. By induction hypothesis, for every subterm $t : \tau$ (not headed by a free variable) of some $s_i : \sigma_i$, we have $\sigma_i \geq_{\mathcal{T}_S} \tau$, and hence $\sigma \geq_{\mathcal{T}_S} \tau$. Note that we have considered all possible subterms (not headed by a free variable) of s.

2. $s = \lambda x.u$, with $\sigma = \alpha \rightarrow \beta$. By compatibility $\sigma \geq_{\mathcal{T}_S} \alpha$ and $\sigma \geq_{\mathcal{T}_S} \beta$. By induction hypothesis for every subterm $t : \tau$ of $u : \beta$ not below a free variable, $\beta \geq_{\mathcal{T}_S} \tau$ and hence $\sigma \geq_{\mathcal{T}_S} \tau$. The only new free variable of u (wrt. s) is x. Therefore, we need to ensure that for all subterms $t : \tau$ below some occurrence of x, we also have $\sigma \geq_{\mathcal{T}_S} \tau$. Let α be $\alpha_1 \rightarrow \ldots \alpha_n \rightarrow \alpha_{n+1}$, with $n \geq 0$. Assume there is a subterm of u of the form $x(u_1, \ldots, u_n)$. By compatibility, $\sigma \geq_{\mathcal{T}_S} \alpha \geq_{\mathcal{T}_S} \alpha_i$ for all i and by induction hypothesis for every subterm $t : \tau$ (not below a free variable) of some u_i $\alpha_i \geq_{\mathcal{T}_S} \tau$ and hence $\sigma \geq_{\mathcal{T}_S} \tau$. □

There is a tradeoff between the granularity and the compatibility of the ordering on types. This is why we provide with two different orderings satisfying the compatibility properties. The first is a recursive path ordering on type expressions. This is a fine grain ordering, thus compatibility may therefore be hard to achieve. The second ordering identifies many types, allowing us to ensure compatibility easily, but its strict part compares fewer types.

4.1 Recursive Path Ordering on Types

As already noticed in the context of algebraic terms, the recursive path ordering itself is a good candidate for the type ordering. Condition (ii) is always satisfied (the comparison is strict), and condition (i) is easily checked when the signature $\mathcal{F}$ is finite. The signature to be considered for the type ordering is the set of basic types plus the arrow operator. Usually, it is better to take $\rightarrow$ smaller than any basic type, although there is no obligation. The only requirement is to provide a precedence $\geq_{\mathcal{S}}$ on $\mathcal{S} \cup \{\rightarrow\}$, and a status for $\rightarrow$. The obtained ordering is quite powerful, hence it will allow us to compare many terms by type.

Example 1 : Sorting
We use the following precedences:

$List >_{\mathcal{S}} Nat$,
$\{max, min\} >_{\mathcal{F}} \{0, s\}$,
$insert >_{\mathcal{F}} cons$, $sort >_{\mathcal{F}} \{nil, insert\}$,
$\{ascending\_sort, descending\_sort\} >_{\mathcal{F}} sort$,
$insert \in Lex$ (right to left).

Example 2 : Mapcar
$\mathcal{S} = \{Nat, List\}$,
$\mathcal{F}_{List} = \{nil\}, \mathcal{F}_{Nat \times List \rightarrow List} = \{cons\}, \mathcal{F}_{(Nat \rightarrow Nat) \times List \rightarrow List} = \{map\}$,
$\mathcal{X}_{Nat \rightarrow Nat} = \{X\}$

$$map(\lambda x.X(x), nil) \rightarrow nil$$
$$map(\lambda x.X(x), cons(n, l)) \rightarrow cons(X(n), map(\lambda x.X(x), l))$$

The termination proof may use the following precedences:

$List >_{\mathcal{S}} Nat$, $List >_{\mathcal{S}} \rightarrow$, $map >_{\mathcal{F}} cons$, $map \in Mul$.

Example 3 : Maplist
$\mathcal{S} = \{Nat, List\}$,

$\mathcal{F}_{List} = \{nil\}, \mathcal{F}_{Nat \times List \to List} = \{cons\}, \mathcal{F}_{(Nat \to Nat) \times List \to List} = \{fcons\}$,
$\mathcal{F}_{List \times Nat \to List} = \{fmap\}$,
$\mathcal{X}_{Nat \to Nat} = \{X\}$

$$fmap(nil, n) \to nil$$
$$fmap(fcons(\lambda x.X(x), L), n) \to cons(X(n), fmap(L, n))$$

The termination proof may use the following precedences:

$$List >_{\mathcal{S}} Nat, \quad List >_{\mathcal{S}} \to, \qquad fmap >_{\mathcal{F}} cons, \qquad fmap \in Mul.$$

4.2 Sort Ordering

The second ordering is again generated by a precedence $\geq_{\mathcal{S}}$ on the set of basic types. It compares type expressions according to the maximal basic type occurring in them, that is

$$\sigma \geq_{\mathcal{T}_S} \tau \text{ iff } max(\sigma) \geq_{\mathcal{S}} max(\tau)$$

where $max(\sigma)$ is the maximal (wrt. $\geq_{\mathcal{S}}$) basic type occuring in σ.

Example 4 : Maplist_to_list

$\mathcal{S} = \{Nat, List\}$,
$\mathcal{F}_{List} = \{nil\}, \mathcal{F}_{Nat \times List \to List} = \{cons\}, \mathcal{F}_{(List \to Nat) \times List \to List} = \{fcons\}$,
$\mathcal{F}_{List \times Nat \to List} = \{fmap\}$.

$$fmap(nil, s) \to nil$$
$$fmap(fcons(\lambda x.X(x), L), s) \to cons(X(s), fmap(L, s))$$

The termination proof may use the following precedences:

$$List >_{\mathcal{S}} \{Nat, \to\}, \qquad fmap >_{\mathcal{F}} cons, \qquad fmap \in Mul$$

Note that since $List \to Nat$ is necessarily strictly bigger than $List$ for a recursive path ordering, $fcons$ would not fulfil the compatibility property with respect to any recursive path ordering on types.

5 Discussion

Three recent papers and a phd thesis discuss termination of higher-order rewrite rules, among which two give methods based on orderings for higher-order terms. In [10], the user is responsible for proving the monotonicity property of the ordering used, in the form of proof obligations that he or she has to verify. Besides, the resulting ordering is still weak, assuming in particular that left-hand sides are patterns in the sense of Miller. The method described in [3] is much more powerful, since it allows to prove termination of cut-elimination calculi, to the price of loosing control on the amount of verifications to be performed. On the other hand, [9] describes a computable ordering in the same spirit as ours, based on a first-order interpretation of terms in η-long β-normal form. According to [10] who give a counter example, this ordering may not be well-founded, but the same authors believe that the ordering defined in [8] is correct. It is also restricted to patterns in left-hand sides, a restriction that we do not need, but is equipped with a powerful notion of higher-order subterm, allowing to state that $v(x, u)$ is a subterm of $rec(S(x), u, \lambda yz.v)$. However, this notion of subterm is not enough to deal with the following example of primitive recursion of higher type over the natural numbers in Peano notation:

$$rec(0, u, \lambda yz.v(y, z)) \to u$$
$$rec(S(x), u, \lambda yz.v(y, z)) \to v(x, rec(x, u, \lambda yz.v(y, z)))$$

Indeed, our ordering cannot deal with this example either, because our notion of compatibility is defined in terms of the first-order notion of subterm: given a type γ, the higher-order variable v has type $Nat \times \gamma \to \gamma$, and Gödel's recursor rec has type $Nat \times \gamma \times (Nat \times \gamma \to \gamma) \to \gamma$. Since γ cannot be bigger than $Nat \times \gamma \to \gamma$ in the ordering on types, compatibility requires all types to be equal, and the variable v cannot be made smaller by type comparison. The very reason of this failure is that we implicitely consider $\lambda yz.v(x, y)$ as a subterm of $rec(x, u, \lambda yz.v(y, z))$. Applying $\lambda yz.v(x, y)$ to inputs of the appropriate type as in the definition of the higher-order subterm, results in a term of type γ, and compatibility becomes satisfied. The use of higher-order subterms therefore results in a sharper notion of compatibility of an operator f in terms of the output type (instead of the type itself) of each of its inputs.

On the other hand, our ordering is already powerful enough to treat a variety of examples, as we have shown in section 4. For all these examples, the use of type information was essential. As a matter of fact, even the first example, *sorting*, cannot be proved terminating by using the orderings of [9, 8], which fail to check the second *insert* rule.

6 Conclusion

We have described an ordering for higher-order terms in η-long β-normal form, which enables us to automatically prove termination properties of higher-order rewrite rules in this setting. This ordering extends two distinct orderings to typed terms, an ordering on function symbols and an ordering on types. As a result of this structure similar to that of the recursive path ordering for first-order terms, the ordering is easy to implement and to use in practice, and indeed, we have demonstrated its applicability by giving several practical examples. Improving over previous attempts, the ordering does not assume that left-hand sides of rules are patterns. It requires instead that the ordering on types is compatible with the signature, a quite restrictive property indeed.

However, we believe that we can do a lot better by incorporating to our ordering a notion of higher-order subterm as the one proposed in [8]. For this, we need to show that the embedding relation defined by an appropriate subterm ordering for higher-order terms is a well-order: this would allow us to generalize the present work quite smoothly. We are currently progressing in this direction which should yield what we think should be the true generalization of the recursive path ordering to this higher-order setting.

References

1. Henk Barendregt. *Handbook of Theoretical Computer Science*, volume B, chapter Functional Programming and Lambda Calculus, pages 321–364. North-Holland, 1990. J. van Leeuwen ed.
2. Henk Barendregt. *Handbook of Logic in Computer Science*, chapter Typed lambda calculi. Oxford Univ. Press, 1993. eds. Abramsky et al.
3. Jaco Van de Pol and Helmut Schwichtenberg. Strict functional for termination proofs. In *Proceedings of the International Conference on Typed Lambda Calculi and Applications, Edinburgh, Great Britain*, 1995.
4. Nachum Dershowitz. Orderings for term rewriting systems. *Theoretical Computer Science*, 17(3):279–301, March 1982.
5. Nachum Dershowitz and Jean-Pierre Jouannaud. Rewrite systems. In J. van Leeuwen, editor, *Handbook of Theoretical Computer Science*, volume B, pages 243–309. North-Holland, 1990.
6. Maribel Fernández and Jean-Pierre Jouannaud. Modular termination of term rewriting systems revisited. In Egidio Astesiano, Gianni Reggio, and Andrzej Tarlecki, editors, *Recent Trends in Data Type Specification*, volume 906 of *Lecture Notes in Computer Science*. Springer-Verlag, 1995. Refereed selection of papers presented at ADT'94.
7. Deepak Kapur and Han Tao Zhang. An overview of the rewrite rule laboratory (RRL). In *Proc. 3rd Rewriting Techniques and Applications, Chapel Hill, LNCS 355*, pages 559–563. Springer-Verlag, 1989.
8. Carlos Loría-Sáenz. *A Theoretical Framework for Reasoning about Program Construction based on Extensions of Rewrite Systems*. PhD thesis, Fachbereich Informatik der Universität Kaiserslautern, 1993.
9. Carlos Loría-Sáenz and Joachim Steinbach. Termination of combined (rewrite and λ-calculus) systems. In *Proc. 3rd Int. Workshop on Conditional Term Rewriting Systems, Pont-à-Mousson, LNCS 656*, volume 656 of *Lecture Notes in Computer Science*, pages 143–147. Springer-Verlag, 1992.
10. Olav Lysne and Javier Piris. A termination ordering for higher order rewrite systems. In *Proc. 6th Rewriting Techniques and Applications, Kaiserslautern, LNCS 914*, Kaiserslautern, Germany, 1995.
11. Claude Marché. Normalised rewriting and normalised completion. In *Proceedings of the Ninth Annual IEEE Symposium on Logic in Computer Science*, Paris, France, July 1994. IEEE Comp. Soc. Press.
12. Tobias Nipkow. Higher order critical pairs. In *Proc. IEEE Symp. on Logic in Comp. Science*, Amsterdam, 1991.
13. Pilar Nivela and Robert Nieuwenhuis. Practical results on the saturation of full first-order clauses: Experiments with the saturate system. (system description). In C. Kirchner, editor, *5th International Conference on Rewriting Techniques and Applications*, LNCS 690, Montreal, Canada, June 16–18, 1993. Springer-Verlag.

Higher-Order Superposition for Dependent Types *

Roberto Virga

Carnegie Mellon University, Pittsburgh PA 15213, USA

Abstract. We describe a proof of the Critical Pair Lemma for Plotkin's LF calculus [4]. Our approach basically follows the one used by Nipkow [12] for the simply-typed case, though substantial modifications and some additional theoretical machinery are needed to ensure well-typedness of rewriting in this richer type system. We conclude the paper presenting some significant applications of the theory.

1 Overview

Higher-order rewriting has always attracted considerable interest for the potentially wide range of application it has on several fields of theoretical computer science, ranging from program transformation [5] to automated theorem proving [13]. Until recently, however, undecidability of higher-order unification discouraged any attempt to lift at least some the most interesting results of the first-order theory to the higher-order setting.

One of the first steps in this direction, to the author's knowledge, is due to Wolfram, who in [22] offers a first definition of rewriting in the simply-typed lambda calculus, and suggests how other related concepts can also be similarly generalized to this framework. However, no indication is given as what additional restrictions it is necessary to impose to overcome the undecidability results and to make these notions of practical interest.

The most important result, from a computational standpoint, may be considered a paper by Nipkow, published the same year [12]: by imposing some restrictions to the form of rules, he was is able to prove an analogue of the Critical Pair Lemma. Nipkow's work has inspired a lot of activity the area of higher-order rewriting, and contributed to a series of important results, such as Prehofer's work on higher-order narrowing [18], or Loria's study of conditional higher-order rewriting [8].

In this paper we extend Nipkow's proof to the LF calculus; here the possibility of indexing types by terms, while providing enormous flexibility of representation, it also creates considerable problems. In particular, unlike the simply-typed case, replacing an expression with another of the same type may in some cases produce an ill-typed overall expression. For this reason we introduce the notion of *(type) dependency relation*, and use it to obtain a formulation of rewriting which preserves well-typedness of expressions.

* This work was supported by NSF Grant CCR-9303383.

The paper is organized as follows: section two is used to introduce some basic terminology; section three defines the notions of higher-order rewriting and congruence modulo a set of (higher-order) rules, and explores the relation between the two; in section four we give a definition of critical pair, and use it to prove a version of the Critical Pair Lemma for the calculus. We show some applications of rewriting with dependent types in section five, and we finally conclude by briefly mentioning some promising directions of future research. Due to the excessive complexity, as well as lack of space, proofs will be omitted in most cases; the results presented are however proved in full detail in [21].

2 Preliminaries

In order to make this paper more self-contained, we briefly introduce Plotkin's LF calculus; an interested reader may refer to [14] for a more exhaustive presentation.

Definition 1. The LF calculus is a three-level calculus for *terms*, *type families*, and *kinds*

$$\begin{array}{ll} \textit{Kinds} & K := \text{type} \mid \Pi x : A.K \\ \textit{Families} & A := a \mid \Pi x : A.B \mid AM \\ \textit{Terms} & M := c \mid x \mid \lambda x : A.M \mid MN \end{array}$$

In the following, K denotes kinds, A, B families, M, N terms; a will be used to indicate type constants, c for constants at the level of terms, x, y, z for variables.

We will make use of the usual notions of α, β and η-reductions. These, although defined on terms, extend naturally by congruence to type families and kinds. All objects will be considered equal modulo α-conversion. We will denote by $\equiv$ the smallest equivalence relation including α-, β-, and η-reductions.

By $[N/x]M$ ($[N/x]A$, $[N/x]K$ respectively) we intend, as usual, the replacement of all the free occurrences of x by N inside M (A, K, respectively). As usual, α-conversion will be used, if necessary, to ensure the that no free variable occurrence is captured inside the scope of a quantifier.

The notation $\mathcal{FV}(E)$ and $\mathcal{BV}(E)$ is used to denote the set of free and bound variables, respectively, in E, where E is a term, a type family or a kind.

Definition 2. To define the class of well-typed kinds, type families, and terms we make use of signatures and contexts:

$$\begin{array}{ll} \textit{Signatures} & \Sigma := \cdot \mid \Sigma, a : K \mid \Sigma, c : A \\ \textit{Contexts} & \Gamma := \cdot \mid \Gamma, x : A \end{array}$$

We will use Γ and Δ to range over contexts.

Well-formed expressions are then constructed accordingly to the judgements

$$\Gamma \vdash_{\Sigma} M : A$$
$$\Gamma \vdash_{\Sigma} A : K$$
$$\Gamma \vdash_{\Sigma} K \; \textit{Kind}$$

These, in turn, are defined in terms of the auxiliary judgements

$$\vdash \Sigma\ Sig$$
$$\vdash_\Sigma \Gamma\ Ctx$$

which specify how valid signatures and contexts are formed.

The rules for the calculus are listed below:

$$\frac{\Sigma(c)=A}{\Gamma\vdash_\Sigma c:A} \qquad \frac{\Gamma(x)=A}{\Gamma\vdash_\Sigma x:A} \qquad \frac{\Gamma\vdash_\Sigma M:A \quad A\equiv A' \quad \Gamma\vdash_\Sigma A':\text{type}}{\Gamma\vdash_\Sigma M:A'}$$

$$\frac{\Gamma\vdash_\Sigma M:\Pi x:A.B \quad \Gamma\vdash_\Sigma N:A}{\Gamma\vdash_\Sigma MN:[N/x]B} \qquad \frac{\Gamma\vdash_\Sigma A:\text{type} \quad \Gamma,x:A\vdash_\Sigma M:B}{\Gamma\vdash_\Sigma \lambda x:A.M:\Pi x:A.B}$$

$$\frac{\Sigma(a)=K}{\Gamma\vdash_\Sigma a:K} \qquad \frac{\Gamma\vdash_\Sigma A:K \quad K\equiv K' \quad \Gamma\vdash_\Sigma K'\ Kind}{\Gamma\vdash_\Sigma A:K'}$$

$$\frac{\Gamma\vdash_\Sigma A:\Pi x:B.K \quad \Gamma\vdash_\Sigma M:B}{\Gamma\vdash_\Sigma AM:[M/x]K} \qquad \frac{\Gamma\vdash_\Sigma A:\text{type} \quad \Gamma,x:A\vdash_\Sigma B:\text{type}}{\Gamma\vdash_\Sigma \Pi x:A.B:\text{type}}$$

$$\frac{}{\Gamma\vdash_\Sigma \text{type}\ Kind} \qquad \frac{\Gamma\vdash_\Sigma A:\text{type} \quad \Gamma,x:A\vdash_\Sigma K\ Kind}{\Gamma\vdash_\Sigma \Pi x:A.K\ Kind}$$

$$\frac{}{\vdash_\Sigma \cdot\ Ctx} \qquad \frac{\vdash_\Sigma \Gamma\ Ctx \quad \Gamma\vdash_\Sigma A:\text{type}}{\vdash_\Sigma \Gamma,x:A\ Ctx}$$

$$\frac{}{\vdash \cdot\ Sig}$$

$$\frac{\vdash_\Sigma K\ Kind \quad \vdash \Sigma\ Sig}{\vdash \Sigma,a:K\ Sig} \qquad \frac{\vdash_\Sigma A:\text{type} \quad \Gamma\vdash \Sigma\ Sig}{\vdash \Sigma,c:A\ Sig}$$

We will use $M\overline{N}$ to denote the repeated application $MN_1N_2\ldots N_n$; similarly for type families. The notation $[\overline{N}/\overline{x}]$ will stand for the repeated replacement $[N_n/x_n]\ldots[N_1/x_1]$.

Differently from the simply-typed lambda-calculus, in the LF calculus replacing a subterm with another of the same type inside a term may affect the type of the overall expression. This is illustrated by the following:

Example 1. Consider the following representation of a fragment of arithmetic:

$$\mathbf{nat} : \mathbf{type}$$

$$\mathbf{0} : \mathbf{nat}$$
$$\mathbf{s} : \mathbf{nat} \Rightarrow \mathbf{nat}$$
$$+ : \mathbf{nat} \Rightarrow (\mathbf{nat} \Rightarrow \mathbf{nat})$$

where we used the notation $A \Rightarrow B$ and $A \Rightarrow K$ for the abstractions $\Pi x : A.B$ and $\Pi x : A.K$, respectively, where $x \notin \mathcal{FV}(B)$ and $x \notin \mathcal{FV}(K)$.

We want now to formalize the (first-order) predicate "n is even", together with some inference rules that allow us to decide if a number is even:

$$\begin{aligned} \mathbf{o} &: \mathbf{type} \\ \mathbf{proof} &: \mathbf{o} \Rightarrow \mathbf{type} \\ \mathbf{even} &: \mathbf{nat} \Rightarrow \mathbf{o} \end{aligned}$$

$$\begin{aligned} \mathbf{even_0} &: \mathbf{proof(even\ 0)} \\ \mathbf{even_{ss}} &: \Pi x : \mathbf{nat}.\ (\mathbf{proof(even}\ x) \Rightarrow \mathbf{proof(even\ (s\ (s}\ x)))) \\ \mathbf{even_+} &: \Pi x : \mathbf{nat}.\ \Pi y : \mathbf{nat}.\ (\mathbf{proof(even}\ x) \Rightarrow (\mathbf{proof(even}\ y) \Rightarrow \mathbf{proof(even\ (+}\ x\ y)))) \\ \mathbf{even_{s+}} &: \Pi x : \mathbf{nat}.\ \Pi y : \mathbf{nat}.\ (\mathbf{proof(even\ (+}\ x\ y)) \Rightarrow \mathbf{proof(even\ (+\ (s}\ x)\ (\mathbf{s}\ y)))) \end{aligned}$$

According to this signature, the term

$$\mathbf{even_+\ 0\ (+\ 0\ 0)\ even_0\ (even_+\ 0\ 0\ even_0\ even_0)}$$

is well-typed, but rewriting $(+\ \mathbf{0}\ \mathbf{0})$ into $\mathbf{0}$ (both of type $\mathbf{nat}$) yields

$$\mathbf{even_+\ 0\ 0\ even_0\ (even_+\ 0\ 0\ even_0\ even_0)}$$

which is not.

In defining a notion of rewriting, we must therefore be careful to rule out all these pathological cases leading to ill-typed expressions.

From a close analysis, it appears that all these cases derive from a common problem, namely that, by use of the application rule

$$\frac{\Gamma \vdash_\Sigma M : \Pi x : A.B \quad \Gamma \vdash_\Sigma N : A}{\Gamma \vdash_\Sigma M\ N : [N/x]B},$$

the rewritten term is propagated inside a type. Hence, a way to ensure well-typedness is to allow rewriting only inside those terms whose type does not contain terms which can be, in turn, rewritten. The notion of type dependency relation provides a clean and formal way to extract this information from a LF signature.

Definition 3. Define

$$\mathrm{head}(\Pi x_1 : A_1 \ldots \Pi x_n : A_n.a\,\overline{M}) = a,$$

let Σ_0 be a signature, a pair $\prec_0 = (\prec_0^A, \prec_0^M)$ of binary transitive relations over the set of type constants of Σ_0 is called a *dependency relation* if it satisfies the following conditions:

- $a_i \prec_0^A a$ if $\Sigma_0(a) = \Pi x_1 : A_1 \ldots \Pi x_n : A_n.\mathrm{type}$, $\mathrm{head}(A_i) = a_i$, $1 \le i \le n$;
- $a \prec_0^A a'$ if, for some b, $a \prec_0^A b \prec_0^M a'$ or $a \prec_0^M b \prec_0^A a'$;
- $a \prec_0^M b$ if $a \prec_0^A b$;
- $\vdash^{\prec_0} \Sigma_0\ Sig$;

where $\vdash^{\prec_0} \Sigma\ Sig$ is defined recursively using the judgements

$$\Gamma \vdash^{\prec_0}_{\Sigma} M : A$$
$$\Gamma \vdash^{\prec_0}_{\Sigma} A : K$$
$$\Gamma \vdash^{\prec_0}_{\Sigma} K\ Kind$$
$$\vdash^{\prec_0}_{\Sigma} \Gamma\ Ctx$$

by an inference system very similar to the one for general LF calculus, but with an additional side condition in the rules for abstraction:

$$\frac{\Gamma \vdash^{\prec_0}_{\Sigma} A\text{:type} \quad \Gamma,x{:}A \vdash^{\prec_0}_{\Sigma} B\text{:type}}{\Gamma \vdash^{\prec_0}_{\Sigma} \Pi x{:}A.B\text{:type}}\,* \qquad \frac{\Gamma \vdash^{\prec_0}_{\Sigma} A\text{:type} \quad \Gamma,x{:}A \vdash^{\prec_0}_{\Sigma} M{:}B}{\Gamma \vdash^{\prec_0}_{\Sigma} \lambda x{:}A.M{:}\Pi x{:}A.B}\,*$$

* head$(A) \prec^M_0$ head(B) or head$(A) =$ head(B)

By abuse of notation, given two type families A, B, we will write $A \prec^A B$ and $A \prec^M B$ for head$(A) \prec^A$ head(B) and head$(A) \prec^M$ head(B), respectively. We will use $A \preceq^M_{\Sigma} B$ to say that $A \prec^M B$ or $head(A) = head(B)$.

The idea underlying the introduction of the relations $\prec^A$ and $\prec^M$ is to restrict, using the $\vdash^{\preceq}_{\Sigma}$ judgements, the generation of valid terms and type families to those which preserve the dependencies satisfied by the signature Σ; in particular, we want terms of type A to be allowed to appear inside B only if $A \prec^A B$, and, similarly, terms of type A will be subterms of terms of type B only if $A \preceq^M B$.

When looking for a dependency relation, we will usually prefer coarser ones, so that the class of dependency-preserving terms (i.e. terms well typed according to the $\vdash^{\preceq}_{\Sigma}$ judgement) is as wide as possible. In practice, given a derivation of $\vdash \Sigma\ Sig$, we will try to determine the least $\prec$ such that $\vdash^{\prec} \Sigma\ Sig$ holds.

Example 1. In our previous example about even numbers, the following is easily seen to be a dependency relation:

$$\prec = (\{\mathbf{nat} \prec^A \mathbf{proof}, \mathbf{o} \prec^A \mathbf{proof}\}, \{\mathbf{nat} \prec^M \mathbf{o}, \mathbf{nat} \prec^A \mathbf{proof}, \mathbf{o} \prec^M \mathbf{proof}\})$$

The condition $\mathbf{o} \prec^A \mathbf{proof}$ comes from the type of **proof**; $\mathbf{nat} \prec^M \mathbf{o}$ is obtained from type checking on **even**; finally $\mathbf{nat} \prec^A \mathbf{proof}$ since $\prec^A \supseteq \prec^M \cdot \prec^A$. All the other pairs in $\prec^M$ follow from $\prec^M \supseteq \prec^A$.

From now on, we will assume that a signature Σ and a dependency relation $\prec$ for it have been fixed. Also sometimes, when mentioning a contex Γ we will tacitly assume it is well-typed and dependency-preserving, i.e. $\vdash^{\preceq}_{\Sigma} \Gamma\ Ctx$.

Most basic properties of the LF calculus relativize to dependency-preserving terms. We list a few of them:

Proposition 4 (Substitution). *Let* $\Gamma \vdash^{\preceq}_{\Sigma} N : C$, *then:*

1. *if* $\Gamma, y : C, \Delta \vdash^{\preceq}_{\Sigma} M : A$ *then* $\Gamma, [N/y]\Delta \vdash^{\preceq}_{\Sigma} [N/y]M : [N/y]A$;

2. if $\Gamma, y : C, \Delta \vdash^{\preceq}_{\Sigma} A : K$ *then* $\Gamma, [N/y]\Delta \vdash^{\preceq}_{\Sigma} [N/y]A : [N/y]K$;
3. if $\Gamma, y : C, \Delta \vdash^{\preceq}_{\Sigma} K\ Kind$ *then* $\Gamma, [N/y]\Delta \vdash^{\preceq}_{\Sigma} [N/y]K\ Kind$.

Proposition 5 (Weakening). *Let* $\Sigma' \subseteq \Sigma$, $\Gamma' \subseteq \Gamma$, *and* $\vdash^{\preceq}_{\Sigma} \Gamma\ Ctx$.

1. *If* $\Gamma' \vdash^{\preceq}_{\Sigma'} M : A$ *then* $\Gamma \vdash^{\preceq}_{\Sigma} M : A$.
2. *If* $\Gamma' \vdash^{\preceq}_{\Sigma'} A : K$ *then* $\Gamma \vdash^{\preceq}_{\Sigma} A : K$.
3. *If* $\Gamma' \vdash^{\preceq}_{\Sigma'} K\ Kind$ *then* $\Gamma \vdash^{\preceq}_{\Sigma} K\ Kind$.

Proposition 6. *If* $\Gamma \vdash^{\preceq}_{\Sigma} M : A$ *and* N *is a subterm of* M*, then there is* $\Gamma' \supseteq \Gamma$ *and type* A' *such that* $\Gamma' \vdash^{\preceq}_{\Sigma} N : A'$.

In the rest of this paper, we will write $\Gamma(M, N)$ and $A(M, N)$ for the context Γ' and type A', respectively, obtained by the Proposition above.

The following result clarifies the motivating property of the two relations $\prec^A$ and $\prec^M$:

Lemma 7. *Let* $\vdash^{\preceq}_{\Sigma} \Gamma, x : C, \Delta\ Ctx$,

1. *if* $\Gamma, x : C, \Delta \vdash^{\preceq}_{\Sigma} A : K$ *and* $x \in \mathcal{FV}(A)$ *then* $C \prec^A A$;
2. *if* $\Gamma, x : C, \Delta \vdash^{\preceq}_{\Sigma} M : A$ *and* $x \in \mathcal{FV}(M)$ *then* $C \preceq^M_{\Sigma} A$.

Definition 8. Environments are expressions with a "hole", which we will denote by $\circ$, constructed according to the following syntax:

$$\textit{Environments} \qquad E := \circ \mid \lambda x : A.E \mid M\ E \mid E\ N$$

Well-typed environments are constructed by means of the judgement

$$\Gamma \vdash^{\preceq}_{\Sigma} E[\![\Gamma_\circ \vdash \circ : A_\circ]\!] : A,$$

and the rules

$$\frac{\Gamma_\circ \vdash^{\preceq}_{\Sigma} A_\circ\text{:type} \quad \Gamma_\circ \subseteq \Gamma}{\Gamma \vdash^{\preceq}_{\Sigma} \circ\ [\![\Gamma_\circ \vdash \circ : A_\circ]\!] : A_\circ} \qquad \frac{\Gamma \vdash^{\preceq}_{\Sigma} E[\![\Gamma_\circ \vdash \circ : A_\circ]\!] : A \quad A \equiv B \quad \Gamma \vdash^{\preceq}_{\Sigma} B\text{:type}}{\Gamma \vdash^{\preceq}_{\Sigma} E[\![\Gamma_\circ \vdash \circ : A_\circ]\!] : B}$$

$$\frac{\Gamma \vdash^{\preceq}_{\Sigma} E[\![\Gamma_\circ \vdash \circ : A_\circ]\!] : \Pi x{:}A.B \quad \Gamma \vdash^{\preceq}_{\Sigma} N : A}{\Gamma \vdash^{\preceq}_{\Sigma} (E[\![\Gamma_\circ \vdash \circ : A_\circ]\!])\ N : [N/x]B}$$

$$\frac{\Gamma \vdash^{\preceq}_{\Sigma} M : \Pi x{:}A.B \quad \Gamma \vdash^{\preceq}_{\Sigma} E[\![\Gamma_\circ \vdash \circ : A_\circ]\!] : A}{\Gamma \vdash^{\preceq}_{\Sigma} M\ (E[\![\Gamma_\circ \vdash \circ : A_\circ]\!]) : B} \quad A_\circ \not\prec^A B$$

$$\frac{\Gamma \vdash^{\preceq}_{\Sigma} A\text{:type} \quad \Gamma, x{:}A \vdash^{\preceq}_{\Sigma} E[\![\Gamma_\circ \vdash \circ : A_\circ]\!] : B}{\Gamma \vdash^{\preceq}_{\Sigma} \lambda x{:}A.E[\![\Gamma_\circ \vdash \circ : A_\circ]\!] : \Pi x{:}A.B} \quad A \preceq^M_{\Sigma} B$$

The side condition $A_\circ \not\prec^A B$ in the application rule enforces our requirement that, whenever we substitute a term for the hole, the effect of this substitution does not propagate to the type.

Example The environment

$$\mathbf{even}_+\ \mathbf{0}\ (\circ\ [\![\vdash \circ : \mathbf{nat}]\!]),$$

and therefore also

$$\mathbf{even}_+\ \mathbf{0}\ (\circ\ [\![\vdash \circ : \mathbf{nat}]\!])\ (\mathbf{even}_+\ \mathbf{0}\ \mathbf{0}\ \mathbf{even}_0\ \mathbf{even}_0)$$

are not well-typed. This because in the application

$$\frac{\vdash^{\prec}_{\Sigma}\mathbf{even}_+\ 0{:}\Pi y{:}\mathbf{nat}.(\mathbf{proof}(\mathbf{even}\ 0)\Rightarrow(\mathbf{proof}(\mathbf{even}\ y)\Rightarrow\mathbf{proof}(\mathbf{even}\ (+\ 0\ y))))\quad \vdash^{\prec}_{\Sigma}\circ\ [\![\vdash\circ{:}\mathbf{nat}]\!]{:}\mathbf{nat}}{\vdash^{\prec}_{\Sigma}\mathbf{even}_+\ 0\ (\circ\ [\![\vdash\circ{:}\mathbf{nat}]\!]){:}\mathbf{proof}(\mathbf{even}\ 0)\Rightarrow(\mathbf{proof}(\mathbf{even}\ \circ)\Rightarrow\mathbf{proof}(\mathbf{even}\ (+\ 0\ \circ)))}$$

the side condition $\mathbf{nat} \not\prec^A \mathbf{proof}$ is violated.

Given an environment E and a term M, we will write $E[\![M]\!]$ for the term obtained by replacing the $\circ$ with M.

As expected, when the hole is replaced by an expression of compatible type, environments always produce well-typed expressions:

Lemma 9. *If* $\Gamma \vdash^{\prec}_{\Sigma} E[\![\Gamma_\circ \vdash \circ : A_\circ]\!] : A$*, and* $\Delta \vdash^{\prec}_{\Sigma} M : A_\circ$ *with* $\Delta \subseteq \Gamma_\circ$*, then* $\Gamma \vdash^{\prec}_{\Sigma} E[\![M]\!] : A$*.*

In [9], the definition of substitution makes use of the existence and uniqueness of long $\beta\eta$ normal forms. In the LF calculus, these find an analogue in the concept of canonical form:

Definition 10. We define canonical forms for terms and type families by the judgements

$$\begin{array}{ll} \Gamma \vdash_\Sigma M \Downarrow A & M \text{ is canonical of type } A \\ \Gamma \vdash_\Sigma A \Downarrow \text{type} & A \text{ is a canonical type} \end{array}$$

$$\begin{array}{ll} \Gamma \vdash_\Sigma M \downarrow A & M \text{ is atomic of type } A \\ \Gamma \vdash_\Sigma A \downarrow K & A \text{ is atomic of kind } K \end{array}$$

formed according to the following inference rules:

$$\frac{\Gamma \vdash_\Sigma A \Downarrow \text{type} \quad \Gamma, x{:}A \vdash_\Sigma M \Downarrow B}{\Gamma \vdash_\Sigma \lambda x{:}A.M \Downarrow \Pi x{:}A.B} \qquad \frac{\Gamma \vdash_\Sigma M \Downarrow A \quad A \equiv B \quad \Gamma \vdash_\Sigma B{:}\text{type}}{\Gamma \vdash_\Sigma M \Downarrow B}$$

$$\frac{\Gamma \vdash_\Sigma A \downarrow \text{type} \quad \Gamma \vdash_\Sigma M \downarrow A}{\Gamma \vdash_\Sigma M \Downarrow A}$$

$$\frac{\Sigma(c) = A}{\Gamma \vdash_\Sigma c \downarrow A} \qquad \frac{\Gamma(x) = A}{\Gamma \vdash_\Sigma x \downarrow A} \qquad \frac{\Gamma \vdash_\Sigma M \downarrow A \quad A \equiv B \quad \Gamma \vdash_\Sigma B{:}\text{type}}{\Gamma \vdash_\Sigma M \downarrow B}$$

$$\frac{\Gamma \vdash_\Sigma M \downarrow \Pi x{:}A.B \quad \Gamma \vdash_\Sigma N \Downarrow A}{\Gamma \vdash_\Sigma M\ N \downarrow [N/x]B}$$

$$\frac{\Gamma \vdash_\Sigma A \Downarrow \text{type} \quad \Gamma, x{:}A \vdash_\Sigma B \Downarrow \text{type}}{\Gamma \vdash_\Sigma \Pi x{:}A.B \Downarrow \text{type}} \qquad \frac{\Gamma \vdash_\Sigma A \downarrow \text{type}}{\Gamma \vdash_\Sigma A \Downarrow \text{type}}$$

$$\frac{\Sigma(a)=K}{\Gamma \vdash_{\Sigma} a \downarrow K} \qquad \frac{\Gamma \vdash_{\Sigma} A \downarrow K \quad K \equiv K' \quad \Gamma \vdash_{\Sigma} K'\ Kind}{\Gamma \vdash_{\Sigma} A \downarrow K'}$$

$$\frac{\Gamma \vdash_{\Sigma} A \downarrow \Pi x{:}B.K \quad \Gamma \vdash_{\Sigma} M \Downarrow B}{\Gamma \vdash_{\Sigma} A\ M \downarrow [M/x]K}$$

We will make use of the abbreviations:

$$\Gamma \vdash_{\Sigma}^{\preceq} M \Downarrow A \overset{\text{def}}{\Longleftrightarrow} \Gamma \vdash_{\Sigma} M \Downarrow A \text{ and } \Gamma \vdash_{\Sigma}^{\preceq} M : A$$

$$\Gamma \vdash_{\Sigma}^{\preceq} A \Downarrow \text{type} \overset{\text{def}}{\Longleftrightarrow} \Gamma \vdash_{\Sigma} A \Downarrow \text{type and } \Gamma \vdash_{\Sigma}^{\preceq} A : \text{type}$$

and similarly for $\Gamma \vdash_{\Sigma}^{\preceq} M \downarrow A$ and $\Gamma \vdash_{\Sigma}^{\preceq} A \downarrow K$.

The following holds:

Theorem 11. *Let* $\vdash_{\Sigma} \Gamma\ Ctx$.

1. *If* $\Gamma \vdash_{\Sigma} M : A$ *then there is a unique* M' *such that* $M' \equiv M$ *and* $\Gamma \vdash_{\Sigma} M' \Downarrow A$.
2. *If* $\Gamma \vdash_{\Sigma} A : \text{type}$ *then there is a unique* A' *such that* $A \equiv A'$ *and* $\Gamma \vdash_{\Sigma} A' \Downarrow \text{type}$.

Proof. These facts can be proved for generic LF expressions, i.e. when $\vdash_{\Sigma}$ instead of $\vdash_{\Sigma}^{\preceq}$ is considered; see [1, 3, 20]. In [21] it is shown that they relativize to dependencies.

Given a well-typed term M or a type family A, we will denote their canonical form by $M_{\Downarrow}$ and $A_{\Downarrow}$, respectively.

Definition 12. Given two contexts Γ and Δ, a substitution from Γ to Δ is a type-preserving, finite-support mapping from variables to terms $\theta : \Gamma \rightharpoondown \Delta$ formed according to the following rules:

$$\frac{}{\cdot{:}\cdot \rightharpoondown \Delta} \qquad \frac{\{\overline{x} \mapsto \overline{M}\}{:}\Gamma \rightharpoondown \Delta \quad \Delta \vdash_{\Sigma} N \Downarrow [\overline{M}/\overline{x}]A}{\{\overline{x} \mapsto \overline{M}, y \mapsto N\}{:}(\Gamma, y{:}A) \rightharpoondown \Delta}$$

Similarly, dependencies-preserving substitution are also defined:

$$\frac{}{\cdot{:}\cdot \overset{\preceq}{\rightharpoondown} \Delta} \qquad \frac{\{\overline{x} \mapsto \overline{M}\}{:}\Gamma \overset{\preceq}{\rightharpoondown} \Delta \quad \Delta \vdash_{\Sigma}^{\preceq} N \Downarrow [\overline{M}/\overline{x}]A}{\{\overline{x} \mapsto \overline{M}, y \mapsto N\}{:}(\Gamma, y{:}A) \overset{\preceq}{\rightharpoondown} \Delta}$$

Definition 13. Given any well-typed term $\Gamma \vdash_{\Sigma} M : A$ and substitution $\theta = \{\overline{x} \mapsto \overline{N}\} : \Gamma \rightharpoondown \Delta$, define θM to be the (unique) canonical form of

$$\Delta \vdash_{\Sigma} (\lambda \overline{x} : \overline{B}.M)\ \overline{N} : [\overline{N}/\overline{x}]A$$

Note that here, in analogy to [9], we define the result of a substitution application to be a canonical term.

Definition 14.

1. Given two substitutions $\theta_1 = \{\overline{x} \mapsto \overline{M}\} : \Gamma_1 \rightharpoondown \Gamma_2$ and $\theta_2 : \Gamma_2 \rightharpoondown \Gamma_3$, the *composition* $\theta_2 \circ \theta_1$ is the substitution $\{\overline{x} \mapsto \overline{\theta_2 M}\} : \Gamma_1 \rightharpoondown \Gamma_3$.
2. A substitution $\theta = \{\overline{x} \mapsto \overline{M}\} : \Gamma \rightharpoondown \Delta$ is a *renaming* if all the terms M_i are (convertible to) distinct variables.
3. A substitution $\theta_1 : \Gamma \rightharpoondown \Delta$ is said to be *more general* than $\theta_2 : \Gamma \rightharpoondown \Delta'$ if there is $\rho : \Delta \rightharpoondown \Delta'$ such that $\theta_2 = \rho \circ \theta_1$.
4. Given two well typed terms $\Gamma \vdash_\Sigma M : A$ and $\Gamma \vdash_\Sigma N : A'$, a substitution $\theta : \Gamma \rightharpoondown \Delta$ is said to be a *unifier* of M and N if $\theta M = \theta N$; M and N are then said to unify.

The class of dependency-preserving terms is closed with respect to substitution:

Proposition 15. *If $\Gamma \vdash^{\preceq}_\Sigma M : A$ and $\theta = \{\overline{x} \mapsto \overline{N}\} : \Gamma \overset{\preceq}{\rightharpoondown} \Delta$ then $\Delta \vdash^{\preceq}_\Sigma \theta M : [\overline{N}/\overline{x}]A$.*

Corollary 16. *If $\theta_1 : \Gamma_1 \overset{\preceq}{\rightharpoondown} \Gamma_2$ and $\theta_2 : \Gamma_2 \overset{\preceq}{\rightharpoondown} \Gamma_3$, then $\theta_2 \circ \theta_1 : \Gamma_1 \overset{\preceq}{\rightharpoondown} \Gamma_3$.*

One particular class of terms for which unification is decidable are patterns [10]; the definition derives, almost unchanged, from the simply-typed case [15].

Definition 17. A canonical term $\Gamma \vdash_\Sigma M \Downarrow A$ is said to be a pattern if each $x \in \mathrm{dom}\,\Gamma$ can appear in M and A only applied to terms η-equivalent to distinct bound variables.

Theorem 18. *Unification of patterns is decidable; if two patterns unify, there is a unique (up to conversion) most general unifier.*

Proof. See [15].

3 Higher-Order Term Rewriting

In this section we extend the notion of term rewriting system and rewriting relation to a higher-order setting with dependent types.

Definition 19. A rewrite rule $\Gamma \vdash^{\preceq}_\Sigma l \to r : A$ is a pair of well typed terms such that

- $\Gamma \vdash^{\preceq}_\Sigma l \Downarrow A$ is a pattern, $\Gamma \vdash^{\preceq}_\Sigma r : A$,
- $\Gamma \vdash^{\preceq}_\Sigma A \downarrow \mathrm{type}$,
- $\mathcal{FV}(l) \supseteq \mathcal{FV}(r)$.

A Higher-order Term Rewriting System (HTRS) R is a finite set of rewrite rules, such that, for each pair of rules $\Gamma_1 \vdash^{\preceq}_\Sigma l_1 \to r_1 : A_1, \Gamma_2 \vdash^{\preceq}_\Sigma l_2 \to r_2 : A_2 \in R$, $A_1 \not\prec^A A_2$.

The condition above translates to the requirement that it is not possible to use a rule to rewrite the type of another. This is therefore consistent with the original goal to define rewriting in such a way that it does not modify types, and hence preserve well-typedness of expressions.

Definition 20. Given a HTRS R and two terms $\Gamma \vdash^{\preceq}_{\Sigma} M : A$ and $\Gamma \vdash^{\preceq}_{\Sigma} N : A$ we define R-rewriting as follows:

$$\Gamma \vdash^{\preceq}_{\Sigma} M \xrightarrow{R} N : A \overset{\text{def}}{\Longleftrightarrow} \begin{array}{l} M_{\Downarrow} = E[\![\theta l]\!], N_{\Downarrow} = E[\![\theta r]\!] \\ \text{for some } (\Delta \vdash l \to r : B) \in R, \theta : \Delta \preceq\!\!\!\to \Gamma(M_{\Downarrow}, \theta l), \\ \text{and } \Gamma \vdash^{\preceq}_{\Sigma} E[\![\Gamma(M_{\Downarrow}, \theta l) \vdash \circ : A(M_{\Downarrow}, \theta l)]\!] : A. \end{array}$$

We furthermore define R-conversion as the judgement $\Gamma \vdash^{\preceq}_{\Sigma} M \overset{R}{\longleftrightarrow} N : A$ formed according to the following rules:

$$\frac{\Gamma \vdash^{\preceq}_{\Sigma} M{:}A \quad M \equiv N \quad \Gamma \vdash^{\preceq}_{\Sigma} N{:}A}{\Gamma \vdash^{\preceq}_{\Sigma} M \overset{R}{\longleftrightarrow} N{:}A} \qquad \frac{\Gamma \vdash^{\preceq}_{\Sigma} M \overset{R}{\longrightarrow} N{:}A}{\Gamma \vdash^{\preceq}_{\Sigma} M \overset{R}{\longleftrightarrow} N{:}A}$$

$$\frac{\Gamma \vdash^{\preceq}_{\Sigma} M \overset{R}{\longleftrightarrow} N{:}A}{\Gamma \vdash^{\preceq}_{\Sigma} N \overset{R}{\longleftrightarrow} M{:}A} \qquad \frac{\Gamma \vdash^{\preceq}_{\Sigma} M \overset{R}{\longleftrightarrow} N'{:}A \quad \Gamma \vdash^{\preceq}_{\Sigma} N' \overset{R}{\longleftrightarrow} N{:}A}{\Gamma \vdash^{\preceq}_{\Sigma} M \overset{R}{\longleftrightarrow} N{:}A}$$

In addition to R-conversion, a more natural notion of equality modulo R can be defined, as the smallest congruence relation containing all instances of R, and closed with respect to conversion:

Definition 21. Let R be a HTRS, congruence modulo R is defined by the judgement

$$\Gamma \vdash^{\preceq}_{\Sigma} M \overset{R}{=} N : A \rhd \mathcal{D} \qquad M \text{ and } N \text{ of type } A \text{ are congruent modulo } R$$

where $\mathcal{D}$ is a set of type constants used to keep track of the dependency constraints. The rules associated to this judgement are the following:

$$\frac{\Gamma \vdash^{\preceq}_{\Sigma} M{:}A}{\Gamma \vdash^{\preceq}_{\Sigma} M \overset{R}{=} M{:}A \rhd \emptyset} \qquad \frac{\Gamma \vdash^{\preceq}_{\Sigma} M \overset{R}{=} N{:}A \rhd \mathcal{D}}{\Gamma \vdash^{\preceq}_{\Sigma} N \overset{R}{=} M{:}A \rhd \mathcal{D}} \qquad \frac{\Gamma \vdash^{\preceq}_{\Sigma} M \overset{R}{=} N'{:}A \rhd \mathcal{D} \quad \Gamma \vdash^{\preceq}_{\Sigma} N' \overset{R}{=} N{:}A \rhd \mathcal{D}'}{\Gamma \vdash^{\preceq}_{\Sigma} M \overset{R}{=} N{:}A \rhd (\mathcal{D} \cup \mathcal{D}')}$$

$$\frac{\Delta \vdash^{\preceq}_{\Sigma} l \to r{:}A \in R \quad \theta{:}\Delta \preceq\!\!\!\to \Gamma}{\Gamma \vdash^{\preceq}_{\Sigma} \theta l \overset{R}{=} \theta r{:}\ \theta A \rhd \text{head}(A)} \qquad \frac{\Gamma \vdash^{\preceq}_{\Sigma} A{:}\text{type} \quad \Gamma, x{:}A \vdash^{\preceq}_{\Sigma} M \overset{R}{=} N{:}B \rhd \mathcal{D}}{\Gamma \vdash^{\preceq}_{\Sigma} \lambda x{:}A.M \overset{R}{=} \lambda x{:}A.N{:}\Pi x{:}A.B \rhd \mathcal{D}}\ A \preceq^{M}_{\Sigma} B$$

$$\frac{\Gamma \vdash^{\preceq}_{\Sigma} M \overset{R}{=} M'{:}\Pi x{:}A.B \rhd \mathcal{D} \quad \Gamma \vdash^{\preceq}_{\Sigma} N \overset{R}{=} N'{:}A \rhd \mathcal{D}'}{\Gamma \vdash^{\preceq}_{\Sigma} M\ N \overset{R}{=} M'\ N'{:}[N/x]B \rhd (\mathcal{D} \cup \mathcal{D}')}\ a \not\prec^{A} B \text{ for all } a \in \mathcal{D}'$$

$$\frac{\Gamma \vdash^{\preceq}_{\Sigma} M \overset{R}{=} N'{:}A \rhd \mathcal{D} \quad N' \equiv N \quad \Gamma \vdash^{\preceq}_{\Sigma} N'{:}A}{\Gamma \vdash^{\preceq}_{\Sigma} M \overset{R}{=} N{:}A \rhd \mathcal{D}}$$

The only place the set of dependencies $\mathcal{D}$ above plays a role is in the application rule: there, it restricts the rule to those cases where well-typedness of both sides is guaranteed. An analogous set can be defined for R-rewriting:

Definition 22. The set of dependency constraints generated by a R-rewriting step is defined as

$$(\Gamma \vdash_{\Sigma}^{\preceq} M \xrightarrow{R} N : A) \triangleright \{\text{head}(B)\}$$

if $(\Delta \vdash_{\Sigma}^{\preceq} l \to r : B) \in R$ was the rewriting rule used in its definition.

This definition is extended to R-conversion:

$$\frac{\Gamma \vdash_{\Sigma}^{\preceq} M:A \quad M \equiv N \quad \Gamma \vdash_{\Sigma}^{\preceq} N:A}{(\Gamma \vdash_{\Sigma}^{\preceq} M \xleftrightarrow{R} N:A) \triangleright \emptyset} \qquad \frac{(\Gamma \vdash_{\Sigma}^{\preceq} M \xrightarrow{R} N:A) \triangleright \mathcal{D}}{(\Gamma \vdash_{\Sigma}^{\preceq} M \xleftrightarrow{R} N:A) \triangleright \mathcal{D}}$$

$$\frac{(\Gamma \vdash_{\Sigma}^{\preceq} M \xleftrightarrow{R} N:A) \triangleright \mathcal{D}}{(\Gamma \vdash_{\Sigma}^{\preceq} N \xleftrightarrow{R} M:A) \triangleright \mathcal{D}} \qquad \frac{(\Gamma \vdash_{\Sigma}^{\preceq} M \xleftrightarrow{R} N':A) \triangleright \mathcal{D} \quad (\Gamma \vdash_{\Sigma}^{\preceq} N' \xleftrightarrow{R} N:A) \triangleright \mathcal{D}'}{(\Gamma \vdash_{\Sigma}^{\preceq} M \xleftrightarrow{R} N:A) \triangleright (\mathcal{D} \cup \mathcal{D}')}$$

This allows us to prove:

Theorem 23. *Let R be a HTRS, then for all M, N,*

$$(\Gamma \vdash_{\Sigma}^{\preceq} M \xleftrightarrow{R} N : A) \triangleright \mathcal{D} \Leftrightarrow \Gamma \vdash_{\Sigma}^{\preceq} M \stackrel{R}{=} N : A \triangleright \mathcal{D}.$$

4 Critical Pairs

As in the first order case, the check for local confluence of $\xrightarrow{R}$ goes through the search for critical pairs generated by the rules of the HTRS R. The definition of critical pairs here, however, is complicated by the presence of dependent types.

Definition 24. Let $\theta : \Gamma \xrightarrow{\preceq} \Delta$ be a substitution, an atomic term $\Gamma \vdash_{\Sigma} M \downarrow A$ is said to be stable for θ if $M = h\,\overline{N}$ where h is either a constant c or a variable $x \notin \text{supp}(\theta)$.

Stability implies that the head of a canonical term is preserved by the application of a substitution, i.e. that $\theta(h\,\overline{N}) = h\,\overline{\theta N}$.

Definition 25. Let $\theta = \{\overline{x} \mapsto \overline{M}\} : \Gamma \xrightarrow{\preceq} \Delta$ be a substitution, an environment $\Gamma \vdash_{\Sigma}^{\preceq} E[\![\Gamma_\circ \vdash \circ : A_\circ]\!] : A$ is stable for θ if whenever the rule

$$\frac{\Gamma \vdash_{\Sigma}^{\preceq} M_1 : \Pi x{:}A.B \quad \Gamma \vdash_{\Sigma}^{\preceq} E_2[\![\Gamma_\circ \vdash \circ : A_\circ]\!] : A}{\Gamma \vdash_{\Sigma}^{\preceq} M_1(E_2[\![\Gamma_\circ \vdash \circ : A_\circ]\!]) : B} \quad A_\circ \not\preceq^A B$$

is applied, $\Gamma \vdash_{\Sigma}^{\preceq} M \downarrow \Pi x : A.B$ and M is stable for θ.

Since the application rule in a stable environment is applied to stable terms, one expects that when the substitution θ is applied, most of the original structure is preserved; the following lemma shows that this is actually the case:

Lemma 26. *Let*

$$\theta = \{\overline{x} \mapsto \overline{M}\} : \Gamma \overset{\preceq}{\rightarrow} \Delta$$
$$\Gamma \vdash^{\preceq}_{\Sigma} E[\![\Gamma_\circ \vdash \circ : A_\circ]\!] : A \text{ stable for } \theta,$$
$$\Gamma_\circ \vdash^{\preceq}_{\Sigma} M_\circ \Downarrow A_\circ, \qquad \Gamma_\circ \vdash^{\preceq}_{\Sigma} A_\circ \downarrow \text{type},$$

and $M = E[\![M_\circ]\!]$*, then there are*

$$\theta' : \Gamma_\circ \overset{\preceq}{\rightarrow} \Delta_\circ \text{ with } \theta' \doteq \theta,$$
$$\Delta \vdash^{\preceq}_{\Sigma} E'[\![\Delta_\circ \vdash \circ : [\overline{M}/\overline{x}]A_\circ]\!] : [\overline{M}/\overline{x}]A$$

such that:

1. *if* $\Gamma \vdash^{\preceq}_{\Sigma} E[\![M_\circ]\!] \Downarrow A$ *then* $\theta M = E'[\![\theta' M_\circ]\!]$ *and* $\Delta \vdash^{\preceq}_{\Sigma} E'[\![\theta' M_\circ]\!] \Downarrow [\overline{M}/\overline{x}]A$;
2. *if* $\Gamma \vdash^{\preceq}_{\Sigma} E[\![M_\circ]\!] \downarrow A$ *then* $\theta M \to^*_\eta E'[\![\theta' M_\circ]\!]$ *and* $\Delta \vdash^{\preceq}_{\Sigma} E'[\![\theta' M_\circ]\!] \downarrow [\overline{M}/\overline{x}]A$.

We will write $E(\theta, M_\circ)$ and $\theta(E, M_\circ)$ to denote the environments E' and substitutions θ' obtained from Lemma 26.(1).

Definition 27 (Critical Pair). Let R be a HTRS, $\Gamma_1 \vdash^{\preceq}_{\Sigma} l_1 \to r_1 : C_1$, $\Gamma_2 \vdash^{\preceq}_{\Sigma} l_2 \to r_2 : C_2$ two rules in R, $\theta_1 : \Gamma_1 \overset{\preceq}{\rightarrow} \Delta$, $\theta_2 : \Gamma_2 \overset{\preceq}{\rightarrow} \Delta$, $\theta_1 = \{\overline{x} \mapsto \overline{N}\}$, and $\Gamma_1 \vdash^{\preceq}_{\Sigma} E[\![\Gamma_\circ \vdash \circ : A_\circ]\!] : A$ such that $l_1 = E[\![M_\circ]\!]$, $M_\circ$ not η-equivalent to a variable in domΓ, $\theta_1(E_1, M_\circ)M_\circ = \theta_2 l_2$, then

$$\Delta \vdash^{\preceq}_{\Sigma} < E(\theta_1, M_\circ)[\![\theta_2 r_2]\!], \theta_1 r_1 >: [\overline{N}/\overline{x}]C_1$$

is a *critical pair*

Remark. By applying a renaming substitution and using α-conversion, we can assume, without loss of generality, $\Gamma_1(M_\circ) \cap \Gamma_2 = \emptyset$. Then by Weakening it is easily verified that $\theta_1(E_1, M_\circ) \cup \theta_2 : \Gamma_1(M_\circ), \Gamma_2 \overset{\preceq}{\rightarrow} \Delta$ can be chosen to be the most general unifier of $M_\circ$ and l_2, and the definition above appears as a generalization of the familiar one for first-order TRSs.

Using the definition above, the following can be proved:

Theorem 28 (Critical Pair Lemma). *Let R be a HTRS, if* $\Gamma \vdash^{\preceq}_{\Sigma} M \overset{R}{\rightarrow} N_1 : A$ *and* $\Gamma \vdash^{\preceq}_{\Sigma} M \overset{R}{\rightarrow} N_2 : A$ *then either there is a critical pair in R, or there are rewriting sequences* $\Gamma \vdash^{\preceq}_{\Sigma} N_1^{(i)} \overset{R}{\rightarrow} N_1^{(i+1)}$ $(0 \leq i < n_1)$, $\Gamma \vdash^{\preceq}_{\Sigma} N_2^{(i)} \overset{R}{\rightarrow} N_2^{(i+1)}$ $(0 \leq i < n_2)$ *such that* $N_1^{(0)} = N_1$, $N_2^{(0)} = N_2$, $N_1^{(n_1)} \equiv N_2^{(n_2)}$.

5 Applications

In this section we briefly mention a few applications of higher order rewriting with dependent types.

Lambda calculus with simple types The simply-typed lambda calculus can be easily formalized within LF. We will need two type families: one, called **type**, for types, and the second, **term**, indexed by objects of the first, for terms.

$$\begin{aligned} \textbf{type} &: \text{type} \\ \textbf{arrow} &: \textbf{type} \Rightarrow (\textbf{type} \Rightarrow \text{type}) \end{aligned}$$

$$\begin{aligned} \textbf{term} &: \textbf{type} \Rightarrow \text{type} \\ \textbf{lambda} &: \Pi x : \textbf{type}.\Pi y : \textbf{type}.(((\textbf{term}\ x) \Rightarrow (\textbf{term}\ y)) \Rightarrow \textbf{term}(\textbf{arrow}\ x\ y)) \\ \textbf{app} &: \Pi x : \textbf{type}.\Pi y : \textbf{type}.((\textbf{term}(\textbf{arrow}\ x\ y)) \Rightarrow ((\textbf{term}\ x) \Rightarrow (\textbf{term}\ y))) \end{aligned}$$

β- and η-reductions can then be expressed by the two rewrite rules

$$\begin{aligned} \Gamma_1 \vdash^{\prec}_{\Sigma} (\textbf{app}\ A\ B\ (\textbf{lambda}\ A\ B\ (\lambda x : (\textbf{term}\ A).F\ x))\ U) \rightarrow (F\ U) : \textbf{term}\ B \\ \Gamma_2 \vdash^{\prec}_{\Sigma} \textbf{lambda}\ A\ B\ (\lambda x : (\textbf{term}\ A).\textbf{app}\ A\ B\ G\ x) \rightarrow G : \textbf{term}\ (\textbf{arrow}\ A\ B) \end{aligned}$$

where

$$\begin{aligned} \Gamma_1 &= A : \textbf{type}, B : \textbf{type}, F : (\textbf{term}\ A) \Rightarrow (\textbf{term}\ B), U : \textbf{term}\ A \\ \Gamma_2 &= A : \textbf{type}, B : \textbf{type}, G : \textbf{term}\ (\textbf{arrow}\ A\ B) \end{aligned}$$

Using the critical pair criterion one can easily check that the system is locally confluent. Since it is also known to be terminating, we conclude by Newman's Lemma [11] that it is confluent.

Category Theory To represent categories we define types for objects and morphisms:

$$\begin{aligned} \textbf{categ} &: \text{type} \\ \textbf{object} &: \textbf{categ} \Rightarrow \text{type} \\ \textbf{morph} &: \Pi x : \textbf{categ}.((\textbf{object}\ x) \Rightarrow (\textbf{object}\ x)) \end{aligned}$$

$$\begin{aligned} \textbf{o} &: \Pi x : \textbf{categ}\,.\,\Pi u : (\textbf{object}\ x)\,.\,\Pi v : (\textbf{object}\ x)\,.\,\Pi w : (\textbf{object}\ x)\,. \\ &\qquad ((\textbf{morph}\ x\ v\ w) \Rightarrow ((\textbf{morph}\ x\ u\ v) \Rightarrow (\textbf{morph}\ x\ u\ w))) \\ \textbf{id} &: \Pi x : \textbf{categ}\,.\,\Pi u : (\textbf{object}\ x)\,.\,\textbf{morph}\ x\ u\ u \end{aligned}$$

The basic axioms can be then formalized by the rewrite system

$$\begin{aligned} \Gamma_1 \vdash^{\prec}_{\Sigma} (\textbf{o}\ x\ u\ u\ v\ f\ (\textbf{id}\ x\ u)) \rightarrow f : \textbf{morph}\ x\ u\ v \\ \Gamma_1 \vdash^{\prec}_{\Sigma} (\textbf{o}\ x\ u\ v\ v\ (\textbf{id}\ x\ v)\ f) \rightarrow f : \textbf{morph}\ x\ u\ v \\ \Gamma_2 \vdash^{\prec}_{\Sigma} (\textbf{o}\ x\ u\ w\ z\ h\ (\textbf{o}\ x\ u\ v\ w\ g\ f)) \rightarrow (\textbf{o}\ x\ u\ v\ z\ (\textbf{o}\ x\ u\ w\ z\ h\ g)\ f) : \textbf{morph}\ x\ u\ z \end{aligned}$$

where

$$\begin{aligned} \Gamma_1 &= x : \textbf{categ}, u : (\textbf{object}\ x), v : (\textbf{object}\ x), f : (\textbf{morph}\ x\ u\ v) \\ \Gamma_2 &= x : \textbf{categ}, u : (\textbf{object}\ x), v : (\textbf{object}\ x), w : (\textbf{object}\ x), z : (\textbf{object}\ x), \\ &\qquad f : (\textbf{morph}\ x\ u\ v), g : (\textbf{morph}\ x\ v\ w), h : (\textbf{morph}\ x\ w\ z). \end{aligned}$$

More complex notions of category theory can be similarly represented: terminating and confluent HTRSs for natural transformations, adjunctions, and monads are presented in [2].

Cut Elimination Theorem In [16], F. Pfenning gives a LF representation of the cut elimination theorem for both intuitionistic and classical sequent calculi. It turns out that is possible to transform all the cases in this proof into rewrite rules, yielding a (terminating) HTRS. While this is not confluent, each of the (nontrivial) critical pairs appears to correspond to a different case of commutativity of couples of rules of the sequent calculus.

6 Future Developments

While the Critical Pair Lemma gives us a criterion to check for local confluence of a HTRS, we are are also interested in general methods to test for termination. Two methods have been recently proposed [6, 17], and it is our hope that they can be adapted to dependent types. Also, the same notion of dependency relation has been used to prove well foundedness of proofs by structural induction in LF [19]; this suggests that it might be useful in proving termination of HTRSs as well.

Another interesting direction of research would be to define, on the same line of [9], rewriting modulo an equational theory. This might allow to circumvent the restrictions imposed by the dependencies: a single HTRS could be decomposed into several ones, each involving disjoint sets of base types. The proof of confluence could then proceed by stages: as soon as one component HTRS has been proved terminating and confluent, it becomes part of the underlying equational theory on which the confluence of the next one is tested.

7 Acknowledgments

I would like to thank F. Pfenning for his help, suggestions, and support. I also thank E. Rohwedder and W. Gehrke for their valuable comments.

References

1. Coquand, T. *An algorithm for Testing Conversion in Type Theory.* Logical Frameworks, Cambridge University Press, 1991, pages 155-279
2. Gehrke, W., *Decidability Results For Categorical Notions Related to Monads by Rewriting Techniques* Ph.D. Thesis, Johannes Kepler Universität, Linz, 1995
3. Geuvers, H. *The Church-Rosser Property for $\beta\eta$-Reduction in Typed λ-Calculi.* Proceedings of the 7th Annual IEEE Symposium on Logic in Computer Science (LICS), 1992, pages 453-460
4. Harper, R., Honsell F., Plotkin, G. *A framework for Defining Logics.* Journal of the Association for Computing Machinery, January 1993, pages 143-184
5. Huet, G.P., Lang, B. *Proving and Applying Program Transformations Expressed with Second-Order Patterns* Acta Informatica 11, 1978, pages 31-55
6. Kahrs, D. *Towards a Domain Theory for Termination Proofs.* Proceedings of the 6th International Conference on Rewriting Techniques and Applications (RTA), 1995, pages 241-255

7. Knuth, D.E., Bendix, P.B. *Simple Word Problems in Universal Algebra.* Computational Problems in Abstract Algebra, Pergamon Press, 1972, pages 263-297
8. Loría-Sáenz, C. A. *A Theoretical Framework for Reasoning about Program Construction Based on Extensions of Rewrite Systems* Ph.D. Thesis, Universität Kaiserslautern, 1993
9. Mayr, R., Nipkow, T. *Higher-Order Rewrite Systems and their Confluence.* Technical Report TUM-I9433, Technische Universität München, 1994
10. Miller, D. *A Logic Programming Language With Lambda abstraction, Function Variables, and Simple Unification.* LFCS Report Series, University of Edinburgh, 1991, pages 253-281
11. Newman, M.H.A. *On theories with a combinatorial definition of 'equivalence'* Annals of Mathematics, 43(2), 1942, pages 223-243
12. Nipkow, T. *Higher-Order Critical Pairs.* Proceedings of the 5th IEEE Conference of Logic In Computer Science (LICS), 1990, pages 342-348
13. Paulson, L.C. *The Foundation of a Generic Theorem Prover* Journal of Automated Reasoning, vol. 5, 1989, pages 363-397
14. Pfenning, F. *Logic Programming in the LF Logical Framework.* G. Huet, G. Plotkin ed., Logical Frameworks, Cambridge University Press, 1991, pages 149-181
15. Pfenning, F. *Unification and anti-unification in the Calculus of Constructions.*, Proceedings of the 6th IEEE Conference of Logic In Computer Science (LICS), 1991, pages 149-181
16. Pfenning, F. *A Structural Proof of Cut Elimination and Its Representation in a Logic Framework* Technical Report CMU-CS-94-218, Carnegie Mellon University, 1994
17. Pol, J. *Termination Proofs for Higher-Order Rewrite Systems*, J. Heering, K. Meinke, B. Moller, T. Nipkow ed., Higher Order Algebra, Logic and Term Rewriting (HOA),Lecture Notes in Computer Science, vol 816, 1994, pages 305-325
18. Prehofer, C. *Solving Higher-Order Equations.*, Technical Report, Technische Universität München, 1994
19. Rohwedder, E. , Pfenning, F. *Mode and Termination Analysis for Higher-Order Logic.*, to appear at the 1996 European Symposium on Programming (ESOP)
20. Salvesen, A. *The Church-Rosser Property for Pure Systems with $\beta\eta$-Reduction.* Technical Report, University of Oslo, 1992
21. Virga, R. *Higher-Order Superposition for Dependent Types*, Technical Report CMU-CS-95-150, Carnegie Mellon University, 1995 (*http://www.cs.cmu.edu/afs/cs.cmu.edu/user/rvirga/Web/dep-rel.ps*)
22. Wolfram, D.A *Rewriting, and Equational Unification: the Higher-Order Cases* Proceedings of the 4th International Conference on Rewriting Techniques and Applications (RTA), 1991, pages 25-36

Higher-Order Narrowing with Definitional Trees

Michael Hanus[1] and Christian Prehofer[2]

[1] Informatik II, RWTH Aachen, D-52056 Aachen, Germany
hanus@informatik.rwth-aachen.de
[2] Fakultät für Informatik, TU München, D-80290 München, Germany
prehofer@informatik.tu-muenchen.de

Abstract. Functional logic languages with a sound and complete operational semantics are mainly based on narrowing. Due to the huge search space of simple narrowing, steadily improved narrowing strategies have been developed in the past. Needed narrowing is currently the best narrowing strategy for first-order functional logic programs due to its optimality properties w.r.t. the length of derivations and the number of computed solutions. In this paper, we extend the needed narrowing strategy to higher-order functions and λ-terms as data structures. By the use of definitional trees, our strategy computes only incomparable solutions. Thus, it is the first calculus for higher-order functional logic programming which provides for such an optimality result. Since we allow higher-order logical variables denoting λ-terms, applications go beyond current functional and logic programming languages.

1 Introduction

Functional logic languages [7] with a sound and complete operational semantics are mainly based on narrowing. Narrowing, originally introduced in automated theorem proving [20], is used to *solve* goals by finding appropriate values for variables occurring in arguments of functions. A *narrowing step* instantiates variables in a goal and applies a reduction step to a redex of the instantiated goal. The instantiation of goal variables is usually computed by unifying a subterm of the goal with the left-hand side of some rule.

Example 1. Consider the following rules defining the less-or-equal predicate on natural numbers which are represented by terms built from 0 and s:

$$0 \leq X \to true$$
$$s(X) \leq 0 \to false$$
$$s(X) \leq s(Y) \to X \leq Y$$

To solve the goal $s(X) \leq Y$, we perform a first narrowing step by instantiating Y to $s(Y_1)$ and applying the third rule, and a second narrowing step by instantiating X to 0 and applying the first rule:

$$s(X) \leq Y \quad \leadsto_{\{Y \mapsto s(Y_1)\}} \quad X \leq Y_1 \quad \leadsto_{\{X \mapsto 0\}} \quad true$$

Since the goal is reduced to *true*, the computed solution is $\{X \mapsto 0, Y \mapsto s(Y_1)\}$.

Due to the huge search space of simple narrowing, steadily improved narrowing strategies have been developed in the past. *Needed narrowing* [2] is based on the idea to evaluate only subterms which are *needed* in order to compute some result. For instance, in a goal $t_1 \le t_2$, it is always necessary to evaluate t_1 (to some head normal form) since all three rules in Example 1 have a non-variable first argument. On the other hand, the evaluation of t_2 is only needed if t_1 is of the form $s(\cdots)$. Thus, if t_1 is a free variable, needed narrowing instantiates it to a constructor, here 0 or s. Depending on this instantiation, either the first rule is applied or the second argument t_2 is evaluated. Needed narrowing is the currently best narrowing strategy for first-order functional logic programs due to its optimality properties w.r.t. the length of derivations and the number of computed solutions [2]. Moreover, it can be efficiently implemented by pattern-matching and unification due to its local computation of a narrowing step (see, e.g., [8]).

In this paper, we extend the needed narrowing strategy to higher-order functions and λ-terms as data structures. We introduce a class of higher-order inductively sequential rewrite rules which can be defined via definitional trees. Although this class is a restriction of general higher-order rewrite systems, it covers higher-order functional languages. As higher-order rewrite steps can be expensive in general, we show that finding a redex with inductively sequential rules can be performed as in the first-order case.

Since our narrowing calculus LNT is oriented towards previous work on higher-order narrowing [19], we show in the first part that LNT coincides with needed narrowing in the first-order case. For the higher-order case, we show soundness and completeness with respect to higher-order needed reductions, which we define via definitional trees. Furthermore, we show that the calculus is optimal w.r.t. the solutions computed, i.e., no solution is produced twice. Optimality of higher-order reductions is subject of current research. It is however shown that higher-order needed reductions are in fact needed for reduction to a constructor normal form.

This strategy is the first calculus for higher-order functional logic programming which provides for optimality results. Moreover, it falls back to the optimal needed narrowing strategy if the higher-order features are not used, i.e., our calculus is a conservative extension of an optimal first-order narrowing calculus. Since we allow higher-order logical variables denoting λ-terms, applications go beyond current functional and logic programming languages. In general, our calculus can compute solutions for variables of functional type. Although this is very powerful, we show that the incurring higher-order unification can sometimes be avoided by techniques similar to [4]. Due to lack of space, some details and the proofs are omitted. They can be found in [9].

2 Preliminaries

We briefly introduce the simply typed λ-calculus (see e.g. [10]). We assume the following **variable conventions**:

- F, G, H, P, X, Y denote free variables,
- a, b, c, f, g (function) constants, and

– x, y, z bound variables.

Type judgments are written as $t : \tau$. Further, we often use s and t for terms and u, v, w for constants or bound variables. The set of types $\mathcal{T}$ for the simply typed λ-terms is generated by a set $\mathcal{T}_0$ of base types (e.g., int, bool) and the function type constructor $\rightarrow$. The syntax for **λ-terms** is given by

$$t \;=\; F \mid x \mid c \mid \lambda x.t \mid (t_1\, t_2)$$

A list of syntactic objects $s_1, \ldots, s_n$ where $n \geq 0$ is abbreviated by $\overline{s_n}$. For instance, n-fold abstraction and application are written as $\lambda\overline{x_n}.s = \lambda x_1 \ldots \lambda x_n.s$ and $a(\overline{s_n}) = ((\cdots(a\; s_1)\cdots)\; s_n)$, respectively. **Substitutions** are finite mappings from variables to terms, denoted by $\{\overline{X_n \mapsto t_n}\}$, and extend homomorphically from variables to terms. Free and bound variables of a term t will be denoted as $\mathcal{FV}(t)$ and $\mathcal{BV}(t)$, respectively. A term t is **ground** if $\mathcal{FV}(t) = \{\}$. The **conversions in λ-calculus** are defined as:

– **α-conversion:** $\lambda x.t =_\alpha \lambda y.(\{x \mapsto y\}t)$,
– **β-conversion:** $(\lambda x.s)t =_\beta \{x \mapsto t\}s$, and
– **η-conversion:** if $x \notin \mathcal{FV}(t)$, then $\lambda x.(tx) =_\eta t$.

The long $\beta\eta$-normal form [14] of a term t, denoted by $t\updownarrow_\beta^\eta$, is the η-expanded form of the β-normal form of t. It is well known [10] that $s =_{\alpha\beta\eta} t$ iff $s\updownarrow_\beta^\eta =_\alpha t\updownarrow_\beta^\eta$. As long $\beta\eta$-normal forms exist for typed λ-terms, we will in general assume that terms are in long $\beta\eta$-normal form. For brevity, we may write variables in η-normal form, e.g., X instead of $\lambda\overline{x_n}.X(\overline{x_n})$. We assume that the transformation into long $\beta\eta$-normal form is an implicit operation, e.g., when applying a substitution to a term.

A substitution θ is in long $\beta\eta$-normal form if all terms in the image of θ are in long $\beta\eta$-normal form. The convention that α-equivalent terms are identified and that free and bound variables are kept disjoint (see also [5]) is used in the following. Furthermore, we assume that bound variables with different binders have different names. Define $\mathcal{D}om(\theta) = \{X \mid \theta X \neq X\}$ and $\mathcal{R}ng(\theta) = \bigcup_{X \in \mathcal{D}om(\theta)} \mathcal{FV}(\theta X)$. Two **substitutions are equal on a set of variables** W, written as $\theta =_W \theta'$, if $\theta\alpha = \theta'\alpha$ for all $\alpha \in W$. The restriction of a substitution to a set of variables W is defined as $\theta_{|W}\alpha = \theta\alpha$ if $\alpha \in W$ and $\theta_{|W}\alpha = \alpha$ otherwise. A substitution θ is **idempotent** iff $\theta = \theta\theta$. We will in general assume that substitutions are idempotent. A substitution θ' is more general than θ, written as $\theta' \leq \theta$, if $\theta = \sigma\theta'$ for some substitution σ. We describe positions in λ-terms by sequences over natural numbers. The subterm at a **position** p in a λ-term t is denoted by $t|_p$. A term t with the subterm at position p replaced by s is written as $t[s]_p$.

A term t in β-normal form is called a **higher-order pattern** if every free occurrence of a variable F is in a subterm $F(\overline{u_n})$ of t such that the $\overline{u_n}$ are η-equivalent to a list of distinct bound variables. Unification of patterns is decidable and a most general unifier exists if they are unifiable [12]. Examples are $\lambda x, y.F(x, y)$ and $\lambda x.f(G(\lambda z.x(z)))$.

A rewrite rule [14] is a pair $l \rightarrow r$ such that l is a higher-order pattern but not a free variable, l and r are long $\beta\eta$-normal forms of the same base type, and

$\mathcal{FV}(l) \supseteq \mathcal{FV}(r)$. Assuming a rule $l \rightarrow r$ and a position p in a term s in long $\beta\eta$-normal form, a **rewrite step** from s to t is defined as

$$s \longrightarrow_{p,\theta}^{l\rightarrow r} t \;\Leftrightarrow\; s|_p = \theta l \wedge t = s[\theta r]_p.$$

For a rewrite step we often omit some of the parameters $l \rightarrow r, p$ and θ. It is a standard assumption in functional logic programming that constant symbols are divided into free **constructor symbols** and defined symbols. A symbol f is called a **defined symbol** or **operation**, if a rule $f(\cdots) \rightarrow t$ exists. A **constructor term** is a term without defined symbols. Constructor symbols and constructor terms are denoted by c and d. A term $f(\overline{t_n})$ is called **operation-rooted** (respectively **constructor-rooted**) if f is a defined symbol (respectively constructor). A **higher-order rewrite system (HRS)** $\mathcal{R}$ is a set of rewrite rules. A term is in **$\mathcal{R}$-normal form** if no rule from $\mathcal{R}$ applies and a substitution θ is **$\mathcal{R}$-normalized** if all terms in the image of θ are in $\mathcal{R}$-normal form.

By applying rewrite steps, we can compute the *value* of a functional expression. However, in the presence of free variables, we have to compute values for these free variables such that the instantiated expression is reducible. This is the motivation for narrowing which will be precisely defined in the following sections. Narrowing is intended to *solve* goals, where a **goal** is an expression of Boolean type that should be reduced to the constant *true*. This is general enough to cover the equation solving capabilities of current functional logic languages with a lazy operational semantics, like BABEL [13] or K-LEAF [6], since the strict equality $\approx$[1] can be defined as a binary operation by a set of orthogonal rewrite rules (see [2, 6, 13] for more details about strict equality). An important consequence of this restriction on goals is the fact that during the successful rewriting of a goal the topmost symbol is always an operation or the constant *true*. This property will be used to simplify the narrowing calculus.

Notice that a subterm $s|_p$ may contain free variables which used to be bourd in s. For rewriting it is possible to ignore this, as only matching of a left-hand side of a rewrite rule is needed. For narrowing, we need unification and hence we use the following construction to lift a rule into a binding context to facilitate the technical treatment. An **$\overline{x_k}$-lifter** of a term t **away from** W is a substitution $\sigma = \{F \mapsto (\rho F)(\overline{x_k}) \mid F \in \mathcal{FV}(t)\}$ where ρ is a renaming such that $\mathcal{D}om(\rho) = \mathcal{FV}(t)$, $\mathcal{R}ng(\rho) \cap W = \{\}$ and $\rho F : \tau_1 \rightarrow \cdots \rightarrow \tau_k \rightarrow \tau$ if $x_1 : \tau_1, \ldots, x_k : \tau_k$ and $F : \tau$. A term t (rewrite rule $l \rightarrow r$) is $\overline{x_k}$-lifted if an $\overline{x_k}$-lifter has been applied to t (l and r). For example, $\{G \mapsto G'(x)\}$ is an x-lifter of $g(G)$ away from any W not containing G'.

3 First-Order Definitional Trees

Definitional trees are introduced in [1] to define efficient normalization strategies for (first-order) term rewriting. The idea is to represent all rules for a defined

[1] The **strict equality** $t \approx t'$ holds if t and t' are reducible to the same ground constructor term. Note that normal forms may not exist in general due to non-terminating rewrite rules.

symbol in a tree and to control the selection of the next redex by this tree. This technique is extended to narrowing in [2]. We will extend definitional trees to the higher-order case in order to obtain a similar strategy for higher-order narrowing. To state a clear relationship between the first-order and the higher-order case, we review the first-order case in this section and present the needed narrowing calculus in a new form. Thus, we assume in this section that all terms are first-order, i.e., λ-abstractions and functional variables do not occur.

Traditionally [7], a term t is **narrowed** into a term t' if there exist a non-variable position p in t (i.e., $t|_p$ is not a free variable), a variant $l \to r$ of a rewrite rule with $\mathcal{FV}(t) \cap \mathcal{FV}(l \to r) = \{\}$ and a most general unifier σ of $t|_p$ and l such that $t = \sigma(t[r]_p)$. In this case we write $t \leadsto_\sigma t'$. We write $t_0 \leadsto^*_\sigma t_n$ if there is a narrowing derivation $t_0 \leadsto_{\sigma_1} t_1 \leadsto_{\sigma_2} \cdots \leadsto_{\sigma_n} t_n$ with $\sigma = \sigma_n \cdots \sigma_2 \sigma_1$. In order to compute all solutions by narrowing, we have to apply all rules at all non-variable subterms in parallel. Since this simple method leads to a huge and often infinite search space, many improvements have been proposed in the past (see [7] for a survey). A **narrowing strategy** determines the position where the next narrowing step should be applied. As shown in [2], an optimal narrowing strategy can be obtained by dropping the requirement for most general unifiers and controlling the instantiation of variables and selection of narrowing positions by a data structure, called definitional tree. $\mathcal{T}$ is a **definitional tree** with pattern π iff its depth is finite and one of the following cases holds:

$\mathcal{T} = rule(l \to r)$, where $l \to r$ is a variant of a rule in $\mathcal{R}$ such that $l = \pi$.

$\mathcal{T} = branch(\pi, o, \overline{\mathcal{T}_k})$, where o is an occurrence of a variable in π, $\overline{c_k}$ are different constructors of the type of $\pi|_o$ ($k > 0$), and, for $i = 1, \ldots, k$, $\mathcal{T}_i$ is a definitional tree with pattern $\pi[c_i(\overline{X_{n_i}})]_o$, where n_i is the arity of c_i and $\overline{X_{n_i}}$ are new distinct variables.

A **definitional tree** of an n-ary function f is a definitional tree $\mathcal{T}$ with pattern $f(\overline{X_n})$, where $\overline{X_n}$ are distinct variables, such that for each rule $l \to r$ with $l = f(\overline{t_n})$ there is a node $rule(l' \to r')$ in $\mathcal{T}$ with l variant of l'.[2] For instance, the rules in Example 1 can be represented by the following definitional tree:

$$\begin{array}{l} branch(X \le Y, 1, rule(0 \le Y \to true), \\ \qquad branch(s(X') \le Y, 2, rule(s(X') \le 0 \to false), \\ \qquad\qquad rule(s(X') \le s(Y') \to X' \le Y'))) \end{array}$$

A definitional tree starts always with the most general pattern for a defined symbol and branches on the instantiation of a variable to constructor-headed terms, here 0 and $s(X')$. It is essential that each rewrite rule occurs only once as a leaf of the tree. Thus, when evaluating the arguments of a term $f(\overline{t_n})$ to constructor terms, the tree can be incrementally traversed to find the matching rule.

A function f is called **inductively sequential** if there exists a definitional tree of f such that each *rule* node corresponds to exactly one rule of the rewrite system $\mathcal{R}$. The term rewriting system $\mathcal{R}$ is called inductively sequential if each function defined by $\mathcal{R}$ is inductively sequential.

---

[2] This corresponds to Antoy's notion [1] except that we ignore *exempt* nodes.

A definitional tree defines a strategy to apply narrowing steps.[3] To narrow a term t, we consider the definitional tree $\mathcal{T}$ of the outermost function symbol of t (note that, by our restriction on goals, the outermost symbol is always a Boolean function). If $\mathcal{T} = rule(l \to r)$, we apply the rule $l \to r$ to t. If $\mathcal{T} = branch(\pi, o, \overline{\mathcal{T}_k})$, we consider the subterm $t|_o$. If $t|_o$ has a function symbol at the top, we narrow this subterm (to a head normal form) by recursively applying our strategy to $t|_o$. If $t|_o$ has a constructor symbol at the top, we narrow t with $\mathcal{T}_j$, where the pattern of $\mathcal{T}_j$ unifies with t. If $t|_o$ is a variable, we non-deterministically select a subtree $\mathcal{T}_j$, instantiate $t|_o$ to the constructor of the pattern of $\mathcal{T}_j$ at position o, and narrow this instance of t with $\mathcal{T}_j$. This strategy is called **needed narrowing** [2] and is the currently best narrowing strategy due to its optimality w.r.t. the length of derivations (if terms are shared) and the number of computed solutions.

In order to extend this strategy to higher-order functions, another representation is required since it is shown in [17] that the direct application of narrowing steps to inner subterms should be avoided in the presence of λ-bound variables. For this purpose we transform the needed narrowing calculus into a lazy narrowing calculus in the spirit of Martelli/Montanari's inference rules. In a first step, we integrate the definitional trees into the rewrite rules by extending the language of terms and providing *case* constructs to express the concrete narrowing strategy. A **case expression** has the form

$$case\ X\ of\ c_1(\overline{X_{n_1}}) : \mathcal{X}_1, \ldots, c_k(\overline{X_{n_k}}) : \mathcal{X}_k$$

where X is a variable, $c_1, \ldots, c_k$ are different constructors of the type of X, and $\mathcal{X}_1, \ldots, \mathcal{X}_k$ are terms possibly containing case expressions. Using such case expressions, each inductively sequential function symbol can be defined by exactly one rewrite rule. For instance, the rules for the function $\leq$ defined in Example 1 are represented by the following rule:

$$X \leq Y \ \to \ case\ X\ of\ 0 : true,\ s(X_1) : (case\ Y\ of\ 0 : false,\ s(Y_1) : X_1 \leq Y_1)$$

To be more precise, we translate a definitional tree $\mathcal{T}$ into a term with case expressions by the use of the function $dtc(\mathcal{T})$ which is defined as follows:

$$\begin{aligned} dtc(rule(l \to r)) &= r \\ dtc(branch(\pi, o, \overline{\mathcal{T}_k})) &= case\ \pi|_o\ of\ \pi_1|_o : dtc(\mathcal{T}_1), \ldots, \pi_k|_o : dtc(\mathcal{T}_k) \\ & \quad \text{where } \pi_i \text{ is the pattern of } \mathcal{T}_i \end{aligned}$$

If $\mathcal{T}$ is the definitional tree with pattern $f(\overline{X_n})$ of the n-ary function f, then $f(\overline{X_n}) \to dtc(\mathcal{T})$ is the new rewrite rule for f. A case expression $case\ X\ of\ \overline{p_n : \mathcal{X}_n}$ can be considered as a function with arity $2n + 1$ where the semantics is defined by the following n rewrite rules:[4]

$$case\ p_i\ of\ \overline{p_n : X_n} \to X_i \quad (i = 1, \ldots, n)$$

[3] Due to lack of space, we omit a precise definition which can be found in [2].

[4] To be more precise, different *case* functions are needed for case expressions with different patterns, i.e., the case functions should be indexed by the case patterns. However, for the sake of readability, we do not write these indices and allow the overloading of the *case* function symbols.

Bind

$$e \to^? Z, G \Rightarrow^\sigma \sigma(G)$$

if e is not a case term and $\sigma = \{Z \mapsto e\}$

Case Select

$$case\ c(\overline{t_n})\ of\ \overline{p_k : \mathcal{X}_k} \to^? Z, G \Rightarrow^\sigma \sigma(\mathcal{X}_i) \to^? Z,\ G$$

where $p_i = c(\overline{X_n})$ and $\sigma = \{\overline{X_n \mapsto t_n}\}$

Case Guess

$$case\ X\ of\ \overline{p_k : \mathcal{X}_k} \to^? Z, G \Rightarrow^\sigma \sigma(\mathcal{X}_i) \to^? Z,\ \sigma(G)$$

where $\sigma = \{X \mapsto p_i\}$

Case Eval

$$case\ f(\overline{t_n})\ of\ \overline{p_k : \mathcal{X}_k} \to^? Z, G \Rightarrow^\sigma \sigma(\mathcal{X}) \to^? X,\ case\ X\ of\ \overline{p_k : \mathcal{X}_k} \to^? Z, G$$

if $f(\overline{X_n}) \to \mathcal{X} \in \mathcal{R}'$ is a rule with fresh variables, $\sigma = \{\overline{X_n \mapsto t_n}\}$, and X is a fresh variable

Fig. 1. Calculus LNT for lazy narrowing with definitional trees in the first-order case

In the following, we denote by $\mathcal{R}$ an inductively sequential rewrite system, by $\mathcal{R}'$ its translated version containing exactly one rewrite rule for each function defined by $\mathcal{R}$, and by $\mathcal{R}_c$ the additional *case* rewrite rules. The following theorem states that needed narrowing w.r.t. $\mathcal{R}$ and leftmost-outermost narrowing w.r.t. $\mathcal{R}' \cup \mathcal{R}_c$ are equivalent, where **leftmost-outermost** means that the selected subterm is the leftmost-outermost one among all possible narrowing positions.[5]

Theorem 1. *Let t be a term with a Boolean function at the top. For each needed narrowing derivation $t \leadsto^*_\sigma true$ w.r.t. $\mathcal{R}$ there exists a leftmost-outermost narrowing derivation $t \leadsto^*_{\sigma'} true$ w.r.t. $\mathcal{R}' \cup \mathcal{R}_c$ with $\sigma =_{\mathcal{FV}(t)} \sigma'$, and vice versa.*

As mentioned above, in the higher-order case we need a narrowing calculus which always applies narrowing steps to the outermost function symbol which is often different from the leftmost-outermost narrowing position. For this purpose, we transform a leftmost-outermost narrowing derivation w.r.t. $\mathcal{R}' \cup \mathcal{R}_c$ into a derivation on a **goal system** G (a sequence of goals of the form $t \to^? X$) where narrowing rules are only applied to the outermost function symbol of the leftmost goal. This is the purpose of the inference system LNT shown in Figure 1. The **Bind** rule propagates a term to the subsequent case expression. The **Case** rules correspond to the case distinction in the definition of needed narrowing, where the narrowing of a function is integrated in the **Case Eval** rule. Note that the only possible non-determinism during computation with these inference rules is in the **Case Guess** rule. Since we are interested in solving goals by reduction to *true*, we assume that the **initial goal** has always the form $case\ t\ of\ true : true \to^? T$. We use this representation in order to provide a calculus with few inference rules. Note that $T \mapsto true$ if such a goal can be reduced to the empty goal system.

[5] A position p is **leftmost-outermost** in a set P of positions if there is no $p' \in P$ with p' prefix of p, or $p' = q \cdot i \cdot q'$ and $p = q \cdot j \cdot q''$ and $i < j$.

Theorem 2. *Let t be a term with a Boolean function at the top and X a fresh variable. For each leftmost-outermost narrowing derivation* $t \rightsquigarrow_{\sigma}^{*} true$ *w.r.t.* $\mathcal{R}' \cup \mathcal{R}_c$ *there exists a LNT-derivation* $case\ t\ of\ true : true \rightarrow^{?} X \stackrel{*}{\Rightarrow}_{\sigma'} true \rightarrow^{?} X$ *w.r.t.* $\mathcal{R}'$ *such that* $\sigma' =_{\mathcal{FV}(t)} \sigma$*, and vice versa.*

Theorems 1 and 2 imply the equivalence of needed narrowing and the calculus LNT. Since we will extend LNT to higher-order functions in the next section, the results in this section show that our higher-order calculus is a conservative extension of an optimal first-order narrowing strategy.

4 Higher-Order Definitional Trees

In the following we extend first-order definitional trees to the higher-order case. To generalize from the first-order case, it is useful to recall the main ideas: When evaluating the arguments of a term $f(\overline{t_n})$ to constructor terms, the definitional tree can be incrementally traversed to find the (single) matching rule. It is essential that each branching depends on only one subterm (or argument to the function) and that for each rigid term (non-variable headed), a single branch can be chosen. For this purpose, we need further restrictions in the higher-order case, where we employ λ-terms as data structure, e.g., higher-order terms with bound variables in the left-hand sides. For instance, we permit the rules

$$\begin{array}{ll} diff(\lambda y.y, X) & \rightarrow 1 \\ diff(\lambda y.sin(F(y)), X) & \rightarrow cos(F(X)) * diff(\lambda y.F(y), X) \\ diff(\lambda y.ln(F(y)), X) & \rightarrow diff(\lambda y.F(y), X)/F(X) \end{array}$$

where $diff(F, X)$ computes the differential of F at X.

A **shallow pattern** is a linear term of the form $\lambda\overline{x_n}.v(\overline{H_m(\overline{x_n})})$. We will use shallow patterns for branching in trees. In contrast to the first-order case, v can also be a bound variable.

Definition 3. $\mathcal{T}$ is a **higher-order definitional tree** (*hdt*) iff its depth is finite and one of the following cases holds:

- $\mathcal{T} = p_f : case\ X\ of\ \overline{\mathcal{T}_n}$
- $\mathcal{T} = p_f : rhs$,

where p_f are shallow patterns with fresh variables, X is a free variable and $\overline{\mathcal{T}_n}$ are *hdts* in the first case, and *rhs* is a term (representing the right-hand side of a rule). Moreover, all shallow patterns of the *hdts* $\overline{\mathcal{T}_n}$ must be pairwise non-unifiable.

We write *hdts* as $p_f : \mathcal{X}$, where $\mathcal{X}$ stands for a case expression or a term. To simplify technicalities, rewrite rules $f(\overline{X_n}) \rightarrow \mathcal{X}$ are identified with the *hdt* $f(\overline{X_n}) : \mathcal{X}$. With this latter form of a rule, we can relate rules to the usual notation as follows. The **selector** of a tree $\mathcal{T}$ of the form $\mathcal{T} = p_f : \mathcal{X}$ is defined as $sel(\mathcal{T}) = p_f$. For a node $\mathcal{T}'$ in a tree $\mathcal{T}$, the constraints in the case expressions on the path to it determine a term, which is recursively defined by the pattern function $pat_{\mathcal{T}}(\mathcal{T}')$:

$$pat_{\mathcal{T}}(\mathcal{T}') = \begin{cases} sel(\mathcal{T}') & \text{if } \mathcal{T} = \mathcal{T}' \text{ (i.e., } \mathcal{T}' \text{ is the root)} \\ \{X \mapsto sel(\mathcal{T}')\}pat_{\mathcal{T}}(\mathcal{T}'') & \text{if } \mathcal{T}' \text{ has parent } \mathcal{T}'' = p_f : case\ X\ of\ \overline{\mathcal{T}_n} \end{cases}$$

Each branch variable must belong to the pattern of this node, i.e., for each node $\mathcal{T}' = p_f : case\ X\ of\ \overline{\mathcal{T}_n}$ in a tree $\mathcal{T}$, X is a free variable of $pat_{\mathcal{T}}(\mathcal{T}')$. Furthermore, each leaf $\mathcal{T}' = p : rhs$ of a *hdt* $\mathcal{T}$ is required to correspond to a rewrite rule $l \to r$, i.e., $pat_{\mathcal{T}}(\mathcal{T}') \to rhs$ is a variant of $l \to r$. $\mathcal{T}$ is called ***hdt* of a function** f if for all rewrite rules of f there is exactly one corresponding leaf in $\mathcal{T}$.

As in the first-order case, rewrite rules must be **constructor based.** This means that in a *hdt* only the outermost pattern has a defined symbol. An HRS, for all of which defined symbols *hdts* exits, is called **inductively sequential**.

For instance, the rules for *diff* above have the *hdt*

$$\begin{aligned} diff(F,X) \to case\ F\ of\ & \lambda y.y && : 1, \\ & \lambda y.sin(F'(y)) && : cos(F'(X)) * diff(\lambda y.F'(y), X), \\ & \lambda y.ln(F'(y)) && : diff(\lambda y.F'(y), X)/F'(X) \end{aligned}$$

Note that free variables in left-hand sides must have all bound variables of the current scope as arguments. Such terms are called **fully extended.** This important restriction, which also occurs in [16], allows to find redices as in the first-order case, and furthermore simplifies narrowing. For instance, Flex-Flex pairs do not arise here, in contrast to the full higher-order case [18, 19]. Consider an example for some non-overlapping rewrite rules which do not have a *hdt*:

$$\begin{aligned} f(\lambda x.c(x)) &\to a \\ f(\lambda x.H) &\to b \end{aligned}$$

The problem is that for rewriting a term with these rules the full term must be scanned. For example, if the argument to f is the rigid term $\lambda x.c(G(t))$, it is not possible to commit to one of the rules (or branches of a tree) before checking if the bound variable x occurs inside t. In general, this may lead to an unexpected complexity w.r.t. the term size for evaluation via rewriting.

We define the $\overline{x_k}$-lifting of *hdts* by schematically applying the $\overline{x_k}$-lifter to all terms in the tree, i.e., to all patterns, right-hand sides, and free variables in cases.

5 Narrowing with Higher-Order Definitional Trees

In the higher-order case, the rules of LNT of Section 3 must be extended to account for several new cases. Compared to the first-order case, we need to maintain binding environments and higher-order free variables, possibly with arguments, which are handled by higher-order unification. For this purpose, the Imitation, the Function Guess and the Projection rules have been added in Figure 2. These three new rules, to which we refer as the Guess Rules, are the only ones to compute substitutions for the variables in the case constructs. The Case Guess rule of the first-order case can be retained by applying Imitation plus Case Select. The Imitation and Projection rules are taken from higher-order unification and compute a partial binding for some variable. The Function Guess rule covers the case of non-constructor solutions, which may occur for higher-order variables. It thus enables the synthesis of functions from existing ones. Note that the selection of a binding in this rule is only restricted by the types occurring. For all rules, we assume that newly introduced variables are fresh, as in the first-order case.

Bind

$$e \to^? Z, G \quad \Rightarrow^{\{\}} \quad \sigma(G)$$
where $\sigma = \{Z \mapsto e\}$ and e is not a case term

Case Select

$$\lambda\overline{x_k}.case\ \lambda\overline{y_l}.v(\overline{t_m})\ of\ \overline{p_n : \mathcal{X}_n} \to^? Z, G \quad \Rightarrow^{\{\}} \quad \lambda\overline{x_k}.\sigma(\mathcal{X}_i) \to^? Z, G$$
if $p_i = \lambda\overline{y_l}.v(\overline{X_m(\overline{x_k}, \overline{y_l})})$ and $\sigma = \{\overline{X_m \mapsto \lambda\overline{x_k}, \overline{y_l}.t_m}\}$

Imitation

$$\lambda\overline{x_k}.case\ \lambda\overline{y_l}.X(\overline{t_m})\ of\ \overline{p_n : \mathcal{X}_n} \to^? Z, G \quad \Rightarrow^{\sigma} \quad \sigma(\lambda\overline{x_k}.case\ \lambda\overline{y_l}.X(\overline{t_m})\ of\ \overline{p_n : \mathcal{X}_n} \to^? Z, G)$$
if $p_i = \lambda\overline{y_l}.c(\overline{X_o(\overline{x_k}, \overline{y_l})})$ and $\sigma = \{X \mapsto \lambda\overline{x_m}.c(\overline{H_o(\overline{x_m})})\}$

Function Guess

$$\lambda\overline{x_k}.case\ \lambda\overline{y_l}.X(\overline{t_m})\ of\ \overline{p_n : \mathcal{X}_n} \to^? Z, G \quad \Rightarrow^{\sigma} \quad \sigma(\lambda\overline{x_k}.case\ \lambda\overline{y_l}.X(\overline{t_m})\ of\ \overline{p_n : \mathcal{X}_n} \to^? Z, G)$$
if $\lambda\overline{x_k}, \overline{y_l}.X(\overline{t_m})$ is not a higher-order pattern,
$\sigma = \{X \mapsto \lambda\overline{x_m}.f(\overline{H_o(\overline{x_m})})\}$, and f is a defined function

Projection

$$\lambda\overline{x_k}.case\ \lambda\overline{y_l}.X(\overline{t_m})\ of\ \overline{p_n : \mathcal{X}_n} \to^? Z, G \quad \Rightarrow^{\sigma} \quad \sigma(\lambda\overline{x_k}.case\ \lambda\overline{y_l}.X(\overline{t_m})\ of\ \overline{p_n : \mathcal{X}_n} \to^? Z, G)$$
where $\sigma = \{X \mapsto \lambda\overline{x_m}.x_i(\overline{H_o(\overline{x_m})})\}$

Case Eval

$$\lambda\overline{x_k}.case\ \lambda\overline{y_l}.f(\overline{t_m})\ of\ \overline{p_n : \mathcal{X}_n} \to^? Z, G \quad \Rightarrow^{\{\}} \quad \lambda\overline{x_k}, \overline{y_l}.\sigma(\mathcal{X}) \to^? X,\ \lambda\overline{x_k}.case\ \lambda\overline{y_l}.X(\overline{x_k}, \overline{y_l})\ of\ \overline{p_n : \mathcal{X}_n} \to^? Z, G$$
where $\sigma = \{\overline{X_m \mapsto \lambda\overline{x_k}, \overline{y_l}.t_m}\}$, and
$f(\overline{X_m(\overline{x_k}, \overline{y_l})}) \to \mathcal{X}$ is a $\overline{x_k}, \overline{y_l}$-lifted rule

Fig. 2. System LNT for needed narrowing in the higher-order case

Notice that for goals where only higher-order patterns occur, there is no choice between Projection and Imitation and furthermore Function Guess does not apply. This special case is refined later in Section 8.

For a sequence $\Rightarrow^{\theta_1} \cdots \Rightarrow^{\theta_n}$ of LNT steps, we write $\stackrel{*}{\Rightarrow}^{\theta}$, where $\theta = \theta_n \cdots \theta_1$. In contrast to the calculus in Section 3 not all substitutions are recorded for $\stackrel{*}{\Rightarrow}$; only the ones produced by guessing are needed for the technical treatment. Informally, all other substitutions only concern intermediate (or auxiliary) variables similar to [18].

As in the first-order case, we consider only reductions to the dedicated constant *true*. This is general enough to cover reductions to a term without defined symbols c, since a reduction $t \stackrel{*}{\longrightarrow} c$ can be modeled by $f(t) \stackrel{*}{\longrightarrow} true$ with the additional rule $f(c) \to true$ and a new symbol f. Hence we assume that solving a goal $t \to^? true$ is initiated with the **initial goal** $I(t) = case\ t\ of\ true : true \to^? X$.

As an example, consider the goal $\lambda x.diff(\lambda y.sin(F(x, y)), x) \to^? \lambda x.cos(x)$ w.r.t. the rules for *diff* and the *hdt* for the function $*$:

$$X * Y \to case\ Y\ of\ 1 : X, s(Y') : X + X * Y'$$

To solve the above goal, we simply add the rule $f(\lambda x.cos(x)) \to true$ to solve the following goal. Since each computation step only affects the two leftmost goals, we often omit the others.

$$case\ f(\lambda x.diff(\lambda y.sin(F(x, y)), x))\ of\ true : true \to^? X_1$$

$\Rightarrow_{Case\ Eval}$

$case\ \lambda x.diff(\lambda y.sin(F(x,y)), x)\ of\ cos : true \rightarrow^? X_2,$
$case\ X_2\ of\ true : true \rightarrow^? X_1$

$\Rightarrow_{Case\ Eval}$

$\lambda x.case\ \lambda y.sin(F(x,y))\ of \ldots, \lambda y.sin(G(x,y)) : \ldots, \ldots \rightarrow^? X_3,$
$case\ X_3\ of\ cos : true \rightarrow^? X_2, case\ X_2\ of\ true : true \rightarrow^? X_1$

$\Rightarrow_{Case\ Select}$

$\lambda x.cos(F(x,x)) * diff(\lambda y.F(x,y), x) \rightarrow^? X_3, case\ X_3\ of\ cos : true \rightarrow^? X_2, \ldots$

$\Rightarrow_{Bind}$

$case\ \lambda x.cos(F(x,x)) * diff(\lambda y.F(x,y), x)\ of\ cos : true \rightarrow^? X_2, \ldots$

$\Rightarrow_{Case\ Eval}$

$\lambda x.case\ diff(\lambda y.F(x,y), x)\ of\ 1 : cos(F(x,x)), \ldots \rightarrow^? X_3', \ldots$

$\Rightarrow_{Case\ Eval}$

$\lambda x.case\ \lambda y.F(x,y)\ of\ \lambda y.y : 1, \ldots \rightarrow^? X_4, \lambda x.case\ X_4(x)\ of\ 1 : cos(F(x,x)), \ldots$

$\Rightarrow^{\{F \mapsto \lambda x,y.y\}}_{Projection}$

$\lambda x.case\ \lambda y.y\ of\ \lambda y.y : 1, \ldots \rightarrow^? X_4, \lambda x.case\ X_4(x)\ of\ 1 : cos(x), \ldots \rightarrow^? X_3', \ldots$

$\Rightarrow_{Case\ Select}$

$\lambda x.1 \rightarrow^? X_4, \lambda x.case\ X_4(x)\ of\ 1 : cos(x), \ldots \rightarrow^? X_3', \ldots$

$\Rightarrow_{Bind}$

$\lambda x.case\ 1\ of\ 1 : cos(x), \ldots \rightarrow^? X_3', case\ X_3'\ of\ cos : true \rightarrow^? X_2, \ldots$

$\Rightarrow_{Case\ Select} \Rightarrow_{Bind} \Rightarrow_{Case\ Select} \Rightarrow_{Bind}$

$case\ true\ of\ true : true \rightarrow^? X_1 \quad \Rightarrow_{Case\ Select} \quad true \rightarrow^? X_1 \quad \Rightarrow_{Bind} \quad \{\}$

Thus, the computed solution is $\{F \mapsto \lambda x, y.y\}$.

6 Correctness and Completeness

As in the first-order case, we show completeness w.r.t. needed reductions. We first define needed reductions and then lift needed reductions to narrowing. In the following we assume an inductively sequential HRS $\mathcal{R}$ and assume LNT is invoked with the corresponding definitional trees.

For our purpose it is convenient to define needed reductions via LNT. Then we show that they are in fact needed. For modeling rewriting, the Guess rules are not needed: For LNT we have $S \stackrel{*}{\Rightarrow}{}^{\{\}}_{LNT} S'$ if and only if no Guess rules are used in the reduction. Hence no narrowing is performed. This can also be seen as an implementation of a particular rewriting strategy.

In order to relate a system of LNT goals to a term, we associate a position p with each case construct and a substitution θ for all newly introduced variables on the right. For each case expression $\mathcal{T} = case\ X\ of\ \ldots$ in a rule $\mathcal{T}' = f(\overline{X_n}) \rightarrow \mathcal{X}$ we attach the position p of X in the left-hand side of the corresponding rewrite rule. Formally, we define a function $l_{\mathcal{T}}$ such that $l_{\mathcal{T}}(f(\overline{X_n}) : \mathcal{X})$ yields the **labeled tree** for a rule $\mathcal{T} = f(\overline{X_n}) \rightarrow \mathcal{X}$:

- $l_{\mathcal{T}}(p_f : case\ X\ of\ \overline{\mathcal{T}_n}) = p_f : case_p\ X\ of\ \overline{l_{\mathcal{T}}(\mathcal{T}_n)}$
  where p is the position of X in $pat_{\mathcal{T}}(p_f : case\ X\ of\ \overline{\mathcal{T}_n})$
- $l_{\mathcal{T}}(p_f : r) = p_f : r$

We assume in the following that definitional trees for some inductively sequential HRS $\mathcal{R}$ are labeled.

The following invariant will allow us to relate a goal system with a term:

Theorem 4. *For an initial goal with* $case_\epsilon\ t\ of\ true : true \rightarrow^? X_1 \stackrel{*}{\Rightarrow}{}^{\{\}}_{LNT} S$, *S is of one of the following two forms:*

1. $\lambda\overline{x}.case_{p_n}\ s\ of\ \ldots \rightarrow^? X_n, \lambda\overline{x}.case_{p_{n-1}}\ \lambda\overline{y}.X_n(\overline{x},\overline{y})\ of\ \ldots \rightarrow^? X_{n-1}, \ldots,$
   $\lambda\overline{x}.case_{p_2}\ \lambda\overline{y}.X_3(\overline{x},\overline{y})\ of\ \ldots \rightarrow^? X_2,\ case_{p_1}\ X_2\ of\ true : true \rightarrow^? X_1$
2. $r \rightarrow^? X_{n+1}, \lambda\overline{x}.case_{p_n}\ \lambda\overline{y}.X_{n+1}(\overline{x},\overline{y})\ of\ \ldots \rightarrow^? X_n,$
   $\lambda\overline{x}.case_{p_{n-1}}\ \lambda\overline{y}.X_n(\overline{x},\overline{y})\ of\ \ldots \rightarrow^? X_{n-1}, \ldots,$
   $\lambda\overline{x}.case_{p_2}\ \lambda\overline{y}.X_3(\overline{x},\overline{y})\ of\ \ldots \rightarrow^? X_2,\ case_{p_1}\ X_2\ of\ true : true \rightarrow^? X_1$

Furthermore, all $\overline{X_{n+1}}$ *are distinct and each variable* X_i *occurs only as shown above, i.e. at most twice in* $\ldots, e \rightarrow^? X_i, case\ X_i\ of \ldots$.

Notice that the second form in the above theorem is created by a Case Select rule application, which may reduce a case term to a non-case term, or by Case Eval with a rule $f(\overline{X_n}) \rightarrow r$. As only the Bind rule applies on such systems, they are immediately reduced to the first form. As we will see, the Bind rule corresponds to the replacement which is part of a rewrite step. Since we now know the precise form of goal systems which may occur, bound variables as arguments and binders are often omitted in goal systems for brevity.

The next goal is to relate LNT and rewriting. For a goal system S, we write $S\!\downarrow$ for the normal form obtained by applying Case Eval and Case Select.

Definition 5. We define an **associated substitution** for each goal system inductively on $\stackrel{*}{\Rightarrow}_{LNT}$:

- For an initial goal system of the form $S = case_\epsilon\ t\ of\ true : true \rightarrow^? X$, we define the associated substitution $\theta_S = \{X \mapsto t\}$.
- For the Case Eval rule on $S = \lambda\overline{x}.case_p\ \lambda\overline{y}.f(\overline{t})\ of \ldots \rightarrow^? X, G$ with

  $$S \Rightarrow \lambda\overline{x},\overline{y}.\sigma(\mathcal{X}') \rightarrow^? X', \lambda\overline{x}.case_p\ \lambda\overline{y}.X'(\overline{x},\overline{y})\ of\ \ldots \rightarrow^? X, G =: S'$$

  we define $\theta_{S'} = \theta_S \cup \{X' \mapsto \lambda\overline{x}.(\theta_S X)|_p\}$.

For all other rules, the associated substitution is unchanged.

For a goal system S we write the associated substitution as θ_S. Notice that the associated substitution is not a "solution" as used in the completeness result and only serves to reconstruct the original term.

We can translate a goal system produced by LNT into one term as follows. The idea is that $case_p\ t\ of\ \ldots \rightarrow^? X$ should be interpreted as the replacement of the case term t at position p in $\theta_S X$, i.e., $(\theta_S X)[t]_p$. Extending this to goal systems yields the following definition:

Definition 6. For a goal system S of the form

$$[r \rightarrow^? X,]\ \lambda\overline{x}.case_{p_n}\ s\ of\ \ldots \rightarrow^? X_n, \ldots, case_{p_1}\ X_2\ of\ true : true \rightarrow^? X_1$$

(where $[r \rightarrow^? X,]$ is optional) with associated substitution θ we define the **associated term** $T(S)$ as $(\theta X_1)[(\theta X_2)[\ldots(\theta X_n(\overline{x}))[\theta s]_{p_n} \ldots]_{p_2}]_{p_1}$.

For instance, if we start with a goal system $S_1 = case_\epsilon\ t\ of\ true : true \rightarrow^? X$, then $T(S_1) = t$.

For a goal system S, we write $Bind(S)$ to denote the result of applying the Case Bind rule. Notice that the substitution of the Bind rule only affects the two leftmost goals.

Lemma 7. *Let $S = I(t)$. If $S\downarrow$ is of the form of Invariant 2, then $t = T(S\downarrow)$ is reducible at position $p = p_1 \cdots p_n$. Furthermore, if $t \longrightarrow_p t'$, then $I(t')\downarrow = Bind(S\downarrow)\downarrow$.*

Now, we can define needed reductions:

Definition 8. A term t has a needed redex p if $I(t)\downarrow$ is of Invariant 2 with $p = p_1 \cdots p_n$.

It remains to show that needed reductions are indeed needed to compute a constructor headed term.

Theorem 9. *If t reduces to true, then t has a needed redex at position p and t must be reduced at p eventually. Otherwise, t is not reducible to true.*

The next desirable result is to show that needed reductions are normalizing. This is suggested from related works [15, 11], but is beyond the scope of this paper.

For a goal system S, we call the variables that do not occur in $T(S)$ **dummies**. In particular, all variables on the right and all variables in selectors in patterns of some tree in S are dummies.

Lemma 10. *If $S \stackrel{*}{\Rightarrow}{}^{\theta}_{LNT} \{\}$, then $\theta S \stackrel{*}{\Rightarrow}{}^{\{\}}_{LNT} \{\}$.*

Theorem 11 (Correctness of LNT). *If $I(t) \stackrel{*}{\Rightarrow}{}^{\theta}_{LNT} \{\}$ for a term t, then $\theta t \stackrel{*}{\longrightarrow} true$.*

We first state completeness in terms of LNT reductions.

Lemma 12. *If $\theta S \stackrel{*}{\Rightarrow}{}^{\{\}}_{LNT} \{\}$ and θ is in $\mathcal{R}$-normal form and contains no dummies of S,[6] then $S \stackrel{*}{\Rightarrow}{}^{\theta'}_{LNT} \{\}$ with $\theta' \leq \theta$.*

Theorem 13 (Completeness of LNT). *If $\theta t \stackrel{*}{\longrightarrow} true$ and θ is in $\mathcal{R}$-normal form, then $I(t) \stackrel{*}{\Rightarrow}{}^{\theta'}_{LNT} \{\}$ with $\theta' \leq \theta$.*

7 Optimality regarding Solutions

We show here another important aspect, namely uniqueness of the solutions computed. Compared to the more general case in [19], optimality of solutions is possible here, since we only evaluate to constructor-headed terms. For this to hold for all subgoals in a narrowing process, our requirement of constructor-based rules is also essential. For these reasons, we never have to chose between Case Select and Case Eval in our setting and optimality follows easily from the corresponding result of higher-order unification.

[6] I.e., $\mathcal{FV}(\theta) \cap \mathcal{FV}(S) = \mathcal{FV}(T(S))$

Theorem 14 (Optimality). *If $I(t) \stackrel{*}{\Rightarrow}^{\theta}_{LNT} \{\}$ and $I(t) \stackrel{*}{\Rightarrow}^{\theta'}_{LNT} \{\}$ are two different derivations, then θ and θ' are incomparable.*

It is also conjectured that our notion of needed reductions is optimal (this is subject to current research [16, 15, 3]). Note, however, that sharing is needed for optimality, as shown for the first-order case in [2].

8 Avoiding Function Synthesis

Although the synthesis of functional objects by full higher-order unification in LNT is very powerful, it can also be expensive and operationally complex. There is an interesting restriction on rewrite rules which entails that full higher-order unification is not needed in LNT for (quasi) first-order goals.

We show that the corresponding result in [4] is easy to see in our context, although lifting over binders obscures the results somewhat unnecessarily. Lifting may instantiate a first-order variable by a higher-order one, but this is only needed to handle the context correctly.

A term t is **quasi first-order** if t is a higher-order pattern without free higher-order variables. A rule $f(\overline{X_n}) \rightarrow \mathcal{X}$ is called **weakly higher-order**, if every higher-order free variable which occurs in $\mathcal{X}$ is in $\{\overline{X_n}\}$. In other words, higher-order variables may only occur directly below the root and are immediately eliminated when *hdts* are introduced in the Case Eval rule.

Theorem 15. *If $I(t) \stackrel{*}{\Rightarrow}_{LNT} S$ where t is quasi first-order w.r.t. weakly higher-order rules, then $T(S)$ is quasi first-order.*

As a trivial consequence of the last result, Function Guess and Projection do not apply and Imitation is only used as in the first-order case.

9 Conclusions

We have presented an effective model for the integration of functional and logic programming with completeness and optimality results. Since we do not require terminating rewrite rules and permit higher-order logical variables and λ-abstractions, our strategy is a suitable basis for truly higher-order functional logic languages. Moreover, our strategy reduces to an optimal first-order strategy if the higher-order features are not used. Further work will focus on adapting the explicit model for sharing using goal systems from [19] to this refined context.

References

1. S. Antoy. Definitional trees. In *Proc. of the 3rd International Conference on Algebraic and Logic Programming*, pages 143–157. Springer LNCS 632, 1992.
2. S. Antoy, R. Echahed, and M. Hanus. A needed narrowing strategy. In *Proc. 21st ACM Symposium on Principles of Programming Languages*, pages 268–279, Portland, 1994.

3. Andrea Asperti and Cosimo Laneve. Interaction systems I: The theory of optimal reductions. *Mathematical Structures in Computer Science*, 4:457–504, 1994.
4. J. Avenhaus and C. A. Loría-Sáenz. Higher-order conditional rewriting and narrowing. In Jean-Pierre Jouannaud, editor, *1st International Conference on Constraints in Computational Logics*, München, Germany, September 1994. Springer LNCS 845.
5. Hendrik Pieter Barendregt. *The Lambda Calculus, its Syntax and Semantics*. North Holland, 2nd edition, 1984.
6. E. Giovannetti, G. Levi, C. Moiso, and C. Palamidessi. Kernel LEAF: A logic plus functional language. *Journal of Computer and System Sciences*, 42(2):139–185, 1991.
7. M. Hanus. The integration of functions into logic programming: From theory to practice. *Journal of Logic Programming*, 19&20:583–628, 1994.
8. M. Hanus. Efficient translation of lazy functional logic programs into Prolog. In *Proc. Fifth International Workshop on Logic Program Synthesis and Transformation*, pages 252–266. Springer LNCS 1048, 1995.
9. M. Hanus and C. Prehofer. Higher-order narrowing with definitional trees. Technical report 96-2, RWTH Aachen, 1996.
10. J.R. Hindley and J. P. Seldin. *Introduction to Combinators and λ-Calculus*. Cambridge University Press, 1986.
11. Jan Willem Klop. *Combinatory Reduction Systems*. Mathematical Centre Tracts 127. Mathematisch Centrum, Amsterdam, 1980.
12. Dale Miller. A logic programming language with lambda-abstraction, function variables, and simple unification. *J. Logic and Computation*, 1:497–536, 1991.
13. J.J. Moreno-Navarro and M. Rodríguez-Artalejo. Logic programming with functions and predicates: The language BABEL. *Journal of Logic Programming*, 12:191–223, 1992.
14. Tobias Nipkow. Higher-order critical pairs. In *Proc. 6th IEEE Symp. Logic in Computer Science*, pages 342–349, 1991.
15. Vincent van Oostrom. *Confluence for Abstract and Higher-Order Rewriting*. PhD thesis, Vrije Universiteit, 1994. Amsterdam.
16. Vincent van Oostrom. Higher-order families, 1996. In this volume.
17. Christian Prehofer. Higher-order narrowing. In *Proc. Ninth Annual IEEE Symposium on Logic in Computer Science*, pages 507–516. IEEE Computer Society Press, 1994.
18. Christian Prehofer. A Call-by-Need Strategy for Higher-Order Functional-Logic Programming. In J. Lloyd, editor, *Logic Programming. Proc. of the 1995 International Symposium*, pages 147–161. MIT Press, 1995.
19. Christian Prehofer. *Solving Higher-order Equations: From Logic to Programming.* PhD thesis, TU München, 1995. Also appeared as Technical Report I9508.
20. J.R. Slagle. Automated theorem-proving for theories with simplifiers, commutativity, and associativity. *Journal of the ACM*, 21(4):622–642, 1974.

Design of a Proof Assistant

Gérard Huet
INRIA -Rocquencourt
Domaine de Voluceau
Rocquencourt B.P. 105
78153 Le Chesnay Cedex
Gerard.Huet@inria.fr

Abstract. We discuss a few architectural design decisions for a general purpose proof assistant, combining a programmable tactics-based proof-checker, a sequent calculus search engine based on logic programming with higher-order unification constraints, a library browser managing modular mathematical developments, and a user interface allowing structural selection in formulas displayed in readable notation. The talk is illustrated with concrete experience issued from various versions of the Coq Proof Assistant for Type Theory. It is intended as a discussion platform for the QED collaborative endeavor.

A Compiler for Nondeterministic Term Rewriting Systems

Marian Vittek

INRIA-Lorraine & CRIN
615, rue du Jardin Botanique, BP 101
54602 Villers-lès-Nancy Cedex, FRANCE

ILOG
9, rue de Verdun, BP 85
94253 Gentilly Cedex, FRANCE

E-mail: vittek@loria.fr, vittek@ilog.fr

Abstract

This work presents the design and the implementation of a compiler for the ELAN specification language. The language is based on rewriting logic and permits, in particular, the combination of computations where deterministic evaluations are mixed with a nondeterministic search for solutions. The implementation combines compilation methods of term rewriting systems, functional and logic programming languages, and some new original techniques producing, in summary, an efficient code in an imperative language. The efficiency of the compiler is demonstrated on experimental results.

1 Introduction

The use of term rewriting in software development is natural in many areas such as computer algebra, constraint solving or compiler development. Several programming languages such as OBJ or ASF+SDF use term rewriting as the engine for the execution of their programs. In these languages the rewriting rules are seen as oriented equations between terms, rewriting itself is a *simplification* of a term inside its equivalence class into the *canonical form*. This point of view is too restrictive for many practical applications. Some more free interpretations of term rewriting rules can be found for example in [JK91, Frü95]. In particular, rewriting logic [MOM93] proposes a semantic background where term rewriting is seen as a sequence of *transitions* which starts with an initial term t and transforms it to its *result form*. In rewriting logic a query of the form $t \rightarrow^* x$ leads to the search of all terms x, such that t can be rewritten to x. Rewriting becomes nondeterministic in the sense that there can be several result forms starting from one initial term.

The use of rewriting logic raises new interesting problems concerning the efficient implementation of *nondeterministic rewriting*. We call nondeterministic rewriting the process that starts from an initial term and looks for all terms to which it can be rewritten. This search is obviously implemented by backtracking where some branches of the search space may be pruned by additional conditions. The implementation of nondeterministic rewriting recalls the implementation of logic programming languages, the significant difference is due to the fact that the rewriting rules can be applied inside the terms. Also the formalism we use to prune the search space is different from that of logic programming languages.

In this paper we discuss the possibilities of efficient implementation of nondeterministic rewriting by compilation into an imperative programming language. In particular, we want to present the techniques we have used in the compiler of the ELAN language [Vit94, KKV95]. ELAN is a logical framework whose specification language is entirely based on term rewriting. It is used for the specification and study of different constraint solvers, logic programming languages, and their combinations. Semantically, it is based on a specialization of rewriting logic called *computational system* [KKV95]. It introduces a notion of *strategy* which permits, in particular, the formalization of algorithms combining deterministic and nondeterministic computations. We will briefly present the language in the following section.

The main originality of the paper is the presentation of the ELAN compiler, namely the first presentation (to the author's best knowledge) of a compilation scheme for nondeterministic rewriting. The presented compiler transforms rewriting systems into C programs compiled then by a standard compiler. A new technique is defined for compiling the specific control flow in programs during the backtracking. Our method preserves the efficiency of deterministic computations and can be of more general interest, for example, it can be interesting to test it in implementations of constraint solvers, of the WAM and Prolog-like languages. The experimental results, presented at the end of the paper, show that the nondeterministic rewriting can be implemented as efficiently as the best current implementations of functional and logic programming languages. Briefly, on classical benchmarks taken from functional programming we have obtained on average results slightly better than SML compiler of New Jersey [AM87]. On other benchmarks, testing backtracking, we have obtained significant speed-up compared to ECLiPSe [MS+93].

The paper is organized as follows: We start by a brief presentation of the ELAN language, then we discuss methods for the efficient compilation of both deterministic and nondeterministic rewriting, we present in particular several optimizations of the generated code and the implementation of the library realizing backtracking. We finish the paper by presentation of some experimental results and by a brief conclusion.

2 The ELAN Language

We present only briefly, on simple examples, the language main features, more detailed description can be found in [Vit94, KKV95]. Similarly to algebraic specification languages like OBJ or ASF+SDF, a *program* is composed from *modules*, each of them defines its own signature, labelled rewriting rules and *strategies* controlling the applications of rules. In the rest of the paper, we use the term "strategy" meaning a piece of code of ELAN's program. We are aware that this term becomes overloaded in the context of the term rewriting, where it has its specific meaning. Terms in ELAN can be written in a mix-fix syntax defined by a many sorted signature. A module can *import* other modules and a *parametrization* is possible and realized (for the moment) by a textual preprocessing. The rewriting rules can be conditional and a special kind of *local assignment* is permitted inside the rules. A special formalism is used to define strategies. Strategies describe sequences of elementary transformations (i.e. applications of rewriting rules) from initial (*input*) terms to resulting (*output*) terms. The strategies are constructed using a particular formalism permitting applying a rule (and testing its applicability), making a loop and sequencing. The rewriting rules from a strategy are applied at the head position of the term which is not really a limitation since applications inside terms can be simulated using local assignments. A program can contain definitions of several strategies, one of them has to be designed as being the *main* strategy. When executing the program, the main strategy is applied on the input term.

The language contains built-in boolean, integer and floating point arithmetics. Based on practical experience, rewrite rules are divided into two groups: the labelled rewrite rules, whose application is controlled by user-defined strategies, and the non labelled rules, whose application is controlled by a default *normalization strategy*, which consists in applying non-labelled rules at leftmost-innermost positions of a term until the normal form is reached. The normalization strategy is used with rules defining deterministic functions and is applied after each reduction produced by a labelled rewrite rule. This corresponds to the intuition that, after each application of a labelled rewrite rule, functions introduced by the right-hand side of the rule must be evaluated.

In the rest of the section we introduce and illustrate on examples some important features of the language.

Examples

Let us take for the first example the *append* function on lists. Let us suppose that we have defined a signature containing the constant *nil* and the binary symbols *cons* and *append*. The following code defines the function appending two lists:

```
[]    append(nil,y)          => y                     end
[]    append(cons(x,y),z)    => cons(x,append(y,z))   end
```

In this syntax, the rewriting rules begin with their label inside [] brackets. If there is no label mentioned (like here) the rules are applied according to the built-in normalization strategy. This means that the intended semantics of the evaluation is functional. The key word **end** is used to end definitions of rewriting rules.

In the second example, we define a nondeterministic strategy **range** which returns the n results: $n, n-1, \cdots, 1$ when applied to an integer n. We define first the following conditional rewriting rule:

```
[range_rule] x      => x-1       if x>1                end
```

We use this rule to define the strategy **range** which, when applied to n, returns n itself, then it returns the result of one application of the rule **range_rule** on n, then the result of two applications of the rule, etc until the rule is no longer applicable. In this strategy we will use two elementary strategy constructors: **dont care choose** provides an application of the first applicable rewriting rule from a given list and **iterate-enditerate** (a nondeterministic loop constructor) which when applied to a term t returns t itself; then after a backtrack it returns the result of application of its sub-strategy to t; after another backtrack it returns the result of two applications of its sub-strategy, etc, until no more application is possible. In other words, the iteration constructor provides a loop making at each pass a nondeterministic branching between breaking and continuing the loop. The definition of the strategy **range** is:

```
strategy range
  iterate     dont care choose(range_rule)     enditerate
end of strategy
```

Definitions of strategies begin with the key word `strategy` following by the name of the strategy. Strategies are ended by the phrase `end of strategy`.

A last example consists in a program providing each possible insertions of an element into a given list. For example, an insertion of the term c into the list $a.b.nil$ (the . here is an infix notation for the *cons* operator) gives three results: $c.a.b.nil$, $a.c.b.nil$ and $a.b.c.nil$. In this example we suppose we have defined the binary symbol *insert* and the ternary symbol *ins*, and consider the rewriting rules (where the symbols `e,e1,e2,l,l1,l2` stand for variables):

```
[i1] insert(e , l)          => ins(e , nil , l)                 end
[i2] ins(e , l1 , l2)       => append(l1 , e.l2)                end
[i3] ins(e1 ,l1 , e2.l2)    => ins(e1 , append(l1 , e2.nil) ,l2) end
```

For a given list L and a given element a, all possible insertions of a into L can be obtained by applying first the rule `i1` to the term $insert(a, L)$ and then, while it is possible, and in a nondeterministic manner the rules `i2,i3`. During the loop the transformed term is of the form $ins(e, l1, l2)$ and the invariant of the loop is that $append(l1, l2)$ is equal to the original list L. In other words, successive applications of the third rule cut the original list L into two pieces $l1$ and $l2$. An application of the second rule creates the list $l1.a.l2$ and terminates the loop (as no other rule will be further applicable). The strategy starting with an application of rule `i1` and continuing by repeatedly applying rules `i2,i3` in a nondeterministic manner can be written in ELAN as:

```
strategy insert
  dont care choose(i1)
  while    dont know choose(i2 i3)    endwhile
end of strategy
```

This strategy uses the **dont know choose** construction which provides a nondeterministic application of rewriting rules (exploring all the possibilities) and the **while-endwhile** loop, which applies its sub-strategy until no more application is possible. As opposed to the **iterate** loop, **while** returns only "final" results, it returns only terms to which no further application of its sub-strategy is possible. The strategy `insert` illustrates also the *sequencing* of two sub-strategies, the final results are obtained by application of the **while-endwhile** loop to the results of the **dont care choose** sub-strategy.

Note that other strategies can give the same results as the previous one. One such strategy is for example:

```
strategy insert2
  dont care choose(i1)
  iterate   dont care choose(i3) enditerate
  dont care choose(i2)
end of strategy
```

This strategy first applies rule `i1`, then it iteratively applies rule `i3`, and after each iteration it gives a result by final application of rule `i2`.

3 Compiling Term Rewriting with Strategies

Compilers of term rewriting systems provide a significant speed-up of execution compared to interpreters. In our case, the additional formalism of strategies contain possibilities of nondeterministic computations which makes it more difficult to implement than simple conditional term rewriting system. The design of the general architecture of our compiler is influenced mainly by the search of trade-offs between efficiency of deterministic and of nondeterministic computations. In practical experiences we have observed that even the programs using massive nondeterminism spent a large part of run time in deterministic evaluations. For example, algorithms used in a variety of constraint solvers, provide deterministic propagation of changes after each nondeterministic step. In our compiler we give then priority to the efficient implementation of deterministic computations.

The general idea of our compiler is to transform a given ELAN program into a C program, which receives an input term t and computes the results of application of the program's main strategy to t.

The compiler transforms each strategy S into a C function (named str_S) of one argument. An application of a strategy S to a term t is compiled into a call to the function str_S whose argument is a pointer to t. The function returns the pointer to the resulting term. It is obvious that this scheme of compilation works well for deterministic strategies, in the nondeterministic case, when the strategy S can return several results, the situation is more complicated.

3.1 Deterministic Computations

We present first in this section the method (refined by several optimizations) we use for compilation of deterministic strategies and we discuss the general non-deterministic case later in section 3.2. As we have just mentioned, each strategy S is compiled into a C function *str_S*. This function is built according to the structure of the original strategy, in particular, the sequencing of sub-strategies is compiled into a concatenation of parts of C code and the **while** construction is compiled into a loop. The most interesting thing is the compilation of the elementary strategy **dont care choose**$(\ell_1, \cdots, \ell_n)$. This strategy, when applied to a term t, selects the first of the rules $\ell_1, \cdots, \ell_n$ which can be applied to t, it matches t with the left hand side of the rule, instantiates its variables and replaces t by the right hand side of the selected rule. The naive compilation of this process gives us a sequence of n parts of code corresponding to application of each rewriting rule. Each part starts with a compilation of the matching algorithm for the corresponding rule. A successful matching instantiates the variables of the left hand side and the code continues by evaluating the conditions and the local affectations. Then it continues by freeing the part of the input term corresponding to the left hand side of the rewriting rule and finally by the construction of the right hand side of the rule. If the matching fails, a condition was evaluated to false or there is no local affectation of variables the computation continues on the part corresponding to the next rewriting rule. If no rule is applicable a call of a special function *fail* is generated (see also the section 3.2 of the paper).

Several refinings of this general schema are possible. We present now those we have implemented in our compiler.

Many to one matching

The first possible optimization concerns the compilation of the matching algorithm. All the rewriting rules are known at compile time. Matching of left hand sides of rules to one unknown input term can be pre-compiled using some existing algorithm. The resulting code gives the set of applicable rules in a very efficient manner. Several works are concerned with this or similar problems, among others [HO82, Aug85, Vit90, KL91]. In the ELAN compiler we have implemented two of them, namely [Aug85] and [Vit90].

Reusing parts of terms

Another optimization comes from the Berlin project OPAL [DFG+94]. The main idea is to reuse parts of left hand sides of rules to construct the right hand sides when applying a rewriting rule. In the case when both sides of a rewriting rule are of approximately the same size, a significant speed-up can be gained. Let us take for example the rewriting rule: $append(cons(x,y),z) \rightarrow cons(x, append(y,z))$ and apply it to the term: $append(cons(a,nil), cons(b,nil))$. In the rewriting rule, the size of the left hand side is exactly the same as the size of the right hand side. Once the rule matches a term, we know that the term to reduce is of the form *append*(*cons*(x, y), z). Note that after the reduction this part of the reduced term is of no further use, it is considered as garbage and is freed. We can construct efficiently the resulting term *cons*(x, *append*(y, z)) by re-using this garbage. The next figure shows that in this case only two affectations of pointers are necessary to provide the reduction.

However, this optimization is not possible if some parts of the reduced term are shared. To detect easily whether a node is shared or not we use reference counters indicating how many times a term is referenced. The reference counters are also used in the garbage collection. The rewriting rules are known during compilation, so the possibilities of reusing their parts can be pre-computed at compile time.

Collecting rules with the same head symbol

A special optimization concerns the non labelled rules which are applied with the built-in normalization strategy. This optimization used for example in [Kap87] consists of regrouping the non labelled rules with the same head symbol on the left hand sides. For each functional symbol f of arity n the collected rules are compiled into a C function fun_f of n arguments. This function when applied to the terms $t_1, \cdots, t_n$ returns the result of applying the normalization strategy to the term $f(t_1, \cdots, t_n)$. Remember that the built-in normalization strategy is used after each application of a rewriting rule. There is no reason to construct first the right hand side of the applied rule and to normalise the resulting term only after this. Using the functions fun_f, both steps can be made together, so the construction of the right hand side can be compiled into nested calls of fun_f functions. This optimization is illustrated on the example in the section 3.1.

Further optimizations

Several further optimizations are implemented in the ELAN compiler. In particular the strong typing of the language permits us to directly represent the numeric values. No additional information is stored in terms to determine whether a value is a pointer or numeric value. Numerical expressions are built-in and they are compiled directly into C expressions. To decrease the time spent to maintain the reference counters, no reference counting is provided on the constants and numeric values. All the functional constants are stored in a special part of the memory, they are never freed and multiple occurences of the same constant are always shared, so at run-time no constant needs to be created. This optimization helps, because in the average case, the constants represent approximately one half of the symbols in a term. The compiler provides also the tail recursion and the tail recursion modulo constructor application optimizations, which are compiled into loops.

Example of the generated code

Let's take two rules for computing the n-th Fibonacci number.

```
[] fib(x,y,0)          => y                        end
[] fib(x,y,z)          => fib(y,x+y,z-1)           end
```

These rules have no label, they are applied with the built-in normalization strategy. Using these two rules, any term $fib(0,1,n)$ where n is a natural number will be rewritten to the n-th Fibonacci number. Note also that the normalization strategy always applies the first applicable rule.

Several optimizations come in while compiling these two rules. As the rules are applied with the built-in normalization strategy and they have the same functional symbol fib at the head of left hand sides, they are compiled into a function fun_fib of three arguments. The body of the function starts with the many-to-one matching (in this case only a test whether the third argument is zero or not). Two possibilities correspond to the application of each of these rewriting rules. No reference counting occurs in this example, because all concerned terms are numerical values. For the same reason, no freeing of left hand sides of rules is needed. The tail recursion optimization occurs in the construction of the right hand side of the second rule.

The resulting code in C, and then compiled to SPARC assembler is:

```
#define PLUS(a,b) ((int) a)+((int) b)
#define MINUS(a,b) ((int) a)-((int) b)

struct term *fun_fib(v1,v2,v3)
struct term *v1,*v2,*v3;
{ beginlabel:
  switch((int) v3){
  case 0 :  return(v2);
  default: {
    struct term *sv2,*sv1;
    sv1 = MINUS(v3,1);
    sv2 = PLUS(v1,v2);
    v1 = v2;  v2 = sv2; v3 = sv1;
    goto beginlabel;
} } }
```

```
_fun_fib:
        b       LY2
        tst     %o2
LY1:    mov     %o1,%o0
        mov     %o3,%o1
        dec     %o2
        tst     %o2
LY2:    bne,a   LY1
        add     %o0,%o1,%o3
        retl
        add     %g0,%o1,%o0
```

Note, that the normalization using the two rewriting rules is compiled in a cycle where at each pass (corresponding to one application of a rewriting rule) only two register movings, one addition instruction, one decrementation and one test of zero are executed.

3.2 Nondeterministic Search

The nondeterminism in ELAN programs occurs when using one of the strategy constructors: **dont know choose** or **iterate**. It is implemented by backtracking which at the moment, where two rewriting rules can be applied in a nondeterministic manner, applies the first one and continues the execution until a result term is obtained or until some sub-strategy fails. After this, it returns back, it recovers the state of the evaluation where it was at the moment of the choice and it continues the evaluation exploring the second branch.

To compile this specific control flow we have implemented a pair of functions, named setChoicePoint and fail. The function setChoicePoint when called returns zero and the computation continues. Then when the function fail is called, it provides a jump into the last call of setChoicePoint and returns the integer 1. These functions may remind the reader of the pair of standard C functions setjmp and longjmp providing so-called long jump between functions. However, the longjmp can be used only in a function called from the function setting setjmp. Our functions have not such a limitation which makes them more difficult to implement. We present this point in section 3.2 of the paper. In the rest of the paper we talk about *setting a choice point* when calling the function setChoicePoint.

Once having these two functions, the general scheme of compilation of nondeterministic computations becomes easy. Each time we have two possibilities to explore in a nondeterministic manner (for example to apply two rewriting rules ℓ_1, ℓ_2), the compiler generates a call to the function setChoicePoint and a test of its result value. The first possibility (the rule ℓ_1) is then compiled into the branch corresponding to the result zero, the second one (the rule ℓ_2) into the other branch. I.e. the nondeterministic application of two rewriting rules ℓ_1, ℓ_2, gives the code: `if (setChoicePoint()) {` *apply*(ℓ_2) `} else {` *apply*(ℓ_1) `}`.

Nondeterministic strategies

We can now extend the compilation schema from the section 3 and to define how the nondeterministic strategy constructors are compiled. Similarly to its deterministic equivalent, the strategy **dont know choose**$(\ell_1, \cdots, \ell_n)$ is compiled into a sequence of parts, each part corresponding to a compilation of the corresponding rewriting rule. The main difference from the deterministic case is that each part starts with a call to the function setChoicePoint and provides a jump to the next part, if this call returns one. After all parts a call to the function fail is generated. We can remark at this point that the many-to-one matching optimization is possible in the nondeterministic case and is implemented in the current version of the compiler. The **iterate** constructor is compiled into an infinite loop containing the line `if (! setChoicePoint()) break;` followed by the code corresponding to the sub-strategy of **iterate**. The first generated line means that the function setChoicePoint is called inside the loop and the loop is broken if the result of this call is not equal to zero. It is easy to see that the compilation of both strategies satisfies the expected control flow as presented in the section 2.

Saving the working memory

A particular problem arises during the nondeterministic computations. Suppose, for example, that we have defined the rewriting rules:

$$\begin{array}{lll} \ell_1: & f(x) & \rightarrow g(x) \\ \ell_2: & f(x) & \rightarrow x \\ \ell_3: & g(h(x)) & \rightarrow h(g(x)) \end{array}$$

and we apply the strategy **dont know choose**(ℓ_1, ℓ_2)**dont care choose**(ℓ_3) on the term $f(h(a))$. This evaluation sets the choice point between the first two rules, applies the first one and then the third one. This gives the first result $h(g(a))$. This computation is shown in the following figure:

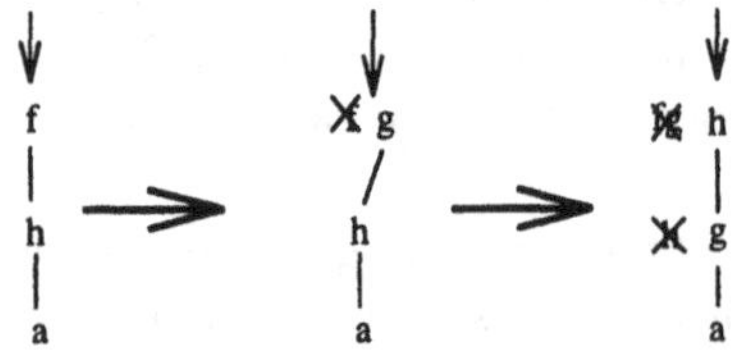

After having obtained the first result the function fail is executed to explore other possibilities. The execution of fail provokes a jump to the last choice point and the execution has to continue by an application of the second rule ℓ_2 on the original term $f(h(a))$. However, this term does not exist anymore in the memory. The problem is that the original method of compilation is not adapted to nondeterministic computations and it destroys the terms which could be needed later in other branches of the computation.

In our implementation we have solved this problem by a special compilation of the rewriting rules applied by the **dont know choose** strategy. Contrary to the deterministic case such an application do not free the term corresponding to the left hand side of the rewriting rule. This implies on the other hand, that this term would be never freed. For this reason we have introduced a special data structure called *Trail.* The Trail contains pointers to the term on which the strategy **dont know choose** was applied. At the moment of setting the choice point a special *choice point mark* is pushed into Trail. If a fail occurs, the terms pushed into the Trail after the last choice point mark are freed, and are deleted (together with the choice point mark) from the Trail.

The invariant valid during the computation is the following: if we free the current resulting term and terms pushed into the Trail after the corresponding choice point mark, we will obtain the state of the memory as it was at the moment of setting of the corresponding choice point.

Let us take again the computational system from the last example and apply it to the term $f(h(a))$. The figure 1 shows the correct computation until having obtained the first result. In this figure, the reference counter (if different from 1) is displayed as the small index of the corresponding functional symbol. The figure shows a computation where one nondeterministic step (i.e. without freeing the left hand side of the rule) is provided followed by one deterministic

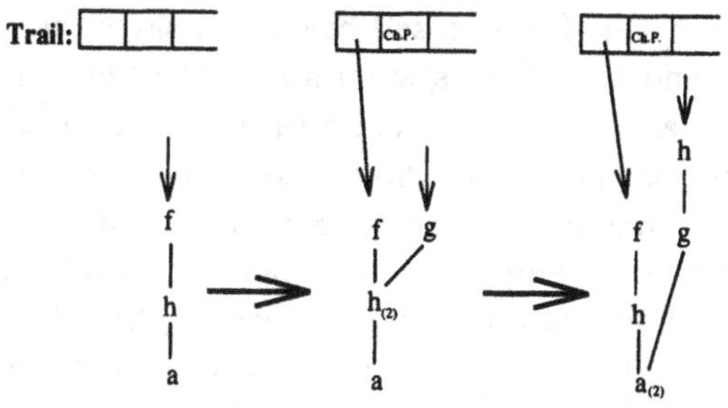

Figure 1.

application. Notice that only a needed part of the original term is copied and that the reusing of parts of terms is possible in deterministic computations (in this case in the term $g(h(a))$ we have reused the g packet to create the term $g(a)$) at its place. If we continue in the execution of this example then first the resulting term $h(g(a))$ will be freed, then (as there is no term in Trail after the choice point mark) only the choice point mark will be deleted from Trail and the evaluation will continue by the application of the rule ℓ_2 to $f(h(a))$ giving the term $h(a)$. After this the application of the rule ℓ_3 fails and all terms will be freed.

Recovering the Stack

The important part of the realization of the ELAN compiler is the implementation of the functions setChoicePoint and fail, supporting the backtracking. It is a very technical part, containing mainly the saving and recovering of machine registers and the system stack of the process.

The two functions behave similarly to the standard functions setjmp and longjmp providing long jumps. In order to better explain the problems we have met, we present first the implementation of these standard C functions. We call the *goal function* the function calling setjmp (or setChoicePoint) and the *failing function* the function calling longjmp (or fail). The *stack frame* of a function is a part of the system stack where the arguments and local variables of the function are stored. The *system stack pointer* is a machine register pointing to the top of the system stack.

The standard implementation of the long jumps (in a simplified version) is the following: the function setjmp saves the machine registers, its return address and the system stack pointer; the function longjmp recovers the saved machine registers, system stack pointer and returns to the address saved by setjmp. This implementation implies that the stack frame of the goal function has to exist at the moment of execution of longjmp. We need to eliminate this restriction as the fail in ELAN can occur in any strategy even if the strategy setting the choice point has finished (and freed its stack frame). In practice it means that (besides the job done by setjmp and longjmp) at the moment of the fail we also need to recover the system stack of the process. The naive implementation would then be the following: the function setChoicePoint saves the machine registers, its return address and the whole system stack; the function fail recovers the system stack, the machine registers and returns to the saved address. In this implementation, the saving of the whole system stack is too expensive, in the average case only a small part of the system stack needs to be changed at the moment of failure. For example, let us suppose that we have a function f_0 calling the setChoicePoint and a function f_1 calling first f_0 and then fail. An execution of f_1 creates the stack frame of f_1 in the system stack. Then f_1 calls f_0, this pushes the stack frame of f_0 onto the stack. So, when the choice point is set two stack frames (f_1 and f_0) are on the stack. After this, when leaving f_0 its stack frame is freed and execution continues in f_1 by fail. But, at this moment the stack contains the stack frame of f_1. So, to reconstitute the stack as it was at the moment of the choice only the stack frame of f_0 has to be pushed onto the current system stack.

The example illustrates the fact that it is useless to copy the whole system stack because only the stack frames of some functions are concerned. Our implementation of the setChoicePoint uses this idea. Because of the lack of the space and because the subject is very technical, we do not explain the implementation details. The main idea consists of implementing a special *handle function* which saves the top stack frame of the system stack. Return addresses of nondeterministic functions are successively (first by setChoicePoint and then by the handle function itself) modified to point to this handle function. This guarantees that the handle function is called each time a nondeterministic function executes the return instruction (and frees its stack frame). These calls save the corresponding stack frames which are then used to reconstitute the original system stack by the fail function.

The implementation is quite technical, it is done in assembler, as there is no direct access to machine registers from the C programming language. It represents about 200 lines of code and is currently working on the SPARC-architecture and on the processors Intel 80x86.

4 Comparing to the WAM

The Warren Abstract Machine (WAM) [War83] used to implement Prolog-like languages is a well known architecture providing nondeterministic computations. For this reason we have decided to compare our implementation to this abstract architecture. We are not going to compare the generated code, this would not be possible as the two implementations implement two very different languages. We provide rather a conceptual comparison of the organisation of the main data structures used during the nondeterministic search. In both architectures there are three main data structures: *Heap* is the "working memory" containing the bodies of the terms; *Stack* stores function arguments and local variables (and choice points in the WAM) and *Trail* contains some specific information used during the backtracking. An additional data structure is used in our implementation to store the choice points and the stack frames of nondeterministic functions.

Several differences between both architectures can be seen on these data structures: The Heap in the WAM is a LIFO (Last In First Out) data structure, it increases while setting the choice points and decreases at the moment of fail. In our implementation the Heap is a stable piece of the memory handled by the reference counting garbage collector.

The Stack has a very similar function in the WAM and in our implementation. Nevertheless, in our implementation the Stack is directly the system stack of the process (and the top of the Stack is obviously in machine registers). During the nondeterministic computations the freed stack frames are saved into a special additional data structure from where they are recovered at the moment of fail. This double copying is avoided in the WAM where, after the setting of a choice point the Stack does not decrease and no stack frame is freed. We did not made this optimization, because in our case this non-standard behaviour of the system stack can provoke problems when using standard C compilers with the register optimizations.

The Trail is in both cases (the WAM and the ELAN compiler) an additional LIFO data structure. The WAM's Trail contains pointers to variables which have to be un-installed when a fail occurs, in our implementation the Trail contains pointers to terms which have to be freed when a fail occurs.

5 Experimental Results

We are aware of the difficulties of trying to compare different software using experimental results which can be sensitive to the choice of computer architecture and benchmarks. In this section we present only a few experimental results to illustrate the level of efficiency which can be obtained by the presented method of compilation. Contrary to possible expectations, we do not compare our implementation to some other compilers of term rewriting. In general, these systems compile term rewriting into functional language and it seems evident that they can not supersede the efficiency of programs written directly in a functional language.

In particular, we compare here several benchmarks executed by the ELAN compiler, Standard ML compiler of New-Jersey [AM87] Version 0.93 (for deterministic benchmarks) and ECLiPSe [MS+93] Version 3.5.1 (for nondeterministic benchmarks). ECLiPSe is an ECRC implementation of a Prolog extension. The figure 2 summarises the execution times (in seconds) measured on a Sun-4 workstation for the following benchmarks: *fib* - the naive implementation of the n-th Fibonacci number; *nrev* - the naive reverse of a list of size n; *primes* - computes the list of prime numbers from 1 to n; *lrev* - reverse in linear time of a list of size n; *perm* - computes all permutations of a list of size n; *queens* - the n queens on the chessboard problem. The notation $n * problem$ means that the *problem* was executed n times and the total time of these executions was measured.

The performance of the compiler can be partially explained by the use of the assembler library for backtracking and by the reference counting garbage

Problem	*SML − NJ*	*ELAN*	*ECLiPSe*
$fib(33)$	8.4	8.4	
$nrev(5000)$	17.19	5.7	
$primes(50000)$	12.68	7.8	
$10 * lrev(100000)$	4.08	2.8	
$100000 * lrev(100)$	4.01	11.3	
$perm(8)$		1.8	2.86
$queens(8)$		0.4	2.25

Figure 2: Experimental results.

collector, which permits reusing parts of terms of left hand sides of rewriting rules to build right hand sides without producing garbage. The biggest advantage of these two techniques is that no data structure for storing the "living" variables is needed to be maintained for garbage collection. This allows us to store variables directly in machine registers and to obtain a speed-up due to the good register optimization in compiled programs. On the other hand reference counting needs an active procedure of freeing garbage (if any) and can then slow the execution time.

6 Summary

In this paper we have presented a compiler for the ELAN programming language. The language permits us to combine deterministic and nondeterministic computations using the formalism of term rewriting systems. The resulting implementation uses a reference counting garbage collector, and do not use any additional stack (beyond the system stack) to store function's arguments and local variables. A new technique was developed to compile the non-standard control flow during the backtracking. The main theoretical contribution of this implementation is the combination of nondeterministic search with the efficient implementation techniques of deterministic rewriting without losing efficiency.

The implementation of the compiler represents an important task, it consists of about 12000 lines of (we think, intelligent) C++ code. Beyond the few presented benchmarks, the compiler has been tested on several non-trivial tasks with satisfactory results.

Acknowledgement: Many thanks to all persons contributing to this work, in particular to Peter Borovanský, Claude and Hélène Kirchner, and Pierre-Etienne Moreau.

References

[AM87] A. W. Appel and D. B. MacQueen. A Standard ML Compiler. In *Proceedings of the Conference on Functional Programming Languages and Com-*

puter Architecture, volume 274 of *Lecture Notes in Computer Science*, pages 301–324, Portland, Oregon, USA, September 14–16, 1987. Springer-Verlag.

[Aug85] L. Augustsson. Compiling pattern matching. In *Proceedings 2nd Conference on Functional Programming Languages and Computer Architecture, Nancy (France)*, volume 201 of *Lecture Notes in Computer Science*, Nancy (France), 1985. Springer-Verlag.

[DFG+94] K. Didrich, A. Fett, C. Gerke, W. Grieskamp, and P. Pepper. OPAL: Design and implementation of an algebraic programming language. In J. Gutknecht, editor, *Programming Languages and System Architectures PLSA'94*, volume 782 of *Lecture Notes in Computer Science*, pages 228–244. Springer-Verlag, March 1994.

[Frü95] T. Frühwirth. Constraint handling rules. In A. Podelski, editor, *Constraint Programming: Basics and Trends*, volume 910 of *Lecture Notes in Computer Science*. Springer-Verlag, March 1995.

[HO82] C. M. Hoffmann and M. J. O'Donnell. Pattern matching in trees. *Journal of the ACM*, 29(1):68–95, 1982.

[JK91] J.-P. Jouannaud and C. Kirchner. Solving equations in abstract algebras: a rule-based survey of unification. In J.-L. Lassez and G. Plotkin, editors, *Computational Logic. Essays in honor of Alan Robinson*, chapter 8, pages 257–321. The MIT press, Cambridge (MA, USA), 1991.

[Kap87] S. Kaplan. A compiler for conditional term rewriting system. In P. Lescanne, editor, *Proceedings 2nd Conference on Rewriting Techniques and Applications, Bordeaux (France)*, volume 256 of *Lecture Notes in Computer Science*, pages 25–41, Bordeaux (France), May 1987. Springer-Verlag.

[KKV95] C. Kirchner, H. Kirchner, and M. Vittek. Designing constraint logic programming languages using computational systems. In P. Van Hentenryck and V. Saraswat, editors, *Principles and Practice of Constraint Programming. The Newport Papers.*, pages 131–158. The MIT press, 1995.

[KL91] E. Kounalis and D. Lugiez. Compilation of pattern matching with associative commutative functions. In *16th Colloquium on Trees in Algebra and Programming*, volume 493 of *Lecture Notes in Computer Science*, pages 57–73. Springer-Verlag, 1991.

[MOM93] N. Martì-Oliet and J. Meseguer. Rewriting logic as a logical and semantical framework. Technical report, SRI International, May 1993.

[MS+93] M. Meier, J. Schimpf, et al. ECLiPSe User Manual. Technical report ECRC-93-6, ECRC, Munich (Germany), 1993.

[Vit90] M. Vittek. An efficient many-to-one unification algorithm for linear terms. (in Slovak language). In *Proceedings of the First Czechoslovak Logic Programming Conference*, 1990.

[Vit94] M. Vittek. *ELAN: Un cadre logique pour le prototypage de langages de programmation avec contraintes.* Thèse de Doctorat d'Université, Université Henri Poincaré - Nancy 1, October 1994.

[War83] D. H. D. Warren. An Abstract PROLOG Instruction Set. Technical Report 309, Artificial Intelligence Center, Computer Science and Technology Division, SRI International, Menlo Park, CA, October 1983.

Combinatory Reduction Systems with Explicit Substitution that Preserve Strong Normalisation

Roel Bloo[1] and Kristoffer H. Rose[2]

[1] Eindhoven University of Technology, PO-Box 513, NL–5600 MB Eindhoven‡
[2] BRICS, Dept. of Computer Science, University of Aarhus, DK–8000 Århus C §

Abstract. We generalise the notion of explicit substitution from the λ-calculus to *higher order rewriting*, realised by combinatory reduction systems (CRSs). For every confluent CRS, R, we construct an explicit substitution variant, Rx, which we prove confluent.

We identify a large subset of the CRSs, the *structure-preserving CRSs*, and show for any structure-preserving CRS R that Rx preserves strong normalisation of R.

We believe that this is a significant first step towards providing a methodology for reasoning about the operational properties of higher-order rewriting in general, and higher-order program transformations in particular, since confluence ensures correctness of such transformations and preservation of strong normalisation ensures that the transformations are always safe, in both cases independently of the used reduction strategy.

1 Introduction

Klop (1980) developed *combinatory reduction systems* (CRSs) to provide a syntactic model for reasoning more directly about general rewriting with binding than is possible using encodings into λ-calculus. Although operational, the CRS model shares with λ-calculus the problem that it is not implementable with constant overhead: counting β-reduction steps $(\lambda x.M)N \to M[x := N]$ does not include the size of the abstraction body M. Hence these models are not well suited as computational models for studying algorithms and implementations.

For the λ-calculus this has traditionally been addressed by defining 'abstract machines' (Landin 1964), however, such machines restrict the evaluation sequence to particular reduction strategies and thus make comparative studies and reasoning about program transformations difficult. Recently, a better solution has been proposed, namely the study of explicit (or stepwise) substitution

‡ E-mail: *bloo@win.tue.nl*, www ⟨URL: *http://www.win.tue.nl/win/cs/fm/bloo*⟩.
§ E-mail: *krisrose@brics.dk*, www ⟨URL: *http://www.brics.dk/~krisrose*⟩.

(Abadi, Cardelli, Curien and Lévy 1991) where each reduction step corresponds to a 'realistic' atomic computation and it remains possible to vary the used reduction strategy. One has to be careful that the 'refined' explicit substitution calculi preserve the desired properties of the λ-calculus; in particular termination (strong normalisation) is difficult (Melliès 1995).

This paper generalises explicit substitution to CRSs. There is a technical problem, though: the explicit substitution tradition quoted above is based on λ-calculus with indices à la de Bruijn (1972) but CRSs use 'real' variables in an essential way. Hence in this paper we study how the *named explicit substitution* principle of Rose (1992) can be applied to CRSs, by systematising the way this was done for the λxgc-calculus of Bloo and Rose (1995), which we reproduce as a case study. We assume familiarity with the λ-calculus (Barendregt 1984).

As one of the referees kindly pointed out to us, the idea of explicit substitution in higher order rewrite systems has already been studied by Duggan (1993). He only treats one specific higher order typed λ-calculus and does not prove a PSN result, whereas our approach is general and untyped. In fact, since Duggan has rules for composition of substitution similar to those of Melliès (1995), his calculus will not have PSN.

We commence in section 2 by a thorough introduction to CRSs. We then show in section 3 how one can 'explicify' substitution for arbitrary CRSs such that confluence is preserved; in section 4, we show that this construction even preserves strong normalisation for a large class of CRSs that includes most CRSs usually studied.

2 Combinatory Reduction Systems

Combinatory reduction systems (CRSs) form an expressive class of reduction systems over inductively defined terms extended with the variable binding notion of λ-calculus by formalizing precisely the intuitive notion of substitution without extra constraints such as typing, algebraic conventions, *etc.* We study CRSs in this paper because they constitute a generalisation of the rewriting done by functional programming 'evaluation steps.'

The CRS formalism was invented by Klop (1980) for a systematic treatment of combinations of term rewrite systems (TRS) with the λ-calculus, inspired by the 'definable extensions of the λ-calculus' of Aczel (1978). However, CRSs can also be understood as a form of 'higher order rewriting' (Nipkow 1991; van Oostrom and van Raamsdonk 1995).

This section gives an introduction to CRSs. The presentation is a concise adaption of the (highly recommended) survey of Klop, van Oostrom and van Raamsdonk (1993), with only a slight change of notation to facilitate induction over syntax.

Definition 1 (combinatory reduction systems).

1. An *alphabet* is a set of *function symbols* $A, B, C, F, G, \ldots$ each annotated with a *fixed arity* (notation F^n).

2. The corresponding *preterms*, denoted $t, s, \ldots$, have the inductive form

$$t ::= x \mid [x]t \mid F^n(t_1, \ldots, t_n) \mid Z^n(t_1, \ldots, t_n)$$

where $x, y, z, \ldots$ are used to denote *variables* and X, Y, Z to denote *metavariables*, each with an explicit arity superscript as indicated.[5] The four different preterm forms are called *variable*, *metaabstraction*, *construction*, and *metaapplication* of a *metavariable*, respectively.
3. We denote the *set of metavariables* occuring in a preterm t as $\text{mv}(t)$.
4. A preterm is *closed* if $\text{fv}(t) = \varnothing$ where $\text{fv}(x) = \{x\}$, $\text{fv}([x]t) = \text{fv}(t) \backslash \{x\}$, and $\text{fv}(F^n(t_1, \ldots, t_n)) = \text{fv}(Z^n(t_1, \ldots, t_n)) = \text{fv}(t_1) \cup \cdots \cup \text{fv}(t_n)$.
5. Metaterms are closed preterms considered *modulo renaming of (bound) variables*: we take as implicit the usual α-equivalence denoted $\equiv$ and defined inductively by $x \equiv x$, $[x]t \equiv [y]s$ if $t[x{:=}z] \equiv s[y{:=}z]$ for $z \notin \text{fv}(s) \cup \text{fv}(t)$, and $F^n(s_1, \ldots, s_n) \equiv F^n(t_1, \ldots, t_n)$ as well as $Z^n(s_1, \ldots, s_n) \equiv Z^n(t_1, \ldots, t_n)$ if $s_i \equiv t_i$ for each i; the renaming $t[y{:=}z]$ is defined the usual way by $x[y{:=}z] = z$ if $x = y$, $x[y{:=}z] = x$ if $x \neq y$, $([x]t)[y{:=}z] = [x']t[x{:=}x'][y{:=}z]$ with $x' \notin \text{fv}([x]t) \cup \{y, z\}$, $F^n(t_1, \ldots, t_n)[y{:=}z] = F^n(t_1[y{:=}z], \ldots, t_n[y{:=}z])$, and $Z^n(t_1, \ldots, t_n)[y{:=}z] = Z^n(t_1[y{:=}z], \ldots, t_n[y{:=}z])$.
6. A *term* is a metaterm without metavariables (but possibly including metaabstraction which is then called *abstraction*).
7. *Rewrite rules*, written $p \to r$, have the following restrictions:
   - the LHS (left hand side) p must be a *pattern*: it should be a construction, *i.e.*, the root of p is a function symbol, furthermore p should be closed and arguments of metaapplications in p should be distinct variables.
   - the RHS (right hand side) r must be a *contractor* of the LHS by which we mean that $\text{mv}(p) \supseteq \text{mv}(r)$.
8. A CRS is an alphabet together with a set of rewrite rules.

Notation 2 (syntactic restrictions). We will sometimes define the preterms of a CRS by an inductive definition such as

$$a ::= x \mid L(a) \mid A(B(a_1), [x]a_2)$$

From such a definition it is easily seen that the alphabet of the defined CRS is $\{L^1, A^2, B^1\}$. However, more importantly, the declaration restricts the free term formation such that we only need to use the specified forms in inductive arguments, *e.g.*, it can be seen that B will only occur as the first component of an A-construction. We will use such *restricted (pre/meta)-terms* freely when it is clear that the defined *restricted CRS* subsystem is closed with respect to reduction.

Remark (term rewriting systems). A CRS restricted to not allow metaabstraction at all is a *term rewrite system* (TRS, also known as *first order rewriting systems*). TRS rules consequently have only 0-ary metavariables (in TRS literature these are just called "variables" since there are no bound variables in the CRS sense).

[5] Thus for each particular alphabet the definition of preterms is finite and inductive.

Example 1 (λ-calculus). The ordinary untyped $\lambda\beta$-calculus is described by the CRS with alphabet $\{\lambda^1, @^2\}$ restricted by $t ::= x \mid \lambda([x]t) \mid @(t_1, t_2)$ (to get rid of terms like $[x]x$ and $[x](\lambda x)$), and the single rule

$$@^2(\lambda^1([x]Z^1(x)), Y^0()) \to Z^1(Y^0()) \qquad (\beta)$$

One can verify easily that (β) will reduce a restricted term to another restricted term.

The term $Z^1(Y^0())$ on the righthand side of (β) corresponds to the usual definition by substitution in that the bound variable to be substituted, x, is represented implicitly on the right side through the use of the metavariable Z^1 – informally we could have written $Z^1(Y^0())$ with ordinary substitution as something like $(Z^1(x))[x{:=}Y^0()]$.

So the λ-term $(\lambda x.yx)y$ corresponds to the CRS term $@(\lambda([x]@(y,x)), y)$ and reduces by (β) to $@(y,y)$ if $Z^1(x)$ is matched with $@(y,x)$.

Notation 3 (CRS abbreviations). We will use the usual CRS abbreviations:

- the arity superscript of function symbols and metavariables is omitted when obvious, and we omit the () after zero-ary symbols,
- $[x,y,z]t$ abbreviates the nested metaabstraction $[x][y][z]t$,
- $Fxyz.t$ abbreviates 'curried F-abstraction' $F([x](F([y](F([z]t)))))$,
- st abbreviates 'application' $@(s,t)$ (when it has no other interpretation) where $@^2$ is then included as a function symbol, and
- $\vec{x}_{(n)}$, $\vec{Z}_{(n)}$, and $\vec{t}_{(n)}$, abbreviate the sequences $x_1, \ldots, x_n$, $Z_1, \ldots, Z_n$, and $t_1, \ldots, t_n$, respectively (we omit the $\cdot_{(n)}$ subscript when redundant).

We use () to disambiguate where needed, and let application associate to the left and bind closer than abstraction – this allows ordinary conventions of rewriting and λ-calculus to be followed, *e.g.*, $\lambda xyz.xz(yz)$ denotes the rather unwieldy $\lambda^1([x](\lambda^1([y](\lambda^1([z]@^2(@^2(x,z), @^2(y,z)))))))$.

Example 2 (λ-calculus, readable CRS). Using the above abbreviations we can express the $\lambda\beta$-calculus in a more usual notation: the following CRS is exactly the same as the one in Example 1 above:

$$(\lambda x.Z(x))Y \to Z(Y) \qquad (\beta)$$

The substitution concept of CRS is reminiscent of a two-level λ-calculus in that metavariables are always applied to the list of terms that should be substituted into its body. Metavariables are therefore instantiated to 'substitute-abstractions' denoted $\underline{\lambda}\vec{x}.t$ and the resulting 'substitute-redexes' play the rôle of substitution.

Definition 4 (substitution). A *valuation* σ is a map that maps each metavariable Z^n to a *substitute* $\underline{\lambda}(\vec{x}_{(n)}).t$ where the x_i are distinct and t is a preterm. Valuations are homomorphically extended to metaterms: $\sigma(t)$ denotes the result of first inserting $\sigma(Z)$ for each metavariable Z in t and then replacing all the resulting *substitutions* $(\underline{\lambda}(\vec{x}_{(n)}).t)(\vec{t}_{(n)})$ by $t[x_1{:=}t_1,\ldots,x_n{:=}t_n]$ defined inductively by

$$
\begin{aligned}
x_i[\vec{x}:=\vec{t}\,] &\equiv t_i \\
y[\vec{x}:=\vec{t}\,] &\equiv y \qquad y \notin \{\vec{x}\} \\
([y]t)[\vec{x}:=\vec{t}\,] &\equiv [y](t[\vec{x}:=\vec{t}\,]) \qquad y \notin \{\vec{x}\} \\
([x_i]t)[\vec{x}:=\vec{t}\,] &\equiv [x_i](t[x_1{:=}t_1,\ldots,x_{i-1}{:=}t_{i-1},x_{i+1}{:=}t_{i+1},\ldots,x_n{:=}t_n]) \\
F^m(\vec{s})[\vec{x}:=\vec{t}\,] &\equiv F^m(s_1[\vec{x}:=\vec{t}\,],\ldots,s_m[\vec{x}:=\vec{t}\,]) \\
Z^m(\vec{s})[\vec{x}:=\vec{t}\,] &\equiv Z^m(s_1[\vec{x}:=\vec{t}\,],\ldots,s_m[\vec{x}:=\vec{t}\,])
\end{aligned}
$$

(the last case exists because one metavariable may be mapped to another when we allow reduction of metaterms). We say that s *matches* t when there exists a valuation σ such that $\sigma(s) \equiv t$.

A lot of complexity is hidden in the requirement that valuations be 'homomorphically extended' to metaterms because of the risk of name clashes. This is solved by the following definition which turns out to be a sufficient restriction for avoiding name conflicts.

Definition 5 (safeness).

1. The *bound variables* of a preterm, $\mathrm{bv}(t)$, are defined inductively as $\mathrm{bv}(x) = \varnothing$, $\mathrm{bv}([x]t) = \{x\} \cup \mathrm{bv}(t)$, $\mathrm{bv}(F^n(\vec{t}_{(n)})) = \mathrm{bv}(Z^n(\vec{t}_{(n)})) = \mathrm{bv}(t_1) \cup \cdots \cup \mathrm{bv}(t_n)$.
2. The rewrite rule $p \to t$ is *safe for the valuation* σ if for p and t considered as preterms
$$\forall Z \in \mathrm{mv}(p)\ \forall x \in \mathrm{fv}(\sigma(Z)) : x \notin (\mathrm{bv}(p) \cup \mathrm{bv}(t))$$
3. The valuation σ is *safe with respect to itself* if
$$\forall Z, Z' : \mathrm{fv}(\sigma(Z)) \cap \mathrm{bv}(\sigma(Z')) = \varnothing$$

Thus a CRS inherits the implicit complexity of the λ-calculus renaming, and resolves it in the same way by a generalised form of *variable convention*:

Convention 6 (variable convention). Any valuation used is assumed safe with respect to itself, and any rule it will be used with is assumed safe with respect to it.

Clearly a safe variant can be obtained for any valuation in any context by renaming of some bound variables. This renaming is harmless since we consider metaterms modulo renaming.

Remark. It may seem contradictory that we discuss free variables at all considering that all metaterms are closed. This is because we may 'reduce under binding': a redex occurrence can easily be rooted inside an abstraction and thus have locally free variables.

Definition 7 (match). Given a rule $p \to r$, some valuation σ (assumed safe in all contexts below, of course) defined such that $\sigma(p)$ is a term, and some context $C[\,]$. Then

1. $C[\sigma(p)]$ is *reducible*, $\sigma(p)$ is the *redex*, and $C[\,]$ is its *occurrence*.
2. $C[\sigma(r)]$ is the *contractum* of the rule, and
3. the pair $C[\sigma(p)] \to C[\sigma(t)]$ is a *rewrite* of the rule.

(in all cases we add "with match valuation σ" if appropriate). If $\sigma(p)$ is allowed to be a *metaterm* then we correspondingly define *metaredex*, *metacontractum*, and *metarewrite*, in fact we will use *metaX* to designate the property X of metarewriting.

Definition 8 (reduction). For a CRS R, *R-reduction* is the relation $\xrightarrow[R]{}$ generated by all rewrites possible with rewrites using rules from R. $\twoheadrightarrow_R$ is the symmetric closure of $\twoheadrightarrow_R$ and $=_R$ is the symmetric, reflexive, and transitive closure of $\xrightarrow[R]{}$.

3 Explicit Substitutes

In this section we show how the explicit substitution idea developed for the λ-calculus can be generalised to CRS systems, and in particular we show that there is a translation from an explicit substitution CRS to the original CRS.

This brings us part of the way towards being able to use the CRS reduction count as a complexity measure in that we eliminate 'deep substitution'. The technique used is the same as for the λ-calculus: to perform substitution in a stepwise manner, or, put differently, to change metaredexes to use 'explicit substitutes', such that only *local term knowledge* is used in the rewriting.

First we demonstrate the idea as it was developed for a particular CRS, namely the λ-calculus. Then we identify a subclass of CRSs that has 'explicit substitution' and show that every confluent CRS can be transformed into a confluent CRS in this class.

Example 3 (λxgc-reduction as CRS). λxgc is the CRS over terms

$$t ::= x \mid \lambda x.t \mid t_1 t_2 \mid \Sigma([x]t_1, t_2)$$

with λxgc-CRS rules

$$(\lambda x.Z(x))Y \to \Sigma([x]Z(x), Y) \qquad \text{(b)}$$

$$\Sigma([x]x, Y) \to Y \qquad \text{(xv)}$$

$$\Sigma([x]Z, Y) \to Z \qquad \text{(xgc)}$$

$$\Sigma([x]\lambda y.Z(x,y), Y) \to \lambda y.\Sigma([x]Z(x,y), Y) \qquad \text{(xab)}$$

$$\Sigma([x]\,(Z_1(x))(Z_2(x)), Y) \to (\Sigma([x]Z_1(x), Y))(\Sigma([x]Z_2(x), Y)) \qquad \text{(xap)}$$

It is instructive to compare this system to the definition of λxgc in Bloo and Rose (1995): they are identical except for syntax conventions (for instance the λxgc-term $x\langle x := \lambda y.y\rangle$ corresponds to $\Sigma([x]x, \lambda y.y)$).

Furthermore, the requirement that all metaterms are closed prohibits free variables in CRS rules, which means that all free variables must be 'hidden' inside metavariables (to which they are not given as parameters). This means that we cannot distinguish between substituting a free variable (λxgc rule (xvgc)) and the more general garbage collection (λxgc rule (gc)): both are special cases of the rule (xgc) above.

This is not an orthogonal CRS. Yet it is confluent as proven in Bloo and Rose (1995) and as a consequence of the following.

The key observation in the development for the λ-calculus is that no knowledge of the 'depth' of terms is needed in order to reduce the rules. In the example rules above this is manifest in the fact that all metaapplications on both LHS and RHS have the ***same variables on both sides*** which means that no substitution is needed because it would be a trivial substitution. This is formalised as follows.

Definition 9 (explicit substitution CRS). A CRS R is an *explicit substitution CRS* or simply *ESCRS*, if all metaapplications in the RHS of a rule occur in the form $Z(\vec{x})$ such that $Z(\vec{x})$ also occurs in the LHS of that same rule.[6] The individual metaapplications in RHSs obeying this will be called *explicit metaapplications*.

Since all metavariables of a CRS rule must occur in the LHS in the form $Z(\vec{x})$ this definition means that each metaapplication of Z in that rule is metaapplied to the same list of variables as in the LHS. Recall that the intention is to avoid having to perform substitution. Here are some small sample CRSs that are and are not explicit.

Example 4 (explicit and nonexplicit CRSs). 1. $A([x,y]B(X(x),Y)) \to X(Y)$ *is not* an ESCRS because we have to substitute Y for any occurrence of x in whatever matched $X(x)$.
2. $A([x,y]B(x,y)) \to A([x,y]B(C,x))$ *is* an ESCRS because it contains no metaaplications!
3. $A([x,y]B(X(x,y))) \to A([x]X(x,x))$ *is not* an ESCRS because we need to change one of the variables *inside* what matched $X(x,y)$.

Another interesting observation which we can carry over from the study of explicit substitution for the λ-calculus is that substitution does not depend on the context in which it is created. This insight can be used to *create an ESCRS automatically from a CRS* in a manner that ensures that confluence is preserved by simply 'unfolding' the definition of substitutes (Definition 4) into the new rules.

Definition 10 (CRS explicification). Given a CRS R with alphabet F_i^n. The ESCRS Rx is obtained by the steps listed in Fig. 1. If R defined the relation $\to$ then we will denote the relation defined by Rx as $\xrightarrow[\text{ie}]{}$; the subrelation consisting of

[6] This implies that the variables in $\vec{x}$ are distinct

only the introduction rules (with name (r-x)) is denoted $\underset{\mathrm{i}}{\rightarrow}$, and the subrelation containing only the substitution distribution and elimination rules (with names (x-$*$)) is denoted $\underset{\mathrm{e}}{\rightarrow}$. Note that there are no rules for interaction between two substitutions.

Example 5. The system λx generated this way for the λ-calculus with the rule

$$(\lambda x.Z(x))Y \to Z(Y) \qquad (\beta)$$

is the following:[7]

$$\begin{aligned}
(\lambda x.Z(x))Y &\to \Sigma([x]Z(x), Y) && (\beta\text{-x})\\
\Sigma([x](Z_1(x))(Z_2(x)), Y) &\to (\Sigma([x]Z_1(x), Y))(\Sigma([x]Z_2(x), Y)) && (\text{x-@})\\
\Sigma([x]\lambda(Z(x)), Y) &\to \lambda(\Sigma([x]Z(x), Y)) && (\text{x-}\lambda)\\
\Sigma([x]x, Y) &\to Y && (\text{xv})\\
\Sigma([x]Z, Y) &\to Z && (\text{xgc})\\
\Sigma([x,y]Z(x,y), Y) &\to [y]\Sigma([x]Z(x,y), Y) && (\text{xma})
\end{aligned}$$

It is the same as the λxgc CRS shown above except that the abstraction distribution rule (xab) has been split into two steps: (x-λ) and (xma). As a consequence, a restricted term need not reduce to a restricted term (but another reduction step can fix this). To prevent this, one can define the explicification more cautiously for CRSs with restricted terms (this means that some $\underset{\mathrm{e}}{\rightarrow}$ steps are forced to be followed by other $\underset{\mathrm{e}}{\rightarrow}$ steps).

Proposition 11. *For any CRS R, Rx is an ESCRS.*

Remark. The procedure is *idempotent*: when applied to an ESCRS nothing is added since no non-explicit metaabstractions exist. Also notice that the elimination and distribution rules only depend on the alphabet.

The remainder of this section is devoted to showing that an ESCRS is a conservative extension of the original CRS.

Proposition 12. *For a confluent CRS* $\rightarrow$*,* $\underset{\mathrm{e}}{\rightarrow}$ *is confluent and strongly normalising.*

Proof sketch. Completeness of $\underset{\mathrm{e}}{\rightarrow}$ is shown by first establishing $\underset{\mathrm{e}}{\rightarrow}$ SN by defining a map dominating the longest reduction length similarly as for λxgc in Bloo and Rose (1995); $\underset{\mathrm{e}}{\rightarrow}$ LC follows from a simple investigation of the critical pairs between the (xgc-n) rules and the other rules (this amounts to understanding that 'garbage collection' can be postponed without risk). □

It is not difficult to extend this result to reduction on metaterms.

[7] Generated automatically from (β) by the program developed by the second author.

Restricted terms. The restricted terms of the CRS Rx are defined by extending the syntax for R with the clause $\Sigma^{n+1}([\vec{x}]t, \vec{t})$ where $\Sigma^2, \ldots$ is a series of new function symbols added to the alphabet as needed in the substitution introduction rules below; here (and below) unmarked vectors such as $\vec{x}$ and $\vec{t}$ are assumed to have length n. Terms that do not contain subterms of the form $\Sigma^{n+1}([\vec{x}]s, \vec{t})$ will be called *pure*.

Substitution introduction. For each rule (r) of R construct a new rule (r-x) of Rx by replacing in the RHS all non-explicit metaapplications $Z^n(\vec{t})$ by the construction

$$\Sigma^{n+1}([\vec{x}]Z^n(\vec{x}_{(n)}), \vec{t}_{(n)})$$

Hence the arities of non-explicit metaapplications decide which new function symbols we need.

Stepwise substitution distribution. For each Σ^{n+1} symbol add a rule

$$\Sigma^{n+1}([\vec{x}][y]Z(\vec{x}, y), \vec{X}) \to [y]\Sigma([\vec{x}]Z(\vec{x}, y), \vec{X}) \qquad \text{(xma-}n\text{)}$$

and for each possible Σ^{n+1}, F^m pair add a rule

$$\Sigma^{n+1}([\vec{x}]F^m(Z_1(\vec{x}), \ldots, Z_m(\vec{x})), \vec{X}) \qquad \text{(x-}F^m\text{-}n\text{)}$$
$$\to F^m(\Sigma^{n+1}([\vec{x}]Z_1(\vec{x}), \vec{X}), \ldots, \Sigma^{n+1}([\vec{x}]Z_m(\vec{x}), \vec{X}))$$

Substitution elimination. For each Σ^{n+1} add for each $i \in \{1, \ldots, n\}$ two rules

$$\Sigma^{n+1}([\vec{x}]x_i, \vec{X}) \to X_i \qquad \text{(xv-}n\text{-}i\text{)}$$

$$\Sigma^{n+1}([\vec{x}]Z(\vec{x}\,'), \vec{X}) \to \begin{cases} Z & \text{if } n = 1 \\ \Sigma^n([\vec{x}\,']Z(\vec{x}\,'), \vec{X}\,') & \text{if } n > 1 \end{cases} \qquad \text{(xgc-}n\text{-}i\text{)}$$

where

$$\vec{x}\,' = (x_1, \ldots, x_{i-1}, x_{i+1}, \ldots, x_n)$$
$$\vec{X}\,' = (X_1, \ldots, X_{i-1}, X_{i+1}, \ldots, X_n)$$

(thus the LHS of (xgc-n-i) includes the abstraction for x_i in the variable list and the corresponding element X_i of the substitution body but not in the parameter list $Z(\vec{x}\,')$; the RHS excludes x_i in the metaabstraction and X_i in the right hand side).

We write $\xrightarrow[\text{xgc}]{}$ for the union of all (xgc-n-i) rules.

Fig. 1. Explicification of CRS R into ESCRS Rx.

Next we relate single reductions and then build the components of the proof of multiple reduction equivalence (in this paper nf e(t) denotes the unique $\underset{e}{\rightarrow}$-nf of t, and $\underset{e}{\twoheadrightarrow\!\!|}$ the restriction of $\underset{e}{\twoheadrightarrow}$ to reductions to normal forms).

Lemma 13 (representation). *For terms* t, t_1,

$$\mathrm{nf\,e}(\Sigma([\vec{x}]t, \vec{t})) \equiv \mathrm{nf\,e}(t)[\vec{x} := \mathrm{nf\,e}(\vec{t})]$$

(where we mean parallel substitution).

Proof. This is the 'substitution lemma' of the λ-calculus in disguise; first we prove it (by induction on the number of symbols in the sequence $t, t_1, \ldots, t_n$) for pure terms t, then the Lemma is an easy consequence. □

Lemma 14 (projection & injection). *1. For terms* s, t,
.

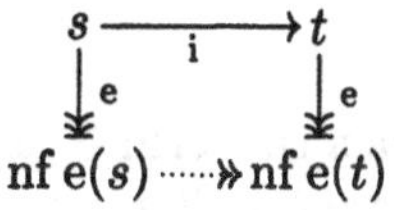

2. For pure terms s, t,
.

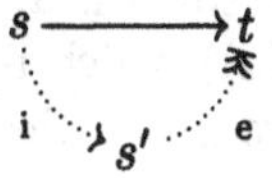

Proof. 1 is by induction over the structure of Rx-metaterms, using Lemma 13; 2 is a simple consequence of Lemma 13 and the fact that the R-rules and Rx-introduction rules have the same redexes. □

Theorem 15. *For R-terms s, t, $s \underset{ie}{\twoheadrightarrow} t$ iff $s \twoheadrightarrow t$.*

Proof. First observe that the R-terms s, t are in e-normal form when considered as Rx-terms. Then use Lemma 14:

Case $\Leftarrow$: Assume $s \twoheadrightarrow t$; the case then follows by induction on the length of the $\twoheadrightarrow$-reduction, using Lemma 14.2 in each step.

Case $\Rightarrow$: Assume $s \underset{ie}{\twoheadrightarrow} t$ and $s, t \in R$. We will do induction on the length of the $\underset{ie}{\twoheadrightarrow}$-reduction and prove

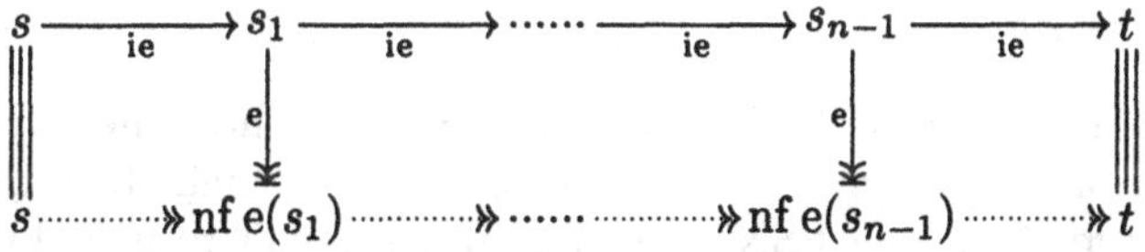

Each $\underset{ie}{\rightarrow}$-step is either $\underset{i}{\rightarrow}$ or $\underset{e}{\rightarrow}$ for which we need Lemma 14.1 and confluence of $\underset{e}{\rightarrow}$, respectively. □

An easy consequence of all this is the main result of this section.

Corollary 16. *If R is confluent then Rx is confluent.*

Proof. If $t \underset{ie}{\twoheadrightarrow} s_1$ and $t \underset{ie}{\twoheadrightarrow} s_2$ then by Lemma 14.1 we have both $\mathrm{nf\,e}(t) \twoheadrightarrow \mathrm{nf\,e}(s_1)$ and $\mathrm{nf\,e}(t) \twoheadrightarrow \mathrm{nf\,e}(s_2)$, now use confluence of $\twoheadrightarrow$ and Theorem 15. □

Several additional aspects of explicification of CRSs are discussed in Rose (1996).

4 Preservation of Strong Normalisation

In this section we investigate the termination behaviour of an ESCRS with respect to the corresponding CRS. We show that for a large subclass of CRSs, explicifying the reduction preserves strong normalisation of terms.

First we show by some examples that not all CRSs have the PSN property, then we define the subclass of *structure preserving CRSs* and show PSN for it.

Definition 17. We say that an explicification Rx has PSN if $\mathrm{SN}_R \subseteq \mathrm{SN}_{R\mathrm{x}}$.

Example 6. Consider the CRS R_1:

$$F(a) \to F(a)$$
$$G([x]X(x), Y) \to X(F(Y))$$

Then the term $G([x]a, a)$ is SN since its only reduct is a. But in the ESCRS R_1x, the term $G([x]a, a)$ can reduce to $\Sigma([x]a, F(a))$ which reduces to itself.

We see that R_1x does not have PSN. Two properties of R_1 can be indicated for causing this failure of PSN:

- R_1 has a circular rule, and
- R_1 has a rule that creates new structure as argument of a meta-application.

The second property is absent in λ-calculus; indeed the proof of PSN for λxgc (see Bloo and Rose 1995) depends on the fact that newly created substitutions contain subterms that were already present in the term before these substitutions were created.

Example 7. Consider the CRS R_2, an extension of λ-calculus with the 3-ary symbol F and the rule $F(\lambda x.X(x), \lambda y.Y(y), Z) \;\to\; X(Y(Z))$ Then the term $F(\lambda x.I, \lambda y.yy, \lambda z.zz)$ is strongly normalising since its only reduct is $\lambda x.I$. But in R_2x, $F(\lambda x.I, \lambda y.yy, \lambda z.zz)$ reduces to $\Sigma([x]I, \Sigma([y]yy, \lambda z.zz))$ which reduces in three steps to $\Sigma([x]I, (\lambda z.zz)(\lambda z.zz))$; a term with Ω as subterm. Hence R_2x does not have PSN.

We see that an ESCRS Rx may fail PSN if R has rules that create new structure as an argument of a metaapplication. We shall show that this is the only reason for failure of PSN. Therefore it seems fair to introduce a name for CRSs that do not create such new structure.

Definition 18. A CRS is called *structure preserving* if, for any rule, any argument of any metaapplication in the RHS is a true subterm of the LHS of that rule.

Note that λ-calculus is structure preserving whereas R_1 and R_2 are not.

We start our proof of PSN for structure preserving CRSs by considering (similar to PSN for λxgc in Bloo and Rose 1995) a calculus in between CRSs and ESCRSs.

For the rest of this section, let R be a CRS and Rx the corresponding ESCRS.

Definition 19. 1. A substitution $\Sigma([\vec{x}]t', \vec{t})$ contains *garbage* if, for some i, $x_i \notin \mathrm{fv}(t')$.

2. An *R*x term is called *garbage-free* if it contains no garbage.
3. *Garbage-free reduction* is $\xrightarrow[\mathrm{gf}]{} = \xrightarrow[\mathrm{ie}]{} \cdot \xrightarrow[\mathrm{xgc}]{}\!\!\!\!\twoheadrightarrow$, that is, a $\xrightarrow[\mathrm{gf}]{}$ step consists of some $\xrightarrow[\mathrm{ie}]{}$ reduction followed by complete garbage collection.
4. nf xgc(t) is used to denote the xgc-normal form of t.

Lemma 20. *1.* $\Sigma^{n+1}([\vec{y}_{(n)}]\Sigma^{m+1}([\vec{x}_{(m)}]s, \vec{t}_{(m)}), \vec{u}_{(n)}) \overset{}{\underset{\mathrm{ie}}{\twoheadleftarrow\!\!\!\twoheadrightarrow}}$
$\Sigma^{m+1}([\vec{x}]\Sigma^{n+1}([\vec{y}_{(n)}]s, \vec{u}_{(n)}), \Sigma^{n+1}([\vec{y}_{(n)}]t_1, \vec{u}_{(n)}), \ldots, \Sigma^{n+1}([\vec{y}_{(n)}]t_m, \vec{u}_{(n)}))$.

2. If t is garbage-free and $t \xrightarrow[\mathrm{i}]{} s$ *then* nf e(t, ⸍ nf e(s).
3. $\mathrm{SN}_R \subseteq \mathrm{SN}_{Rgf}$.

Proof. 1. Use Lemma 13 and the substitution lemma for parallel substitution, *i.e.*, for pure terms $s', \vec{t}', \vec{u}'$,
$s'[\vec{x}_{(m)}{:=}\vec{t}'_{(m)}][\vec{y}{:=}\vec{u}'] \equiv s'[\vec{y}{:=}\vec{u}'][x_1{:=}t'_1[\vec{y}{:=}\vec{u}'], \ldots, x_m{:=}t'_m[\vec{y}{:=}\vec{u}']]$.

2. We prove this by induction on the structure of t. We treat one case: $t \equiv \Sigma([\vec{x}]s, \vec{u})$. The reduction must take place inside s or one of u_i. If it is inside a u_i then since t is garbage-free, nf e(u_i) will be substituted somewhere in nf e(t) $\equiv$ nf e(s)$[\vec{x} {:=}$ nf e$(\vec{u})]$, hence the reduction does not disappear.
3. We project garbage-free reductions to R-reductions: any garbage-free reduction is of the form $t_1\, (\xrightarrow[\mathrm{e}]{} \cdot \xrightarrow[\mathrm{xgc}]{}\!\!\!\!\twoheadrightarrow)^*\, t_2 \xrightarrow[\mathrm{i}]{} \cdot \xrightarrow[\mathrm{xgc}]{}\!\!\!\!\twoheadrightarrow t_3\, (\xrightarrow[\mathrm{e}]{} \cdot \xrightarrow[\mathrm{xgc}]{}\!\!\!\!\twoheadrightarrow)^*\, t_4 \xrightarrow[\mathrm{i}]{} \cdot \xrightarrow[\mathrm{xgc}]{}\!\!\!\!\twoheadrightarrow t_5 \cdots$ (since $\xrightarrow[\mathrm{e}]{}$ is SN); then we project to get a reduction nf e(t_1) $\equiv$ nf e(t_2) $\overset{+}{\twoheadrightarrow}$ nf e(t_3) $\equiv$ nf e(t_4) $\overset{+}{\twoheadrightarrow}$ nf e(t_5) $\cdots$. Now if the first reduction is infinite then its projection is infinite, too. □

Now we subdivide *R*x-reduction into two disjoint parts, reductions that are related to garbage and the others:

Definition 21. *Garbage-reduction* is defined as the union of $\xrightarrow[\mathrm{xgc}]{}$ and the contextual closure of the following rules:

$$\Sigma([\vec{x}]t, \vec{s}) \to \Sigma([\vec{x}]t, \vec{s}\,')$$
$$\text{if } s_i \xrightarrow[\mathrm{ie}]{} s'_i,\ x_i \notin \mathrm{fv}(\mathrm{nf\,xgc}(t)) \text{ and } \vec{s}\,' = (s_1, \ldots, s'_i, \ldots, s_n)$$
$$\Sigma([\vec{x}]F^m(\vec{t}), \vec{s}) \to F^m(\Sigma([\vec{x}]t_1, \vec{s}), \ldots, \Sigma([\vec{x}]t_m, \vec{s}))$$
$$\text{if for some } i,\ x_i \notin \mathrm{fv}(\mathrm{nf\,xgc}(F^m(\vec{t})))$$
$$\Sigma([\vec{x}][y]t, \vec{s}) \to [y]\Sigma([\vec{x}]t, \vec{s})$$
$$\text{if for some } i,\ x_i \notin \mathrm{fv}(\mathrm{nf\,xgc}([y]t))$$

Note that we use the free variable expression fv(nf xgc(·)) to ensure that garbage collection does not create new garbage-reduction redexes. Note also that in the last two rules it is only required that one of the x_i doesn't occur in fv(nf xgc(·)). Therefore garbage-reduction should be understood as 'all reductions that affect garbage'.

Outside-garbage-reduction is defined as any reduction which is not garbage-reduction; this is equivalent to saying that the contracted redex has no descendant in the xgc-normalform.

With this we can prove the following by induction on the structure of terms.

Proposition 22. *If* $t \underset{\text{ie}}{\rightarrow} s$ *is outside garbage then* $\text{nf}\,\text{xgc}(t) \rightarrow \text{nf}\,\text{xgc}(s)$.

Definition 23. We say s_i *is body of a substitution in* t if for some $t', x, \vec{s}$, $\Sigma([\vec{x}]t', \vec{s})$ is a subterm of t. The predicate $\text{subSN}(t)$ should be read to be *all bodies of substitutions in t are strongly normalising for* $\underset{\text{ie}}{\rightarrow}$*-reduction.*

The following lemma expresses our intuition about garbage-reduction.

Lemma 24. *1. If* $\text{subSN}(t)$ *and* $t \underset{\text{ie}}{\rightarrow} s$ *is garbage-reduction, then* $\text{subSN}(s)$.
2. If $\text{subSN}(t)$ *then t is strongly normalising for garbage-reduction.*

Proof. 1. Induction on the structure of t.
2. Let $h_1(t)$ denote the maximal number of $\underset{\text{ie}}{\rightarrow}$-reduction steps that t can perform (finite if t is $\underset{\text{ie}}{\rightarrow}$-SN). Define h_2 by

$$\begin{aligned} h_2(x) &= 1 \\ h_2([x]t) &= h_2(t) + 1 \\ h_2(F^m(t_1, \ldots, t_m)) &= h_2(t_1) + \cdots + h_2(t_m) + 1 \\ h_2(\Sigma([\vec{x}]t, \vec{s})) &= h_2(t) \times \left(\sum_i (h_1(s_i)) + 1 \right) \end{aligned}$$

Then one can show: if $\text{subSN}(t)$ then $h_2(t)$ is well-defined and finite; if $\text{subSN}(t)$ and $t \underset{\text{ie}}{\rightarrow} s$ is garbage-reduction then $h_2(t) > h_2(s)$. □

Definition 25. Define for all Rx-terms t, $\#\text{gf}(t)$ to be the maximum length of garbage-free reduction paths starting in $\text{nf}\,\text{xgc}(t)$. Note that $\#\text{gf}(t)$ can be infinite.

With this we can express our main result.

Theorem 26. *Let R be a structure preserving CRS with rewrite relation* $\rightarrow$*, let Rx be the explicification of R, and let t be an Rx-term.*
If $\#\text{gf}(t) < \infty$ *and* $\text{subSN}(t)$ *then t is strongly normalising for* $\underset{\text{ie}}{\rightarrow}$*-reduction.*

Proof. Induction on $\#\text{gf}(M)$. If $\#\text{gf}(t) = 0$ then t can only do garbage reductions, hence by Lemma 24.2, t is $\underset{\text{ie}}{\rightarrow}$-SN.

Now suppose $\#\text{gf}(t) > 0$ and we know that for all terms t' such that $\text{subSN}(t')$ and $\#\text{gf}(t') < \#\text{gf}(t)$, t' is $\underset{\text{ie}}{\rightarrow}$-SN. Knowing this, we can prove by induction on the structure of the term t that for any $\underset{\text{ie}}{\rightarrow}$-reduct t' of t, $\text{subSN}(t')$. For this we only need to consider one-step reducts of t. We treat some cases:

Case $t \equiv F^m(t_1, \cdots, t_m) \underset{\text{ie}}{\rightarrow} F^m(t_1, \cdots, t'_m) \equiv t'$. Then $\text{subSN}(t_m)$, $\#\text{gf}(t_m) \leq \#\text{gf}(t)$ so by the second induction hypothesis (the structure of t_m is simpler than the structure of t), $\text{subSN}(t'_m)$, hence $\text{subSN}(t')$.

Case $t \equiv \Sigma([\vec{x}]x_i, \vec{s}) \underset{\text{ie}}{\rightarrow} s_i$. Then subSN($t$) implies subSN($s_i$).

Case t reduces at the root by an introduction step to t'. Now since R is structure preserving, all substitutions $\Sigma([\vec{x}]s, \vec{s}')$ in t' were either present in t, hence all its s_i' are $\underset{\text{ie}}{\rightarrow}$-SN, or s_i' was a true subterm of t. Consider these s_i': subSN(s_i') since subSN(t). Furthermore, since s_i' is a true subterm of t, either s_i' is subterm of garbage in t or $\#\text{gf}(s_i') < \#\text{gf}(t)$. In the first subcase s_i' is $\underset{\text{ie}}{\rightarrow}$-SN since subSN($t$), in the second subcase s_i' is $\underset{\text{ie}}{\rightarrow}$-SN by the first induction hypothesis.

Since garbage-reduction is strongly normalising, any reduction from t must either be finite or start like $t \underset{\text{ie}}{\twoheadrightarrow} t'' \underset{\text{ie}}{\rightarrow} t'$ where the first part is garbage-reduction and $t'' \underset{\text{ie}}{\rightarrow} t'$ is outside-garbage-reduction. Then $\#\text{gf}(t) = \#\text{gf}(t'') > \#\text{gf}(t')$ and by what we just proved, subSN(t'), hence by the induction hypothesis, t' is $\underset{\text{ie}}{\rightarrow}$-SN. Therefore, t is $\underset{\text{ie}}{\rightarrow}$-SN. □

Corollary 27 (PSN for Rx). *Let R be a structure preserving CRS with rewrite relation* $\rightarrow$ *and let Rx be its explicification. An R-term is strongly normalising for* $\rightarrow$*-reduction if and only if it is strongly normalising for* $\underset{\text{ie}}{\rightarrow}$*-reduction.*

Proof. **Case** $\Rightarrow$. If t is an R-term then subSN(t) and if t is strongly normalising for $\rightarrow$-reduction then by Lemma 20.3, $\#\text{gf}(t) < \infty$. Now use Theorem 26.

Case $\Leftarrow$. By Lemma 14.2 infinite $\rightarrow$-reductions induce infinite $\underset{\text{ie}}{\rightarrow}$-ones. □

5 Conclusions

We have generalised the notion of explicit substitution to CRS, *cf.* Klop et al. (1993, problem 15(h)), and shown that the derived ESCRS systems inherit the essential properties of the original CRS, notably confluence, and that strong normalisation is preserved for a particular large subset of CRSs.

This leads to several interesting considerations, mostly generalising problems known from explicit substitution for λ-calculus. The following are especially promising:

- Investigate whether the technique is applicable to other forms of higher order rewriting, in particular the notion of 'substitution calculus' (van Oostrom and van Raamsdonk 1995) suggests that one could study 'abstract explicit substitution.'
- Integration of sharing and cyclic substitution (Rose 1992; Ariola and Klop 1994). Some progress has been made, in particular the relation to functional programming languages and in general constructing realistic notions of 'computational models' based on ESCRS (Rose 1996). This requires extensions to the CRS formalism because the *matching time* must also be taken into account.
- Derive abstract machines 'implementing' orthogonal CRS through their ESCRS; in particular investigate the use of a namefree notation (de Bruijn 1972) similar to Duggan's (1993).

References

Abàdi, M., Cardelli, L., Curien, P.-L. and Lévy, J.-J. (1991). Explicit substitutions. *Journal of Functional Programming* 1(4): 375–416.

Aczel, P. (1978). A general Church-Rosser theorem. *Technical report.* Univ. of Manchester.

Ariola, Z. M. and Klop, J. W. (1994). Cyclic lambda graph rewriting. *Proceedings, Ninth Annual IEEE Symposium on Logic in Computer Science.* IEEE Computer Society Press. Paris, France. pp. 416–425. full version forthcoming (Ariola and Klop 1995).

Ariola, Z. M. and Klop, J. W. (1995). Lambda calculus with explicit recursion. Personal Communication.

Barendregt, H. P. (1984). *The Lambda Calculus: Its Syntax and Semantics.* Revised edn. North-Holland.

Bloo, R. and Rose, K. H. (1995). Preservation of strong normalisation in named lambda calculi with explicit substitution and garbage collection. *CSN '95 - Computer Science in the Netherlands.* pp. 62–72. ⟨URL: *ftp://ftp.diku.dk/diku/semantics/papers/D-246.ps*⟩

de Bruijn, N. G. (1972). Lambda calculus notation with nameless dummies, a tool for automatic formula manipulation with application to the Church-Rosser theorem. *Koninklijke Nederlandse Akademie van Wetenschappen, Series A, Mathematical Sciences* 75: 381–392. Also chapter C.2 of (Nederpelt, Geuvers and de Vrijer 1994).

Duggan, D. (1993). Higher-order substitution. *UW TR CS-93-44.* Dept. of Computer Science, University of Waterloo. Waterloo, Ontario, Canada N2L 3G1. ⟨URL: *http://nuada.uwaterloo.ca/~dduggan/papers/*⟩

Klop, J. W. (1980). *Combinatory Reduction Systems.* PhD thesis. University of Utrecht. Also available as Mathematical Centre Tracts 127.

Klop, J. W., van Oostrom, V. and van Raamsdonk, F. (1993). Combinatory reduction systems: Introduction and survey. *Theoretical Computer Science* 121: 279–308.

Landin, P. J. (1964). The mechanical evaluation of expressions. *Computer Journal* 6: 308–320.

Melliès, P.-A. (1995). Typed λ-calculi with explicit substitution may not terminate. *In* Dezani, M. (ed.), *Int. Conf. on Typed Lambda Calculus and Applications.* LNCS. U of Edinburgh. Springer-Verlag. Edinburgh, Scotland. pp. 328–334.

Nederpelt, R. P., Geuvers, J. H. and de Vrijer, R. C. (eds) (1994). *Selected Papers on Automath.* Vol. 133 of *Studies in Logic.* North-Holland.

Nipkow, T. (1991). Higher-order critical pairs. *Proceedings, Sixth Annual IEEE Symposium on Logic in Computer Science.* IEEE Computer Society Press. Amsterdam, The Netherlands. pp. 342–349.

Rose, K. H. (1992). Explicit cyclic substitutions. *In* Rusinowitch, M. and Rémy, J.-L. (eds), *CTRS '92—3rd International Workshop on Conditional Term Rewriting Systems.* Number 656 in *LNCS.* Springer-Verlag. Pont-a-Mousson, France. pp. 36–50. ⟨URL: *ftp://ftp.diku.dk/diku/semantics/papers/D-143.ps*⟩

Rose, K. H. (1996). *Operational Reduction Models for Functional Programming Languages.* PhD thesis. DIKU (University of Copenhagen). Universitetsparken 1, DK-2100 København Ø. DIKU report 96/1.

van Oostrom, V. and van Raamsdonk, F. (1995). Weak orthogonality implies confluence: the higher-order case. *Technical Report CS-R9501.* CWI.

Confluence Properties of Extensional and Non-Extensional λ-Calculi with Explicit Substitutions (Extended Abstract)

Delia Kesner

CNRS and LRI, Bât 490, Université Paris-Sud - 91405 Orsay Cedex, France.
e-mail:Delia.Kesner@lri.fr

Abstract. This paper studies confluence properties of extensional and non-extensional λ-calculi with explicit substitutions, where extensionality is interpreted by η-expansion. For that, we propose a general scheme for explicit substitutions which describes those abstract properties that are sufficient to guarantee confluence. Our general scheme makes it possible to treat at the same time many well-known calculi such as λ_σ, $\lambda_{\sigma_\Uparrow}$ and λ_υ, or some other new calculi that we propose in this paper. We also show for those calculi not fitting in the general scheme that can be translated to another one fitting the scheme, such as λ_s, how to reason about confluence properties of their extensional and non-extensional versions.

1 Introduction

The λ-calculus is a convenient framework to study functional programming, where the evaluation process is modeled by β-reduction. The main mechanism used to perform β-reduction is *substitution*, which is a meta-level operation in classical λ-calculus as in λ-calculus à la de Bruijn whereas it is incorporated into the language when using the formalism of λ-calculi with explicit substitutions.

When working with functions, an *extensional* equality is also necessary to reason about programs. Extensionality means that whenever two programs yield the same result for every possible argument, they are equal. The classical extensional axiom in the theory of λ-calculus is the η-equality, written as $\lambda x.Mx =_\eta M$, if x is not free in M.

This equality can be operationally interpreted from left to right, as the classical η-contraction rule, or in the other way round [36, 33, 23], as an $\widehat{\eta}$-expansion. The traditional contractive way breaks confluence in many λ-calculi [6, 12], while the $\widehat{\eta}$-expansion can be combined with many other higher-order reduction rules [11, 2, 15, 24, 12, 13], by preserving confluence and strong normalization.

The main goal of this paper is to study *confluence* properties of those extensional and non-extensional λ-calculi with explicit substitutions which are designed to implement the λ-calculus à la de Bruijn. To guarantee the correctness of the extensional calculi studied in this paper, we first show that the combination of β-reduction and $\widehat{\eta}$-expansion yields a confluent reduction relation when working with de Bruijn's notation. The rest of the paper is devoted to λ-calculi with explicit substitutions, for which we keep the classical definition of $Beta$-reduction associated to β-reduction, and define the $\widehat{Eta}$-expansion rule associated to the $\widehat{\eta}$-expansion one, this rule being more natural than all the contractive interpretations given in the literature [19, 20, 37, 5]. We study confluence properties of the reduction relation associated to the $Beta$-reduction alone as well as those associated to the combination of $Beta$-reduction and $\widehat{Eta}$-expansion.

Since we are interested in many different λ-calculi with explicit substitutions, which are either well-known in the literature (such as λ_σ [1], $\lambda_{\sigma_\Uparrow}$ [22], λ_υ [29]) or constitute new proposals given in this paper, we develop an "abstract" proof that allows to handle in a simple and general way all these calculi, by a simple instantiation of the proof on each case-study. This is done by extracting the necessary conditions needed for the proofs, then formulating a notion of "general scheme" for λ-calculi with explicit substitution, and finally verifying that every calculus in the paper (well-known or new) matches this general scheme. For those calculi not fitting in the general scheme, such as λ_s [27], that can be translated to another one fitting the scheme, we also give a proof technique allowing to derive the confluence property of the combination of $Beta$-reduction with $\widehat{Eta}$-expansion.

The paper is organized as follows. In Section 2 we recall the λ-calculus à la de Bruijn and we define the associated $\widehat{\eta}$-expansion rule. We prove that the combination of β-reduction and $\widehat{\eta}$-expansion yields a confluent reduction relation in the *typed* λ-calculus à la de Bruijn.

In Section 3 we introduce a general scheme for λ-calculi with explicit substitutions, which is defined to have a concrete structure of terms, but it does not specify the *full* behavior of *all* the substitution constructors. We define an *extensional* version for this general scheme using the notion of $\widehat{Eta}$-expansion associated to that of $\widehat{\eta}$-expansion in classical λ-calculus, which is shown to be correct with respect to the corresponding equational axiomatization. We develop abstract proofs of confluence for the extensional and non-extensional versions of the calculi fitting the general scheme.

In Section 4 we apply the method to some well-known and new λ-calculi with explicit substitutions by just verifying that these calculi fit in the general scheme defined in section 3. Finally, in section 5 we show that $Beta \cup \widehat{Eta}$ is also confluent in λ_s, and we outline a general method to do the same for calculi not fitting the general scheme that can be translated to our scheme. We conclude in section 6.

For details on the technical proofs we refer the reader to [25].

2 The λ-calculus à la de Bruijn

When using the β-reduction rule to model evaluation in classical λ-calculus, bound variables need to be renamed in order to ensure the correctness of the substitution operation. Thus substitution is not really defined on terms but on α-equivalence classes.

A classical way to avoid α-conversion problems is to use the de Bruijn's notation [9, 10] for λ-terms, where names of variables are replaced by natural numbers. Hence, the set of first-order representations of λ-terms, called here *pure terms* or simply *terms*, is defined by the following grammar:

$$Naturals\ n ::= 1 \mid n+1 \qquad Pure\ Terms\ a ::= \underline{n} \mid aa \mid \lambda a$$

A given occurrence u of a bound variable, say x, is replaced by the number of symbols λ whose occurrences are between the binder of this x and u. For example, $\lambda x.\lambda y.x(\lambda z.zx)y$ is written as $\lambda(\lambda(\underline{2}(\lambda(\underline{1}\ \underline{3}))\underline{1}))$. Free variables are represented w.r.t. a given context of variables in such a way that an occurrence of a variable $\underline{n}$ represents the $(n-m)$-th free variables of the context when $n > m$ and there are m symbols λ surrounding this occurrence n. For example, the term $\lambda x.(y\ z)$ is written as $\lambda(\underline{2}\ \underline{3})$ with respect to the context y, z.

To avoid confusion we will note classical λ-terms with capital letters $M, N, \ldots$ and de Bruijn's terms with lower case letters $a, b, \ldots$

Definition 1 Contexts and applied terms. A *context* is a term containing a special symbol $\Box$ denoting a hole. We shall note a context as $C[\,]$ and the textual replacement of the hole by a term a as $C[a]$. Thus, $C[a]$ denotes a term. The subterm a is defined to be *applied* in any term having the form $C[(a\ b)]$.

Definition 2 β-reduction. β-reduction is defined to be the reflexive-transitive closure of the reduction step $(\lambda a)b \longrightarrow_\beta a\{1 \leftarrow b\}$.

The meta-level operation between brackets behaves as expected: for example, $(\lambda(\lambda((\underline{5}\ \underline{2})\ \underline{1})))\lambda(\underline{3}\ \underline{1})$ β-reduces to the term $\lambda((\underline{5}\ \underline{2})\ \underline{1})\{1 \leftarrow \lambda(\underline{3}\ \underline{1})\}$ which is equal to $\lambda((\underline{4}\ (\lambda(\underline{4}\ \underline{1})))\ \underline{1})$.

Type information can be added to this formalism to model the *typed* λ-calculus. It will be kept in an *environment*, defined as a list of types $A_1 \ldots A_n.nil$. The *typing rules* are the following:

$$\frac{}{A,\Gamma \vdash \underline{1} : A} \qquad \frac{\Gamma \vdash \underline{n} : B}{A,\Gamma \vdash \underline{n+1} : B} \qquad \frac{A,\Gamma \vdash b : B}{\Gamma \vdash \lambda A.b : A \rightarrow B} \qquad \frac{\Gamma \vdash a : A \rightarrow B \qquad \Gamma \vdash b : A}{\Gamma \vdash ab : B}$$

We say that a *is of type* A, written $a : A$, if there exists Γ such that $\Gamma \vdash a : A$ is derivable from the typing rules above.

2.1 Handling η-reduction

By far, the best known extensional equality in λ-calculus is the η-axiom, written as $\lambda x : A.Mx =_\eta M$, provided x is not free in M. This equality captures the fact that both functions, $\lambda x : A.Mx$ and M, return the same result when applied to the same argument N in any context $C[\ ]$, *i.e.*, $C[(\lambda x : A.Mx)N] =_\beta C[MN]$.

When one wants to turn the η-equality into a rule there are two different choices: either from left to right as a *contraction*, called η-contraction, or in the other way round as an *expansion*, called η-expansion or $\widehat{\eta}$-expansion, depending on whether some other restrictions are imposed to its application.

The η-axiom has traditionally been turned into a contraction. Such an interpretation is well behaved in the simply typed λ-calculus as it preserves confluence [35], but it is not in many other λ-calculi [6, 12].

Fortunately, expansions can be combined with many other higher-order reduction rules [11, 2, 15, 24, 12, 13]; all these combinations preserve confluence and strong normalization. For that, application of the η-expansion has to be restricted by some conditions in order to guarantee the strong normalization property, and thus the restricted reduction relation, called $\widehat{\eta}$-expansion, is no more a congruence on terms.

The η-equality in the calculus à la de Bruijn is intended to express the fact that for any context $C[\ ]$, the de Bruijn's representations of two terms $C[\lambda x.Mx]$ and $C[M]$ are equal. In terms of representation of variables, this means that all the free variables in M (that may be bound with respect to $C[\ ]$) traverse one more λ when M is replaced by $\lambda x.Mx$, suggesting in this way that a term a is not η-equivalent to $\lambda(a\ \underline{1})$ because of the adjustments to be made on the free variables of a. For example, the term $\lambda(\underline{2}\ \underline{1})$, placed in a context $\lambda[\ ]$ is η-equivalent to the term $\lambda\underline{1}$ and not to $\lambda\underline{2}$. This is not surprising since $\lambda(\lambda(\underline{2}\ \underline{1}))$ is the de Bruijn's representation of $\lambda y.\lambda x.yx$, which is η-equivalent to $\lambda y.y$, represented by $\lambda\underline{1}$. This condition can be expressed by first defining a^+ as the term obtained by lifting any free variable of a by 1, and then by defining η-equality as follows:

Definition 3 η-equality. Let a and b be pure terms. Then $\lambda(a\ \underline{1}) =_\eta b$, if $a = b^+$.

Now, the *η-contraction* is obtained by orienting the previous equality from left to right, while the *η-expansion* is obtained by orienting the equation into the other way round. Analogously to what is done in classical λ-calculus to guarantee strong normalization of extensional expansions [11], we can now define a conditional $\widehat{\eta}$-expansion as follows:

Definition 4 The conditional $\widehat{\eta}$-expansion. The conditional $\widehat{\eta}$-expansion is defined to be the reflexive-transitive closure of the following reduction step:

$$C[a] \longrightarrow_{\widehat{\eta}} C[\lambda A.(a^+\ \underline{1})] \qquad \text{if} \begin{cases} a \text{ is of type } A \rightarrow B \\ a \text{ is not a } \lambda\text{-abstraction} \\ a \text{ is not applied in } C[a] \end{cases}$$

Exactly as in the case of the simple typed λ-calculus, the rule enjoys the subject reduction property and is adequate, *i.e.*, any η-equality can be generated by the reflexive, symmetric and transitive closure of β-reduction plus the conditional $\widehat{\eta}$-expansion [11, 25]. From now on, the conditional $\widehat{\eta}$-expansion will be just called *$\widehat{\eta}$-expansion*.

2.2 Confluence of $\beta\widehat{\eta}$-reduction

We show now that the combination of β-reduction and $\widehat{\eta}$-expansion yields a confluent relation in the typed λ-calculus à la de Bruijn. For that, we will use the following abstract theorem proposed in [14] which allows to derive the confluence property for the combination of two different reduction relation R_1, R_2.

Proposition 5 Sufficient conditions for confluence. *Let R_1 and R_2 be two confluent reduction relations such that R_1 is strongly normalizing and, for all terms a, b and c such that $a \longrightarrow_{R_1} b$ and $a \longrightarrow_{R_2} c$, there is a term d such that $c \longrightarrow^{+}_{R_1} d$ and $b \longrightarrow^{*}_{R_2} d$ (local commutation property). Then $R_1 \cup R_2$ is confluent.*

Now, to prove that $\beta\widehat{\eta}$ is confluent, it is sufficient to take $R_1 = \beta$ and $R_2 = \widehat{\eta}$ in proposition 5, then to verify the hypothesis of the statement. As β-reduction is confluent and strongly normalizing in typed λ-calculus à la de Bruijn [3, 17] and $\widehat{\eta}$-expansion is confluent [11], we are just left to show the local commutation property, which can be proved by inspecting all the critical pairs between β and $\widehat{\eta}$. The proof proceeds exactly as in [11], but we refer the interested reader to [25] for a proof with de Bruijn's indices. Now, we are ready to conclude

Theorem 6. $\longrightarrow^{*}_{\beta\widehat{\eta}}$ *is confluent in the typed λ-calculus à la de Bruijn.*

3 A general scheme for explicit substitutions

When substitutions are specified by a meta-level operation, as in classical λ-calculus, an external mechanism takes place each time a β-redex needs to be reduced. The approach is very different in λ-calculi with explicit substitutions where the manipulation of substitutions is incorporated in an explicitly way to the calculus via a set of rewrite rules.

In this section we introduce a *general scheme for λ-calculi with explicit substitutions* which is defined to have a concrete structure of terms, but does not specify the *full* behavior of *all* the substitution constructors. The intended meaning of this general scheme is to extract from the various λ-calculi with explicit substitutions existing in the literature a uniform description of their specifications and a set of common features needed to reason about confluence. We also define the notion of $\widehat{Eta}$-expansion associated to that of $\widehat{\eta}$-expansion in classical λ-calculus, and show that the definition is correct with respect to the corresponding equational axiomatization. The "abstract" specification given in this section will be sufficient to show that both $Beta$ and $Beta \cup \widehat{Eta}$ are confluent reduction relations in many λ-calculi with explicit substitutions such as λ_σ [1], $\lambda_{\sigma_\Uparrow}$ [22], and λ_υ [29]. Moreover, the general scheme proposed here can also be used to show confluence properties of two *new* λ-calculi with explicit substitutions fitting this abstract specification: the λ_d and the λ_{dn} calculi, both described in section 4.

3.1 Syntax

Definition 7 Substitution signatures. Let us consider two distinguished symbols $\mathcal{T}$ (for terms) and $\mathcal{S}$ (for substitutions). A *substitution declaration* is a (possibly empty) word over the alphabet $\{\mathcal{T}, \mathcal{S}\}$. A *substitution signature* is defined to be a signature Σ (a set of symbols) such that every symbol in Σ is equipped with an arity n and a declaration of length n. We usually write $\xi : \langle n, \sigma_1 \ldots \sigma_n \rangle$ if ξ has arity n and declaration $\sigma_1 \ldots \sigma_n$.

Definition 8 Substitution language. The set of objects over a substitution signature Σ is defined to be the union of objects of sort $\mathcal{T}$ and $\mathcal{S}$. They are constructed in the following way :

- If n is a natural number, then $\underline{n}$, called a *variable*, is of sort $\mathcal{T}$.
- If a and b are of sort $\mathcal{T}$, then $(a\ b)$, called an *application*, is of sort $\mathcal{T}$.
- If a is of sort $\mathcal{T}$, then $\lambda(a)$, called an *abstraction*, is of sort $\mathcal{T}$.
- If a is of sort $\mathcal{T}$ and s is of sort $\mathcal{S}$, then $a[s]$, called a *closure*, is of sort $\mathcal{T}$.
- If every f_i is of sort σ_i, and $\xi : \langle n, \sigma_1 \ldots \sigma_n \rangle$, then $\xi(f_1, \ldots, f_n)$ is of sort $\mathcal{S}$.

For each substitution language W, the set of objects of sort $\mathcal{T}$ (resp. $\mathcal{S}$) is denoted by Λ^t_W (resp. Λ^s_W), and called *the set of terms (resp. substitutions) of W*. We write Λ_W for $\Lambda^t_W \cup \Lambda^s_W$.

For example, the signature Σ associated to the substitution language of the v-calculus [29] is the set $\{\#, \Uparrow, \uparrow\}$, where $\# : \langle 1, \mathcal{T}\rangle$, $\Uparrow: \langle 1, \mathcal{S}\rangle$ and $\uparrow: \langle 0, \epsilon\rangle$. The signature Σ associated to the substitution language of the σ-calculus [1] is the set $\{., \circ, id, \uparrow\}$, where $. : \langle 2, \mathcal{TS}\rangle$, $\circ : \langle 2, \mathcal{SS}\rangle$, $id : \langle 0, \epsilon\rangle$ and $\uparrow: \langle 0, \epsilon\rangle$.

We now introduce the rewriting rules of the general scheme for λ-calculi with explicit substitutions. We start with the *Beta* rule that is the main mechanism in these λ-calculi: it is used to initiate the computation and to explicitly introduce substitutions in the terms to be evaluated. The left-hand side of the *Beta* rule corresponds to a β-redex $(\lambda a)b$ while the right-hand side must be an expression used to denote the term a where the index $\underline{1}$ is replaced by the term b, the index $\underline{2}$ by $\underline{1}$, the index $\underline{3}$ by $\underline{2}$, etc. This is done in different ways according to the substitution language of the corresponding calculus, but we can, in general, write this expression as $a[cons^W(b)]$, where $cons^W$ is a function from terms to substitutions that must be defined for each λ-calculus W. The *Beta* rule of the general scheme can then be expressed as [1]:

$$(Beta) \qquad (\lambda a)b \longrightarrow a[cons^W(b)]$$

For example, the $cons^v$ function corresponding to the λ_v-calculus is $cons^v(b) = \#(b)$, while the $cons^\sigma$ function corresponding to the λ_σ-calculus is $cons^\sigma(b) = b.id$.

The second rule of the general scheme, called the *App* rule, is used to distribute a substitution to both subterms of an application term:

$$(App) \qquad (a\ b)[s] \longrightarrow (a[s]\ b[s])$$

The third rule, called *Lambda*, applies when a substitution goes under a λ constructor, so that the left-hand side is a redex $(\lambda a)[s]$, while the right-hand side is written as $\lambda(a[lift^W(s)])$, where $lift^W$ is a function from substitutions to substitutions and must be defined for each λ-calculus W [2].

$$(Lambda) \qquad (\lambda a)[s] \longrightarrow \lambda(a[lift^W(s)])$$

As an example, $lift^v(s) = \Uparrow(s)$ and $lift^\sigma(s) = \underline{1}.(s \circ \uparrow)$.

Definition 9 Substitution calculus. A rewrite rule $l \to r$ is *sort-preserving* if r is of sort $\mathcal{K}$ when l is of sort $\mathcal{K}$. A *Substitution Calculus*[3] (SC) consists of a signature containing the substitution constant $\uparrow: \langle 0, \epsilon\rangle$, which is called a *shift-constant* and will be used to denote extensional equalities, a lift-function, a cons-function, and a set of sort-preserving rewriting rules containing *App* and *Lambda* (but not *Beta*).

Notation 10 We write simply W for the set of rewriting rules of the SC W, and λ_W for the set $W \cup Beta$. The notations $\longrightarrow_{\mathcal{R}}$ and $=_{\mathcal{R}}$ are respectively used to denote $\mathcal{R}$-reduction and $\mathcal{R}$-equality. For every function h, we define h_i (for $i \geq 0$) as $h_0(s) = s$ and $h_{n+1}(s) = h(h_n(s))$.

The rewriting rules *Beta*, *App* and *Lambda* are necessary to describe some relations between terms and substitutions, but they are not sufficient to express all of them. In particular, we want to prove confluence of some reduction relations associated to all the λ-calculi satisfying our general scheme, so we have to impose some additional conditions on the set of rewriting rules of the SC. These conditions are mainly inspired from the various proofs of confluence existing in the literature for the relations $\longrightarrow_{\lambda_W}$.

Definition 11 Basic conditions. A substitution calculus W is said to be *basic* (written BSC) if it satisfies the following conditions:

---

[1] Since the right hand side of the *Beta* rule depends on the substitution calculus W, we should denote this rule as $Beta_W$, but we prefer to omit the index W to make easier the notation.

[2] The same remark done for the *Beta* rule applies here.

[3] Another notion of substitution calculus can be found in [38].

1. W is strongly normalizing[4].

2. W is confluent.

3. W-normal forms of terms are pure terms.

4. $W(a\ b) = (W(a)\ W(b))$ and $W(\lambda a) = \lambda W(a)$.

5. For any substitution s in W, $\underline{1}[lift^W(s)] =_W \underline{1}$ and for any $m \geq 1$, $\underline{m+1}[lift^W(s)] =_W \underline{m}[s][\uparrow]$.

6. For any term k in W, $\underline{1}[cons^W(k)] =_W k$ and for any $m \geq 1$, $\underline{m+1}[cons^W(k)] =_W \underline{m}$

7. For any variable $\underline{m}$ in W we have $\underline{m}[\uparrow] =_W \underline{m+1}$.

From conditions 1 and 2 in definition 11 we deduce the existence and uniqueness of W-normal forms, denoted by $W(\ )$ [5]. This, together with condition 3 guarantees that for every object a in Λ_W and every pure term b such that $W(a) = b$, then $a \longrightarrow^*_W b$. This property will be used in several lemmas of the paper.

The type system associated to each SC depends on the substitution function symbols of its signature. However, there is a set of *common* typing rules in all these systems, which is:

$$\frac{}{A,\Gamma \vdash \underline{1} : A} \qquad \frac{\Gamma \vdash \underline{n} : B}{A,\Gamma \vdash \underline{n+1} : B} \qquad \frac{\Gamma \vdash a : A \rightarrow B \qquad \Gamma \vdash b : A}{\Gamma \vdash ab : B}$$

$$\frac{}{A,\Gamma \vdash \uparrow \rhd \Gamma} \qquad \frac{\Gamma \vdash a : A \qquad \Delta \vdash s \rhd \Gamma}{\Delta \vdash a[s] : A} \qquad \frac{A,\Gamma \vdash b : B}{\Gamma \vdash \lambda A.b : A \rightarrow B}$$

3.2 Handling Eta-reduction

The standard equation corresponding to η-equality in classical λ-calculus is usually written in the formalism of λ-calculi with explicit substitutions as the axiom:

$$(Eta) \qquad \lambda(a[\uparrow]\ \underline{1}) = a$$

where $\uparrow$ is the substitution constant which was assumed to be in the signature of every SC.

The relation between $\widehat{\eta}$ and $\widehat{Eta}$ can be stated using the following property:

Lemma 12. *Let W be a BSC and let a be a pure term. Then $W(a[\uparrow])$ is the term a^+.*

When turning the Eta-axiom into a reduction rule some problems arise. If we orient this equation from left to right as the rewriting rule $\lambda(a[\uparrow]\ \underline{1}) \longrightarrow a$, an infinite set of critical pairs is generated. As a consequence, the rule is often expressed as the *conditional* rule [19, 20, 37]:

$$(Eta_1) \qquad \lambda(a\ \underline{1}) \longrightarrow b \qquad \text{if } a =_W b[\uparrow]$$

However, the condition $a =_W b[\uparrow]$ depends on the particular definition of W, and may be difficult (or expensive) to be verified each time that an Eta_1-reduction is performed.

There is another *unconditional* rewriting rule associated to the Eta-axiom, proposed by Briaud [5], expressed in our syntax as follows:

$$(Eta_2) \qquad \lambda(a\ \underline{1}) \longrightarrow a[cons^W(\perp)]$$

---

[4] The well-known substitution calculi appearing in the literature are all strongly normalizing, and moreover, standard proof techniques like polynomial orders are usually sufficient to show this property. However, when adding the *Beta* rule, strong normalization is not evident, and in may cases it does not hold, even in a typed framework [32].

[5] Even if existence of unique normal forms can also be deduced from *weak normalization* and confluence, we prefer to require a substitution calculus to have the strong normalization property to guarantee that any strategy terminates when computing pure terms.

where $\perp$ is a *new* constant added to the set of terms. This rule can be expressed in classical λ-calculus as:

$$(Eta_3) \qquad \lambda x.(M\ x) \longrightarrow M\{x \leftarrow \perp\}$$

The η-contraction rule in classical λ-calculus coincides with the Eta_3-rule only if the variable x is not free in M. Similarly, the Eta_2-rule coincides with the conditional Eta_1-rule if the variable represented by $\underline{1}$ is not free in the term a. Otherwise, the Eta_1-rule is not allowed (because the condition is not verified), but Eta_2 is. The intended meaning of the constant $\perp$ is to denote something that is not a term, *i.e.*, a meaningless term. For this reason, every normal form involving $\perp$ has to be discharged, and this requires some kind of backtracking in the computation process, which is, as we know, an expensive operation.

The Eta_2-rule can also be interpreted as the following *conditional* rule:

$$(Eta_2') \qquad \lambda(a\ \underline{1}) \longrightarrow a[cons^W(\perp)], \qquad \text{if } \perp \notin W(a[cons^W(\perp)])$$

This leads to perform a verification before applying the rule, since one has to verify that the symbol $\perp$ does not appear in the W-normal of the term $a[cons^W(\perp)]$. Therefore, this solution is still expensive by means of computation steps and, exactly as for the Eta_1-rule, depends on the particular definition of the substitution calculus W.

Fortunately, there is still another reading of the *Eta*-axiom that avoids these problems, it corresponds to the *unrestricted Eta*-expansion:

$$(Eta) \qquad a \longrightarrow \lambda(a[\uparrow]\ \underline{1})$$

As explained in section 2.1, the expansive interpretation of the η-axiom has been very successful in these last years, mainly because it has been shown to be compatible with many other higher-order rules. This suggests that it would also be a good solution to define *extensional* versions of λ-calculi with explicit substitutions containing the *expansive* interpretations of the *Eta*-axiom.

As the unrestricted *Eta*-expansion is not strongly normalizing, one has to restrict its application, exactly as in the case of the $\widehat{\eta}$-expansion rule, by imposing some conditions to guarantee termination.

Definition 13 Applied-Terms and Lambda-Abstractions. A term a is a *Lambda-Abstraction* if either $a = \lambda b$, or $a = b[s]$ and b is a Lambda-Abstraction. Similarly, let $C[\,]$ be any context and s any substitution. A subterm a is said to be an *Applied-Term* in $C[a]$ if it is applied in $C[a]$; while a is said to be an *Applied-Term* in $C[a[s]]$ if it is an Applied-Term in $C[a]$.

For example, $(\lambda\underline{1})$ and $(\lambda\underline{1})[\uparrow][\uparrow]$ are Lambda-Abstractions, and $\underline{1}$ is an Applied-Term in $(\underline{1}\ \underline{2})$ and $(\underline{1}[\uparrow]\ \underline{2})$.

We now present the conditional $\widehat{Eta}$-expansion rule, remark that the relation generated by this rule is no longer a congruence, as in the case of λ-calculus.

Definition 14. The conditional $\widehat{Eta}$-expansion rule is defined to be the reflexive-transitive closure of the following reduction step:

$$C[a] \longrightarrow_{\widehat{Eta}} C[\lambda A.(a[\uparrow]\ \underline{1})], \text{ if } \begin{cases} a \text{ is of type } A \rightarrow B \\ a \text{ is not a Lambda-Abstraction} \\ a \text{ is not an Applied-Term in } C[a] \end{cases}$$

The *extensional* version of W is the calculus containing the rules W, *Beta* and $\widehat{Eta}$. We note $\longrightarrow_{\lambda_W \cup \widehat{Eta}}$ the reduction relation associated to the *extensional* substitution calculus W.

Lemma 15 Subject reduction for $\widehat{Eta}$. *If $\Gamma \vdash a : A$ and $a \longrightarrow_{\widehat{Eta}} b$, then $\Gamma \vdash b : A$.*

Notice that if a subterm a is not defined to be an Applied-Term in $C[(a[s]\ b)]$, then the $\widehat{Eta}$-expansion rule will not be terminating as the following infinite reduction sequence shows:

$$\underline{a} \longrightarrow_{\widehat{Eta}} \lambda(\underline{a}[\uparrow]\ \underline{1}) \longrightarrow_{\widehat{Eta}} \lambda((\lambda(a[\uparrow]\ \underline{1}))[\uparrow]\ \underline{1})\ldots$$

Lemma 16 Strong normalization of $\widehat{Eta}$. *The reduction $\longrightarrow_{\widehat{Eta}}$ is strongly normalizing.*

Proof. Using a decreasing measure as defined in [34].

It is also worth noticing that even if a term a is not a Lambda-Abstraction according to definition 13, its W-normal form may be one: for example $\underline{1}[cons^W(\lambda\underline{1})]$ is not a Lambda-Abstraction but $W(\underline{1}[cons^W(\lambda\underline{1})]) = \lambda\underline{1}$ is. The same happens with the notion of Applied-Terms. This remark suggests that one could also use a different notion of restriction in definition 14, saying that a term a is a Lambda-Abstraction if $a =_W \lambda b$. This alternative notion of restricted expansion coincides exactly with that of simply typed λ-calculus, but introduces at the same time a condition that depends on the particular definition of W, exactly as in the case of the Eta_1-rule previously mentioned. Even if our approach introduces a conditional rule in definition 14, the restriction does not depend at all on the particular theory generated by the substitution calculus. On the other hand, there is no backtracking when applying this rule as in the case of the Eta_3-contraction rule.

The $\widehat{Eta}$-expansion generates the same equational theory as Eta_1, even if it seems more restrictive because of the syntactic conditions to be verified.

Theorem 17. *Let W be a BSC. Then any Eta-equality $a =_{Eta} b$ can be generated by the reflexive, symmetric and transitive closure of $\longrightarrow_{W\cup Beta\cup\widehat{Eta}}$.*

3.3 Confluence properties

We show in this section that extensional and non-extensional basic substitution calculi are confluent. For the non-extensional case, we use the *interpretation method* [18], that is the standard technique used to prove confluence of λ-calculi with explicit substitutions. When dealing with extensional rules, the interpretation method has to be slighty modified, resulting in the *generalized interpretation method*, to prove that $Beta$-reduction together with $\widehat{Eta}$-expansion preserve confluence of any SC. It is also worth noticing that standard techniques, like the Tait and Martin-Löf's parallel moves lemma, do not work when dealing with restricted expansions, this is the reason we prefer to use directly the interpretation method, even for the non-extensional versions of our λ-calculi. According to the philosophy of this paper, we extract the necessary conditions to be added to the basic conditions stated in definition 11 in order to verify the properties required by the interpretation methods. These conditions are very simple to understand and easy to prove as they just concern the interaction between variables and substitutions of the substitution language.

Definition 18 General scheme. We say that a BSC W obeys the *general scheme* iff for every variable $\underline{m} \in \Lambda_W^t$ and every function symbol $\xi \in \Sigma$ of arity q one of the two following cases holds:

- There is a variable $\underline{n}$, indices $1 \leq i_1, \ldots, i_p \leq q$ $(p \geq 0)$ and substitutions $u_1, \ldots, u_k$ $(k \geq 0)$ such that for all $s_1 \ldots s_q$ we have $\underline{m}[\xi(s_1, \ldots, s_q)] =_W \underline{n}[s_{i_1}] \ldots [s_{i_p}][u_1] \ldots [u_k]$
- There is an index i $(1 \leq i \leq q)$ such that for all $s_1 \ldots s_q$ we have $\underline{m}[\xi(s_1, \ldots, s_q)] =_W s_i$

We assume these equations to be well-typed, in the sense that whenever the first case holds, then $s_{i_1}, \ldots, s_{i_p}$ are substitutions, and whenever the second case holds, then s_i is a term.

This condition says that the behavior of any substitution $s = \xi(s_1, \ldots, s_q)$ with respect to a variable $\underline{m}$ is only determined by the constructor ξ and not at all by the other components $s_1 \ldots s_q$. In both cases, we use the equality $=_W$ instead of the rewrite relation $\longrightarrow_W$ because sometimes the property is verified by a rewrite step $\longrightarrow_W$ and others by ${}_W\!\longleftarrow$: indeed, in the σ-calculus, we have $\underline{m}[s \circ t]\ {}_{Clos}\!\longleftarrow \underline{m}[s][t]$ and not $\underline{m}[s \circ t] \longrightarrow_{Clos} \underline{m}[s][t]$, while, for example in the λ_v-calculus, we have $\underline{m}[\uparrow] \longrightarrow_{VarShift} \underline{m+1}$. The general scheme also makes easier to reason by induction on the structure of an object.

We are now ready to apply the interpretation method which allows to reason about confluence in a quite modular way, by splitting an entire reduction relation R into two different and disjoint relations R_1 and R_2.

Lemma 19 Interpretation method [18]. *Let $R = R_1 \cup R_2$, where R_1 is a confluent and strongly normalizing reduction relation and R_2 an arbitrary reduction relation. If there exists a reduction relation R' on the set of R_1-normal forms such that*

$$R' \subseteq R^* \text{ and } (a \longrightarrow_{R_2} b \text{ implies } R_1(a) \longrightarrow_{R'} R_1(b))$$

then if R' is confluent, R is also confluent.

When showing the confluence property for any relation $\longrightarrow_{\lambda_W}$, one usually takes R' as $\longrightarrow^*_\beta$, R_1 as $\longrightarrow_W$ and R_2 as $\longrightarrow_{Beta}$. As every BSC W is confluent and strongly normalizing, and β-reduction is only defined on W-normal forms (that are pure terms), one is left to show that

$$\longrightarrow^*_\beta \subseteq \longrightarrow^*_{\lambda_W} \text{ and } (a \longrightarrow_{Beta} b \text{ implies } W(a) \longrightarrow^*_\beta W(b))$$

The first property is quite simple to prove whereas the second one is the essential part of the general abstract proof that distills the different techniques appearing in the literature. It is also worth noticing that the property concerns only terms because β-reduction is not defined on substitutions. The key case to prove that $a \longrightarrow_{Beta} b$ implies $W(a) \longrightarrow^*_\beta W(b)$ is when a and b are closures $c[s]$ and $c[s']$ such that $s \longrightarrow_{Beta} s'$. In all the proofs appearing in the litterature this is done by inspecting all the possible cases, whereas in our case we use a similar statement for substitutions (which results in the second point of the following lemma), and also the general scheme condition (which allows to reason by induction on the structure of objects).

Lemma 20. *Let W be a BSC having the general scheme and let $p \in \Lambda_W$. If $p \longrightarrow_{Beta} p'$, then*
1) if p is a term, then $W(p) \longrightarrow^*_\beta W(p')$
2) for every pure term d such that $d[p]$ is a term, and every $n \geq 0$, then
$W(d[lift^W_n(p)]) \longrightarrow^*_\beta W(d[lift^W_n(p')])$

Proof. The proof proceeds by induction on the structure of p, uses the fact that W has the general scheme, and a meta-substitution lemma stating that $a[cons^W(b)][s] =_W a[lift^W(s)][cons^W(b[s])]$, for any pure term a, any term $b \in \Lambda^t_W$ and any $n \geq 0$. We refer the reader to [25] for details.

Lemma 21. *Let W be a BSC. If $a \longrightarrow^*_\beta b$, then $a \longrightarrow^*_{\lambda_W} b$.*

Proof. The proof proceeds by induction on the number of reduction steps from a to b. We only show here the base case. Let $a \longrightarrow_\beta b$. Then $a = C[(\lambda c)d]$ and $b = C[c\{1 \leftarrow d\}]$. Since $W[c\{1 \leftarrow d\}]$ is equal to $W(c[cons^W(d)])$, then $a = C[(\lambda c)d] \longrightarrow_{Beta} C[c[cons^W(d)]] \longrightarrow^*_W C[c\{1 \leftarrow d\}]$.

Theorem 22 λ_W is confluent. *For every BSC W satisfying the general scheme, the relation λ_W is confluent.*

Proof. Using lemma 19, where R' is $\longrightarrow^*_\beta$, R_1 is $\longrightarrow_W$ and R_2 is $\longrightarrow_{Beta}$. The two properties required by the hypothesis of the lemma come from lemma 21 and lemma 20.

When $\widehat{Eta}$-expansions are also considered in the reduction system, the interpretation method is no longer useful because the second condition required by lemma 19 does not always hold, as the following example shows:

Example 1. Let us consider the extensional λ_υ-calculus and the following $\widehat{Eta}$-expansion step $a = \underline{1}[\#(\lambda\underline{1})] \longrightarrow_{\widehat{Eta}} (\lambda(\underline{1}[\uparrow]\ \underline{1}))[\#(\lambda\underline{1})] = b$. Then $W(a) = \lambda\underline{1}$ and $W(b) = \lambda((\lambda\underline{1})\ \underline{1})$, so neither $W(a) \longrightarrow^*_{\widehat{\eta}} W(b)$, nor $W(a) \longrightarrow^*_{\beta\widehat{\eta}} W(b)$. In fact, $W(a)$ is a $\beta\widehat{\eta}$-normal form so it cannot be reduced at all.

As the previous example suggests, the second condition required by the interpretation method can be weakened to recover confluence as follows:

$$a \longrightarrow_{R_2} b \text{ implies } R_1(a) =_{R'} R_1(b)$$

As a consequence, lemma 19 becomes a particular case of the following one:

Lemma 23 Generalized Interpretation Method. *Let $R = R_1 \cup R_2$, where R_1 is a confluent and strongly normalizing reduction relation and R_2 an arbitrary reduction relation. If there exists a reduction relation R' on the set of R_1-normal forms such that*

$$R' \subseteq R^* \text{ and } (a \longrightarrow_{R_2} b \text{ implies } R_1(a) =_{R'} R_1(b))$$

then if R' is confluent, R is also confluent.

When showing confluence of any relation $\longrightarrow_{\lambda_W \cup \widehat{Eta}}$, one usually takes R' as $\longrightarrow^*_{\beta\widehat{\eta}}$, R_1 as $\longrightarrow_W$ and R_2 as $\longrightarrow_{Beta \cup \widehat{Eta}}$. As every BSC W is confluent and strongly normalizing, and $\beta \cup \widehat{\eta}$-reduction is only defined on W-normal forms (that are pure terms), one is left to show the two properties required by the lemma. In particular, we will show that

$$\longrightarrow^*_{\beta\widehat{\eta}} \subseteq \longrightarrow^*_{\lambda_W \cup \widehat{Eta}} \text{ and } (a \longrightarrow_{Beta \cup \widehat{Eta}} b \text{ implies } W(a) \longrightarrow^*_{\widehat{\eta}}\ {}_{\beta}{}^{*}\!\!\longleftarrow W(b))$$

This is in fact stronger than what is required by lemma 23, but we think that this formulation is more useful to understand the interaction between $\widehat{Eta}$-expansion, terms and explicit substitutions. Exactly as in the case of the confluence proof of $\longrightarrow_{\lambda_W}$, the first property is quite simple to prove whereas the second one is the essential part of the general abstract proof, it can be summarized by the following lemma.

Lemma 24. *Let W be a BSC having the general scheme and let $p \in \Lambda_W$. If $p \longrightarrow_{\widehat{Eta}} p'$, then*
1) if p is a term, then $W(p) \longrightarrow^*_{\widehat{\eta}}\ {}_{\beta}{}^{*}\!\!\longleftarrow W(p')$
2) for every pure term d such that $d[p]$ is a term, and every $n \geq 0$, then
$W(d[lift_n^W(p)]) \longrightarrow^*_{\widehat{\eta}}\ {}_{\beta}{}^{*}\!\!\longleftarrow W(d[lift_n^W(p')])$

Now, by lemma 20 together with lemma 24 we obtain

Corollary 25. *Let W be BSC having the general scheme and let a be a term of W such that $a \longrightarrow_{Beta \cup \widehat{Eta}} b$. Then $W(a) \longrightarrow^*_{\beta\widehat{\eta}}\ {}_{\beta\widehat{\eta}}{}^{*}\!\!\longleftarrow W(b)$.*

Lemma 26. *Let W be a BSC and let a be a pure term. Then $a \longrightarrow_{\widehat{\eta}} b$ implies $a \longrightarrow^*_{W \cup \widehat{Eta}} b$.*

Proof. Let $C[a] \longrightarrow_{\widehat{\eta}} C[\lambda(a^+\ \underline{1})]$, where $a \longrightarrow_{\widehat{\eta}} \lambda(a^+\ \underline{1})$. Then a is not a λ-abstraction and is not applied to another term. By definition $a \longrightarrow_{\widehat{Eta}} \lambda(a[\uparrow]\ \underline{1})$, and by lemma 12 $W(a[\uparrow])$ is exactly a^+, so that $\lambda(a[\uparrow]\ \underline{1}) \longrightarrow^*_W \lambda(W(a[\uparrow])\ \underline{1}) = \lambda(a^+\ \underline{1})$ which implies $a \longrightarrow^*_{W \cup \widehat{Eta}} \lambda(a^+\ \underline{1})$ and concludes the proof.

Now, by lemma 26 together with lemma 21 we obtain

Corollary 27. *Let W be a BSC and let a be a pure term. Then $a \longrightarrow^*_{\beta\widehat{\eta}} b$ implies $a \longrightarrow^*_{\lambda_W \cup \widehat{Eta}} b$.*

Theorem 28 $\lambda_W \cup \widehat{Eta}$ is confluent. *For every BSC W having the general scheme, the relation $\lambda_W \cup \widehat{Eta}$ is confluent.*

Proof. By the generalized interpretation method (lemma 23), where R' is $\longrightarrow^*_{\beta\widehat{\eta}}$, R_1 is $\longrightarrow_W$ and R_2 is $\longrightarrow_{Beta \cup \widehat{Eta}}$. Note that $\longrightarrow_W$ is confluent and strongly normalizing by conditions 1 and 2, the two other properties required by the hypothesis of the lemma come from Corollary 27 and Corollary 25.

4 Some λ-calculi fitting the general scheme

In this section we apply our method to some well-known λ-calculi with explicit substitutions such as λ_v, λ_σ and $\lambda_{\sigma_\Uparrow}$ and also to some new calculi that we proposed here, namely, λ_d and λ_{dn}. For that, we have just to associate functions $lift^W$ and $cons^W$ to each calculus W, and then verify not only the existence of the *Lambda, App* and *Beta* rule, but also conditions required by definitions 11 (basic conditions) and 18 (general scheme).

The λ_σ, $\lambda_{\sigma_\Uparrow}$ and λ_v calculi

In the λ_σ-calculus [1], terms and substitutions are defined by the grammar

$$(Terms)\ \ a ::= \underline{1} \mid aa \mid \lambda a \mid a[s] \qquad (Substitutions)\ \ s ::= id \mid a.s \mid \uparrow \mid s \circ s$$

As a consequence, any variable $\underline{n+1}$ (for $n \geq 1$) is represented by $\underline{1}[\uparrow^n] = \underline{1}[\underbrace{\uparrow \circ(\uparrow \circ(\ldots \circ \uparrow))}_{n\ times}]$, which becomes in this way a pure term.

The lift-function is defined by $lift^\sigma(s) = \underline{1}.(s \circ \uparrow)$ and the cons-function by $cons^\sigma(b) = b.id$. The reduction rules are the following:

$$\begin{array}{llcl}
(Beta) & (\lambda a)b & \longrightarrow & a[b.id] \\
(App) & (a\,b)[s] & \longrightarrow & (a[s]\ b[s]) \\
(Lambda) & (\lambda a)[s] & \longrightarrow & \lambda(a[\underline{1}.(s \circ \uparrow)]) \\
(Clos) & (a[s])[t] & \longrightarrow & a[s \circ t] \\
(VarId) & \underline{1}[id] & \longrightarrow & \underline{1} \\
(VarCons) & \underline{1}[a.s] & \longrightarrow & a \\
(IdL) & id \circ s & \longrightarrow & s \\
(ShiftId) & \uparrow \circ id & \longrightarrow & \uparrow \\
(ShiftCons) & \uparrow \circ(a.s) & \longrightarrow & s \\
(Ass) & (s_1 \circ s_2) \circ s_3 & \longrightarrow & s_1 \circ (s_2 \circ s_3) \\
(Map) & (a.s) \circ t & \longrightarrow & a[t].(s \circ t)
\end{array}$$

The implementation of the lift-function is much simpler in the $\lambda_{\sigma_\Uparrow}$-calculus [22, 7]: it only uses a unary substitution constructor instead of the two constants and two operators used in the case of λ_σ. Terms and substitutions of the $\lambda_{\sigma_\Uparrow}$-calculus can be defined by the following grammar:

$$(Terms)\ \ a ::= \underline{n} \mid aa \mid \lambda a \mid a[s] \qquad (Substitutions)\ \ s ::= id \mid a.s \mid \Uparrow(s) \mid \uparrow \mid s \circ s$$

The lift-function is defined by $lift^{\sigma_\Uparrow}(s) = \Uparrow(s)$ and the cons-function by $cons^{\sigma_\Uparrow}(b) = b.id$. Reduction rules of the calculus are the following:

$$\begin{array}{llcl}
(Beta) & (\lambda a)b & \longrightarrow & a[b.id] \\
(App) & (a\,b)[s] & \longrightarrow & (a[s]\ b[s]) \\
(Lambda) & (\lambda a)[s] & \longrightarrow & \lambda(a[\Uparrow(s)]) \\
(Clos) & (a[s])[t] & \longrightarrow & a[s \circ t] \\
(VarShift1) & \underline{n}[\uparrow] & \longrightarrow & \underline{n+1} \\
(VarShift2) & \underline{n}[\uparrow \circ s] & \longrightarrow & \underline{n+1}[s] \\
(FVar) & \underline{1}[a.s] & \longrightarrow & a \\
(FVarLift1) & \underline{1}[\Uparrow(s)] & \longrightarrow & \underline{1} \\
(FVarLift2) & \underline{1}[\Uparrow(s) \circ t] & \longrightarrow & \underline{1}[t] \\
(RVar) & \underline{n+1}[a.s] & \longrightarrow & \underline{n}[s] \\
(RVarLift1) & \underline{n+1}[\Uparrow(s)] & \longrightarrow & \underline{n}[s \circ \uparrow] \\
(RVarLift2) & \underline{n+1}[\Uparrow(s) \circ t] & \longrightarrow & \underline{n}[s \circ (\uparrow \circ t)]
\end{array}
\qquad
\begin{array}{llcl}
(Ass) & (s_1 \circ s_2) \circ s_3 & \longrightarrow & s_1 \circ (s_2 \circ s_3) \\
(Map) & (a.s) \circ t & \longrightarrow & a[t].(s \circ t) \\
(Shift) & \uparrow \circ(a.s) & \longrightarrow & s \\
(ShiftLift1) & \uparrow \circ \Uparrow(s) & \longrightarrow & s \circ \uparrow \\
(ShiftLift2) & \uparrow \circ(\Uparrow(s) \circ t) & \longrightarrow & s \circ (\uparrow \circ t) \\
(Lift1) & \Uparrow(s) \circ \Uparrow(t) & \longrightarrow & \Uparrow(s \circ t) \\
(Lift2) & \Uparrow(s) \circ (\Uparrow(t) \circ u) & \longrightarrow & \Uparrow(s \circ t) \circ u \\
(LiftEnv) & \Uparrow(s) \circ (a.t) & \longrightarrow & a.(s \circ t) \\
(IdL) & id \circ s & \longrightarrow & s \\
(IdR) & s \circ id & \longrightarrow & s \\
(LiftId) & \Uparrow(id) & \longrightarrow & id \\
(Id) & a[id] & \longrightarrow & a
\end{array}$$

In a different spirit, Pierre Lescanne [29] introduces the λ_v-calculus, which is, in some sense, the *minimal* calculus of explicit substitutions that satisfies the basic conditions in definition 11. As a consequence, it can be derived from our general scheme in a very direct way: we have just to associate a unary substitution constructor to the cons-function $cons^v$, and another one to the the lift-function

$lift^{\upsilon}$, then any of the three last basic conditions becomes a rewrite rule; whereas conditions on substitutions in definition 18 can be immediately deduced.

Terms and substitutions of the λ_{υ}-calculus can be defined by the following grammar:

$$(Terms)\ a ::= \underline{n} \mid aa \mid \lambda a \mid a[s] \qquad (Substitutions)\ s ::= \#(a) \mid \Uparrow(s) \mid \uparrow$$

The lift-function is defined by $lift^{\upsilon}(s) = \Uparrow(s)$ and the cons-function by $cons^{\upsilon}(b) = \#(b)$. We use here # instead of the / symbol introduced in [37] and used in [29]. The reduction rules are:

$$\begin{array}{llll@{\qquad}llll}
(Beta) & (\lambda a)b & \longrightarrow & a[\#(b)] & (App) & (a\,b)[s] & \longrightarrow & (a[s]\,b[s]) \\
(Lambda) & (\lambda a)[s] & \longrightarrow & \lambda(a[\Uparrow(s)]) & (FVar) & \underline{1}[\#(a)] & \longrightarrow & a \\
(RVar) & \underline{n+1}[\#(a)] & \longrightarrow & \underline{n} & (FVarLift) & \underline{1}[\Uparrow(s)] & \longrightarrow & \underline{1} \\
(RVarLift) & \underline{n+1}[\Uparrow(s)] & \longrightarrow & \underline{n}[s][\uparrow] & (VarShift) & \underline{n}[\uparrow] & \longrightarrow & \underline{n+1}
\end{array}$$

The λ_d and λ_{dn} calculi

Mainly inspired from the λ_{τ}-calculus in [37], which was in turn inspired by [16], we propose here the λ_d-calculus by putting together the nice properties of the three previous substitution calculi: we just use unary substitution operators for the lift-function and the cons-function, keeping composition of substitutions which is one the main features needed to describe different implementations of functional programming. Terms and substitutions are defined by

$$(Terms)\ a ::= \underline{1} \mid aa \mid \lambda a \mid a[s] \qquad (Substitutions)\ s ::= id \mid \#(a) \mid \Uparrow(s) \mid \uparrow \mid s \circ s$$

We represent, exactly as in the case of the λ_{σ}-calculus, any variable $\underline{n+1}$ (for $n \geq 1$) by $\underline{1}[\uparrow^n]$.

The functions $lift^d$ and $cons^d$ are defined by $lift^d(s) = \Uparrow(s)$ and $cons^d(b) = \#(b)$. The reduction rules are the following ones:

$$\begin{array}{llll@{\qquad}llll}
(Beta) & (\lambda a)b & \longrightarrow & a[\#(b)] & (App) & (a\,b)[s] & \longrightarrow & (a[s]\,b[s]) \\
(Lambda) & (\lambda a)[s] & \longrightarrow & \lambda(a[\Uparrow(s)]) & (Clos) & (a[s])[t] & \longrightarrow & a[s \circ t] \\
(FVar1) & \underline{1}[\#(a)] & \longrightarrow & a & (FVar2) & \underline{1}[\#(a) \circ s] & \longrightarrow & a[s] \\
(FVarLift1) & \underline{1}[\Uparrow(s)] & \longrightarrow & \underline{1} & (FVarLift2) & \underline{1}[\Uparrow(s) \circ t] & \longrightarrow & \underline{1}[t] \\
(Shift1) & \uparrow \circ \#(a) & \longrightarrow & id & (Shift2) & \uparrow \circ (\#(a) \circ s) & \longrightarrow & s \\
(ShiftLift1) & \uparrow \circ \Uparrow(s) & \longrightarrow & s \circ \uparrow & (ShiftLift2) & \uparrow \circ (\Uparrow(s) \circ t) & \longrightarrow & s \circ (\uparrow \circ t) \\
(Lift1) & \Uparrow(s) \circ \Uparrow(t) & \longrightarrow & \Uparrow(s \circ t) & (Lift2) & \Uparrow(s) \circ (\Uparrow(t) \circ u) & \longrightarrow & \Uparrow(s \circ t) \circ u \\
(IdL) & id \circ s & \longrightarrow & s & (IdR) & s \circ id & \longrightarrow & s \\
(LiftId) & \Uparrow(id) & \longrightarrow & id & (Id) & a[id] & \longrightarrow & a \\
(Ass) & (s_1 \circ s_2) \circ s_3 & \longrightarrow & s_1 \circ (s_2 \circ s_3) & & & &
\end{array}$$

Note that the $MapEnv$ rule of the λ_{τ}-calculus in [37] $\#(a) \circ s \longrightarrow \Uparrow(s) \circ \#(a[s])$ is replaced here by $FVar2$ and $Shift2$. This may be in principle superfluous, but is essential to make our calculus fit in the general scheme. This difference makes it possible to prove confluence and strong normalization of d, while confluence remains still as a conjecture in the case of the τ-calculus and strong normalization does not hold [28]. However, the rule $MapEnv$ is essential if one wants to recover confluence on open terms [6], and is at the same time, as explained by [32] and [4], the cause of non termination in many λ-calculi with explicit substitutions. It is then natural to conjecture that λ_d preserves β-strong normalization.

Theorem 29. *The d-calculus is locally confluent and strongly normalizing.*

Proof. The proof of local confluence can be done automatically, for example by using CIME [31]. For strong normalization, we know that the $\sigma_{\Uparrow}$-calculus is strongly normalizing [19], so it is sufficient to interpret the d-calculus into the $\sigma_{\Uparrow}$-calculus in the following way:

Let $\mathcal{T}$ be a function from objects in Λ_d into objects in $\Lambda_{\sigma_{\Uparrow}}$ defined to be the identity on all the objects, but on substitutions of the form $\#(a)$, where $\mathcal{T}(\#(a))$ is equal to $\mathcal{T}(a).id$.

We can show by case-analysis that $a \longrightarrow_d b$ implies $\mathcal{T}(a) \longrightarrow^{+}_{\sigma_{\Uparrow}} \mathcal{T}(b)$, so that strong normalization of $\sigma_{\Uparrow}$ implies that of d.

[6] Indeed, the open term $((\lambda X)a)[s]$ reduces to both $X[\#(a) \circ s]$ and $X[\Uparrow(s) \circ \#(a[s])]$, which have no common reduct in λ_d but can be joined in the λ_{τ}-calculus proposed in [37].

The λ_{dn}-calculus is just λ_d plus natural numbers to represent variables. It is a natural extension of λ_d which also satisfies the abstract properties required by the general scheme.

The sets of terms and substitutions are defined as follows:

$$(Terms)\ a ::= \underline{n} \mid aa \mid \lambda a \mid a[s] \qquad (Substitutions)\ s ::= id \mid \#(a) \mid \Uparrow(s) \mid \uparrow \mid s \circ s$$

The function $lift^{dn}$ (resp. $cons^{dn}$) is defined exactly as $lift^{d}$ (resp. $cons^{d}$). We add the following set of rules to those of the λ_d-calculus.

$$\begin{array}{llll}
(VarShift1) & \underline{n}[\uparrow] \longrightarrow \underline{n+1} & (VarShift2) & \underline{n}[\uparrow \circ s] \longrightarrow \underline{n+1}[s] \\
(RVar) & \underline{n+1}[\#(a)] \longrightarrow \underline{n} & (RVarLift1) & \underline{n+1}[\Uparrow(s)] \longrightarrow \underline{n}[s \circ \uparrow] \\
(RVarLift2) & \underline{n+1}[\Uparrow(s) \circ t] \longrightarrow \underline{n}[s \circ (\uparrow \circ t)] & (RMap) & \underline{n+1}[\#(a) \circ s] \longrightarrow \underline{n}[s]
\end{array}$$

Theorem 30. *The dn-calculus is locally confluent and strongly normalizing.*

Proof. The proof of local confluence can be done automatically, for example by using CIME [31]. For strong normalization, we proceed exactly as in theorem 29.

Theorem 31 Special cases of the general scheme. *The non-extensional and extensional versions of the λ_σ, $\lambda_{\sigma_\Uparrow}$, λ_v, λ_d and λ_{dn} calculi are all confluent.*

Proof. The proof comes from theorem 22 and theorem 28. Since *Lambda*, *App* and *Beta* are well defined according to the definition of each cons-function and lift-function, we are left to show that these calculi are all basic (definition 11) and satisfy the general scheme (definition 18).

- Basic Conditions:
  - The proofs of strong normalization can be found in [21, 8] for σ, in [22] for $\sigma_\Uparrow$ and in [29] for v. Strong normalization for d (resp. dn) follows from theorem 29 (resp. theorem 30).
  - Confluence comes from local confluence and strong normalization by Newman's lemma.
  - σ-normal forms of terms are pure terms by [1]. The same happens for $\sigma_\Uparrow$ (see [22]) and v (see [29]). For the d and dn calculi, an induction on the structure of a suffices (see [25] for details).
  - Conditions 4, 5, 6 and 7 in definition 11 are straightforward in all the cases.
- General Scheme: we have to verify that for every variable $\underline{n}$ and every constructor ξ one of the cases described in definition 18 holds. By a simple inspection, we can observe in all these calculi that the behavior of id, $\uparrow$, $\circ$ and $\Uparrow$ corresponds to the first case of the definition, while . and $\#$ corresponds to the second case for the variable $\underline{1}$ and to the first case for any other variable $\underline{m+1}$.

5 Deriving confluence properties of other calculi

Our method can also be applied to λ-calculi that do not fit our definition of SC but that can be translated to some other substitution calculi. In particular, we show that the non-extensional and extensional versions of the λ_s-calculus [27] are confluent on closed terms.

Terms and substitutions of the λ_s-calculus are given by the following grammar:

$$(Terms)\ a ::= \underline{n} \mid aa \mid \lambda a \mid a\sigma^i b \mid \varphi^i_k a$$

The reduction rules are:

$$\begin{array}{lll}
(\sigma\text{-}generation) & (\lambda a)b & \longrightarrow a\sigma^1 b \\
(\sigma\text{-}\lambda\text{-}generation) & (\lambda a)\sigma^j b & \longrightarrow \lambda(a\sigma^{j+1}b) \\
(\sigma\text{-}destruction) & \underline{n}\sigma^j b & \longrightarrow \begin{cases} \underline{n-1} & \text{if } n > j \\ \varphi^j_0 b & \text{if } n = j \\ \underline{n} & \text{if } n < j \end{cases} \\
(\sigma\text{-}app\text{-}transition) & (a\,b)\sigma^j c & \longrightarrow (a\sigma^j c)(b\sigma^j c) \\
(\Phi\text{-}\lambda\text{-}transition) & \varphi^i_k(\lambda a) & \longrightarrow \lambda(\varphi^i_{k+1} a) \\
(\Phi\text{-}app\text{-}transition) & \varphi^i_k(a\,b) & \longrightarrow (\varphi^i_k a)(\varphi^i_k b) \\
(\Phi\text{-}destruction) & \varphi^i_k \underline{n} & \longrightarrow \begin{cases} \underline{n+i-1} & \text{if } n > k \\ \underline{n} & \text{if } n \le k \end{cases}
\end{array}$$

Even if this calculus does not fit in the general scheme defined in this paper, it turns out that it can be translated into a substitution calculus by preserving the desired confluence properties. In particular, λ_s turns out to be confluent as shown in [27], and, on the other hand, we can add an $\widehat{Eta}$-expansion rule to the λ_s-calculus preserving confluence of the whole reduction system. In order to define the $\widehat{Eta}$-rule in the λ_s-calculus, we first need the notions of Applied-Terms and Lambda-Abstractions introduced in definition 13.

Definition 32 Applied-Terms and Lambda-Abstractions. A term a is a *Lambda-Abstraction* if either it is λb; or it is equal to $b\sigma^i c$ or $\varphi^i_k b$ and b is a Lambda-Abstraction. Similarly, a subterm a is said to be an *Applied-Term* in $C[a]$ if it is applied in $C[a]$; while a is said to be an *Applied-Term* in $C[a\sigma^i c]$ (resp. in $C[\varphi^i_k a]$) if a is an Applied-Term in $C[a]$.

We are now ready to define $\widehat{Eta}$-expansions in the λ_s-calculus:

Definition 33 $\widehat{Eta}$-expansion in λ_s. The condition $\widehat{Eta}$-expansion in λ_s is defined to be the reflexive-transitive closure of the following reduction step:

$$C[a] \longrightarrow_{\widehat{Eta}} C[\lambda((\varphi^2_0 a)\ \underline{1})], \text{ if } \begin{cases} a : A \to B \\ a \text{ is not a Lambda-Abstraction} \\ a \text{ is not an Applied-Term in } C[a] \end{cases}$$

As expected, β-reduction and $\widehat{\eta}$-expansion can be simulated in the $\lambda_s \cup \widehat{Eta}$-calculus:

Theorem 34. *Let a be a pure term. Then $a \longrightarrow_{\beta\widehat{\eta}} b$ implies $a \longrightarrow^*_{\lambda_s \cup \widehat{Eta}} b$.*

Proof. If $a \longrightarrow_\beta b$, then the property holds by lemma 11 in [27]. Let $C[a] \longrightarrow_{\widehat{\eta}} C[\lambda(a^+\ \underline{1})]$, where $a \longrightarrow_{\widehat{\eta}} \lambda(a^+\ \underline{1})$. Then a is not a λ-abstraction and is not applied to another term, so by definition $a \longrightarrow_{\widehat{Eta}} \lambda((\varphi^2_0 a)\ \underline{1})$. By lemma 10 in [27] we have $\varphi^2_0 a \longrightarrow^*_s U^2_0(s(a)))$, but $s(a) = a$ since a is a pure term, and $U^2_0(a) = a^+$, which concludes the proof.

The λ_s-calculus has already been shown to be confluent in [27], so the aim here is to show that $\lambda_s \cup \widehat{Eta}$ is also confluent. We will use the following properties:

- s is strongly normalizing.
- s-normal forms of terms are pure terms.
- If a and b are pure terms, then $a \longrightarrow_{\beta\widehat{\eta}} b$ implies $a \longrightarrow^*_{\lambda_s \cup \widehat{Eta}} b$.
- There is a translation $\mathcal{T}$ from Λ^t_s to terms of some SC W such that $\mathcal{T}$ is the identity on pure terms and $a \longrightarrow_{\lambda_s \cup \widehat{Eta}} b$ implies $\mathcal{T}(a) \longrightarrow^*_{\lambda_W \cup \widehat{Eta}} \mathcal{T}(b)$.

We claim that these properties are sufficient to show that $\lambda_s \cup \widehat{Eta}$ is confluent. Indeed,

Proof. Let a be a term such that $b\ {}_{\lambda_s \cup \widehat{Eta}}{}^*\!\longleftarrow a \longrightarrow^*_{\lambda_s \cup \widehat{Eta}} c$. Since s is strongly normalizing, we can reduce b and c to their s-normal forms so that $s(b) = b'\ {}_{\lambda_s \cup \widehat{Eta}}{}^*\!\longleftarrow a \longrightarrow^*_{\lambda_s \cup \widehat{Eta}} c' = s(c)$. By the fourth hypothesis $\mathcal{T}(b')\ {}_{\lambda_W \cup \widehat{Eta}}{}^*\!\longleftarrow \mathcal{T}(a) \longrightarrow^*_{\lambda_W \cup \widehat{Eta}} \mathcal{T}(c')$, and by corollary 25 $W(\mathcal{T}(b')) \longrightarrow^*_{\beta\widehat{\eta}} k_1\ {}_{\beta\widehat{\eta}}{}^*\!\longleftarrow W(\mathcal{T}(a))$ and $W(\mathcal{T}(a)) \longrightarrow^*_{\beta\widehat{\eta}} k_2\ {}_{\beta\widehat{\eta}}{}^*\!\longleftarrow W(\mathcal{T}(c'))$, so that $k_1 \longrightarrow^*_{\beta\widehat{\eta}} k\ {}_{\beta\widehat{\eta}}{}^*\!\longleftarrow k_2$ by confluence of $\longrightarrow^*_{\beta\widehat{\eta}}$ (theorem 6). Since b' and c' are pure terms by the second hypothesis, then $\mathcal{T}(b') = b'$ and $\mathcal{T}(c') = c'$ hold by the fourth hypothesis and $W(b') = b'$ and $W(c') = c'$ hold by definition of substitution calculi. We then have $b' \longrightarrow^*_{\beta\widehat{\eta}} k\ {}_{\beta\widehat{\eta}}{}^*\!\longleftarrow c'$, and by the third hypothesis we obtain $b' \longrightarrow^*_{\lambda_s \cup \widehat{Eta}} k\ {}_{\lambda_s \cup \widehat{Eta}}{}^*\!\longleftarrow c'$ which concludes the proof.

Now, since s is strongly normalizing by Corollary 1 in [27], s-normal forms of terms are pure terms by lemma 12 in [26] and whenever a and b are pure terms, then $a \longrightarrow_{\beta\widehat{\eta}} b$ implies $a \longrightarrow^*_{\lambda_s \cup \widehat{Eta}} b$ by theorem 34, then we are left to show that there is a translation $\mathcal{T}$ satisfying the required properties.

As showed in [27], the λ_s-calculus has a nice translation $\mathcal{T}$ into the λ_υ-calculus that allows also to derive the confluence of $\lambda_s \cup \widehat{Eta}$ via the following property:

Proposition 35. *If* $a \longrightarrow_{\lambda_s \cup \widehat{Eta}} b$*, then* $\mathcal{T}(a) \longrightarrow^*_{\lambda_\upsilon \cup \widehat{Eta}} \mathcal{T}(b)$.

Proof. If $a \longrightarrow_{\lambda_s \cup \widehat{Eta}} b$ is not a root reduction, then we can proceed by induction on the structure of a. For that, it is important to notice that only root expansions are translated into root expansions, so that the inductive proof concerning this case is straightforward. If $a \longrightarrow_{\lambda_s \cup \widehat{Eta}} b$ is a root reduction, we proceed by case-analysis.

We can now finally obtain the following:

Theorem 36. $\longrightarrow^*_{\lambda_s \cup \widehat{Eta}}$ *is confluent.*

6 Conclusion

We give a general and homogeneous treatment of λ-calculi with explicit substitutions. Such treatment is essential in the field of implementation of functional programming because of the growing number of such calculi proposed in the literature. The major contributions of this paper can be summarized by the following points:

- We propose a general scheme for λ-calculi with explicit substitutions which allows to reason in an abstract way and to deal with many different calculi. In particular, we are able to deal with λ_σ, $\lambda_{\sigma_\Uparrow}$ and λ_υ, between others, using the same formalism and tools.
- We study confluence properties of extensional and non-extensional λ-calculi with explicit substitutions, where extensionality is interpreted by η-expansion. This reading of extensionality has never been studied before in the framework of explicit substitutions, and it turns out to be much more natural and less complex than previous interpretations via η-contraction.
- We derive two *new* calculi with explicit substitutions having nice properties. In particular, they have a composition operator for substitutions and simple constructors to implement all the other kind of substitutions. We conjecture that those calculi preserve β-strong normalization.

For those few calculi not fitting in the general scheme (such as λ_s [27]) that can be translated into a substitution calculus, we also showed how to reason about confluence of the combination of $Beta$-reduction with $\widehat{Eta}$-expansion. This is in some sense a generalization of the technique proposed via the general scheme.

We think that an abstract approach in the spirit of the one proposed in this paper would also be useful to study confluence properties on *open terms* and preservation of β-strong normalization, the challenge being the definition of an appropriate general scheme associated to those properties.

Acknowledgments

I would like to thank Pierre Lescanne and Gilles Dowek for interesting discussions, Roberto Di Cosmo for careful proofreading and useful comments, and Alejandro Ríos and Paul-André Mellies for explaining me some key points in the theory of calculi with explicit subtitutions.

References

[1] M. Abadi, L. Cardelli, P-L. Curien, and J-J. Lévy. Explicit substitutions. *JFP*, 4(1):375–416, 1991.

[2] Y. Akama. On mints' reductions for ccc-calculus. In *TLCA*, LNCS 664, 1993.

[3] H. Barendregt. *The Lambda Calculus; Its syntax and Semantics (revised edition)*. North Holland, 1984.

[4] Z-E-A. Benaissa and D. Briaud and P. Lescanne and J. Rouyer-Degli. λ_υ, a calculus of explicit substitutions which preserves strong normalisation. Available from `http://www.loria.fr/ lescanne/publications.html`. 1995.

[5] D. Briaud. An explicit *eta* rewrite rule. In *TLCA*, LNCS 902, 1995.

[6] P-L. Curien and R. Di Cosmo. A confluent reduction system for the λ-calculus with surjective pairing and terminal object. In *ICALP*, LNCS 510, 1991.

[7] P-L. Curien, T. Hardin, and J-J. Lévy. Confluence properties of weak and strong calculi of explicit substitutions. Technical Report 1617, INRIA Rocquencourt, 1992.

[8] P-L. Curien, T. Hardin, and A. Ríos. Strong normalisation of substitutions. In *MFCS'92*, LNCS 629, 1992.

[9] N. de Bruijn. Lambda-calculus notation with nameless dummies, a tool for automatic formula manipulation, with application to the church-rosser theorem. *Indag. Mat.*, 5(35):381–392, 1972.

[10] N. de Bruijn. Lambda-calculus notation with namefree formulas involving symbols that represent reference transforming mappings. *Indag. Mat.*, (40):384–356, 1978.

[11] Roberto Di Cosmo and Delia Kesner. A confluent reduction for the extensional typed $\lambda-$calculus with pairs, sums, recursion and terminal object. In *ICALP*, LNCS 700, 1993.

[12] Roberto Di Cosmo and Delia Kesner. Combining first order algebraic rewriting systems, recursion and extensional typed lambda calculi. In *ICALP*, LNCS 820, 1994.

[13] R. Di Cosmo and D. Kesner. Rewriting with extensional polymorphic λ-calculus. In *CSL*, 1995.

[14] R. Di Cosmo and A. Piperno. Expanding extensional polymorphism. In *TLCA*, LNCS 902, 1995.

[15] D. Dougherty. Some lambda calculi with categorical sums and products. In *RTA*, LNCS 690, 1993.

[16] Thomas Ehrhard. *Une sémantique catégorique des types dépendants. Application au calcul des constructions.* Thèse de doctorat, Université de Paris VII, 1988.

[17] J-Y. Girard, Y. Lafont, and P. Taylor. *Proofs and Types*. Cambridge University Press, 1990.

[18] T. Hardin. *Résultats de confluence pour les règles fortes de la logique combinatoire catégorique et liens avec les lambda-calculs.* Thèse de doctorat, Université de Paris VII, 1987.

[19] T. Hardin. η-reduction for explicit substitutions. In *ALP'92*, LNCS 632, 1992.

[20] T. Hardin. Eta-conversion for the languages of explicit substitutions. *AAECC*, 5:317–341, 1994.

[21] T. Hardin and A. Laville. Proof of termination of the rewriting system subst on c.c.l. *TCS*, 1986.

[22] T. Hardin and J-J. Lévy. A confluent calculus of substitutions. In *France-Japan Art. Int. and Comp. Sci. Symp.*, 1989.

[23] G. Huet. *Résolution d'équations dans les langages d'ordre* $1, 2, \ldots, \omega$. Thèse de doctorat d'état, Université Paris VII, 1976.

[24] C. Barry Jay and N. Ghani. The virtues of eta-expansion. *JFP*, 5(2):135–154, 1995.

[25] D. Kesner. Confluence properties of extensional and non-extensional λ-calculi with explicit substitutions, 1995. Available as `ftp://ftp.lri.fr/LRI/articles/kesner/explicit.ps.gz`.

[26] F. Kamareddine and A. Ríos. The confluence of the λs_e-calculus via a generalized interpretation method, 1995. Draft.

[27] F. Kamareddine and A. Ríos. A λ-calculus à la de bruijn with explicit substitutions. In *PLILP*, LNCS 982, 1995.

[28] P. Lescanne. Personal Communication.

[29] P. Lescanne. From λ_σ to λ_ν, a journey through calculi of explicit substitutions. In *POPL*, pages 60–69. ACM, 1994.

[30] P. Lescanne and J. Rouyer-Degli. The calculus of explicit substitutions $\lambda\nu$. Technical Report, INRIA, Lorraine, 1994.

[31] C. Marché. *Réécriture modulo une théorie présentée par un système convergent et décidabilité des problèmes du mot dans certains classes de théories équationnelles.* PhD thesis, Université Paris-Sud, Orsay, 1993.

[32] P-A. Mellies. Typed λ-calculi with explicit substitutions may not terminate. In *TLCA*, LNCS 902, 1995.

[33] G. Mints. Closed categories and the theory of proofs. *Zap. Nauch. Semin. Leningradskogo*, 68:83–114, 1977.

[34] G. Mints. Teorija categorii i teoria dokazatelstv.I. *Aktualnye problemy logiki i metodologii nauky*, pages 252–278, 1979.

[35] G. Pottinger. The Church Rosser Theorem for the Typed lambda-calculus with Surjective Pairing. *Notre Dame Jour. of Formal Logic*, 22(3):264–268, 1981.

[36] D. Prawitz. Ideas and results in proof theory. *Proceedings of the 2nd Scandinavian Logic Symposium*, pages 235–307, 1971.

[37] A. Ríos. *Contribution à l'étude des λ-calculus avec substitutions explicites.* Thèse de doctorat, Université de Paris VII, 1993.

[38] V. van Oostrom and F. van Raamsdonk. Weak orthogonality implies confluence: the higher-order case. In *LICS*, 1994

On the Power of Simple Diagrams

Roberto Di Cosmo

DMI-LIENS (CNRS URA 1327)
Ecole Normale Supérieure
45, Rue d'Ulm
75230 Paris, France
e-mail:dicosmo@dmi.ens.fr

Abstract. In this paper we focus on a set of abstract lemmas that are easy to apply and turn out to be quite valuable in order to establish confluence and/or normalization modularly, especially when adding rewriting rules for extensional equalities to various calculi. We show the usefulness of the lemmas by applying them to various systems, ranging from simply typed lambda calculus to higher order lambda calculi, for which we can establish systematically confluence and/or normalization (or decidability of equality) in a simple way. Many result are new, but we also discuss systems for which our technique allows to provide a much simpler proof than what can be found in the literature.

1 Introduction

During a recent investigation of confluence and normalization properties of polymorphic lambda calculus with an expansive version of the η rule, we came across a nice lemma that gives a simple but quite powerful sufficient condition to check the Church Rosser property for a compound rewriting system in a modular way, providing something of a dual to the usual well-known sufficient condition for the Hindley-Rosen Lemma. Also, under some additional assumptions, it allows to check strong normalization in a modular way. This lemma turns out to allow quite simple and elegant modular proofs of confluence and/or strong normalization for many rewriting systems associated to various lambda calculi.

Our purpose here is to present the lemma and give a survey of applications not only to the case of adding extensional equalities as conditional expansions but also as contractions. More precisely, we will apply it to prove:

- confluence and strong normalization for simple typed lambda calculus with expansive η and SP, also in the presence of *terminal object* and *iteration*
- confluence and strong normalization for the monadic calculus from [26]
- confluence for the polymorphic lambda calculus with expansive η and SP, also in the presence of *algebraic term rewriting systems*
- confluence for Girard's F^ω with expansive η, even with *algebraic term rewriting systems*
- confluence and strong normalization of the polymorphic extensional typed lambda calculus with Axiom C and contractive η from [23]

Of these results, the confluence and normalization for the monadic calculus, confluence for polymorphic lambda calculus with expansions and algebraic TRS's and confluence for Girard's F^ω with expansions with or without algebraic TRS's are, to the author's best knowledge, entirely new, while for the other results the proofs presented here are quite simpler than the previously published ones known to this author.

2 Brief Survey and the Commutation Lemma

First of all, let us recall some basic notation from rewriting theory that we will be using along the exposition.

Notation 1 (ARS) *An* abstract reduction system *is a pair* $\langle A, \xrightarrow{R} \rangle$ *of a set A and a binary relation* $\xrightarrow{R}$ *on A. The transitive reflexive closure of a relation* $\xrightarrow{R}$ *is denoted by* $\overset{R}{\twoheadrightarrow}$, *while* $\xrightarrow[=]{R}$ *denotes the reflexive closure of* $\xrightarrow{R}$. *When working with different ARS's* $\langle A, \xrightarrow{R} \rangle$ $\langle A, \xrightarrow{S} \rangle$ *share the same set A, we will often just talk about reductions* $\xrightarrow{R}$ *and* $\xrightarrow{S}$ *or even R and S. Also,* $R \cup S$ *denotes the reduction obtained as the union of R and S.*

Definition 2 Commutation of reductions. Two reductions $\xrightarrow{R}$ and $\xrightarrow{S}$ *commute* with each other if the following diagram holds:

$$\forall a, b, c \in \mathcal{A}, \exists d \in \mathcal{A} \quad \begin{array}{ccc} a & \xrightarrow{R} & c \\ \downarrow S & & \downarrow S \\ b & \xrightarrow{R} & d \end{array}$$

Definition 3 Confluence. A reduction $\xrightarrow{R}$ is *confluent* if $\overset{R}{\twoheadrightarrow}$ commutes with itself, and is *weakly (or locally) confluent* if the following diagram holds:

$$\forall a, b, c \in \mathcal{A}, \exists d \in \mathcal{A} \quad \begin{array}{ccc} a & \overset{R}{\twoheadrightarrow} & c \\ \downarrow S & & \downarrow S \\ b & \overset{R}{\twoheadrightarrow} & d \end{array}$$

Definition 4 Normalization. For an ARS $\langle A, \xrightarrow{R} \rangle$, we say that $\xrightarrow{R}$ is *strongly normalizing* if, for all $a \in A$, all reduction sequences starting form a are finite. An *R-normal form* is an element $a \in A$ such that no reduction out of it is possible. Also, $\xrightarrow{R}$ is *weakly normalizing* if, for all $a \in A$, there is a finite reduction sequence out of a leading to an R-normal form.

2.1 Modularity of confluence

One of the most known lemmas for showing confluence of rewriting system (especially when they are associated to various lambda calculi) is the following one, due to Hindley and Rosen:

Lemma 5 Hindley-Rosen ([4], section 3). *If* $\xrightarrow{R}$ *and* $\xrightarrow{S}$ *are confluent, and* $\overset{R}{\twoheadrightarrow}$ *and* $\overset{S}{\twoheadrightarrow}$ *commute with each other, then* $R \cup S$ *is confluent.*

Since establishing the commutation directly is often a very difficult task, because one has to cope with arbitrarily long S and R reduction sequences, one does not really use this lemma directly, but a via simpler precondition to commutation:

Lemma 6 usual sufficient condition for commutation. *If, whenever* $M \xrightarrow{R} M'$ *and* $M \xrightarrow{S} M''$, *there exist* M''' *s.t.* $M' \overset{S}{\twoheadrightarrow} M'''$ *and* $M'' \xrightarrow[=]{R} M'''$, *then* $\overset{R}{\twoheadrightarrow}$ *and* $\overset{S}{\twoheadrightarrow}$ *commute with each other.*

The condition imposed here to use *at most* one step of R reduction to close the diagram is quite restrictive, and is not satisfied for example in the presence of *restricted expansion rules*, that have become quite relevant today for handling extensionality in various lambda calculi (see for example [1, 15, 11, 9, 22]). This restriction is necessary if one does not know anything else about the two systems R and S, as a nice counterexample based on a never ending diagram chase from [4] shows:

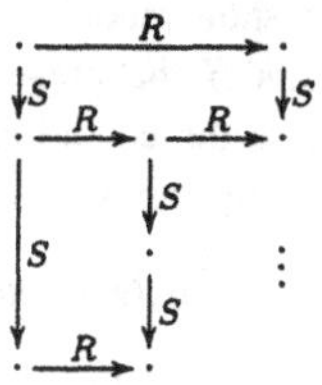

But this very counterexample suggest that, if R is a strongly normalizing system, then we can use a dual condition to the previous one: instead of imposing to use *at most* one step of R reduction ($\xrightarrow[=]{R}$) to close the diagram, one can ask for using *at least* one step of R reduction ($\xrightarrow[+]{R}\!\!\!\!\rightarrow$). This key observation is at the basis of our original lemma as it was stated in [14], which has a simple, but quite interesting proof (the original lemma assumed implicitly that R is finitely branching, but the version here has not such a restriction, thanks to a very helpful discussion with Pierre Lescanne).

Lemma 7 Commutation Lemma: a dual sufficient condition for commutation from [14]. *Let $\langle \mathcal{A}, \xrightarrow{R} \rangle$ and $\langle \mathcal{A}, \xrightarrow{S} \rangle$ be two abstract reduction systems, where R is strongly normalizing. Let the following diagram hold*

(DPG) $\qquad \forall a, b, c \in \mathcal{A}, \exists d \in \mathcal{A}$

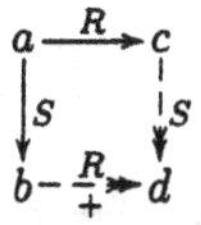

Then $\xrightarrow{R}\!\!\!\!\rightarrow$ *and* $\xrightarrow{S}\!\!\!\!\rightarrow$ *commute.*

Proof. Since R is a strongly normalizing rewriting system, we have a well-founded order $<$ on $\mathcal{A}$ by setting $a_1 < a_2$ if $a_2 \xrightarrow{R} a_1$. Also, let us denote $dist(a_1, a_2)$ the length of a given S-reduction sequence from a_1 to a_2. The proof then proceeds by well-founded induction on pairs $(b, dist(a, b))$, ordered lexicographically. Indeed, if b is an R-normal form and $dist(a, b) = 0$, then the lemma trivially holds. Otherwise, by hypothesis, there exist a', a'', a''' as in the following diagram.

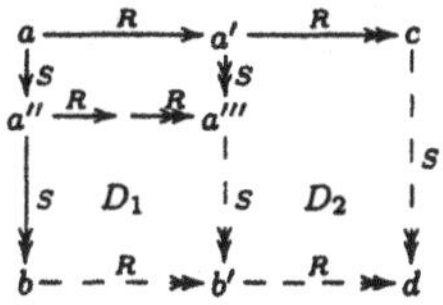

We can now apply the inductive hypothesis to the diagram D_1, since

$$(b, dist(a'', b)) <_{lex} (b, dist(a, b)).$$

Finally, we observe that $b \xrightarrow[+]{R}\!\!\!\!\rightarrow b'$, just composing the diagram in the hypothesis down from a.

Hence we can apply the inductive hypothesis to the diagram D_2, since

$$(b', dist(a', b')) <_{lex} (b, dist(a, b)),$$

and we are done.

Alfons Geser remarked this very same property in his PhD Thesis (see [17], page 38, remark after the proof sketch), where the (DPG) diagram is read as *R strictly locally commutes over S^-1*.

Remark. Notice that for (DPG) to hold, it must be the case that the relation $\xleftarrow{S}$ (the inverse of $\xrightarrow{S}$) preserve R-normal forms. This is a simple precondition that can be useful to discover that (DPG) does not hold: for example, if S is the usual η-contraction (see for example [4] for a discussion) and R is simple typed β, then $xy \xleftarrow{S} (\lambda z : A.xz)y$ and (DPG) does not hold.

2.2 Modularity of confluence and/or termination

In[1] Akama gives an interesting lemma to show modularity of both confluence and termination, by requiring some additional conditions on R and S, that presents the same difficulty as Hindley-Rosen's lemma, when one tries to use it directly, as the condition on S-normal forms requires to handle arbitrarily long S-reduction sequences in the hypothesis:

Lemma 8 [1]. *Let R and S be confluent and strongly normalizing reductions, s.t.*

$$\forall a, b \quad (a \xrightarrow{R} b) \quad \textit{implies} \quad (a^S \xrightarrow{R}\!\!\!\!\rightarrow b^S),$$

where a^S and b^S are the S-normal forms of a and b, respectively; then $R \cup S$ is also confluent and strongly normalizing.

Here too, we can help improve the situation with a simpler precondition:

Lemma 9 preconditions for modularity of confluence and/or normalization.
Let $\langle \mathcal{A}, \xrightarrow{R} \rangle$ and $\langle \mathcal{A}, \xrightarrow{S} \rangle$ be abstract reduction systems, where R-reduction is strongly normalizing. Let the following diagram hold

$$\forall a, b, c \in \mathcal{A}, \exists d \in \mathcal{A} \quad \begin{array}{ccc} a & \xrightarrow{R} & c \\ {\scriptstyle S}\downarrow & & \downarrow{\scriptstyle S} \\ b & \xrightarrow[+]{R}\!\!\!\!\rightarrow & d \end{array}$$

Then (as seen in 7) $\xrightarrow{R}\!\!\!\!\rightarrow$ and $\xrightarrow{S}\!\!\!\!\rightarrow$ commute and furthermore

- *(i) if R preserves S normal forms (let $S{\downarrow}$ denote reduction to S normal form), then*

$$\forall a, b, c \in \mathcal{A}, \exists d \in \mathcal{A} \quad \begin{array}{ccc} a & \xrightarrow{R}\!\!\!\!\rightarrow & c \\ {\scriptstyle S\downarrow}\downarrow & & \downarrow{\scriptstyle S\downarrow} \\ b & \xrightarrow{R}\!\!\!\!\rightarrow & d \end{array}$$

- *(ii) if S normal forms are unique and R preserves S normal forms, then*

$$\forall a, b, c, d \in \mathcal{A} \quad \begin{array}{ccc} a & \xrightarrow{R} & c \\ {\scriptstyle S\downarrow}\downarrow & & \downarrow{\scriptstyle S\downarrow} \\ b & \xrightarrow[+]{R}\!\!\!\!\rightarrow & d \end{array}$$

Proof. The first property can be shown by using 7. As for the second property, notice that by iterating 7 we can obtain:

$$\forall a, b, c \in \mathcal{A}, \exists d \in \mathcal{A} \quad \begin{array}{ccc} a & \xrightarrow{R} & c \\ {\scriptstyle S\downarrow}\downarrow & & \downarrow{\scriptstyle S\downarrow} \\ b & \xrightarrow[+]{R}\!\!\!\!\rightarrow & d' \end{array}$$

Where d' is an S-normal form because R preserves S-normal forms. But then, by unicity of S-normal forms, $d = d'$ and we are done.

The last item tells us that to check the commutation property required by Akama's lemma, which is a global property, as it involves arbitrarily long reduction sequences in the hypothesis, one can resort to just checking the same local condition we had before for commutation, which are usually boring but simple tasks, when R is strongly normalizing, S is confluent (which implies uniqueness of normal forms) *and* R preserves S-normal forms (the first two conditions beeing anyway part of the hypothesis of Akama's lemma). This gives

Corollary 10 Simplified Akama's Lemma. *Let S and R be confluent and strongly normalizing reductions, s.t.*

$$\forall a,b,c \in \mathcal{A}, \exists d \in \mathcal{A} \quad \begin{array}{ccc} a & \xrightarrow{R} & c \\ \downarrow S & & \downarrow S \\ b & \overset{R}{\underset{+}{\dashrightarrow}} & d \end{array}$$

and R preserves S-normal forms: then $S \cup R$ is also confluent and strongly normalizing.

3 Variations of the Lemma that do not work

We can now wonder if it is possible to relax a little the hypothesis of the lemmas, to allow empty R steps at least in some cases. Indeed, in some cases one is interested in combinations of rewriting systems that *both* contain erasers, i.e. rules that can erase redexes in the other system (like for example, contractive η together with β), and this prevents the many-step commutation required as an hypothesis by the lemma.

Consider the following example (the long $=$ signs mean equality of elements):

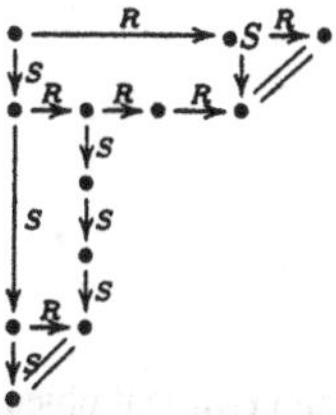

The strong normalization of R and S do not help here, since the newly built diagram can be exactly identical to the starting one, and one never gets to actually close it.

This is indeed a *counterexample* that rules out a whole bunch of possible even very weak relaxations of the hypothesis in the Lemma, detailed here.

- Allow empty R reduction only when also the closing S reduction is empty, that is reformulating the hypothesis as follows:

$$R\ \mathrm{SN}, \quad \forall a,b,c \in \mathcal{A}, \exists d \in \mathcal{A} \quad \begin{array}{ccc} a & \xrightarrow{R} & c \\ \downarrow S & & \downarrow S \\ b & \overset{R}{\underset{+}{\dashrightarrow}} & d \end{array} \quad or \quad \begin{array}{ccc} a & \xrightarrow{R} & b \\ \downarrow S & & \| \\ b & = & b \end{array}$$

  The example above is a counterexample: the only empty R reductions correspond to empty S reductions there.

- One can think that assuming also S strongly normalizing and allowing only simultaneously empty reductions the commutation property may hold. That is, using the following hypothesis:

$$R\ \mathrm{SN}, \quad S\ \mathrm{SN}, \quad \forall a,b,c \in \mathcal{A}, \exists d \in \mathcal{A} \quad \begin{array}{ccc} a & \xrightarrow{R} & c \\ \downarrow S & & +\downarrow S \\ b & \overset{R}{\underset{+}{\dashrightarrow}} & d \end{array} \quad or \quad \begin{array}{ccc} a & \xrightarrow{R} & b \\ \downarrow S & & \| \\ b & = & b \end{array}$$

  Again, the example above respects all the conditions: there are empty S reductions only where empty R reductions appear and vice-versa.

4 Applications : simple typed lambda calculus with expansive η and SP

As a first simple application of the lemma, consider the typed lambda calculus $\lambda^1\beta\eta\pi*$ for Cartesian Closed Categories: this consists of β, η, π, SP and a rule Top that collapses all terms of a special type T into a single constant $*$ (with both η and SP taken as expansions). A discussion of the conditional expansion rules falls outside the scope of this work (the interested reader will find a thorough discussion and motivation for example in [11]), but let us just point out that using the traditional contractive rules for η and SP, the system as it is not even confluent, and one has to go through a lot of hassle to complete it to a confluent one [10]. It is worth noting that the same problem for confluence comes up with algebraic rewriting rules for constant functions like $f(x) \longrightarrow a$.

$$
\begin{array}{lll}
(\beta) & (\lambda x : A.M)N \xrightarrow{\beta} M[N/x] & \\
(\pi_i) & \pi_i\langle M_1, M_2\rangle \xrightarrow{\pi_i} M_i, & \text{for } i = 1,2 \\
(SP) & M \xrightarrow{SP} \langle \pi_1(M), \pi_2(M)\rangle, & \text{if } \begin{cases} M : A \times B \\ M \text{ is not a pair and is not projected} \end{cases} \\
(\eta) & M \xrightarrow{\eta} \lambda x : A.Mx, & \text{if } \begin{cases} x\ fresh \\ M : A \Rightarrow C \\ M \text{ is not a } \lambda\text{-abstraction} \\ M \text{ is not applied} \end{cases} \\
(Top) & M \xrightarrow{Top} *, & \text{if } M : T \text{ and } M \not\equiv *
\end{array}
$$

Table 1. Reduction system for simple typed lambda calculus with expansions and terminal object.

There have been many different proofs of confluence and strong normalization in the literature for this calculus (or some variations of it) (for example [1, 15, 11, 9, 22]), but all of them are essentially technically complex exercises, with only [1, 11] using some kind of modular technique, yet requiring a serious amount of work.

Here our lemma suggests the following proof.

Theorem 11. *Simple typed λ-calculus with expansions and terminal object is confluent and strongly normalizing.*

Proof. It is easy to verify that rules η and SP do not erase any redex, while the rules β and π and Top preserve the normal forms of η and SP. Then it is quite natural to set $R = \beta \cup \pi \cup Top$ and $S = \eta \cup SP$, and try to apply our lemma 9. This boils down to checking a small subset of the diagrams one should check for the local confluence of the whole system (which is not a very easy task, because the reduction is no longer a congruence, but is unavoidable in any other proof technique[1]).

Then, since confluence and strong normalization for the two separate subsystems are already well known (and easy to show with traditional techniques), we can finally apply Akama's lemma and get confluence and normalization for the full system.

This gives an extremely simple and straightforward proof which is way easier than the already published ones.

[1] Actually, one can simply go over the relevant cases in [11], where local confluence is checked in detail, and verify that the *at least one step* condition is indeed respected.

4.1 Handling Iteration

As was originally remarked in [1], one is faced with serious technical difficulties when trying to use *directly* Akama's lemma to handle a weaker computational principle, namely iteration:

$$It(a, f, 0) \longrightarrow a \qquad It(a, f, S(e)) \longrightarrow f(It(a, f, e))$$

Indeed, one gets involved in a complex technical analysis of the shape of expansive normal forms that does not behave well when we add iteration.

Nevertheless, here again our simple precondition applies with no difficulty, and one gets confluence and strong normalization (local confluence is easy to check even with expansions, as the only nontrivial divergence, namely an expansion of f, can be closed by using β).

It is worth recalling here that using a modular technique presented in [12], it is now quite easy to show that the previous systems stays confluent if we add a recursion operator.

5 The monadic calculus for database query languages

This calculus, that arises from category theoretic considerations and forms the basis for an elegant database query language, was first introduced in [26]. An equivalent calculus NRC (see table 3)*without* these two last features has been proven confluent and strongly normalizing by Woong in his PhD thesis [28]. It contains a subset of the simple typed lambda calculus we have seen above, as it provides a limited form of β reduction (arguments of functions cannot be functions themselves), an equality axiom for the terminal object and the extensional equality axiom for pairs (SP) and functions (η).

$$\frac{}{\{\} : \{s\}} \qquad \frac{e : s}{\{e\} : \{s\}} \qquad \frac{\{e_1\} : \{s\} \quad \{e_2\} : \{s\}}{\{e_1 \cup e_2\} : \{s\}} \qquad \frac{\{e_1\} : \{s\} \quad \{e_2\} : \{t\}}{\bigcup\{e_1 | x \in e_2\} : \{s\}}$$

Table 2. The typing rules for sets in NRC

But it also provides constructors and operations to manipulate *sets* of values (terms and types for sets ($\{\}$), union ($\cup$) and a form of set comprehension ($\bigcup\{e_1 | x \in e_2\}$).
We are now able to state our result:

Theorem 12. *The reduction system for the monadic calulus with expansive η and SP is confluent and strongly normalizing.*

Proof. Take R to be the system proved CR and SN by Woong (that is the system of table 3 without expansions), and S to be expansive SP and η rules alone. The (DPG) diagram is easily checked, as expansive SP and η does not erase any R redex. Since R is SN and $SP \cup \eta$ is known to be CR and SN, this is enough to get confluence for the system with expansive SP using 7. It is very easy to check that R preserves $SP \cup \eta$ expansive normal forms: all rules in R preserve types (this ensure that no new redex due to types is created) and no rule can move a subterm from a position where an expansion is not legal to one where it is legal (the substitution rules can destroy expansion redexes, but not create them). So we get also strong normalization for the full system, using 9.

$$
\begin{array}{lll}
(\beta) & (\lambda x:A.M)N \xrightarrow{\beta} M[N/x] & (A \text{ not a functional type}) \\
(\pi_i) & \pi_i\langle M_1, M_2\rangle \xrightarrow{\pi_i} M_i, & \text{for } i = 1,2 \\
(SP) & M \xrightarrow{SP} \langle \pi_1(M), \pi_2(M)\rangle, & \text{if } \begin{cases} M : A \times B \\ M \text{ is not a pair and is not projected} \end{cases} \\
(\eta) & M \xrightarrow{\eta} \lambda x:A.Mx, & \text{if } \begin{cases} x\ fresh \\ M : A \Rightarrow C \\ M \text{ is not a } \lambda\text{-abstraction} \\ M \text{ is not applied} \end{cases} \\
(Top) & M \xrightarrow{Top} *, & \text{if } M : T \text{ and } M \not\equiv *
\end{array}
$$

$(Set\ monad\ operations)$

$$
\begin{array}{ll}
(empty) & \bigcup\{e|x \in \emptyset\} \longrightarrow \emptyset \\
(flat) & \bigcup\{e_1|x \in \{e_2\}\} \longrightarrow e_1[e_2/x] \\
(distrib) & \bigcup\{e|x \in (e_1 \cup e_2)\} \longrightarrow \bigcup\{e|x \in e_1\} \cup \bigcup\{e|x \in e_2\} \\
(assoc) & \bigcup\{e_1|x \in \bigcup\{e_2|y \in e_3\}\} \longrightarrow \bigcup\{\bigcup\{e_1|x \in e_2\}|y \in e_3\}
\end{array}
$$

Table 3. The reduction system for the monadic query calculus NRC

6 The polymorphic lambda calculus with expansive SP, η and η^2

The polymorphic lambda calculus (also known as Girard's System F, see [20]) adds to the simple typed lambda calculus the possibility of taking types as parameters, via type abstraction $\Lambda X.M$ and type application $M[A]$. The essential features from the rewriting point of view are a new β^2 rule that is analogous to β, but operates on types, and a *contractive* extensional rule η^2_c:

$$
\begin{array}{ll}
(\beta^2) & (\Lambda X.M)[A] \xrightarrow{\beta^2} M[A/X] \\
(\eta^2_c) & (\Lambda X.M[X]) \xrightarrow{\eta^2_c} M \quad (\text{if } X \notin FTV(M))
\end{array}
$$

where $FTV(M)$ is the set of free type variables of M.
For the same reasons why expansions are recognized as a necessity for first order calculi, one would also like better to use an *expansive* rule for η^2

$$
(\eta^2)\ M \xrightarrow{\eta^2} (\Lambda X.M[X]) \text{ if } \begin{cases} X fresh \\ M : \forall X.A \\ M \text{ is not a polymorphic } \lambda\text{-abstraction} \\ M \text{ is not applied} \end{cases}
$$

Now, our simple lemmas allow us to derive in a very straightforward way the confluence of this system with expansion rules.

Theorem 13 Confluence with expansions. *The polymorphic lambda calculus with expansive SP, η and η^2 is confluent.*

Proof. First of all, notice that $SP \cup \eta \cup \eta^2$ is confluent, as it enjoys the diamond property. Now, for the full calculus, take R to be the usual polymorphic lambda calculus without expansion rules, which we know is confluent and strongly normalizing, and let S be the system made up of the expansion rules alone (SP, η and η^2). It is an easy task to check (DPG), as the only new cases are due to η^2 and β^2 (see [13]), and the expansion rules do not erase R redexes. Again, we can apply 7, and confluence for the full system follows.

It should be noted that the strategy consisting in doing all non-expansive steps first and then only expansions is normalizing, so this very simple proof (that gives us confluence) is already enough both for getting decidability of equality and getting the unicity of polymorphic $\beta\eta$-long normal forms, which is useful in higher order unification [21].

6.1 Handling confluent algebraic term rewriting systems (TRS's)

It is also possible to go on further and show that whenever we have a canonical (that is, confluent and strongly normalizing) algebraic TRS, then it can be added to system F with expansion rules, preserving decidability of equality. One important property we will use is the following, that holds for arbitrary TRS's:

Lemma 14 Algebraic reduction commutes with reduction to expansive normal form. *Let M, M' be arbitrary terms, and M^E, M'^E be their repective expansive normal forms. Then whenever $M \xrightarrow{\mathcal{T}} M'$, we have $M^E \xrightarrow{\mathcal{T}}\!\!\!\!\rightarrow M'^E$.*

Proof. A simple induction on the structure of terms, using in the crucial case the fact (proven by induction on the structure of algebraic terms) that $(A[M/x])^E = A[M^E/x]$ for any *algebraic* term A.

Now, we will first show a simple and self-contained proof technique that works only in the case that the rewriting system is also *left-linear* (i.e. when variables occur at most once in the l.h.s. of any algebraic rewriting rule):

Theorem 15 Expansive System F plus left-linear TRS's. *Let $\mathcal{T}$ be a left-linear algebraic TRS which is confluent and strongly normalizing. Then System F with expansions together with $\mathcal{T}$ forms a confluent system.*

Proof. We already established that (DPG) holds taking system F as the horizontal system and expansions as the vertical one. Lemma 14 shows that (DPG) holds also taking the left linear algebraic system $\mathcal{T}$ as the horizontal reduction and expansions as the vertical reduction. Taken together, these two facts give

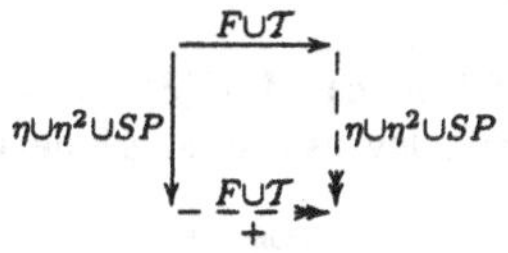

We know from [6, 8] that combining the non-extensional simply typed lambda calculus with a confluent first-order algebraic rewriting system preserves confluence. On the other hand, this combination yields a strongly normalizing system when the algebraic one is [7, 25]. This is enough to apply lemma 7 and obtain confluence of F with expansions together with $\mathcal{T}$.

Corollary 16. *System F together with a left-linear canonical TRS is a decidable system.*

Proof. The expansions preserve also algebraic normal forms (because the system is left linear), and the strategy consisting in going to $F \cup \mathcal{T}$ normal form first and then normalize w.r.t. the expansion rules is normalizing. This, together with confluence, gives a decision procedure for equality.

Handling non left-linear TRS's

The restriction to left-linear TRS's is imposed here by the necessity to ensure that (DPG) holds, which cannot be the case in the presence of non-left-linear rules: a vertical reduction could destroy an horizontal redex. But it is possible to raise this restriction by using some technical results from [8]:

there it is shown that algebraic reductions commute with reduction to normal form in F without extensional rules(which we write here $F \downarrow$)

$$
\begin{array}{ccc}
 & \xrightarrow{\quad T \quad} & \\
F\downarrow & & \bigg\downarrow F\downarrow \\
 & \xrightarrow[\quad T \quad]{} &
\end{array}
$$

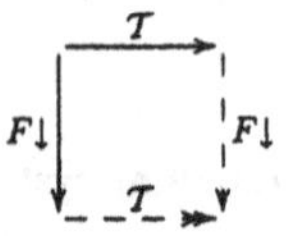

We can show the same result w.r.t. expansion rules.

Lemma 17 Expansions commute with reduction to F normal form. *Reduction to F normal form commutes w.r.t. expansion rules, i.e. the following diagram holds:*

$$
\begin{array}{ccc}
 & \xrightarrow{\quad \eta \cup SP \quad} & \\
F\downarrow & & \bigg\downarrow F\downarrow \\
 & \xrightarrow[\quad \eta \cup SP \quad]{} &
\end{array}
$$

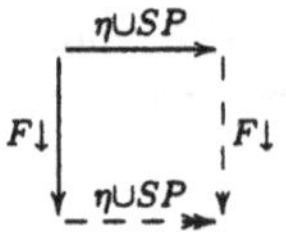

Proof. We have shown above, by establishing (DPG) and using our commutation lemma, that expansions commute with the reductions in F without extensional rules, that is

$$
\begin{array}{ccc}
 & \xrightarrow{\quad \eta \cup SP \quad} & \\
F & & \bigg\downarrow F \\
 & \xrightarrow[\quad \eta \cup SP \quad]{} &
\end{array}
$$

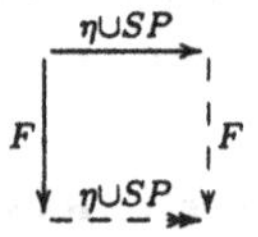

Now the result is a direct consequence of the fact that expansions preserve F-normal forms (the restriction are there exactly to insure this).

We can now state the main result:

Theorem 18 Expansive System F with confluent TRS's. *System F plus expansion rules plus an arbitrary confluent TRS T is confluent.*

Proof. Lemmas 17 together with 14 and lemma 4.1 of [8] (which states that algebraic reduction commutes with reduction to β normal form) allow us to establish the following simulation property:

$$
\begin{array}{ccc}
 & \xrightarrow{\quad F \cup T \cup \eta \cup SP \quad} & \\
F\downarrow & & \bigg\downarrow F\downarrow \\
 & \xrightarrow[\quad T \cup \eta \cup SP \quad]{} &
\end{array}
$$

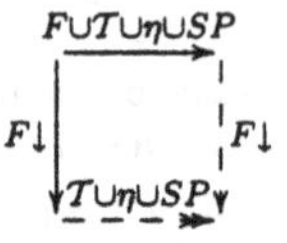

since $F \downarrow$ is confluent, this allows to reduce the confluence of $F \cup T \cup \eta \cup SP$ to confluence of $T \cup \eta \cup SP$, which can be in turn reduced, due to the confluence of expansion rules, to confluence of T via the simulation established in 14. Bu T is confluent by hypothesis, and we are done.

It is worth noting that the normal forms in this rewriting system are exactly Huet's second order *long $\beta\eta$ normal forms*.

7 Girard's F^ω with expansion rules

A quite surprising fact, the proof strategy we used to show decidability of F plus expansion rules even in the presence of canonical left linear TRS's can be used with no changes at all to show decidability of Girard's F^ω with expansive η, even with left linear canonical TRS's added. We do not fully introduce here the syntax and typing judgements for System F^ω (see [16] for a detailed introduction to the topic), but let's recall that this system is basically System F with a simple typed lambda calculus *over its types*, the types of the types being now called *kinds*. More formally, kinds, types and terms are defined by the following grammar:

$$\begin{array}{rl}(Kinds) & K := *|K \to K \\ (Types) & T := t|A|T\Rightarrow T|\forall t : K.T|\lambda t : K.T|T\,T \\ (Terms) & M := x|\lambda x : T.M|M\,M|\Lambda t : K.M|M[T]\end{array}$$

and one only works with those types that kind-check and terms that type-check w.r.t. appropriate kinding and typing rules (here we follow essentially the presentation from [16]).

$$\frac{\Gamma, t : K_1 \vdash s : K_2}{\Gamma \vdash (\lambda t : K_1.s) : K_1 \to K_2} \qquad \frac{\Gamma \vdash t : K_1 \to K_2 \quad \Gamma \vdash s : K_1}{\Gamma \vdash ts : K_2}$$

$$\frac{\Gamma, t : * \vdash s : *}{\Gamma \vdash \forall t : *.s : *} \qquad \frac{\Gamma \vdash t : * \quad \Gamma \vdash s : *}{\Gamma \vdash t \Rightarrow s : *}$$

Table 4. Kinding judgements

Over the types, that now form a simple typed lambda calculus, we have the usual β and η equality, that we turn into rewriting by choosing the usual β-reduction and restricted expansion rule for η. Once the well-kinded types are defined, one defines the well-typed terms as in table 5.

$$\frac{\Gamma, x : t_1 \vdash M : t_2}{\Gamma \vdash (\lambda x : t_1.M) : t_1 \Rightarrow t_2} \qquad \frac{\Gamma \vdash M : t_1 \Rightarrow t_2 \quad \Gamma \vdash N : t_1}{\Gamma \vdash MN : t_2}$$

$$\frac{\Gamma, t_1 : K \vdash M : t_2}{\Gamma \vdash \Lambda t_1 : K.M : \forall t_1 : K.t_2} \qquad \frac{\Gamma \vdash M : \forall t_1 : K.t_2 \quad \Gamma \vdash s : K}{\Gamma \vdash M[s] : t_2[s/t_1]}$$

$$\frac{\Gamma \vdash M : t \quad t =_{\beta\eta} s}{\Gamma \vdash M : s}$$

Table 5. Typing judgements

Over terms, one has the usual β reduction, both for term application and for type application. The most remarkable fact is that now a term has no longer a *unique* type, and this is a fact that we need to consider when defining expansion rules.

We have no difficulty in writing the higher order η-expansion rule by simply generalizing the one for System F:

$$(\eta^\omega)\ M \xrightarrow{\eta^\omega} (\Lambda t : K.M[t]) \text{ if } \begin{cases} t\ fresh \\ M : (\forall t : K.A) \\ M \text{ is not a polymorphic } \lambda\text{-abstraction} \\ M \text{ is not applied} \end{cases}$$

But for the first order expansion, due to the type conversion rules, the usual η expansion rule taken alone is now not even confluent, as it can be the case that:

$$\lambda x : A'.Mx \xleftarrow{\eta} M \xrightarrow{\eta} \lambda x : A.Mx$$

where we only know that $A =_{\beta\eta} A'$ in the type-conversion relation.
For this reason, we chose to work with a somewhat more restrictive rule, that only allow expansion with types in normal form w.r.t. the simple typed lambda calculus over types.

$$(\overline{\eta})\ M \xrightarrow{\eta} \lambda x : A.Mx, \text{ if } \begin{cases} x\ fresh \\ M : A \Rightarrow C, \textit{with } A \Rightarrow C \textit{ in type normal form} \\ M \text{ is not a } \lambda\text{-abstraction} \\ M \text{ is not applied} \end{cases}$$

Let's call F^{ω}_{exp} the rewriting system composed by the usual rules for F^{ω} plus expansive η and η^{ω}, and call $F^{\omega}_{\overline{exp}}$ the system F^{ω}_{exp} with our limited expansion rule $\overline{\eta}$ instead of η. The choice of a limited version of η expansion does not make us loose any equality.

Lemma 19 $F^{\omega}_{\overline{exp}}$ and F^{ω}_{exp} vs. F^{ω}-equality. *The reflexive, symmetric and transitive closure of $\xrightarrow{F^{\omega}_{exp}}$ generates the usual equality over terms of F^{ω}. The same holds for $\xrightarrow{F^{\omega}_{\overline{exp}}}$.*

Proof. This comes from the fact that all η equalities $M = \lambda x : A.Mx$ that seem to be forbidden by our restrictions on the expansions can be obtained either by β-reduction of $\lambda x : A.Mx$ (both for F^{ω}_{exp} and $F^{\omega}_{\overline{exp}}$) or by the *type reduction* (which we know is confluent) of A (needed for $F^{\omega}_{\overline{exp}}$).

Now, for this system, we can use the same proof strategy as for System F:

Theorem 20 Confluence with expansions. *System $F^{\omega}_{\overline{exp}}$ is confluent and weakly normalizing (thus decidable).*

Proof. The proof proceeds exactly as for System F (the only novelty is the need to show that $\eta \cup \eta^{\omega}$ is confluent, which is trivial as they enjoy the diamond property).

Much in the same way as for System F, we can then also establish the following:

Theorem 21 System $F^{\omega}_{\overline{exp}}$ plus left-linear TRS's. *Let T be a left-linear algebraic TRS which is confluent and strongly normalizing. Then $F^{\omega}_{\overline{exp}} \cup T$ forms a confluent and weakly normalizing (thus decidable) system.*

Indeed, we can now even prove the following:

Corollary 22 Confluence with general η-expansion. *The system F^{ω}_{exp} (where η is not restricted to type normal forms) is confluent and weakly normalizing.*

Proof. Consider a divergence $M' \twoheadleftarrow M \twoheadrightarrow M''$ in the system F^{ω}_{exp}. This means that $M' = M''$, and since the equality generated by F^{ω}_{exp} is the same as the usual one for F^{ω}, we have that $M' \xrightarrow{F^{\omega}_{\overline{exp}}}\!\!\!\!\!\rightarrow M''' \twoheadleftarrow_{F^{\omega}_{\overline{exp}}} M''$, and since an expansion on type-normal form is a special case of the non-restricted one, this is also $M' \xrightarrow{F^{\omega}_{exp}}\!\!\!\!\!\rightarrow M''' \twoheadleftarrow_{F^{\omega}_{exp}} M''$.
As for normalization, the same strategy as for $F^{\omega}_{\overline{exp}}$ will obviously do.

Corollary 23. *The union of the system F^{ω}_{exp} with a canonical left-linear TRS is confluent and weakly normalizing (hence decidable).*

8 The polymorphic lambda calculus with Axiom C

This calculus stems from a promising new analysis of parametricity proposed in [23], where it is shown that it is sound to add the following axiom C to the polymorphic lambda calculus (system F):

$$(Axiom\ C) \qquad \frac{\Gamma| - M : \forall X.\alpha, \quad X \notin FV(\Gamma) \cup FV(\alpha)}{M\sigma = M\tau}$$

Where $FV(M)$ is the set of free variables of M. It has been long open the problem to prove that the equational theory of the resulting system F_C is decidable, which can be done for example showing that the usual reduction rules for system F plus the following new ones form a confluent and normalizing system:

$$(\beta^2_C)\ M[\sigma/X] \longrightarrow M[\forall X.X/X]\ (M:\alpha, X \notin FTV(\alpha), \sigma \neq \forall X.X)$$
$$(\eta^2_C)\quad \Lambda X.M[\forall X.X] \longrightarrow M \quad (M:\forall Y.\alpha, Y \notin FV(\alpha), X \notin FV(M))$$

Only recently in [5] it has been proved that this system is indeed CR and SN, using a non modular approach. We show here how, using our simple lemma, we can get the decidability of equality in F_C in a very straightforward manner (via confluence and weak normalization). Let us start with the system F_C without the extensional rules η^2 and η^2_C. We apply our technique taking system F without η^2 (we will denote it F') as R (the horizontal reduction) and just β^2_C as S (the vertical reduction).

Lemma 24. *System F' plus β^2_C is confluent and strongly normalizing.*

Proof. The two systems are separately confluent and strongly normalizing (normalization for β^2_C is trivial as each reduction strictly decreases the number of redexes, while confluence comes from a rather sophisticated result in [23], but again this is out of the scope of the present paper). The commutation can be easily checked, and the *at least one step* is guaranteed by the fact that β^2_C does not erase redexes of F', as no reduction in this system depends on the particular form of a type (which is not the case of η^2). Finally, it is easily seen that system F' preserves β^2_C normal forms. Then, we can apply our lemma 9 and Akama's lemma and we are done.

Then we focus on a restricted version of the rules η^2_C and η^2:

$$(\eta^{2\,\prime}_C)\ \Lambda X.M[\forall X.X] \longrightarrow M \text{ if } \begin{cases} X \notin FTV(M) \\ M \neq \Lambda Z.M' \text{ with } Z \notin FTV(M') \\ \Lambda X.M[\forall X.X] \text{ is not applied to the type } \forall X.X \end{cases}$$

$$(\eta^{2\prime})\quad \Lambda X.M[X] \longrightarrow M \quad \text{if } \begin{cases} X \notin FTV(M) \\ M \neq \Lambda Z.M' \\ \Lambda X.M[X] \text{ is not applied to a type} \end{cases}$$

Lemma 25. *The system $\eta^{2\prime} \cup \eta^{2\,\prime}_C$ is strongly normalizing and confluent.*

Proof. Strong normalization is trivial, as the rules decrease the number of Λ's in a term. Confluence is also easy, as the system has the diamond property.

We are now in a position to state the main results:

Theorem 26. *The rewriting system for F_C is confluent.*

Proof. For confluence, take R as system $F' \cup \beta_C$ and S as $\eta^{2\prime} \cup \eta^{2\,\prime}_C$: it is easy to check the (DPG) diagram, where the at least one step is guaranteed by the restrictions imposed on $\eta^{2\prime}$ and $\eta^{2\,\prime}_C$, and then we get confluence of the system $F' \cup \beta_C \cup \eta^{2\prime} \cup \eta^{2\,\prime}_C$ using lemma 7. But it is quite easy to check that if $M \xrightarrow{\eta^2_C} M'$, then we have either $M \xrightarrow{\eta^{2\,\prime}_C} M'$ or $M \xrightarrow{\beta^2} M'$, and that if $M \xrightarrow{\eta^2} M'$, then either $M \xrightarrow{\eta^{2\prime}} M'$or $M \xrightarrow{\beta^2} M'$, so $F' \cup \beta_C \cup \eta^{2\prime} \cup \eta^{2\,\prime}_C$ is the same as $F \cup \beta_C \cup \eta^2_C$ and we are done.

To show that equality in F_C is decidable, it is enough to provide a normalizing strategy (like the one that does $\eta^2 \cup \beta^2_C \cup \eta^2_C$ after F'), but we are able to show more:

Theorem 27. *The rewriting system for F_C is strongly normalizing.*

Proof. Since β^2 does not preserve η^2_C normal forms, we cannot obtain strong normalization *directly* from our lemma, but the commutation we have shown using our lemma between β^2_C and F' allow to obtain the result indirectly via a sort of postponement of $\eta^2 \cup \eta^2_C$. Indeed, in the system F_C η^2 can be postponed to any other rule, while it is possible to show that from any infinite reduction containing η^2_C one can build an infinite reduction not containing it. The only case when η^2_C cannot be simply postponed arises when we have a reduction sequence

$$C[(\Lambda X.(\Lambda Y.M)[\forall X.X])[A]] \xrightarrow{\eta^2_C} C[(\Lambda Y.M)[A]] \xrightarrow{\beta^2} C[M[A/Y]]$$

and then the only thing we can do to perform β^2 first is either

$$C[(\Lambda X.(\Lambda Y.M)[\forall X.X])[A]] \xrightarrow{\beta^2} C[(\Lambda X.M[\forall X.X/Y])[A]] \xrightarrow{\beta^2} C[M[\forall X.X/Y]]$$

where the last step uses the fact that $X \notin FTV(M)$, or

$$C[(\Lambda X.(\Lambda Y.M)[\forall X.X])[A]] \xrightarrow{\beta^2} C[(\Lambda Y.M)[\forall X.X]] \xrightarrow{\beta^2} C[M[\forall X.X/Y]]$$

where the first step uses the fact that $X \notin FTV(M)$. In any case, we did not achieve a real postponement, as we do not get to $C[M[A/Y]]$. Nevertheless, remark that an infinite reduction sequence can be projected via β^2_C into another infinite reduction sequence (using (DPG) as established in 24 this is quite easy), and then we can proceed as follows to build an infinite sequence without η^2_C from an infinite sequence containing it: postpone the rule whenever possible, and when it is not possible we can build the diagram

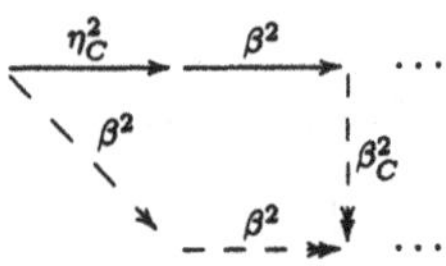

where we have managed to bring to front at least one β^2 step, while still having an infinite sequence available (the one projected via β^2_C is still infinite). This is enough to reduce normalization of F_C to the already known normalization for F.

9 Conclusions

We have studied a few lemmas for proving the commutation of two rewriting relations and/or the preservation of strong normalization. Despite their extreme simplicity, we showed that they can be of great utility in proving confluence and/or normalization of many rewriting systems associated to various typed lambda calculi, especially (but not only) when one needs to use expansive rewriting rules for η and surjective pairing in order to get a confluent system in the presence of rules like Top or of general algebraic rewriting systems. The major advantages of the lemmas are the simplicity of the preconditions that one needs to establish. This has allowed us to collect in just one paper a survey of results that, with the traditional approaches, would have required (or have required, for the old results like the simple typed lambda calculus), a full paper by themselves. It is worth mentioning that what we presented here is also a relevant contribution to the study of expansion rules in rewriting with typed lambda calculi, which are now widely used.

Acknowledgements I am endebted to Delia Kesner, for many discussions and comments on the whole work, and to Adolfo Piperno for many pleasurable discussions on the rewriting lemma.

References

1. Y. Akama. On Mints' reductions for ccc-Calculus. In *TLCA*, n. 664 in LNCS, pages 1–12. Springer Verlag, 1993.
2. F. Barbanera. Combining term-rewriting and type-assignment systems. In *3rd It. Conf. on TCS*, 1989.
3. F. Barbanera, M. Fernandez, and H. Geuvers. Modularity of strong normalization and confluence in the algebraic-λ-cube. In *LICS*, Paris, 1994.
4. H. Barendregt. *The Lambda Calculus; Its syntax and Semantics (revised edition)*. North Holland, 1984.
5. G. Bellè. Syntactical properties of an extension of girard's system f where types can be taken as "generic" inputs. 1995. Available as `ftp://idefix.disi.unige.it/pub/gbelle/systemFC.ps.Z`.
6. V. Breazu-Tannen. Combining algebra and higher order types. In *LICS*, pages 82–90, July 1988.
7. V. Breazu-Tannen and J. Gallier. Polymorphic rewriting preserves algebraic strong normalization. *TCS*, 83:3–28, 1991.
8. V. Breazu-Tannen and J. Gallier. Polymorphic rewiting preserves algebraic confluence. *Inf. and Comp.*, 114:1–29, 1994.
9. D. Cubric. On free CCC. Distributed on the `types` mailing list, 1992.
10. P.-L. Curien and R. Di Cosmo. A confluent reduction system for the λ-calculus with surjective pairing and terminal object. *JFP*, 1995. To appear. A preliminary version appeared in *ICALP* 91.
11. R. Di Cosmo and D. Kesner. Simulating expansions without expansions. *MSCS*, 4:1–48, 1994.
12. R. Di Cosmo and D. Kesner. Combining algebraic rewriting, extensional lambda calculi and fixpoints. *TCS*, 1995. To appear.
13. R. Di Cosmo and D. Kesner. Rewriting with polymorphic extensional λ-calculus. In *CSL'95 (extended abstract)*, 1995. Full version accepted for CSL95 Proceedings, to appear in 1996.
14. R. Di Cosmo and A. Piperno. Expanding extensional polymorphism. In M. Dezani-Ciancaglini and G. Plotkin, editors, *TLCA*, volume 902 of *LNCS*, pages 139–153, Apr. 1995.
15. D. J. Dougherty. Some lambda calculi with categorical sums and products. In *RTA*, 1993.
16. J. Gallier. *On Girard's "Candidats de Reductibilité"*, pages 123–203. Logic and Computer Science. Academic Press, 1990.
17. A. Geser. *Relative termination*. Dissertation, Fakultät für Mathematik und Informatik, Universität Passau, Germany, 1990.
18. N. Ghani. $\beta\eta$-equality for coproducts. In M. Dezani-Ciancaglini and G. Plotkin, editors, *TLCA*, volume 902 of *LNCS*, 1995.
19. N. Ghani. Extensionality and polymorphism. University of Edimburgh, Submitted, 1995.
20. J.-Y. Girard, Y. Lafont, and P. Taylor. *Proofs and Types*. Cambridge University Press, 1990.
21. G. Huet. Résolution d'équations dans les langages d'ordre $1, 2, \ldots, \omega$. *Thèse d'Etat, Université Paris VII*, 1976.
22. C. B. Jay and N. Ghani. The Virtues of Eta-expansion. *JFP*, 5(2):135–154, Apr. 1995.
23. G. Longo, K. Milsted, and S. Soloviev. The Genericity Theorem and effective Parametricity in Polymorphic lambda-calculus. *TCS*, 121:323–349, 1993.
24. G. Mints. Teorija categorii i teoria dokazatelstv.I. *Aktualnye problemy logiki i metodologii nauky*, pages 252–278, 1979.
25. M. Okada. Strong normalizability for the combined system of the types lambda calculus and an arbitrary convergent term rewrite system. In *Symp. Symb. and Alg. Comp.*, 1989.
26. V. Tannen, P. Buneman, and L. Wong. Naturally embedded query languages. In *4th Int. Conf. on Database Theory*, n. 646 in LNCS, 1992. Available as `ftp://www.cis.upenn.edu/pub/papers/db-research/icdt92.dvi.Z`.
27. V. van Oostrom. Developing developments. Draft, 1994.
28. L. Wong. *Querying nested collections*. PhD thesis, University of Pennsylvania, 1994. Available as `ftp://www.cis.upenn.edu/pub/papers/db-research/limsoonphd.ps.Z`.

Coherence for Sharing Proof Nets *

S. Guerrini[1], S. Martini[2], A. Masini[1]

[1] Dipartimento di Informatica, Università di Pisa,
Corso Italia, 40, I-56125 Pisa – Italy; guerrini,masini@di.unipi.it.
[2] Dipartimento di Matematica e Informatica, Università di Udine,
Via delle Scienze, 206, I-33100 Udine – Italy; martini@dimi.uniud.it.

ABSTRACT: Sharing graphs are a way of representing linear logic proof-nets in such a way that their reduction never duplicates a redex. In their usual presentations, they present a problem of coherence: if the proof-net N reduces by standard cut-elimination to N', then, by reducing the sharing graph of N we do *not* obtain the sharing graph of N'. We solve this problem by changing the way the information is coded into sharing graphs and introducing a new reduction rule (*absorption*). The rewriting system is confluent and terminating.

1 Introduction

Implementations of functional languages based on graph rewriting need sophisticated techniques to control the runtime duplication of subgraphs. From a theoretical point of view, we know after [Lév78] that given a normalizable λ-term there is an optimal (in the number of beta-reductions) reduction strategy to reach the normal form. Since, however, it is a parallel strategy (counting as a single step the simultaneous reduction of several redexes, those belonging to the same *family*), how to implement this strategy remained open until Lamping [Lam90] introduced his *sharing graphs*.

Sharing graphs are based on three main ideas. First, any time a duplication seems required (e.g., when a bound variable appears several times in the body of a term), it is not actually performed; it is instead indicated (in a somewhat lazy way) by specific (new) nodes in the graph (*fans*, in Lamping's terminology). Second, special reduction rules are added to perform the actual duplication in a controlled way (a redex will be never duplicated). Finally (and non trivially), there is a way to mark the boundary of the subgraph where duplication has to happen (again new nodes, the *brackets*). The reduction then proceeds in a distributed and asynchronous way, firing locally those reduction rules which apply. The crucial properties to show are then: (i) this asynchronous process terminates (if the term has a normal form); (ii) the normal form is (a possibly shared representative of) the normal form we would have reached we had done the reduction in the standard way; and (iii) no useless duplication is ever done (i.e., optimality of beta-reduction).

* Partially supported by: HCM Project CHRX-CT93-0046 and CNR GNSAGA (Guerrini,Martini); by BRA 8130 LOMAPS (Masini); by MURST 40% “Modelli della computazione e dei linguaggi di programmazione”.

Following Lamping's breakthrough, several papers generalized and improved his result. First, Gonthier, Abadi, and Lévy [GAL92a, GAL92b] realized that Lamping's method was in fact a way to reduce linear logic proof-nets [Gir87] and that the information needed to mark the boundary of the subgraph to be duplicated, was a local and distributed representation of the (global) notion of (linear logic) "box". Asperti showed how the same problems might be approached from a categorical point of view [Asp95b], and Asperti and Laneve generalized the theory to the "interaction systems" [AL93]. The relations with the geometry of interaction are investigated in [ADLR94].

Sharing graphs present a problem of coherence. Suppose that the proof-net (or lambda-term) N reduces by standard cut-elimination (beta-reduction) to N'. Then, by reducing the sharing graph corresponding to N we do ***not*** obtain the sharing graph corresponding (in the given translation) to N'. The recovering of the proof-net N' is instead obtained by the so-called ***read-back*** process, a semantically based procedure *external* to the reduction system, which essentially computes the equivalence quotient of all the sharing graphs representing the same proof-net (term). A first contribution towards the solution of this problem is the notion of safeness in [Asp95]. In presence of certain safety conditions (which may be computed along the computation) some additional reductions may be performed, allowing a further simplification of the net.

We adopt, instead, a different approach. The main contribution of this paper is a solution to the coherence problem (for restricted proof-nets, see below) obtained by changing the way the information is coded into sharing graphs. This is achieved via two technical tools: (i) a new reduction rule (***absorption***) allowing a simplification of the net in some critical cases; (ii) a clear separation of the logical and control information in the representation of a net. The logical information takes the form of levels on the formulas of the proof-net; control is expressed by unifying fans and brackets into one single node (*mux*). It is this separation to allow the formulation of the absorption reduction and to enforce coherence.

Our results, like those of most of the literature, hold for restricted proof-nets, where weakening is not allowed. It should be clear that any approach to cut-elimination based on a *local* graph exploration may work only on connected components. If the syntax allows, during reduction, the creation of distinct components out of a single connected graph, then any local approach is bound to fail. This is why we ban weakening from our logic (cf. also [GAL92b]). A different solution is to allow weakening, but also to change the logic; e.g., take intuitionistic logic coded inside linear logic; this is (typed) λ-calculus, treated in [Gue95].

The insight needed to introduce our new techniques came from the proof theory of modal logics. In the context of proof-nets, the already mentioned notion of box is necessary to ensure soundness of the introduction of a modal connective (the of-course "!") and to allow the proper reduction of the proof-net during the cut-elimination process. A box is a global, explicitly given notion: each occurrence of an of-course connective in the proof-net "comes together" with a certain subgraph, its box. In [MM95]—applying to linear logic ideas and techniques previously developed for modal logic, see [MM96]—we discovered that a different, straightforward approach was possible, labelling with natural number indexes the formulas of the proof-net. The approach of [MM95], moreover, allowed a clear recognition, at any time, of the boundary of the box. This suggested our new, simple absorption rule. The approach has been applied to the optimal reduction of lambda terms in [Gue95], where the main algebraic techniques necessary to prove its correctness are developed. A generalization of the technique and detailed proofs may be found in Guerrini's thesis [Gue96].

Finally, we would like to attract the attention of the reader to our formalization of proof-nets as hypergraphs. We believe it an improvement over the current formulation, allowing a good mastering of the concepts and techniques needed in the field.

2 Levelled nets, proof-nets, reduction

We introduce in this section the net concepts we will use in the sequel. The most standard notions are that of restricted proof-structure and proof-net (Definitions 3 and 5; restricted in that weakening is not allowed), though given here as hypergraph (consistently with the presentation of [Gir87], but unlike most literature) and with levels instead of boxes (see [MM95] for the equivalence with the box approach). Proof-structures are special cases of *levelled-nets* (or ℓ-nets, Definition 1), which may contain additional links, responsible for duplication (*mux*'s and their duals *demux*'s; a single mux would correspond, in Lamping's approach, to one fan and several brackets). By *formula*, we mean a multiplicative-exponential linear logic formula; an *indexed* formula is a formula decorated with a non negative integer, the *level* of the formula.

Definition 1. An *ℓ-net* is a finite connected hypergraph whose nodes are labelled with indexed formulas and hyperedges (also called *links*) are labelled from the set $\{\text{cut}, \text{ax}, \wp, \otimes, !, ?\} \cup \{mux[i] \mid i \geq 0\} \cup \{demux[i] \mid i \geq 0\}$; the integer i in (de)muxes is the *threshold* of the link. Allowed links and nodes are drawn in Figure 1. The source nodes of a link are its *premises*; the target nodes are the *conclusions*. Premises and conclusions are assumed to be distinguishable (i.e., we will have *left/right* premises, i-th conclusion and so on), with the exception of ?-links. In an ℓ-net, each node must be conclusion of exactly one link and premise of at most one link; those nodes that are not premises of any link are the *net conclusions*; unary (de)muxes are also called *lifts*.

We assume that ℓ-net axioms have only atomic conclusions. Such a restriction does not decrease the expressive power of ℓ-nets. However, it would be possible to have a more economic representation of nets, allowing axioms with non exponential conclusions [Gue96].

Remark 2. Figure 2 states the correspondence between our ℓ-nets and the nets of [GAL92b, Asp95b] (see also Remark 7). A (de)mux with n auxiliary ports corresponds, in Asperti's notation, to a tree of fans with n leaves followed by

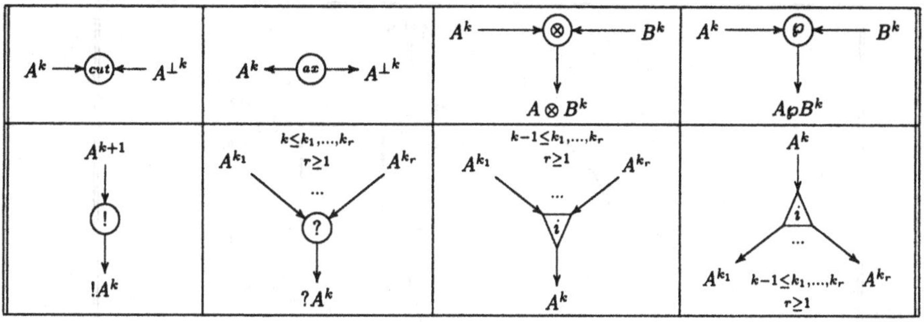

Fig. 1. ℓ-net links

a chain of brackets closed at the top by a croissant, one chain for each leaf. The length of the chain is given by the offsets of the corresponding port (i.e., the difference between the level of the formula assigned to such a port and the one assigned to the principal one) increased by 1. The top of Figure 2 shows the binary case (the triangle on the right side of the equivalence is then a fan and not a mux). A ?-link with a conclusion at level k corresponds to a bracket with an Asperti index equal to k (Gonthier index would be 0) followed by a configuration analogous to that of a mux with threshold k and conclusion at level $k+1$ (cf. the $\triangleright_{exp}$ rule). The corresponding binary case is drawn at the bottom-left of Figure 2. An !-link is just a bracket indexed as the bottom bracket of a corresponding ?-link.

Definition 3. A *restricted proof-structure* is an ℓ-net without (de)muxes.

Definition 4. Let Π be a restricted proof-structure and let A^k be a premise of an !-link; we call *box* of A^k a sub-hypergraph $bx_\Pi[A^k]$ of Π verifying the following properties:

1. $A^k \in bx_\Pi[A^k]$ (A^k is the *principal door* of $bx_\Pi[A^k]$);
2. $bx_\Pi[A^k]$ is a restricted proof-structure;
3. each net conclusion of $bx_\Pi[A^k]$ different from the principal door is a premise, in Π, of a ?-link with conclusion at level $j < k$ (such ?-premises are the *secondary doors* of the box);
4. for each $B^j \in \Pi$, if $B^j \in bx_\Pi[A^k]$, then $j \geq k$.

We denote by $BX[\Pi]$ the set of boxes of Π. Because of the definition of ℓ-net, boxes are connected. By this we see that each !-premise node has at most one associated box.

Definition 5. Let Π be a restricted proof-structure. Π is a *restricted proof-net* iff all the net conclusions have level 0 and, after erasing all levels from the

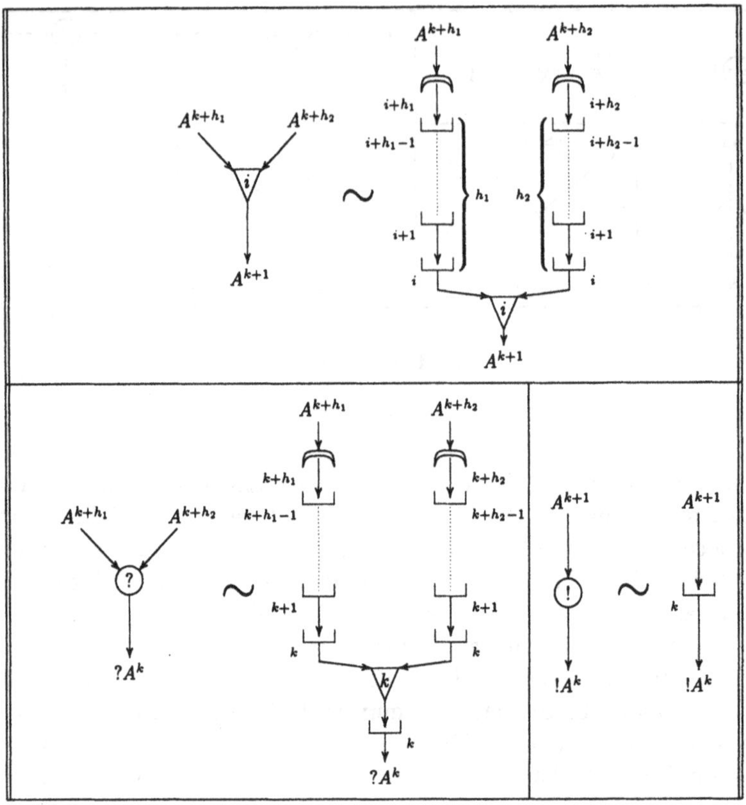

Fig. 2. Correspondence between ℓ-nets and sharing graphs

formulas, the resulting proof-structure *à la Girard*, equipped with $BX[\Pi]$ as set of boxes, verifies (one of) the correctness criteria [Gir87] for multiplicative-exponential proof-nets.

Theorem 6. *Let S be a weakening-free proof-net à la Girard, equipped with a given set of boxes, with conclusions $A_1, \ldots, A_m$. Then there is a restricted proof-net (as defined in this paper) S^* with conclusions $A_1^0, \ldots, A_m^0$, obtained by assigning to each node of S a level corresponding to the number of boxes that contain that node.*

2.1 Reduction

ℓ-nets may be used to implement a local and asynchronous version of the standard cut-elimination procedure (i.e., of the cut-elimination as defined in [Gir87]) for proof-nets. The elimination of ***propositional*** cuts (i.e., those formed by pairs tensor/par and axiom/cut) is directly mirrored in the corresponding rules. Figure 3 shows how to perform ***standard exponential cut-elimination***. Observe, first, that the box $\Pi1$ is (globally) duplicated. Second, after the reduction the different copies of $\Pi1$ may have been put inside other boxes (this happens when the ?-node is a secondary door of another box). The notation $\Pi1[k_i - k]$ means that all the levels of $\Pi1$ have been incremented by $k_i - k$.

Levels and (de)muxes are designed to take care in a local way of both these aspects of the exponential reduction: multiple premises handle (incremental) duplication, while the threshold handles the (incremental) *reindexing* of the box—the re-computation of the new level of its nodes.

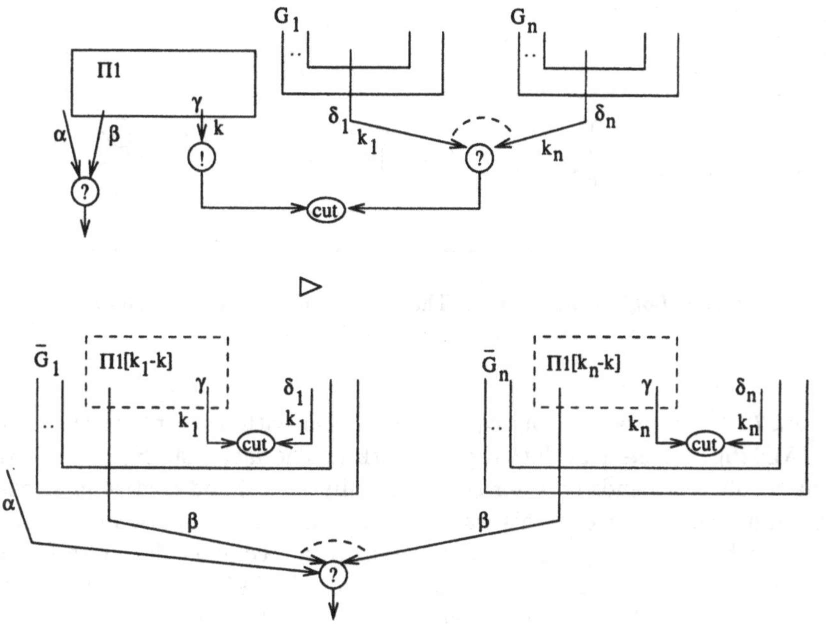

Fig. 3. Exponential cut reduction

We distinguish the rules in two kinds: the logical (or β) rules (Figure 4), where interaction happens through a cut-link (corresponding to a logical cut-elimination step); and the π rules (Figures 5, 6, and 7), when one of the interacting nodes is a mux/demux (corresponding to a step of incremental duplication and/or reindexing).

The set $\pi_{opt} = \pi - \triangleright_{dup}$ contains the only rules allowed during an *optimal* reduction (see Section 2.2). We stress the presence of the *absorption* rule ($\triangleright_{abs}$), corresponding to the case when the mux reaches the border of a box (through one of its secondary doors) and has therefore exhausted its job. It is motivated by the proof theoretical work in [MM95, MM96] (see also Section 5) and it is a special case of a safe reduction [Asp95].

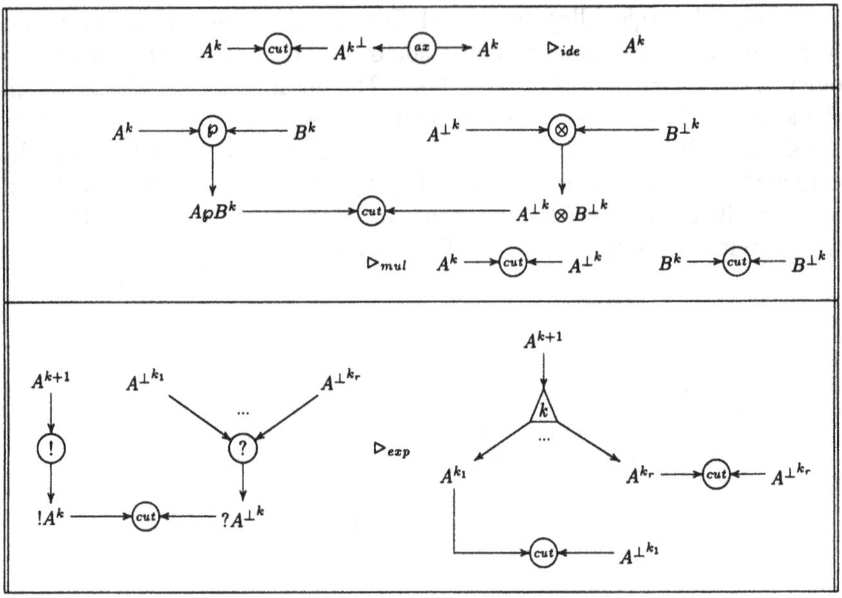

Fig. 4. Logical (or β) rules. The symmetric cases are not shown.

Remark 7. Any rule of π_{opt}, but $\rhd_{abs}$, is admissible with respect to the reductions of [GAL92b] and the translation of Remark 2. The fact that $\rhd_{abs}$ is not valid in that context depends on their choice to unify logical and control information in the same nodes, since in this way it is impossible to recognise in a local way whether a bracket configuration corresponds to a secondary door of a box (see also Section 5). If one sticks to the notation of [GAL92b], the solution is that indicated in [Asp95]: add another tag to each node, to record its "safeness".

Remark 8. Interactions between muxes are allowed only between mux/demux pairs in which the mux conclusion is the demux premise, i.e., connected through their principal ports as interaction nets (see π_{swap} and π_{anh}). Correspondingly, a non-identity logical link interacts with a demux when its conclusion (i.e., its principal port) is the demux premise (compare π_{odup} with π_{swap}). But, generalizing the rules present in [Asp95b], even a mux may interact with a logical link (see π_{dup}) when its conclusion is a premise of a logical link. An identity link behaves as a straight connection whose only purpose it to invert link orientation, so a cut-link interacts with a mux when one of its premise is a conclusion of the mux, and vice versa for the ax-link/demux case (see π_{idup}). The inversion implied by an identity link reflects in the mux/demux switching implied by a π_{idup} interaction.

Remark 9. It is impossible for a mux to reach a net conclusion. Let i be the threshold of a (de)mux, and let A^k be its (premise)conclusion; the fact follows

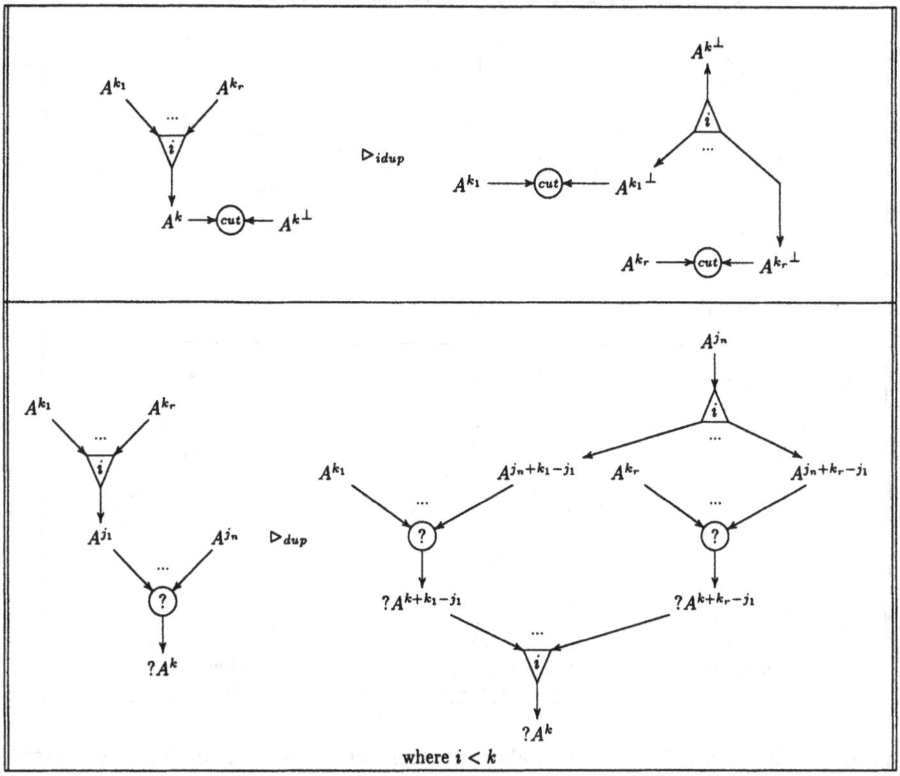

Fig. 5. Duplication rules, I. The following cases are not shown: in $\triangleright_{idup}$ the dual rule (demux/ax); in $\triangleright_{dup}$ the cases where interaction happens through another premise of the ?-link; in $\triangleright_{dup}$ the cases where the logical link is $\otimes$, $\wp$, !, instead of why-not (?).

since the relation $k > i$ is an invariant under reduction and any net conclusion has level 0.

2.2 Optimality

Optimality for the β reduction of λ-calculus has been studied by Lévy [Lév78, Lév80]. An analogous analysis may be performed in the case of proof-nets (see [GAL92b], or [AL93]). By a suitable labelling of (standard) proof-nets, we may define a Lévy labelled rewriting system for proof-nets, in which, as in the λ-calculus, the residuals of a cut have all the same label and new labels appear only when new cuts are created during reduction. Starting from a labelled proof-net N in which all nodes have different labels, we say that two cuts (not necessarily belonging to the same reduct of N) are in the same *Lévy family* iff they have the same label. A *family reduction* is a sequence of parallel rewritings $R_1 R_2 \ldots$

where $i_1 = \cdots = i_s = i$, and $j_1 = j + k_1 - n, \ldots, j_r = j + k_r - n$ when $i < j$,
$i_1 = i + h_1 - n, \ldots, i_s = i + h_s - n$ and $j_1 = \cdots = j_r = j$, when $i > j$.

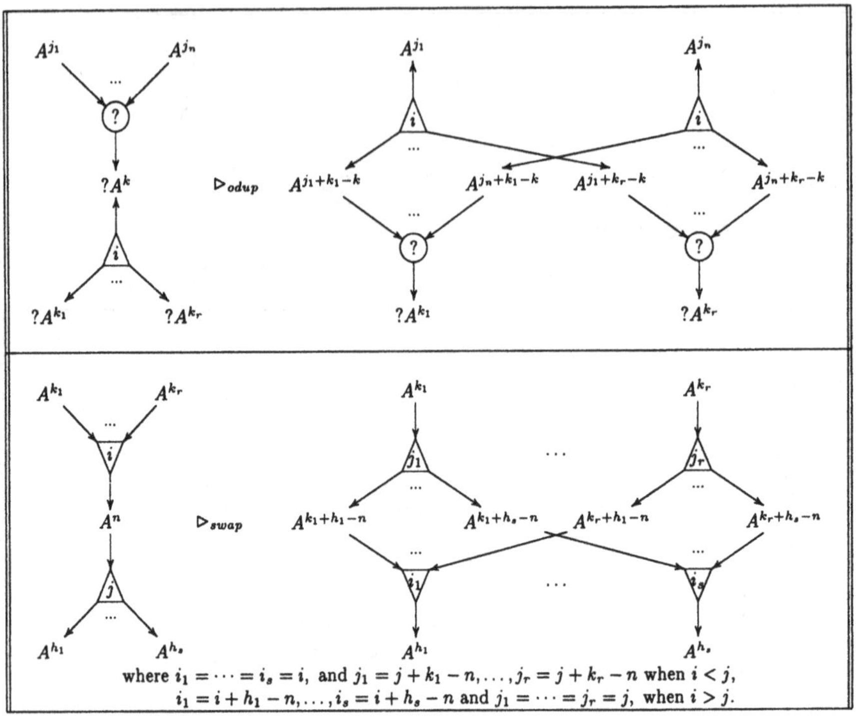

Fig. 6. Duplication rules, II. The following cases are not shown: in $\triangleright_{odup}$ the cases where the logical link is $\otimes$, $\wp$, !, instead of why-not (?).

s.t. all the cuts in R_i are in the same family. A *complete* reduction is a sequence of rewritings where at each step are reduced *all* the cuts of the same family (i.e., if r and r' are two cuts in the same family, then $r \in R_i$ implies $r' \in R_i$). Finally, a *call-by-need reduction* of N is a sequence of rewritings where at any step we reduce at least a needed cut—a cut which appears (more precisely, a residual of which appears) in any rewriting sequence starting from N. Main argument of Lévy [Lév80] is that, in the case of λ-calculus, the optimal cost of the reduction of a λ-term may be taken as the number of β reductions of a call-by-need complete family reduction (in the λ-calculus case, a call-by-need strategy is left-most-outer-most). We assume the same measure (β contractions) for proof-nets.

It is important to observe that a redex of a restricted proof-net is always *needed*. This is not surprising, since without weakenings it is impossible to have redexes belonging to subgraphs that will be erased (i.e., not needed redexes). Therefore, all reduction strategies are effective call-by-need strategies.

We stress that the solution presented in this paper to the coherence problem is motivated by pure proof theoretical considerations. We have not studied the

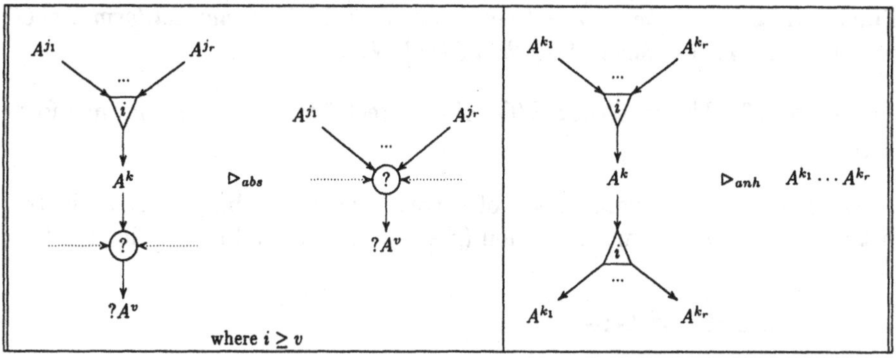

Fig. 7. Simplification rules

efficiency of our approach compared with the others approaches. Finding a good measure for the computational complexity of asynchronous and local reductions in proof-nets (and λ-calculus) is an important open problem, outside the scope of the present paper (e.g., [Asp96, LM96]).

3 Coherence

We state in this section our main results, namely that the reduction rules $\beta + \pi$ solve the coherence problem for ℓ-nets. This is not trivial, since the rules may be fired in any order (logical and non-logical reductions will be in general interleaved). Our proof strategy, analogous to the one used in [Gue95] for the λ-calculus, is to simulate ℓ-nets over proof-nets. Via a (long and technical) detour through an algebraic semantics for ℓ-nets we prove the following main theorems. For the sake of their statement, let an ℓ-net G be *correct* iff there exists a restricted proof-net N s.t. $N \rhd^* G$; informally, an ℓ-net is correct if it represents a restricted proof-net.

Theorem 10. *Let G be a correct ℓ-net.*

1. *The π rules are strongly normalizing and confluent on G. The π normal form of G is a restricted proof-net.*
2. *The $\beta + \pi$ rewriting rules are strongly normalizing and confluent on G. The $\beta + \pi$ normal form of G is a restricted proof-net.*
3. *The π normal form of G reduces by standard cut-elimination to its $\beta + \pi$ normal form.*

Theorem 11. *The $\beta + \pi_{opt}$ rewriting rules are Lévy optimal.*

Confluence of $\beta + \pi$ implies thus the following.

Theorem 12. *Let G be a correct ℓ-net and N be its $\beta+\pi$ normal form. Let G' be a $\beta+\pi_{opt}$ normal form of G, then $G' \rhd_{\pi}^{*} N$.*

Definition 13. The *read-back* $\mathcal{R}(G)$ of a correct ℓ-net G is the π normal form of G.

By Theorem 12, normalization of correct ℓ-nets may be performed in two distinct steps: first optimal reduction ($\beta+\pi_{opt}$), then read-back reduction (π).

4 The inside of ℓ-nets

We give in this section a more detailed overview of the way the results of the previous section are obtained.

The technical core of the approach is an algebraic semantics of ℓ-nets, which cannot be presented here for lack of space. It may be found in [Gue96], which we refer to also for the statements below without a proof.

4.1 Sharing morphisms

Definition 14. An *s-morphism* is a surjective graph homomorphism $M : G_0 \to G_1$ of ℓ-nets which preserves the link and node labels (i.e., the type of links and the levels of nodes) and the names of the link ports, and is injective when restricted to the net-conclusions.

If $M : G_0 \to G_1$, then G_1 is equal in all respects to G_0 but for the number of premises of (de)mux and ?-links (e.g., a k-ary mux may be mapped to one with $k' \geq k$ premises). G_0 may thus be seen as a "less shared instance" of G_1; we write $G_0 \prec G_1$ when there exists an s-morphism from G_0 to G_1.

We need the concept of *uℓ-net*, an ℓ-net whose (de)muxes have a single (conclusion)premise. Over uℓ-nets we define a notion of reduction that lives midway between standard proof-net reduction (global duplication + boxes redrawing) and ℓ-net reduction. While the π rules are unchanged (though always applied with unary muxes), the β rule for the exponential cut is formulated with a global duplication of boxes (computed using the algebraic semantics to extend Definition 4 to uℓ-nets) without any modification of the involved levels, and the introduction of a lift for any duplicated box. We write $G \rhd_{\beta_u} G'$ for *the uℓ-net G reduces, by a β uℓ-net reduction, to the uℓ-net G'.*

We will use uℓ-net reduction to simulate ℓ-net reduction. The crucial properties of uℓ-nets are expressed in the following statements (see [Gue96] for proofs and more details).

Proposition 15. *If G is a correct ℓ-net, then there is a unique correct uℓ-net G^u (the* least shared instance *of G) such that $G^u \prec G$.*

Proposition 16. *Let G be a correct uℓ-net.*

1. *There is no infinite π reduction of G.*

2. *G has a unique π normal form, which we indicate with $\mathcal{R}(G)$.*
3. *$\mathcal{R}(G)$ is a restricted proof-net.*

Proposition 17. *Let G be a correct uℓ-net and let $G \rhd_{\beta_u} G_1$. The uℓ-net G_1 is correct and $\mathcal{R}(G) \rhd \mathcal{R}(G_1)$ by the standard proof-net reduction of the same redex.*

Strong normalization of standard proof-net reduction of (restricted) proof-nets implies thus the following.

Corollary 18. *The reduction relation $\pi + \beta_u$ is strongly normalizing on correct uℓ-nets.*

4.2 Correctness of ℓ-net reduction

We may now simulate π and β reduction of ℓ-nets over uℓ-nets.

Lemma 19. *Let G_0 be a correct ℓ-net for which there exists a correct uℓ-net G_0^u s.t. $G_0^u \prec G_0$. If $G_0 \rhd_\pi G_1$, there exists $G_0^u \rhd_\pi^+ G_1^u$ s.t $G_1^u \prec G_1$.*

Proof. (Sketch) Let M be the s-morphism between G_0^u and G_0 and let r be a redex of G_0. The counterimage $M^{-1}(r)$ of r w.r.t. M is a set of redexes that may contain only a case of critical pair: two lifts pointing to the premises of the same ?-link. If the redex r is a duplication, the algebraic semantics (note that G_0^u is correct) allows to prove that such two lifts must be equal and then that such a critical pair is confluent. Hence, let us execute in any order the redexes of G_0^u in $M^{-1}(r)$ (closing as previoulsy stated the critical pairs present in it), the result is G_1^u. It is also not difficult to see that the s-morphism between G_1^u and G_1 maps any residual of a link v of G_0^u to the residual of $M(v)$.

Proposition 20. *Let G be a correct ℓ-net with least shared instance G^u.*

1. *There is no infinite π reduction of G.*
2. *G has a unique π normal form. Moreover, this π normal form is $\mathcal{R}(G^u)$.*

Proof. (Sketch) (1) By Proposition 16, G^u strongly normalizes by π reduction to the restricted proof-net $\mathcal{R}(G^u)$. By Lemma 19, the existence of an infinite π reduction of G would contradict the strong normalization of G^u.
(2) The π normal form $\mathcal{R}(G^u)$ of G^u does not contain lifts (by Proposition 16 it is a restricted proof-net). Let now N be any π normal form of the ℓ-net G. Observe that $\mathcal{R}(G^u) \prec N$, by Lemma 19, and thus also N does not contain muxes, for a sharing-morphism preserves links. Hence it is an uℓ-net. Some thought shows that this implies $\mathcal{R}(G^u) = N$.

From the previous lemma we get Theorem 10(1). We now simulate ℓ-net β reduction on β_u reduction of uℓ-nets.

Proposition 21. *Let G_0 be a correct ℓ-net for which there exists a correct uℓ-net G_0^u s.t. $G_0^u \prec G_0$. If $G_0 \rhd_\beta G_1$, there exists $G_0^u \rhd_{\beta_u}^+ G_1^u$ s.t G_1^u is correct and $G_1^u \prec G_1$.*

Proof. (Sketch) Let $M : G_0^u \to G_0$ and let r be a β redex of G_0. The unshared reduction corresponding to the reduction of r is a development of the set of redexes $M^{-1}(r)$ (a development of a set of β redex of a proof-net is the analougus of a development of a set of β redexes for the λ-calculus). The s-morphism between the $u\ell$-net G_1^u obtained in this way and G_1 is the one mapping any residual of a link l of G_0^u to the residual of its image $M(l)$ (see the detailed proof given in [Gue96] for the λ-calculus case).

We finally prove Theorem 10(2-3).

Theorem 22. *Let G be a correct ℓ-net.*

2. *The $\beta + \pi$ rewriting rules are strongly normalizing and confluent on G. The $\beta + \pi$ normal form of G is a restricted proof-net.*
3. *The π normal form of G reduces by standard cut-elimination to its $\beta + \pi$ normal form.*

Proof. (Sketch) Assume $G \rhd_\beta^* G_1 \rhd_\pi^* G_2$, and let G^u be the least shared instance of G. By 21 and 19 we have a corresponding unshared reduction $G^u \rhd_{\beta_u}^* G_1^u \rhd_\pi^* G_2^u$. Moreover, by 17 and 21, $\mathcal{R}(G) \rhd^* \mathcal{R}(G_1)$ by a standard proof-net reduction. By Proposition 20, $\mathcal{R}(G_1) = \mathcal{R}(G_2)$, and the π reduction of the previous pair cannot be infinite. Thus, any reduction of G may be decomposed in an alternating sequence of a non empty β reduction and of a finite number of π rewritings. Since each element of such a sequence corresponds to a non-empty sequence of β standard proof-net rewritings, the alternating sequence cannot be infinite, for otherwise we would have an infinite reduction of a proof-net. This establishes both strong normalization and (3). Moreover, we conclude the uniqueness of the $\beta + \pi$ normal form and then the confluence of $\beta + \pi$. In fact, by Proposition 16 and Proposition 20 we see that any $\beta + \pi$ normal form of G is a restricted proof-net, that is, it is the (unique) normal form of $\mathcal{R}(G)$ under standard proof-net reduction.

5 Conclusions

We have presented in this paper a solution to the coherence problem for the sharing graph representation of (restricted) proof-nets and their computations. This result has been made possible by a change in the representation of the nets. As discussed in Remarks 2 and 7, there is a rather simple correspondence between our approach (levels on formulas and only one kind of control nodes—(de)muxes) and the one established in the literature (levels on nodes, two kinds of control nodes—fans and brackets). This shift of notation, however, is crucial and responds to a deep conceptual issue: separating logic from control. The level of a formula, indeed, is a logical information, necessary to ensure not only the correctness of the reduction, but even the static correctness of a net. This has been clear since our previous work on levelled approaches to modal and linear proof theory [MM95, MM96]. In the case of this paper, levels belong to the logic and (de)muxes and their reduction rules belong to control. It is this separation to make coherence possible. In the standard approach, instead, logic and control are blurred together. There is more uniformity of notation, but the price to be paid is the difficulty to recognize in a local way the border of boxes, that is to eventually guarantee coherence. A different solution is that of the safe reductions of [Asp95], of which our absorption is a special case.

It remains to address the problem of full proof-nets, where weakening is allowed. Weakening in linear logic can produce boxes whose contents are disconnected. Such boxes can be also generated by the cut-elimination procedure, even starting from proof-nets whose boxes are connected. The crucial case is that of a box whose principal door has as premise a weakening link, and hence it needs a separate component S (that must be a proof-net) to be a valid conclusion of the box. This separate component yields the secondary doors of the box. Now, any attempt to reindex/duplicate the box through its principal door will not reach the disconnected net S. Observe that this problem is shared by all the approaches proposed so far, as any local graph rewriting procedure cannot deal with disconnected components. There is a simple way to bypass this problem, e.g., by restricting the proof-net syntax to generate interaction systems (this means for example to be able to code typed λ-calculus, intuitionistic linear logic and so on). We claim, however, that a solution to the general case will call for an extension of the proof-net syntax in order to avoid the formation of disconnected boxes. Research in this direction is ongoing.

Acknowledgments

We are happy to thank Andrea Asperti, for the many discussions, Laurent Regnier, for many detailed remarks on the subject of this paper, and an anonymous referee, for help in improving presentation.

References

[ADLR94] Andrea Asperti, Vincent Danos, Cosimo Laneve, and Laurent Regnier. Paths in the lambda-calculus: three years of communications without understanding. In *Proc. of 9th Symposium on Logic in Computer Science*, pages 426–436, Paris, France, July 1994. IEEE.

[AL93] Andrea Asperti and Cosimo Laneve. Interaction systems. In *Int. Workshop on Higher Order Algebra, Logic and Term Rewriting*, 1993.

[Asp95b] Andrea Asperti. Linear logic, comonads and optimal reductions. *Fundamenta infomaticae*, 22:3–22, 1995.

[Asp95] Andrea Asperti. $\delta\circ!\varepsilon = 1$: Optimizing optimal λ-calculus implementations. In Jieh Hsiang, editor, *Rewriting Techniques and Applications, 6th International Conference, RTA-95*, LNCS 914, pages 102–116, Kaiserslautern, Germany, April 5–7, 1995. Springer-Verlag.

[Asp96] Andrea Asperti. On the complexity of beta-reduction. In *POPL*, St. Petersburg Beach, Florida, 1996. ACM.

[GAL92a] Georges Gonthier, Martín Abadi, and Jean-Jacques Lévy. The geometry of optimal lambda reduction. In *Proc. of Nineteenth Principles of Programming Languages (POPL)*, pages 15–26. ACM, January 1992.

[GAL92b] Georges Gonthier, Martín Abadi, and Jean-Jacques Lévy. Linear logic without boxes. In *Proc. of 7th Symposium on Logic in Computer Science*, pages 223–234, Santa Cruz, CA, June 1992. IEEE.

[Gir87] Jean-Yves Girard. Linear logic. *Theoretical Computer Science*, 50:1–102, 1987.

[Gue95] Stefano Guerrini. Sharing-graphs, sharing-morphisms, and (optimal) λ-graph reductions. In Z. Khasidashvili, editor, *1st Tbilisi Symposium on Logic, Language, and Computation*, CSLI Lecture Notes (to appear). Tblisi, Georgia, October 1995.

[Gue96] Stefano Guerrini. *Theoretical and Practical Aspects of Optimal Implementations of Functional Languages.* PhD thesis, Dottorato di Ricerca in Informatica, Pisa–Udine, January 1996.

[Lam90] John Lamping. An algorithm for optimal lambda calculus reduction. In *Principles of Programming Languages (POPL)*, pages 16–30. ACM, 1990.

[Lév78] Jean-Jacques Lévy. *Réductions Correctes et Optimales dans le lambda-calcul.* PhD Thesis, Université Paris VII, 1978.

[Lév80] Jean-Jacques Lévy. Optimal reductions in the lambda-calculus. In Jonathan P. Seldin and J. Roger Hindley, editors, *To H.B. Curry: Essays on Combinatory Logic, Lambda Calculus and Formalism*, pages 159–191. Academic Press, 1980.

[LM96] Julia L. Lawall and Harry G. Mairson. Optimality and inefficiency: What isn't a cost model of the lambda calculus? In *1996 ACM International Conference on Functional Programming*, 1996.

[MM96] Simone Martini and Andrea Masini. A computational interpretation of modal proofs. In H. Wansing, editor, *Proof theory of Modal Logics.* Kluwer, 1996. To appear.

[MM95] Simone Martini and Andrea Masini. On the fine structure of the exponential rule. In J.-Y. Girard, Y. Lafont, and L. Regnier, editors, *Advances in Linear Logic*, volume 222 of London Mathematical Society Lecture Note Series, pages 197–210. Cambridge University Press, 1995. Proceedings the 1993 Cornell Linear Logic Workshop.

Modularity of Termination in Term Graph Rewriting

M. R. K. Krishna Rao*
Max-Planck-Institut für Informatik,
Im Stadtwald, 66123 Saarbrücken, Germany.
e-mail: **krishna@mpi-sb.mpg.de**

Abstract

Term rewriting is generally implemented using graph rewriting for efficiency reasons. Graph rewriting allows sharing of common structures thereby saving both time and space. This implementation is sound in the sense that computation of a normal form of a graph yields a normal form of the corresponding term. In this paper, we study modularity of termination of the graph reduction. Unlike in the case of term rewriting, termination is modular in graph rewriting for a large class of systems. Our results generalize the results of Plump [14] and Kurihara and Ohuchi [10].

1 Introduction

Term rewriting is often implemented using graph rewriting to cut down the evaluation costs. Graph (directed acyclic) representation of terms facilitate sharing of structures – unlike the tree representation – and hence saves space and avoids the repetition of computations. This implementation is both sound and complete in the following sense. If a graph G reduces to G' then the term corresponding to G rewrites to the term corresponding to G' (soundness) and two graphs are convertible if and only if the corresponding terms are convertible (completeness). One of the nice fallouts of this is that the computation of a normal form of a given graph yields a normal form of the corresponding term.

A graph rewriting step using a non-right-linear rewrite rule does not make multiple copies of the subgraphs corresponding to non-linear variables, but enforces sharing of these subgraphs – however it does not enforce identification of two equal subterms (subgraphs) of the right-hand side term of the rule. Due to this enforced sharing, certain properties of the given TRS are not reflected in the graph rewriting implementation. The following list indicates how subtle the relation between term rewriting and term graph rewriting is. Here, $\Rrightarrow_{\mathcal{R}}$ denotes the term graph rewriting relation induced by TRS $\mathcal{R}$.

1. Confluence of $\mathcal{R}$ does not imply confluence of $\Rrightarrow_{\mathcal{R}}$ (see [15, 8]).

*On leave from Tata Institute of Fundamental Research, Bombay

2. Weak normalization (WN) of $\mathcal{R}$ does not imply WN of $\Rrightarrow_{\mathcal{R}}$ (see [13, 8]).

3. Termination of $\Rrightarrow_{\mathcal{R}}$ does not imply termination of $\mathcal{R}$ (see [15]).

4. Confluence is modular in term rewriting [16] but not modular in term graph rewriting (for direct sum).

5. Termination is not modular in term rewriting [17] but modular in term graph rewriting (for direct sum).

The study of properties which are preserved under combinations of systems (called modular properties) is of both theoretical and practical importance. In particular, modularity results facilitate (i) incrementality in the synthesis of systems and (ii) divide-and-conquer approach in the analysis of systems. The fragile relationship between term rewriting and term graph rewriting – in particular, the above statements 4 and 5 which show that modularity results in term graph rewriting for direct-sum are quite the opposite of the modularity results in term rewriting – makes it imperative to investigate modular aspects of term graph rewriting rigorously.

In this paper, we study modularity of termination in graph rewriting and consider hierarchical combinations, where functions defined in one system are used as built-ins in the other system. The best results known about modularity of termination in term rewriting [9, 6, 2, 3] need that (i) the two systems are confluent and terminating or (ii) termination of both the systems is provable by simplification orderings (i.e., simple termination). In contrast, we show that for modularity of termination in term graph rewriting, neither confluence nor simple termination is needed. Our results generalize the existing results in the literature [14, 10]; see section 6.

2 Preliminaries

We assume that the reader is familiar with the basic terminology of term rewriting systems and give definitions only when they are required. The notations not defined in the paper can be found in Dershowitz and Jouannaud [1], Klop [5] or Plump [15].

In the following, $\mathcal{T}(\Sigma, X)$ denotes the set of terms constructed from a set of function symbols Σ and a countable set of variables X. For each variable x, $arity(x) = 0$. We use the (possibly with some subscripts) symbols a, b, c, d to denote constants, f, g, h to denote functions of arity at least one and x, y, z to denote variables. We recall the following definitions from Plump [14, 15].

A *hypergraph* G over Σ is a system $\langle V_G, E_G, s_G, t_G, l_G \rangle$, where V_G, E_G are finite sets of nodes and hyperedges, $s_G : E_G \to V_G$, $t_G : E_G \to V_G^*$ are mappings that assign a source node and a string of target nodes to each hyperedge, and $l_G : E_G \to \Sigma \cup X$ is a mapping that labels each hyperedge e such that $arity(l_G(e))$ is the length of $t_G(e)$.

A node v is a *predecessor* of a node v' if there is an edge e with source v such that v' occur in $t_G(e)$. The relations $<_G$ and $\leq_G$ are the transitive and reflexive-transitive closures of the predecessor relation. We say v' is below v when $v \leq_G v'$. For each node v, G/v is the subhypergraph of G consisting of all the nodes v' with $v \leq_G v'$ and all the edges outgoing from these nodes.

A hypergraph G over Σ is a *collapsed tree* if (1) there is a node $root_G$ such that $root_G \leq_G v$ for each node v, (2) the predecessor relation of G is acyclic and (3) each node has a unique outgoing edge. A collapsed tree is also refered to as a term graph in the sequel.

Let G be a collapsed tree. Then the mapping $term_G : V_G \rightarrow T(\Sigma, X)$ is defined as $term_G(v) = l_G(e)$ if $t_G(e)$ is an empty string ϵ and $term_G(v) = l_G(e)(term_G(v_1), \ldots, term_G(v_n))$ if $t_G(e) = v_1 \ldots v_n$, where e is the unique edge with source v. In the following $term(G)$ stands for $term_G(root_G)$.

For a collapsed tree G, the mapping $node_G : Pos(term(G)) \rightarrow V_G$ (relating positions/subterms of term and the nodes/subgraphs in a collapsed tree representing that term) is defined as (i) $node_G(\epsilon) = root_G$ and (ii) $node_G(i.\pi) = node_{G/v_i}(\pi)$, where $v_1 \cdots v_n$ is the target string of the hyperedge with source $root_G$ and $Pos(t)$ is the set of positions in t.

A collapsed tree G is a *tree with shared variables* if (1) for each node v, $indegree_G(v) > 1$ implies $term_G(v) \in X$ and (2) for all nodes v, v', $term_G(v) = term_G(v') \in X$ implies $v = v'$. Here, $indegree_G(v)$ is the number of occurrences of v in the target strings.
In the following, $\Diamond t$ denotes a tree with shared variables such that $term_G(\Diamond t) = t$ and $\underline{G}$ denotes the hypergraph obtained from G by removing all the edges labelled with variables.

Let G, H be hypergraphs. A *hypergraph morphism* $g : G \rightarrow H$ is a pair of mappings $\langle g_v : V_G \rightarrow V_H,\ g_e : E_G \rightarrow E_H \rangle$ that preserve sources, targets and labels, i.e., $s_H \circ g_e = g_v \circ s_G$, $t_H \circ g_e = g_v^* \circ t_G$ and $l_H \circ g_e = l_G$.[1]

Definition 1 (evaluation step) Let G_1, G_2 be collapsed trees. Then there is an *evaluation step* from G_1 to G_2, denoted by $G_1 \Rrightarrow_{\mathcal{E}} G_2$, if there is a rule $l \rightarrow r \in \mathcal{R}$ and hypergraph morphism $g : \underline{\Diamond l} \rightarrow G_1$ such that G_2 is isomorphic to the collapsed tree constructed as follows:

1. Remove hyperedge outgoing from $g_v(root_{\Diamond l})$, yielding a hypergraph G'.
2. Build the disjoint union $G' + \underline{\Diamond r}$ and
   - identify $g_v(root_{\Diamond l})$ with $root_{\Diamond r}$ (i.e., merge the two nodes into one),
   - for each pair $\langle u, u' \rangle \in V_{\Diamond l} \times V_{\Diamond r}$ with $term_{\Diamond l}(u) = term_{\Diamond r}(u') \in X$, identify $g_v(u)$ with u'.

   Let G'' be the resulting hypergraph.
3. Remove garbage, resulting a collapsed tree $G''/root_G$.

[1] Given a mapping $f : A \rightarrow B$, $f^* : A^* \rightarrow B^*$ sends ϵ to ϵ and $a_1 \ldots a_n$ to $f(a_1) \ldots f(a_n)$.

For evaluations with non-left-linear rules, we need to 'fold' collapsed trees.

Definition 2 (folding step) Let G_1, G_2 be collapsed trees. Then there is a *folding step* $G_1 \Rrightarrow_{\mathcal{F}} G_2$ if there are distinct edges $e, e' \in E_{G_1}$ with $l_{G_1}(e) = l_{G_1}(e')$, $t_{G_1}(e) = t_{G_1}(e')$, and G_2 is isomorphic to the collapsed tree obtained from G_1 by identifying e with e' and $s_{G_1}(e)$ with $s_{G_1}(e')$.

We denote the relation $\Rrightarrow_{\mathcal{E}} \cup \Rrightarrow_{\mathcal{F}}$ by $\Rrightarrow_{\mathcal{R}}$ and omit the subscript if it does not lead to any confusion.

Example 1 This figure shows an evaluation step on a collapsed tree C representing term $(((0+\mathbf{x})\times(0+\mathbf{x}))+\mathbf{x})$ with rewrite rule $\mathbf{x}\times(\mathbf{y}+\mathbf{z}) \to (\mathbf{x}\times\mathbf{y})+(\mathbf{x}\times\mathbf{z})$. Here, *the hyperedges are represented by boxes and the nodes are represented by circles.* The morphism locating the left-hand side $\underline{\Diamond(\mathbf{x}\times(\mathbf{y}+\mathbf{z}))}$ identifies the nodes representing $\mathbf{x}$ and $(\mathbf{y}+\mathbf{z})$ with the node representing $(0+\mathbf{x})$ in C. In the examples below, we simplify the pictures of collapsed trees by deleting the nodes and replacing every hyperedge having n target nodes by n arcs, without introducing any confusion.

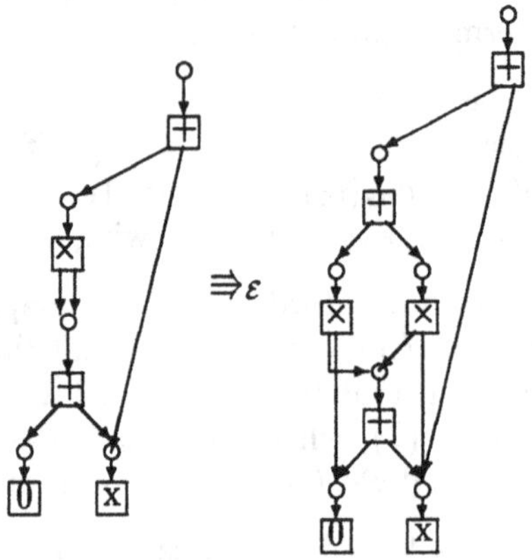

We need the following definitions in the sequel.

Definition 3 The set $D_{\mathcal{R}}$ of *defined* symbols of a term rewriting system $\mathcal{R}(\mathcal{F}, R)$ is defined as $\{root(l) \mid l \to r \in R\}$ and the set $C_{\mathcal{R}}$ of *constructor* symbols of $\mathcal{R}(\mathcal{F}, R)$ is defined as $\mathcal{F} - D_{\mathcal{R}}$.

To show the defined and constructor symbols explicitly, we often write the above TRS as $\mathcal{R}(D_{\mathcal{R}}, C_{\mathcal{R}}, R)$ and omit the subscript when such omission does not cause any confusion.

Definition 4 (dependency relation $\succeq_d$ over defined symbols)
The dependency relation of a rewrite system $\mathcal{R}(D, C, R)$ is the smallest quasi-order $\succeq_d$ over D satisfying the condition: $f \succeq_d g$ *if there is a rule* $l \to r \in R$ *such that* $f = root(l)$ *and* g *occurs in* r.

We say that a defined symbol $f \in D$ *depends on* a defined symbol $g \in D$ if $f \succeq_d g$. The set of symbols depending on a set of symbols S is defined as $\{f \mid f \succeq_d g \text{ and } g \in S\}$.

Notions for Modularity

In the following, we consider union of two term rewriting systems $\mathcal{R}_0(D_0 \uplus D, C_0, R_0)$ and $\mathcal{R}_1(D_1 \uplus D, C_1, R_1)$ sharing some function symbols and rules $R_0 \cap R_1 = \{l \to r \mid root(l) \in D\}$. To define the notion of *rank*, we paint the symbols in black, white and transparent as follows. The symbols of D_0 are black, those of D_1 are white and others (including variables) are transparent. Each transparent symbol in a term takes the colour of its surroundings (i.e., the symbols above it) if there is any. A term t with $root(t) \in D_0$ (resp. D_1) is a top black (resp. white) term and a term with transparent root is a top transparent term.

Definition 5 Any term t can be uniquely written as $C[\![t_1, \cdots, t_n]\!]$, $n \geq 0$ such that for each $i \in [1, n]$, (1) $root(t_i)$ and $root(t)$ are in different colour and (2) t_i is a maximal subterm of t with that property.

Definition 6 The *rank* of a term $t \equiv C[\![t_1, \cdots, t_n]\!]$, $n \geq 0$ is defined as:

$$\begin{aligned} rank(t) &= 1 + max(\{rank(t_i) \mid 1 \leq i \leq n\}) && \text{if } root(t) \in D_0 \cup D_1, \\ &= max(\{rank(t_i) \mid 1 \leq i \leq n\}) && \text{otherwise.} \end{aligned}$$

The *rank* of a term graph G is defined as $rank(G) = rank(term(G))$.

Example 2 Consider the following two systems.

$\mathcal{R}_0$: `mult(0,y)` → `0`	$\mathcal{R}_1$: `fib(0)` → `0`
`mult(s(x),y)` → `add(y,mult(x,y))`	`fib(s(0))` → `s(0)`
	`fib(s(s(x)))` → `add(fib(x),fib(s(x)))`
`add(0,y)` → `y`	`add(0,y)` → `y`
`add(s(x),y)` → `s(add(x,y))`	`add(s(x),y)` → `s(add(x,y))`

The ranks of terms `add(s(0),s(s(0)))`, `mult(s(x), y)`, `add(y,mult(x, y))` and `mult(fib(s(x)), fib(s(y))))` are 0, 1, 1 and 2 respectively. □

Termination of term graph rewriting is preserved under signature extensions.

Theorem 1 If the graph-reduction relation $\Rrightarrow_{\mathcal{R}}$ of a TRS $\mathcal{R}(\mathcal{F}, R)$ is noetherian then the graph-reduction relation $\Rrightarrow_{\mathcal{R}'}$ of TRS $\mathcal{R}'(\mathcal{F} \uplus \mathcal{F}', R)$ is noetherian too.

Proof: Easy[2]. □

Notation: Exploiting the above theorem, we slightly abuse the notation in the sequel by using $\Rrightarrow_{\mathcal{R}_i}$ to denote the graph-reduction relation of the signature-extension $\mathcal{R}'_i(D \cup D_0 \cup D_1 \cup C_0 \cup C_1, R_i)$, $i \in [0, 1]$.

The following definition and lemma are needed in the sequel.

Definition 7 We define a *subgraph* relation $\Rrightarrow_{sub}$ over collapsed trees as follows: $G \Rrightarrow_{sub} G'$ if and only if $G' \equiv G/v$ for some non-root node $v \in V_G$.

Lemma 1 Let S be a set of collapsed trees and $\mathcal{R}$ be a TRS with graph rewrite relation $\Rrightarrow_{\mathcal{R}}$. Then, *the relation* $\Rrightarrow_{\mathcal{R}} \cup \Rrightarrow_{sub}$ *is noetherian over* S *if and only if* $\Rrightarrow_{\mathcal{R}}$ *is noetherian over* S.

Proof : There must be infinitely many $\Rrightarrow_{\mathcal{R}}$-steps in an infinite derivation of $\Rrightarrow_{\mathcal{R}} \cup \Rrightarrow_{sub}$. Since the subgraph-steps do not creat new redex positions, one can get an infinite derivation of $\Rrightarrow_{\mathcal{R}}$ from an infinite derivation of $\Rrightarrow_{\mathcal{R}} \cup \Rrightarrow_{sub}$ by just omitting the subgraph-steps. □

[2]In fact this theorem follows from Plump's result on termination of crosswise disjoint union. However, the proof of this theorem is much simpler than the proof for crosswise disjoint union.

3 Crosswise Independent Unions

In this section, we study modularity of termination for crosswise independent unions in graph rewriting.

Definition 8 We say that two TRSs $\mathcal{R}_0(D_0 \uplus D, C_0, R_0)$ and $\mathcal{R}_1(D_1 \uplus D, C_1, R_1)$ are *crosswise independent* if *(i)* $R_0 \cap R_1 = \{l \to r \in R_0 \cup R_1 \mid root(l) \in D\}$ *and (ii)* $f_i \not\geq_d f_{1-i}$ *for each* $f_i \in D_i \cup D$ *and* $f_{1-i} \in D_{1-i}$, *where* $i \in \{0, 1\}$.
We say that $\mathcal{R}_0 \cup \mathcal{R}_1$ *is a crosswise independent union if* $\mathcal{R}_0$ *and* $\mathcal{R}_1$ *are crosswise independent.*

The notion of crosswise independent union is a generalization of constructor sharing (ao. [4, 10]) and composable unions (ao. [11, 12]). In the following, we consider two crosswise independent systems $\mathcal{R}_0(D_0 \uplus D, C_0, R_0)$ and $\mathcal{R}_1(D_1 \uplus D, C_1, R_1)$ such that $\Rrightarrow_{\mathcal{R}_0}$ and $\Rrightarrow_{\mathcal{R}_1}$ are **terminating.** We denote the combined system $\mathcal{R}_0 \cup \mathcal{R}_1$ by $\mathcal{R}$.

The following two lemmas are useful.

Lemma 2 If $\mathcal{R}_0$ and $\mathcal{R}_1$ are crosswise independent, then $G \Rrightarrow_{\mathcal{R}} G'$ implies $rank(G) \geq rank(G')$.

Definition 9 The relation $\Rrightarrow_{sub_i}$, $i \in [0, 1]$ over collapsed trees is defined as $(\Rrightarrow_{\mathcal{R}_i} \cup \Rrightarrow_{sub})^+$. The multiset extension of $\Rrightarrow_{sub_i}$ is denoted by $\Rrightarrow^m_{sub_i}$.

By Lemma 1, it follows that $\Rrightarrow_{sub_i}$ and $\Rrightarrow^m_{sub_i}$ are noetherian.

Lemma 3 The relations $\Rrightarrow_{sub_i}$ and $\Rrightarrow^m_{sub_i}$ are noetherian for $i \in [0, 1]$.

Now, we prove that $\Rrightarrow_{\mathcal{R}}$ is terminating. The proof is by induction on rank. A top transparent term can be uniquely written as $C[t_1, \cdots, t_n]$ such that C is a context of transparent symbols and t_i are top black/white terms.

Definition 10 For a top transparent graph G with $term(G) \equiv C[t_1, \cdots, t_n]$ such that C is a context of transparent symbols and each t_i is a top black/white term occurring at position p_i, we define

- **(top)**: The top of G (denoted $top(G)$) is defined as *the collapsed tree obtained from G by replacing the (unique) hyperedges outgoing from the nodes* $node_G(p_1)$, $\cdots$, $node_G(p_n)$ *by the hyperedges representing* $\Box$ *and removing the garbage.*

- **(aliens)**: The multiset of aliens in G is defined as $aliens(G) = \{G/v \mid v \in V\}$, where V is the set $\{node_G(p_i) \mid 1 \leq i \leq n$ and $node_G(p_i)$ is not strictly below $node_G(p_j)$ for any $j \neq i\}$. The multiset of top black and top white aliens of G are denoted by $A_0(G)$ and $A_1(G)$ respectively.

- **(inner/outer reductions)**: We say an evaluation step $G \Rrightarrow_{\mathcal{E}} G'$ is *inner* if the reduction took place in an element of $aliens(G)$ (i.e., below some node $v \in V$), otherwise it is an outer reduction. A folding step $G \Rrightarrow_{\mathcal{F}} G'$ is *inner* if at least one of the two identified (merged) hyperedges is from $aliens(G)$, otherwise it is an outer reduction.

Note that $top(G)$ and the aliens $A_0(G)$ and $A_1(G)$ may share some parts of G.

The following lemma helps in ignoring folding steps in the proofs below.

Lemma 4 If $G \Rrightarrow G'$ is an outer reduction and it is a folding step, then (i) $aliens(G') = aliens(G)$ and (ii) $top(G) \Rrightarrow top(G')$.

Proof: A folding step identifies two hyperedges only when their target strings are identical and the graph remains the same except that two hyperedges are identified (merged). Since both the identified hyperedges are in $top(G)$, the aliens are not disturbed. Therefore $aliens(G') = aliens(G)$ and $top(G) \Rrightarrow top(G')$. □

The following characteristic lemma about graph reductions is repeatedly used in the sequel.

Lemma 5 If $G \Rrightarrow G'$ is an outer reduction involving an evaluation step over top transparent graphs G and G', then $aliens(G) \succeq_{sub} aliens(G')$, where $\succ_{sub}$ is the multiset extension of $\Rrightarrow_{sub}$.

Proof: The applicable rewrite rules are $\{l \to r \mid root(l) \in D\}$ and no function symbols from $D_0 \cup D_1$ occur in the right-hand sides of these rules. Therefore, no new subgraphs with root in $D_0 \cup D_1$ are created in any outer reduction. Further, some hyperedges in G corresponding to function symbols from $D_0 \cup D_1$ occurring in the left-hand side of the applied rule might be deleted in the garbage collection. The lemma follows from these observations and the fact that no subgraph of an alien is again an alien (see V in Def. 10). □

We first show that $\Rrightarrow_{\mathcal{R}}$ is noetherian over collapsed trees of rank 1. For this purpose, a noetherian relation $\succ$ is defined over the set of top transparent collapsed trees of rank 1.

Definition 11 The relation $\succ$ over the set of top transparent collapsed trees of rank 1 is defined as: $G \succ G'$ if and only if

(a) $A_0(G) \Rrightarrow^m_{sub_0} A_0(G')$ or
(b) $A_0(G) = A_0(G')$ and $A_1(G) \Rrightarrow^m_{sub_1} A_1(G')$ or
(c) $A_0(G) = A_0(G')$, $A_1(G) = A_1(G')$ and $G \Rrightarrow_{\mathcal{R}_0 \cap \mathcal{R}_1} G'$.

Lemma 6 The relation $\succ$ over the set of top transparent collapsed trees of rank at most 1 is noetherian.

Proof: By Lemma 3, $\Rrightarrow_{sub_0}$ and $\Rrightarrow_{sub_1}$ and their multiset-extensions are noetherian. Since the only rewrite rules in $\mathcal{R}_0 \cap \mathcal{R}_1$ are $\{l \to r \mid root(l) \in D\}$ (a subsystem of $\mathcal{R}_i$, $i \in [0,1]$), the relation $\Rrightarrow_{\mathcal{R}_0 \cap \mathcal{R}_1}$ is noetherian. Therefore, $\succ$ is noetherian as it is a lexicographic extension of three noetherian relations. □

Theorem 2 The reduction relation $\Rrightarrow_{\mathcal{R}}$ is noetherian over collapsed trees of rank at most 1.

Proof : The theorem obviously holds for collapsed trees of rank 0 as the only rewrite rules applicable on them are $\{l \to r \mid root(l) \in D\}$ (a subsystem of $\mathcal{R}_i$, $i \in [0,1]$). We only have to consider collapsed trees of rank 1. Assume to the contrary that there is an infinite derivation $G_1 \Rrightarrow_{\mathcal{R}} G_2 \Rrightarrow_{\mathcal{R}} \cdots$ over collapsed trees of rank 1. If $root(term(G_k)) \in D_i$, $i \in [0,1]$ for some k, it is clear that each step after that is a $\Rrightarrow_{\mathcal{R}_i}$-step as any top black (white) collapsed tree of rank 1 does not contain any white (resp. black) symbols. That is, if $root(term(G_k)) \in D_i$, there is an infinite derivation $G_k \Rrightarrow_{\mathcal{R}_i} G_{k+1} \Rrightarrow_{\mathcal{R}_i} G_{k+2} \Rrightarrow_{\mathcal{R}_i} \cdots$, contradicting the termination of $\Rrightarrow_{\mathcal{R}_i}$. Therefore, each G_k , $k \geq 0$ is top transparent.

We prove that there can be no infinite derivation $G_1 \Rrightarrow_{\mathcal{R}} G_2 \Rrightarrow_{\mathcal{R}} G_3 \Rrightarrow_{\mathcal{R}} \cdots$ over top transparent collapsed trees of rank 1 by showing that $G \Rrightarrow_{\mathcal{R}} G'$ implies $G \succ G'$. If the reduction took place in $A_0(G)$, it is obvious that $A_0(G) \Rrightarrow^m_{sub_0} A_0(G')$. Similarly, $A_1(G) \Rrightarrow^m_{sub_1} A_1(G')$ and $A_0(G) = A_0(G')$ if the reduction took place in $A_1(G)$ but not in (any part shared with) $A_0(G)$. In both these cases $G \succ G'$. If $G \Rrightarrow_{\mathcal{R}} G'$ is an outer reduction, it is clear that $G \Rrightarrow_{\mathcal{R}_0 \cap \mathcal{R}_1} G'$ and $aliens(G) \succeq_{sub} aliens(G')$ by Lemma 5. Now, it is easy to see that one of the 3 requirements of Def. 11 holds and hence $G \succ G'$. □

Now, we prove that $\Rrightarrow_{\mathcal{R}}$ is noetherian on the set of collapsed trees of arbitrary rank by induction. First, we prove that there is no infinite derivation from a top black collapsed tree of rank k if $\Rrightarrow_{\mathcal{R}}$ is noetherian on the set of collapsed trees of rank less than k. The proof is similar for top white collapsed trees. We need the following definition and lemma.

Definition 12 The relation $\Rrightarrow_{sub_{01}}$ over collapsed trees is defined as $(\Rrightarrow_{\mathcal{R}} \cup \Rrightarrow_{sub})^+$. The multiset extension of $\Rrightarrow_{sub_{01}}$ is denoted by $\Rrightarrow^m_{sub_{01}}$.

Lemma 7 The relations $\Rrightarrow_{sub_{01}}$ and $\Rrightarrow^m_{sub_{01}}$ are noetherian over collapsed trees of rank less than k if $\Rrightarrow_{\mathcal{R}}$ is noetherian over collapsed trees of rank less than k.

Any term t of rank $k > 1$ with $root(t) \notin D_1$ can be written as $C_b[t_1, \cdots, t_n]$ in a unique way, where C_b is a context of black and transparent symbols and $root(t_i) \in D_1$ for each $i \in [1,n]$. Notions of top_0 and $aliens_0$ can be defined for top black/transparent collapsed trees of rank k similar to the notions *top* and *aliens* defined in Def. 10. Note that the (top white) aliens of such a collapsed tree are of rank less than k.

Theorem 3 If the reduction relation $\Rrightarrow_{\mathcal{R}}$ is noetherian over collapsed trees of rank less than k, *there is no infinite* $\Rrightarrow_{\mathcal{R}}$ *derivation starting from a top black collapsed tree of rank* k.

Proof : Since white-aliens of a top black collapsed tree of rank k are of rank less than k, there cannot be a top white collapsed tree in an infinite $\Rrightarrow_{\mathcal{R}}$ derivation starting from a top black collapsed tree of rank k. So, the notions top_0 and $aliens_0$ are well-defined for each collapsed tree in the derivation. Now, we show that there cannot be an infinite derivation by proving that $G \Rrightarrow_{\mathcal{R}} G'$ implies: (i)

$aliens_0(G) \Rrightarrow^m_{sub_{01}} aliens_0(G')$ or (ii) $aliens_0(G') = aliens_0(G)$ and $G \Rrightarrow_{\mathcal{R}_0} G'$. Since, $\Rrightarrow_{sub_{01}}$ is noetherian over collapsed trees of rank less than k and $\Rrightarrow_{\mathcal{R}_0}$ is noetherian, it follows that there cannot be an infinite $\Rrightarrow_{\mathcal{R}}$ derivation starting with a top black collapsed tree of rank k.

If $G \Rrightarrow_{\mathcal{R}} G'$ took place in an alien of G, it is obvious that $aliens_0(G) \Rrightarrow^m_{sub_{01}} aliens_0(G')$. In the other case, it is clear that $G \Rrightarrow_{\mathcal{R}_0} G'$ and $aliens_0(G) \succeq_{sub} aliens_0(G')$. This implies that either (i) or (ii) above holds. □

Now, we prove the result for arbitrary collapsed trees of rank k.

Theorem 4 If the reduction relation $\Rrightarrow_{\mathcal{R}}$ is noetherian over collapsed trees of rank less than k, then $\Rrightarrow_{\mathcal{R}}$ *is noetherian over collapsed trees of rank* k *as well.*

Proof: By the above lemma, $\Rrightarrow_{\mathcal{R}}$ is noetherian over top black (white) collapsed trees of rank k. As in Theorem 2, every tree in an infinite $\Rrightarrow_{\mathcal{R}}$ derivation starting with a top transparent collapsed tree of rank k is top transparent. We can prove that there cannot be an infinite $\Rrightarrow_{\mathcal{R}}$ derivation over top transparent collapsed trees of rank k by showing that $G \Rrightarrow_{\mathcal{R}} G'$ implies (a) $A_0(G) \Rrightarrow^m_{sub_{01}} A_0(G')$ or (b) $A_0(G) = A_0(G')$ and $A_1(G) \Rrightarrow^m_{sub_{01}} A_1(G')$ or (c) $A_0(G) = A_0(G')$, $A_1(G) = A_1(G')$ and $G \Rrightarrow_{\mathcal{R}_0 \cup \mathcal{R}_1} G'$. The proof of this fact runs on the same lines as in Theorem 2. □

From the above two theorems, we get the main result of this section.

Theorem 5 Let $\mathcal{R}_0$ and $\mathcal{R}_1$ be two crosswise independent systems with graph rewrite relations $\Rrightarrow_{\mathcal{R}_0}$ and $\Rrightarrow_{\mathcal{R}_1}$. Then, $\Rrightarrow_{\mathcal{R}_0 \cup \mathcal{R}_1}$ *terminates if and only if both* $\Rrightarrow_{\mathcal{R}_0}$ *and* $\Rrightarrow_{\mathcal{R}_1}$ *terminate.*

4 Hierarchical Combinations

In this section, we define a class of hierarchical combinations for which the modularity of termination is studied in the next section. Before defining this class, we show that termination of graph reduction is not modular for hierarchical combinations in general.

Example 3 It is easy to see that the following two systems $\mathcal{R}_0$ and $\mathcal{R}_1$ are terminating and hence the graph reductions $\Rrightarrow_{\mathcal{R}_0}$ and $\Rrightarrow_{\mathcal{R}_0}$ are terminating as well.

$\mathcal{R}_0 : \mathtt{f(x)} \to \mathtt{x}$ $\qquad\qquad$ $\mathcal{R}_1 : \mathtt{h(a)} \to \mathtt{h(f(a))}$

But the combined system has a cyclic derivation: $\mathtt{h(a)} \Rrightarrow_{\mathcal{R}_1} \mathtt{h(f(a))} \Rrightarrow_{\mathcal{R}_0} \mathtt{h(a)} \cdots$ □

The class of combinations considered in this paper is even more general than hierarchical combinations as well as crosswise independent unions, i.e., defined symbols of system $\mathcal{R}_0$ can occur in both left- and right-hand sides of rules in $\mathcal{R}_1$ and defined symbols of $\mathcal{R}_1$ can occur in left-hand sides (but not right-hand sides) of rules in $\mathcal{R}_0$. Such combinations arise while analyzing systems produced

by completion procedures and are refered to as super-hierarchical combinations. See [9, 7] for further discussion on the motivation for these combinations.
In the following, we consider super-hierarchical combinations of two systems $\mathcal{R}_0(D_0 \uplus D, C_0, R_0)$ and $\mathcal{R}_1(D_1 \uplus D, C_1, R_1)$ sharing some symbols and rules $R_0 \cap R_1 = \{l \to r \mid root(l) \in D\}$.

Notation: For discussions in the sequel, it is convenient to classify defined symbols in $D_1 \uplus D$ into two sets (i) $D_1^0 = \{ f \mid f \in (D_1 \uplus D)$ and $f \succeq_d D_0 \}$ consisting of function symbols depending on D_0 and $D_1^1 = (D_1 \uplus D) - D_1^0$ consisting of function symbols not depending on D_0. We denote the set of constructors $(C_0 \cup C_1) - (D_0 \cup D_1 \cup D)$ of the combined system by *Constr*.

The following definition characterizes the main class of super-hierarchical combinations we are interested in.

Definition 13 A term rewriting system $\mathcal{R}_1(D_1 \uplus D, C_1, R_1)$ is a *generalized nice-extension** of another term rewriting system $\mathcal{R}_0(D_0 \uplus D, C_0, R_0)$ if the following conditions are satisfied:

1. $D_0 \cap D_1 = \phi$ and $R_0 \cap R_1 = \{l \to r \mid root(l) \in D\}$.
2. $\forall f \in (D_0 \uplus D)$, $\forall g \in D_1$, $f \not\succeq_d g$ (i.e., $\mathcal{R}_0 \cup \mathcal{R}_1$ is a super-hierarchical combination).
3. Each rewrite rule $l \to r \in R_1$ satisfies the following condition:
   (H) : For every subterm s of r, if $root(s) \in D_1^0$, then s contains no function symbol (in $D_0 \cup D_1^0$) depending on D_0 except at the outermost level (of s).

The third (and the main) condition essentially says that the nesting of defined symbols from D_1^0 is not allowed in the right-hand side terms of rules and no symbol from D_0 occurs below D_1^0-symbols.

The following lemma characterizes the rewrite rules in generalized nice-extension*s.

Lemma 8 *If $\mathcal{R}_1$ is a generalized nice-extension* of $\mathcal{R}_0$ then for each rule $l \to r \in R_1$, r is of the form $C[t_1, \ldots, t_n]$, where C is a context without any D_1^0-symbols, $root(t_i) \in D_1^0$ and no proper subterm of t_i contains any function symbol depending on D_0 for each $i \in [1, n]$.*

Proof: Follows from the condition (H) of Definition 13. □

5 Termination of Nice extensions

In this section, we establish the modularity of termination for generalized nice-extension*s. In the following, we consider two systems $\mathcal{R}_0(D_0 \uplus D, C_0, R_0)$ and $\mathcal{R}_1(D_1 \uplus D, C_1, R_1)$ such that (i) the graph rewrite relations $\Rrightarrow_{\mathcal{R}_0}$ and $\Rrightarrow_{\mathcal{R}_1}$ are terminating, (ii) $\mathcal{R}_1$ is a generalized nice-extension* of $\mathcal{R}_0$ and (iii) function symbols from D_1^0 occur in l only at the outermost level for any rule $l \to r$. We denote the combined system $\mathcal{R}_0 \cup \mathcal{R}_1$ by $\mathcal{R}$. Now, we define a measure, which does not increase after a reduction in generalized nice-extension*s.

Definition 14 The *level* of a term t is defined inductively as follows:

(i)	$level(t) = 0$ if t is a variable or a constant not in D_1^0.	
(ii)	$level(t) = 1$ if t is a constant in D_1^0	
(iii)	$level(f(t_1, \cdots, t_n)) = max(\{level(t_j) \mid j \in [1, n]\})$,	if $f \notin D_1^0$.
(iv)	$level(f(t_1, \cdots, t_n)) = 1 + max(\{level(t_j) \mid j \in [1, n]\})$,	if $f \in D_1^0$.

The *level* of a term graph G is defined as $level(term(G))$. The following two lemmas are easy.

Lemma 9 *$level(r) \leq level(l) \leq 1$ for each rule $l \rightarrow r$ in $\mathcal{R}_0 \cup \mathcal{R}_1$.*

Lemma 10 *If $G \Rrightarrow_{\mathcal{R}} G'$, then $level(G) \geq level(G')$.*

5.1 Collapsed trees of level 0

Collapsed trees of level 0 contain function symbols from $Constr \cup D_0 \cup D_1^1$ and the function symbols D_1^0 are not reachable from these collapsed trees. Therefore the rules applicable on these collapsed trees are those in $\mathcal{R}_0 \cup \mathcal{R}_1'$, where $\mathcal{R}_1' = \{l \rightarrow r \in R_1 \mid root(l) \in D_1^1\}$. It is easy to see that $\mathcal{R}_0$ and $\mathcal{R}_1'$ are crosswise independent and hence $\Rrightarrow_{\mathcal{R}_0 \cup \mathcal{R}_1'}$ is terminating by Theorem 5.

Theorem 6 The graph reduction relation $\Rrightarrow_{\mathcal{R}}$ is noetherian over collapsed trees of level 0.

Definition 15 We define a relation $\Rrightarrow_{sub_{01'}}$ over collapsed trees as $(\Rrightarrow_{\mathcal{R}_0 \cup \mathcal{R}_1'} \cup \Rrightarrow_{sub})^+$. The multiset extension of $\Rrightarrow_{sub_{01'}}$ is denoted by $\Rrightarrow_{sub_{01'}}^m$.

By lemma 1, the relation $\Rrightarrow_{sub_{01'}}$ is noetherian.

5.2 Collapsed trees of level 1

We first consider collapsed trees of level 1 with root in D_1^0. A term t of level 1 with $root(t) \in D_1^0$ can be uniquely written as $C[t_1, \cdots, t_n]$, $n \geq 0$ such that C is a context of function symbols in $Constr \cup D \cup D_1$, t_i occurs at position p_i and $root(t_i) \in D_0$ for each $i \in [1, n]$. For a collapsed tree G representing the above t, $D_0sub(G)$ denotes the multiset of subgraphs $\{G/v \mid v \in V\}$, where V is the set $\{node_G(p_i) \mid 1 \leq i \leq n$ and $node_G(p_i)$ is not below $node_G(p_j)$ for any $j \neq i\}$.

Definition 16 The relation $\succ_1$ over the set of collapsed trees of level 1 with outermost function symbol in D_1^0 is defined as: $G \succ_1 G'$ if and only if

(a) $D_0sub(G) \Rrightarrow_{sub_{01'}}^m D_0sub(G')$ or
(b) $D_0sub(G) = D_0sub(G')$ and $G \Rrightarrow_{sub_1} G'$.

The relation $\succ_1$ is noetherian as both $\Rrightarrow_{sub_1}$ and $\Rrightarrow_{sub_{01'}}$ are noetherian.

A term t of level 1 can be uniquely written as $C[t_1, \cdots, t_n]$, $n \geq 0$ such that C is a context of function symbols in $Constr \cup D_0 \cup D_1^1$ and $root(t_i) \in D_1^0$ for each $i \in [1, n]$. For a collapsed tree G representing the above t, $D_1^0 sub(G)$ denotes the multiset of subgraphs of G corresponding to the subterms $t_1, \cdots, t_n$. Note that D_1^0-symbols are not nested in any term of level 1 and we do not need to use V here unlike in defining $D_0 sub(G)$.

Lemma 11 If G and G' are two collapsed trees of level 1 with $root(term(G)) \in D_1^0$ and $G \Rrightarrow_{\mathcal{R}} G'$ then $D_1^0 sub(G) \gg_1 D_1^0 sub(G')$, where $\gg_1$ is the multiset-extension of $\succ_1$.

Proof : First of all note that $D_1^0 sub(G) = \{G\}$. If the reduction took place in an element of $D_0 sub(G)$, it is obvious that (i) $D_1^0 sub(G') = \{G'\}$ and (ii) $D_0 sub(G) \Rrightarrow^m_{sub_{01'}} D_0 sub(G')$ and hence $G \succ_1 G'$. Therefore $D_1^0 sub(G) \gg_1 D_1^0 sub(G')$. If the reduction took place outside the subgraphs in $D_0 sub(G)$, we have two subcases: the reduction took place (1) below the root of G or (2) at the root.

Subcase (1): If the reduction took place below the root, $D_1^0 sub(G') = \{G'\}$ and either the reduction step is a folding step or the applied rule $l \to r \in \mathcal{R}_1'$. In either case, $G \Rrightarrow_{\mathcal{R}_1} G'$ and no hyperedges corresponding to functions in D_0 are added, i.e., $D_0 sub(G) = D_0 sub(G')$ or $D_0 sub(G) \Rrightarrow^m_{sub_{01'}} D_0 sub(G')$. Therefore, $G \succ_1 G'$ and hence $D_1^0 sub(G) = \{G\} \gg_1 \{G'\} = D_1^0 sub(G')$.

Subcase (2): If the reduction took place at the root of G, $D_1^0 sub(G') = \{G_1, \cdots, G_m\}$, $m \geq 0$ such that $D_0 sub(G_i) = D_0 sub(G')$ or $D_0 sub(G) \Rrightarrow^m_{sub_{01'}} D_0 sub(G_i)$ for each $i \in [1, m]$ (note: by condition (H) of Definition 13, D_0 symbols do not occur in right-sides of rules in $\mathcal{R}_1$ *below* D_1^0 *symbols*). Further, it is easy to see that $G \Rrightarrow_{sub_1} G_i$ for each $i \in [1, m]$. To sum up, $G \succ_1 G_i$ for each $i \in [1, m]$ and hence $D_1^0 sub(G) = \{G\} \gg_1 D_1^0 sub(G')$. □

Now, we are in a position to show that $\Rrightarrow_{\mathcal{R}}$ is noetherian over collapsed trees of level 1.

Theorem 7 The reduction relation $\Rrightarrow_{\mathcal{R}}$ is noetherian over collapsed trees of level 1.

Proof : We prove this by showing that $G \Rrightarrow_{\mathcal{R}} G'$ implies (a) $D_1^0 sub(G) \gg_1 D_1^0 sub(G')$ or (b) $D_1^0 sub(G) = D_1^0 sub(G')$ and $G \Rrightarrow_{\mathcal{R}_0 \cup \mathcal{R}_1'} G'$. Since both $\gg_1$ and $\Rrightarrow_{\mathcal{R}_0 \cup \mathcal{R}_1'}$ are noetherian, it follows that $\Rrightarrow_{\mathcal{R}}$ is noetherian.

There are two cases: (1) the reduction took place in an element of $D_1^0 sub(G)$ or (2) the reduction took place outside the subgraphs in $D_1^0 sub(G)$. By the above lemma $D_1^0 sub(G) \gg_1 D_1^0 sub(G')$ in case (1). Consider case (2). If the reduction took place outside the subgraphs in $D_1^0 sub(G)$, either the reduction step is a folding step or the applied rule $l \to r \in \mathcal{R}_0 \cup \mathcal{R}_1'$. In either case, $G \Rrightarrow_{\mathcal{R}_0 \cup \mathcal{R}_1'} G'$ and no hyperedges corresponding to functions in D_1^0 are added, i.e., $D_1^0 sub(G') = D_0 sub(G)$ or $D_1^0 sub(G) \gg_1 D_1^0 sub(G')$. This completes the proof. □

5.3 Collapsed trees of level greater than 1

Definition 17 A term t of level k can be uniquely written as $C[t_1, \cdots, t_n]$, $n \geq 0$ such that C is a context of level 1, t_i occurs at position p_i, $root(t_i) \in D_1^0$ and $rank(t_i) < k$ for each $i \in [1, n]$. For a collapsed tree G representing the above t,

- $D_1^0 sub_k(G)$ denotes the multiset of subgraphs $\{G/v \mid v \in V\}$, where V is the set $\{node_G(p_i) \mid 1 \leq i \leq n$ and $node_G(p_i)$ is not below $node_G(p_j)$ for any $j \neq i\}$.
- $cap_k(G)$ denotes the collapsed tree obtained from G by replacing the (unique) hyperedges outgoing from the nodes $node_G(p_1), \cdots, node_G(p_n)$ by the hyperedges representing $\Box$ and removing the garbage.

We prove that $\Rrightarrow_{\mathcal{R}}$ is noetherian over collapsed trees of level k assuming that $\Rrightarrow_{\mathcal{R}}$ is noetherian over collapsed trees of level less than k. We define a noetherian relation $\succ_k$ over collapsed trees of level $< k$ with the outermost symbol in D_1^0 as $G \succ_k G'$ if and only if there is a G'' such that (i) $G \Rrightarrow_{\mathcal{R}} G''$, (ii) $G' \equiv G''/v$ for some node in G'' and (iii) $root(term(G')) \in D_1^0$. The multiset extension of $\succ_k$ is denoted by $\gg_k$.

Theorem 8 If the reduction relation $\Rrightarrow_{\mathcal{R}}$ is noetherian over collapsed trees of level less than k, then $\Rrightarrow_{\mathcal{R}}$ *is noetherian over collapsed trees of level* k *as well.*

Proof : We show that a reduction $G \Rrightarrow_{\mathcal{R}} G'$ over collapsed trees of level k implies (i) $D_1^0 sub_k(G) \gg_k D_1^0 sub_k(G')$ or (ii) $D_1^0 sub_k(G) = D_1^0 sub_k(G')$ and $cap_k(G) \Rrightarrow_{\mathcal{R}} cap_k(G')$. Since $\gg_k$ is noetherian over collapsed trees of level less than k with the outermost symbol in D_1^0 and $\Rrightarrow_{\mathcal{R}}$ is noetherian over collapsed trees of level 1, it follows that $\Rrightarrow_{\mathcal{R}}$ is noetherian over collapsed trees of level k.

Consider a reduction $G \Rrightarrow_{\mathcal{R}} G'$ over collapsed trees of level k. If the reduction took place in an element of $D_1^0 sub_k(G)$ it is obvious that $D_1^0 sub_k(G) \gg_k D_1^0 sub_k(G')$. Since D_1^0 symbols do not occur in left-sides of rules except at the outermost level and nesting of D_1^0 symbols is not allowed in right-sides, it follows that $D_1^0 sub_k(G') \subseteq D_1^0 sub_k(G)$ and $cap_k(G) \Rrightarrow_{\mathcal{R}} cap_k(G')$ if the reduction took place outside the subgraphs in $D_1^0 sub_k(G)$. That is, $D_1^0 sub_k(G) \gg_k D_1^0 sub_k(G')$ or $D_1^0 sub_k(G) = D_1^0 sub_k(G')$ and $cap_k(G) \Rrightarrow_{\mathcal{R}} cap_k(G')$. This completes the proof. $\Box$

Now, we are in a position to establish one of the main results of the paper.

Theorem 9 Let $\mathcal{R}_0$ and $\mathcal{R}_1$ be two term rewriting systems such that (i) $\Rrightarrow_{\mathcal{R}_0}$ and $\Rrightarrow_{\mathcal{R}_1}$ are terminating, (ii) $\mathcal{R}_1$ is a generalized nice extension* of $\mathcal{R}_0$ and (iii) function symbols from D_1^0 occur in l only at the outermost level for any rule $l \to r \in R_1$. Then *the reduction relation* $\Rrightarrow_{\mathcal{R}_0 \cup \mathcal{R}_1}$ *is terminating as well.*

Proof: Follows by induction from the above two theorems. $\Box$

The condition (iii) above is only used in Theorem 8. In our proof, this condition is very essential to establish that $cap_k(G) \Rrightarrow_{\mathcal{R}} cap_k(G')$ if the reduction took place in $cap_k(G)$. Without this condition, $cap_k(G')$ can possibly contain some function symbols from $D_1^0 sub_k(G)$ when a D_1^0 symbol occurs in the left-hand side of the rewrite rule applied.

6 Comparison with Related Works

Plump [14] proved modularity of termination in graph rewriting for crosswise disjoint systems.

Definition 18 Two TRSs $\mathcal{R}_0$ and $\mathcal{R}_1$ are *crosswise disjoint* if the function symbol in the left-sides of $\mathcal{R}_i$ do not occur in the right-sides of $\mathcal{R}_{1-i}$ for $i \in [0,1]$.

Theorem 10 **(Plump** [14]**)** Let $\mathcal{R}_0$ and $\mathcal{R}_1$ be two crosswise disjoint systems. Then $\Rrightarrow_{\mathcal{R}_0 \cup \mathcal{R}_1}$ *terminates if and only if both* $\Rrightarrow_{\mathcal{R}_0}$ *and* $\Rrightarrow_{\mathcal{R}_1}$ *terminate.*

Kurihara and Ohuchi [10] proved modularity of termination in graph rewriting for constructor sharing systems (which share constructors but not defined symbols).

Theorem 11 **(Kurihara and Ohuchi** [10]**)** Let $\mathcal{R}_0$ and $\mathcal{R}_1$ be two TRSs sharing constructors. Then $\Rrightarrow_{\mathcal{R}_0 \cup \mathcal{R}_1}$ *terminates if and only if both* $\Rrightarrow_{\mathcal{R}_0}$ *and* $\Rrightarrow_{\mathcal{R}_1}$ *terminate.*

Note that Theorem 11 is not a generalization of Theorem 10 as crosswise disjoint systems do not forbid sharing of defined symbols. To have a theorem which is generalization of Theorem 10, Kurihara and Ohuchi allow a set $\mathcal{B}$ of defined symbols to be shared provided those symbols (in $\mathcal{B}$) occur only in left-sides of $\mathcal{R}_0 \cup \mathcal{R}_1$.

Theorem 12 **(Kurihara and Ohuchi** [10]**)** Let TRS $\mathcal{R}_0(D_0 \uplus \mathcal{B}, C_0, R_0)$ and $\mathcal{R}_1(D_1 \uplus \mathcal{B}, C_1, R_1)$ be two TRSs such that (i) $D_0 \cap D_1 = D_0 \cap C_1 = C_0 \cap D_1 = \phi$ and (ii) symbols in $\mathcal{B}$ occur only in left-sides of rules in $R_0 \cup R_1$. Then $\Rrightarrow_{\mathcal{R}_0 \cup \mathcal{R}_1}$ *terminates if and only if both* $\Rrightarrow_{\mathcal{R}_0}$ *and* $\Rrightarrow_{\mathcal{R}_1}$ *terminate.*

The proof of this theorem can be sketched as follows. Since graph rewriting does not copy subgraphs and $\mathcal{B}$-symbols do not occur in right-sides of the rewrite rules, $G \Rrightarrow G'$ implies $\#(G) \geq \#(G')$, where $\#(G)$ denotes the number of occurrences of $\mathcal{B}$-symbols in G. Therefore, in any derivation, the number of such occurrences (in collapsed tree) remain constant after a finite number of steps. That is, after a finite number of steps, the rewrite rules in $S = \{l \to r \mid root(l) \in \mathcal{B}\}$ are not applied. Since $(\mathcal{R}_0 \cup \mathcal{R}_1) - S$ is a union of two constructor sharing TRSs, its graph rewrite relation terminates by Theorem 11. Hence there cannot be an infinite $\Rrightarrow_{\mathcal{R}_0 \cup \mathcal{R}_1}$ derivation.

This idea works for our results as well, leading to the following theorem.

Theorem 13 Let $\mathcal{R}_0(D_0 \uplus D \uplus \mathcal{B}, C_0, R_0)$ and $\mathcal{R}_1(D_1 \uplus D \uplus \mathcal{B}, C_1, R_1)$ be two term rewriting systems such that (i) $\Rrightarrow_{\mathcal{R}_0}$ and $\Rrightarrow_{\mathcal{R}_1}$ are terminating, (ii) $\mathcal{R}_1 - \{l \to r \mid root(l) \in \mathcal{B}\}$ is a generalized nice-extension* of $\mathcal{R}_0 - \{l \to r \mid root(l) \in \mathcal{B}\}$, (iii) function symbols from D_1^0 occur in l only at the outermost level for any rule $l \to r \in R_1$ and (iv) symbols in $\mathcal{B}$ occur only left-sides of rules in $R_0 \cup R_1$. Then $\Rrightarrow_{\mathcal{R}_0 \cup \mathcal{R}_1}$ *is terminating as well.*

This theorem is not only a generalization of theorems 10, 11 and 12 but also more powerful than them as hierarchical combinations are very natural and occur in practice very often than the combinations considered in those theorems. In fact, the above theorem can be extended for the class of proper-extensions considered in [9].

7 Conclusion

In this paper, we investigate certain theoretical aspects of graph implementations of term rewriting which are relevant to implementations of functional programming. In particular, we study modular aspects and show that modularity of termination in term graph rewriting needs neither confluence nor simple termination – in sharp contrast to the case of pure term rewriting. Finally, a comparison with related works is provided.

Acknowledgements: I would like to thank Detlef Plump and Harald Ganzinger for carefully reading the paper and scrutinizing the proofs.

References

[1] N. Dershowitz and J.-P. Jouannaud (1990), *Rewrite Systems*, in J. van Leeuwen (ed.), *Handbook of Theoretical Computer Science*, Vol. **B**, pp. 243-320.

[2] N. Dershowitz (1992), *Hierarchical termination*, draft, Hebrew University, Dec.. 1992. Revised version in Proc. CTRS'94, LNCS **968**, Springer-Verlag.

[3] M. Fernandez and J.P. Jouannaud (1995), *Modular termination of term rewriting systems revisited*, Proc. COMPASS workshop on ADT, LNCS **906**, pp. 255-273.

[4] B.Gramlich (1994), *Generalized sufficient conditions for modular termination of rewriting*, in AAECC **5**, pp. 131-158.

[5] J.W. Klop (1992), *Term Rewriting Systems*, in S. Abramsky, D. Gabbay and T. Maibaum (ed.), *Handbook of Logic in Computer Science*, Vol. **2**.

[6] M.R.K. Krishna Rao (1994), *Simple termination of hierarchical combinations of term rewriting systems*, Proc. of TACS'94, LNCS **789**, pp. 203-223.

[7] M.R.K. Krishna Rao (1995), *Semi-completeness of hierarchical and super-hierarchical combinations of term rewriting systems*, Proc. of TAPSOFT'95, LNCS **915**, pp. 379-393.

[8] M.R.K. Krishna Rao (1995), *Graph reducibility of term rewriting systems*, Proc. of MFCS'95, LNCS **969**, pp. 371-381.

[9] M.R.K. Krishna Rao (1995), *Modular proofs for completeness of hierarchical term rewriting systems*, Theoretical Computer Science **151**, pp. 487-512.

[10] M. Kurihara and A. Ohuchi (1995), *Modularity in noncopying term rewriting*, Theoretical Computer Science **152**, pp. 139-169.

[11] A. Middeldorp and Y. Toyama (1993), *Completeness of combinations of constructor systems*, *J. Symb. Comp.* **15**, pp. 331-348.

[12] E. Ohlebusch (1994), *Modular properties of composable term rewriting systems*, Ph.D. Thesis, University of Bielefeld.

[13] D. Plump (1990), *Graph-reducible term rewriting systems*, Proc. 4th workshop on graph grammars and their applications to Computer Science, LNCS **532**, pp. 622-636.

[14] D. Plump (1992), *Collapsed tree rewriting: completeness, confluence and modularity*, Proc. CTRS'92, LNCS **656**, pp. 97-112.

[15] D. Plump (1993), *Evaluation of functional expressions by hypergraph rewriting*, Ph.D. Thesis, University of Bremen.

[16] Y. Toyama (1987), *On the Church-Rosser property for the direct sum of term rewriting systems*, JACM **34**, pp. 128-143.

[17] Y. Toyama (1987), *Counterexamples to termination for the direct sum of term rewriting systems*, Information Processing Letters, IPL **25**, pp. 141-143.

Confluence of Terminating Conditional Rewrite Systems Revisited*

Bernhard Gramlich[1] and Claus-Peter Wirth[2]

[1] INRIA Lorraine, 615, rue du Jardin Botanique, BP 101
54602 Villers-lès-Nancy, France
gramlich@loria.fr
[2] Fachbereich Informatik, Universität Kaiserslautern
67653 Kaiserslautern, Germany
wirth@informatik.uni-kl.de

Abstract. We present a new and powerful criterion for confluence of terminating (terms in) join conditional term rewriting systems. This criterion is based on a certain joinability property for *shared parallel critical peaks* and does neither require the systems to be decreasing nor left-linear nor normal, but only terminating.

1 Introduction and Overview

We investigate sufficient criteria for confluence of terminating join conditional term rewriting systems (CTRSs for short). It is well-known that several basic results from unconditional term rewriting do not hold for the conditional case. In particular, in contrast to the unconditional case, local confluence of CTRSs is not equivalent to joinability of all (conditional) critical pairs. In other words, this means that variable overlaps may be critical, too. Even under the assumption of termination this may happen ([5]), i.e., there are terminating CTRSs which have joinable critical pairs but are not (locally) confluent. That means joinability of all critical pairs does not suffice any more for inferring confluence of terminating CTRSs via Newman's Lemma. The problem is reflected somehow in the fact that reasonable proof attempts for showing confluence of terminating systems with joinable critical pairs either have to require

- a strengthened termination assumption (which enables a justified inductive reasoning also when recursing into the conditions), or
- some syntactical restrictions on the rules and / or strengthened forms of joinability for critical pairs (which are exploited in an inductive proof based on the ordinary termination assumption).

Our approach falls into the second category. The basically new idea is to consider as critical divergences not only (feasible instances of) ordinary (conditional) critical peaks consisting of two conflicting ordinary rewrite steps, but also and more generally (feasible instances of) *shared parallel* (conditional) critical peaks consisting of an ordinary root reduction step and a *shared parallel* reduction

* This research was supported in part by 'DFG, SFB 314 D4'.

step which simultaneously contracts several parallel critical occurrences of the same redex all of which are critical w.r.t. to the ordinary root reduction step. Roughly speaking, this idea is motivated by the fact that (the recursive analysis of) a reduction step in the variable part of a rule instance naturally gives rise to a corresponding shared parallel reduction step in the corresponding variable parts of the conditions, due to multiple occurrences of the respective variable in the conditions. Yet, the definition of appropriate joinability conditions for shared parallel critical peaks requires a thorough analysis of the proof-technical requirements when trying to prove confluence of terminating systems. The (inductive) proof of the technical key result, Theorem 6, is fairly involved. Therefore we have tried to present it in a carefully structured and modular way, exhibiting the crucial arguments in sufficient detail. This clear proof structure then enables us to derive several consequences and extensions in a relatively straightforward manner.

The structure of the paper is as follows. After recalling some basics for CTRSs and introducing the crucial notion of shared parallel critical peaks in section 2 we review in section 3 the most important results on confluence of terminating CTRSs, and discuss a motivating example. In the main section 4 we first define the needed shared parallel critical peak property and prove the central Theorem 6. Subsequently, we develop some consequences and extensions, and present illustrative examples. Finally, in section 5 we briefly summarize the main contributions of our approach in view of other known results and related work.

2 Preliminaries

We assume familiarity with the basic no(ta)tions, terminology and theory of term rewriting (cf. e.g. [4], [10]).

The set of terms over some given signature $\mathcal{F}$ and some (disjoint) infinite set $\mathcal{V}$ of variables is denoted by $\mathcal{T}(\mathcal{F},\mathcal{V})$.

Positions (in terms) are defined as usual, and denoted by $p, q, \pi, \ldots$. They are ordered by the prefix ordering $\leq$ as usual. The 'empty' position is denoted by λ. If $p \leq q$ we say that p is *above* q (or q is *below* p). Two positions p and q are said to be *parallel* (or *independent, disjoint*), denoted by $p \parallel q$, if neither $p \leq q$ nor $q \leq p$. These notations extend in a straightforward way to sets of positions denoted by $\Pi, \Pi', \ldots$. Furthermore we also use mixed notations like $p \leq \Pi$ with the obvious meaning (i.e., $\forall \pi \in \Pi : p \leq \pi$).

The set of positions of a term s is denoted by $Pos(s)$. The sets of variable positions and of non-variable, i.e., function symbol, positions of s are denoted by $\mathcal{V}Pos(s)$ and $\mathcal{F}Pos(s)$, respectively. The subterm of s at some position $p \in Pos(s)$ is denoted by s/p. The result of replacing in s the subterm at position $p \in Pos(s)$ by t is denoted by $s[p \leftarrow t]$. If the same term t is to substituted for all $p \in P$, $P \subseteq Pos(s)$ (with all $p \in P$ mutually parallel), then we write $s[p \leftarrow t \,|\, p \in P]$.

Definition 1. (conditional term rewriting system)
A *join conditional term rewriting system* (CTRS for short) over some signature $\mathcal{F}$ consists of a set $\mathcal{R}$ of *conditional rewrite rules* of the form $l \rightarrow r \Longleftarrow P$

where P is a conjunction of equational conditions (where equality is interpreted as joinability) $s_i \downarrow t_i$ $(1 \le i \le n)$, with $l, r, s_i, t_i, \in \mathcal{T}(\mathcal{F}, \mathcal{V})$. To simplify the discussion we require $l \notin \mathcal{V}$ and $Var(r) \subseteq Var(l)$, i.e., no variables as left-hand sides and no extra variables on right-hand sides. Rules without conditions (i.e., with $n = 0$) will be written as $l \to r$. The rewrite relation $\to_{\mathcal{R}}$ induced by $\mathcal{R}$ is inductively defined as follows: Let $\mathcal{R}_0 = \emptyset$, and $\mathcal{R}_{i+1} = \{l\sigma \to r\sigma \mid (l \to r \Longleftarrow P) \in \mathcal{R}, u\sigma \downarrow_{\mathcal{R}_i} v\sigma \text{ for all } (u \downarrow v) \text{ in } P\}$. Note that $\mathcal{R}_i \subseteq \mathcal{R}_{i+1}$, for all $i \ge 0$. Then: $s \to_{\mathcal{R}} t$ if $s \to_{\mathcal{R}_i} t$ for some $i \ge 0$, hence $\to_{\mathcal{R}} = \bigcup_{i \ge 0} \to_{\mathcal{R}_i}$. Instead of $\to_{\mathcal{R}}$ we shall also simply use $\to$.

If $s \to_{\mathcal{R}} t$ then the *depth* of $s \to_{\mathcal{R}} t$ is defined to be the minimal n with $s \to_{\mathcal{R}_n} t$. If the depth of $s \to_{\mathcal{R}} t$ is less than or equal to n we denote this by $s \xrightarrow{n}_{\mathcal{R}} t$.

$P\downarrow$ means joinability of all conditions in P, and $P\sigma$ means that all conditions in P are instantiated by σ. Furthermore, we sometimes subscript reduction steps by additional information as in $s \to_{p,\sigma,l\to r \Leftarrow P} t$. We shall also freely use mirrored versions of arrows with subscripts like $t \;{}_{p,\sigma,l\to r\Leftarrow P}\!\leftarrow s$ with the obvious meaning.

Remark 2. **(encoding of conditions via an equality predicate)**
Note that instead of a CTRS $\mathcal{R}$ over some signature $\mathcal{F}$ one may — within a many-sorted framework — consider the extended system $\mathcal{R}' := \mathcal{R} \uplus \{eq(x,x) \to true\}$ over the extended signature $\mathcal{F}' := \mathcal{F} \uplus \{eq, true\}$. Here, eq is a fresh binary function symbol of a new sort, and $true$ a fresh constant of this new sort (with x a variable of the 'old' sort). Then it is easily shown that $\mathcal{R}'$ is a conservative extension of $\mathcal{R}$ in the following sense: for all 'old' terms s, t, i.e., with $s, t \in \mathcal{T}(\mathcal{F}, \mathcal{V})$, we have:[3]

- $s \xrightarrow{n}_{\mathcal{R}} t \iff s \xrightarrow{n}_{\mathcal{R}'} t$,
- $s \to_{\mathcal{R}} t \iff s \to_{\mathcal{R}'} t$,
- $s \downarrow^n_{\mathcal{R}} t \iff eq(s,t) \downarrow^n_{\mathcal{R}'} true$ (for $n \ge 1$),
- $eq(s,t) \xrightarrow{n}{}^*_{\mathcal{R}'} eq(u,v) \iff s \xrightarrow{n}{}^*_{\mathcal{R}} u \wedge t \xrightarrow{n}{}^*_{\mathcal{R}} v$,
- $eq(s,t) \xrightarrow{n}{}^*_{\mathcal{R}'} true \iff \exists w : eq(s,t) \xrightarrow{n}{}^*_{\mathcal{R}} eq(w,w) \to_{\mathcal{R}'} true$ (for $n \ge 1$),

From these properties it is straightforward to infer that properties like termination, confluence, local confluence and joinability of critical pairs as well as the set of critical pairs / peaks are not affected by considering $\mathcal{R}'$ instead of $\mathcal{R}$, or vice versa. Note in particular, that the equivalence $s \downarrow^n_{\mathcal{R}} t \iff eq(s,t) \downarrow^n_{\mathcal{R}'} true$ (for $n \ge 1$) means: $s \downarrow^n_{\mathcal{R}} t \iff eq(s,t) \xrightarrow{n}{}^*_{\mathcal{R}'} true$, since $true$ is irreducible.

Conditional rewriting is inherently much more complicated than unconditional rewriting. Intuitively, the main reason is that for applying some rule $l \to r \Longleftarrow P$ the appropriately instantiated conditions must be verified recursively using the reduction relation again. This may lead to a non-terminating evaluation process for the conditions, even for terminating systems. In fact, the rewrite relation (and reducibility) may be undecidable even for (finite) CTRSs without extra variables which are terminating and confluent ([8], cf. also [13]).

[3] Note that $s \downarrow^n_{\mathcal{R}} t$ is to denote that the depth of $s \downarrow_{\mathcal{R}} t$ is at most n.

In order to ensure decidability of the basic notions like reducibility one has to impose a stronger condition than termination: A CTRS $\mathcal{R}$ is said to be *decreasing* ([5]) if there exists a well-founded partial ordering $>$ extending the reduction relation and the proper subterm ordering such that $l\sigma > s_i\sigma$ and $l\sigma > t_i\sigma$, for every rule $l \to r \Longleftarrow s_1 \downarrow t_1, \ldots, s_n \downarrow t_n$ in $\mathcal{R}$ and every substitution σ.

We need to be a bit more precise with the notion of *critical peak / pair* than it is usually done: Our critical peak conditions to be developed crucially rely on some additional information (namely, the positions of the 'inner' shared redexes contracted) which gets lost if only the resulting *(conditional) critical pair* is considered. The *parallel reduction relation* on terms (induced by $\to_{\mathcal{R}} = \to$ for some CTRS $\mathcal{R}$) is defined as usual, and denoted by $\dashv\!\!\vdash\!\!\!\to$.

Definition 3. (shared parallel critical peaks and related notions)
Let $\mathcal{R}$ be a CTRS, and let $l_1 \to r_1 \Longleftarrow P_1$, $l_2 \to r_2 \Longleftarrow P_2$ be two rewrite rules of $\mathcal{R}$ which have no variables in common. Let $\Pi \subseteq \mathcal{F}Pos(l_2)$ be a non-empty set of parallel non-variable positions of l_2 such that l_1 and all l_2/π, $\pi \in \Pi$, are (simultaneously) unifiable with mgu σ. Then the 6-tuple $\langle t_1, Q_1, t_2, Q_2, u, \Pi\rangle = \langle (l_2[\pi \leftarrow r_1 \mid \pi \in \Pi])\sigma, P_1\sigma, r_2\sigma, P_2\sigma, l_2\sigma, \Pi\rangle$ is said to be a *shared parallel (conditional) critical peak* of $\mathcal{R}$ (obtained by overlapping the rule $l_1 \to r_1 \Longleftarrow P_1$ into $l_2 \to r_2 \Longleftarrow P_2$ simultaneously at all positions from Π). The corresponding *shared parallel (conditional) critical pair* is obtained by ignoring the overlap u and the set Π of parallel overlap positions, written as $\langle t_1 = t_2\rangle \Longleftarrow Q_1, Q_2$. However, we exclude the case where $l_1 \to r_1 \Longleftarrow P_1$, $l_2 \to r_2 \Longleftarrow P_2$ are renamed versions of the same rule of $\mathcal{R}$ and $\Pi = \{\lambda\}$, i.e., we do not overlap a rule with itself at root position (since this gives only rise to trivial (conditional) divergences, due to $Var(r_i) \subseteq Var(l_i)$). For any substitution τ, $\langle t_1', Q_1', t_2', Q_2', u', \Pi\rangle = \langle t_1\tau, Q_1\tau, t_2\tau, Q_2\tau, u\tau, \Pi\rangle$ is said to be an instance of $\langle t_1, Q_1, t_2, Q_2, u, \Pi\rangle$. If, for an instance $I = \langle t_1', Q_1', t_2', Q_2', u', \Pi\rangle$, Q_1' and Q_2' are satisfied, i.e., if $Q_1' \downarrow_{\mathcal{R}}$ and $Q_2' \downarrow_{\mathcal{R}}$ hold, then I is called *feasible*, and *infeasible* otherwise. If I is feasible, its corresponding *critical divergence* is given by the quadruple $\langle t_1', t_2', u', \Pi\rangle$ which – for the sake of readability – is also denoted by $t_1' \;{}_{\Pi}\!\!\leftarrow\!\!\dashv\!\!\vdash u' \to_{\lambda} t_2'$. A critical divergence $\langle t_1', t_2', u', \Pi\rangle$ is *joinable*, if $t_1' \downarrow_{\mathcal{R}} t_2'$. The instance $I = \langle t_1', Q_1', t_2', Q_2', u', \Pi\rangle$ is *joinable* if it is infeasible or satisfies $t_1' \downarrow_{\mathcal{R}} t_2'$. A shared parallel (conditional) critical peak $\langle t_1, Q_1, t_2, Q_2, u, \Pi\rangle$ is said to be *outside* (or a *(conditional) critical overlay*) if $\Pi = \{\lambda\}$. Otherwise, i.e., if some $\pi \in \Pi$ is strictly below the root ($\pi > \lambda$) (which implies $\pi > \lambda$ for all $\pi \in \Pi$), it is said to be *inside*. It is said to be *joinable* if all its instances are joinable. Ordinary *(conditional) critical peaks* are obtained as a special case in the above definition, namely by requiring that Π is a singleton set. If every shared parallel critical peak of $\mathcal{R}$ is a critical overlay, $\mathcal{R}$ is said to be an *overlay CTRS*. $\mathcal{R}$ *has joinable critical peaks* (or *pairs*) if all (feasible) instances of all critical peaks (pairs) are joinable. $\mathcal{R}$ is *shallow confluent* ([5]) if for all $m, n \geq 0$ and all terms s, t, u with $s \overset{m}{\to}{}^* t$, $s \overset{n}{\to}{}^* u$ there exists a term v such that $t \overset{n}{\to}{}^* v$ and $u \overset{m}{\to}{}^* v$. An (ordinary) critical peak of $\mathcal{R}$ is *shallow joinable* if for each feasible instance of it the corresponding critical divergence $t_1 \leftarrow u \to t_2$ is shallow joinable, i.e., if $u \overset{m}{\to} t_1$ and $u \overset{n}{\to} t_2$, then there exists t_3 with $t_1 \overset{n}{\to}{}^* t_3$ and $t_2 \overset{m}{\to}{}^* t_3$. $\mathcal{R}$ is said to be *normal* if for every rule $(\, l \to r \Longleftarrow s_1 \downarrow t_1, \ldots, s_n \downarrow t_n\,) \in \mathcal{R}$ and $1 \leq i \leq n$, s_i or t_i is a ground term that is irreducible w.r.t. $\mathcal{R}_u = \{l \to r \mid \exists (l \to r \Longleftarrow P) \in \mathcal{R}\}$.

Note that testing joinability of (shared parallel) conditional critical peaks is in general much more difficult than in the unconditional case since one has to consider all feasible instances.

3 Known Results and Motivation

As already mentioned, joinability of critical pairs is not sufficient for (local) confluence of terminating CTRSs ([5]). On the positive side the following results are known.

Theorem 4. *([5]) Let $\mathcal{R}$ be a CTRS. Then the following properties hold:*

(1) If $\mathcal{R}$ is decreasing and has joinable critical peaks, then it is confluent.
(2) If $\mathcal{R}$ is terminating, left-linear, normal and has shallow joinable critical peaks, then it is (shallow) confluent.
*(3) If $\mathcal{R}$ is a terminating overlay system with joinable critical peaks, then it is confluent (***overlay confluence criterion***).*

According to our introductory classification the underlying approach for result (1) above essentially works by enabling the classical inductive proof technique via a strengthened termination property: The decreasingness assumption justifies the necessary application(s) of the induction hypothesis when recursing into conditions of applied rules (for verifying that variable overlaps are not critical).

Result (2) imposes (quite severe) syntactical restrictions on the form of the rules, and requires a particular form of joinability for (ordinary) critical peaks. (3) is syntactically less restrictive concerning the form of the rules, but only admits critical overlays.

In essence, our main result will be a substantially generalized (local and global) version of the overlay confluence criterion (3). In order to provide some intuition for the basic problems and motivation for our approach let us give a simple, but instructive example.

Example 1. The CTRS

$$\mathcal{R} = \begin{cases} f(a,a) \to b & \\ a \to b & \\ f(b,x) \to b & \Leftarrow \quad f(x,x) \downarrow b \\ f(x,b) \to b & \Leftarrow \quad f(x,x) \downarrow b \end{cases}$$

is terminating (but obviously not decreasing). It has two (symmetric) outside critical peaks (between the last two rules) with no feasible instances at all, and the two inside critical peaks $f(b,a) \;{}_1\!\leftarrow f(a,a) \to_\lambda b$ and $f(a,b) \;{}_2\!\leftarrow f(a,a) \to_\lambda b$ both of which are joinable from left to right: $f(b,a) \to b$, $f(a,b) \to b$, because in both cases the third or fourth rule, respectively, is applicable due to $f(a,a) \to b$ (using the first rule), hence $f(a,a) \downarrow b$. However, $\mathcal{R}$ is not (locally) confluent. For instance, we have

$$l\sigma' = f(b,b) \;{}_2\!\leftarrow f(b,a) = l\sigma \to_\lambda r\sigma = b\,,$$

where the rule $l \to r \Leftarrow P$ applied in the right step is $f(b,x) \to b \Leftarrow f(x,x) \downarrow b$, with matching substitution $\sigma = \{x \mapsto a\}$, and where $\sigma' = \{x \mapsto b\}$. But the two reducts $f(b,b)$ and b are both irreducible. In particular, $l\sigma' \to_{\lambda,\sigma',l\to r\Leftarrow P} r\sigma'$ does not hold. Intuitively, the reason for that is that recursively checking the condition $(P\sigma')\downarrow$ leads to the *shared parallel critical peak*

$$f(b,b)\ {}_{\{1,2\}}\!\leftarrow\!\!\!\!\!\!\!\shortparallel\!\!\! - f(a,a) \to_\lambda b$$

which has a duplicated critical redex and which is not joinable. In other words, a variable overlap has become critical by duplication of the contracted (terminating) redex a in the condition. This suggests to prevent such situations in advance by incorporating a priori such critical situations into the definition of the relevant critical divergences to be analyzed, and naturally leads to the notion of shared parallel critical peaks.

4 Main Results

Now we define the property of shared parallel critical peaks which will be shown to suffice for inferring confluence for terminating (terms in given) CTRSs. Here, given a CTRS $\mathcal{R}$, a term s is said to be *terminating* or *strongly normalizing* (SN(s) for short) if there is no infinite ($\mathcal{R}$-) reduction sequence $s \to s_1 \to s_2 \to \ldots$. Consequently, $\mathcal{R}$ (and $\to$) is terminating if every term is terminating.

Definition 5. (quasi-overlay joinability)
Let $\mathcal{R}$ be a CTRS. Let $I = \langle t_1', Q_1', t_2', Q_2', u', \Pi\rangle$ be a feasible instance of a shared parallel critical peak of $\mathcal{R}$. Then we say that I (and its corresponding critical divergence $t_1'\ {}_\Pi\!\leftarrow\!\!\!\!\!\!\shortparallel\!\!\! - u' \to_\lambda t_2'$) is *quasi-overlay joinable* if it is joinable as follows: There exists some t_3' with $t_1' \to^* t_3'$ and $t_2' \to^*_{<_s} t_3'$, where $s := u'/\pi$ for any $\pi \in \Pi$ (note that s does not depend on which $\pi \in \Pi$ we choose). Here the subscript $_{<_s}$ means that in the reduction sequence $t_2' \to^* t_3'$ only redexes are allowed to be contracted which are strictly smaller than s w.r.t. $>:= (\to \cup \rhd_{st})^+$ (i.e., if $s(\to \cup \rhd_{st})^+ w$ for any redex w contracted in $t_2' \to^* t_3'$). I is said to be *innermost* if no proper subterm of $s = u'/\pi$ (for $\pi \in \Pi$) is reducible (w.r.t. $\mathcal{R}$). A shared parallel critical peak is said to be *quasi-overlay joinable* if all its feasible instances are quasi-overlay joinable. $\mathcal{R}$ *has quasi-overlay joinable shared parallel critical peaks* if all its shared parallel critical peaks are quasi-overlay joinable.

Let us introduce the following abbreviation (*).

all feasible innermost instances of all shared parallel critical peaks of $\mathcal{R}$ are quasi-overlay joinable	(*)

Now we are prepared to state and prove the following central result, which in essence is a substantially generalized local version of [5, Lemma 2] (but with a proof that is different in important details).

Theorem 6. (technical key result)
Let $\mathcal{R}$ be a CTRS satisfying (*). Let $\mathcal{R}' = \mathcal{R} \uplus \{eq(x,x) \to true\}$ (as in Remark 2). Then the following localized confluence property holds:
$\forall s \in \mathcal{T}(\mathcal{F},\mathcal{V}), SN(s)\ \forall t \in \mathcal{T}(\mathcal{F},\mathcal{V})\ \forall u,v \in \mathcal{T}(\mathcal{F}',\mathcal{V})\ \forall \Pi, [\forall \pi \in \Pi : u/\pi = s]:$

$$\left.\begin{array}{l} u \to^*_{\mathcal{R}'} v \\ s \to^*_{\mathcal{R}} t \end{array}\right\} \implies u[\pi \leftarrow t \,|\, \pi \in \Pi] \downarrow_{\mathcal{R}'} v$$

Proof. Let $\bar{s} \in \mathcal{T}(\mathcal{F},\mathcal{V})$ be a terminating term, i.e., with $\mathrm{SN}(\bar{s})$. We have to show:

(I) $\forall t \in \mathcal{T}(\mathcal{F},\mathcal{V})$ $\forall u,v \in \mathcal{T}(\mathcal{F}',\mathcal{V})$ $\forall \Pi, [\forall \pi \in \Pi : u/\pi = \bar{s}]$:

$$\left.\begin{array}{l} u \to^*_{\mathcal{R}'} v \\ \bar{s} \to^*_{\mathcal{R}} t \end{array}\right\} \implies u[\pi \leftarrow t \,|\, \pi \in \Pi] \downarrow_{\mathcal{R}'} v$$

Now, instead of (I) we shall prove the following strengthened version

(II) $\forall s,t \in \mathcal{T}(\mathcal{F},\mathcal{V}), \bar{s} \geq_1 s$ $\forall u,v \in \mathcal{T}(\mathcal{F}',\mathcal{V})$ $\forall \Pi, [\forall \pi \in \Pi : u/\pi = s]$:

$$\left.\begin{array}{l} u \to^*_{\mathcal{R}'} v \\ s \to^*_{\mathcal{R}} t \end{array}\right\} \implies u[\pi \leftarrow t \,|\, \pi \in \Pi] \downarrow_{\mathcal{R}'} v$$

by induction. Here the partial ordering $>_1$ (which depends on $\bar{s}$!) is defined by $>_1 := (\to \cup \rhd_{st})^+{}_{\mathrm{below}\ \bar{s}}$, where — for some binary (ordering) relation R — $R_{\mathrm{below}\ a}$ is defined by $R \cap (\{b \,|\, aR^*b\}^2)$. Note that $>_1$ is well-founded due to $\mathrm{SN}(\bar{s})$ which is easily seen by standard arguments. We shall prove (II) by induction, using the following complexity measure $M(s,t,u,v,\Pi)$ for $s \in \mathcal{T}(\mathcal{F},\mathcal{V})$ with $\bar{s} \geq_1 s$, $t \in \mathcal{T}(\mathcal{F},\mathcal{V})$, $u,v \in \mathcal{T}(\mathcal{F}',\mathcal{V})$ and Π, such that $u/\pi = s$ for all $\pi \in \Pi$, and $u \to^*_{\mathcal{R}'} v$:

$$M(s,t,u,v,\Pi) = \langle s,n,k \rangle\,,$$

where

$$n = n(u,v) = \min\{m \,|\, u \overset{m}{\to}{}^*_{\mathcal{R}'} v\}$$

and

$$k = k(u,v,n) = \min\{l \,|\, u \overset{n}{\to}{}^l_{\mathcal{R}'} v\}\,.$$

These triples $\langle s,n,k \rangle$ are compared using the lexicographic combination $\succ$ of the orderings $>_1$, $>_2$ and $>_3$, where $>_2$ and $>_3$ are the usual ordering $>$ on natural numbers. Now, by well-foundedness of $>_1$ (and of $>$) $\succ$ is well-founded, too. Subsequently, for the sake of readability we shall often omit the subscripts $\mathcal{R}$ and $\mathcal{R}'$, respectively, in notations like $s \to^*_{\mathcal{R}} t$ and $u \to^*_{\mathcal{R}'} v$ (when they are clear from the context).

The rest of the proof is by a complete case analysis using induction w.r.t. the well-founded ordering $\succ$. We distinguish the following cases:

(1) If $u = v$ (which implies $n = k = 0$) or $s = t$, then we are trivially done.

(2) Otherwise, we may suppose

$$u \overset{n}{\to}_{p,\sigma,l \to r \Leftarrow P} u' \overset{n}{\to}{}^{k-1} v$$

and

$$s \to_{q,\tau,l_1 \to r_1 \Leftarrow P_1} s' \to^* t$$

for $n \geq 1$ minimal with $u \overset{n}{\to}{}^* v$, and $k \geq 1$ minimal with $u \overset{n}{\to}{}^k v$.[4] For the remaining cases it suffices to show

---

[4] Note that $n' = \min\{m \,|\, u' \overset{m}{\to}{}^* v\}$, $k' = \min\{l \,|\, u' \overset{n'}{\to}{}^l v\}$ and n, k are related as follows: either $n' < n$ or else $n' = n$ and $k' < k$. For that reason, one may apply the induction hypothesis in situations of the form $u' \to^* v$, $s \to^* t$ such that $u'/\pi' = s$ for all $\pi' \in \Pi'$ (for some other set Π' of mutually disjoint positions) for inferring $u'[\pi' \leftarrow t \,|\, \pi' \in \Pi'] \downarrow v$, because of a decrease of the measure in the second or third component.

$$u[\pi \leftarrow s' \mid \pi \in \Pi] \downarrow v$$

because then, induction via a decrease in the first component ($s >_1 s'$ because of $s \to s'$) yields

$$u \mathrel{+\!\!\!\!\rightarrow} u[\pi \leftarrow s' \mid \pi \in \Pi] \mathrel{+\!\!\!\!\rightarrow}^* u[\pi \leftarrow t \mid \pi \in \Pi] \downarrow v$$

as desired (this is illustrated in Fig. 1).

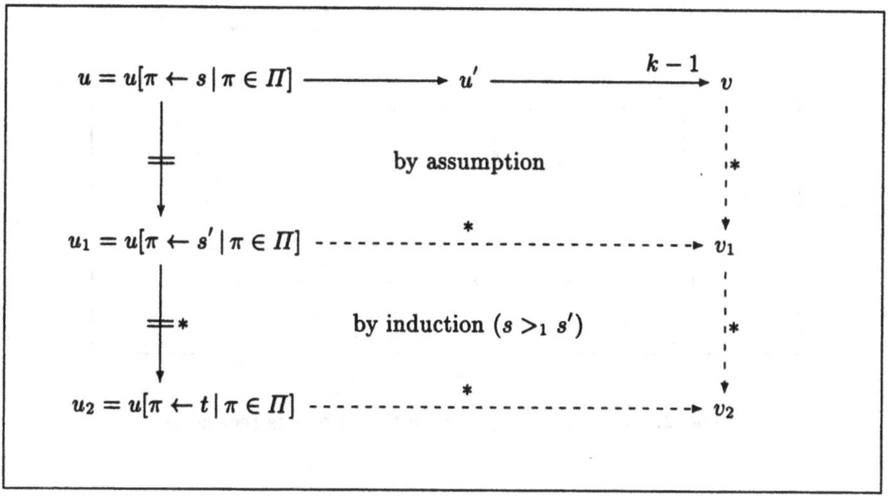

Fig. 1. Case **(2)**: $u[\pi \leftarrow s' \mid \pi \in \Pi] \downarrow v$ suffices for showing $u[\pi \leftarrow t \mid \pi \in \Pi] \downarrow v$

(2.1) Next we consider the case that a proper subterm of s is reducible (this case is illustrated in Fig. 2). Hence, let $s/q' = \hat{s} \to \hat{s}'$ for some $q' > \lambda$. Then we get (cf. the upper part of the diagram)

$$u = u[\pi \leftarrow s \mid \pi \in \Pi] = u[\pi q' \leftarrow \hat{s} \mid \pi \in \Pi] \mathrel{+\!\!\!\!\rightarrow} u[\pi q' \leftarrow \hat{s}' \mid \pi \in \Pi] =: u_2$$

by a shared parallel contraction of the redexes $\hat{s}$ in u into $\hat{s}'$. By induction (due to $s \rhd_{st} \hat{s}$, hence $s >_1 \hat{s}$) we conclude that there exists some v_2 with

$$u_2 = u[\pi q' \leftarrow \hat{s}' \mid \pi \in \Pi] \to^* v_2 \; {}^*\!\!\leftarrow v \,.$$

For the left part of the diagram in Fig. 2, where we have

$$u = u[\pi \leftarrow s \mid \pi \in \Pi] \mathrel{+\!\!\!\!\rightarrow} u[\pi \leftarrow s' \mid \pi \in \Pi] = u_1$$

by a shared parallel contraction of the redex s into s', we consider the extracted divergence

$$s[q' \leftarrow \hat{s}'] \leftarrow s[q' \leftarrow \hat{s}] = s \to s' \,.$$

By induction (taking $\hat{s}$, $\hat{s}'$, s, s', and $\{q'\}$ instead of s, t, u, v and Π, respectively), which is justified due to $s \rhd_{st} \hat{s}$ and hence $s >_1 \hat{s}$, we obtain $s[q' \leftarrow \hat{s}'] \downarrow s'$, i.e., there exists some s'' with

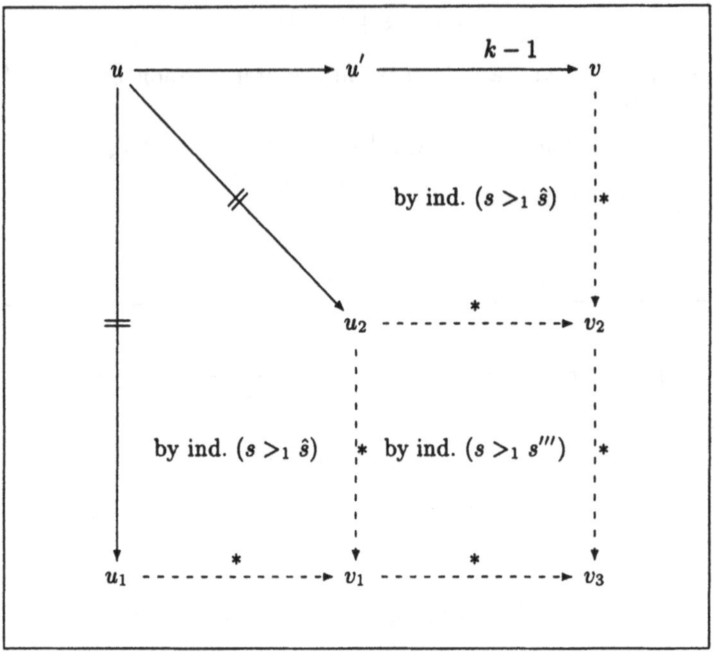

Fig. 2. Case **(2.1)** A proper subterm of s is reducible

$$s' \to^* s'' \;{}^*\!\!\leftarrow s[q' \leftarrow \hat{s}'] \, .$$

Consequently, we also get

$$u_1 = u[\pi \leftarrow s' \mid \pi \in \Pi] \to^* u[\pi \leftarrow s'' \mid \pi \in \Pi] =: v_1$$

and

$$u_2 = u[\pi \leftarrow s[q' \leftarrow \hat{s}'] \mid \pi \in \Pi] \to^* u[\pi \leftarrow s'' \mid \pi \in \Pi] = v_1 \, .$$

Finally, for closing the diagram (cf. its lower right part) we appeal again to the induction hypothesis (taking $s''' := s[q' \leftarrow \hat{s}']$, s'', u_2, v_2 and Π instead of s, t, u, v and Π, respectively). This is justified because of $s \to s''' \to^* s''$ (i.e., $s \to_{\mathcal{R}} s''' \to^*_{\mathcal{R}} s''$ due to $s \in \mathcal{T}(\mathcal{F},\mathcal{V})$, $s''' \in \mathcal{T}(\mathcal{F},\mathcal{V})$) and thus $s >_1 s'''$, and yields some v_3 with $v_1 \to^* v_3 \;{}^*\!\!\leftarrow v_2$ as desired.

(2.2) For the remaining case we may assume that no proper subterm of s is reducible. This implies $q = \lambda$, i.e., $s = l_1\tau$ is an innermost redex which is contracted to $r_1\tau = s'$ using the rule $l_1 \to r_1 \Leftarrow P_1$. Consequently, the redex contraction in $u \overset{n}{\to}_{\sigma,p,l\to r \Leftarrow P} u'$ at position p is either above some positions $\pi' \in \Pi' \subseteq \Pi$ of the shared redexes contracted in the shared parallel step $u \mathrel{-\!\!\!\Vert\!\!\!\to}_{\Pi} u[\pi \leftarrow s' \mid \pi \in \Pi]$, or disjoint from (all of) them. The latter case is no problem (and is also subsumed by the proof of the former), whereas in the first case the overlapping positions may be further partitioned into a "shared parallel variable overlap part" and a "shared parallel critical overlap part". In order to cope with the "shared parallel critical overlap part" the global joinability assumption for shared parallel critical

peaks of $\mathcal{R}$ will be essential. Now we have the following situation:
$p \leq \Pi' \neq \emptyset$, $\Pi' \subseteq \Pi$, $p \parallel (\Pi \backslash \Pi')$ **(some occurrences of the shared parallel redex are below the single redex**, cf. Fig. 3): For a precise argumentation

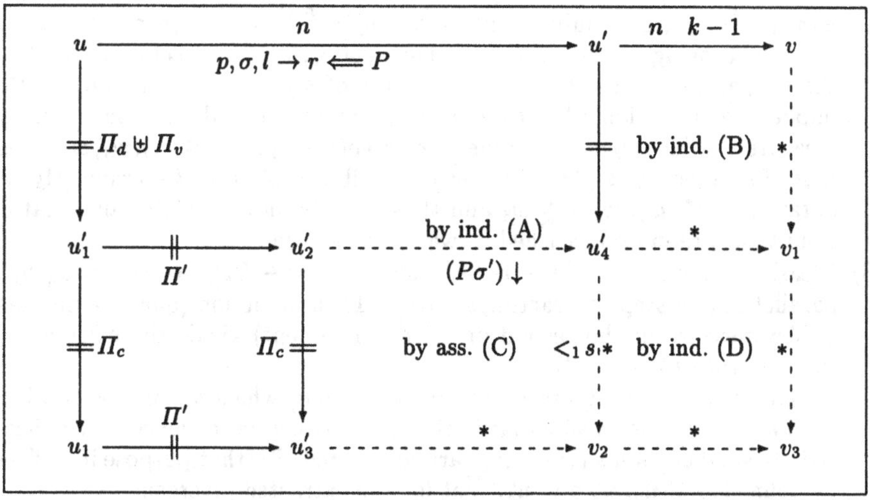

Fig. 3. Case **(2.2)** Some occurrences of the shared parallel redex are strictly below the single redex

we introduce the following definitions:

- $\Pi_x := \{pp'p'' \in \Pi \mid l/p' = x\}$, for $x \in Var(l)$
- $\Pi_v := \{\pi \in \Pi \mid \exists x \in Var(l) : \pi \in \Pi_x\}$
- $\Pi_d := \{\pi \in \Pi \mid \pi \parallel p\}$
- $\Pi_c := \{\pi \in \Pi \mid \exists p' \in \mathcal{F}Pos(l) : \pi = pp'\}$
- $\Pi = \Pi_d \uplus \Pi_v \uplus \Pi_c$
- $\Pi' := \{p\bar{p}p'' \mid \exists p' : \exists x \in Var(l) : (l/p' = x = l/\bar{p} \wedge pp'p'' \in \Pi)\} \setminus \Pi_v$
- $u = u[\pi \leftarrow s \mid \pi \in \Pi]$
- $u' = u[p \leftarrow r\sigma]$
- $x\sigma' := (x\sigma)[p'' \leftarrow s' \mid \exists p' : (l/p' = x \wedge pp'p'' \in \Pi)]$
- $u_1 = u[\pi \leftarrow s' \mid \pi \in \Pi]$
- $u_1' := u[\pi \leftarrow s' \mid \pi \in \Pi_d \uplus \Pi_v]$
- $u_2' := u[\pi \leftarrow s' \mid \pi \in \Pi_d][p \leftarrow l\sigma']$
- $u_3' := u_2'[\pi \leftarrow s' \mid \pi \in \Pi_c]$
- $u_4' := u[\pi \leftarrow s' \mid \pi \in \Pi_d][p \leftarrow r\sigma']$
- $v_2 := u_3'[p \leftarrow w] = u_4'[p \leftarrow w]$ (here w is yet to be determined)

Now, according to Fig. 3 there are four non-trivial parts to be verified, namely (A)-(D). The other reductions are easily checked using the above definitions. In particular, we observe that the shared parallel reductions $u_1' \mathrel{+\!\!\!+\!\!\!\!\rightarrow} u_2'$ and $u_1 \mathrel{+\!\!\!+\!\!\!\!\rightarrow} u_3'$ cope with a potential non-left-linearity of the rule $l \to r \Longleftarrow P$, i.e., these reductions restore an instance of the left-hand side l at position p which may have been destroyed by the shared parallel reduction from u to u'_1.

(A) We have to verify the step $u'_2 \rightarrow_{p,\sigma',l\rightarrow r\Leftarrow P} u'_4$. By definition we know $u'_2/p = l\sigma'$, $u'_4/p = r\sigma'$. Hence it suffices to show $(P\sigma')\downarrow$, i.e., $w_1\sigma' \downarrow w_2\sigma'$ for all conditions $w_1 \downarrow w_2$ in P. From $u \overset{n}{\rightarrow}_{p,\sigma,l\rightarrow r\Leftarrow P} u'$ we know $w_1\sigma \downarrow^{n-1} w_2\sigma$, or, equivalently, $eq(w_1,w_2)\sigma \overset{n-1^*}{\rightarrow}_{\mathcal{R}'} true$ (with the case of $n-1=0$ being trivial). Since we have $eq(w_1,w_2)\sigma \twoheadrightarrow eq(w_1,w_2)\sigma'$ by a shared parallel contraction of occurrences of s in $eq(w_1,w_2)\sigma$ into s', this implies by induction (due to a decrease in the second component in the measure): $eq(w_1,w_2)\sigma' \downarrow_{\mathcal{R}'} true$, hence $eq(w_1,w_2)\sigma' \rightarrow^*_{\mathcal{R}} eq(w_3,w_3) \rightarrow_{\mathcal{R}'} true$, for some $w_3 \in \mathcal{T}(\mathcal{F},\mathcal{V})$, by irreducibility of $true$. Consequently, we obtain $w_1 \rightarrow^*_{\mathcal{R}} w_3$, $w_2 \rightarrow^*_{\mathcal{R}} w_3$ and thus $w_1\sigma' \downarrow_{\mathcal{R}} w_2\sigma'$. This means, that all conditions are indeed satisfied as was to be shown.

(B) Clearly we have $u' = u[p \leftarrow r\sigma] \twoheadrightarrow u[\pi \leftarrow s' \mid \pi \in \Pi_d][p \leftarrow r\sigma'] = u'_4$ by a parallel shared step contracting s into s'. Then induction (due to a decrease of the measure in the second or third component) yields the existence of some v_1 with $u'_4 \rightarrow^* v_1 \; {}^*\!\!\leftarrow v$.

(C) We have to show that there exists a reduct v_2 of u'_3 which can also be obtained from u'_4, but in such a way that in the latter reduction sequence only redexes strictly smaller than s (w.r.t. $>_1$) are contracted. For that purpose it suffices, by definition of u'_2, u'_3 and u'_4, that for the extracted divergence

$$u'_3/p \twoheadleftarrow u'_2/p \rightarrow u'_4/p\,,$$

i.e., for

$$(l\sigma')[\pi'_c \leftarrow s' \mid p\pi'_c \in \Pi_c] \twoheadleftarrow l\sigma' \rightarrow r\sigma'\;,$$

we can find a common reduct of $u'_3/p = (l\sigma')[\pi'_c \leftarrow s' \mid p\pi'_c \in \Pi_c]$ and $u'_4/p = r\sigma'$ which can be reached from the latter by contracting only redexes strictly smaller than s (w.r.t. $>_1$). Since by construction the above divergence is a feasible innermost[5] instance of a shared parallel critical peak of $\mathcal{R}$ (determined by overlapping $l_1 \rightarrow r_1 \Longleftarrow P_1$ into $l \rightarrow r \Longleftarrow P$), the global joinability assumption for such shared parallel critical peaks indeed ensures this special form of joinability.

(D) Finally, we have to show that the divergence $v_2 \; {}^*\!\!\leftarrow u'_4 \rightarrow^* v_1$ can be closed by finding a common reduct v_3. This is possible by repeatedly[6] applying induction, justified by a decrease in the first component of the measure, since only redexes strictly smaller than s (w.r.t. $>_1$) are contracted in the reduction sequence from u'_4 to v_2 (cf. (C)). Hence we are done.

□

Next we shall discuss crucial aspects of this central result and its proof, thus deriving various interesting generalizations and consequences.

First of all we observe that in the above proof the case of a (possibly critical) overlay between the rules $l \rightarrow r \Longleftarrow P$ and $l_1 \rightarrow r_1 \Longleftarrow P_1$, i.e., for $p \in \Pi$,

[5] Note that by assumption no proper subterm of $s = l\sigma'/\pi'_c$ (for all π'_c with $p\pi'_c \in \Pi_c$) is reducible!

[6] Doing this completely formally requires an additional (locally nested) induction on the length of the derivation $u'_4 \rightarrow^* v_2$.

is implicitly contained in case (2). In that case we have $\Pi_d = \Pi_v = \emptyset$, $\Pi = \Pi_c = \{p\}$ and the diagram in Fig. 3 collapses according to the identifications $u = u_1' = u_2'$, $u_1 = u_3'$, $\sigma' = \sigma$. Furthermore, the shared parallel step $u_1' \Vdash\!\!\!\!\rightarrow u_1$ (as well as $u_2' \Vdash\!\!\!\!\rightarrow u_3'$) actually is an ordinary reduction at position p, i.e., the extracted divergence

$$u_3'/p = r_1\tau \;{}_{\lambda}\!\leftarrow l_1\tau = s = u_2'/p = l\sigma \rightarrow_{\lambda} r\sigma = u_4'/p$$

corresponds to a (feasible) instance of the critical overlay of $\mathcal{R}$ between the rules $l \rightarrow r \Longleftarrow P$ and $l_1 \rightarrow r_1 \Longleftarrow P_1$. Consequently, if there exists a common reduct v_4 (which is equal to v_2/p) of u_3'/p and u_4'/p, as it is guaranteed by the global assumption, then the imposed ordering restriction for the reduction sequence $u_4'/p \rightarrow^* v_2/p$, namely that all contracted redexes are strictly smaller than s (w.r.t. $>_1$), is vacuously satisfied. This follows from $u_2'/p = s \rightarrow_{\lambda} u_4'/p$ and hence $u_2'/p = s >_1 u_4'/p$ by definition of $>_1$. In other words, this observation makes clear that for critical overlays of $\mathcal{R}$ joinability is sufficient without any further restriction.

Secondly, we observe that by definition condition (*) in Theorem 6 obviously holds if $\mathcal{R}$ has quasi-overlay joinable shared parallel critical peaks. Hence, any subsequent result depending on (*) also holds under the latter slightly more restrictive precondition.

As an easy consequence of Theorem 6 we now obtain the following local criterion for confluence of terminating terms in a CTRS.

Theorem 7. (local criterion for confluence of terminating terms) *Let $\mathcal{R}$ be a CTRS satisfying (*). Then any terminating term s is confluent, i.e., if SN(s) and $t_1 \;{}^*\!\!\leftarrow s \rightarrow^* t_2$ then $t_1 \downarrow t_2$.*

Proof. We simply apply Theorem 6 choosing $u = s$, $t = t_1$, $v = t_2$ and $\Pi = \{\lambda\}$ (observing that 'proper' $\mathcal{R}'$-reductions, i.e., using the $\mathcal{R}'$-rule $eq(x, x) \rightarrow true$ are not needed in $t_1 \downarrow_{\mathcal{R}'} t_2$). □

A corollary of the local criterion in Theorem 7 is the following global result.

Theorem 8. (global criterion for confluence of terminating CTRSs) *Any terminating CTRS satisfying (*) is confluent.*

Corollary 9. *Any terminating CTRS with quasi-overlay joinable shared parallel critical peaks is confluent.*

For instance, the system $\mathcal{R}' = \mathcal{R} \cup \{f(x, x) \rightarrow x \Longleftarrow x \downarrow b\}$ with $\mathcal{R}$ as in Example 1 is easily shown to be confluent by applying Theorem 8 (or Corollary 9) whereas none of the results of Theorem 4 is applicable.

If all critical peaks of some CTRS $\mathcal{R}$ are overlays, then, according to our observation above, the ordering restriction imposed on the joinability requirement in (*) is vacuously satisfied. Hence, as a special case of Theorem 8 we get the well-known overlay confluence criterion of Theorem 4(3). If a divergence is a feasible instance of a shared parallel critical peak, then the ordering requirement is vacuously satisfied if we have joinability from left to right, i.e., if $t_1 \rightarrow^* t_2$.

Moreover, we observe that, by definition of (*), feasible non-innermost instances of shared parallel critical peaks can be safely ignored. In this sense, the above Theorems 7, 8 constitute critical peak criteria for confluence of CTRSs (in a local and global version, respectively) in the spirit of well-known "critical peak criteria" for confluence of unconditional TRSs as for instance described in [9], [2] (these criteria allow to ignore certain critical pairs when testing for confluence).

Finally, we now show how to generalize the results obtained by making use of orderings. Up to now we have only argued relative to the ordering $(\rightarrow \cup \rhd_{st})^+$. Henceforth, we shall consider the case that termination of $\mathcal{R}$ is shown by some well-founded ordering $\succ$ on terms (i.e., $\rightarrow \subseteq \succ$) which is stable w.r.t. contexts. First we generalize the definition of the quasi-overlay joinability notions introduced in Definition 5 by parameterizing the fixed ordering used there.

Definition 10. ($\succ$-quasi-overlay joinability)
The quasi-overlay joinability notions introduced in Definition 5 are generalized into corresponding $\succ$-quasi-overlay joinability notions simply by replacing $\rightarrow$ with $\succ$, i.e., the original $> = (\rightarrow \cup \rhd_{st})^+$ now becomes $> = (\succ \cup \rhd_{st})^+$.

Note that according to this new definition the old notion of quasi-overlay joinability now means $\rightarrow$-quasi-overlay joinability. Next we define (**) by

all feasible innermost instances of all shared parallel critical peaks of $\mathcal{R}$ are $\succ$-quasi-overlay joinable	(**)

and obtain the following generalization of Theorem 8.

Theorem 11. (generalized confluence criterion)
Let $\mathcal{R}$ be a CTRS such that $\rightarrow \subseteq \succ$ for some well-founded ordering $\succ$ on terms which is stable w.r.t. contexts. If $\mathcal{R}$ satisfies (**) then it is confluent.

Proof. It suffices to prove the local version, i.e., to show confluence below some arbitrary term s which, by assumption, must be terminating. The proof is virtually the same as for Theorem 7, namely via the corresponding version of Theorem 6. The only difference is that instead of $>_1 = (\rightarrow \cup \rhd_{st})^+{}_{\text{below } s}$ we employ $>_1 := (\succ \cup \rhd_{st})^+{}_{\text{below } s}$. Since $\succ$ is stable w.r.t. contexts, $>_1$ is well-founded. □

Corollary 12. *Let $\mathcal{R}$ be a CTRS such that $\rightarrow \subseteq \succ$ for some well-founded ordering $\succ$ on terms which is stable w.r.t. contexts. If $\mathcal{R}$ has $\succ$-quasi-overlay joinable shared parallel critical peaks then it is confluent.*

To see the benefits of Theorem 11, let us give a simple example.

Example 2. The CTRS

$$\mathcal{R} = \begin{cases} f(x,x) \rightarrow g(x,x) & \\ a \rightarrow b & \\ h(f(x,x)) \rightarrow a & \\ h(g(x,y)) \rightarrow b & \Longleftarrow \quad h(f(x,y)) \downarrow b \end{cases}$$

is terminating via the recursive path ordering $>$ induced by the following precedence $>_{\mathcal{F}}$: $f >_{\mathcal{F}} g >_{\mathcal{F}} a >_{\mathcal{F}} b$. There is only one shared parallel (inside) critical peak of $\mathcal{R}$, obtained by overlapping the first into the third rule at position 1: $h(g(x,x))\ {}_1{\leftarrow} h(f(x,x)) \rightarrow_\lambda a$ which is joinable as follows: $h(g(x,x)) \rightarrow b \leftarrow a$. We observe that for the redex contraction $a \rightarrow b$ here, the ordering requirement in (**) means to verify that the inner redex $f(x,x)$ in the overlap term $h(f(x,x))$ is strictly greater (w.r.t. $>_1 = (> \cup \rhd_{st})^+$) than the redex a contracted to establish joinability. This does indeed hold due to $f(x,x) > a$. Applying Theorem 11 (or Corollary 12) yields confluence of $\mathcal{R}$. Observe that Theorem 8 is not applicable here, since $f(x,x)\ (\rightarrow \cup \rhd_{st})^+\ a$ does not hold. We note that $\mathcal{R}$ is neither an overlay CTRS, nor left-linear, nor decreasing. The latter follows since any decreasing ordering $\succ$ for $\mathcal{R}$ would have to satisfy $h(g(x,x)) \succ h(f(x,x)) \succ h(g(x,x))$, due to the last and the first rule, which contradicts irreflexivity. Hence, all other known confluence criteria, in particular those of Theorem 4, are not applicable.

In view of the conditions (*) and (**) both of which rely on joinability properties of shared parallel critical peaks, one may ask whether the corresponding properties for all ordinary critical peaks would already suffice for the results proved above. Actually, this is not the case, even for the case of terminating systems with left-to-right joinable critical peaks. This is witnessed by Example 1 above.

Finally let us remark that it is not difficult to give examples of terminating CTRSs that are confluent but where confluence cannot be shown by any of the presented criteria.

5 Conclusion and Related Work

Summarizing, we have succeeded in developing a new approach for verifying confluence of terminating (terms in) conditional rewrite systems. It is based on the notion of shared parallel critical peaks, and on an appropriate generalization of the notion of 'overlay joinability'. In fact, originally our approach was motivated by the result of [5] (cf. Theorem 4(3) above) in the following sense: We wanted to understand the crucial properties needed for the approach of [5] to work. Two main aspects turned out to be crucial for the presented generalization:

- A localized version of the overlay confluence criterion of [5] (Theorem 4(3)), which only requires a local termination assumption: This result was already obtained in [6], using an induction ordering (similar to the one in [13]) different from the one used in the proof of the corresponding [5, Lemma 2].
- The observation that shared parallel critical peaks constitute the natural candidates for capturing the relevant critical divergences to be taken into account.

Finally, let us briefly mention some related work. In [12], besides several other extensions of known results (also on non-terminating CTRSs), it is shown that the essential ideas and results of our approach also carry over to the more general (and technically more involved) setting of *constructor-based positive/negative CTRSs*. That the notion of *parallel critical peaks*, which is the "unshared" version of *shared parallel critical peaks*, may also be useful is shown in [7] where a sufficient parallel critical peak based condition for confluence of possibly non-terminating, unconditional left-linear TRSs is presented.

Further interesting confluence criteria for CTRSs which have not yet been mentioned can be found in [1], [3] and [11] (the latter two dealing with non-terminating systems).

Acknowledgements: We would like to thank Paul Taylor for his diagrams and the referees for some useful comments.

References

1. J. Avenhaus and C. Loría-Sáenz. On conditional rewrite systems with extra variables and deterministic logic programs. In F. Pfenning, ed., *Proc. 5th LPAR*, **LNAI** 822, pp. 215–229, Springer-Verlag, 1994.
2. L. Bachmair and N. Dershowitz. Critical pair criteria for completion. *Journal of Symbolic Computation*, 6(1):1–18, 1988.
3. J. Bergstra and J. Klop. Conditional rewrite rules: Confluence and termination. *Journal of Computer and System Sciences*, 32:323–362, 1986.
4. N. Dershowitz and J.-P. Jouannaud. Rewrite systems. In J. van Leeuwen, ed., *Formal models and semantics, Handbook of Theoretical Computer Science*, vol. B, ch. 6, pp. 243–320. Elsevier - The MIT Press, 1990.
5. N. Dershowitz, M. Okada, and G. Sivakumar. Confluence of conditional rewrite systems. In S. Kaplan and J.-P. Jouannaud, eds., *Proc. 1st CTRS (1987)*, **LNCS** 308, pp. 31–44, Springer-Verlag, 1988.
6. B. Gramlich. On termination and confluence of conditional rewrite systems. In N. Dershowitz and N. Lindenstrauss, eds., *Proc. 4th CTRS (1994)*, **LNCS** 968, pp. 166–185. Springer-Verlag, 1995.
7. B. Gramlich. Confluence without termination via parallel critical pairs. In H. Kirchner, ed., *Proc. 21st CAAP*, **LNCS** 1059, pp. 211–225. Springer-Verlag, 1996.
8. S. Kaplan. Conditional rewrite rules. *TCS*, 33:175–193, 1984.
9. D. Kapur, D. Musser, and P. Narendran. Only prime superpositions need be considered in the Knuth-Bendix completion procedure. *JSC*, 1988(6):19–36, 1988.
10. J. W. Klop. Term rewriting systems. In S. Abramsky, D. Gabbay, and T. Maibaum, eds. , *Handbook of Logic in Computer Science*, vol. 2, ch. 1, pp. 2–117. Clarendon Press, Oxford, 1992.
11. T. Suzuki, A. Middeldorp, and T. Ida. Level-confluence of conditional rewrite systems with extra variables in right-hand sides. In J. Hsiang, ed., *Proc. 6th RTA*, **LNCS** 914, pp. 179–193, Kaiserslautern, Springer-Verlag, 1995.
12. C.-P. Wirth. Syntactic confluence criteria for constructor-based positive/negative-conditional term rewriting systems. SEKI-Report SR-95-09, Fachbereich Informatik, Universität Kaiserslautern, 1995.
13. C.-P. Wirth and B. Gramlich. A constructor-based approach for positive/negative conditional equational specifications. *JSC*, 17:51–90, 1994.

Applications of Rewrite Techniques in Monoids and Rings

Klaus Madlener
Universität Kaiserslautern
67663 Kaiserslautern
madlener@informatik.uni-kl.de

Abstract. The concept of algebraic simplification is of great importance for the field of symbolic computation in computer algebra. In this talk we review some applications of rewrite techniques in monoids and groups, in particular for solving the word and the subgroup problems by string rewriting- and prefix string rewriting systems. Restricted confluence is often sufficient for solving these and related problems.

We present a survey of results and applications of Noetherian systems that are confluent on one equivalence class. In particular decidability and specialized completion procedures as well as the computational and descriptive power of various classes of string rewriting systems will be discussed.

We review some fundamental concepts and properties of reduction rings in the spirit of Buchberger. The techniques for presenting monoids or groups by string rewriting systems are used to define several types of reduction in monoid and group rings. Gröbner bases in this setting arise naturally as generalizations of the corresponding known notions in the commutative and some non-commutative cases. Depending on the used reduction notion different types of Gröbner bases can be considered and hence different standard representations of the ideal elements in terms of the basis are obtained.

The connection of the word and subgroup problems and the corresponding congruence problem leads naturally to the concepts of saturation and completion in these rings for monoids having a finite convergent presentation by a semi-Thue system. For certain presentations, including free groups and context-free groups, the existence of finite Gröbner bases for finitely generated right ideals can be guaranteed and procedures to compute them following the standard Gröbner bases computation exist.

Compositional Term Rewriting: An Algebraic Proof of Toyama's Theorem

Christoph Lüth *

Universität Bremen — FB 3
Postfach 330440
28334 Bremen
Germany
cxl@informatik.uni-bremen.de
Phone: +49 (421) 218 7585, Fax: +49 (421) 218 3054

Abstract. This article proposes a compositional semantics for term rewriting systems, i.e. a semantics preserving structuring operations such as the disjoint union. The semantics is based on the categorical construct of a monad, adapting the treatment of universal algebra in category theory to term rewriting systems.
As an example, the preservation of confluence under the disjoint union of two term rewriting systems is shown, obtaining an algebraic proof of Toyama's theorem, generalised slightly to term rewriting systems introducing variables on the right-hand side of the rules.

1 Introduction

Term rewriting has long been recognised as an important tool for reasoning in algebraic (and other) specifications. Specifications occurring in practice tend to be very large, so structuring operations are used to construct large specifications from smaller ones ([ST88, EM85] etc.). Unfortunately the interaction of the structuring operations with term rewriting systems is not at all clear, since there has been no way to obtain the semantics of a term rewriting system for a structured specification by composing the semantics of the term rewriting systems for its component specifications.

Of particular interest is the question how properties like confluence, termination and completeness are preserved by these structuring operations.

In this article, following some preliminaries, we will show how to obtain a compositional semantics by generalising the categorical treatment of universal algebra, and argue why this semantics can be rightly called "compositional" (Section 2). We will then consider the disjoint union of two term rewriting systems (Section 3), corresponding to the coproduct of two monads, show how to construct this coproduct, and use this construction to show that the coproduct of two confluent monads is confluent.

* This research was supported by EPSRC grant GR/H73103 and the COMPASS basic research working group while the author was affiliated with Edinburgh University.

1.1 Preliminaries

We assume a working knowledge of term rewriting systems, and category theory as gained from the first five chapters of [Mac71] (the notation and terminology of which will be used here, and to which we will often refer). Although this work involves enriched categories, no knowledge of them is either assumed or even necessary for a basic understanding of what follows;[2] a gentler introduction into enriched category theory than the somewhat demanding standard text [Kel82] is [Bor94, Chapter 6].

This article is an extract of the author's forthcoming thesis [Lü96]. Without referring to it explicitly in the following, the thesis will present the material of the present article, some of which can only be adumbrated due to length limitations, in far more detail.

I would like to thank Don Sannella, Stefan Kahrs and Neil Ghani for many stimulating discussions during the preparation of this work, and Burkhardt Wolff and two of the anonymous referees for helpful comments on the presentation.

2 Using Monads to Model Term Rewriting

2.1 Why Monads?

Recall that a monad $\mathsf{T} = \langle T, \eta, \mu \rangle$ on a category $\mathcal{C}$ is given by an endofunctor $T : \mathcal{C} \to \mathcal{C}$, called the *action*, and two natural transformations, $\eta : 1_{\mathcal{C}} \Rightarrow T$, called the *unit*, and $\mu : TT \Rightarrow T$, called the *multiplication* of the monad, satisfying the *monad laws*: $\mu \cdot T\eta = 1_{\mathcal{C}} = \mu \cdot \eta_T$, and $\mu \cdot T\mu = \mu \cdot \mu_T$.

To motivate the use of monads to model term rewriting systems, consider how a monad $\mathsf{T} = \langle T, \eta, \mu \rangle$ on the category **Set** of all (small) sets and functions between them captures the way terms are built:

- for a set X, we can consider TX to be the term algebra (the set of terms built over the variables X);
- then the unit $\eta_X : X \to TX$ describes how to make elements of X into variables (i.e. terms);
- and the multiplication $\mu : TTX \to TX$ describes how to substitute terms for variables: given a set $Y = \{ y_1, \ldots, y_n \}$ of variables and $t_1, \ldots, t_n \in TX$ (n terms built over X), there is an obvious map $\sigma : Y \to TX$ with $\sigma(y_i) \stackrel{def}{=} t_i$; then for $s \in TY$ (a term built over Y), the substitution $s[t_i/y_i]$ of y_i with t_i, written $s[t_1, \ldots, t_n]$ in the following, is defined as $s[t_1, \ldots, t_n] \stackrel{def}{=} \mu_X(T\sigma(s))$.

The monad laws mean that this substitution is associative, and that substituting a term into a variable, and a variable for itself, yields the identity (in an informal notation, $x[t/x] = t$ and $t[x/x] = t$). It turns out this is all one needs for universal algebra (see [Man76]).

By adding a reduction structure, we will extend this to term rewriting systems, but let us first see how to treat signatures.

[2] At some points, footnotes will point out technical details and side issues which the casual reader can safely ignore.

2.2 Modelling Signatures

In the following, let Ω be a (single sorted) signature or operator domain, given by a set Ω_0 of operators equipped with a function $ar : \Omega_0 \to \mathbb{N}$ giving for each operator f its *arity*, $ar(f)$. If X is a set, the term algebra $T_\Omega(X)$ contains terms over X, formed either by taking a variable $x \in X$ to the term $'x \in T_\Omega(X)$[3], or by applying an operation $\omega \in \Omega$, then $\omega(t_1, \ldots, t_n) \in T_\Omega(X)$ if $t_1, \ldots, t_n \in T_\Omega(X)$ and $ar(\omega) = n$. (Here and in the following, we use $\omega \in \Omega$ as an abbreviation for $\omega \in \Omega_0$.) A signature Ω gives rise to a monad T_Ω on **Set**:

Definition 1. Given a signature Ω, the monad $\mathsf{T}_\Omega \stackrel{def}{=} \langle T_\Omega, \eta, \mu\rangle$ is defined as follows:

- the action maps a set X to the term algebra $T_\Omega(X)$, and a morphism $f : X \to Y$ to its *lifting* $f^* : T_\Omega(X) \to T_\Omega(Y)$ defined inductively on the terms as follows:

$$f^*('x) \stackrel{def}{=} {}'fx$$
$$f^*(e(t_1, \ldots, t_n)) \stackrel{def}{=} e(f^*(t_1), \ldots, f^*(t_n))$$

- the unit η_X maps $x \in X$ to $'x \in T_\Omega(X)$;
- the substitution $\mu_X : T_\Omega(T_\Omega(X)) \to T_\Omega(X)$ is defined as follows:

$$\mu_X(e(t_1, \ldots, t_n)) \stackrel{def}{=} e(\mu_X(t_1), \ldots, \mu_X(t_n))$$
$$\mu_X('x) \stackrel{def}{=} x$$

One routinely checks (using familiar structural induction on the terms) the functoriality of the action T_Ω, naturality of η and μ and that they satisfy the monad laws.

2.3 Modelling Term Rewriting Systems

The above extends to an equational presentation (Ω, E) (i.e. a signature Ω with equations E); then $T_{(\Omega,E)}$ maps X to the quotient term algebra (see [Man76] for the details). To model term rewriting systems, we need to extend the set TX with a reduction structure between the elements. To model many-step reductions, this structure needs to be transitive and reflexive. Hence, TX should be a category or preorder (a transitive and reflexive binary relation, or equivalently a category with at most one morphism between any two objects), the objects of which are the terms and the morphisms of which model the reduction; in the former case, we distinguish different reductions between the same terms ("named reductions").

Since the action T is an endofunctor, the variables X have to form a category or preorder as well. This corresponds to reductions between variables (called

[3] The reader may wonder about the reason for the notation for variables; later on we will consider terms built over terms, and we will have to distinguish between terms like $'x$ and $''x$, or even $'\mathtt{G}('x)$ and $\mathtt{G}(''x)$.

variable rewrites). In other words, we should be able to assume more about variables than merely their existence: for if a context like $X = \{x, y, z\}$ is just a way of modelling the assumption that there are three entities x, y and z to build terms with, then to model reductions there has to be a way of assuming that there are reductions between them.

This entails a more general form of rewrite rules, called *generalised rewrite rules*, in which one can impose conditions on the variables.

Definition 2. A *generalised rewrite rule* in a signature Ω is given by a triple (X, l, r), written as $(X \vdash l \to r)$, where $X = (X_0, \leq)$ is a finite preorder and $l, r \in T_\Omega(X_0)$ are terms.

For example, given the preorder $X \stackrel{def}{=} (\{x, y, z\}, \leq)$, ordered as $x \leq z, y \leq z$ and the signature $\Omega = \{\mathtt{F}, \mathtt{G}\}$ (with $\mathtt{F}$ binary and $\mathtt{G}$ unary), the rule $(X \vdash \mathtt{F}('x, 'y) \to \mathtt{G}('z))$ means that only if we can instantiate x and y with terms t_1 and t_2 which have a common reduct t_3 (which is the instantiation of z), is there a reduction from $\mathtt{F}(t_1, t_2)$ to $\mathtt{G}(t_3)$.

It should be emphasized that this is a conservative extension of the traditional definition of rewrite rules: they are just a special case of Def. 2 with the preorder being the identity relation. The greater generality of Def. 2 is not actually needed until one constructs a mapping from monads to term rewriting systems (see Sec. 2.4). Note also that we do not require the variables occurring in the right-hand side r to occur in the left-hand side l.

We are now going to show how to model the reduction order on the terms generated by a set of generalised rewrite rules by a preorder. The category **Pre** in which we will model term rewriting systems has as its objects preorders, and as morphisms $f : (X, \leq) \to (Y, \preccurlyeq)$ between two preorders maps $f : X \to Y$ respecting the preorder (i.e. $x \leq y \Rightarrow fx \preccurlyeq fy$). Preorder morphisms can be ordered pointwise: given $f, g : (X, \leq) \to (Y, \preccurlyeq)$ then $f \leq g$ iff $\forall x \in X. fx \preccurlyeq gx$. Hence the set of preorder morphisms between two preorders $(X, \leq)$ and $(Y, \preccurlyeq)$ forms in turn a preorder. One says that the category **Pre** is *closed*.[4]

The crucial categorical insight when extending Def. 1 is that it is not sufficient to merely define a monad on **Pre**, but that this monad has to respect the closed structure of **Pre** (i.e. the order on the morphisms); in other words, it has to be an *enriched* monad in the sense of [Kel82].

The analogue of the term algebra for a term rewriting system is the *term reduction algebra*. It is freely generated by three rules (in Table 1 below):

- every variable rewrite is a reduction in the term reduction algebra (rule [VAR]);
- the operations in Ω have to preserve the reduction (rule [PRE]; repeated application of this rule builds contexts);

[4] To be precise, *monoidal closed* [Kel82]. This is a particular instance of a general phenomenon: for example, the set of functors between two categories $\mathcal{X}$ and $\mathcal{Y}$ are the objects of a category the morphisms of which are the natural transformations between the functors: the functor category $[\mathcal{X}, \mathcal{Y}]$.

– and the variables in a rewrite rule can be instantiated with terms, provided they satisfy the variable rewrites (rule [INST]).

Definition 3. Given a term rewriting system $\Theta = (\Omega, R)$ and a preorder $X = (X_0, \leq)$, the *term reduction algebra* on X is the smallest preorder $(T_\Omega(X_0), \leq)$ on the terms over X_0 satisfying the implications in Table 1, where $t[t_1, \ldots, t_n]$ is the substitution of the n variables in $t \in T_\Omega(Y)$ with terms $t_1, \ldots, t_n$ defined above (in Sec. 2.1).

$$[\text{VAR}] \quad \frac{x \leq y}{{}'x \leq {}'y} \; x, y \in X_0$$

$$[\text{PRE}] \quad \frac{t_1 \leq s_1, \ldots, t_n \leq s_n}{\omega(t_1, \ldots, t_n) \leq \omega(s_1, \ldots, s_n)} \; \omega \in \Omega, ar(\omega) = n$$

$$[\text{INST}] \quad \frac{\begin{array}{c}(Y \vdash l \to r) \in R, Y = (\{y_1, \ldots, y_n\}, \preccurlyeq) \\ \forall i = 1, \ldots, n \, \forall j = 1, \ldots n. \; y_i \preccurlyeq y_j \Rightarrow t_i \leq t_j\end{array}}{l[t_1, \ldots, t_n] \leq r[t_1, \ldots, t_n]} \; t_1, \ldots, t_n \in T_\Omega(X)$$

Table 1. Definition of the Reduction Preorder.

Definition 4. Given a term rewriting system $\Theta = (\Omega, R)$, the monad $\mathsf{T}_\Theta = \langle T_\Theta, \eta, \mu \rangle$ is defined as follows:

- its action T_Θ maps a preorder $(X, \leq)$ to the term reduction algebra $(T_\Omega(X), \leq)$ from Def. 3, and a preorder morphism f to its lifting f^* from Def. 1;
- its unit η and multiplication μ are as in Def. 1.

It has to be shown (by structural induction) that T_Θ is a **Pre**-enriched functor by showing that f^* is a preorder morphism (i.e. $s \leq t \Rightarrow f^*(s) \leq f^*(t)$), and that the lifting respects the pointwise order on the morphisms (i.e. if $\forall x \in X \,.\, fx \leq gx$ then $\forall t \in T_\Omega(X) \,.\, f^*(t) \leq g^*(t)$); and further that η and μ as defined above are preorder morphisms (the former is trivial, the latter requires another easy induction). Then the monad laws follow from Def. 1, and T_Θ is a **Pre**-enriched monad.

2.4 Compositionality

As observed by Goguen and Burstall [GB92], most structuring operations for algebraic specifications are colimits, either in the category of syntactic presentations (here, term rewriting systems), or in the category of semantic representations (here, monads). "Compositionality of the semantics" means that the mapping from the syntax to the semantics should preserve these colimits; for this, it is sufficient that the mapping is (or extends to) a left adjoint functor, and use the general fact that left adjoints preserve colimits [Mac71, Section V.5]. We will omit the details of this construction here since they are not needed in the following.

2.5 Finiteness

A signature as defined above in which the arities of all the operations are finite is called *finitary*. A monad T_Ω arising from a finitary signature Ω preserves a special kind of colimit, called filtered or directed (see [Mac71, Section IX.1]). In fact, we have an even stronger result: the monad T_Θ is ***strongly finitary***, meaning it preserves ***weakly filtered diagrams***, where for any two objects X, Y there is an object Z and morphisms $f : X \to Z$ and $g : Y \to Z$.

3 Disjoint Union and the Preservation of Confluence

The disjoint union of two term rewriting systems is given by the coproduct in the category **TRS** (just as the disjoint union of two sets is given by the coproduct in **Set**); by the compositionality, the theory of the coproduct is the same as the coproduct of the theories, i.e. $\mathsf{T}_{\Theta_1+\Theta_2} \cong \mathsf{T}_{\Theta_1} + \mathsf{T}_{\Theta_2}$. In this section, we are going to construct the coproduct on the right side of this isomorphism — the coproduct of two monads — and will use this to give a categorical account of Toyama's theorem by showing that the coproduct of two confluent monads (monads arising from confluent term rewriting systems) is confluent as well.

We will also switch to the more general case of monads on the category **Cat** of all small categories, of which the case above (preorders) is a special case. Given $\mathsf{T}_1 = \langle T_1, \eta_1, \mu_1\rangle, \mathsf{T}_2 = \langle T_2, \eta_2, \mu_2\rangle$ on **Cat**, we define their coproduct by its universal property: a monad $\mathsf{T}_{1+2} = \langle T, \eta, \mu\rangle$ such that there are two monad morphisms $\iota_1 : \mathsf{T}_1 \to \mathsf{T}_{1+2}, \iota_2 : \mathsf{T}_2 \to \mathsf{T}_{1+2}$, and for any other monad $\mathsf{S} = \langle S, \eta_S, \mu_S\rangle$ with monad morphisms $\alpha : \mathsf{T}_1 \to \mathsf{S}$, $\beta : \mathsf{T}_2 \to \mathsf{S}$, there is a unique monad morphism $[\alpha, \beta] : \mathsf{T}_{1+2} \to \mathsf{S}$ such that $\alpha = [\alpha, \beta]\cdot\iota_1$ and $\beta = [\alpha, \beta]\cdot\iota_2$.[5]

This coproduct monad is defined pointwise. For every category $\mathcal{X}$, the action T will map $\mathcal{X}$ to the colimit of a diagram describing the combinations of T_1 and T_2.

To motivate the construction, consider two monads on the category **Set** given by signatures Ω_1, Ω_2. Then the coproduct of T_{Ω_1} and T_{Ω_2} should map a set X to the set of all terms built from operations of $\Omega_1 + \Omega_2$. Terms from $T_{\Omega_1+\Omega_2}(X)$

[5] We have omitted the definitions of the category **TRS** of term rewriting systems and *Mon*(**Cat**) of monads on **Cat** here. The morphisms of the latter are natural transformations respecting the unit and multiplication (*monad morphisms*, see [BW85, Section 3.6]). It is actually a **Cat**-enriched category (or 2-category [KS74]), so the colimit has to have an additional colimiting property on 2-cells: given two pairs of monad morphisms $\alpha, \alpha' : \mathsf{T}_1 \to \mathsf{S}$, $\beta, \beta' : \mathsf{T}_1 \to \mathsf{S}$ and two *modifications* (see [KS74]) $\gamma : \alpha \to \alpha', \delta : \beta \to \beta'$, there is a modification $[\gamma, \delta] : [\alpha, \beta] \to [\alpha', \beta']$.

can be decomposed into *layers* of terms from $T_{\Omega_1}(X)$ and $T_{\Omega_2}(X)$ (*aliens* or *principal subterms*) (see e.g. [KM+94] for the definition and the notation). We forego the introduction of holes and principal subterms, and take the notion of a layer as primitive in so far as every application of the functor T_1 or T_2 corresponds to one layer; i.e. it takes $t_1, \ldots, t_n$ to $C[\![t_1, \ldots, t_n]\!]$. This is because we can build term algebras on top of term algebras; for example, the elements of $T_{\Omega_1}(T_{\Omega_2}(X))$ correspond (roughly) to terms of rank two. However, in term algebras like $T_{\Omega_2}(T_{\Omega_1}(T_{\Omega_2}(X)))$ we will have terms from $T_{\Omega_2}(X)$ treated as variables in $T_{\Omega_1}(X)$ inserted into terms of $T_{\Omega_2}(X)$, which should be equivalent to a term from $T_{\Omega_2}(X)$; for example, if $F \in \Omega_2$, then the terms $F(\texttt{''}F(\texttt{'}x))$ and $F(F(\texttt{'}x))$ should be equivalent. This identification is called "collapsing layers".

Hence, the coproduct will be given by the disjoint union of all the term algebras

$$\begin{aligned} T_{\Omega_1+\Omega_2}(X) \stackrel{def}{=} X + T_{\Omega_1}(X) + T_{\Omega_2}(X) + T_{\Omega_1}(T_{\Omega_2}(X)) + T_{\Omega_2}(T_{\Omega_1}(X)) + \\ T_{\Omega_1}(T_{\Omega_2}(T_{\Omega_1}(X))) + T_{\Omega_2}(T_{\Omega_1}(T_{\Omega_2}(X))) + \ldots \end{aligned}$$

quotiented by a suitable equivalence relation, affected by the unit and the multiplication: the unit identifies all the variables from X in the different term algebras, and the multiplication collapses layers as described above. We arrive at the definition of the action T as the colimit of a diagram which has all the combinations of T_1 and T_2 as objects, and all morphisms which can be formed using the unit and multiplication of the two monads as morphisms. We are now going to define this diagram formally.

3.1 The Functor $D_{\mathcal{X}}$

In the following, the graph $\mathcal{G}$ will define the diagram giving all possible combinations of η and μ in a generic fashion (i.e. independent of $\mathcal{X}$). The functor $D_{\mathcal{X}}$ will map this scheme to a specific diagram over $\mathcal{X}$. We use the alphabet $\mathcal{L} \stackrel{def}{=} \{1, 2\}$, and the words $W \stackrel{def}{=} \mathcal{L}^*$ over that alphabet. The functor $D_{\mathcal{X}}$ will be a functor from the *free category* $\mathcal{F}(\mathcal{G})$ of the graph $\mathcal{G}$, which has vertices of $\mathcal{G}$ as objects and paths in $\mathcal{G}$ as morphisms (see [Mac71, pg.50]), into **Cat**. First, for all $w \in W$ the functor $T^w : \mathbf{Cat} \to \mathbf{Cat}$ is defined as follows:

$$\begin{aligned} T^{\varepsilon} &\stackrel{def}{=} 1_{\mathbf{Cat}} \\ T^{jv} &\stackrel{def}{=} T_j T^v \quad \text{where } j \in \mathcal{L}, v \in W \end{aligned}$$

The graph $\mathcal{G}$ has two different classes of vertices, $E_E(\mathcal{G})$ and $E_M(\mathcal{G})$ (corresponding to units and multiplication respectively), which are explicitly distinguished since we need to refer to them later on:

$$\begin{aligned} \text{Vertices:} \quad V(\mathcal{G}) &\stackrel{def}{=} W \\ \text{Edges:} \quad E_E(\mathcal{G}) &\stackrel{def}{=} \{\, \mathtt{e}^w_{j,v} : wv \to wjv \mid w, v \in W, j \in \mathcal{L} \,\} \\ E_M(\mathcal{G}) &\stackrel{def}{=} \{\, \mathtt{m}^w_{j,v} : wjjv \to wjv \mid w, v \in W, j \in \mathcal{L} \,\} \\ E(\mathcal{G}) &\stackrel{def}{=} E_E(\mathcal{G}) \cup E_M(\mathcal{G}) \end{aligned}$$

The graphs $\mathcal{G}_E$ and $\mathcal{G}_M$ are the subgraphs of $\mathcal{G}$ with the same edges, but only $E_E(\mathcal{G})$ and $E_M(\mathcal{G})$, respectively, as vertices.

For a category $\mathcal{X} \in \mathbf{Cat}$, we define the functor $D_\mathcal{X} : \mathcal{F}(\mathcal{G}) \to \mathbf{Cat}$ by mapping the vertices and edges of $\mathcal{G}$ to the underlying graph of $\mathbf{Cat}$ as follows:

$$\begin{array}{ll} \text{On the vertices:} & D_\mathcal{X}(w) \stackrel{def}{=} T^w(\mathcal{X}) \\ \text{On the edges:} & D_\mathcal{X}(\mathrm{e}^w_{j,v}) \stackrel{def}{=} T^w(\eta_{j,T^v(\mathcal{X})}) \\ & D_\mathcal{X}(\mathrm{m}^w_{j,v}) \stackrel{def}{=} T^w(\mu_{j,T^v(\mathcal{X})}) \end{array}$$

3.2 The Coproduct Monad

The coproduct monad $\mathsf{T}_{1+2} = \langle T, \eta, \mu \rangle$ is defined as follows:

- The action T maps a category $\mathcal{X}$ to the colimit $colim\, D_\mathcal{X}$ of the functor $D_\mathcal{X}$. Given a functor $F : \mathcal{X} \to \mathcal{Y}$, we can precompose the colimiting cone over $D_\mathcal{Y}$ with F, and since all components of $D_\mathcal{X}$ and $D_\mathcal{Y}$ are natural transformations, this yields a cone over $D_\mathcal{X}$, and hence by the colimiting property of $colim D_\mathcal{X}$, there is a functor $!_F : colim\, D_\mathcal{X} \to colim\, D_\mathcal{Y}$. The action maps F to this unique functor $!_F$. Similarly, a natural transformation $\alpha : F \Rightarrow G$ induces a natural transformation $!_\alpha :!_F \Rightarrow !_G$, which describes the action on natural transformations.[6]
- The unit η is given by the component of the colimiting cone over $D_\mathcal{X}$ at $\mathcal{X}$;
- The multiplication μ relies on the fact that T_1 and T_2 preserve weakly filtered colimits, and that $D_\mathcal{X}$ is weakly filtered. $TT\mathcal{X}$ is a colimit of a functor which maps $w \in W$ to $T^w T\mathcal{X}$, then $T^w T\mathcal{X} = T^w colim\, D_\mathcal{X} \cong colim\, T^w D_\mathcal{X}$; now $T^w D_\mathcal{X}$ is again a part of $D_\mathcal{X}$, and we can form a cone over that diagram by using the colimiting cone over $D_\mathcal{X}$, which induces a morphism $! : TT\mathcal{X} \to T\mathcal{X}$ (by the colimiting property of $TT\mathcal{X}$).

Verifying the monad laws and the universal property is a case of diagram chasing the details of which would take us well outside the scope of this paper.

Category theory also tells us how the colimit is computed using coproducts and coequalizers. Applying the dual of Theorem 2 in [Mac71, pg. 109], the colimit of $D_\mathcal{X}$ is given by the coequalizer of Diagram 1, where on the left side, we have

$$\coprod_{d:T^u\mathcal{X} \to T^v\mathcal{X} \in D_\mathcal{X}} T^u\mathcal{X} \underset{G}{\overset{F}{\rightrightarrows}} \coprod_{w \in W} T^w\mathcal{X} \tag{1}$$

for any morphism $d : T^u\mathcal{X} \to T^v\mathcal{X}$ in the image of $D_\mathcal{X}$ (with $u, v \in W$) the component $T^u\mathcal{X}$ of the coproduct, and the two functors F and G are defined as $F(T^u\mathcal{X}) \stackrel{def}{=} \iota_u(T^u\mathcal{X})$, $G(T^u\mathcal{X}) \stackrel{def}{=} \iota_v(d(T^u\mathcal{X}))$ where ι_u and ι_v are the injections into the coproduct on the right.

In general, given two categories $\mathcal{X}$ and $\mathcal{Y}$, and two functors $F, G : \mathcal{X} \to \mathcal{Y}$ between them, their coequalizer is a category $\mathcal{Z}$, and a functor $Q : \mathcal{Y} \to \mathcal{Z}$, where $\mathcal{Z}$ is defined as follows (see [Gra74, Chapter I.1]):

[6] This follows since all components of $\mathcal{G}$ are 2-natural transformations, and from the colimit property of $colim\, D_\mathcal{X}$ on 2-cells.

- The objects are the objects of $\mathcal{Y}$, quotiented by the equivalence closure $\equiv$ of the relation $\sim$ defined as $x \sim y \Leftrightarrow \exists z \in \mathcal{X} \,.\, Fz = x, Gz = y$.
- The morphisms are sequences $<f_1, \ldots, f_n>$ of morphisms f_i from $\mathcal{Y}$ such that $\delta_s(f_i) \equiv \delta_t(f_{i-1})$ (where for a morphism α, $\delta_s(\alpha)$ is its source, and $\delta_t(\alpha)$ its target), quotiented by the smallest equivalence relation $\equiv$ compatible with composition in $\mathcal{Y}$ such that $<f, g> \equiv <g \cdot f>$ if f, g are composable in $\mathcal{Y}$, and $<Fh> \equiv <Gh>$ for all morphisms h in $\mathcal{X}$.

3.3 Preservation of Confluence for Coequalizers of Functors

We are now going to find general conditions under which the coequalizing category $\mathcal{Z}$ above is confluent. We will obtain a general result which we can subsequently specialise to Diagram 1. First of all, we have to define confluence for categories and monads: the first is a straightforward generalization of the usual definition, the second has to take variable rewrites into account, spans of which have to be completed by variable rewrites.

Definition 5. A category $\mathcal{C}$ is *confluent* if for any two morphisms $\alpha : x \to x_1, \beta : x \to x_2$ there are morphisms $\gamma : x_1 \to z, \delta : x_2 \to z$ such that $\gamma \cdot \alpha = \delta \cdot \beta$.

A monad $\mathsf{T} = \langle T, \eta, \mu \rangle$ on **Cat** is *confluent* if $T\mathcal{X}$ is confluent whenever $\mathcal{X}$ is.

By an easy induction, one shows that this coincides with the usual definition of confluence (i.e. if a category $\mathcal{X}$ is confluent and the term rewriting system Θ is confluent, then $T_\Theta(\mathcal{X})$ is confluent).

Let us try to characterize sufficient conditions for the confluence of the coequalising category $\mathcal{Z}$. Since the morphisms in $\mathcal{Z}$ are equivalence classes of sequences of morphisms in $\mathcal{Y}$, we can complete any span of these sequences if for any two morphisms in $\mathcal{Y}$ the source of which is equal under the coequalising functor Q we can find another two morphisms in $\mathcal{Y}$ such that their composition is equal under Q — a one-step completion of $\mathcal{Y}$ with respect to the functor Q:

Definition 6. Given a functor $Q : \mathcal{Y} \to \mathcal{Z}$, the category $\mathcal{Y}$ has the *one-step completion property with respect to* Q, written $\mathcal{Y} \models_Q \diamond$, if for all morphisms $\alpha : x \to x'$, $\beta : y \to y'$ in $\mathcal{Y}$ such that $Qx = Qy$ there are morphisms $\gamma : v \to v', \delta : w \to w'$ in $\mathcal{Y}$ such that $Q\gamma \cdot Q\alpha = Q\delta \cdot Q\beta$.

Lemma 7. *Let $Q : \mathcal{Y} \to \mathcal{Z}$ be the coequalizer of two functors $F, G : \mathcal{X} \to \mathcal{Y}$ in* **Cat**. *If $\mathcal{Y}$ is confluent and $\mathcal{Y} \models_Q \diamond$, then $\mathcal{Z}$ is confluent.*

Proof. Given two morphisms $\alpha = [<\alpha_1, \ldots, \alpha_n>]$ and $\beta = [<\beta_1, \ldots, \beta_m>]$ in $\mathcal{Z}$ with the same source (i.e. $Q(\delta_s(\beta_1)) = Q(\delta_s(\alpha_1)))$. Then (since $\mathcal{Y} \models_Q \diamond$) there are β'_1, α'_1 such that $Q(\beta'_1) \cdot Q(\alpha_1) = Q(\alpha'_1) \cdot Q(\beta_1)$. By induction on the length n and m of α and β, respectively, we obtain completions $\alpha' \stackrel{def}{=} [<\alpha_1^{(m)}, \ldots, \alpha_n^{(m)}>]$, $\beta' \stackrel{def}{=} [<\beta_1^{(n)}, \ldots, \beta_m^{(n)}>]$ such that $\beta' \cdot \alpha = \alpha' \cdot \beta$. □

To show $\mathcal{Y} \models_Q \diamond$ and hence confluence of $\mathcal{Z}$, we introduce the notion of a *witness*. The idea is that for two morphisms the sources of which are equal under Q, we find two equivalent morphisms which form a span in $\mathcal{Y}$ which by confluence of $\mathcal{Y}$ can be completed. Given a functor $Q : \mathcal{Y} \to \mathcal{Z}$, we say an object $x \in \mathcal{Y}$ is a *witness* of an object $y \in \mathcal{Y}$ with respect to Q, written $x \operatorname{wit}_Q y$, if $Qx = Qy$ and for all morphisms $\beta : y \to y'$ in $\mathcal{Y}$, there is a morphism $\alpha : x \to x'$ such that $Q\alpha = Q\beta$; in other words, for all morphisms the source of which is y there is an equivalent one the source of which is x. If now any two equivalent objects have a common witness, then $\mathcal{Z}$ will be confluent, thus to prove of confluence it is sufficient to prove the existence of a common witness:

Lemma 8. *Given the coequalizer $Q : \mathcal{Y} \to \mathcal{Z}$ of two functors $F, G : \mathcal{X} \to \mathcal{Y}$. If $\mathcal{Y}$ is confluent and for all $x, y \in \mathcal{Y}$ s.t. $Qx = Qy$ there is a common witness $z \in \mathcal{Y}$ such that $z \operatorname{wit}_Q x$ and $z \operatorname{wit}_Q y$ then $\mathcal{Z}$ is confluent.*

Proof. We show that $\mathcal{Y} \models_Q \diamond$ and use Lemma 7: given any two morphisms $\alpha : x \to x'$, $\beta : y \to y'$ such that $Qx = Qy$, there is a common witness $z \in \mathcal{Y}$, hence there are $\alpha' : z \to z'$, $\beta' : z \to z''$ such that $Q\alpha' = Q\alpha, Q\beta' = Q\beta$, which by confluence of $\mathcal{Y}$ have a completion $\gamma : z' \to u, \delta : z'' \to u$ such that $\gamma \cdot \alpha' = \delta \cdot \beta'$, hence (since Q preserves composition) $Q\gamma \cdot Q\alpha' = Q\delta \cdot Q\beta'$, and $Q\gamma \cdot Q\alpha = Q\delta \cdot Q\beta$. □

The existence of a common witness is shown by constructing a binary relation $\preccurlyeq$ on the objects of $\mathcal{Y}$, compatible with the equivalence relation, such that $x \preccurlyeq y$ implies that x is a witness of y. Such a relation is called a *witness relation*:

Definition 9. Given the coequalizer $Q : \mathcal{Y} \to \mathcal{Z}$ of two functors $F, G : \mathcal{X} \to \mathcal{Y}$, a binary relation $\preccurlyeq$ on the objects of $\mathcal{Y}$ is a *witness relation* if it satisfies the following four properties:

(i) $x \preccurlyeq y \Rightarrow x \operatorname{wit}_Q y$;
(ii) For all $x \in \mathcal{X}$ there is $y \in \mathcal{Y}$ such that $y \preccurlyeq Fx$ and $y \preccurlyeq Gx$;
(iii) $\preccurlyeq$ is transitive;
(iv) $\preccurlyeq$ has *filtered lower bounds*: if $x \preccurlyeq z$ and $y \preccurlyeq z$, then there is $w \in \mathcal{Y}$ such that $w \preccurlyeq x$ and $w \preccurlyeq y$.

Lemma 10. *Given the coequalizer $Q : \mathcal{Y} \to \mathcal{Z}$ of two functors $F, G : \mathcal{X} \to \mathcal{Y}$, if there is a witness relation $\preccurlyeq$ on the objects of $\mathcal{Y}$, and $\mathcal{Y}$ is confluent, then $\mathcal{Z}$ is confluent.*

Proof. Given $x \equiv y$, we show there is a z such that $z \preccurlyeq x$ and $z \preccurlyeq y$, then by the first property $z \operatorname{wit}_Q x$ and $z \operatorname{wit}_Q y$, and by Lemma 8 $\mathcal{Z}$ is confluent. If $x \equiv y$, then

- either there is a $u \in \mathcal{X}$ such that $Fu = x, Gu = y$, then by the second property, there is $z \in \mathcal{Y}$ such that $z \preccurlyeq x$ and $z \preccurlyeq y$;

- or they are made equivalent by the equivalence closure, of which the symmetric and reflexive closure are trivial, so only the transitive closure remains: there is $z \in \mathcal{Y}$ s.t. $x \equiv z, z \equiv y$, and we can assume that there is $u \in \mathcal{Y}$ s.t. $u \preccurlyeq x, u \preccurlyeq z$ and $v \in \mathcal{Y}$ s.t. $v \preccurlyeq z, v \preccurlyeq y$. Since $\preccurlyeq$ has filtered lower bounds, there is a $w \in \mathcal{Y}$ such that $w \preccurlyeq u$ and $w \preccurlyeq v$, and by transitivity $w \preccurlyeq x$ and $w \preccurlyeq y$, hence $u \preccurlyeq x$ and $u \preccurlyeq y$.

□

3.4 Confluence of the Coproduct Monad

To show that T_{1+2} is confluent, it now suffices to construct a witness relation for $\coprod_{w \in W} T^w \mathcal{X}$ with respect to the coequalizer Q of F and G in Diagram 1; by an easy induction on w, all $T^w \mathcal{X}$ are confluent and thus the coproduct is confluent as well, and we can apply Lemma 10. We will need to make the following two assumptions about the two monads T_1 and T_2: that they are non-expanding, and that their units are monomorphisms (in **Cat**); in particular, that their object function is injective. The first corresponds to the restriction to term rewriting systems in which the left-hand side of the rules is not a variable; and the second is more technical and means that two terms $'x$ and $'y$ are equal only if x and y are equal.

We first define non-expanding monads:

Definition 11. A functor $F : \mathcal{X} \to \mathcal{Y}$ is *non-expanding*, if for all objects $x \in \mathcal{X}$ and all morphisms $\alpha : Fx \to y'$ in $\mathcal{Y}$ there is a morphism $\beta : x \to x'$ in $\mathcal{X}$ such that $F\beta = \alpha$.

A monad $\mathsf{T} = \langle T, \eta, \mu \rangle$ on **Cat** is non-expanding if all components $\eta_{\mathcal{X}} : \mathcal{X} \to T\mathcal{X}$ of the unit are non-expanding, and the action preserves this: for any non-expanding functor $F : \mathcal{X} \to \mathcal{Y}$, $TF : T\mathcal{X} \to T\mathcal{Y}$ is non-expanding as well.

That a term rewriting system Θ which does not contain expanding rules (a rule $(X \vdash l \to r)$ in which $l = {'x}$) gives rise to a monad T_Θ which is non-expanding in the sense above is shown by easy induction on the rules in Def. 3. Further, the unit is a monomorphism, since by definition (i.e. the freeness of the term algebra) $'x = {'y}$ implies $x = y$.

For convenience, we introduce the notational shortcuts $\eta^w_{j,v} \stackrel{def}{=} T^w(\eta_{j,T^v})$ and $\mu^w_{j,v} \stackrel{def}{=} T^w(\mu_{j,T^v})$, for $w, v \in W$ and $j \in \mathcal{L}$. We are now going to construct the witness relation:

Definition 12. The relation $\prec$ on the objects of $\coprod_{w \in W} T^w \mathcal{X}$ is defined to be the smallest relation such that for all $w \in W$ and $x \in T^w \mathcal{X}$,

$$\forall u, v \in W, j \in \mathcal{L} \,.\, w = uv \Rightarrow x \prec \eta^u_{j,v}(x)$$
$$\forall u, v \in W, j \in \mathcal{L} \,.\, w = ujjv \Rightarrow \mu^u_{j,v}(x) \prec x$$

The relation $\preceq$ is defined to be the reflexive-transitive closure of $\prec$.

To show that $\preceq$ is a witness relation, we go through the four properties of Def. 9 in turn.

(i) We show that $x \prec y \Rightarrow x \operatorname{wit}_Q y$, from which $x \preceq y \Rightarrow x \operatorname{wit}_Q y$ follows by a simple induction. (Note that every object trivially witnesses itself, taking care of the reflexive closure.) If $x \prec y$, there are two cases:
- if $y = \eta^w_{j,v}(x)$, then since $\eta^w_{j,v}$ is non-expanding, there is an $\alpha : x \to x'$ for all $\beta : \eta^w_{j,v}x \to y'$ with $Q\alpha = Q\beta$;
- if $x = \mu^r_{i,s}(y)$, then there is $\mu^r_{i,s}(\beta)$ for all $\beta : y \to y'$.

Hence x is a witness of y with respect to Q.

(ii) We have show that for all $d : T^u\mathcal{X} \to T^v\mathcal{X}$ in the image of $D_\mathcal{X}$ and all $x \in T^u\mathcal{X}$, there is a $w \in W$, $y \in T^w\mathcal{X}$ such that $y \operatorname{wit}_Q F(x)$ and $y \operatorname{wit}_Q G(x)$, with $F(x) = \iota_u(x) = x$; and $G(x) = \iota_v(d(x)) = d(x)$.
By Lemma 14 below, for all morphisms $d : T^u\mathcal{X} \to T^v\mathcal{X}$ in the image of $D_\mathcal{X}$ there are morphisms e in $\mathcal{F}(\mathcal{G}_E)$ and m in $\mathcal{F}(\mathcal{G}_M)$ such that $d = D_\mathcal{X}(e) \cdot D_\mathcal{X}(m)$. Let $d_\eta \stackrel{def}{=} D_\mathcal{X}(e)$, $d_\mu \stackrel{def}{=} D_\mathcal{X}(m)$, then $y \stackrel{def}{=} d_\mu(x)$, and by a simple induction, $y \preceq d_\eta(y)$ and $d_\mu(x) \preceq x$, hence $y \preceq d_\eta d_\mu(x) = d(x) = G(x)$ and $y = d_\mu(x) \preceq x = F(x)$.

(iii) Transitivity is trivial.

(iv) To show the existence of filtered lower bounds for $\preceq$, we show that $\prec$ has filtered lower bounds. From this, we obtain the existence of filtered lower bounds for $\preceq$ by another simple induction (a "tiling" process like the proof of Lemma 7).
Given x, y, z such that $x \prec z$ and $y \prec z$, we have to show there is u s.t. $u \prec x$ and $u \prec y$. By the definition of $\prec$, there are four cases to consider, two of which are symmetric; in particular, these are (for some $w, v, r, s \in W$, $i, j \in \mathcal{L}$):
1. $z = \eta^w_{j,v}(x)$ and $z = \eta^r_{i,s}(y)$;
2. $z = \eta^w_{j,v}(x)$ and $\mu^r_{i,s}(z) = y$ and its symmetric case;
3. $x = \mu^w_{j,v}(z)$ and $y = \mu^r_{i,s}(z)$.

The existence of u follows from the three properties of the morphisms in the image of $D_\mathcal{X}$ given by Lemma 13 below. For example, in the second case, $y = \mu^r_{i,s}(\eta^w_{j,v}(x))$; then either $\mu^r_{i,s} \cdot \eta^w_{j,v} = 1_{T^{wv}\mathcal{X}}$ and $x = y$, hence $u \stackrel{def}{=} x = y$, or there are $w', v', r', s' \in W$ such that $\mu^r_{i,s} \cdot \eta^w_{j,v} = \eta^{w'}_{j,v'} \cdot \mu^{r'}_{i,s'}$, then $u \stackrel{def}{=} \mu^{r'}_{i,s'}(x)$ with $u \preceq \eta^{w'}_{j,v'} \mu^{r'}_{i,s'}(x) = \mu^r_{i,s} \eta^w_{j,v}(x) = y$ and $u = \mu^{r'}{}_{i,s'}(x) \preceq x$.

It remains to show the two lemmas needed above:

Lemma 13. *In the following, let $w, v, r, s \in W$ and $i, j \in \mathcal{L}$:*

(i) *Given $\mu^w_{i,v}, \mu^r_{j,s}$ such that $wiiv = rjjs$, then either $w = r$, $i = j$, $v = s$, or there are $w', v', r', s' \in W$ such that $\mu^{w'}_{j,v'} \cdot \mu^w_{i,v} = \mu^{r'}_{i,s'} \cdot \mu^r_{j,s}$.*

(ii) *Given $\eta^w_{j,v}, \eta^r_{i,s}$ such that $wjv = ris$, and given $y \in T^{wv}\mathcal{X}, z \in T^{rs}\mathcal{X}$ such that $\eta^w_{j,v}(y) = \eta^r_{i,s}(z)$, there is $u \in W, x \in T^u\mathcal{X}$, and w', v', r', s' such that $\eta^{w'}_{i,v'}(x) = y$, $\eta^{w'}_{i,v'}(x) = z$.*

(iii) *Given $\eta^w_{j,v}, \mu^s_{i,t}$ such that $wjv = siit$, then there are either $r', s', w', v' \in W$ s.t. $\mu^s_{i,t} \cdot \eta^w_{j,v} = \eta^{w'}_{j,v'} \cdot \mu^{s'}_{i,t'}$, or $\mu^s_{i,t} \cdot \eta^w_{j,v} = 1_{wv}$.*

Proof. The idea of the proof is that either the two morphisms commute over each other by the naturality of μ and η, or we can use the monad laws (associativity in the first case, the unit laws in the third case).

The proofs rely on the algebra of words over the language W, and a careful case distinction. Briefly, given a word $u \in W$ such that $u = wxv$ and $u = rys$ (with $r, s, w, v, x, y \in W$) we call the occurrence of x and y *independent* if we can find a word $z \in W$ such that $w = ryz$ and $s = zxv$ (there is of course a symmetric case). Above, x and y correspond to ii and jj in the first case; j and i in the second, and j and ii in the third.

If x and y are independent we can construct a naturality square such that the two morphisms commute over each other. For example, in the first case, assume that there is a $z \in W$ s.t. $w = rjjz$ and $s = ziiv$. Then let $w' \stackrel{def}{=} r$, $v' \stackrel{def}{=} ziv$, $r' \stackrel{def}{=} rjz$ and $s' = v$, and by applying T^r to the naturality square of μ_j (Diagram 2), we obtain $\mu^r_{j,ziv} \cdot \mu^{rjjz}_{i,v} = \mu^{rjz}_{i,v} \cdot \mu^r_{j,ziiv}$, hence (by definition of w',v',r',and s') $\mu^{w'}_{j,v'} \cdot \mu^{w}_{i,v} = \mu^{r'}_{i,s'} \cdot \mu^{r}_{j,s}$.

$$\begin{array}{ccc} T^{jjziiv}\mathcal{X} & \xrightarrow{\mu_{j,ziiv}} & T^{jziiv}\mathcal{X} \\ \mu^{jjz}_{i,v}\big\downarrow & & \big\downarrow\mu^{jz}_{i,v} \\ T^{jjziv}\mathcal{X} & \xrightarrow[\mu_{j,ziv}]{} & T^{jziv}\mathcal{X} \end{array} \qquad (2)$$

In the second case, this square is completed starting from the target (that would be T^{jzv} for the square in Diagram 2), hence the requirement that the units are monomorphisms (to be more specific, have left inverses).

If on the other hand x and y are not independent, then in the first case we use the associativity of the multiplication; in the second case, they are equal; and in the third case, multplication and unit cancel each other out by the unit law. □

Lemma 14. *For all morphisms d in the image of $D_{\mathcal{X}}$, there are morphisms e in $\mathcal{F}(\mathcal{G}_E)$, m in $\mathcal{F}(\mathcal{G}_M)$ such that $d = D_{\mathcal{X}}(e) \cdot D_{\mathcal{X}}(m)$.*

Proof. For d as above there is a path p in $\mathcal{G}$ such that $D_{\mathcal{X}}(p) = d$. The lemma is shown by induction on the length of p, using the third case of Lemma 13, which here means that if in a path p there is an edge from $E_E(\mathcal{G})$ followed by one from $E_M(\mathcal{G})$, we can always find another path p' s.t. $D_{\mathcal{X}}(p) = D_{\mathcal{X}}(p')$ in which either none of these edges occur (they cancel each other out), or an edge from $E_M(\mathcal{G})$ is followed by an edge from $E_E(\mathcal{G})$. Hence, for all paths p we can find a path q s.t. $D_{\mathcal{X}}(p) = D_{\mathcal{X}}(q)$ and q consists of edges from $E_M(\mathcal{G})$ (the path m above) followed by edges from $E_E(\mathcal{G})$ (the path e). □

We conclude that $\preceq$ is indeed a witness relation for $\coprod_{w \in W} T^w \mathcal{X}$ with respect to the coequalizer Q in Diagram 1, hence $T\mathcal{X}$ is confluent if $\mathcal{X}$ is, and hence T is confluent, under the assumption that T_1 and T_2 are confluent, non-expanding and their units are monomorphisms. Call such monads *regular*, then we have the main theorem:

Theorem 15. *The coproduct of two confluent regular monads is confluent.*

The original theorem by Toyama [Toy87] of course does not consider categories (corresponding to named reductions); it corresponds to Theorem 15 for two confluent, regular monads on **Pre**. It is obtained as a corollary from that theorem by observing that the category **Pre** of preorders is a reflexive subcategory of **Cat**. Then given two monads on **Pre**, we can (under the inclusion) consider them to be monads on **Cat**, apply the construction and proof, and obtain a monad which in turn is a monad on **Pre** for which Theorem 15 holds.

Theorem 15 is more general than Toyama's theorem. Since neither the construction of the monad nor the proof rely on the fact that all variables on the right side of a rewriting rule occur on the left (one readily checks that the monad given by such a term rewriting system is regular, in particular non-expanding, in the sense defined above), the proposition above extends Toyama's theorem to these term rewriting systems. Furthermore, it is valid for generalized rewrite rules (Def. 2), which can be considered a very limited form of conditional rewriting.

The original proof (and its simplified version [KM+94]) proceeds by induction on the rank of terms (hence it would not work for rewriting rules with extra variables on the right where the rank can increase arbitrarily). The proof presented here uses the algebraic properties of the combination of the term rewriting systems (as given by Def. 12 and Lemmas 13 and 14). Hence, although the proof is based on the same ideas as [Toy87] and [KM+94], the actual technique employed is different.

The condition that the term rewriting systems are non-expanding is essential, since Theorem 15 does not hold for expanding term rewriting systems. Consider two systems with rules $'x \to \mathtt{A}('x)$ and $\mathtt{B}(\mathtt{C}('y)) \to \mathtt{C}(\mathtt{B}('y))$ (where all operations are unary), then in their combination there is the incompletable span

$$\mathtt{B}(\mathtt{A}(\mathtt{C}('z))) \leftarrow \mathtt{B}(\mathtt{C}('z)) \to \mathtt{C}(\mathtt{B}('z)) \ .$$

The condition can be replaced by requiring that all expanding rewrites are contractible again.

4 Conclusions and Further Work

We have introduced a semantics for term rewriting systems based on the categorical treatment of universal algebra which is compositional in the sense that it is a free construction. We have shown how to use this semantics to give a categorical account of Toyama's theorem, which slightly generalises the original.

The semantics gives a clean distinction between the structure modelling the process of closing the reduction structure under context and substitution (given by the monad) and the choice of the mathematical structure used to model the reduction (preorders or categories; other possibilities include Sesqui-categories [Ste94], or graphs or binary relations to model the one-step reduction). It can handle some forms of non-standard rewriting as well. For example, combining the treatment of equational presentations and term rewriting systems, we obtain a model for rewriting modulo an arbitrary set of equations by a monad on **Pre**. However, this monad will not preserve all weakly filtered diagrams, and so the coproduct will have to be constructed differently.

Further work to appear in the author's thesis includes consideration of other structuring operations. Shared operations are modelled by the coequalizer of two monads. Restricting ourselves to systems sharing only constructors (this corresponds to coequalizers in which the two functors F, G are non-expanding) we should be able to recover results along the lines of [Ohl94].

References

[Bor94] Francis Borceux. *Handbook of Categorical Algebra 2: Categories and Structures.* Number 51 in Encyclopedia of Mathematics and its Applications. Cambridge University Press, 1994.

[BW85] M. Barr and C. Wells. *Toposes, Triples and Theories.* Number 278 in Grundlehren der mathematischen Wissenschaften. Springer Verlag, 1985.

[EM85] H. Ehrig and B. Mahr. *Fundamentals of Algebraic Specification 1: Equations and Initial Semantics*, volume 6 of *EATCS Monographs on Theoretical Computer Science.* Springer Verlag, 1985.

[GB92] J. A. Goguen and R. Burstall. Institutions: Abstract model theory for specification and programming. *Journal of the ACM*, 39:95– 146, 1992.

[Gra74] John W. Gray. *Formal Category Theory: Adjointness for 2-Categories.* Number 391 in Lecture Notes in Mathematics. Springer Verlag, 1974.

[Kel82] G. M. Kelly. *Basic Concepts of Enriched Category Theory*, volume 64 of *LMS Lecture Note Series.* Cambridge University Press, 1982.

[KM+94] J. W. Klop, A. Middeldorp, Y. Toyama, and R. de Vrijer. A simplified proof of Toyama's theorem. *Information Processing Letters*, 49:101–109, 1994.

[KS74] G. M. Kelly and Ross Street. Review of the elements of 2-categories. In *Category Seminar Sydney 1972/73*, number 420 in Lecture Notes in Mathematics, pages 75–103. Springer Verlag, 1974.

[Lü96] Christoph Lüth. *Compositional Categorical Term Rewriting in Structured Algebraic Specifications.* PhD thesis, University of Edinburgh, 1996. Forthcoming.

[Mac71] S. Mac Lane. *Categories for the Working Mathematician*, volume 5 of *Graduate Texts in Mathematics.* Springer Verlag, 1971.

[Man76] Ernest G. Manes. *Algebraic Theories*, volume 26 of *Graduate Texts in Mathematics.* Springer Verlag, 1976.

[Ohl94] Enno Ohlenbusch. On the modularity of confluence of constructor-sharing term rewriting systems. In Sophie Tison, editor, *Trees in Algebra and Programming — CAAP 94*, LNCS 787. Springer Verlag, April 1994.

[ST88] D. Sannella and A. Tarlecki. Specifications in an arbitrary institution. *Information and Computation*, 76(2/3):165–210, Feb/Mar 1988.

[Ste94] John G. Stell. Modelling term rewriting systems by Sesqui-categories. Technical Report TR94-02, Keele Unversity, January 1994.

[Toy87] Y. Toyama. On the Church-Rosser property for the direct sum of term rewriting systems. *Journal of the ACM*, 34(1):128–143, 1987.

The First-Order Theory of One-Step Rewriting is Undecidable

Ralf Treinen*

Laboratoire de Recherche en Informatique (LRI), Bât. 490
Université de Paris-Sud, F-91405 Orsay cedex, France
email: treinen@lri.fr, web: http://www.lri.fr/~treinen

Abstract. The theory of one-step rewriting for a given rewrite system R and signature Σ is the first-order theory of the following structure: Its universe consists of all Σ-ground terms, and its only predicate is the relation "x rewrites to y in one step by R". The structure contains no function symbols and no equality. We show that there is no algorithm deciding the $\exists^*\forall^*$-fragment of this theory for an arbitrary rewrite system. The proof uses both non-linear and non-shallow rewrite rules.
As a refinement of the proof, we show that the $\exists^*\forall^*$-fragment of the first-order theory of encompassment (reducibility by rewrite rules) together with one-step rewriting by the rule $f(x) \to g(x)$ is undecidable.

1 Introduction

The problem of decidability of the first-order theory of one-step rewriting was posed in [CCD93]. It has been mentioned in the list of open problems in rewriting in 1993 [DJK93] and in 1995 [DJK95].

The hope that this theory might be decidable was based on the observation that important properties which are decidable for arbitrary rewrite systems can be expressed in this logic, while undecidable properties of rewrite systems seemed not to be expressible in it. Let us first consider two decidable properties which can be expressed in the theory of one-step rewriting: strong confluence and ground reducibility.

A rewrite system R is *strongly confluent* ([DJ90], this definition differs from the one given in [Hue80]) if

$$\forall x, y_1, y_2\, (x \to y_1 \wedge x \to y_2 \Rightarrow \exists z\, (y_1 \overset{=}{\to} z \wedge y_2 \overset{=}{\to} z))$$

where $x \to y$ means that x rewrites to y in exactly one step of R, and $y \overset{=}{\to} z$ means $y = z \vee y \to z$. The system R is *strongly ground confluent* if the above property holds when x is restricted to range over all *ground* terms. It is easy to see that R is strongly confluent iff it is strongly ground confluent in a signature

* Supported by the *Human Capital and Mobility Programme* of the European Union, under the contracts *SOL* (CHRX-CT92-0053) and *CONSOLE* (CHRX-CT94-0495).

extended by new constants. This property can be expressed in the logic of one-step rewriting, since R is strongly ground confluent if

$$\forall x, y_1, y_2\, (x \to y_1 \wedge x \to y_2 \Rightarrow \exists z\, (y_1 \to z \wedge y_2 \to z))$$

holds in the structure of ground terms where $\to$ is the one-step rewriting by the system $R \cup \{x \to x\}$. Note that, as an easy consequence of the Critical Pair Lemma [KB70], strong confluence (and hence strong ground confluence) is decidable.

A term t is *ground-reducible* by a rewrite system R if each of its ground instances is reducible by R. This can be expressed in a slight extension of our logic, where we have different relations $\to_R$ for different rewrite systems R. Using the additional rewrite system $S = \{t \to t\}$, we can express ground reducibility of t by

$$\forall x\, (x \to_S x \Rightarrow \exists z\, (x \to_R z))$$

Decidability of ground reducibility has been shown in [Pla85].

It was observed by [Jac95] that in the special case of a signature containing constants and unary function symbols only (so-called *string rewriting systems* or *semi-Thue systems*), the theory of one-step rewriting by any rewriting system can be translated to $WS1S$, the weak monadic second order logic of one successor function, and is hence decidable (see [Tho90] for a survey of the results on $WS1S$). One can use this translation to show that the predicate "$x \xrightarrow{*} y$", that is "x rewrites to y in some finite number of steps", can not be expressed in the theory of one-step rewriting (this idea is due to [Jac95]). This is a consequence of the fact that ground confluence of a string rewriting system can be expressed in the logic with the predicate "$x \xrightarrow{*} y$" and hence should be decidable if "$x \xrightarrow{*} y$" can be expressed in the theory of one-step rewriting. Ground confluence of string rewriting systems is however undecidable [BO93][2]. Hence it seems that undecidable properties like confluence or weak termination can not be expressed in the logic of one-step rewriting since they require the "$x \xrightarrow{*} y$" predicate.

Using tree automata techniques, several results have been obtained which have been considered steps towards the decidability of one-step rewriting. The first-order theory of rewriting by a *ground* term rewriting system has been shown decidable in [DT90]. To be precise, for a given ground term rewriting system R (that is all left and right hand sides of the rules are ground) the structure of all ground terms, where all terms are available as constants, with the predicates "$x \to y$", $x \xrightarrow{*} y$" and "$x \xrightarrow{\parallel} y$" (parallel one-step rewriting) is decidable.

For an arbitrary rewrite systems, the decidability of the theory of encompassment was shown in [CCD93]. This means that for given rewrite systems $R_1, \ldots, R_n$ and regular tree languages $L_1, \ldots, L_n$ the structure of ground terms, where all terms are available as constants, with the unary predicates "x is reducible by the rewrite system R_i" and "x is in L_i", is decidable.

Note that the theory of the structure consisting of the universe of ground terms together with the predicate "$x \xrightarrow{*} y$" is undecidable in general (even in

[2] In [BO93], the term "confluence" has been used for what we call "ground confluence".

the restricted case of unary function symbols) by the undecidability of the ground confluence of string rewriting systems [BO93].

The first result of this paper is that there is no algorithm which decides for any rewrite system R the $\exists^*\forall^*$-fragment of the theory of one-step rewriting by R. We construct, for a given instance P of the Post Correspondence Problem, a rewrite system R_P such that solvability of P is equivalent to the validity of a special sentence in the structure of one-step rewriting by R. The system R_P uses non-shallow and non-linear rules, but every rule of R_P is shallow *or* linear. The formula corresponding to the solvability of P uses both positive and negative literals. This encoding of the Post Correspondence Problem is based on ideas similar to those used in [Tre92].

Our second result concerns the question of decidability of the theory of encompassment plus "simple" classes of rewriting systems. We show that there is no algorithm which decides for any finite set M of terms the $\exists^*\forall^*$-fragment of the theory of the structure of ground-terms, equipped with the predicates "x encompasses t", for any $t \in M$, and the predicate "x rewrites in one step to y by the rule $f(x) \to g(x)$". This rule is syntactically simple: it is linear (there are no multiple variable occurrence on either side), it is non-overlapping (there are non-trivial critical pairs) and it is shallow (all variables occur at most at depth 1). Furthermore, this rule has nice semantic properties: it is uniformly confluent (confluent and all derivations with the same source and target have the same length) and it is terminating.

An alternative proof of the undecidability of one-step rewriting has been given by Sergei Vorobyov [Vor95]. He defines *one particular* rewrite system R and shows the undecidability of the full first-order theory of one-step rewriting by R. He considers, however, the structure where all the function symbols of the signature are available in the language (this is not the case with our result), and he does not attempt to characterize a "simple" undecidable fragment of the theory.

2 Preliminaries

We summarize the main notions used in this paper, see [DJ90] for an overview of rewriting. We write a signature as a set of function symbols, where we specify (following the PROLOG tradition) the arity of the function symbols after a "/"-sign. The set of terms build over a signature Σ and set X of variables is denoted as $T(\Sigma, X)$, we write $T(\Sigma) = T(\Sigma, \emptyset)$ for the set of *Σ-ground terms.*

We say that a term t encompasses a term s if there is a subterm of t which is an instance of s. In other words, t encompasses s if any rewrite rule with left-hand side s reduces t.

We consider first-order predicate logic *without* equality. The *$\exists^*\forall^*$-fragment* of a theory T is the subset of T of all sentences having a prenex normal form of the form

$$\exists x_1, \ldots, x_n \forall y_1, \ldots, y_m\, Q$$

where Q contains no quantifier.

We denote concatenation of words by juxtaposition. The length of a word w is written as $|w|$, and w_i, where $1 \leq i \leq |w|$, is the i-th symbol of w, that is $w = w_1 \dots w_{|w|}$. We write $v < w$ if v is a proper prefix of w.

An instance of the *Post Correspondence Problem (PCP)* is a finite set of pairs of non-empty binary words $\{(p_i, q_i) \mid 1 \leq i \leq n, p_i, q_i \in \{a,b\}^+\}$. A solution of P is a finite non-empty sequence $(i_1, \dots, i_m) \in \{1, \dots, n\}^+$ such that

$$p_{i_1} \cdots p_{i_m} = q_{i_1} \cdots q_{i_m}$$

It is undecidable whether an instance of the PCP has a solution [Pos46].

3 One-Step Rewriting

Definition 1. Let Σ be a signature and R be a Σ-rewrite system. The structure $\mathcal{A}_{\Sigma,R}$ is defined as follows: The language of $\mathcal{A}_{\Sigma,R}$ contains no constants or function symbols, and its only predicate symbol is the binary predicate symbol $\rightarrow$. The universe of $\mathcal{A}_{\Sigma,R}$ is the set $T(\Sigma)$, and $t \rightarrow s$ holds in $\mathcal{A}_{\Sigma,R}$ iff t rewrites to s in one rewriting step of R.

Theorem 2. *There is no algorithm which decides for any signature Σ and Σ-rewrite system R the $\exists^*\forall^*$-fragment of the theory of $\mathcal{A}_{\Sigma,R}$.*

The proof of this theorem is subject of this section. We show how to reduce the solvability of an instance of the Post-Correspondence Problem (PCP) to the validity of some $\exists^*\forall^*$-sentence in $\mathcal{A}_{\Sigma,R}$ for some signature Σ and rewrite system R. All constructions and proofs are parameterized by the given instance of the PCP. For the sake of convenience, we now fix this instance for the rest of the paper to be

$$P = \{(p_i, q_i) \mid 1 \leq i \leq n\}$$

Words from $\{a, b\}^*$ can easily be encoded in $T(\Sigma)$. First we define an application of a word from $\{a, b\}$ to an arbitrary term $t \in T(\Sigma)$ inductively by

$$\begin{aligned} \epsilon(t) &= t \\ wa(t) &= a(w(t)) \\ wb(t) &= b(w(t)) \end{aligned}$$

Note that, for the case of $a(t)$ and $b(t)$, this coincides with the definition of the operations in $\mathcal{A}_{\Sigma,R}$. A word $w \in \{a, b\}^*$ is now represented by the term $w(\epsilon)$. Note that

- the empty word is represented by the term ϵ,
- the encoding is injective, that is equality of words translates to equality of their respective representations,
- and $w(t)$ represents the word vw iff t represents the word v.

The idea is to encode a solution $(i_1, \dots, i_m)$ of P by the term depicted in Figure 1.

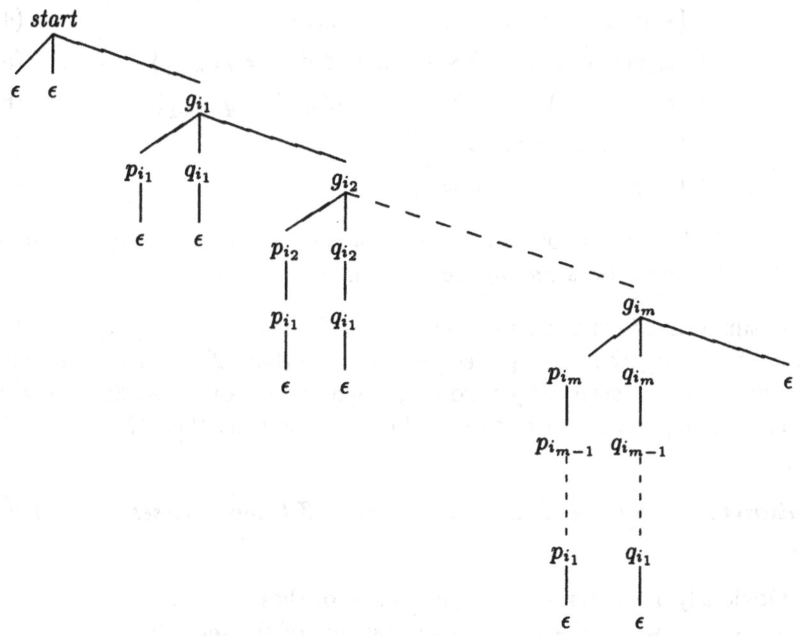

Fig. 1. Representation of the solution $(i_1, \ldots, i_m)$ of P.

Definition 3. The signature Σ_P is

$$\{\epsilon/0, a/1, b/1, start/3\} \cup \{g_i/3, k_i/3, h_{i,j}/5, eq_i/2 \mid 1 \leq i, j \leq n, \}$$

A Σ_P-ground term t is called a P-term if

- $t \in T(\{\epsilon, a, b\})$ or
- t is of one of the forms

$$g_{i_1}(p_{i_1}(r_1), q_{i_1}(s_1), \ldots, g_{i_m}(p_{i_m}(r_m), q_{i_m}(s_m), \epsilon) \ldots)$$
$$start(\epsilon, \epsilon, g_{i_1}(p_{i_1}(r_1), q_{i_1}(s_1), \ldots, g_{i_m}(p_{i_m}(r_m), q_{i_m}(s_m), \epsilon) \ldots))$$

where $1 \leq i_1, \ldots, i_m \leq n$, $r_i, s_i \in T(\{\epsilon, a, b\})$, and if t contains *start* then $m \geq 1$.

In particular, the term depicted in Figure 1 is a P-term.

Definition 4. The set $\bar{P}$ is defined as follows:

$$\bar{P} := \{k_i(x,y), h_{i,j}(x,y,x',y',z), eq_i(x,y) \mid 1 \leq i,j \leq n\} \quad (1)$$
$$\cup\ \{a(h(\bar{z})), b(h(\bar{z})) \mid h \notin \{\epsilon, a, b\}\} \quad (2)$$
$$\cup\ \{g_i(x,y,h(\bar{z})) \mid 1 \leq i \leq n, h \notin \{\epsilon, g_1, \ldots, g_n\}\} \quad (3)$$

$$\cup\ \{start(x,y,h(\bar{z})) \mid h \notin \{g_1,\dots,g_n\}\} \tag{4}$$
$$\cup\ \{g_i(p(h(\bar{x})),y,z) \mid 1 \le i \le n, p < p_i, h \ne p_{i_{|p|+1}}\} \tag{5}$$
$$\cup\ \{g_i(x,q(h(\bar{y})),z) \mid 1 \le i \le n, q < q_i, h \ne q_{i_{|q|+1}}\} \tag{6}$$
$$\cup\ \{start(h(\bar{x}),y,z) \mid h \ne \epsilon\} \tag{7}$$
$$\cup\ \{start(x,h(\bar{y}),z) \mid h \ne \epsilon\} \tag{8}$$

Proposition 5. *If a term t contains the symbol start at a position different from the root, then t encompasses one of the terms in $\bar{P}$.*

Proof: Assume that t contains a subterm of the form $f(\dots, start(\dots),\dots)$. If f is one of k_i, $h_{i,j}$ or eq_i then (1) applies. If f is a or b then (2) applies, and f can not be ϵ since ϵ is a constant. If f is some g_i then (5), (6) or (3) apply, where in the first two cases p, resp. q are taken to be ϵ. If f is *start* then (7), (8) or (4) apply. □

Proposition 6. *A term $t \in T(\Sigma_P)$ is a P-term iff t encompasses none of the terms in $\bar{P}$.*

Proof: Obviously, no P-term encompasses any of these terms.

Let t be a term which does not encompass any of the terms in $\bar{P}$. By (1), t can contain only the symbols $\{\epsilon, a, b, start, g_1, \dots, g_n\}$. If t does not contain a g_i or *start* then it is in $T(\{\epsilon,a,b\})$ and hence a P-term.

The only possible occurrence of *start* in t is, by Proposition 5, the root, and the first and second arguments of *start* must be ϵ by (7) and (8). By (2), (5), (6), (7) and (8) a symbol g_i can only occur at the root or as the third argument of *start* or some g_j. Hence, if t contains some g_i then it must be of one of the forms

$$g_{i_1}(r_1, s_1, \dots, g_{i_m}(r_m, s_m, \epsilon)\dots)$$
$$start(\epsilon, \epsilon, g_{i_1}(r_1 s_1, \dots, g_{i_m}(r_m, s_m), \epsilon)\dots))$$

with $m \ge 0$ and $1 \le i_1, \dots, i_m \le n$. By (5), r_k must be of the form $p_{i_k}(v_k)$, where by (2) $v_k \in T(\{\epsilon,a,b\})$, for any $1 \le k \le m$. Analogously, by (6), r_k must be of the form $q_{i_k}(w_k)$, where by (2) $w_k \in T(\{\epsilon,a,b\})$ for $1 \le k \le m$.

Finally, by (4), t cannot be $start(\epsilon,\epsilon,\epsilon)$. □

Definition 7. The rewrite system R_P consists of the following rules:

$$t \to t \qquad \text{where } t \in \bar{P} \tag{9}$$
$$start(\epsilon,\epsilon,g_i(p_i(x),q_i(y),z)) \to k_i(x,y,z) \tag{10}$$
$$k_i(\epsilon,\epsilon,z) \to start(\epsilon,\epsilon,g_i(p_i(\epsilon),q_i(\epsilon),z)) \tag{11}$$
$$g_i(x,y,g_j(p_j(x'),q_j(y'),z)) \to h_{i,j}(x,y,x',y',z) \tag{12}$$
$$h_{i,j}(x,y,x,y,z) \to g_i(x,y,g_j(p_j(x),q_j(y),z)) \tag{13}$$
$$g_i(x,y,\epsilon) \to eq_i(x,y) \tag{14}$$
$$eq_i(x,x) \to g_i(x,x,\epsilon) \tag{15}$$
$$start(x,y,z) \to start(x,y,g_1(p_1(\epsilon),q_1(\epsilon),z)) \tag{16}$$

where $1 \leq i, j \leq n$.

Note the non-linearity of the rules (11), (13) and (15). In the following, we use the abbreviation

$$\Phi(x) ::= \neg x \to x$$

Proposition 8. *$\mathcal{A}_{\Sigma_P, R_P}, \alpha \models \Phi(x)$ iff $\alpha(x)$ is a P-term.*

Proof: This is an immediate consequence of Proposition 6, since no rule but the ones of (9) can rewrite a term to itself. □

Proposition 9. *$\mathcal{A}_{\Sigma_P, R_P}, \alpha \models \exists x' \, (\Phi(x) \wedge x \to x' \wedge \Phi(x'))$ iff $\alpha(x)$ is a P-term with root symbol start.*

Proof: If $\alpha(x)$ is a P-term with root symbol *start*, then it rewrites with rule (16) at the root to another P-term, hence the claim follows from Proposition 8.

Let $\mathcal{A}_{\Sigma_P, R_P}, \alpha \models \Phi(x) \wedge x \to x' \wedge \Phi(x')$. By Proposition 8, $\alpha(x)$ and $\alpha(x')$ are P-terms, and by definition of Φ they are different. Since the only way to rewrite a P-term to another P-term is to apply rule (16), $\alpha(x)$ must contain the symbol *start*. By Definition of P-term, *start* is the root symbol of $\alpha(x)$. □

Lemma 10. *P is solvable iff*

$$\mathcal{A}_{\Sigma_P, R_P} \models \exists x \left(\underbrace{\exists x' \, (\Phi(x) \wedge x \to x' \wedge \Phi(x'))}_{(17)} \wedge \underbrace{\forall y \, ((x \to y \wedge \neg\Phi(y)) \Rightarrow y \to x)}_{(18)} \right)$$

Proof: Let $(i_1, \ldots, i_m)$ be a solution of P. Consider the term

$$t = start(\epsilon, \epsilon, g_{i_1}(r_1, s_1, \ldots, g_{i_m}(r_m, s_m, \epsilon) \ldots)$$

where

$$r_k = p_{i_k}(p_{i_{k-1}}(\cdots(p_{i_1}(\epsilon))\cdots))$$
$$s_k = q_{i_k}(q_{i_{k-1}}(\cdots(q_{i_1}(\epsilon))\cdots))$$

for $1 \leq k \leq m$ (this is the term shown in Figure 1). Choose $\alpha(x) = t$. Since t is a P-term and since t rewrites with rule (16) to another P-term, (17) is satisfied by Proposition 8. There are only three sorts of rules that can rewrite t to a non-P-term.

1. Rules from (10) rewrite t to

$$k_{i_1}(\epsilon, \epsilon, g_{i_2}(r_2, s_2, \ldots, g_{i_m}(r_m, s_m, \epsilon) \ldots))$$

   which can be rewritten to t by a rule from (11).
2. Rules from (12) rewrite t to

$$start(\epsilon, \epsilon, g_{i_1}(r_1, s_1, \ldots, h_{i_k, i_{k+1}}(r_k, s_k, r_k, s_k, g_{i_{k+2}}(r_{k+2}, s_{k+2}, \ldots, g_{i_m}(r_m, s_m, \epsilon) \ldots)) \ldots))$$

   which can be rewritten to t by a rule from (13).

3. Rules from (14) rewrite t to

$$start(\epsilon, \epsilon, g_{i_1}(r_1, s_1, \dots, g_{i_{m-1}}(r_{m-1}, s_{m-1}, eq_{i_m}(r_m, r_m)) \dots))$$

which can be rewritten to t by a rule from 15.

Hence, (18) is also satisfied.

Let t be a term satisfying (17) and (18). By Proposition 9, t is a P-term of the form

$$t = start(\epsilon, \epsilon, g_{i_1}(p_{i_1}(r_1), q_{i_1}(s_1), \dots, g_{i_m}(p_{i_m}(r_m), q_{i_m}(s_m), \epsilon) \dots))$$

with $m \geq 1$. It remains to show that

1. $r_1 = p_{i_1}(\epsilon)$ and $s_1 = q_{i_1}(\epsilon)$,
2. $r_{k+1} = p_{i_k}(r_k)$ and $s_{k+1} = q_{i_k}(s_k)$ for all $1 \leq k \leq m-1$, and that
3. $p_{i_m}(r_m) = q_{i_m}(s_m)$.

With the rules (10), (12) and (14) the term t rewrites in one step to the terms

$$k_{i_1}(r_1, s_1, g_{i_2}(p_{i_2}(r_2), q_{i_2}(s_2), \dots, g_{i_m}(p_{i_m}(r_m), q_{i_m}(s_m), \epsilon) \dots)) \quad (19)$$

$$\begin{aligned} &start(\epsilon, \epsilon, g_{i_1}(p_{i_1}(r_1), q_{i_1}(s_1), \dots, \\ &\qquad h_{i_k, i_{k+1}}(p_{i_k}(r_k), q_{i_k}(s_k), r_{k+1}, s_{k+1}, \dots, \\ &\qquad g_{i_m}(p_{i_m}(r_m), q_{i_m}(s_m), \epsilon) \dots) \dots)) \end{aligned} \quad (20)$$

$$start(\epsilon, \epsilon, g_{i_1}(p_{i_1}(r_1), q_{i_1}(s_1), \dots, eq_{i_m}(p_{i_m}(r_m), q_{i_m}(s_m)) \dots)) \quad (21)$$

all of which are no P-terms since they contain k_i, $h_{i,j}$ or eq_i. By (18), the term (19) rewrites to t in one step. This is only possible using rule (11), hence 1. must hold. Similarly, 2. holds since (20) rewrites to t, which is only possible with rule (13), and 3. holds since (21) rewrites to t, which is only possible with rule (15). □

4 Encompassment with Linear One-Step Rewriting

Definition 11. Let Δ be the signature $\{\epsilon/0, a/1, b/1, f/1, g/1, h/3\}$ and let M be a subset of $T(\Delta, X)$. The structure $\mathcal{B}_M$ is defined as follows: The language of $\mathcal{B}_M$ contains no constants or function symbols, and its only predicate symbols are the unary symbols Ψ_u for every $u \in M$ and the binary predicate symbol $\rightarrow$. The universe of $\mathcal{B}_M$ is the set $T(\Delta)$, $\Psi_u(t)$ holds in $\mathcal{B}_M$ if t encompasses u, and $t \rightarrow s$ holds in $\mathcal{B}_M$ iff t rewrites to s in one rewriting step of $f(x) \rightarrow g(x)$.

Theorem 12. *There is no algorithm which decides for any finite set $M \subseteq T(\Delta, X)$ the $\exists^*\forall^*$-fragment of the theory of $\mathcal{B}_M$.*

We will construct, for every instance P of the PCP, a finite set $M \subseteq T(\Delta, X)$ such that P is solvable iff a certain $\exists^*\forall^*$-sentence is valid in $\mathcal{B}_M$. We fix an instance of the PCP:

$$P = \{(p_i, q_i) \mid 1 \leq i \leq n\}$$

We define a first set of terms

$$\begin{aligned} M_1 := &\ \{g(x)\} && (22)\\ \cup &\ \{a(f(x)), a(h(\bar{x})), b(f(x)), b(h(\bar{x}))\} && (23)\\ \cup &\ \{h(h(\bar{x}), y, z), h(f(x), y, z), h(x, h(\bar{y}), z), h(x, f(y), z)\} && (24)\\ \cup &\ \{h(x, y, h(\bar{z})), h(x, y, a(z)), h(x, y, b(z))\} && (25)\\ \cup &\ \{f(\epsilon), f(a(x)), f(b(x))\} && (26)\\ \cup &\ \{f(f(f(x))), h(x, y, f(f(z)))\} && (27) \end{aligned}$$

Definition 13. A term $t \in T(\Delta, X)$ is a *list* if it is of the form

$$f(f(h(\epsilon, \epsilon, f(h(r_1, s_1, \ldots, f(h(r_m, s_m, \epsilon)) \ldots)))))$$

where $m \geq 1$, $r_i, s_i \in T(\{\epsilon, a, b\})$ for $1 \leq i \leq m$ and $r_m = s_m$.

We now introduce the abbreviations

$$\mathit{list}(x) := \bigwedge_{u \in M_1} \neg \Psi_u(x) \wedge \Psi_{f(f(h(\epsilon,\epsilon,z)))}(x) \wedge \Psi_{h(x,y,f(h(v,v,\epsilon)))}(x)$$

Proposition 14. *$\mathcal{B}_P, \alpha \models \mathit{list}(x)$ iff $\alpha(x)$ is a list.*

Proof: This is very similar to the proof of Proposition 6. Note that (22) means that t may contain ϵ, a, b, f and h only, (23) that any son of a or b is in $T(\{\epsilon, a, b\})$, (24) that the first two sons of h are in $T(\{\epsilon, a, b\})$, (25) that the last son of h is f or ϵ, and (26) that every son of f is f or h. By (27), h and f alternate, but there might be $f(f(\cdot)$ at the root of t. □

We now define a second set M_P of terms. In contrast to M_1, this set depends on the instance P of the PCP.

$$M_P := \{g(f(x))\} \cup \{g(h(x, y, f(h(p_i(x), q_i(y), z)))) \mid 1 \leq i \leq m\}$$

Lemma 15. *P is solvable iff*

$$\mathcal{B}_M \models \exists x \left(\mathit{list}(x) \wedge \forall y \,(x \to y \Rightarrow \bigvee_{u \in M_P} \Psi_u(y))\right)$$

The proof is analogous to the proof of Lemma 10.

5 Conclusions

There are two important special classes of rewrite systems where decidability of the first-order theory of one-step rewriting is not yet known:

1. (left)-linear rewrite systems and
2. (left)-shallow rewrite systems.

Furthermore, decidability of the $\exists^*$-fragment as well as of the positive theory of one-step rewriting are still open.

I'm very grateful to Hubert Comon who pointed me to this problem, to Florent Jacquemard who suggested substantial improvements on the first version of the proof, to an anonymous referee for his very helpful comments and suggestions, and to Max Dauchet for his kind support.

References

[BO93] Ronald V. Book and Friedrich Otto. *String-Rewriting Systems.* Texts and Monographs in Computer Science. Springer-Verlag, 1993.

[CCD93] Anne-Cécile Caron, Jean-Luc Coquide, and Max Dauchet. Encompassment properties and automata with constraints. In Kirchner [Kir93], pages 328–342.

[DJ90] Nachum Dershowitz and Jean-Pierre Jouannaud. Rewrite systems. In van Leeuwen [vL90], chapter 6, pages 243–320.

[DJK93] Nachum Dershowitz, Jean-Pierre Jouannaud, and Jan Willem Klop. More problems in rewriting. In Kirchner [Kir93], pages 468–487.

[DJK95] Nachum Dershowitz, Jean-Pierre Jouannaud, and Jan Willem Klop. Problems in rewriting III. In Jieh Hsiang, editor, *Rewriting Techniques and Applications,* Lecture Notes in Computer Science, vol. 914, pages 457–471. Springer-Verlag, April 1995.

[DT90] Max Dauchet and Sophie Tison. The theory of ground rewrite systems is decidable. In *Proceedings of the Fifth Annual IEEE Symposium on Logic in Computer Science,* pages 242–256. IEEE Computer Society Press, 1990.

[Hue80] Gérard Huet. Confluent reductions: Abstract properties and applications to term rewriting systems. *Journal of the ACM,* 27(4):797–821, October 1980.

[Jac95] Florent Jacquemard. Personel Communication, December 1995.

[KB70] Donald E. Knuth and Peter B. Bendix. Simple word problems in universal algebras. In J. Leech, editor, *Computational Problems in Abstract Algebra,* pages 263–297. Pergamon Press, 1970.

[Kir93] Claude Kirchner, editor. *Rewriting Techniques and Applications, 5th International Conference, RTA-93,* Lecture Notes in Computer Science, vol. 690, Montreal, Canada, 1993. Springer Verlag.

[Pla85] David A. Plaisted. Semantic confluence tests and completion methods. *Information and Computation,* 65(2/3):182–215, 1985.

[Pos46] Emil L. Post. A variant of a recursively unsolvable problem. *Bulletin of the AMS,* 52:264–268, 1946.

[Tho90] Wolfgang Thomas. Automata on infinite objects. In van Leeuwen [vL90], chapter 4, pages 133–191.

[Tre92] Ralf Treinen. A new method for undecidability proofs of first order theories. *Journal of Symbolic Computation*, 14(5):437–457, November 1992.

[vL90] Jan van Leeuwen, editor. *Handbook of Theoretical Computer Science*, volume B - Formal Models and Semantics. Elsevier Science Publishers and The MIT Press, 1990.

[Vor95] Sergei Vorobyov. Elementary theory of one-step rewriting is undecidable (note). Draft, 1995.

An Algorithm for Distributive Unification

Manfred Schmidt-Schauß
Fachbereich Informatik, Postfach 11 19 32,
J.W.-Goethe Universität Frankfurt,
60054 Frankfurt, Germany
E-mail: schauss@informatik.uni-frankfurt.de

Abstract
The purpose of this paper is to describe a decision algorithm for unifiability of equations w.r.t. the equational theory of two distributive axioms: x*(y+z) = x*y + x*z and (x+y)*z = x*z + y*z. The algorithm is described as a set of non-deterministic transformation rules. The equations given as input are eventually transformed into a conjunction of two further problems: One is an AC1-unification-problem with linear constant restrictions. The other one is a second-order unification problem that can be transformed into a word-unification problem and then can be decided using Makanin's decision algorithm. Since the algorithm terminates, this is a solution for an open problem in the field of unification.
One spin-off is an algorithm that decides the word-problem w.r.t. D in polynomial time. This is the basis for an NP-algorithm for D-matching, hence D-matching is NP-complete.

Introduction
Unification (solving equations) in equationally defined theories has several applications in computer science. An overview and further references can be found in [Si89], [KiC89], [BS94]. Since 1982, there was interest in developing unification algorithms for special equational theories, in particular, if distributive axioms are present. These distributive axioms are very common in algebraic structures and every-day mathematics, for example in solving Diophantine equations. Solving equations in these structures is a hard task, for example there is no algorithm for solving Diophantine equations. P. Szabó [Sz82] has considered unification in several equational theories where some axioms from the Peano set of axioms are dropped (not the distributive ones), proved undecidability results for unification w.r.t. several equational theories where the axioms are a subset of the Peano-axioms, a minimal set of axioms being two-sided distributivity plus associativity of addition. Peter Szabó left open the question of a unification algorithm for the theory D, where all axioms but the two distributive ones are dropped. Recent work on D-unification was done by E. Contejean [Con93], where an AC1-based unification algorithm for the subset of product terms is given, and also a (non-terminating) set of rules for D-unification .

Tidén and Arnborg [TA87] investigated other subsets of the Peano axioms motivated by the occurrence of distributive axioms in a modelling of communicating processes [BK85, BW90]. In [TA87] there is a unification algorithm for one distributive axiom, and also complexity results for unification in the presence of distributive axioms. In particular they showed that there is another small set of axioms, one-sided distributivity, associativity of addition and a multiplicative unit, for which unification is undecidable. The author gave an algorithm for the theory of one distributive axiom with a multiplicative unit [Sch93].

Another area where unification in a theory with a one-sided distributive axiom is of interest is retrieval of functions by similarity of their type [Ri90], which is closely related to unification in cartesian closed categories [NPS93].

The intention of this paper is to give a description of the algorithm for deciding D-unifiability and to give also a description of the used methods for solving this problem. Lack of space prevents to include a detailed theoretical justification. More details are in the references [Sch94a, Sch94b, Sch95]. The algorithm given in this paper is based on [Sch94b] and [Sch95], which is an improved version of [Sch94a]. This reworking has removed some flaws in [Sch94a], which affect also the D-unification algorithm in step 3 of 4.5. I am quite convinced that the algorithm is correct. A paper containing a complete and detailed proof is in preparation.

The paper is structured as follows: first we give a decision algorithm for unification of terms over the algebra of 1-sums using AC1-unification with linear constant restrictions. Section 2 is devoted to clarifying the structure of free D-algebras. In section 3 we show that D-unification can be solved if unifiability w.r.t. $=_F$, a related theory, can be decided. In section 4 we give a decision algorithm for unification problems w.r.t. $=_F$.

Preliminaries

We use a signature S_D containing the (infix) binary symbols + and *. Furthermore there may be infinitely many constants, also called free constants. Sometimes the signature is extended to S_{D1} by the constant 1. The theory of two-sided distributivity (D) w.r.t. S_D has the two axioms:

$$(x+y)*z = x*z + y*z \quad \text{and} \quad z*(x+y) = z*x + z*y$$

We denote equality of terms in the free term algebra by $=_D$. If the axioms for a multiplicative unit 1*x = x*1 = x are also present, then we speak of the theory D1 (w.r.t. S_{D1}) and denote equality by $=_{D1}$.

Some known properties of D are: the cardinality of an equivalence class of $=_D$ is finite, D-unification is NP-hard [TA87] and the number of most general unifiers may be infinite [Sz82]. A complete unification algorithm based on AC1-unification for equational systems consisting only of products has been given by Contejean [Con93].

We use the axioms also as a term-rewriting system by directing the axioms to transform terms into a "sum of products": $(x+y)*z \rightarrow x*z + y*z$; $z*(x+y) \rightarrow z*x + z*y$. In the theory D1, we also have the rewrite rules $x*1 \rightarrow x$ and $1*x \rightarrow x$.

Terms that can't be further simplified are called **irreducible**. The two TRS´es are terminating, but not confluent, since there are D-equal sums of products, that are not syntactically equal, for example (a+b)*(c+d) can be simplified to the two irreducible sums of products (a*c + a*d) + (b*c + b*d) and (a*c + b*c) + (a*d + b*d). This example serves as a counterexample for some naïve ideas for D-unification procedures.

Homomorphisms from the algebra of terms into the natural numbers can be used as sizes of terms, such that D-equal terms have the same value. If the value of the homomorphism on variables and constants is greater than 1, then the size of a term is always greater than the size of its proper subterms. If the value of the homomorphism on variables and constants is exactly 1, then this homomorphism counts the leaves of the irreducible representative.

We will denote a position in a term as π, the subterm of t at position π by $t|_\pi$, and the replacement of the subterm of t at position π by s as $t[\pi \leftarrow s]$.

1. Unification of Constant-Free D1-Terms

The purpose of this section is to provide a decision algorithm for constant-free D1-terms. Later it will turn out that this is one key method in solving the D-unification problem.

We will use the **algebra of 1-sums,** I_{D1}. This algebra is the initial term algebra for the theory D1. Note that every term in I_{D1} has a representative that consists of 1's and +'es only, these elements are called **1-sums.**

It is not hard to see that * on I_{D1} satisfies the axioms for an Abelian monoid (i.e., AC1(*)).

A 1-sum $s \neq_{D1} 1$ is called **prime**, if there is no nontrivial product representation $s =_{D1} s_1 * s_2$. A 1-sum s' is a **factor** of s, if $s =_{D1} s' * s''$ for some non-trivial s''. It can be shown that elements in I_{D1} have a **unique factorisation**. In other words, the algebra I_{D1} is a free Abelian monoid with the prime 1-sums as free generators. The notion of a **greatest common divisor** can be used in the obvious way.

The following facts are helpful for constructing a unification algorithm: The term s+t is prime, provided s and t are 1-sums and have no common factor. Furthermore, prime 1-sums permit +-decomposition. I.e., If s_1, s_2, t_1, t_2 are 1-sums and if $s_1 + s_2$ is prime, then $s_1 + s_2 =_{D1} t_1 + t_2 \Rightarrow s_1 =_{D1} t_1$ and $s_2 =_{D1} t_2$.

Now we present a unification algorithm for multi-equations over the algebra of 1-sums. The terms that are permitted in equations are terms from the free D1-term algebra without free constants. The algorithm is a set of non-deterministic transformation rules for systems Γ of multi-equations and constraints:

The permitted constraints in Γ are of the form $x < y$, $x \leq y$ for variables. The corresponding reflexive, transitive closure is denoted by $\leq_\Gamma$, and the strict part of the ordering as $<_\Gamma$. We have constraints of the form prime(x). In the AC1-unification step, the algorithm has to respect linear constant restrictions.

A ground substitution θ is a **unifier** of Γ, if it unifies every multi-equation in Γ, and if for every constraint $y \leq x$: $\text{size}(\theta y) \leq \text{size}(\theta x)$, for $y < x$: $\text{size}(\theta y) < \text{size}(\theta x)$, and if for a constraint prime(y) the term θy is a prime 1-sum.

1.1 Algorithm UNIFY-1S (for unifying equations over the algebra of 1-sums).

Step 1: Unfold every sum.

$$\frac{\{\{t[s_1 + s_2]\} \cup M\} \cup \Gamma}{\{\{t[x]\} \cup M, \{x, y_1+y_2\}, \{y_1, s_1\}, \{y_2, s_2\}\}\} \cup \Gamma}$$

where x, y_1, y_2 are a new variables.

Step 2:

The following control is used. All rules but Identify-Primes are applied until no one is applicable. In this case, we can apply Identify-Primes and again use the rules, or go to the next step. The final situation is that all +-symbols are in multi-equations that are marked as prime, and those multi-equations contain at most one top-level variable and at most one + -symbol.

Merge

$$\frac{\{M_1, M_2\} \cup \Gamma}{\{M_1 \cup M_2\} \cup \Gamma}$$

if M_1 and M_2 contain a common variable.

Variable replacement

$$\frac{\{\{x, y, M\}\} \cup \Gamma}{\{\{x, \{y \to x\}M\}\} \cup \{y \to x\}\Gamma}$$

Clash If there is a multi-equation $\{1, s+t\} \cup M$, then FAIL.

Decomp-plus

$$\frac{\{\{s_1 + s_2, t_1 + t_2\} \cup M\} \cup \Gamma}{\{\{s_1 + s_2\} \cup M\}, \{s_1, t_1\}, \{s_2, t_2\}\} \cup \Gamma}$$

if M is marked as prime.

Decomp-Mix

$\{\{s_1 + s_2\} \cup M\} \cup \Gamma$

$\{\{s_1, x*x_1\}, \{s_2, x*x_2\}, \{x*y\} \cup M\}, \{y, x_1+x_2\}\} \cup \Gamma, \; x_1 < y, x_2 < y, \;$ prime(y)

If M is not marked as prime. The variables x,y, x_1, x_2 are new ones

Identify-primes: $\{M_1, M_2\} \cup \Gamma$

$\{M_1 \cup M_2\} \cup \Gamma$ — if M_1 and M_2 are marked as prime.

Step 3. Guess a total quasi-ordering $\leq'_\Gamma \supseteq \leq_\Gamma$ on all the variables in Γ.
If for some variables x,y: $x < y$ is in Γ and $y \leq'_\Gamma x$, then FAIL.

Step 4. Construct the following AC1-unification problem.
Let Γ_{AC1} consist of all multi-equations that are not marked prime. All top-level variables in multi-equations marked as primes are considered as constants.
Furthermore, there are constraints on the occurrences of constants in variables (These are called linear constant restrictions in [BS91]): If $x <'_\Gamma a$, then a should not occur in σx for every unifier σ.
If the AC1-system Γ_{AC1} with linear constant restrictions is unifiable , then the algorithm stops with "unifiable", otherwise with FAIL. ♦

1.2 Theorem. The algorithm **UNIFY-1S** is a non-deterministic decision algorithm for unification in the free term algebra over 1-sums as well as for the unification of constant-free S_{D1}-terms. Since AC1-unification with linear constant restrictions is NP-hard [BS91], we have also that the unification problem for constant-free D1-unification problems is NP-complete.

Note that this does not give any information about the unification of constant-free S_D-terms.

1.3 Example: Is there a unifier of $x*x + y*y = z*z$ over the algebra of 1-sums?
We make the transformations by adding equations and replacing the sum. This gives three equations: $x*x = x_1*x_2$, $y*y = x_1*x_3$, $z*z = x_1*v$, $v = x_2 + x_3$, prime(v), $x_2 < v$, $x_3 < v$.
The AC1-problem is: $x*x = x_1*x_2$, $y*y = x_1*x_3$, $z*z = x_1*a$, together with a linear constant restrictions, such that a does not occur in x_2 nor in x_3. It is easy to see that this AC1-problem is not unifiable, since x_1 must be instantiated with an odd number of a's, hence x_2 and x_3 must also be instantiated with an odd number of a's. However, this contradicts the constant restrictions for x_2 and x_3. Hence the equation $x*x + y*y = z*z$ is not unifiable over the algebra of 1-sums. ♦

2. Structure of free D-algebras

The example $(a+a)*b =_D a*(b+b)$ for constants a,b shows that D-unification can't use a naïve decomposition method for *, since $(a+a) \neq_D a$. However, if we could write this as $((1+1)*a)*b =_D a*((1+1)*b)$, then there is a chance for a decomposition that decomposes products modulo the 1-sums. This is indeed possible, however, only for a subset of D-terms, namely the terms that can be represented as a non-trivial product.

We have to investigate the operation of 1-sums on S_D-terms, but have to be careful, since we do not want to deal with all terms that are available in the S_{D1}-signature. Thus we extend the algebra by permitting products (using the operator •) between 1-sums and D-terms. Let o, o_i be 1-sums and let the operation be defined as follows:

$(o_1+o_2)\bullet t \quad := o_1\bullet t + o_2\bullet t$

$1\bullet t \quad := t$

$(o_1 * o_2)\bullet t) \quad := o_1\bullet(o_2\bullet t)$

Thus every expression o•t can be evaluated to a D-term (a term in the free D-algebra). This operation generates a new equality relation on D-terms, which is denoted by $=_F$. Note that $s =_D t$ implies $s =_F t$. The converse is false:

2.1 Example. This (minimal) example shows that there are terms s,t, such that $\neg(s =_F t \Rightarrow s =_D t)$, and furthermore that the cancellation rule $s*t_1 =_D s*t_2 \Rightarrow t_1 =_D t_2$ does not hold.
We have ((a+a)+ ((a+a)+(a+a))) * b $=_D$ ((a+(a+a)) + (a+(a+a))) * b, which can be seen by some applications of distributive axioms, but ((a+a)+ ((a+a)+(a+a))) $\neq_D$ ((a+(a+a)) + (a+(a+a))). However, we have ((1+1)+((1+1)+(1+1)))•a $=_D$ ((a+a)+((a+a)+(a+a))) and ((1+(1+1)) + (1+(1+1)))•a = ((a+(a+a)) + (a+(a+a))). Since ((1+1)+((1+1)+(1+1))) $=_{D1}$ (1+1)*(1+(1+1)) $=_{D1}$ ((1+(1+1)) + (1+(1+1))), the equation ((a+a)+ ((a+a)+(a+a))) $=_F$ ((a+(a+a)) + (a+(a+a))) holds.

2.2 Example. This example shows that the equality relation $=_F$ is also different from $=_{D1}$ on D-terms: Multiplying out (((a+1)*(b+1))*c) in two different ways gives: ((a*b)*c+a*c)+(b*c+c) $=_{D1}$ ((a+1)*(b+1))*c $=_{D1}$ ((a*b)*c+b*c)+(a*c+c). Applying distributive axioms on the right term shows that the $=_D$-equivalence class contains exactly two terms, ((a*b)*c+b*c)+(a*c+c) and ((a*b)+b)*c+(a*c+c). There is also no possibility to extract 1-sums. Hence ((a*b)*c+a*c)+(b*c+c) $\neq_F$ ((a*b)*c+b*c)+(a*c+c).

We say a D-term t is **D-prime**, iff $t =_D t_1*t_2$ is impossible for D-terms t_1 and t_2. Otherwise the term is called a **D-product**.

2.3 Lemma [Sch94b] .

i) If s and t are D-products, then $s =_F t \Leftrightarrow s =_D t$.

ii) If s and t are D-terms and o is a 1-sum, then $o\bullet(s*t) =_D (o\bullet s)*t =_D s*(o\bullet t)$.

Since we have clarified the role of • and *, we drop the distinction between • and * in the following, if we are talking about $=_F$-equality.

We say a D-term t has **no 1-sum factor** (is **1-sum free**), iff $t =_F o*s$ for a 1-sum o implies $o =_{D1} 1$. We say a D-term t is **F-prime**, if t is D-prime and 1-sum-free. An **F-factorisation** of a term t is a representation $t =_F o*t_0$, where o is a 1-sum, and t_0 has no 1-sum factor, and either t_0 is F-prime, or $t_0 =_F t_1*t_2$, and t_1 and t_2 are F-factorisations. We say a D-term t has a **unique F-factorisation**, if i) for two F-factorisations $t =_F o_1*t_1$ and $t =_F o_2*t_2$, we have $o_1 =_{D1} o_2$ and $t_1 =_F t_2$, and t_1 has a unique F-factorisation; and ii) for two F-factorisations $t =_F t_1*t_2$ and $t =_F t_3*t_4$, where t_i are 1-sum free, we have $t_1 =_F t_3$ and $t_2 =_F t_4$, and t_i, i=1,...,4 have a unique F-factorisation.

The following fundamental structure theorem for D-algebras holds:
2.4 Theorem [Sch94b] Every D-term has a unique F-factorisation.

A similar theorem has been proved in [Con93] for a related algebra.

2.5 Algorithm. The O- and N-parts t_O and t_N, respectively, of a D-term t can be recursively computed by the following rules. Note that in a sum (s+t) it is not possible that s is a 1-sum and t is a D-term, since then s+t is not a D-term. Furthermore, the result is given in a standardised form

$(s*t)_O = s_O*t_O$

$(s*t)_N = s_N*t_N$

$(s + t)_O = r_O$, where $r_O = \gcd(s_O, t_O)$ if $s_N \neq t_N$

$(s + t)_O = s_O + t_O$ if $s_N = t_N$

$(s+t)_N = s'*s_N + t'*t_N$, where $r_O = \gcd(s_O, t_O)$, $s'*r_O = s_O$ and $t'*r_O = t_O$; if $s_N \neq_F t_N$

$(s+t)_N = s_N = t_N$, if $s_N = t_N$

Note that the computation of gcd(.) is polynomial for 1-sums. As a consequence, the word-problem for D can be solved in polynomial time. As a further consequence it can be shown that D-matching is in NP, and since NP-hardness was shown in [TA87], we have:

2.6 Theorem [Sch94b] D-matching is NP-complete.

2.7 Lemma The *-cancellation rules hold for $=_F$, i.e.,

i) $r*s =_F r*t \Rightarrow s =_F t$

ii) $s*r =_F t*r \Rightarrow s =_F t$

Note that the *-cancellation rules do not hold with respect to $=_D$, see example 2.2.

2.8 Lemma. Let $s_1 + s_2$ be a D-term that is not D-prime, then there are two possibilities:

i) $s_{1,N} =_F s_{2,N}$.

ii) There is a term t with $t =_F s_1 + s_2$ and some position π, such that $t|_\pi = p = p_1 + p_2$ is a D-prime, every superterm of $t|_\pi$ in t is a product, and $s_1 = t[\pi \to p_1]$, $s_2 = t[\pi \to p_2]$.

2.9 Lemma.

i) If a sum $s_1 + s_2$ is D-prime and $s_1+s_2 =_D t_1 + t_2$, then $s_1 =_D t_1$ and $s_2 =_D t_2$.

ii) If a sum $s_1 + s_2$ is F-prime and $s_1+s_2 =_F t_1 + t_2$, then $s_1 =_F t_1$ and $s_2 =_F t_2$.

3. Reduction of D-Unification to F-Unification

This section gives an algorithm that decides D-unification given a decision algorithm for F-unification. These transformation rules have to deal more or less with D-prime terms.

We use as basic data structure a set Γ of labelled multi-equations, i.e., multisets of terms. The possible labels are subsets of {D,F,prime}, but only {D}, {F}, and {D, prime} are used. A substitution σ is a **unifier** of Γ iff the following holds:

i) for every multi-equation $\{s_1,\ldots,s_n\}_F$ the equations $\sigma s_1 =_F \sigma s_2 =_F \ldots =_F \sigma s_n$ hold.

ii) for every multi-equation $\{s_1,\ldots,s_n\}_D$ the equations $\sigma s_1 =_D \sigma s_2 =_D \ldots =_D \sigma s_n$ hold.

iii) for every multi-equation $\{s_1,\ldots,s_n\}_{D,prime}$, $\sigma s_1 =_D \sigma s_2 =_D \ldots =_D \sigma s_n$ and σs_i is a D-prime.

For the input of a system of multi-equations we can always assume that it is unfolded, i.e., every proper subterm is represented by a variable.

3.1 Algorithm for D-unification using $=_F$-unification.

Input is a set of multi-equations that are all labelled {D}. The terms in the multi-equations are D-terms, i.e., no 1-sum is permitted.

Step 1. The following rules are non-deterministically used until application is no longer possible.

Rule "Variable-replacement":
If the multi-equation M is labelled {D} and x,y ∈ M, then remove x from M and replace all occurrences of x by y in all terms of Γ.

Rules (Basic Rules)
"**Merge**": If two multie-equations M and L contain the same variable, then replace them by their union. The label of the union is the union of the labels.
If the resulting label is {D,F}, then replace it by F.
If the resulting label is {D,F,prime}, then FAIL
"**Occur-check**". Stop with FAIL, if the following conditions are satisfied:
There is a cycle $x_1, s_1, \ldots, x_n, s_n, x_{n+1}, s_{n+1}$ such that s_1 is identical with s_{n+1} and x_1 is identical with x_{n+1}; x_i and s_i are in the same multie-quation for all $i=1,\ldots,n$, and $x_{i+1} \in Var(s_i)$ for $i = 1,\ldots,n$, and at least one s_i is not a variable.
"**Trivial**". Delete multi-equations that contain only one element.

Rule Select-Prime
Select some multi-equation M labelled with {D}.
Choose non-deterministically one of the following possibilities:
i) change the label of M from {D} to {F}.
ii) change the label of M from {D} to {D,prime}.

Rule Process-Prime
Select a multi-equation M labelled {D, prime}.
If there is a term t ∈ M, which is a product, then FAIL.
Now let $x_1 + x_2$ and $y_1 + y_2$ be two different nonvariable terms in M.
Remove $x_1 + x_2$ from M and add $\{x_1, y_1\}$ and $\{x_2, y_2\}$ to Γ, and label the new multi-equations with {D}.

Step 2. If there are remaining multi-equations labelled {D,prime}, change their label into {F}.
The result is a set of multi-equations with respect to $=_F$.
If this set is unifiable w.r.t. $=_F$, then return "unifiable", else FAIL. ♦

3.2 Proposition [Sch94b]. The algorithm 3.1 decides D-unifiability of terms if there is a decision algorithm for F-unification.

4. F-Unification using Second-Order Unification and AC1-unification

The result of section 3 shows that we can concentrate on F-unification. The goal of this section is to show that F-unifiability of D-terms can be decided by transforming and decomposing the problem into a second-order problem and an AC1-unification problem. The second order unification problem can be solved using the same methods as for the unification algorithm of stratified second order problems [Sch94a]. Eventually, the system will be split into two main parts: equations between 1-sums, and associative equations. The first will be solved using an AC1-unification algorithm, and the associative equations using Makanin's unification decision algorithm [Ma77].

We extend terms to second-order terms as follows. Assume there is an infinite supply of second-order monadic (function) variables (SO-variables), which we denote by upper-case letters like X, Y, Z. We permit the symbol Ω as a syntactic constant with the meaning that Ω stands for the abstracted variable in a term. For example $f(g(\Omega))$ denotes the function $\lambda x.\ f(g(x))$ mapping a term t to the term $f(g(t))$.

4.1 Definition.

A **parametric term** can be:

i) Ω, the trivial parametric term,

ii) A **basic parametric term** $t*\Omega$ or $\Omega*t$, where t is a 1-sum free second order term (t is called the **parameter**).

iii) A concatenation of two (non-trivial) parametric terms $p \bullet q$. $\bullet$ is used as associative operator.

iv) A power p^n of a (non-trivial) parametric term p, where n is a variable representing a positive natural number.

A **second order term** can be:

i) A variable or a constant,

ii) $s*t$ for second-order terms s and t,

iii) $o*t$, where o is a 1-sum and t is a second-order term.

iv) $X(t)$, where X is a second-order variable and t a second-order term,

v) $p(t)$, where p is a (non-trivial) parametric term and t a second-order term. ♦

A ground product context is either Ω, or a basic parametric term, or $s*p$, or $p*s$, where s is a 1-sum-free ground term, and p a ground product context. The semantics of second order variables is that they stand for a ground product context.

A second-order substitution is a mapping that can be represented by a finite set of pairs (x,t), (n,k) and (X,p), where t is a ground second-order term, n is an integer variable and k an integer value, and p is a ground product context.

The application of a second-order substitution σ to a second-order term is as follows: If (x,t) is a pair in σ, then all x's are replaced by t; if (X,p) is in σ, then every occurrence X(t) is replaced by $p[\Omega \rightarrow t]$; and if (n,k) is in σ, then every occurrence of the variable n is replaced by the integer k. Using the semantics of parametric terms, every ground second order term can be reduced to a ground term that does not contain parametric terms: We reduce as follows: $p_1 \bullet \ldots \bullet p_n(t) \rightarrow p_1 \bullet \ldots \bullet p_{n-1}(p_n(t))$; $(t*\Omega)(s) \rightarrow (t*s)$; $(\Omega*t)(s) \rightarrow (s*t)$; $p^1(t) \rightarrow p(t)$; $p^k(t) \rightarrow p^{k-1}(t)$, if $k > 1$.

4.2 Lemma.

i) For every substitution σ, O-term s_O and N-term t_N, we have $\sigma(X(s_O*s_N)) =_F \sigma(s_O*X(s_N))$

ii) For every substitution σ, we have $\sigma(X(s+t)) =_F \sigma(X(s)) + \sigma(X(t))$

4.3 Lemma. Every 1-sum free ground term s_1+s_2 can be represented as r[p], where r is a ground product context, and $p = p_1+p_2$ is an F-prime. Furthermore $s_1 = r[p_1]$ and $s_2 = r[p_2]$.

4.4 Definition. Let S be a set of second-order terms. For every occurrence π, the second-order-prefix of π is the string of second-order variables on a path from the root to π: If X(s) is a subterm of a top-level term t and has SO-prefix q, then s has SO-prefix qX. The length of this prefix is also denoted as SO-depth(π), or SO-depth(x) for some variable. A set of terms is **stratified**, if for every first-order variable x and for every second-order variable X, all the occurrences of a specified variable have the same second-order-prefixes. Different variables may have different SO-prefixes. Furthermore, the constant Ω should always have empty second-order prefix.

The data structure for the decision algorithm for F-unification is a system Γ that consists of a set of equations, a set of disequations between basic parametric terms, and a set of constraints. The equations can be of three kinds:

i) equations between second order terms,

ii) equations between terms over the algebra of 1-sums (see section 1.)

iii) equations between parametric terms

In addition there is a set of disequations between basic parametric terms and a system of constraints of the form N(x), O(x), or prime(x) for first-order variables x.

We sometimes speak of an equation marked as prime (or N, O, respectively), if it contains a top-level variable x with prime(x), (or O(x), N(x), respectively). In a system Γ of equations and constraints, we denote by $N_\Gamma(x)$, $O_\Gamma(x)$, $prime_\Gamma(x)$, that N(x), O(x), or prime(x), respectively, is in Γ.

The predicates $O_\Gamma()$ and $N_\Gamma()$ can be extended to terms in Γ as follows: If $O_\Gamma(s)$ and $O_\Gamma(t)$, then $O_\Gamma(s*t)$ and $O_\Gamma(s+t)$. Furthermore, we have $O_\Gamma(1)$ for the constant 1. If $N_\Gamma(s)$ and $N_\Gamma(t)$, then $N_\Gamma(s*t)$. If $N_\Gamma(s)$ then $N_\Gamma(X(s))$ and $N_\Gamma(p(s))$. We have always $N_\Gamma(a)$ for free constants a. Note that $N_\Gamma(s)$ and $N_\Gamma(t)$ do not imply $N_\Gamma(s+t)$, since for example $a + a =_F (1+1)*a$.

We distinguish subsystems of Γ as follows: Γ_C is the set of constraints, Γ_T the set of equations between terms, Γ_A the set of equations between parametric terms, Γ_D the set of disequations. The set Γ_T is separated into further disjoint subsystems: $\Gamma_{T,N}$ the set of equations between 1-sum-free terms, i.e. terms with $N_\Gamma(s)$. $\Gamma_{T,O}$ is the set of equations between 1-sums, i.e. of equations s = t, where $O_\Gamma(s)$ and $O_\Gamma(t)$.

A second-order ground substitution σ is a **unifier** of Γ, iff σ solves all equations, σx is a 1-term for $O_\Gamma(x)$, σx is 1-sum free for $N_\Gamma(x)$, σx is a prime for variables x with $prime_\Gamma(x)$, and if $\sigma p \neq \sigma q$ for disequations $p \neq q$. Note that for correctness proofs we have to use a weaker notion of unifier.

4.5 Transformation Algorithm.

Input is an arbitrary system of equations (w.r.t. $=_F$) between D-terms. In particular, at the start of the algorithm, only the part Γ_T is not empty, and there are no parametric terms and no second-order variables. We assume that the system is unfolded in such a way, that all sums appear at top-level. This can easily be achieved by introducing new variables x and replacing subterms of the form s+t with a new x and adding the equation x = s+t to the system.

Step 1.

In this step we first apply Split-Sums until it is no longer applicable. Then we apply the rule Select-N/O until all variables are constrained by O(.) or N(.).

Rule "Split-sums".

Replace every equation $s_1 + s_2 = t_1 + t_2$ by two equations $x = s_1 + s_2$ and $x = t_1 + t_2$, where x is a new variable.

Rule "Select-N/O".

Replace every first order variable x for which no constraint N(x) or O(x) is in Γ, by x_1*x_2, and add $O(x_1)$ and $N(x_2)$, where x_1 and x_2 are new variables.

The situation now is: For every first order variable x, there is either a constraint N(x) or O(x) in the system Γ. Furthermore, all +-symbols appear at the top-level of terms, and there is no equation $s_1 + s_2 = t_1 + t_2$. This means also that (first order) terms are either variables, constants, products or a term s+t, where s,t may be variables, constants or products.
We denote by the suffix O and N the corresponding O- and N-parts of the terms, which can easily be computed adapting the algorithm in 2.5 to terms with variables taking the predicates $N_\Gamma(.)$ and $O_\Gamma(.)$ into account. For free constants a, we have $a_O = 1$.

Step 2 of 4.5

The goal of this step is to eliminate or isolate the +-symbols, and to reduce the number of equations that are neither in $\Gamma_{T,N}$ nor in $\Gamma_{T,O}$. This step may introduce SO-variables, but no parametric terms. The rules should by applied exhaustively.

Rule "Decompose O in products"

If there is an equation $s = t$ in $\Gamma \setminus \Gamma_{T,O}$ where s,t do not contain +, and s_O or t_O is not trivial, then remove $s = t$ from Γ, and add $s_O = t_O$ and $s_N = t_N$ to Γ.

Rule "Decompose O in sums"

If there is an equation $r = s + t$ in $\Gamma \setminus \Gamma_{T,O}$, such that r_O is not trivial, then choose non-deterministically one of the following alternatives:
i) remove $r = s + t$ from Γ,
add $r_O = s_O + t_O$, $r_N = s_N$, $s_N = t_N$ to Γ.
ii) remove $r = s + t$ from Γ,
Add the following equations and constraints to Γ:
$r_N = y*s_N + z*t_N$, $s_O = y*r_O$, $t_O = z*r_O$, O(y), O(z)
where y,z are new variables.

Rule (FAILURE)

If there is an equation $a = s*t$, and a is a free constant, then FAIL.
If there is an equation $a = b$ where a and b are two different free constants, then FAIL.
If there is an equation $a = s + t$, where a is a free constant , then FAIL.

Rule (SOV-Introduction)

If $r = s + t$ is an equation in Γ, and we have N(r), but r is not a prime variable, then remove the equation from Γ,
add $r = X(u)$, $u = s_O*u_1 + t_O*u_2$, prime(u), $X(u_1) = s_N$, $X(u_2) = t_N$, N(u), $N(u_1)$, $N(u_2)$.
where X is a new second-order variable, u, u_1, u_2 are new FO-variables.

End of Step 2.

If no rule is applicable, then we have the following situation: Γ_T can be separated into three disjoint subsystems of equations: Γ_O, Γ_N, Γ_{prime}.

- Γ_O consists of all equations that contain only O-terms, i.e., $\Gamma_O = \Gamma_{T,O}$.
- Γ_N consists of all equations that contain only N-terms and no +-symbol.
- Γ_{prime} consists of all equations of the form $u = s_1*u_1+s_2*u_2$, where u is marked as prime and s_1, t_1 are O-terms, and u_1,u_2 are N-variables with the same second-order prefix as u.

The system Γ_N is a stratified SO-system, where every FO-variable has a SO-prefix of length at most 1, and every SO-variable has an empty SO-prefix. Furthermore for every prime variable u, there is exactly one equation in Γ_{prime}.

Remarks before Step 3.
Now we concentrate on solving the stratified second-order unification problem Γ_N. However, it is not possible to use the algorithm from [Sch94a] as it stands, assuming all prime variables as constants, since we have to take into account that some primes may be equal. An identification step in advance does not help, since then the system may be non-stratified.

Since it exceeds the space restrictions for this paper to give an explicit description of the algorithm in [Sch94a, Sch95], we will give a rough idea what are the essential steps solving stratified SO-systems. There is a basic set of rules:

Replace-Variable. If $x = t$ is an equation in Γ, and x does not occur in t, then remove the equation $x = t$, and replace x by t everywhere in Γ.

Trivial-Equations. Remove equations of the form $x = x$, where x is a variable.

Occur-Check. If there is an equation $x = t$, such that t is not a variable, and x occurs in t, then FAIL: the system is not unifiable.

Decomposition . If $s_1*s_2 = t_1*t_2$ is an equation in Γ_N, then remove the equation and add the equations $s_1 = t_1$, $s_2 = t_2$ to Γ_N.

Constants If $s_1*s_2 = a$ is an equation in Γ, where a is a constant then FAIL.
If $a = b$ is an equation in Γ, where a,b are different constants, then FAIL.
If $a = X(t)$ is in Γ, then remove X from Γ.
If $a = p(t)$ is in Γ, where p is a (non-trivial) parametric term, then FAIL.

Para-Clash. If there is a disequation $p \neq p$ in Γ_D, then FAIL

There are also rules to transform equations, such that every equation has at least one top-level term of the form X(s).

The algorithm to solve stratified SO-systems in [Sch94a, Sch95] has three major steps. The first one is to break SO-cycles, like $X(x) = Y(y)$, $Y(z) = a*X(u))$. This is done by guessing the SO-variables in a careful way top down. Parametric terms may be introduced, for example if a small cycle is to be solved: $X(x) = X(a)*b$ for example has as a solution $X= (\Omega*b)^n$, $x= a*b$.
The next major step after SO-cycles have been removed is to remove the maximal SO-variables.
If all SO-variables have been removed, the remaining equations are only those between parametric terms. The final step is to apply associative unification, i.e., Makanin's decision algorithm.

Now we repeat the definition of SO-cycle, define the new notion of an SO-prime-cycle, and give a modified definition for SOV-cluster.
An **SO-cycle** in Γ is a set of equations $X_i(s_i) = t_i$, $i = 1,\ldots,n$, such that X_i occurs in $t_{i-1(\mathrm{mod}\ n)}$ and at least one occurrence is not at top level.
Since there may be cycles between SO-variables and primes, we need another type of cycle:
An **SO-prime-cycle** in Γ is a set of equations e_i, $i=1,\ldots,n$, every equation is either of the form i) $X_i(s_i) = t_i$ or ii) $x_i = t_i$, with $\mathrm{prime}_\Gamma(x_i)$. Furthermore, in case i) X_i occurs in $t_{i-1(\mathrm{mod}\ n)}$ and in case ii) x_i occurs in $t_{i-1(\mathrm{mod}\ n)}$. At least one prime x_i should occur in the cycle, otherwise it is an SO-cycle.
An **SOV-cluster** is an equivalence class of SO-variables, which is maximal w.r.t to the transitive pre-ordering $\geq^*_{SO}$ generated by the following relations: $X \geq_{SO} Y$, if there is an equation $X(s) = Y(t)$; $X >_{SO} Y$, if $X(s) = t$ is in Γ, and Y occurs in t not at top level; $X >_{SO} x$, if $X(s) = t$ is in Γ, x occurs in t, and $\mathrm{prime}_\Gamma(x)$; $x >_{SO} X$, if $x = s + t$ is in Γ, $\mathrm{prime}_\Gamma(x)$, and X occurs in s+t; $x >_{SO} y$, if $x = s + t$ is in Γ, $\mathrm{prime}_\Gamma(x)$, $\mathrm{prime}_\Gamma(y)$, and y occurs in $s + t$.
It is not necessary to consider the case $x = t$, where x is not a prime, since in this case, we can use variable-replacement.
We have that the ordering $v_1 >_{SO} v_2$ implies $\neg(v_2 \geq^*_{SO} v_1)$ iff there are no SO-prime-cycles.

Step 3. This step should remove the second-order variables from Γ_T.
All rules that are borrowed from [Sch94a, Sch95] operate on Γ_N, Γ_D, Γ_A, but ignore the system Γ_{prime} and treat the different prime variables as different constants. For identification of primes we will describe an extra rule. The steps 3.1 and 3.2 are used like meta-rules. Whenever there is a SO-prime-cycle, then step 3.1 becomes active.

There are background rules that transform the system Γ_N, such that every equations has one term of the form X(s). Therefore we use the method in [Sch94a, Sch95] which decomposes equations of the form p(s) = q(t) and p(s) = t_1*t_2.

Step 3.1 This step eliminates SO-prime-cycles.
Fix an SO-prime-cycle of minimal length. If the length is 1, then either a prime-variable is involved, in which case the algorithm should return FAIL. If in the cycle of length 1 a SO-variable is involved, then use the cycle-elimination of [Sch94a, Sch95].
If the cycle has length > 1, then there are three cases:

i) There are only prime variables involved. Then FAIL.
ii) There are prime variables and SO-variables involved. Then there is some equation of the form X(s) = t[x] in the cycle, where X and x contribute to the cycle, and $prime_{\Gamma}(x)$. Then apply Split-SO-Variable [Sch94a,Sch95] and either the cycle is shortened, or we get an equation, where the depth of the variable x in t is smaller. The exits are that some SO-variable is guessed as Ω or that a shorter SO-prime-cycle is generated. A minimal case is X(s) = x, implying X= Ω.
iii) There are no prime variables involved. Then proceed as in [Sch94a,Sch95]

Since the rules above may guess some SO-variable as trivial, in this case we non-deterministically perform the following rule (as a demon) for the primes that have changed their SO-prefix from one SO-variable to none.
Rule "Identify primes"

> Choose one of the two alternatives
> i) do nothing
> ii) Let x be the prime variable, that has now SO-depth = 0, and let $x = s_1*s_2 + s_3*s_4$ be the equation for x in Γ_{prime}.
> Select some other prime-variable y with SO-depth(y) = 0, and let $y = t_1*t_2 + t_3*t_4$ be the equation for y in Γ_{prime}.
> Remove $x = s_1*s_2 + s_3*s_4$. Replace x by y everywhere.
> Add $s_1 = t_1$, $s_3 = t_3$ to Γ_O. Add $s_2 = t_2$, $s_4 = t_4$ to Γ_N.

Step 3.2 Elimination of SOV-cluster.
This step assumes, that there is no SO-prime-cycle.
From now on, we use also a set $\Gamma_{prime,p}$ for passive prime equations. The set Γ_{prime} contains the active primes. In the beginning all primes and prime equations are active. Maximality will be computed only w.r.t. the active prime variables, even if it is necessary to jump back to step 3.1.
We have two cases:

i) There is a $\geq^*_{SO}$-maximal SO-variable. Then we use the method in [Sch94a, Sch95] to eliminate the SOV-cluster.
ii) There are no $\geq^*_{SO}$-maximal SO-variables, but $\geq^*_{SO}$-maximal primes. In this case, we non-deterministically select some maximal prime equation and move it into the set $\Gamma_{prime,p}$.

Note that only the system consisting of Γ_N and Γ_{prime} without passive prime equations is guaranteed to remain stratified.

The rule "Prime-Identification" is only used for active primes, and thus cannot reintroduce unwanted second-order variables which may be contained in the set $\Gamma_{prime,p}$, but do not occur in Γ_N nor Γ_{prime}. We prevent the reintroduction of SO-variables due to Definition 3.7 in [Sch95], which may identify parametric terms, similarly as in [Sch95], where identification is not necessary, if a basic parametric p that is already in Γ_D, contains some variables that are not in Γ_N nor Γ_{prime}.

Step 4
Now the system Γ_N is empty. In the same way as in [Sch94a, Sch95] we transform Γ_A into an associative unification problem and check unifiability using the algorithm in [Ma77].
If Γ_A is unifiable and if Γ_O is unifiable, then the answer is "unifiable".
Otherwise, the answer is "FAIL". ♦

4.6 Remarks on Termination of algorithm 4.5.
Step 2: The well-founded measure that is strictly decreased in every rule application is as follows: We restrict the measure to equations that are not in Γ_O. μ_1 is the number of +-symbols in $\Gamma \setminus \Gamma_O$, μ_2 is the number of +-symbols in equations that are not prime, μ_3 is the number of +-symbols in equations that contain a top level term with a non-trivial O- and N-part, μ_4 is the number of top level products that have a nontrivial O-and N-part. The well-founded measure is the lexicographical combination $(\mu_1,\mu_2,\mu_3,\mu_4)$.
Step3. Termination follows from [Sch94a, Sch95], the ordering consists of the following main components: #SO-variables in $\Gamma_N \cup \Gamma_{prime}$, #variables in $\Gamma_N \cup \Gamma_{prime}$, #integer variables in $\Gamma_N \cup \Gamma_{prime}$, #primes in Γ_{prime}. ♦

4.7 Theorem. Algorithm 4.5 is a decision algorithm for unifiability of systems of equations w.r.t $=_F$. I.e., for every unifiable system of equations w.r.t. $=_F$, there is some sequence of applications of rules in algorithm 4.5, such that the final answer is "unifiable", and for every system that is not unifiable, the answer will always be FAIL, (or not unifiable). ♦

4.8 Theorem. D-unification is decidable.
The unification algorithm is non-deterministic and finally uses an AC1-unification algorithm with linear constant restriction and the decision algorithm for word equations of Makanin. ♦

Note that the decision algorithm 4.5 cannot be extended to a complete unification algorithm, since the method in [Sch95] has the same drawback. The reason is that SOV-cluster-elimination may increase the number of SO-variables in the whole system Γ (not in the active part), and the mechanism to prevent reintroduction into the active part can only be justified by modifying the unifier in a non-trivial way.

Somw remaining **open questions** are:
i) Give better upper and lower bounds for the complexity of D-unification: The best known lower bound for the complexity of D-unification is that it is NP-hard (TA87).
ii) Give a unification algorithm for D1 or show undecidability of unification w.r.t. D1. Note that the technique developed in this paper does not work, since $a*(a+1) =_{D1} (a+1)*a$, but $a+1 \neq_{D1} a$.

4.9 Example. We want to demonstrate a run of the algorithm for the example $x*x + y*y =_D z*z$. Obviously, this is equivalent to $x*x + y*y =_F z*z$.
Step 1 splits variables into O and N-part:
$(x_1*x_2)* (x_1*x_2) + (y_1*y_2)*(y_1*y_2) = (z_1*z_2)*(z_1*z_2)$ where x_1, y_1, z_1 are O-variables and x_2, y_2, z_2 are N-variables.

Computation of O- and N-part gives the problem:
$(x_1*x_1)*(x_2*x_2) + (y_1*y_1)*(y_2*y_2) = (z_1*z_1)*(z_2*z_2)$
We apply "decompose O in sums". There are two alternatives:
i) $x_1*x_1 + y_1*y_1 = z_1*z_1$, $x_2*x_2 = y_2*y_2$, $y_2*y_2 = z_2*z_2$.
Example 1.3 shows, that the O-part $x_1*x_1 + y_1*y_1 = z_1*z_1$ is not unifiable over the algebra of 1-sums. Hence the result is FAIL.
ii) $x_3*(x_2*x_2) + y_3*(y_2*y_2) = z_2*z_2$, $x_3*z_1*z_1 = x_1*x_1$, $y_3*z_1*z_1 = y_1*y_1$, $O(x_3)$, $O(y_3)$.
SOV-Introduction gives:
$X(u) = z_2*z_2$, $u = x_3*u_1 + y_3*u_2$, $X(u_1) = x_2*x_2$, $X(u_2) = y_2*y_2$, $N(u)$, $prime(u)$, $N(u_1)$, $N(u_2)$,...
We apply elimination of the SOV-cluster $\{X\}$, since there are no SO-prime-cycles.
There are two alternatives
i): $X = \Omega$. This leads to FAIL, since $u = z_2*z_2$ is not unifiable, for a (prime) constant u.
ii) $X = z_2*X'(\Omega)$ (or $X = X'(\Omega)*z_2$). Replacement of X gives:
$z_2*X'(u) = z_2*z_2$, $u = x_3*u_1 + y_3*u_2$, $z_2*X'(u_1) = x_2*x_2$, $z_2*X'(u_2) = y_2*y_2$, ...
Decomposition and Variable-Replacement reduce this to
$X'(u) = z_2$, $u = x_3*u_1 + y_3*u_2$, $X'(u_1) = z_2$, $X'(u_2) = z_2$, ...
Further Variable-Replacement gives the equations
$u = x_3*u_1 + y_3*u_2$, $X'(u_1) = X'(u)$, $X'(u_2) = X'(u)$, ...
Now we can eliminate X' by decomposition, which gives
$u = x_3*u_1 + y_3*u_2$, $u_1 = u$, $u_2 = u$, ...
Now we have the opportunity to apply Prime-Identification, however, there is only one prime.
Variable-Replacement gives $u = x*u + y_3*u$, ... This leads to a FAIL and we can conclude that the equation $x*x + y*y =_D z*z$ is not D-unifiable. ♦

Remark. In [Sch94b] there is a sketch of an argumentation, that unifiability of equations together with linear constant restrictions w.r.t. the theory D is decidable.

Acknowledgements. I would like to thank Hubert Comon for a discussion on second-order systems, and Evelyne Contejean for discussions on D-unification.

Conclusion.

We have provided a decision algorithm for unifiability of equations under the theory of two-sided distributivity, answering a question that was open for some years. The description of the algorithm is rather complex, and requires unifying AC1-equations with linear constant restrictions, a certain kind of second order equations, and finally unifying word equations.
Though this algorithm may be impractical, it demonstrates the power of the tools developed in the field of unification algorithms. Furthermore it provides a theory generated by a subset of the Peano-axioms, which has a decidable unification problem.
The new efficient algorithm for deciding the word problem and the NP-completeness of D-matching may have some practical usage in applications which make use of two-sided distributive axioms

References.

BK85 Bergstra, J.A. and Klop, J.W., Algebra of communicating processes with abstraction. J. theoretical computer science 37, 77-121, (1985)
BS91 Baader, F., Schulz, K.U., General A- and AX-Unification via Optimised Combination Procedures, Proc. Second International Workshop on Word Equations and Related Topics 1991, LNCS 677, pp. 23-42, (1992)
BS92 Baader, F., Schulz, K.U., Unification in the union of disjoint equational theories: Combining decision procedures, Proc. 11th CADE, LNCS 607, Springer-Verlag, pp. 50-65, (1992)
BS94 Baader, F, Siekmann, J., Unification Theory, in D.M. Gabbay, C.J. Hogger, J.A: Robinson (eds.), Handbook of Logic in Artificial Intelligence and Logic Programming, Oxford University Press, (1994)

BW90 Baeten, J.C.M., Weijland, W.P., Process Algebra, Cambridge tracts in theoretical computer science, Cambridge university press, (1990)

Con93 Contejean, E., Solving *-problems modulo Distributivity by a reduction to AC1-Unification, J. of Symbolic Computation 16, pp. 493-521. (1993)

Fa91 Farmer, W., A., Simple second-order languages for which unification is undecidable. Theoretical Computer Science 87, pp. 173-214, (1991)

Gol81 Goldfarb, W. The undecidability of the second-order unification problem, J. TCS 13, pp. 225-230, (1981)

Jaf90 Jaffar, J., Minimal and complete word unification , J. of the ACM, 37, 47-85, (1990)

KN92 Kapur, D., Narendran, Complexity of AC1-unification, JAR 92: pp 261-288, (1992)

KiC89 Kirchner, C. (ed.), Unification, reprint from J. of Symbolic Computation, Academic Press, (1989)

Ma77 Makanin G.S:, The problem of solvability od equations in a free semigroup. Math. Sbornik, 103, 147-236, (1977), english translation in Math USSR Sbornik 32, (1977)

NPS93 Narendran, P., Pfenning, F., Statman, R., On the unification problem in cartesian closed categories, Proc. Logic in Computer Science, 57-63, (1993)

Ri90 Rittri, M., Retrieving library identifiers via equational matching of types, Proc. 10th CADE, Springer Lecture Notes in Computer Science 449, 603- 617, (1990)

Sch89 Schmidt-Schauß, M., Unification in a combination of arbitrary disjoint equational theories, J. Symbolic computation 8, 51-99, (1989)

Sch92 Schmidt-Schauß, M., Some results on unification in distributive equational theories, Internal report 7/92. J.W. Goethe-Universität, Frankfurt am Main, (1992)

Sch93 Schmidt-Schauß, M., Unification under one-sided distributivity with a multiplicative unit, Proc. LPAR 93, Springer LNCS 698, pp. 289-300, (1993)

Sch94a Schmidt-Schauß, M., Unification of Stratified Second-Order Terms, Internal report 12/94, Fachbereich Informatik, Johann Wolfgang Goethe-Universität Frankfurt, (1994)

Sch94b Schmidt-Schauß, M., An Algorithm for Distributive Unification, Internal report 13/94, Fachbereich Informatik, Johann Wolfgang Goethe-Universität Frankfurt, (1994)

Sch95 Schmidt-Schauß, M., Unification of Stratified Second-Order Terms, improved version of Sch94a, submitted for publication, 1995

Su93 Schulz, K.U., Word unification and transformation of generalized equations, J. Automated Reasoning 11, pp. 149-184, (1993)

Si89 Siekmann, J., Unification theory: a survey, in C. Kirchner (ed.), Special issue on unification, Journal of symbolic computation 7, (1989)

Sz82 Szabó, P., Unifikationstheorie erster Ordnung, Dissertation, Karlsruhe, (1982)

TA87 Tiden, E., Arnborg, S., Unification problems with one-sided distributivity, J. Symbolic Computation 3, pp. 183-202, (1987)

On the Termination Problem for One-Rule Semi-Thue System

Géraud Sénizergues

LaBRI
Université de Bordeaux I
351, Cours de la Libération 33405 Talence, France **

Abstract. We solve the u-termination and the termination problems for the one-rule semi-Thue systems S of the form $0^p 1^q \longrightarrow v$, $(p, q \in \mathbb{N} - \{0\}, v \in \{0,1\}^*)$. We obtain a structure theorem about a monoid that we call the *termination-monoid* of S. As a consequence, for every fixed system S of the above form, the termination-problem has a *linear* time-complexity.

Keywords: semi-Thue systems; termination; finite automata; rational monoid; automatic structure;

1 Introduction

The semi-Thue systems are among the simplest type of rewriting systems that occur in the literature: they can be seen as the special case of term rewriting systems where function symbols are of arity 1 only, which implies also that they are linear (with only one variable). Despite this apparent simplicity it has been shown recently that the *termination* and *u-termination* problems (see §2.4 for precise definitions) are both *undecidable* for 3 rules semi-Thue systems ([MS96]). In the case of semi-Thue systems with only *one* rule, these two algorithmic problems are still open. Partial results are obtained in [Kur90, Ges91, DH93, McN94, ZG95].

We show here that for the one rule semi-Thue systems of the form $0^p 1^q \longrightarrow v, (p, q \in \mathbb{N} - \{0\}, v \in \{0,1\}^*)$, these two problems are decidable, thus generalizing the results of [ZG95].

The general idea of our solution is that the termination (resp. u-termination) problem for a system $u \longrightarrow v$ can be reduced to the study of either the set of irreducible words $L_+(S) = \{\beta \in Irr(S) \mid \rho(\beta u) = \infty\}$ or its analogue on the right $R_+(S) = \{\gamma \in Irr(S) \mid \rho(u\gamma) = \infty\}$ (provided u has no self-overlap). We show that for semi-Thue systems of the above form, it is always true that $L_+(S)$ (or $R_+(S)$) is *rational* (Theorem 3.10).

We describe in two steps a way to *construct effectively* a finite automaton $\mathcal{A}_S$ recognizing $L_+(S)$ (or $R_+(S)$):

- we first show that a word w is the initial word of some infinite derivation iff w is the initial word of a *looping* derivation (see §4); this is sufficient to solve the termination problem (theorem 4.7),
- we then show that an integer parameter k_0, which is in some sense the key-parameter allowing to construct $\mathcal{A}_S$, is in fact always smaller than $2 \cdot p$; this second step turns out to be rather tricky, it consists in the detailed inspection of 11 different cases (see §5); it follows that $\mathcal{A}_S$ is constructible and that the u-termination problem is decidable (theorem 5.4).

At last, we study the structure of a monoid $\bar{M}$ expressing in some sense the termination problem for S (therefore, we call it the *termination*-monoid): $\bar{M}$ is the Rees-quotient of $M = X^*/ \xleftrightarrow{*}_S$ by the image in M of the ideal $I_+ = \{w \in \{0,1\}^* \mid w \xrightarrow{\infty}_S\}$. It turns out that when S is not u-terminating, $\bar{M}$ is a *rational* monoid (in the sense of [Sak87, PS90]). This implies that, for every given S, the termination problem is solvable in *linear* time (theorem 6.1 and corollary 6.5).

** mailing adress:LaBRI and UFR Math-info, Université Bordeaux1
351 Cours de la libération -33405- Talence Cedex.
email:ges@labri.u-bordeaux.fr ; fax: 56-84-66-69

2 Preliminaries

2.1 Words

Given an alphabet X, by $(X^*, \cdot, \epsilon)$ we denote the *free monoid* generated by X (where $\cdot$ is the concatenation-product and ϵ is the empty word). Given a word u, by $|u|$ we denote the length of u. X^+ denotes the subset $X^* - \{\epsilon\}$. As $X^*$is embedded in $F(X)$ (the *free group* generated by X) we sometimes use the notation u^{-1} for the *inverse* in $F(X)$ of a word u. A prefix (resp. strict prefix)of a word $u \in X^*$ is any word v such that there exists $w \in X^*$ (resp. $w \in X^+$) fulfilling $u = v \cdot w$. The notions of suffix (resp. strict suffix) are defined similarly. Given $u \in X^*$ and $K \in \mathbb{N}$, we denote by $u^{(K)}$ the suffix of length K of u: either $|u| \leq K$ and $u^{(K)} = u$ or $|u| > K$ and $u = wu^{(K)}$ with $|u^{(K)}| = K$. By $u^{<p}$ we denote the set of all the powers of u with an exponent strictly less than p: $\{u^i \mid 0 \leq i < p\}$. As we deal with termination problems, it will be convenient to consider the monoid X^*_∞ defined by: $X^*_\infty = X^* \cup \{\infty\}$ (∞ is just one new symbol); the product in the monoid X^* is extended to X^*_∞ by the formula: $\forall w \in X^*_\infty, w \cdot \infty = \infty \cdot w = \infty$. One can check that $(X^*_\infty, \cdot, \epsilon)$ is a monoid too.

2.2 Semi-Thue systems

We recall a semi-Thue system over X is a subset $S \subseteq X^* \times X^*$. The one-step derivation generated by S, denoted $\longrightarrow_S$, is the binary relation defined by: $\forall f, g \in X^*, f \longrightarrow_S g$ iff there exists $(u, v) \in S$ and $\alpha, \beta \in X^*$ such that $f = \alpha u \beta, g = \alpha v \beta$. The relations $\xrightarrow{*}_S$ (the derivation generated by S), $\xleftrightarrow{*}_S$(the *congruence* generated by S), ..., are then deduced from $\longrightarrow_S$ as usual. We denote by Irr(S) the set of *irreducible* words: $\mathrm{Irr}(S) = X^* - \bigcup_{(u,v)\in S} X^*uX^*$. The relation ${}_l\!\longrightarrow_S$, the one-step *leftmost derivation* generated by S, is classical. Let us mention that, in the particular case where S consists of only one rule $u \longrightarrow v$, it can be simply defined by: $f\ {}_l\!\longrightarrow_S g \iff \exists r, s \in X^*$ such that $f = rus, g = rvs$ and every decomposition $f = r'us'$ is such that $|r| \leq |r'|$. ${}_l\!\xrightarrow{*}_S$ is the leftmost-derivation generated by S. We note $w \xrightarrow{\infty}_S$ iff there is an infinite derivation starting on w.

We refer the reader to [BO93, DJ91] for more information on rewriting systems.

2.3 Automata

A n-tape *generalized finite automaton* (abbreviated n-g.f.a. in the sequel) is a 5-tuple:

$$\mathcal{A} = < X, Q, \delta, q_0, F >$$

where X is a finite alphabet, the input-alphabet; Q is a finite set, the set of states; q_0 is a distinguished state , the initial state; $F \subseteq Q$ is a set of distinguished states , the final states; δ, the set of transitions, is a subset of $Q \times (X^*)^n \times Q$.

The *one-step move relation* $\longrightarrow_\mathcal{A}$ is the binary relation on Config($\mathcal{A}$) defined by: $(q, \mathbf{u}) \longrightarrow_\mathcal{A} (q', \mathbf{u}') \iff$ $\exists \mathbf{a} \in (X^*)^n$ such that $(q, \mathbf{a}, q') \in \delta$ and $\mathbf{u} = \mathbf{a} \cdot \mathbf{u}'$.
The language recognized by $\mathcal{A}$ is: $\mathrm{L}(\mathcal{A}) = \{\mathbf{u} \in (X^*)^n \mid \exists q \in F, (q_0, \mathbf{u}) \xrightarrow{*}_\mathcal{A} (q, (\epsilon)^n)\}$. For every $\mathbf{u} \in (X^*)^n$, the binary relation $\xrightarrow{\mathbf{u}}_\mathcal{A}$ over Q is defined by: $q \xrightarrow{\mathbf{u}}_\mathcal{A} q' \iff (q, \mathbf{u}) \xrightarrow{*}_\mathcal{A} (q', (\epsilon)^n)$.

One can easily see that the class of languages of the form L($\mathcal{A}$) for some 1-g.f.a. $\mathcal{A}$ is exactly the class of *rational languages* and the class of binary relations of the form L($\mathcal{A}$) for some 2-g.f.a. $\mathcal{A}$ is exactly the class of *rational relations* (see [Ber79, chap.III-IV]).

2.4 Termination problems

We focus here on the two following algorithmic problems.

termination problem : the termination-problem for the alphabet X and the semi-Thue system $S \subseteq X^* \times X^*$ is the following
  instance: $w \in X^*$
  question : does every derivation (mod S) starting on w have finite length ?
    (when the answer is "yes", we say that S *terminates* on w).

uniform termination problem : the uniform-termination problem for a class $\mathcal{S}$ of semi-Thue systems is the following

instance: an alphabet X and a finite semi-Thue system $S \subseteq X^* \times X^*$ which belongs to $\mathcal{S}$.
question : does every derivation (mod S) starting from a word in X^* have finite length ?
(when the answer is "yes" we say that S is *uniformly-terminating*, sometimes abbreviated as u-terminating).

For more information about termination problems, the reader should refer to [Der87, DJ91].

3 The ideal I_+

Let $S : u \longrightarrow v$ be a one-rule semi-Thue system over the alphabet $X = \{0,1\}$. We suppose u has no self-overlap i.e. : $\forall u_1, u_2 \in \{0,1\}^*, u = u_1u_2u_1 \Longrightarrow u_1 = \epsilon$. We define a map $\rho : X^*_\infty \longrightarrow \mathrm{Irr}(S) \bigcup \{\infty\}$ by:

$$w \mapsto \begin{cases} w' & \text{if } w \xrightarrow{*}_S w' \in \mathrm{Irr}(S) \\ \infty & \text{if } w \xrightarrow{\infty}_S \text{ or } w = \infty \end{cases}$$

As u is overlap-free, ρ is well-defined.

Lemma 3.1 *Let $w \in \{0,1\}^*$. The following properties are equivalent*

1. $\rho(w) = \infty$,
2. $\exists \beta \in \mathrm{Irr}(S), \exists \gamma \in \{0,1\}^*, w \,{}_l\!\xrightarrow{*}_S \beta u \gamma$ *and* $\rho(\beta u) = \infty$.

Proof: It is clear that (2) $\Longrightarrow$ (1). Let us suppose that (2) is false. Let us consider the decomposition :

$$w = x_1 \ldots x_i \ldots x_p \text{ where } x_i \in \{0,1\}. \tag{1}$$

Let us consider the sequence of elements of X^*_∞ :

$$w_0 = \epsilon\ ,\ z_0 = w\ ,\ w_{i+1} = \rho(w_i x_{i+1}) \text{ and } z_{i+1} = (x_{i+1})^{-1} z_i \text{ for } 0 \leq i < p.$$

Using decomposition (1) and hypothesis $\neg(2)$, one can show by induction on i that, for every $i \in [0,p]$: $w_i \neq \infty$ and $w \,{}_l\!\xrightarrow{*}_S w_i z_i$. It follows that $\rho(w) = w_p z_p = w_p \neq \infty$. □

Let us define

$L_+(S) = \{\beta \in Irr(S) \mid \rho(\beta u) = \infty\}, L_-(S) = \{\beta \in Irr(S) \mid \rho(\beta u) \neq \infty\}$,
$R_+(S) = \{\gamma \in Irr(S) \mid \rho(u\gamma) = \infty\}, R_-(S) = \{\gamma \in Irr(S) \mid \rho(u\gamma) \neq \infty\}$,
$I_+(S) = \{w \in \{0,1\}^* \mid \rho(w) = \infty\}, I_-(S) = \{w \in \{0,1\}^* \mid \rho(w) \neq \infty\}$.

Corollary 3.2 *:*
1- One of the sets $L_\epsilon(S), R_\epsilon(S), I_\epsilon(S) (\epsilon \in \{+,-\})$ is recursive iff all these sets are recursive
2- S is u-terminating $\Longleftrightarrow L_+(S) = \emptyset \Longleftrightarrow R_+(S) = \emptyset$.

Let us say that a word $w_1 \in X^*$ *crosses* (from left to right) a word $w_2 \in X^+$ iff there exist a leftmost derivation :

$$w_1 \cdot w_2 \,{}_l\!\xrightarrow{*}_S w_3$$

which uses the rightmost letter of w_2.

We say that a word $w \in Irr(S)$ is a *left-separator* iff the following situation is impossible :

$$\exists w_1, w_2, w_3 \in \{0,1\}^*, ww_2 \in \mathrm{Irr}(S), w_1 \cdot ww_2 \xrightarrow{*}_S w_3,$$

where this derivation uses the rightmost letter of w. A notion of *right-separator* can be defined similarly.

In all the remaining we suppose $u = 0^p1^q$ with $p > 0, q > 0$.

Lemma 3.3 *Let $S = 0^p1^q \to v'0$ where $p > 0, q > 0, v' \in \{0,1\}^*$. Let $n \in \mathbb{N} - \{0\}$. One (and only one) of the following cases is true.*

C1: $\forall q' < q, 0^p1^{q'}$ *does not cross* 1^n *and* $\rho(0^p1^{q'}1^n) < \infty$,
C2: $\forall q' < q, 0^p1^{q'}$ *does not cross* 1^n *and* $\rho(0^p1^{q'}1^n) = \infty$,
C3:

$$\exists q' < q \begin{cases} 0^p1^{q'} \text{ crosses } 1^n, \\ \rho(0^p1^{q'}1^n) \neq \infty, \\ \forall q'' < q, q'' \neq q' \Longrightarrow 0^p1^{q''} \text{ does not cross } 1^n \quad \text{and } \rho(0^p1^{q''}1^n) \neq \infty. \end{cases}$$

C4:

$$\exists q' < q \begin{cases} 0^p1^{q'} \text{ crosses } 1^n, \\ \rho(0^p1^{q'}1^n) = \infty, \\ \forall q'' < q', 0^p1^{q''} \text{ does not cross } 1^n \quad \text{and } \rho(0^p1^{q''}1^n) \neq \infty, \\ \forall q'' \in]q', q[, 0^p1^{q''} \text{ does not cross } 1^n \quad \text{and } \rho(0^p1^{q''}1^n) = \infty. \end{cases}$$

Remark. In any case, 0^p1^q has *at most one* strict prefix which crosses 1^n.

Lemma 3.4 *Let $S = 0^p1^q \to v'0$ where $p > 0, q > 0, v' \in \{0,1\}^*1\{0,1\}^*$. Let $n \in \mathbb{N} - \{0\}$ realizing case C3. Let $q'' < q$ such that $0^p1^{q''}$ does not cross 1^n. Then $\rho(0^p1^{q''}1^n0)$ is a left-separator.*

Sketch of proof: Suppose $0^p1^{q'}$ crosses 1^n and $\rho(0^p1^{q'}1^n) \neq \infty$. It shows that

$$n = q - q' \tag{2}$$
$$\text{or } v'0 = v''0^p \text{ for some } v'' \in (0+1)^*. \tag{3}$$

If (2) is true : $\rho(0^p1^{q''}1^n) \in (0+1)^*011^{<q-1}$ and every element of $011^{<q-1}0$ is a left-separator. Hence $\rho(0^p1^{q''}1^n0)$ is a left-separator.
If (3) is true : $\rho(0^p1^{q''}1^n) \in (0+1)^*0^p11^{<q-1}$. Hence $\rho(0^p1^{q''}1^n0)$ is a left-separator. □

Lemma 3.5 *Let $S = 0^p1^q \to 1^rv'0^s$ where $p, q, r, s > 0, v' \in (0^+1^+)^*$, one of the blocks of 0 in $1^rv'0^s$ is not divided by p. Let $w \in 1^rv'0^s1^tv'(0+1)^*$ for some integer $t \geq 0$ such that $v'1^t \neq \epsilon$. Then $\rho(w) \in 1^r0(0+1)^* \cup \{\infty\}$.*

Let us define the sets $M(S), M_+(S), M_-(S)$ by:

$$M(S) = \{f \in X^* \mid \exists n \in \mathbb{N}, f = f_n \cdot f_{n-1} \cdots f_r \cdots f_0, \forall i \in [0,n] f_i \text{ is a strict prefix of } u,$$
$$f_0v \in u(0+1)^* \text{ and } \forall i \in [1,n] f_i\rho(f_{i-1} \cdots f_0u) \in u(0+1)^*\} \cup \{\epsilon\}.$$

$$M_+(S) = M(S) \cap L_+(S), \quad M_-(S) = M(S) \cap L_-(S).$$

Lemma 3.6 $L_+(S) = ((0+1)^*M_+(S)) \cap \mathrm{Irr}(S)$

Hence $L_\epsilon(S)$ is rational iff $M_\epsilon(S)$ is rational (for every $\epsilon \in \{+,-\}$).

Lemma 3.7 *Let $S = 0^p1^q \to 1^rv'0^s$ where $p, q, r, s > 0, v' \in (0^+1^+)^*$, one of the blocks of 0 in $1^rv'0^s$ is not divided by p. Then $M_+(S), M_-(S)$ are rational.*

Sketch of proof: By lemma 3.3, the integer $n = r$ must fulfill one of cases C1-C4. Let us give a description of a generalized f.a. $\mathcal{A}_S$ recognizing $M_+(S)$ in each of these cases.
C1 : $\forall q' < q, 0^p1^{q'}$ does not cross 1^r and $\rho(0^p1^{q'}1^r) < \infty$. Hence $r > q$ and $s < p$. So that $M_+(S) = \emptyset$. The g.f.a. $\mathcal{A}_S$ is trivial.
C2 : $\forall q' < q, 0^p1^{q'}$ does not cross 1^r and $\rho(0^p1^{q'}1^r) = \infty$. Hence $M_+(S) = 0^p1^{<q}$. The g.f.a. $\mathcal{A}_S$ is straightforward.
C3 : $\exists! q' < q, 0^p1^{q'}$ crosses 1^r, and $\rho(0^p1^{q'}1^r) \neq \infty$.

Let us note $\alpha = 0^p1^{q'}$. Let us define : $Q_i = (0^p1^q)1^i (i = 0 \text{ or } r - q \leq i < r)$.
For every $i \in \{0\} \cup [r-q, r[$ we define :

$$k_i = \inf\{k \mid \rho(\alpha^k Q_i) = \infty\} \tag{4}$$

(notice that this definition implies that $[k_i = \infty \iff \forall k, \rho(\alpha^k Q_i) < \infty]$ and also

$$k_o \geq k_{r \dot{-} q} \geq \cdots \geq k_{r-1} \geq 0).$$

Let us define : $P_{i,j} = \rho(\alpha^j Q_i)$ for $i \in \{0\} \cup [r \dot{-} q, r[, 0 \leq j \leq k_i$.
The g.f.a $\mathcal{A}_S$ has the set of states :

$\mathcal{Q}_S = \{P_{i,j} \mid i \in \{0\} \cup [r-q, r[, 0 \leq j \leq k_i\} \cup \{\infty\}$,
(notice that all the states $P_{i,j}$ with $j = k_i < \infty$ are equal to ∞),
its set of transitions δ is:

$$\begin{aligned}
\delta = \{&(P_{i,j+1}, \alpha, P_{i,j}, \mid 0 \leq j \leq k_i - 1 < \infty\} & (5)\\
\cup\ \{&(P_{i,0}, \alpha, P_{i,0}) \mid k_i = \infty\} & (6)\\
\cup\ \{&(P_{\ell,0}, 0^p1^{q''}, P_{i,j}) \mid q \dot{-} r \leq q'' < q, q'' \neq q', \ell = r - q + q''\}, & (7)
\end{aligned}$$

its initial state is: ∞,
its terminal state is: $P_{0,0}$.

One can prove by induction on $|f|$ that, for all $f \in \{0,1\}^*, i \in \{0\} \cup [r \dot{-} q, r[, 0 \leq j \leq k_i$:

$$f \in \mathrm{M}(S) \Longrightarrow \exists P \in \mathcal{Q}_S, P \xrightarrow{f}_{\mathcal{A}_S} P_{0,0}, \tag{8}$$

$$i = 0 \text{ and } P_{i,j} \xrightarrow{f}_{\mathcal{A}_S} P_{i,0} \Longrightarrow f \in \mathrm{M}(S) \text{ and } \rho(fQ_0) = P_{i,j}, \tag{9}$$

$$i \neq 0, k_i = \infty \text{ and } P_{i,0} \xrightarrow{f}_{\mathcal{A}_S} P_{0,0} \Longrightarrow f \in \mathrm{M}(S) \text{ and } \exists k \in \mathbb{N}, \rho(fQ_0) \in P_{i,k}0(0+1)^*, \tag{10}$$

$$i \neq 0, k_i \neq \infty \text{ and } P_{i,j} \xrightarrow{f}_{\mathcal{A}_S} P_{0,0} \Longrightarrow f \in \mathrm{M}(S) \text{ and } \rho(fQ_0) \in P_{i,j}0(0+1)^*. \tag{11}$$

The key-arguments are that, for $i \neq 0$, if $\rho(fQ_0) = P_{i,j}0w$ then
1- $\rho(\alpha f Q_0) = P_{i,j+1}0w$, because, by lemma 3.4, $P_{i,0}0$ is a left-separator;
2- for $q \dot{-} r \leq q'' < q, q'' \neq q', \ell = r - q + q''$, if $\rho(fQ_0) = P_{i,j}0w$, then

$$\begin{aligned}
\rho(0^p1^{q''}fQ_0) &= \rho(0^p1^{q''}P_{i,j}0w) = \rho(0^p1^{q''}P_{i,j}0)w \quad (\text{ because } P_{i,0}0 \text{ is a left-separator})\\
&\in \rho(0^p1^{q''}1^r0(0+1)^*)w \text{ (using lemma 3.5) } = \rho(0^p1^{q''}1^r)0w' \text{ (for some } w' \in (0+1)^*),
\end{aligned}$$

(because $\rho(0^p1^{q''}1^r)0 = P_{\ell,0}0, q' \neq q'' \Longrightarrow \ell \neq 0$, hence $P_{\ell,0}0$ is either a left-separator or $= \infty$)

$$= P_{\ell,0}0w'.$$

By equivalences (8-11),

$$\mathrm{L}(\mathcal{A}_S) = M_+(S).$$

C4 : $\exists! q' < q, 0^p1^{q'}$ crosses 1^r, and $\rho(0^p1^{q'}1^r) = \infty$
The same g.f.a $\mathcal{A}_S$ as in C3 recognizes $L_+(S)$. Let us notice that in this case :

$$(i \geq r - q' \Longrightarrow P_{i,0} = \infty, k_i = 0) \text{ and } (r \dot{-} q \leq i < r - q' \Longrightarrow P_{i,0} \neq \infty, k_i = 1).$$

(see lemma 3.3, C4). □

Lemma 3.8 *Let $S = 0^p1^q \to 0^t1^rv'$ where $p, q, r, t > 0, p > t, q \leq r, v' \in 0(0+1)^* \cup \{\epsilon\}$. Then $\mathrm{M}_+(S)$ is rational.*

Sketch of proof: Given $w \in 0^t1(0+1)^* \cap \mathrm{Irr}(S)$, there exists at most one strict prefix α of 0^p1^q such that αw is reducible. Hence $M_+(S) = \emptyset$ or $M_+(S) = \{\alpha^{k_0}\}$ for some integer k_0.
□

Lemma 3.9 *Let $S = 0^p1^q \to 1^r v' 0^s$, where $p,q,r,s > 0, v' \in (0^+1^+)^*$, every block of 0 in $1^r v' 0^s$ is divided by p and every block of 1 in $1^r v' 0^s$ is divided by q. Then $M_+(S)$ is rational.*

Sketch of proof: If $v' \neq \varepsilon$ then 0^p1^q is factor of v' and $L_+(S) = \mathrm{Irr}(S)$.
If $v' = \varepsilon : S = 0^p1^q \to (1^q)^\lambda(0^p)^\mu$. Then

- if $\lambda \geq 2$ and $\mu \geq 2$, then $\rho(0^p u) = \infty$. One can construct a g.f.a. $\mathcal{A}_S$ recognizing $M_+(S)$ as in lemma 3.7, C2.
- if $\lambda = 1$, then: $\forall n \in \mathbb{N}, \forall i < r = q, \quad \rho((0^p)^n u 1^i) = 1^q 0^{\mu \cdot p \cdot (n+1)} 1^i < \infty$.
  As in lemma 3.7, C1, we have: $M_+(S) = \emptyset$.
- if $\mu = 1$, by the above argument $R_+(S) = \emptyset$, hence by corollary 3.2, point 2, $L_+(S) = \emptyset$, so that $M_+(S) = \emptyset$.

□

Theorem 3.10 *Let $S = 0^p1^q \to v \quad (p > 0, q > 0, v \in \{0,1\}^*)$. Then either $L_+(S), L_-(S)$ are rational or $R_+(S), R_-(S)$ are rational.*

Proof: If ($v \in 1(0+1)^*0$ and v has at least one block of 0 not divided by p) or $v \in 0(0+1)^*$, then S fulfills the hypothesis of one of the lemma 3.7,3.8,3.9, hence $L_\epsilon(S)$ are rational. In every other case where $v \notin 0^* + 1^*$ by a symmetry argument $R_\epsilon(S)$ are rational. In the remaining case where $v \in 0^* + 1^*$, $L_+(S) = R_+(S) = \emptyset$. □

4 Infinite derivations

Lemma 4.1 *Let S fulfilling the hypothesis of lemma 3.7, case C2. Then*
$\forall q' < q, \exists q'' < q, \exists \beta, \gamma \in \{0,1\}^*$ such that $0^p1^{q'}Q_0 \xrightarrow{+}_S \beta(0^p1^{q''}Q_0)\gamma$.

We skip the proof which is analogous to (but simpler than) the proof of lemma 4.3 below.

Lemma 4.2 *Let S fulfilling the hypothesis of lemma 3.7, case C2, and $w \in \{0,1\}^*$. $\rho(w) = \infty \iff \exists q' < q, \exists \beta, \gamma, \beta', \gamma' \in \{0,1\}^*$, $w \xrightarrow{*}_S \beta'(0^p1^{q'}Q_0)\gamma'$ and $0^p1^{q'}Q_0 \xrightarrow{+}_S \beta(0^p1^{q'}Q_0)\gamma$.*

Proof: The non-trivial direction of the equivalence is ($\Longrightarrow$). Let $w \in \{0,1\}^*$, $\rho(w) = \infty$. By lemma 3.1, there exist $\beta'_0 \in \mathrm{Irr}(S), \gamma'_0 \in \{0,1\}^*, w \,{}_l\!\xrightarrow{*}_S \beta'_0 u \gamma'_0$ and $\rho(\beta'_0 u) = \infty$. As $\beta'_0 v$ must be reducible,

$$\beta'_0 = \beta'_1 0^p 1^{q_1} \quad \text{for some } \beta'_1 \in \mathrm{Irr}(S),\ 0 \leq q_1 < q.$$

By lemma 4.1, there exist infinite sequences $(q_k)_{k\geq 1}, (\beta_k)_{k\geq 1}, (\gamma_k)_{k\geq 1}$ such that:

$$0^p1^{q_k}Q_0 \xrightarrow{+}_S \beta_k(0^p1^{q_{k+1}}Q_0)\gamma_k, \qquad \text{for all } k \geq 1.$$

There must exist $k_0 \geq 1, d \geq 1$ such that $q_{k_0+d} = q_{k_0}$. Let us define:

$$q' = q_{k_0},\ \beta = \beta_{k_0}\beta_{k_0+1}\ldots\beta_{k_0+d-1},\ \gamma = \gamma_{k_0+d-1}\ldots\gamma_{k_0+1}\gamma_{k_0},\ \beta' = \beta'_1\beta_1\ldots\beta_{k_0-1},\ \gamma' = \gamma_{k_0-1}\ldots\gamma_1\gamma'_0.$$

We have

$$w \xrightarrow{*}_S \beta'(0^p1^{q'}Q_0)\gamma' \text{ and } 0^p1^{q'}Q_0 \xrightarrow{+}_S \beta(0^p1^{q'}Q_0)\gamma$$

as required. □

Lemma 4.3 *Let S fulfilling the hypothesis of lemma 3.7, case C3 or C4. Let α, Q_i, k_i be as defined in the proof of lemma 3.7. Then*
$\forall i \in \{0\}\cup[r-q, r[$, if $k_i \neq \infty$ then $\exists i' \in \{0\}\cup[r-q, r[, \exists \beta, \gamma \in \{0,1\}^*$ such that $\alpha^{k_i}Q_i \xrightarrow{+}_S \beta(\alpha^{k_{i'}}Q_{i'})\gamma$.

Proof: Suppose $k_i \neq \infty$. $\rho(\alpha^{k_i}Q_i) = \infty$, hence, by lemma 3.1, $\exists \beta_1 \in \mathrm{Irr}(S), \exists \gamma_1 \in \{0,1\}^*$,

$$\alpha^{k_i}Q_i \mapsto^{*}_S \beta_1 u \gamma_1 \text{ and } \rho(\beta_1 u) = \infty. \tag{12}$$

By lemma 3.6, $\beta_1 = \beta_2\beta_3$ with $\beta_3 \in M_+(S)$. Let us consider an accepting computation of $\mathcal{A}_S$ over the word β_3. It must have the form:

$$\infty = P_{i',k_{i'}} \xrightarrow{\alpha^{k_{i'}}}_{\mathcal{A}_S} P_{i',0} \xrightarrow{0^p1^{q''}}_{\mathcal{A}_S} P_{i'',j} \xrightarrow{\beta_4}_{\mathcal{A}_S} P_{0,0} \tag{13}$$

where $i', i'' \in \{0\} \cup [r-q, r[, 0 \neq q'' < q, 0 \neq j < k_{i''}, i' = r-q+q''$ (see definition 7) and $\beta_3 = \alpha^{k_{i'}}0^p1^{q''}\beta_4$. By (12) (13),

$$\begin{aligned}
\alpha^{k_i}Q_i &\xrightarrow{*}_S \beta_1 Q_0 \gamma_1 \xrightarrow{*}_S \beta_2\alpha^{k_{i'}}(0^p1^{q''}\rho(\beta_4Q_0))\gamma_1 \\
&= \beta_2\alpha^{k_{i'}}(0^p1^{q''}1^r0\gamma_2)\gamma_1 \text{ (for some } \gamma_2 \in (0+1)^*\text{, by lemma 3.5)} \\
&= \beta_2\alpha^{k_{i'}}Q_{i'}0\gamma_2\gamma_1.
\end{aligned}$$

Letting $\beta = \beta_2$ and $\gamma = 0\gamma_2\gamma_1$, the lemma is proved. □

Lemma 4.4 *Let S fulfilling the hypothesis of lemma 3.7, case C3 or C4 and $w \in \{0,1\}^*$.*
$\rho(w) = \infty \iff \exists i \in \{0\} \cup [r-q, r[, \exists \beta, \gamma, \beta', \gamma' \in \{0,1\}^*, w \xrightarrow{*}_S \beta'\alpha^{k_i}Q_i\gamma'$ *and* $\alpha^{k_i}Q_i \xrightarrow{+}_S \beta(\alpha^{k_i}Q_i)\gamma$.

Proof: The proof is analogous to that of lemma 4.2: it leans on lemma 3.1, lemma 4.3 and finiteness of $\{0\} \cup [r-q, r[$. □

Lemma 4.5 *Let $S = 0^p1^q \to 0^t1^rv'$, fulfilling the hypothesis of lemma 3.8. Let α, k_0 be as defined in the proof of lemma 3.8 and let us suppose that $k_0 \neq \infty$. Then*
1- $\exists \beta_S, \gamma_S \in \{0,1\}^*$ such that $\alpha^{k_0}Q_0 \xrightarrow{+}_S \beta_S(\alpha^{k_0}Q_0)\gamma_S$.
2- $\forall w \in \{0,1\}^*, \rho(w) = \infty \iff \exists \beta', \gamma' \in \{0,1\}^*, w \xrightarrow{*}_S \beta'(\alpha^{k_0}Q_0)\gamma'$.

Proof: Analogous to the proof of lemma 4.2. □

Lemma 4.6 *Let $S = 0^p1^q \to (1^q)^\lambda(0^p)^\mu$ where $\lambda \geq 2$ and $\mu \geq 2$. Then*
1- $\exists \beta_S, \gamma_S \in \{0,1\}^*$ such that $0^pQ_0 \xrightarrow{+}_S \beta_S(0^pQ_0)\gamma_S$.
2- $\forall w \in \{0,1\}^*, \rho(w) = \infty \iff \exists \beta', \gamma' \in \{0,1\}^*, w \xrightarrow{*}_S \beta'(0^pQ_0)\gamma'$.

Proof: Point (1) is straightforward. Point (2) is a direct consequence of lemma 3.1. □

Theorem 4.7 *Given any system $S = 0^p1^q \to v$ (where $v \in \{0,1\}^*$), and any word $w \in \{0,1\}^*$, one can decide whether S terminates on w or not.*

Proof: The termination problem for a pair (S, w) where S is any finite semi-Thue system over $\{0,1\}$ and w any word over $\{0,1\}$ is semi-decidable. By the above lemmas 4.2, 4.4, 4.5, 4.6, for systems S of the form $0^p1^q \to v$ the non-termination of S on w is also semi-decidable. This proves the theorem. □

5 Computation of the structure of I_+

Our proofs of lemma 3.7, 3.8 and 3.9 consist in describing (abstractly) a finite automaton recognizing the set $\mathrm{M}_+(S)$. This automaton is *constructible* from two data:

- the case that the system S is fulfilling (i.e. cases C1-C4 of lemma 3.7, the hypothesis of lemma 3.8 or the hypothesis of lemma 3.9),
- a finite set of integers $k_0, \ldots, k_{r-1}$ in cases C1-C4 of lemma 3.7 , a single integer k_0 in the case of lemma 3.8.

We will show now that these cases and integers are effectively computable from the system S.

Lemma 5.1 *Let S fulfill the hypothesis of lemma 3.7. The property "w_1 crosses (from left to right) w_2" is decidable.*

Proof: Let u' such that $0^p1^q = u'1$. Let $v = 1^r w_0 0^s$ such that at least one block of 0 in v is not divided by p. For every $w_1, w_2 \in \{0,1\}^*$, w_1 crosses w_2 iff $w_2 = w_2'1$ (for some w_2') and

$$w_1 \cdot w_2' \overset{*}{\longmapsto}_S \beta \cdot u' (\text{ for some } \beta \in \{0,1\}^*) \text{ and } \beta \cdot u' \in \mathrm{Irr}(S). \tag{14}$$

One can then decide this condition (14) by the following algorithm:
1- decide whether $\rho(w_1 \cdot w_2') = \infty$ or not (by theorem 4.7)
2- if $\rho(w_1 \cdot w_2') = \infty$ then w_1 does not cross w_2
3- if $\rho(w_1 \cdot w_2') \neq \infty$ then compute $\rho(w_1 \cdot w_2')$
4- if $\rho(w_1 \cdot w_2')$ does not admit the suffix u' then w_1 does not cross w_2 else w_1 crosses w_2. □

Lemma 5.2 *Let S fulfill the hypothesis of lemma 3.7. One can decide which of cases C1-C4 is fulfilled.*

Proof: Clearly, it is sufficient to decide for every $q' < q$ whether $0^p1^{q'}$ crosses 1^r or not, and whether $\rho(0^p1^{q'+r}) = \infty$ or not. These properties can be decided by lemma 5.1 and theorem 4.7. □

Lemma 5.3 *Let S fulfill the hypothesis of lemma 3.7, case C3 or C4. Then $k_0 \leq k_{r-1}+1$. In particular, $k_0 = \infty \iff k_{r-1} = \infty$.*

Proof: Let α be the unique strict prefix of 0^p1^q which crosses (from left to right)1^r. Suppose that $\alpha^k 0^p 1^q 1^{r-1} \xrightarrow{\infty}_S$. Then, by confluence of S:

$$\alpha^k 1^r v' 0^s 1^{r-1} \xrightarrow{\infty}_S \tag{15}$$

Let us consider the unique integer λ such that $r - q \leq \lambda \cdot q < r$. The $(r-1)-(\lambda \cdot q)$ last symbols of 1^{r-1} cannot be used in this derivation. Hence $\alpha^k 1^r v' 0^s 1^{\lambda \cdot q} \xrightarrow{\infty}_S$, which implies that

$$\alpha^k 0^p 1^q 1^{\lambda \cdot q} \xrightarrow{\infty}_S . \tag{16}$$

Let us consider the integer q' such that $\alpha = 0^p1^{q'}$. Both integers $\lambda \cdot q$ and $q' + r - q$ are divided by q and belong to $[r-q, r[$. Hence

$$\lambda \cdot q = q' + r - q. \tag{17}$$

Hence

$$\begin{aligned} \alpha^{k+1}0^p1^q &\longrightarrow_S \alpha^k(\alpha 1^r v' 0^s) = \alpha^k(0^p 1^{q'+r} v' 0^s) = \alpha^k(0^p 1^q 1^{\lambda \cdot q} v' 0^s) \text{ by equality (17)} \\ &\xrightarrow{\infty}_S \text{ (by derivation (16)).} \end{aligned}$$

We have proved that $k_0 \leq k_{r-1} + 1$. □
By the definition of the k_i and lemma 5.3 we know that

$$k_{r-1} + 1 \geq k_0 \geq k_{r-q} \geq \ldots \geq k_{r-1} \geq 0. \tag{18}$$

Owing to lemma 5.2, the fact that S fulfills case Ci of lemma 3.7 or the hypothesis of lemma j, is decidable.

In cases C1-C4 of lemma 3.7, by the inequalities (18), from the knowledge that $k_0 = \infty$ or any finite upper bound on k_0, one can compute the exact values of all the k_i's and then the automaton $\mathcal{A}_S$.

In the case of lemma 3.8, from the knowledge that $k_0 = \infty$ or any finite upper bound on k_0, one can compute the exact value of k_0, hence an automaton recognizing $\mathrm{M}_+(S)$.

In the case of lemma 3.9, the computation of a finite automaton is straightforward.

Let us consider some one rule semi-Thue system: $S = 0^p1^q \longrightarrow v$, where $p, q > 0, v \in (0+1)^*$ and u is not factor of v. Let us denote by S' the system $S' = 0^q1^p \longrightarrow v'$, where v' is obtained from the mirror image of v by exchanging letters 0 and 1.
The remaining of this section is a discussion which distinguishes 11 main cases D1,...,D8,D'2,D'5,D'6. In every case Di we give the aforementioned bounds and in every case D'i we show that S' fulfills the corresponding case Di. The remaining case where u is factor of v is trivial (then $\mathrm{L}_+(S) = \mathrm{Irr}(S)$).

(We omit here the detailed treatment of cases D6,D7 and D8, see the annex of [Sén96] for more complete calculations; anyway D6 is rather similar to D5 and D7,D8 are easy).

5.1 Case D1: $v = 1^r w_1 1^{\overline{q}} w_2 0^{\overline{p}} w_3 0^s$

with $r, s > 0, w_1 \in (0^+1^+)^* \cdot 0^+, w_2 \in (0^+1^+)^*, w_3 \in 1^+ \cdot (0^+1^+)^*, p \nmid \overline{p}, q \nmid \overline{q}$.
(That is: v contains an *internal* block of 1 not divided by q, followed by an *internal* block of 0 not divided by p). The hypothesis of lemma 3.7 is fulfilled. Let $\alpha = 0^p 1^{q'}$ and $q' + r = \lambda \cdot q \ \ (\lambda \geq 1)$.

$$\begin{aligned}\alpha 0^p 1^q &\longrightarrow_S 0^p 1^{q'+r} w_1 1^{\overline{q}} w_2 0^{\overline{p}} w_3 0^s \longrightarrow_S 1^r w_1 1^{\overline{q}} w_2 (0^{\overline{p}} w_3 0^s 1^{(\lambda-1)\cdot q}) w_1 1^{\overline{q}} w_2) 0^{\overline{p}} w_3 0^s \\ &\xrightarrow{*}_S 1^r w_1 1^{\overline{q}} w_2 \rho(0^{\overline{p}} w_3 0^s 1^{(\lambda-1)\cdot q} w_1 1^{\overline{q}} w_2) 0^{\overline{p}} w_3 0^s .\end{aligned}$$

where

$$\rho(0^{\overline{p}} w_3 0^s 1^{(\lambda-1)\cdot q} w_1 1^{\overline{q}} w_2) \in (\mathrm{Irr}(S) \cap 0(0+1)^* 1) \cup \{\infty\}. \tag{19}$$

As well, for every $k \geq 1$

$$\alpha^k 0^p 1^q \xrightarrow{*}_S 1^r w_1 1^{\overline{q}} w_2 \rho(0^{\overline{p}} w_3 0^s 1^{(\lambda-1)\cdot q} w_1 1^{\overline{q}} w_2)^k 0^{\overline{p}} w_3 0^s .$$

and by (19),

$$1^r w_1 1^{\overline{q}} w_2 \rho(0^{\overline{p}} w_3 0^s 1^{(\lambda-1)\cdot q} w_1 1^{\overline{q}} w_2)^k 0^{\overline{p}} w_3 0^s \in \mathrm{Irr}(S) \cup \{\infty\}.$$

It follows that either $k_0 = 1$ (if $\rho(0^{\overline{p}} w_3 0^s 1^{(\lambda-1)\cdot q} w_1 1^{\overline{q}} w_2) = \infty$)
or $k_0 = \infty$ (if $\rho(0^{\overline{p}} w_3 0^s 1^{(\lambda-1)\cdot q} w_1 1^{\overline{q}} w_2) \neq \infty$).
Conclusion: either $k_0 = 1$ or $k_0 = \infty$.

5.2 Case D2: $v = 1^r w_1 1^{\overline{q}} w_2 0^s$

with $r, s > 0, w_1 \in (0^+1^+)^* \cdot 0^+, w_2 \in (0^+1^+)^*, q \nmid \overline{q}, p \nmid s$.
(That is: v contains an *internal* block of 1 not divided by q and the *right-external* block of 0 is not divided by p). Let $\alpha = 0^p 1^{q'}$ and $q' + r = \lambda \cdot q \ \ (\lambda \geq 1)$. Then, for every $k \geq 1$,

$$\rho(\alpha^k 0^p 1^q) = 1^r w_1 1^{\overline{q}} w_2 \rho(0^s 1^{(\lambda-1)\cdot q} w_1 1^{\overline{q}} w_2)^k 0^s .$$

It follows that either $k_0 = 1$ (if $\rho(0^s 1^{(\lambda-1)\cdot q} w_1 1^{\overline{q}} w_2) = \infty$) or $k_0 = \infty$ (if $\rho(0^s 1^{(\lambda-1)\cdot q} w_1 1^{\overline{q}} w_2) \neq \infty$).
Conclusion: either $k_0 = 1$ or $k_0 = \infty$.

5.3 Case D'2: $v = 1^r w_1 0^{\overline{p}} w_2 0^s$

with $r, s > 0, w_1 \in (0^+1^+)^*, w_2 \in (1^+0^+)^* \cdot 1^+, q \nmid r, p \nmid \overline{p}$. Then S' fulfills case D2.

5.4 Case D3: $v = 1^r w_1 0^{\overline{p}} w_2 1^{\overline{q}} w_3 0^s$

with $r, s > 0, w_1 \in (0^+1^+)^*, w_2 \in (1^+0^+)^*, w_3 \in (0^+1^+)^*, p \nmid \overline{p}, p \mid s, q \nmid \overline{q}, q \mid r$.
(That is: v contains an *internal* block of 0 not divided by p, followed by an *internal* block of 1 not divided by q). We suppose (without loss of generality) that $1^{\overline{q}}$ is the *leftmost* block of 1 in v which is not divided by q and that $0^{\overline{p}}$ is the *rightmost* block of 0 in v which is not divided by p. Let $\alpha = 0^p$ and $r = \lambda \cdot q \ \ (\lambda \geq 1)$.

$$\alpha 0^p 1^q \xrightarrow{2}_S 1^r w_1 0^{\overline{p}} w_2 1^{\overline{q}} w_3 0^s 1^{(\lambda-1)\cdot q} w_1 0^{\overline{p}} w_2 1^{\overline{q}} w_3 0^s \xrightarrow{*}_S 1^r w_1 0^{\overline{p}} w_2 \rho(1^{\overline{q}} w_3 0^s 1^{(\lambda-1)\cdot q} w_1 0^{\overline{p}} w_2 1^{\overline{q}}) w_3 0^s .$$

Owing to the divisibility of r and s, there exist $\mu_1, \mu_2 \in \mathbb{Z}$ and $\gamma_1 \in (0^+1^+)^*, \gamma_2 \in 1^+(0^+1^+)^*$ such that:

$$\rho(1^{\overline{q}} w_3 0^s 1^{(\lambda-1)\cdot q} w_1 0^{\overline{p}} w_2 1^{\overline{q}}) = 1^{\overline{q}+\mu_1 q} \gamma_1 0^{\overline{p}+\mu_2 p} \gamma_2 \text{ or } \rho(1^{\overline{q}} w_3 0^s 1^{(\lambda-1)\cdot q} w_1 0^{\overline{p}} w_2 1^{\overline{q}}) = \infty. \tag{20}$$

It follows that

$$\rho(\alpha 0^p 1^q) = \rho(1^r w_1 0^{\overline{p}} w_2 1^{\overline{q}+\mu_1 q}) \gamma_1 0^{\overline{p}+\mu_2 p} \gamma_2 w_3 0^s \text{ or } \rho(\alpha 0^p 1^q) = \infty. \tag{21}$$

Similarly

$$\alpha^2 0^p 1^q \longrightarrow_S 1^r w_1 0^{\overline{p}} w_2 (1^{\overline{q}} w_3 0^s 1^{(\lambda-1)\cdot q} w_1 0^{\overline{p}} w_2 1^{\overline{q}+\mu_1 q}) \gamma_1 0^{\overline{p}+\mu_2 p} \gamma_2 w_3 0^s \tag{22}$$

$$\xrightarrow{*}_S 1^r w_1 0^{\overline{p}} w_2 \rho(1^{\overline{q}} w_3 0^s 1^{(\lambda-1)\cdot q} w_1 0^{\overline{p}} w_2 1^{\overline{q}+\mu_1 q}) \gamma_1 0^{\overline{p}+\mu_2 p} \gamma_2 w_3 0^s . \tag{23}$$

There exist $\mu_3 \in \mathbb{Z}$ and $\gamma_3 \in 1^+(0^+1^+)^*$ such that:

$$\rho(1^{\overline{q}} w_3 0^s 1^{(\lambda-1)\cdot q} w_1 0^{\overline{p}} w_2 1^{\overline{q}+\mu_1 q}) = 1^{\overline{q}+\mu_1 q}\gamma_1 0^{\overline{p}+\mu_3 p}\gamma_3 \text{ or } \rho(1^{\overline{q}} w_3 0^s 1^{(\lambda-1)\cdot q} w_1 0^{\overline{p}} w_2 1^{\overline{q}+\mu_1 q}) = \infty. \quad (24)$$

It follows that, if $\rho(1^{\overline{q}} w_3 0^s 1^{(\lambda-1)\cdot q} w_1 0^{\overline{p}} w_2 1^{\overline{q}})$, $\rho(1^{\overline{q}} w_3 0^s 1^{(\lambda-1)\cdot q} w_1 0^{\overline{p}} w_2 1^{\overline{q}+\mu_1 q})$ are both finite, then

$$\rho(\alpha^2 0^p 1^q) = \rho(1^r w_1 0^{\overline{p}} w_2 1^{\overline{q}+\mu_1 q})(\gamma_1 0^{\overline{p}+\mu_3 p}\gamma_3)(\gamma_1 0^{\overline{p}+\mu_2 p}\gamma_2) w_3 0^s, \quad (25)$$

and more generally, for every $k \geq 2$,

$$\rho(\alpha^k 0^p 1^q) = \rho(1^r w_1 0^{\overline{p}} w_2 1^{\overline{q}+\mu_1 q})(\gamma_1 0^{\overline{p}+\mu_3 p}\gamma_3)^{k-1}(\gamma_1 0^{\overline{p}+\mu_2 p}\gamma_2) w_3 0^s. \quad (26)$$

Conclusion: $k_0 \leq 2$ or $k_0 = \infty$.

5.5 Case D4: $v = 1^r 0^s$

with $r, s > 0, p \not| s$ and $q \not| r$.
Let $r = \lambda q + r' (0 < r' < q)$, $s = \mu p + s' (0 < s' < p)$, $\alpha = 0^p 1^{q-r'}$. For every $k \geq 0$,

$$\alpha^k 0^p 1^q \xrightarrow{*}_S 1^r 0^s (1^{\lambda \cdot q} 0^s)^k. \quad (27)$$

D4.1: $\lambda = 0$
Then, for every $k \geq 0$, $\rho(\alpha^k 0^p 1^q) = 1^r 0^{(k+1)\cdot s}$. It follows that $k_0 = \infty$.

D4.2: $\mu = 0$
Then, S' fulfills case D4.1, hence $k_0 = \infty$.

D4.3: $\lambda = 1, \mu \geq 2$
Let $k \geq 1$. By (27) and the special value of λ we have

$$\alpha^k 0^p 1^q \xrightarrow{*}_S 1^r 0^s (1^q 0^s)^k = 1^r (0^s 1^q)^k 0^s. \quad (28)$$

Using the fact that $\mu \geq 1$ we get

$$\begin{aligned}
(0^s 1^q)^k \xrightarrow{*}_S (0^{s-p} 1^r 0^s)^k \xrightarrow{*}_S & \ (0^{s'}(1^r 0^s)^\mu)^k & (29)\\
= & \ (0^{s'} 1^r (0^s 1^r)^{\mu-1} 0^s)^k & (30)\\
= & \ 0^{s'} 1^r (0^s 1^r)^{\mu-1} [0^{s+s'} 1^r (0^s 1^r)^{\mu-1}]^{k-1} 0^s & (31)\\
= & \ 0^{s'} 1^r (0^s 1^r)^{\mu-1} [0^{s'} (0^s 1^r)^\mu]^{k-1} 0^s. & (32)
\end{aligned}$$

One can check that $0^s 1^r \xrightarrow{*}_S 0^{s'} 1^r (0^s 1^{r'})^\mu \in \mathrm{Irr}(S)$.
Plugging (32) into (28) and using the derivation just above we obtain

$$\alpha^k 0^p 1^q \xrightarrow{*}_S 1^r 0^{s'} 1^r (0^{s'} 1^r (0^s 1^{r'})^\mu)^{\mu-1} [0^{s'} (0^{s'} 1^r (0^s 1^{r'})^\mu)^\mu]^{k-1} 0^s 0^s. \quad (33)$$

If $2 \cdot s' < p$, the right-handside of (33) is irreducible , hence $k_0 = \infty$.
If $2 \cdot s' > p$, $\rho(0^{2\cdot s'} 1^r) = 0^{2\cdot s'-p} 1^r 0^s 1^{r'}$ so that

$$\rho(\alpha^k 0^p 1^q) = 1^r 0^{s'} 1^r (0^{s'} 1^r (0^s 1^{r'})^\mu)^{\mu-1} [\rho(0^{2\cdot s'} 1^r)(0^s 1^{r'})^\mu (0^{s'} 1^r (0^s 1^{r'})^\mu)^{\mu-1}]^{k-1} 0^s 0^s,$$

hence $k_0 = \infty$. Let us suppose now that $2 \cdot s' = p$. We can rewrite equation (33) as

$$\alpha^k 0^p 1^q \xrightarrow{*}_S \gamma_1 1 0^s 1^{r'} [0^{2\cdot s'} 1^r 0 \gamma_2 1 0^s 1^{r'}]^{k-1} 0^{2\cdot s} \text{ where } \gamma_1 1, 0\gamma_2 1 \in \mathrm{Irr}(S). \quad (34)$$

We then compute:

$$0^{2\cdot s'} 1^r \xrightarrow{*}_S 1^r 0^s 1^{r'}, \quad (35)$$

$$0^s 1^{r+r'} \longrightarrow_S 0^{s-p} 1^r 0^s 1^{2.r'} \longrightarrow_S 0^{s-2p}(1^r 0^s) 1^{r'} 0^s 1^{2.r'} \xrightarrow{*}_S 0^{s'}(1^r 0^s)(1^{r'} 0^s)^{\mu-1} 1^{2.r'},$$

which implies that

$$\rho(0^s 1^{r+r'}) = 0^{s'} 1 \gamma_3, \text{ where } 1\gamma_3 \in \mathrm{Irr}(S). \quad (36)$$

Using (34),(35) and (36) we obtain that for $k \geq 2$

$$\begin{aligned}\alpha^k 0^p 1^q &\xrightarrow{*}_S \gamma_1 1 0^s 1^{r'} [0^{2\cdot s'} 1^r 0 \gamma_2 1 0^s 1^{r'}]^{k-1} 0^{2\cdot s} \\ &\xrightarrow{*}_S \gamma_1 1 0^s 1^{r'} [1^r 0^s 1^{r'} 0 \gamma_2 1 0^s 1^{r'}]^{k-1} 0^{2\cdot s} \\ &= \gamma_1 1 (0^s 1^{r+r'}) [0^s 1^{r'} 0 \gamma_2 1 (0^s 1^{r+r'})]^{k-2} 0^s 1^{r'} 0 \gamma_2 1 0^s 1^{r'} 0^{2\cdot s} \\ &\xrightarrow{*}_S \gamma_1 1 (0^{s'} 1 \gamma_3) [0^s 1^{r'} 0 \gamma_2 1 (0^{s'} 1 \gamma_3)]^{k-2} 0^s 1^{r'} 0 \gamma_2 1 0^s 1^{r'} 0^{2\cdot s} \in \mathrm{Irr}(S),\end{aligned}$$

hence $k_0 = \infty$.

D4.4: $\lambda = \mu = 1$
This subcase is similar to D4.3. Now equation (33) reduces to

$$\alpha^k 0^p 1^q \xrightarrow{*}_S 1^r 0^{s'} 1^r [0^{2s'} 1^r 0^s 1^{r'}]^{k-1} 0^{2s}. \tag{37}$$

If $2 \cdot s' \neq p$, $\rho(\alpha^k 0^p 1^q) = 1^r 0^{s'} 1^r [\rho(0^{2s'} 1^r 0^s 1^{r'})]^{k-1} 0^{2s}$, hence $k_0 = \infty$.
If $2 \cdot s' = p$, assuming $k \geq 2$ and using (37),(35),(36) we get

$$\rho(\alpha^k 0^p 1^q) = 1^r 0^{s'} 1^{2r} [0^s 1^{r'} 0^{s'} 1 \gamma_3]^{k-2} 0^s 1^{r'} 0^s 1^{r'} 0^{2s}.$$

Hence $k_0 = \infty$.

D4.5: $\lambda \geq 2, \mu = 1$ Then S' fulfills case D4.3, hence $k_0 = \infty$.

D4.6: $\lambda \geq 2, \mu \geq 2$
Let $\alpha = 0^p$. Let us consider the derivation

$$\alpha 0^p 1^q \longrightarrow_S \alpha 1^r 0^s \longrightarrow_S 1^r 0^s 1^{r-q} 0^s = 1^r 0^{s-2p} (\alpha 0^p 1^q) 1^{r-2q} 0^s \xrightarrow{\infty}_S .$$

Hence S fulfills the hypothesis of lemma 3.7, case C2.
Conclusion: $k_0 = 1$ or $k_0 = \infty$.

5.6 Case D5: $v = 1^r w_0 0^s$

with $r, s > 0$, $w_0 \in (0^+1^+)^*$, at least one block of 0 in $w_0 0^s$ is not divided by p and every block of 1 is divided by q.
Let us reduce ourselves to the case where $q = 1$ (the value of k_0 in the general case is equal to the value of k_0 for the system obtained by replacing every factor 1^q in u or v by the letter 1): the system under consideration is then $0^p 1 \longrightarrow 1^r w_0 0^s$, where at least one block of 0 in $w_0 0^s$ is not divided by p.
As we exclude the case where u is a factor of v, it follows that every internal block of 0 in v must belong to $0^{<p}$. Let $\alpha = 0^p$.

D5.1: $p > s$
if $r \geq 2$: for every $k \geq 0$

$$\rho(0^{p\cdot k} 0^p 1) = 1^r w_0 0^s (1^{r-1} w_0 0^s)^k.$$

hence $k_0 = \infty$.
if $r = 1$: let us show by induction on $n \geq 1$ that,

$$\forall w \in (10^{<p})^{n-1} 10^*, \rho(0^p w) \in (10^{<p})^* 10^* \tag{38}$$

Let $n = 1$ and $w = 10^m$ for some $m \geq 0$. Then

$$\rho(0^p w) = \rho(0^p 10^m) = 1^r w_0 0^{s+m} \in (10^{<p})^* 10^*.$$

Let $n \geq 1$ and $w = 10^{m_1}10^{m_2}\dots10^{m_n}10^{m_{n+1}}$ where $m_i < p$ (for $i \leq n$) and $m_{n+1} \geq 0$. Then

$$\begin{aligned}\rho(0^p w) &= \rho(0^p 10^{m_1}10^{m_2}\dots10^{m_n}10^{m_{n+1}})\\ &= \rho(1^r w_0 0^{s+m_1}10^{m_2}\dots10^{m_n}10^{m_{n+1}})\\ &= 1^r w_0 0^{s+m_1}10^{m_2}\dots10^{m_n}10^{m_{n+1}}(\text{ if } s+m_1 < p) \text{ or}\\ &= 1^r w_0 0^{s+m_1-p}\rho(0^p 10^{m_2}\dots10^{m_n}10^{m_{n+1}})(\text{ if } p \leq s+m_1 < 2\cdot p)\\ &\in (10^{<p})^* 10^* (\text{ by induction hypothesis }).\end{aligned}$$

Using (38), one can then prove by induction on $k \geq 0$ that

$$\forall k \geq 0, \rho(0^{p\cdot k}0^p 1) \in (10^{<p})^* 10^*. \tag{39}$$

It follows from (39) that $k_0 = \infty$.

D5.2: $p = s$ Let us consider the unique morphism $\varphi : \{0,1\}^* \to \{0,1\}^*$ such that

$$\varphi(0) = 0, \quad \varphi(1) = 1^r w_0.$$

Then , for every $k \geq 0$

$$\rho(\alpha^k 0^p 1) = \varphi^k(1^r w_0)0^{p\cdot(k+1)}.$$

Hence $k_0 = \infty$.

D5.3: $p < s$
if $|v|_1 = 1$: that is $v = 10^s$.
Then, for every $k \geq 0$

$$\rho(\alpha^k 0^p 1) = 10^{s\cdot(k+1)},$$

which shows that $k_0 = \infty$.
if $|v|_1 \geq 2$: let us consider some integer k such that

$$k \cdot s \geq (k+1)\cdot p. \tag{40}$$

Using the fact that $p < s$, one can prove by induction on l that, for every $l \geq 0$,

$$\alpha^l 1 \xrightarrow{*}_S w_l 0^{l\cdot s}, \text{ for some } w_l \in \{0,1\}^*.$$

We obtain that

$$\alpha^k(0^p 1) \longrightarrow_S (\alpha^k 1)1^{r-1}w_0 0^s \xrightarrow{*}_S w_k 0^{k\cdot s}1^{r-1}w_0 0^s,$$

and by (40), $w_k 0^{k\cdot s}1^{r-1}w_0 0^s = \gamma 0^{(k+1)\cdot p}1\delta$ for some $\gamma, \delta \in \{0,1\}^*$. Hence

$$\alpha^k(0^p 1) \xrightarrow{*}_S \gamma\alpha^k(0^p 1)\delta,$$

which shows that for every k fulfilling (40), $\rho(\alpha^k(0^p 1)) = \infty$. Hence $k_0 \leq \lceil p/(s-p)\rceil$.
Conclusion: $k_0 \leq \lceil p/(s-p)\rceil$ or $k_0 = \infty$.
Case D'5: $v = 1^r w_0 0^s$, where $r, s > 0$, at least one block of 1 is not divided by q and every block of 0 is divided by p. Then S' fulfills case D5.
Case D6: $v = 0^t 1^r w_0 0^s$, with $r, s, t > 0, w_0 \in (0^+1^+)^*$. Then $k_0 \leq \lceil p/(s-h)\rceil$ or $k_0 = \infty$.
Case D'6: $v = 1^t 0^r w_0 1^s$, with $r, s, t > 0, w_0 \in (1^+0^+)^*$. Then S' fulfills case D6.
Case D7: $v = 0^t 1^r w_0 1^s$, with $r, s, t > 0, w_0 \in (0^+1^+)^*0^+$. Then $k_0 = 1$ or $k_0 = \infty$.
Case D8: $v = 0^t 1^s$, with $s, t \geq 0$. Then $\mathrm{L}_+(S) = \emptyset$.

By the above discussion the proof of the following theorem is achieved.

Theorem 5.4 *Given any system $S = 0^p 1^q \to v$ (where $p > 0, q > 0, v \in \{0,1\}^*$)*
(1) one can construct either a finite automaton recognizing $\mathrm{L}_+(S)$ (in cases Di, $1 \leq i \leq 8$), or a finite automaton recognizing $\mathrm{R}_+(S)$ (in cases D'2,D'5,D'6).
(2)one can decide whether S is u-terminating or not.

6 The termination monoid

Let us consider a system $S = u \longrightarrow v$, such that u has no self-overlap. We recall that X is the alphabet $\{0,1\}$. We introduce the alphabet $\bar{X} = \{0,1,\infty\}$ and the following monoids:

$$M = X^*/\overset{*}{\longleftrightarrow}_S, \bar{M} = M/\bar{I_+}$$

where $\bar{I_+}$ is the image of the ideal I_+ of X^* in the quotient M by the canonical projection, and $M/\bar{I_+}$ is the so-called Rees-quotient of M by the ideal $\bar{I_+}$. By definition, $\bar{M}$ admits the following presentation over $\bar{X}$:

$$u = v; x \cdot \infty = \infty (\forall x \in \bar{X}); \infty \cdot x = \infty (\forall x \in \bar{X}); w = \infty (\forall w \in I_+). \tag{41}$$

Let us denote by $\Pi : M \longrightarrow \bar{M}$ the canonical projection induced by the Rees-quotient. As S is confluent, I_+ is saturated by relation $\overset{*}{\longleftrightarrow}_S$. It follows that the restriction of Π on $M - \bar{I_+}$ is injective. We denote by $\bar{S} \subseteq \bar{X}^* \times \bar{X}^*$ the set of all pairs of words shown in (41). By the above remark, the subset $\bar{W} = \mathrm{Irr}(S) \cup \{\infty\} \subseteq \bar{X}^*$ is a system of representatives (mod $\overset{*}{\longleftrightarrow}_{\bar{S}}$). Let us define a map $\bar{\rho} : \bar{X}^* \longrightarrow \bar{W}$ by:

$$\forall w \in \bar{X}^*, w \overset{*}{\longleftrightarrow}_{\bar{S}} \bar{\rho}(w) \text{ and } \bar{\rho}(w) \in \bar{W}.$$

Theorem 6.1 *Let $S = 0^p1^q \longrightarrow v$, where $p > 0, q > 0$ and $v \in (0+1)^*$. If S is not u-terminating then $\bar{\rho}$ is a rational function.*

In other words, $\bar{M}$ is a *rational* monoid in the sense of [Sak87, PS90].
The fact that

$$\rho = \bar{\rho} \cap X^*_\infty \times \bar{X}^*, \bar{\rho} = \rho \cup \{(w,\infty) \mid w \in \bar{X}^* \cdot \infty \cdot \bar{X}^*\}$$

shows that $\bar{\rho}$ is rational iff ρ is rational. Hence we are reduced to prove that ρ is rational. By symmetry we can also suppose that v is not in $(1^+0^+)^*1$. For any word $w \in X^*$ we define the map $\rho_w : \bar{W} \longrightarrow \bar{W}$ by

$$\forall w' \in \bar{W}, \ \rho_w(w') = \rho(w' \cdot w).$$

Lemma 6.2 *ρ_u is rational.*

Proof:

$$\rho_u = \{(\beta w_1, \beta w_2) \mid w_1 \in \mathrm{M}_-(S), \beta w_1 \in \mathrm{Irr}(S), \rho(w_1 u) = w_2\}$$
$$\cup \{(\beta w_1, \infty) \mid w_1 \in \mathrm{M}_+(S), \beta w_1 \in \mathrm{Irr}(S)\} \cup \{(\infty,\infty)\},$$

hence it suffices to prove that $\rho_u \cap (\mathrm{M}_-(S) \times \bar{W})$ is rational. If $v \in 0(0+1)^*$, $\mathrm{M}_-(S)$ is finite hence $\rho_u \cap (\mathrm{M}_-(S) \times \bar{W})$ is trivially rational. Let us suppose now that $v = 1^r v' 0^s$ where $r > 0, s > 0, v' \in (0^+1^+)^*$. If S fulfills the hypothesis of lemma 3.7 case C2 or the hypothesis of lemma 3.9, then $\mathrm{M}_-(S)$ is finite too and the same argument applies. It remains to treate the case where S fulfills the hypothesis of lemma 3.7 case C3 or C4 (C1 is impossible because S is supposed to be non u-terminating). Let us suppose case C3 is fulfilled and let $\alpha = 0^p1^{q'}$ be the unique strict prefix of u which crosses 1^r. Let $w \in \mathrm{M}_-(S)$, it must have the form

$$w = \alpha^{k_1}\alpha'_1\alpha^{k_2}\alpha'_2 \ldots \alpha^{k_m}\alpha'_m\alpha^{k_{m+1}} \tag{42}$$

where $m \geq 0, \forall i \in [1, m+1], 0 \leq k_i < k_0$ and $\forall i \in [1,m], \alpha'_i = 0^p1^{q'_i}$ for some $q'_i \neq q'$. Then

$$\rho_u(w) = \rho(\alpha^{k_1}\alpha'_1 1^r)[1^{-r}\rho(\alpha^{k_2}\alpha'_2 1^r)] \ldots [1^{-r}\rho(\alpha^{k_m}\alpha'_m 1^r)][1^{-r}\rho(\alpha^{k_{m+1}}u)], \tag{43}$$

because every $\rho(\alpha^{k_i}\alpha'_i 1^r)$ begins by 1^r0 (by lemma 3.5) and every $\rho(\alpha'_i 1^r 0)$ is a left-separator (by lemma 3.4). Formula (42) (43) show that ρ_u is rational (it is, indeed, a right-to-left *subsequential function* (see [Ber79, p.100] for a definition)). Case C4 is very similar and could be treated in the same way. □

Lemma 6.3 *$\rho_0, \rho_1, \rho_\infty$ are rational functions.*

Proof:

$$\rho_0 = \{(w, w0) \mid w \in \mathrm{Irr}(S)\} \cup \{(\infty,\infty)\}, \ \rho_\infty = \{(w,\infty) \mid w \in \bar{W}\},$$
$$\rho_1 = \{(w, w1) \mid w1 \in \mathrm{Irr}(S)\} \cup \{(w, \rho_u(w1u^{-1})) \mid w1 \in \mathrm{Irr}(S) \cdot u\} \cup \{(\infty,\infty)\}.$$

Considering these formula, ρ_0, ρ_∞ are trivially rational and ρ_1 is rational by lemma 6.2. □

Remark. Lemma 6.3 shows that $\bar{M}$ has an *automatic* structure over the set of generators $\{0, 1, \infty\}$, with set of representatives $\bar{W}$ (in a sense generalizing in a straightforward way the definition of [ECH+92]).

Lemma 6.4 *Let S be a system fulfilling hypothesis of lemma 3.7 case C3 or C4 and non u-terminating. Then there exists an integer K such that $\forall w \in \mathrm{M}_-(S), |\rho(wu)| < K$ or $(\rho(wu))^{(K)}$ is a right-separator .*

Sketch of proof: Let us suppose C3 is fulfilled, let k_0 be the integer associated to S (by hypothesis $k_0 \neq \infty$) and $\alpha = 0^p 1^{q'}$ the word associated to S. Then for every $\alpha_1 = 0^p 1^{q_1}, \alpha_2 = 0^p 1^{q_2}$ with $0 \leq q_i < q, q_i \neq q'$ and every $k_1 < k_0, k_2 < k_0$,

$$\alpha_1 \alpha^{k_1} \alpha_2 \alpha^{k_2} u \xrightarrow{*}_S 1^r v' 0^s (1^{r-q+q_1} v' 0^s)(1^{r-q} v' 0^s)^{k_1} (1^{r-q+q_2} v' 0^s)(1^{r-q} v' 0^s)^{k_2}.$$

By lemma 3.4 $\rho(1^r v' 0^s 1^{r-q+q_1})0$ is a left-separator. The leftmost block of 0, among all the blocks of 0 in $1v'0^s(1^{r-q}v'0^s)^{k_1} 1^{r-q+q_2}$ which are not divided by p, together with the symbol 1 immediately on its left, is a right-separator. It follows that for every $\beta \in (0+1)^*$,

$$\rho(\beta\alpha_1\alpha^{k_1}\alpha_2\alpha^{k_2}u) = [\rho(\beta 1^r v' 0^s 1^{r-q+q_1} 0)(10)^{-1}]\rho(1v'0^s(1^{r-q}v'0^s)^{k_1}(1^{r-q+q_2}v'0^s)(1^{r-q}v'0^s)^{k_2}).$$

where $\rho(1v'0^s(1^{r-q}v'0^s)^{k_1}(1^{r-q+q_2}v'0^s)(1^{r-q}v'0^s)^{k_2})$ is a right-separator. Let us set

$$K_0 = 2 \cdot k_0 \cdot |\, u \,| \text{ and } K = \max\{|\, \rho(wu) \,| \mid w \in \mathrm{M}_-(S), |\, w \,| \leq K_0\} + 1.$$

One can check that every word $w \in \mathrm{M}_-(S)$ of length $\geq K_0$ has the form $\beta\alpha_1\alpha^{k_1}\alpha_2\alpha^{k_2}$ considered above, that $|\alpha_1\alpha^{k_1}\alpha_2\alpha^{k_2}| \leq K_0$ and consequently

$$\rho(1v'0^s(1^{r-q}v'0^s)^{k_1}(1^{r-q+q_2}v'0^s)(1^{r-q}v'0^s)^{k_2})| \leq K.$$

□

Outline of proof of theorem 6.1

Let us notice that, if $w = x_1 x_2 \ldots x_i \ldots x_n$ (where $x_i \in X$) then,

$$\bar{\rho}(w) = \rho_{x_n}(\ldots(\rho_{x_i}(\ldots\rho_{x_2}(\rho_{x_1}(\epsilon))\ldots)\ldots). \tag{44}$$

1- Under the hypothesis of lemma 3.7 case C2, or lemma 3.8 or lemma 3.9, $\mathrm{M}_-(S)$ is finite. Let us set $K = \max\{|w|, w \in \mathrm{M}_-(S)\}$. The i-th step of the calculation (44) consists in computing $\rho(\rho(x_1 x_2 \ldots x_{i-1})x_i)$ and does only use the suffix $\rho(x_1 x_2 \ldots x_{i-1})^{(K)}$. Hence a finite left-to-right subsequential transducer, which keeps in its memory this suffix of length K of the computed part of the argument, can compute $\bar{\rho}$.
2- Under the hypothesis of lemma 3.7 case C3 or C4, the above argument is no more valid. Nevertheless, with the help of lemma 6.2 and lemma 6.4, one can define a finite 2-automaton which recognizes $\bar{\rho}$ (but it is no more right-subsequential as is ρ_u, nor left-subsequential as was $\bar{\rho}$ in part 1 of the proof).□

Corollary 6.5 *Let $S = 0^p 1^q \longrightarrow v$, where $p > 0, q > 0$ and $v \in (0+1)^*$, be a fixed system. Then the termination problem for S can be solved in linear time.*

Proof: If S is u-terminating then the termination problem for S is trivial. Let us suppose now that S is not u-terminating. For every $w \in \{0,1\}^*$, S terminates on w iff $\bar{\rho}(w) \neq \infty$. By theorem 6.1 $\bar{\rho}$ is a rational function, hence it can be computed in linear time (see theorem 5.2 of [Ber79]). □

7 Examples

Let us apply our results and constructions on some particular systems.

Example 1 $S = 0011 \longrightarrow 1111000$. It fulfills case D5 of the discussion of §5, hence $k_0 \leq 2$ or $k_0 = \infty$. We see that $\alpha = 00$. Hence we compute

$$\rho(\alpha 0011) = 1^4 01^4 0^6, (\alpha)^2 0011 \xrightarrow{*}_S 1^4 01^8 [(\alpha)^2 0011] 0^6$$

$$Q_0 = 0011, k_0 = 2; Q_1 = 00111, k_1 = 2; Q_2 = 001111, k_2 = 1; Q_3 = 0011111, k_3 = 1.$$

The automaton $\mathcal{A}_S$ (which recognizes $\mathrm{M}_+(S)$) follows. We show on figure 1 the "trim" version of $\mathcal{A}_S$. Notice that $\infty = P_{0,2} = P_{3,1}$ and that $P_{2,0}$ is *not* co-accessible, hence it does not appear on this schema.

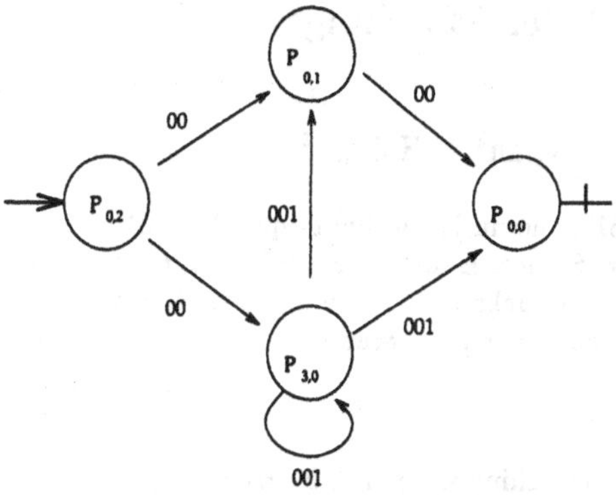

Fig. 1. the g.f.a.$\mathcal{A}_S$.

Example 2 $S = 0^2 1^2 \longrightarrow 1^3 0^5 1 0 1^4 0^3$. It fulfills case D1 of the discussion of §5, hence $k_0 \leq 1$ or $k_0 = \infty$. We see that $\alpha = 001$. Hence we compute $\rho(\alpha 0011) = 1^3(0^5 1 0 1^4 0 1^3 0^5 1 0 1^4 0^3) 0^5 1 0 1^4 0^3$.
We conclude that $k_0 = \infty$, i.e. $M_+(S) = \emptyset$ and S is u-terminating.

Example 3 $S = 0001 \longrightarrow 01011000$. It fulfills case D6.2.2 of the discussion of §5, hence $k_0 \leq \lceil p + h/(s-h) \rceil = 5$ or $k_0 = \infty$. We see that $\alpha = 00$. Hence we compute

$$\rho(\alpha 0001) = (01011)0(01011)^2 0^6, [(\alpha)^2 0001] \xrightarrow{*}_S (01011)0(01011)^3 0(01011)^2 [(\alpha)^2 0001] 1 (01011) 0^6$$

We conclude that $k_0 = 2$. Hence $M_+(S) = \{0^4\}$.
Aknowledgements: I thank Yuri Matiyasevich for useful discussions on these topics and an anonymous referee for pointing out several mistakes in a previous version of the paper.

References

[Ber79] J. Berstel. *Transductions and Context-Free Languages*. Teubner, 1979.

[BO93] R.V. Book and F. Otto. *String Rewriting Systems. Texts and monographs in Computer Science*. Springer-Verlag, 1993.

[Der87] N. Dershowitz. Termination of rewriting. *Journal of Symbolic Computation no 3*, pages 69–116, 1987.

[DH93] N. Dershowitz and C. Hoot. Topics in termination. In *Proceedings of the 5th RTA, edited by C. Kirchner*, pages 198–212. Springer,LNCS 690, 1993.

[DJ91] N. Dershowitz and J.P. Jouannaud. Rewrite Systems. In *Handbook of theoretical computer science, vol.B, Chapter 2*, pages 243–320. Elsevier, 1991.

[ECH+92] D.B.A. Epstein, J.W. Cannon, D.F. Holt, S.V.F. Levy, M.S. Paterson, and W.P. Thurston. *Word processing in groups*. Jones and Bartlett, 1992.

[Ges91] A. Geser. Relative termination. *Report 91-03, Ulmer Informatik-Berichte, Universität Ulm*, 1991.

[Kur90] W. Kurth. Termination und konfluenz von semi-Thue-systemen mit nur einer regel. *Dissertation, Technische Universität Clausthal*, 1990.

[McN94] R. McNaughton. The uniform halting problem for one-rule semi-Thue systems. *Report 94-18 of Rensselaer Polytechnic Institute*, 1994.

[MS96] Y. Matiyasevich and G. Sénizergues. Decision problems for semi-Thue systems with a few rules. *To appear in the proceedings of LICS 96*, 1996.

[PS90] M. Pelletier and J. Sakarovitch. Easy multiplications, II. extensions of rational semigroups. *Information and Computation*, pages 18–59, 1990.

[Sak87] J. Sakarovitch. Easy multiplications, I. the realm of kleene's theorem. *Information and Computation*, pages 173–197, 1987.

[Sén96] G. Sénizergues. The termination and uniform termination problems for one rule of the form $0^p 1^q \longrightarrow v$. *In preparation, preliminary version available by email on request to : ges@labri.u-bordeaux.fr*, 1996.

[ZG95] H. Zantema and A. Geser. A complete characterisation of termination of $0^p 1^q \rightarrow 1^r 0^s$. In *Proceedings RTA95, LNCS 914*, pages 41–55. Springer-Verlag, 1995.

Efficient Second-Order Matching*

Régis Curien[1] Zhenyu Qian[2] Hui Shi[2]

[1] CRIN-CNRS & INRIA-Lorraine, 615, rue du jardin botanique, BP 101
54602 Vandoeuvre-les-Nancy Cedex, France. E-mail: curien@loria.fr
[2] Universität Bremen, FB3 Informatik, Bibliothekstr. 4, 28359 Bremen, Germany
E-mail: {qian,shi}@informatik.uni-bremen.de

Abstract. The standard second-order matching algorithm by Huet may be expansive in matching a flexible-rigid pair. On one hand, many fresh free variables may need to be introduced; on the other hand, attempts are made to match the heading free variable on the flexible side with every "top layer" on the rigid side and every argument of the heading free variable with every subterm covered by the "top layer". We propose a new second-order matching algorithm, which introduces no fresh free variables and just considers some selected "top layers", arguments of the heading free variable and subterms covered by the corresponding "top layers". A first implementation shows that the new algorithm is more efficient both in time and space than the standard one for a great number of matching problems.

1 Introduction

Second-order matching is a useful mechanism. For example, Huet and Lang used second-order matching for program transformations [11]. Boy de la Tour and Caferra [1, 2] used second-order matching to recognize patterns in formulas and to propose lemmas in automatic theorem proving by analogy. Curien followed the similar line to use second-order matching for computing similarities between formulas in automatic analogical proofs [4]. Second-order matching is also used by Kolbe and Walther [12] for reusing proofs. The standard second-order matching algorithm was given by Huet [10] (see also [11]).

Let us use $s \stackrel{\trianglelefteq}{=} t$ to denote a matching problem, where s is a second-order simply typed λ-term (short: term) possibly containing free variables and t a term containing no free variables. An essential case that a second-order matching algorithm should consider is the so-called *flexible-rigid* case, where a matching problem $\lambda\overline{x}.F(\overline{s_m}) \stackrel{\trianglelefteq}{=} \lambda\overline{x}.t$ with F being a free variable should be solved. A term with a free variable at head is called a *flexible* term. If observing the matching process step by step, the standard algorithm may use an imitation rule for the flexible-rigid case, which yields a partial substitution $\{F \mapsto \lambda y_m.a(H_1(\overline{y_m}), \cdots, H_n(\overline{y_m}))\}$, where a is the head of t and $H_1, \cdots, H_n$ are all fresh free variables. If observing the whole matching process the standard algorithm attempts to match F with every "top layer"[3] of t, and every s_i with every subterm covered by a corresponding "top layer". From both aspects as

* Research partially supported by ESPRIT Basic Research WG *COMPASS* 6112 and BMBF Project *UniForM*.

[3] Formally we will define a "top layer" of a term as a context later.

above, the standard algorithm suffers from efficiency problems. The problem with the imitation rule is that it introduces many fresh free variables. In fact, these fresh free variables never need to occur in a final resulting matcher. Thus the efficiency can be increased if they are not introduced at all. The problem with the whole matching process is that many attempts to match F with a "top layer" of t, and to match every s_i with every subterm covered by a "top layer" may fail. Thus the efficiency can be increased when some of the failure cases can be foreseen in some way.

In this paper we propose a new algorithm for second-order matching and proves its soundness and completeness. The new algorithm improves the efficiency of the standard algorithm for the flexible-rigid case $\lambda\overline{x}.F(\overline{s_m}) \stackrel{\triangleleft}{=} \lambda\overline{x}.t$ by directly matching F with a "top layer" of t and solving some matching subproblems consisting of some of $s_1, \cdots, s_m$ and some subterms covered by the "top layer". In addition, the new algorithm does not introduce any fresh free variables and foresees many failure cases in matching subproblems. It should be mentioned that some of the ideas presented in this paper have already been implemented elsewhere, e.g. for inductive proofs in a theorem prover by Boyer and Moore [3]. However, to our knowledge, they have not been studied so systematically and formally as in the current paper.

Theoretically, the new algorithm is by no means worse than the standard one in the sense that for the same original matching problem all matching subproblems encountered during execution of the new algorithm are also encountered during execution of the standard algorithm. However, one may still be wondering whether the increased cost for foreseeing the failure cases in a matching subproblem outweigh the gains in practice. To check this, we implement both Huet's algorithm and the new one. Our measurement shows that the new algorithm has indeed a better performance than Huet's in many cases. In particular, our algorithm is much better for these matching problems $s \stackrel{\triangleleft}{=} t$ where s contains many free variables or t contains many bound variables. Unfortunately, it turns out that our algorithm may have a worse performance than Huet's in the case where many constant symbols (i.e. function symbols with arity 0) occur in t.

The paper is organized as follows. Section 2 introduces some basic not(ta)ions. In Section 3, we review the standard second-order matching algorithm formulated via transformations. The new algorithm is presented via transformations in Section 4. The termination, soundness and completeness of the new algorithm are shown in Section 5. In Section 6 we briefly describe an implementation of the new algorithm and compare it with an implementation of the standard algorithm. We conclude in Section 7.

2 Preliminaries

Types are constructed in the usual way as in simply typed λ-calculus. We use $\mathcal{T}_0$ to denote the set of *base types*. We use $\mathcal{T}$ to denote the set of *types*, and write $\alpha_1 \to \cdots \to \alpha_n \to \beta$ and $\overline{\alpha_n} \to \beta$ for $(\alpha_1 \to \cdots (\alpha_n \to \beta))$. In $\overline{\alpha_n} \to \beta$, β is assumed in $\mathcal{T}_0$. The *order* $O(\alpha)$ of a type α is defined as $O(\alpha) = 1$ for $\alpha \in \mathcal{T}_0$, and $O(\overline{\alpha_n} \to \beta) = max\{O(\alpha_i) \mid 1 \le i \le n\} + 1$ otherwise.

For each $\alpha \in \mathcal{T}$, $\mathcal{C}_\alpha$ and $\mathcal{V}_\alpha$ denote pairwise disjoint denumerable sets of *function symbols* and *variables*, resp. *Constant symbols* are function symbols of base types.

Function symbols and variables are also called *atoms*. We denote $\mathcal{C} = \bigcup_{\alpha\in\mathcal{T}} \mathcal{C}_\alpha$, $\mathcal{V} = \bigcup_{\alpha\in\mathcal{T}} \mathcal{V}_\alpha$ and $\mathcal{A} = \mathcal{C} \cup \mathcal{V}$.

The set $\mathcal{T}_\alpha$ of λ-*terms* (short: *terms*) of type $\alpha \in \mathcal{T}$ is defined by the usual construction of *application* and *abstraction*. Let $\mathcal{T} = \bigcup_{\alpha\in\mathcal{T}} \mathcal{T}_\alpha$. We use $\tau(t)$ to denote the type α for $t \in \mathcal{T}_\alpha$. In an abstraction $\lambda x.t$ the term t is said to be *covered* by the λ-*binder* λx. The term $(\ldots(a\ s_1)\ldots\ s_n)$ may be written as $a(s_1,\ldots,s_n)$, $a(\overline{s_n})$ or $a(\overline{s})$, and $\lambda x_1.\cdots\lambda x_k.t$ as $\lambda\overline{x_k}.t$ or $\lambda\overline{x}.t$.

For a term t we use $|t|$ to denote the number of atoms in t.

Terms are only compared modulo α-conversion. Bound and free variables are defined as usual. Furthermore, we always assume that within one term no λ-binders occur more than once and no variables occur both bound and free, unless otherwise stated. The set of all free variables in a syntactic object O is denoted by $\mathcal{FV}(O)$ and that of all bound variables by $\mathcal{BV}(O)$.

For $\mathcal{X} \in \{\beta, \eta, \beta\eta\}$, we use $\longrightarrow_\mathcal{X}$ to denote one step $\mathcal{X}$-reduction and $=_\mathcal{X}$ the equivalence relation induced by $\longrightarrow_\mathcal{X}$. Let s be a term. Then $s{\downarrow_\mathcal{X}}$ denotes the $\mathcal{X}$-normal form such that $s \longrightarrow^*_\mathcal{X} s{\downarrow_\mathcal{X}}$. If t is a β-normal form, then t must be of the form $\lambda\overline{x}.a(\overline{s_n})$ with $a \in \mathcal{A}$ and each s_i a β-normal form. The atom a is called the *head* and denoted by $\mathcal{H}(t)$. The β-normal form t is called *flexible* if $a \in \mathcal{FV}(t)$ and *rigid* otherwise. A β-normal form $\lambda\overline{x}.a(\overline{s_n})$ may be said to be *long* if $a(\overline{s_n})$ is of a base type and each s_i is long. Let $s{\uparrow_\eta}$ denote the long β-normal form (uniquely) obtained by η-expanding a β-normal form s. For single variable F, $F{\uparrow_\eta}$ may still be written as F. We only consider long β-normal forms in the sequel and thus will use $=$ instead of $=_{\beta\eta}$.

A long β-normal form is said to be *second-order* (or *first-order*) if the types of its free variables are at most of order 2 (or 1, respectively). Huet's second-order matching algorithm works for second-order terms having constants and bound variables of order at most three. In [7], Dowek dropped this restriction.

A *substitution* σ is a function denoted by $\{X_1 \mapsto t_1, \cdots, X_n \mapsto t_n\}$ or $\{\overline{X_n \mapsto t_n}\}$, where $X_i \in \mathcal{V}$, $t_i \in \mathcal{T}$ and $\tau(X_i) = \tau(t_i)$ hold for $i = 1,\ldots,n$, the *domain* is denoted by $\mathcal{D}(\sigma) = \{X_1,\cdots,X_n\}$, and the set of *newly introduced variables* by $\mathcal{I}(\sigma) = \bigcup_{i=1,\cdots,n} \mathcal{FV}(t_i)$. The application of a substitution σ to a term s is written as $\sigma(s)$. It is always assumed in $\sigma(s)$ that the term s have been α-converted such that $\mathcal{BV}(s) \cap \mathcal{I}(\sigma) = \emptyset$, in order to avoid capture of free variables of $\mathcal{I}(\sigma)$ by bound variables of $\mathcal{BV}(s)$. Furthermore, it is always assumed that $\mathcal{BV}(s) \cap \mathcal{D}(\sigma) = \emptyset$, and therefore whenever s is $\lambda x.t$ we have $\sigma(s) = \lambda x.\sigma(t)$ automatically. The *composition* $\sigma\theta$ of two substitutions σ and θ is defined by $(\sigma\theta)(X) = \sigma(\theta(X))$ for every $X \in \mathcal{V}$.

Two substitutions σ and θ are *compatible* if $\sigma(X) = \theta(X)$ holds for all $X \in \mathcal{D}(\sigma) \cap \mathcal{D}(\theta)$. If σ and θ are compatible, then the *union* $\sigma \cup \theta$ are defined as $\sigma \cup \theta(X) = \sigma(X)$ for $X \in \mathcal{D}(\sigma)$, and $\sigma \cup \theta(X) = \theta(X)$ for $X \in \mathcal{D}(\theta)$ and $\sigma \cup \theta(X) = X$ otherwise.

If $\mathcal{W} \subseteq \mathcal{V}$, then the *restriction* $\sigma_{|\mathcal{W}}$ is a substitution defined by $\sigma_{|\mathcal{W}}(X) = \sigma(X)$ for $X \in \mathcal{W}$, $\sigma_{|\mathcal{W}}(X) = X$ otherwise. We use $\sigma_{|-\mathcal{W}}$ to denote $\sigma_{|\mathcal{D}(\sigma)-\mathcal{W}}$.

A substitution σ is said to be *normalized* if $\sigma(X)$ is a long β-normal form for each $X \in \mathcal{D}(\sigma)$. Normalized σ satisfies $(\sigma(t){\downarrow_\beta}){\uparrow_\eta} = \sigma(t){\downarrow_\beta}$ for every long β-normal form t. Only normalized substitutions are considered in this paper.

If $\mathcal{W} \subseteq \mathcal{V}$ and σ and θ are two substitutions, then $\sigma = \theta\ [\mathcal{W}]$ means $\sigma(X) = \theta(X)$ for each $X \in \mathcal{W}$. Furthermore, $\sigma \leq \theta\ [\mathcal{W}]$ means that there is a substitution ρ such that $\rho\sigma = \theta\ [\mathcal{W}]$. $[\mathcal{W}]$ may be omitted if $\mathcal{W} = \mathcal{V}$. For any substitution σ and finite

$\mathcal{W} \supseteq \mathcal{D}(\sigma)$, there always exists a substitution σ' such that $\mathcal{D}(\sigma') \cap \mathcal{I}(\sigma') = \emptyset$, $\mathcal{D}(\sigma) = \mathcal{D}(\sigma')$ and $\sigma \leq \sigma' [\mathcal{W}]$ and $\sigma' \leq \sigma [\mathcal{W}]$. Since $\mathcal{W}$ in question is usually known, we may restrict our attention only to the substitutions like σ' without loss of generality. Note that $\mathcal{D}(\sigma') \cap \mathcal{I}(\sigma') = \emptyset$ implies $\sigma' \sigma' = \sigma'$.

Positions are strings of integers. Let p, q range over positions. The set of all positions of a term t, denoted by $\mathcal{P}os(t)$, consists of all positions corresponding to a subterm of t in the following way, where the root position is the empty string, denoted by Λ:

$$t_{|\Lambda} = t$$
$$(\lambda x.t)_{|1.p} = t_{|p}$$
$$a(t_1, \ldots, t_n)_{|k \cdot p} = (t_k)_{|p} \quad \text{where } 1 \leq k \leq n$$

A position p is *above* q, denoted by $p \leq q$, when p is a prefix of q. We write $p < q$ for $p \leq q$ and $p \neq q$. When $p \not\leq q$ and $q \not\leq p$, p and q are said to be *independent*.

For a term t, independent positions $p_1, \ldots, p_k$ of t and terms $s_1, \cdots, s_k$ with $\tau(t_{|p_i}) = \tau(s_i)$ for $i = 1, \ldots, k$, we use $t[s_1, \cdots, s_k]_{p_1, \ldots, p_k}$ to denote the result of replacing each $t_{|p_i}$ in t by s_i. Furthermore, we may use the special symbols $\Box_1, \cdots, \Box_k$ to denote holes in a term and call a term $t[\Box_1, \cdots, \Box_k]_{p_1, \ldots, p_k}$ a *context*.

In the sequel, we use c, d, e, f, g and h to denote function symbols, a and b atoms, x, y and z bound variables, X, Y, Z, F, G and H free variables, s, t, u and v terms, σ, θ and ρ substitutions, p and q positions. Furthermore, $\sigma(t)$ always denotes $\sigma(t)\downarrow_\beta$, unless stated otherwise.

3   The standard second-order matching

A (second-order) *matching pair* $s \stackrel{\triangleleft}{=} t$ is a pair of second-order terms s and t, where $\tau(s) = \tau(t)$ holds, the term t contains no free variables and the term s may contain free variables whose types are of at most second-order. The term s or t can also be referred as the *left-hand side* or *rigid-hand side* of the matching pair. Since only long η-forms are considered, we may always assume that s and t have the same sequence of outer λ-binders. A (second-order) *matching problem* is a multiset of matching pairs. We use S to denote a matching problem.

A substitution θ is called a *matcher* of $s \stackrel{\triangleleft}{=} t$ if $\theta(s) = t$. A substitution is a matcher of S if and only if it is a matcher of each matching pair in S. A set of matchers of S is said to be *complete* if whenever θ is a matcher of S, there is a matcher σ in the set such that $\sigma \leq \theta [\mathcal{F}V(S)]$ holds.

A matching algorithm can be described via transformations on pairs $\langle S, \theta \rangle$ of matching problems S and substitutions θ. For an input pair $\langle S_0, \{\} \rangle$, the algorithm *succeeds* when there is a sequence of transformations terminating with $\langle \{\}, \sigma \rangle$, in which case σ is a matcher of the initial problem S_0, fails when there exist no sequences of transformations that terminate with a pair of the above form. In the case of failure, S_0 is not matchable.

In this section a second-order matching algorithm is described via the transformations. The transformations are a reformulation of the standard algorithm by Huet [10] (see also [11]). They are in fact a restriction of the corresponding transformations by Snyder and Gallier [19].

The first transformation is the usual simplification rule, which simplifies a matching pair with identical heading symbols on both sides.

$$\langle\{\lambda\overline{x}.a(\overline{s_n}) \stackrel{\triangleleft}{=} \lambda\overline{x}.a(\overline{t_n})\} \cup S, \sigma\rangle \Longrightarrow \langle\{\overline{\lambda\overline{x}.s_n \stackrel{\triangleleft}{=} \lambda\overline{x}.t_n}\} \cup S, \sigma\rangle \qquad \text{(D)}$$

The second rule is the usual imitation rule, which deals with a flexible left-hand side.

$$\langle\{\lambda\overline{x}.F(\overline{s_n}) \stackrel{\triangleleft}{=} \lambda\overline{x}.a(\overline{t_m})\} \cup S, \sigma\rangle \Longrightarrow \langle\{\overline{\lambda\overline{x}.H_m(\overline{\sigma'(s_n)}) \stackrel{\triangleleft}{=} \lambda\overline{x}.t_m}\} \cup \sigma'(S), \sigma'\sigma\rangle \quad \text{(I)}$$

where $\sigma' = \{F \mapsto \lambda\overline{y_n}.a(H_1(\overline{y_n}), \cdots, H_m(\overline{y_n}))\}$, $H_1, \cdots, H_m$ are fresh new free variables of appropriate types.

The third rule is the usual projection rule, which also deals with a flexible left-hand side:

$$\langle\{\lambda\overline{x}.F(\overline{s_n}) \stackrel{\triangleleft}{=} \lambda\overline{x}.t\} \cup S, \sigma\rangle \Longrightarrow \langle\{\lambda\overline{x}.\sigma'(s_i) \stackrel{\triangleleft}{=} \lambda\overline{x}.t\} \cup \sigma'(S), \sigma'\sigma\rangle \qquad \text{(P)}$$

where $\sigma' = \{F \mapsto \lambda\overline{y_n}.y_i\}$ for some $1 \le i \le n$.

This algorithm has the failure case when there is a matching pair $\lambda\overline{x}.a(\overline{s}) \stackrel{\triangleleft}{=} \lambda\overline{x}.b(\overline{t})$ where a is not a free variable and $a \neq b$.

In the sequel we write $\langle S, \sigma\rangle \Longrightarrow_{(R)} \langle S', \sigma'\rangle$ for a step by transformation (R) and $\langle S, \sigma\rangle \Longrightarrow^* \langle S', \sigma'\rangle$ for a finite sequence of transformations.

Let us now see formally why the fresh new free variables $H_1, \cdots, H_m$ introduced in the imitation rule never need to occur in a final resulting matcher.

Lemma 1. *For any matcher θ of $s \stackrel{\triangleleft}{=} t$ there is a matcher σ of $s \stackrel{\triangleleft}{=} t$ such that $\sigma \le \theta\ [\mathcal{FV}(s)]$ and $\mathcal{I}(\sigma) = \emptyset$.*

Proof Let us first prove that for a matcher θ of $s \stackrel{\triangleleft}{=} t$ if $\mathcal{FV}(\theta(F)) \neq \emptyset$ for some $F \in \mathcal{D}(\theta)$ then $\theta_{|-\{F\}}$ is still a matcher of $s \stackrel{\triangleleft}{=} t$. Assume that $\theta(F)$ is of the form $\lambda\overline{y_m}.u$, where $m \ge 0$, and $(\theta_{|-\{F\}})(s) = s'$. Then $\theta(s) = \{F \mapsto \lambda\overline{y_m}.u\}(s')$, since $\mathcal{D}(\theta) \cap \mathcal{I}(\theta) = \emptyset$. If we can show that $F \notin \mathcal{FV}(s')$, then the above assertion holds. Since $\mathcal{FV}(t) = \emptyset$, this problem can be reduced to showing that if $F \in \mathcal{FV}(s')$ and H occurs freely in u, then H also occurs in $\{F \mapsto \lambda\overline{y_m}.u\}(s')$. We prove this by an induction on the structure of s'.

- Let s' be an atom a. Then the above assertion holds trivially.
- Let s' be of the form $\lambda\overline{x_n}.F(\overline{u_m})$. Note that the type of F is of at most second-order. If the type of F is of first-order then $m = 0$. If the type of F is of second-order then the type of each y_i must be first-order. In both cases H occurs in $\{F \mapsto \lambda\overline{y_m}.u\}(s')$.
- Let s' be of the form $\lambda\overline{x_n}.a(\overline{u_k})$, where a is an atom other than F, and u_i contains F for some $1 \le i \le k$. By induction assumption, H occurs $\{F \mapsto \lambda\overline{y_m}.u\}(u_i)$. So, H occurs in $\{F \mapsto \lambda\overline{y_m}.u\}(s')$.

Now assume that θ is an arbitrary matcher of $s \stackrel{\triangleleft}{=} t$ and $\mathcal{W} = \{X \in \mathcal{D}(\theta) \mid \mathcal{FV}(\theta(X)) = \emptyset\} \cap \mathcal{FV}(s)$. Let σ denote $\theta_{|\mathcal{W}}$. Thus $\sigma \le \theta\ [\mathcal{FV}(s)]$ and $\mathcal{I}(\sigma) = \emptyset$ hold. By the above assertion, we know that σ is a matcher of $s \stackrel{\triangleleft}{=} t$. □

The following lemma states formally that the process of the standard algorithm attempts to match F with every "top layer" of t, and every s_i with every subterm covered by a corresponding "top layer".

Lemma 2. Let $\lambda\overline{x}.F(\overline{s_m}) \stackrel{\triangleleft}{=} \lambda\overline{x}.t$ be a matching pair. Assume that $h_1,\cdots,h_k$ are numbers such that $1 \leq h_j \leq m$ for $k \geq 0$ and $j = 1,\ldots,k$, and $q_1,\cdots,q_k$ independent positions of t. Then the standard second-order matching algorithm has a transformation sequence

$$\langle\{\lambda\overline{x}.F(\overline{s_m}) \stackrel{\triangleleft}{=} \lambda\overline{x}.t\},\{\}\rangle \Longrightarrow^* \langle\{\lambda\overline{x}.s_{h_j} \stackrel{\triangleleft}{=} \lambda\overline{x}.t_{|q_j} \mid 1 \leq j \leq k\},\sigma\rangle,$$

where $\sigma(F) = \lambda\overline{y_m}.t[y_{h_1},\cdots,y_{h_k}]_{\overline{q_k}}$,

Proof First of all, we prove that there is always a transformation sequence

$$\langle\{\lambda\overline{x}.F(\overline{s_m}) \stackrel{\triangleleft}{=} \lambda\overline{x}.t\},\{\}\rangle \Longrightarrow^* \langle\{\lambda\overline{x}.G_j(\overline{s_m}) \stackrel{\triangleleft}{=} \lambda\overline{x}.t_{|q_j} \mid 1 \leq j \leq k\},\sigma\rangle,$$

where $G_1,\ldots,G_k$ are fresh free variables, and $\sigma = \{\}$ or $\sigma(F) = \lambda\overline{y_m}.t[G_1(\overline{y_m}),\cdots, G_k(\overline{y_m})]_{\overline{q_k}}$. The proof is easy. In fact, we need only to apply rule (I) repeatedly to $\langle\{\lambda\overline{x}.F(\overline{s_m}) \stackrel{\triangleleft}{=} \lambda\overline{x}.t\},\{\}\rangle$ and the resulting pairs until the resulting pair $\langle\{\lambda\overline{x}.G_j(\overline{s_m}) \stackrel{\triangleleft}{=} \lambda\overline{x}.t_{|q_j} \mid 1 \leq j \leq k\},\sigma\rangle$ is yielded, where $\sigma(F) = \lambda\overline{y_m}.t[G_1(\overline{y_m}),\cdots,G_k(\overline{y_m})]_{\overline{q_k}}$.

Now by applying rule (P) several times, we may easily obtain

$$\langle\{\lambda\overline{x}.G_j(\overline{s_m}) \stackrel{\triangleleft}{=} \lambda\overline{x}.t_{|q_j} \mid 1 \leq j \leq k\},\sigma\rangle \Longrightarrow^* \langle\{\lambda\overline{x}.s_{h_j} \stackrel{\triangleleft}{=} \lambda\overline{x}.t_{|q_j} \mid 1 \leq j \leq k\},\sigma'\rangle,$$

where $\sigma'(F) = \lambda\overline{y_m}.t[y_{h_1},\cdots,y_{h_k}]_{\overline{q_k}}$. Hence the assertion of the lemma holds. □

4 The new efficient algorithm

The new algorithm consists of

- rule (D) in the previous section for rigid-rigid matching pairs, and
- a new rule (FR) for flexible-rigid matching pairs.

Rule (FR) is based on the fact that if $\lambda\overline{x}.F(\overline{s_m})$ is a second-order term then $s_1,\cdots,s_m$ must be of base types. Therefore, if σ is a matcher of $\lambda\overline{x}.F(\overline{s_m}) \stackrel{\triangleleft}{=} \lambda\overline{x}.t$ then each $\sigma(s_i)$ for $1 \leq i \leq m$ will either occur as a subterm in t, or need not be considered at all in proving $\sigma(\lambda\overline{x}.F(\overline{s_m})) = \lambda\overline{x}.t$. Thus we need only to find the occurrences of $\sigma(s_i)$ in t. Indeed, computing a matcher may consist in first constructing new matching pairs composed of s_i and some subterms in t, then computing the matchers for these new matching pairs and finally using these matchers to build a matcher for the original problem.

Which subterms of t should be used to construct the new matching pairs are determined by two observations. The first observation is that for a term $\lambda\overline{x}.u$ and a substitution θ if a bound variable $z \in \{\overline{x}\}$ occurs in $\theta(u)$ then it must also occur in u, since θ introduces no new occurrences of z. This implies that if a matching pair $\lambda\overline{x}.s \stackrel{\triangleleft}{=} \lambda\overline{x}.t$ is matchable and a bound variable $z \in \{\overline{x}\}$ occurs in t then z must also occur in s.

The second observation is that if σ is a matcher of $\lambda\overline{x}.F(\overline{s_m}) \stackrel{\triangleleft}{=} \lambda\overline{x}.t$ then $\sigma(F) = \lambda\overline{y_m}.t[y_{h_1},\ldots y_{h_k}]_{\overline{q_k}}$, where $\overline{q_k}$ are independent positions of t and $1 \le h_j \le m$ holds for $k \ge 0$ and $j = 1,\ldots,k$. Note that

$$\sigma(\lambda\overline{x}.F(\overline{s_m})) \to_\beta \lambda\overline{x}.t[\sigma(s_{h_1}),\ldots,\sigma(s_{h_k})]_{\overline{q_k}}.$$

Therefore, an occurrence of a bound variable $z \in \{\overline{x}\}$ in t must be in $\sigma(s_{h_j})$, i.e. in s_{h_j}, for some $1 \le j \le k$. Thus if p is the position of this occurrence of z in t then $q_j \le p$ holds.

Let us look some simple examples.

The matching pair $\lambda x.F(u) \stackrel{\triangleleft}{=} \lambda x.f(x)$ has no matchers if x does not occur in u.

Let $\lambda x.F(u,x) \stackrel{\triangleleft}{=} \lambda x.g(x,x)$ be a matching pair, where x does not occur in u. Then a matcher σ always satisfies that $\sigma(F) = \lambda\overline{y_2}.g(x,x)[y_2,y_2]_{1,2}$, i.e. $\sigma(F) = \lambda\overline{y_2}.g(y_2,y_2)$. There is no need to consider $\sigma(F) = \lambda\overline{y_2}.g(x,x)[y_2]_\Lambda$, since $\lambda x.x \stackrel{\triangleleft}{=} \lambda x.g(x,x)$ has no matchers.

Let $\lambda x.F(G(x),u) \stackrel{\triangleleft}{=} \lambda x.f(c,x)$ be a matching pair, where u contains no occurrences of x. Let $\sigma(F) = \lambda\overline{y_2}.s$ be any matcher of the matching pair, then y_1 must have an occurrence above 2 in s. So, we only need to consider the following cases:

- $\sigma(F) = \lambda\overline{y_2}.f(c,x)[y_1]_p$ for $p = \Lambda$ or $p = 2$. In fact, if $p = \Lambda$ then $\sigma(F) = \lambda\overline{y_2}.y_1$ and σ must match $\{\lambda x.G(x) \stackrel{\triangleleft}{=} \lambda x.f(c,x)\}$. If $p = 2$ then $\sigma(F) = \lambda\overline{y_2}.f(c,y_1)$ and σ must match $\{\lambda x.G(x) \stackrel{\triangleleft}{=} \lambda x.x\}$.
- $\sigma(F) = \lambda\overline{y_2}.f(c,x)[y_1,y_1]_{p,q}$ for $p = 2$ and $q = 1$. Then $\sigma(F) = \lambda\overline{y_2}.f(y_1,y_1)$ and σ must match $\{\lambda x.G(x) \stackrel{\triangleleft}{=} \lambda x.c, \lambda x.G(x) \stackrel{\triangleleft}{=} \lambda x.x\}$. Since $\{\lambda x.G(x) \stackrel{\triangleleft}{=} \lambda x.c, \lambda x.G(x) \stackrel{\triangleleft}{=} \lambda x.x\}$ is not matchable, there are no matchers in this case.
- $\sigma(F) = \lambda\overline{y_2}.f(c,x)[y_1,y_2]_{p,q}$ for $p = 2$ and $q = 1$. Then $\sigma(F) = \lambda\overline{y_2}.f(y_2,y_1)$ and σ must match $\{\lambda x.u \stackrel{\triangleleft}{=} \lambda x.c, \lambda x.G(x) \stackrel{\triangleleft}{=} \lambda x.x\}$.

The main part of rule (FR) is the function FFR, which computes a set of matchers of a flexible-rigid matching pair as follows.

Function $FFR(\lambda\overline{x}.F(\overline{s_m}) \stackrel{\triangleleft}{=} \lambda\overline{x}.t)$

1. Use the matching algorithm to compute a set M_q^i of matchers of $\lambda\overline{x}.s_i \stackrel{\triangleleft}{=} \lambda\overline{x}.t_{|q}$ for each $1 \le i \le m$ and each position $q \in Pos(t)$ such that $\tau(s_i) = \tau(t_{|q})$, $t_{|q}$ contains at least one bound variable from $\{\overline{x}\}$ and if a bound variable from $\{\overline{x}\}$ occurs in $t_{|q}$ then it also occurs in s_i.

2. Use the matching algorithm to compute a set M_q^i of matchers of $\lambda\overline{x}.s_i \stackrel{\triangleleft}{=} \lambda\overline{x}.t_{|q}$ for each $1 \le i \le m$ and each position $q \in Pos(t)$ such that $\tau(s_i) = \tau(t_{|q})$ and q is independent of all positions p with $\mathcal{H}(t_{|p}) \in \{\overline{x}\}$.

3. Choose each set $\{\overline{q_k}\}$ of independent positions of t with $k \ge 0$. Assume that the elements $\overline{q_k}$ occur in a fixed order. Choose each sequence of numbers $\overline{h_k}$ such that $t[\square,\cdots,\square]_{\overline{q_k}}$ contains no bound variables from $\{\overline{x}\}$ and $M_{q_j}^{h_j}$ is nonempty for $j = 1,\ldots,k$. Choose each substitution $\theta^j \in M_{q_j}^{h_j}$ for each $j = 1,\ldots,k$. Construct a substitution

$$\theta^F = \{F \mapsto \overline{y_m}.t[y_{h_1},\cdots,y_{h_k}]_{\overline{q_k}}\}.$$

If all substitutions $\theta^1, \cdots, \theta^k$, and θ^F are compatible, then construct a substitution

$$\sigma = \theta^1 \cup \cdots \cup \theta^k \cup \theta^F.$$

4. The function FFR stops and returns the set of all substitutions σ constructed in step 3 as the result.

As an example, let us compute $FFR(\lambda\overline{x_2}.F(x_1, x_2, a) \stackrel{\triangleleft}{=} \lambda\overline{x_2}.f(x_1, g(x_1), a))$.

1. The only bound variable in $f(x_1, g(x_1), a))$ on the right is x_1. More precisely, x_1 occurs in $f(x_1, g(x_1), a))$ at the positions $p_1 = 1$ and $p_2 = 2 \cdot 1$ Note that x_1 also occurs in the first argument on the left. The positions Λ, p_1, 2 and p_2 are all positions above p_1 or p_2. Assume that the application of the matching algorithm to the matching pairs yields sets of matchers as follows:

Matching pairs	Sets of matchers
$\lambda\overline{x_2}.x_1 \stackrel{\triangleleft}{=} \lambda\overline{x_2}.f(x_1, g(x_1), a)$	$M^1_\Lambda = \emptyset$
$\lambda\overline{x_2}.x_1 \stackrel{\triangleleft}{=} \lambda\overline{x_2}.x_1$	$M^1_{p_1} = \{\{\}\}$
$\lambda\overline{x_2}.x_1 \stackrel{\triangleleft}{=} \lambda\overline{x_2}.g(x_1)$	$M^1_2 = \emptyset$
$\lambda\overline{x_2}.x_1 \stackrel{\triangleleft}{=} \lambda\overline{x_2}.x_1$	$M^1_{p_2} = \{\{\}\}$.

2. The only position independent of p_1 and p_2 in $f(x_1, g(x_1), a))$ on the right of the original matching pair is $q_1 = 3$. To match each argument on the left with the subterm at q_1 on the right, we apply the matching algorithm to $\lambda\overline{x_2}.x_1 \stackrel{\triangleleft}{=} \lambda\overline{x_2}.a$, $\lambda\overline{x_2}.x_2 \stackrel{\triangleleft}{=} \lambda\overline{x_2}.a$ and $\lambda\overline{x_2}.a \stackrel{\triangleleft}{=} \lambda\overline{x_2}.a$. The resulting sets are $M^1_{q_1} = \emptyset$, $M^2_{q_1} = \emptyset$ and $M^3_{q_1} = \{\{\}\}$.
3. The only sets of independent positions of $f(x_1, g(x_1), a)$ that we need to consider are $\{p_1, p_2\}$ and $\{p_1, p_2, q_1\}$.
   - For $\{p_1, p_2\}$, the sets $M^1_{p_1}$ and $M^1_{p_2}$ are the only nonempty sets in consideration. In this case the sequence of numbers corresponding to p_1, p_2 is $1, 1$. Thus the substitution θ^F is $\{F \mapsto \lambda\overline{y_3}.f(y_1, g(y_1), a)\}$. Since $M^1_{p_1}$ and $M^1_{p_2}$ contain only the identity substitution, we may construct $\sigma_1 = \{F \mapsto \lambda\overline{y_3}.f(y_1, g(y_1), a)\}$.
   - For $\{p_1, p_2, q_1\}$, the sets $M^1_{p_1}$, $M^1_{p_2}$ and $M^3_{q_1}$ are the only nonempty sets in consideration. In this case the sequence of numbers corresponding to p_1, p_2, q_1 is $1, 1, 3$. Thus the substitution θ^F is $\{F \mapsto \lambda\overline{y_3}.f(y_1, g(y_1), y_3)\}$. Since $M^1_{p_1}$, $M^1_{p_2}$ and $M^3_{q_1}$ contain only the identity substitution, we may construct a substitution $\sigma_2 = \{F \mapsto \lambda\overline{y_3}.f(y_1, g(y_1), y_3)\}$.
4. The function FFR returns $\{\sigma_1, \sigma_2\}$.

As another example, let us compute $FFR(\lambda x.F(a, F(x, b)) \stackrel{\triangleleft}{=} \lambda x.f(f(b, x), a))$.

1. The only bound variable occurring in $f(f(b, x), a))$ on the right is x. More precisely it occurs at position $p_1 = 1 \cdot 2$ in $f(f(b, x), a))$. Note that it also occurs in the second argument on the left. The positions Λ, 1 and p_1 are all positions above p_1. The corresponding matching pairs yield the nonempty sets of matchers as follows:

Matching pairs	Sets of matchers
$\lambda x.F(x,b) \stackrel{\trianglelefteq}{=} \lambda x.f(f(b,x),a))$	$M^2_\Lambda = \{\theta_1, \theta_2\}$ where $\theta_1 = \{F \mapsto \lambda\overline{y_2}.f(f(b,y_1),a))\}$
	$\theta_2 = \{F \mapsto \lambda\overline{y_2}.f(f(y_2,y_1),a))\}$
$\lambda x.F(x,b) \stackrel{\trianglelefteq}{=} \lambda x.f(b,x)$	$M^2_1 = \{\theta_3, \theta_4\}$ where $\theta_3 = \{F \mapsto \lambda\overline{y_2}.f(y_2,y_1)\}$,
	$\theta_4 = \{F \mapsto \lambda\overline{y_2}.f(b,y_1)\}$
$\lambda x.F(x,b) \stackrel{\trianglelefteq}{=} \lambda x.x$	$M^2_{p_1} = \{\theta_5\}$ where $\theta_5 = \{F \mapsto \lambda\overline{y_2}.y_1\}$

2. The only position independent of p_1 in $f(f(b,x),a))$ on the right of the original matching pair is $q_1 = 2$ and $q_2 = 1\cdot1\cdot1$. We apply the matching algorithm to the matching pairs $\lambda x.a \stackrel{\trianglelefteq}{=} \lambda x.a$, $\lambda x.F(x,b) \stackrel{\trianglelefteq}{=} \lambda x.a$, $\lambda x.a \stackrel{\trianglelefteq}{=} \lambda x.b$ and $\lambda x.F(x,b) \stackrel{\trianglelefteq}{=} \lambda x.b$. The only nonempty resulting sets of matchers are $M^1_{q_1} = \{\theta_6\}$ where $\theta_6 = \{\}$, $M^2_{q_1} = \{\theta_7\}$ where $\theta_7 = \{F \mapsto \lambda\overline{y_2}.a\}$, $M^1_{q_2} = \emptyset$ and $M^2_{q_2} = \{\theta_8, \theta_9\}$ where $\theta_8 = \{F \mapsto \lambda\overline{y_2}.y_2\}$ and $\theta_9 = \{F \mapsto \lambda\overline{y_2}.b\}$.
3. All sets of independent positions we need to consider are $\{\Lambda\}$, $\{1\}$, $\{1, q_1\}$, $\{p_1\}$, $\{p_1, q_1\}$, $\{p_1, q_2\}$ and $\{p_1, q_1, q_2\}$.
   - For $\{\Lambda\}$, we can choose θ_1 or θ_2 from M^2_Λ. Thus the corresponding sequence of numbers is 2. Hence the substitution θ^F is $\{F \mapsto \lambda\overline{y_2}.y_2\}$. Obviously, θ_1 and θ^F are not compatible, nor θ_2 and θ^F.
   - For $\{1\}$, we can only choose θ_3 or θ_4 from M^2_1. Thus the corresponding sequence of numbers is 2. Hence the substitution θ^F is $\{F \mapsto \lambda\overline{y_2}.f(y_2,a)\}$. It is easy to see that θ_3 and θ^F are not compatible, nor θ_4 and θ^F.
   - For $\{1, q_1\}$, we can first choose θ_3 from M^2_1 and θ_6 from $M^1_{q_1}$. Thus the corresponding sequence of numbers is $2, 1$. Hence the substitution θ^F is $\{F \mapsto \lambda\overline{y_2}.f(y_2,y_1)\}$. Since θ_3 and θ^F are identical and θ_4 is the identity substitution, we construct a resulting substitution $\sigma_1 = \theta_3$. As another possibility we can choose θ_4 from M^2_1 and θ_7 from $M^2_{q_1}$. Thus the corresponding sequence of numbers is $2, 2$. Hence the substitution θ^F is $\{F \mapsto \lambda\overline{y_2}.f(y_2,y_2)\}$. Since θ_7 and θ^F are not compatible, no resulting substitutions can be yielded in this case.
   - For $\{p_1\}$, $\{p_1, q_1\}$, $\{p_1, q_2\}$ and $\{p_1, q_1, q_2\}$, we have to choose θ_5 from $M^2_{p_1}$. Thus the substitution θ^F is $\{F \mapsto \lambda\overline{y_2}.f(\cdots)\}$. Since θ_5 and θ^F are not compatible, no resulting substitutions can be yielded in these cases.
4. The function FFR returns $\{\sigma_1\}$.

Now we formulate rule (FR) as follows:

$$\langle\{\lambda\overline{x}.F(\overline{s_n}) \stackrel{\trianglelefteq}{=} \lambda\overline{x}.t\} \cup S, \sigma\rangle \Longrightarrow \langle\sigma'(S), \sigma'\sigma\rangle \qquad \text{(FR)}$$

where $\sigma' \in FFR(\lambda\overline{x}.F(\overline{s_n}) \stackrel{\trianglelefteq}{=} \lambda\overline{x}.t)$.

5 Termination, soundness and completeness

To prove the termination of the new algorithm we define the complexity measure $CM(S)$ of a matching problem S to be a pair $(\xi_r(S), \xi_l(S))$, where $\xi_r(S)$ is the multiset $\{|t| \mid s \stackrel{\trianglelefteq}{=} t \in S\}$ and $\xi_l(S)$ the multiset $\{|s| \mid s \stackrel{\trianglelefteq}{=} t \in S\}$. The termination proof is based on the standard ordering on multisets of numbers, denoted as $>$, and the lexicographic ordering on pairs, also denoted as $>$.

Theorem 3. The new algorithm always terminates.

Proof The execution of the new algorithm for an input pair $\langle S, \sigma\rangle$, where σ is an arbitrary substitution, can be described as a sequence of applications of rules (D) and (FR) issuing from $\langle S, \sigma\rangle$. Thus the termination of the algorithm follows from that the application of a single rule always terminates and the sequence is always finite. We prove this by an induction on $CM(S)$.

Initially if $CM(S) = (\emptyset, \emptyset)$ then $S = \emptyset$. None of rules (D) and (FR) can be applied. The termination follows trivially.

Assume that S is a nonempty matching problem and rule (D) or (FR) is applicable. First, assume that rule (D) is applicable. Then the sequence is of the form $\langle S, \sigma\rangle \Longrightarrow_{(D)} \langle S', \sigma\rangle \Longrightarrow \cdots$, where $S = \{\lambda\overline{x}.a(\overline{s_n}) \stackrel{\triangleleft}{=} \lambda\overline{x}.a(\overline{t_n})\} \cup S_1$ and $S' = \{\lambda\overline{x}.s_n \stackrel{\triangleleft}{=} \lambda\overline{x}.t_n\} \cup S_1$. The application of (D) is obviously terminating. Since $|\lambda\overline{x}.a(\overline{t_n})| > |\lambda\overline{x}.t_i|$ for all $i = 1, \ldots, n$, we have $CM(S) > CM(S')$. By induction assumption, the algorithm is terminating for the input pair $\langle S', \sigma\rangle$. Hence the algorithm is terminating for the input pair $\langle S, \sigma\rangle$.

Assume that rule (FR) is applicable. Then the sequence is of the form

$$\langle\{\lambda\overline{x}.F(\overline{s_n}) \stackrel{\triangleleft}{=} \lambda\overline{x}.t\} \cup S_1, \sigma\rangle \Longrightarrow_{(FR)} \langle\sigma'(S_1), \sigma'\sigma\rangle \Longrightarrow \cdots$$

for some substitution σ'. The termination of rule (FR) is based on that of the function FFR. In fact, the only sources of non-termination during execution of the function FFR are the two recursive calls to the algorithm in the steps 1 and 2 of the definition of the function FFR. Since both recursive calls have an input matching problem of the form $\lambda\overline{x}.s_i \stackrel{\triangleleft}{=} \lambda\overline{x}.t_{|q}$, where $|t| \geq |t_{|q}|$ and $|F(\overline{s_m})| > |s_i|$ for all $i = 1, \ldots, m$, we have $CM(S) > CM(\{\lambda\overline{x}.s_i \stackrel{\triangleleft}{=} \lambda\overline{x}.t_{|q}\})$. By induction assumption the recursive calls are terminating. Hence the application of rule (FR) is terminating. Since $\sigma'(S_1)$ does not change the right-hand sides in S_1, we have $\xi_r(S) > \xi_r(\sigma'(S_1))$. By induction assumption, the algorithm for the input $\langle\sigma'(S_1), \sigma'\sigma\rangle$ is terminating. Hence the algorithm with the input $\langle S, \sigma\rangle$ is terminating. □

Now we consider the soundness. First, we show that the function FFR is sound in the following sense.

Lemma 4. Each $\sigma \in FFR(\lambda\overline{x}.F(\overline{s_m}) \stackrel{\triangleleft}{=} \lambda\overline{x}.t)$ is a matcher of $\lambda\overline{x_n}.F(\overline{s_m}) \stackrel{\triangleleft}{=} \lambda\overline{x_n}.t$.

Proof We use the notations in the definition of the algorithm. By step 3, σ is of the form $\theta^1 \cup \cdots \cup \theta^k \cup \theta^F$, where $\theta^1, \cdots, \theta^k$ and θ^F are compatible. Note that $\theta^F = \{F \mapsto \lambda y_m.t[y_{h_1}, \ldots, y_{h_k}]_{\overline{q_k}}\}$, each θ^j is a matcher of the problem $\lambda\overline{x}.s_{h_j} \stackrel{\triangleleft}{=} \lambda\overline{x}.t_{|q_j}$ for $j = 1, \ldots, k$, and $\overline{q_k}$ are independent positions of t. Then

$$\sigma(\lambda\overline{x}.F(\overline{s_m})) = \lambda\overline{x}.t[\overline{\theta^k(s_{h_k})}]_{\overline{q_k}} = \lambda\overline{x}.t[\overline{t_{|q_k}}]_{\overline{q_k}} = \lambda\overline{x}.t. \qquad \square$$

Theorem 5. For a matching problem S, if $\langle S, \{\}\rangle \Longrightarrow^* \langle\emptyset, \sigma\rangle$ is a sequence of transformations of the new algorithm, then σ matches S.

Proof Follows from the above lemma and by an induction on the length of the transformation sequence. □

Now we do some preparations for proving the completeness.

Lemma 6. Let σ be a matcher of $\lambda\overline{x}.F(\overline{s_m}) \stackrel{\triangleleft}{=} \lambda\overline{x}.t$. Then for some independent positions $\{\overline{q_k}\}$ of t and some numbers $\overline{h_k}$ such that $1 \le h_j \le m$ for each $j = 1, \ldots, k$, the following holds:

1. *$\sigma(F) = \lambda\overline{y_m}.t[y_{h_1}, \cdots, y_{h_k}]_{\overline{q_k}}$,*
2. *$\sigma(\lambda\overline{x}.s_{h_j}) = \lambda\overline{x}.t_{|q_j}$ for each $j = 1, \ldots, k$, and*
3. *if $\mathcal{H}(t_{|p}) \in \{\overline{x}\}$ for some position p then there are s_{h_j} and q_j with some $1 \le j \le k$ such that $\mathcal{H}(t_{|p})$ occurs in s_{h_j} and $q_j \le p$ holds.*

Proof

1. Follows directly from the fact that the term $\lambda\overline{x}.F(\overline{s_m})$ is second-order and all subterms $\overline{s_m}$ are of base types.
2. Follows directly from the assertion 1.
3. Assume that $\mathcal{H}(t_{|p}) \in \{\overline{x}\}$ for some p. Note that $\sigma(F) = \lambda\overline{y_m}.t[y_{h_1}, \cdots, y_{h_k}]_{\overline{q_k}}$, $\sigma(\lambda\overline{x}.F(\overline{s_m})) = \lambda\overline{x}.t[\overline{\sigma(s_{h_k})}]_{\overline{q_k}}$ and $\sigma(\lambda\overline{x}.F(\overline{s_m})) = \lambda\overline{x}.t$. Since no bound variables from $\{\overline{x}\}$ may occur in $\sigma(X)$ for $X \in \mathcal{D}(\sigma)$, no bound variables from $\{\overline{x}\}$ may occur in $t[y_{h_1}, \cdots, y_{h_k}]_{\overline{q_k}}$. Therefore $\mathcal{H}(t_{|p})$ must occur in some $\sigma(s_{h_j})$ with $1 \le j \le k$. Furthermore, $\mathcal{H}(t_{|p})$ must occur in s_{h_j}. Since $\lambda\overline{x}.t[\overline{\sigma(s_{h_k})}]_{\overline{q_k}} = \lambda\overline{x}.t$, we have $\sigma(s_{h_j}) = t_{|q_j}$. Since $\mathcal{H}(t_{|p})$ occurs in $\sigma(s_{h_j})$, we have $q_j \le p$.

□

A call to a matching algorithm for an input matching problem S is said to be *complete* if whenever θ is a matcher of S the call yields a matcher σ of S such that $\mathcal{I}(\sigma) = \emptyset$, $\mathcal{D}(\sigma) \subseteq \mathcal{FV}(S)$ and $\sigma \le \theta$. A matching algorithm is *complete* if its call for each input matching problem is complete.

Lemma 7. If every call of the matching algorithm in the step 1 or 2 of the definition of the function FFR is complete, then every call to the function FFR is complete.

Proof Consider the call $FFR(\lambda\overline{x}.F(\overline{s_m}) \stackrel{\triangleleft}{=} \lambda\overline{x}.t)$. By Lemma 1, we need only to consider those matchers θ of $\lambda\overline{x}.F(\overline{s_m}) \stackrel{\triangleleft}{=} \lambda\overline{x}.t$ such that $\mathcal{I}(\theta) = \emptyset$.

By Lemma 6-1, $\theta(F) = \lambda\overline{y_m}.t[\overline{y_{h_k}}]_{\overline{q_k}}$ for some independent positions $\overline{q_k}$ of t and some numbers $\overline{h_k}$ such that $1 \le h_j \le m$ for each $j = 1, \ldots, k$. By Lemma 6-2, $\theta(s_{h_j}) = \lambda\overline{x}.t_{|q_j}$ holds for $j = 1, \ldots, k$. By Lemma 6-3, if $\mathcal{H}(t_{|p}) \in \{\overline{x}\}$ for some p then there are s_{h_j} and q_j as above such that $\mathcal{H}(t_{|p})$ occurs in s_{h_j} and $q_j \le p$ holds. This means that the term $\lambda\overline{y_m}.t[\overline{y_{h_k}}]_{\overline{q_k}}$ contains no free occurrences of bound variables from $\{\overline{x}\}$.

Since $\lambda\overline{x}.\theta(s_{h_j}) = \lambda\overline{x}.t_{|q_j}$ for each $1 \le j \le k$, a complete call to the matching algorithm in the step 1 or 2 yields a matcher θ_j of $\lambda\overline{x}.s_{h_j} = \lambda\overline{x}.t_{|q_j}$ such that $\mathcal{I}(\theta_j) = \emptyset$, $\mathcal{D}(\theta_j) \subseteq \mathcal{FV}(\lambda\overline{x}.s_{h_j})$ and $\theta_j \le \theta$. Since $\mathcal{I}(\theta) = \emptyset$, we have that for each $X \in \mathcal{FV}(s_{h_j})$, either $\theta_j(X) = \theta(X)$ or $X \notin \mathcal{D}(\theta_j)$ holds. Thus the substitutions $\theta^1, \cdots, \theta^k$, and θ^F are compatible. Hence we may construct a substitution σ as in step 3 such that $\mathcal{I}(\sigma) = \emptyset$, $\mathcal{D}(\sigma) \subseteq \mathcal{FV}(\lambda\overline{x}.F(\overline{s_m}))$ and $\sigma \le \theta$. □

Now we may prove the completeness result.

Lemma 8. The new matching algorithm is complete.

Proof Let S be a matching problem. By Lemma 1, we need only to consider those matchers θ of S such that $\mathcal{I}(\theta) = \emptyset$. The proof follows by an induction on $CM(S)$.

Initially, if $CM(S) = (\emptyset, \emptyset)$ then $S = \emptyset$. Thus $\{\}$ is a matcher of S as required.

Assume that $S \neq \emptyset$. Since θ is a matcher of S, either rule (D) or (FR) is applicable. If rule (D) is applicable, then $S = \{\lambda\overline{x}.a(\overline{s_n}) \stackrel{\trianglelefteq}{=} \lambda\overline{x}.a(\overline{t_n})\} \cup S_1$. Therefore we have $\langle S, \{\}\rangle \Longrightarrow_{(D)} \langle S', \{\}\rangle$, where $S' = \{\lambda\overline{x}.s_n \stackrel{\trianglelefteq}{=} \lambda\overline{x}.t_n\} \cup S_1$ and θ is a matcher of S'. Since $CM(S) > CM(S')$, by induction assumption, the new algorithm yields a matcher σ of S' as required. The substitution σ is also a matcher σ of S as required.

If rule (FR) is applicable, then $S = \{\lambda\overline{x}.F(\overline{s_n}) \stackrel{\trianglelefteq}{=} \lambda\overline{x}.t\} \cup S_1$. Since $CM(S) > CM(\{\lambda\overline{x}.s_j \stackrel{\trianglelefteq}{=} \lambda\overline{x}.t_{|q}\})$, by induction assumption, every recursive call to the new algorithm in the step 1 or 2 of the definition of the function FFR is complete. By Lemma 7, the call to the function FFR is complete, i.e. it yields a matcher σ of $\lambda\overline{x}.F(\overline{s_n}) \stackrel{\trianglelefteq}{=} \lambda\overline{x}.t$ such that $\mathcal{I}(\sigma) = \emptyset$, $\mathcal{D}(\sigma) \subseteq \mathcal{FV}(\lambda\overline{x}.F(\overline{s_n}))$ and $\sigma \leq \theta$. This implies that $\theta = \sigma \cup \theta_{|-\mathcal{D}(\sigma)}$ and $\theta_{|-\mathcal{D}(\sigma)}$ is a matcher of $\sigma(S_1)$. Note that $\langle S, \{\}\rangle \Longrightarrow_{(FR)} \langle\sigma(S_1), \sigma\rangle$. Since $CM(S) > CM(\sigma(S_1))$, by induction assumption, the new algorithm has a transformation sequence $\langle\sigma(S_1), \{\}\rangle \Longrightarrow^* \langle\emptyset, \sigma_1\rangle$ such that σ_1 is a matcher of $\sigma(S_1)$, $\mathcal{I}(\sigma_1) = \emptyset$, $\mathcal{D}(\sigma_1) \subseteq \mathcal{FV}(\sigma(S_1))$ and $\sigma_1 \leq \theta_{|-\mathcal{D}(\sigma)}$. Hence the algorithm has a transformation sequence $\langle S, \{\}\rangle \Longrightarrow^* \langle\emptyset, \sigma_1\sigma\rangle$, where $\sigma_1\sigma$ is a matcher of S, $\mathcal{I}(\sigma_1\sigma) = \emptyset$, $\mathcal{D}(\sigma_1\sigma) \subseteq \mathcal{FV}(S)$ and $\sigma_1\sigma \leq \theta$. Hence the new algorithm is complete. □

6 Implementation and test results

We have implemented the standard second-order matching algorithm [11] and the new algorithm in SML/NJ [8]. We use the data structures for terms in the theorem prover Isabelle [15]. The sizes of the programs are 359 lines and 571 lines of SML source code, respectively[4]. To compare these two algorithms, more than 40 examples have been tested on a SUN SPARC-Station-20 with 64 megabytes of memory.

Terms in a matching pair always have the same type. A term is a *constant*, a *free variable*, a *bound variable*, an *abstraction*, or an *application*. To avoid the renaming of bound variables, de Bruijn's name-free representation is used.

First, we outline the implementation of the standard second-order matching algorithm. Two main functions are used: the function *simplification* corresponds to rule (D); and the function *flex_rigid* contains two local functions corresponding to rules (P) and (I), respectively. These functions are applied to a matching problem and transform it into a set of new ones. For each new matching problem, this process will be continued, until each matching problem is either a substitution or no functions can be applied to it. All substitutions form the complete set of matchers for the given matching problem.

For the new matching algorithm, a given matching problem will first be simplified using the function *simplification*. The function *flex_rigid* in the standard algorithm is replaced by a new function *FFR*, which contains the local functions *right_bound*,

[4] The programs are available under:
`http://www.informatik.uni-bremen.de/~shi/shi_imp.html`

	Matching pairs	$\mathcal{S}$	$\mathcal{T}_1$	$\mathcal{T}_2$
1	$\lambda\overline{x_2}.F(x_1,x_2,a_1) \overset{\triangleleft}{=} \lambda\overline{x_2}.f(x_1,g(x_1),a_1)$	4	0.24	0.20
2	$\lambda\overline{x_2}.F(x_1,x_2) \overset{\triangleleft}{=} \lambda\overline{x_2}.f(a_1,a_2)$	2	0.20	0.16
3	$\lambda\overline{x_2}.F(G_1(x_1),G_2(x_2)) \overset{\triangleleft}{=} \lambda\overline{x_2}.f(g(a_1),h(a_2,a_3))$	19	0.69	0.56
4	$\lambda\overline{x_3}.F(G_1(x_1),G_2(x_2),G(x_3)) \overset{\triangleleft}{=} \lambda\overline{x_3}.f(x_1,h(a_2,a_3))$	16	0.41	0.33
5	$\lambda\overline{x_3}.F(G_1(x_1),G_2(x_2),G_3(x_3)) \overset{\triangleleft}{=}$ $\lambda\overline{x_3}.f(g(x_1),h_1(x_1,a_1),h_2(a_2,a_3))$	125	1.97	1.38
6	$\lambda\overline{x_3}.F(G_1(x_1),G_2(x_2),G_3(x_3)) \overset{\triangleleft}{=}$ $\lambda\overline{x_3}.f(g_1(x_1),g_2(x_2),h_1(x_1,x_2),h_2(a_1,a_2))$	265	4.38	0.78
7	$\lambda\overline{x_4}.F(G_1(x_1),G_2(x_2),G_3(x_3),G_4(x_4)) \overset{\triangleleft}{=} \lambda\overline{x_4}.f(g_1(x_1),$ $g_2(x_2),g_3(x_3),h_1(a_1,a_2),h_2(x_1,a_3),h_3(x_2,a_4),h_4(x_1,x_2))$	> 10000	577.89	158.99
8	$\lambda\overline{x_3}.F(G_1(x_1),G_2(x_2),G_3(x_3)) \overset{\triangleleft}{=}$ $\lambda\overline{x_3}.f(g_1(x_1),g_2(x_2),h_1(x_1,x_2),h_2(a_1,a_2),h_3(x_2,a_3))$	587	11.85	4.14
9	$\lambda\overline{x_4}.F(G_1(x_1),G_2(x_2),G_3(x_3),G_4(x_4)) \overset{\triangleleft}{=} \lambda\overline{x_4}.f(g_1(x_1),$ $g_2(x_2),g_3(x_3),g_4(x_4),h_1(a_1,a_2),h_2(x_1,a_3))$	3462	150.69	39.75
10	$\lambda\overline{x_3}.F(G_1(x_1),G_2(x_2),G(x_3),a_1) \overset{\triangleleft}{=}$ $\lambda\overline{x_3}.f(g_1(x_1),g_2(x_2),h(x_3,a_2),a_1)$	113	5.78	1.00
11	$\lambda\overline{x_4}.F(G_1(x_1),G_2(x_2),G_3(x_3),G_4(x_4)) \overset{\triangleleft}{=} \lambda\overline{x_4}.f(g_1(x_1),$ $g_2(x_2),h_1(x_1,x_2),h_2(a_1,a_2),h_3(x_2,a_3),h_4(x_1,a_4))$	> 10000	346.26	57.67
12	$\lambda\overline{x_4}.F(G_1(x_1),G_2(x_2),G_3(x_3)) \overset{\triangleleft}{=}$ $\lambda\overline{x_4}.f(g_1(x_1),g_2(x_2),g_3(x_3),g_4(x_4))$	152	3.29	0.20
13	$\lambda\overline{x_4}.F(G_1(x_1),G_2(x_2),G_3(x_3),G_4(x_4)) \overset{\triangleleft}{=}$ $\lambda\overline{x_4}.f(g_1(x_1),g_2(x_2),g_3(x_3),g_4(x_4))$	354	13.50	0.54
14	$\lambda\overline{x_4}.F(G_1(x_1),G_2(x_2),G_3(x_3),G_4(x_4)) \overset{\triangleleft}{=}$ $\lambda\overline{x_4}.f(g_1(x_1),g_2(x_2),g_3(x_3),g_4(x_4),h(a_1,a_2))$	1359	49.86	5.27
15	$\lambda\overline{x_3}.F(G_1(x_1),G_2(x_2),G_3(x_3)) \overset{\triangleleft}{=} \lambda\overline{x_3}.f(g_1(x_1),$ $g_2(x_1),g_3(x_1),h_1(x_1,a_1),h_2(x_1,a_2),h_3(a_3,a_4))$	978	26.90	44.70
16	$\lambda\overline{x_3}.F(G_1(x_1),G_2(x_2),G_3(x_3)) \overset{\triangleleft}{=} \lambda\overline{x_3}.f(g_1(x_1),g_2(x_2),$ $g_3(x_3),h_1(a_1,a_2),h_2(x_1,a_3),h_3(x_2,a_4),h_4(x_1,x_2))$	1704	54.93	81.30

Figure 1. Test results.

right_rest and *composition*, corresponding to the first three steps described in Section 4, respectively. In the functions *right_bound* and *right_rest* the matching algorithm is called recursively.

In order to show how much time performance gain we can get, the above table contains the CPU-time-costs $\mathcal{T}_1$ and $\mathcal{T}_2$ (in seconds) for both algorithms on several examples. In addition, the table contains the total number of fresh free variables $\mathcal{S}$ for the standard algorithm, which indicate to some extent the additional space cost during execution of the standard algorithm.

We can make the following observations and explanations on the data in the table:

- The first group shows that the new algorithm may have a better performance than the standard one even for very simple matching problems. For the given examples, the new algorithm gets about 20% speedup in execution time.
- The second group consists of some typical applications in our program transformation system. The examples show that the more bound variables the right-hand sides in a matching problem have, the bigger improvement the new algorithm has in execution time than the standard one. The reason is that the mechanism for foreseeing the failure branches in the new algorithm is based on occurrences of bound variables. In average, the new algorithm gets about 80% speedup in execution time for the given examples in this group.
- The third group seems to show that the new algorithm may be less efficient than the standard one for the matching problems, whose right-hand sides have much more constant symbols than bound variables. In general, for subterms independent of occurrences of bound variables, the new algorithm may have to consider all possible combinations of matching subproblems in the flexible-rigid case just like the standard algorithm. Therefore any preparations for foreseeing the failure branches would be useless for such subterms. If such subterms are much more than occurrences of bound variables, then the cost for the preparations may not pay off the cost reduction due to cutting the failure branches.

7 Conclusion

We have presented a new second-order matching algorithm. Our implementation shows that the new algorithm can be more efficient than the standard one for many matching problems. The implementation will be used in a prototypical program transformation system [13, 17].

For a certain perspective, the standard second-order matching algorithm is in fact a specialization of an algorithm for unification of arbitrary simply typed λ-terms [9]. Therefore one may ask whether our algorithm can be extended into a second-order equational matching algorithm, which might be more efficient than higher-order equational unification algorithms [18, 14, 16] used for second-order equational matching [5]. Indeed, Curien and Qian proposed such an algorithm for second-order AC matching [6], but have not implemented it. A motivation for designing a second-order AC matching algorithm is to allow usual binary AC logical operators $\vee$ and $\wedge$ in computing similarities of formulas (cf. [4]).

Acknowledgement. We thank the anonymous referees for their corrections and comments.

References

1. T. Boy de la Tour and R. Caferra. Proof analogy in interactive theorem proving: A method to express and use it via second order pattern matching. In *proceedings of AAAI'87*, 1987.

2. T. Boy de la Tour and R. Caferra. A formale approach to some usually informal techniques used in mathematical reasoning. In *ISSAC'88*, pages 402–406. Lecture Notes in Computer Science, 1988.
3. R. S. Boyer and J. S. Moore. A Theorem Prover for a Computational Logic. In *Proc. of the 10th International Conference on Automated Deduction*, 1990.
4. R. Curien. *Outils pour la preuve par analogie.* PhD thesis, Université Henri Poincaré - Nancy 1, January 1995.
5. R. Curien. Second Order E-matching as a Tool for Automated Theorem Proving. In *Proceedings of EPIA'93 (Portugese Conference on Artificial Intelligence) Porto, Portugal.*, volume 727 of *Lecture Notes in Artificial Intelligence*, 93.
6. R. Curien and Z. Qian. Efficiency for second-order matching: the syntactic and AC-cases. Technical report, 1995. Draft paper.
7. G. Dowek. A Second-order Pattern Matching Algorithm in the Cube of Typed λ-calculi. In *Mathematical Fundation of Computer Science*, LNCS 520, 1991.
8. R. Harper, D. MacQueen, and R. Milner. Standard ML. Technical report, Dept. of Cmputer Science, University of Edinburg, 1986.
9. G. Huet. A unification algorithm for typed λ-calculus. *Theoretical Computer Science*, 1:27–57, 1975.
10. G. Huet. *Résolution d'Equations dans les langages d'Ordre 1,2, ...,ω.* Thèse de Doctorat d'Etat, Université de Paris 7 (France), 1976.
11. G. Huet and B. Lang. Proving and applying program transformations expressed with second-order patterns. *Acta Informatica*, 11:31–55, 1978.
12. T. Kolbe and C. Walther. Reusing proofs. In A. Cohn, editor, *ECAI'94, 11th European Conference on Artificial Intelligence*, pages 80 - 84, 1994.
13. B. Krieg-Brüchner, J. Liu, H. Shi, and B. Wolff. Towards correct, effficient and reusable transformational developments. In *"KORSO: Methods, Languages, and Tools for the Construction of Correct Software"*, ages 270–284. LNCS 1009, 1995.
14. T. Nipkow and Z. Qian. Modular higher-order E-unification. In R. Book, editor, *Proc. 4th Int. Conf. Rewriting Techniques and Applications*, pages 200-214. LNCS 488, 1991.
15. L. Paulson. *Isabelle - A Generic Theorem prover.* LNCS 828, 1994.
16. Z. Qian and K. Wang. Higher-order E-unification for arbitrary theories. In K. Apt, ed., *Proc. 1992 Joint Int. Conf. and Symp. on Logic Programming.* MIT Press, 1992.
17. H. Shi. *Extended Matching with Applications to Program Transformation.* PhD thesis, Universität Bremen, 1994.
18. W. Snyder. Higher-order E-unification. In M. Stickel, editor, *Proc. 10th Int. Conf. Automated Deduction*, pages 573–587. Springer-Verlag LNCS 449, 1990.
19. W. Snyder and J. Gallier. Higher-order unification revisited: Complete sets of transformations. *J. Symbolic Computation*, 8(1 & 2):101–140, 1989.

Linear Second-Order Unification*

Jordi Levy

Departament de Llenguatges i Sistemes Informàtics
Universitat Politècnica de Catalunya
http://www-lsi.upc.es/~jlevy

Abstract. We present a new class of second-order unification problems, which we have called *linear*. We deal with completely general second-order typed unification problems, but we restrict the set of unifiers under consideration: they instantiate free variables by linear terms, i.e. terms where any λ-abstractions bind one and only one occurrence of a bound variable. Linear second-order unification properly extends *context unification* studied by Comon and Schmidt-Schauß. We describe a sound and complete procedure for this class of unification problems and we prove termination for three different subcases of them. One of these subcases is obtained requiring Comon's condition, another corresponds to Schmidt-Schauß's condition, (both studied previously for the case of context unification, and applied here to a larger class of problems), and the third one is original, namely that free variables occur at most twice.

1 Introduction

It is well-known that second-order unification is undecidable. However, it is still possible to obtain decidability for some restricted, although practical, classes of problems. That is the case of Miller's *higher-order patterns*. More recently, Comon and Schmidt-Schauß have proposed a new class of second-order unification problems, called *context unification*. They have proved decidability of two different subclasses of these problems, although it is not known if the whole class is decidable. In this paper we extend this class of problems to what we call *linear second-order unification*.

Historically, Robinson and Guard were the first who studied the higher-order unification problem in the sixties. In fact, a student of Guard (Gould [4]), was the first who found a complete second-order matching algorithm. Most of the results of second-order and higher-order unification problems were proved during the seventies. Pietrzykowski [15] described a complete second-order unification procedure, that was later extended to the higher-order case [7], and Huet [6] defined *preunification* (lazy unification) and found a non-redundant procedure for it. Most of the negative results were also discovered during this decade. Independently, Lucchesi [11] and Huet [5] showed that third-order unification is not decidable, later Goldfarb [3] showed that second-order unification is not decidable either. In the nineties, Miller [13] found the first class of decidable higher-order

* This work was partially supported by the ESPRIT Basic Research Action CCL and the project DISCOR (TIC 94-0847-C02-01) funded by the CICYT

unification problems, named ***higher-order pattern*** unification. Such patterns were used by Nipkow [14] to propose a notion of higher-order rewriting, which lead to quite some further research [16, 12, 10].

This paper deals with another class of higher-order unification problems that has caught the attention of some researchers recently, the so called ***context unification*** problems. This is an extension of first-order term unification where variables may denote not only (first-order) terms, but also contexts —terms with a ***hole*** or ***distinguished position***—. Comon [1] studied these problems to solve membership constraints. He proved that context unification is decidable, when any occurrence of the same context variable is always applied to the same term. Schmidt-Schauß [17] also studies the same problem, however he is interested in reducing the problem of unification modulo distributivity to a subset of such context unification problems. He proves that context unification is decidable when terms are ***stratified***. Hence, stratified means that the string of second-order variables we find going from the root of a term to any occurrence of the same variable, is always the same. Finally, our interest on such problem comes from the ***extended critical pair*** problem. This problem arises when trying to apply rewriting techniques to automated deduction in monotonic order theories, using ***bi-rewriting systems*** [8, 9].

However, we deal with an extension of the context unification problem, named ***linear second-order unification***. The generalization comes from two facts:

(i) we consider second-order terms (instead of first-order terms), thus expressions may contain λ-bindings, and

(ii) second-order context variables are not restricted to be unary, they may denote (second-order) terms with more than a ***hole*** or distinguished positions. In other words, second-order variables denote linear second-order terms. Hence, a ***linear term*** is a term whose normal form only contains λ-abstractions where the bound variable occurs once, and only once.

This generalization is motivated by the following problem. The unification problem $F(a) \stackrel{?}{=} G(f(a))$ has two minimum linear second-order unifiers:

$$\sigma_1 = [F \mapsto \lambda x \,.\, G(f(x))]$$
$$\sigma_2 = [F \mapsto \lambda x \,.\, H(x, f(a))][G \mapsto \lambda x \,.\, H(a, x)]$$

However, if we restrict ourselves to unary second-order variables, we can not represent the second minimum unifier. Context unification is infinitary for most of the problems.

This paper is structured as follows. Linear second-order unification problems are defined in section 2. Section 3 describes a linear second-order unification procedure which is proved to be sound and complete in section 4. Then, we prove decidability of such unification problems in three cases. Firstly, when no free variable occurs more than twice (section 5), secondly when a variable is applied to the same term in all its occurrences (section 6), and thirdly when we deal with ***stratified*** terms (section 7). Some of the proofs are long and quite complex, therefore in some cases we have included only a sketch of them.

2 Linear Second-Order Unification

In this section we define the linear second-order (LSO) typed λ-calculus, LSO-unification, and we prove some of its main properties.

We are concerned with a set of types $\mathcal{T} = \bigcup_{n\geq 1} \mathcal{T}^n$, a set of second-order typed variables $\mathcal{V} = \bigcup_{\tau\in\mathcal{T}^2} \mathcal{V}_\tau$, and a set of third-order typed constants $\mathcal{F} = \bigcup_{\tau\in\mathcal{T}^3} \mathcal{F}_\tau$ The inference rules defining well-typed linear-terms are the following ones.

$$\frac{\{x \in \mathcal{V}_\tau\}}{x : \tau} \qquad \frac{\{c \in \mathcal{F}_\tau\}}{c : \tau} \qquad \frac{x : \tau \qquad t : \tau' \qquad \{x \text{ occurs once in } t\}}{\lambda x\,.\,t : \tau \rightarrow \tau'} \qquad \frac{t : \tau \rightarrow \tau' \qquad u : \tau}{t(u) : \tau'}$$

We say that t is a *linear second-order (LSO) term* if $t : \tau$ may be inferred from these rules and $\tau \in \mathcal{T}^2$. Other concepts commonly used in λ-calculus, as free variables $\mathcal{FV}$, bound variables $\mathcal{BV}$, etc. will be used throughout without previous definition. Like in the simply second-order typed λ-calculus, we also consider the β and η equations $(\lambda x\,.\,t)(u) =_\beta t[x \mapsto u]$ and $\lambda x\,.\,t(x) =_\eta t$. Notice that the side condition $x \notin \mathcal{FV}(t)$ is not necessary in the η-equation because, if $\lambda x\,.\,t(x)$ is well-typed, then this condition is ensured. Notice also that these equations, used as rewriting rules, transform well-typed linear terms into linear terms with the same type. The η-long β-normal form of a term t is denoted by $t|_{\beta\eta}$ and has the form $\lambda x_1 \ldots x_n\,.\,a(t_1, \ldots, t_m)$, where a is called the *head* of the term and can be either a free variable, a bound variable or a constant, $a(t_1, \ldots, t_m)$ is a first-order typed term, and $t_1 \ldots t_m$ are also second-order normal terms. Moreover, if a is a bound variable then $m = 0$. We require linearity to prove the following lemma.

Lemma 1. *For any pair of LSO-terms t and u, if $t =_{\beta\eta} u$ then $\mathcal{FV}(t) = \mathcal{FV}(u)$.*

We consider any kind of second-order unification problem, and we only restrict the set of possible unifiers.

Definition 2. A *second-order unification* (SOU) *problem* is a finite set of pairs $\{t_1 \stackrel{?}{=} u_1, \ldots, t_n \stackrel{?}{=} u_n\}$, where t_i and u_i are —not necessarily linear— second-order typed terms, and have the same type, for any $i \in [1..n]$.
A *LSO-substitution* σ is an idempotent and type preserving morphism between terms such that its *domain*, defined by $\mathcal{D}om(\sigma) \stackrel{def}{=} \{X \mid X \neq \sigma(X)\}$, is finite and for any $X \in \mathcal{D}om(\sigma)$, $\sigma(X)$ is a $\beta\eta$-normal LSO-term.
As usual, given a pair of substitutions σ, ρ, we say that $\sigma \preceq \rho$ if there exists a substitution τ such that $\rho = \tau \circ \sigma$. We say that σ is a *minimum substitution* (w.r.t. a set of them) if for any other substitution ρ of the set we have $\sigma \preceq \rho$ or $\rho \not\preceq \sigma$. The set of *free variables of a substitution* is defined as $\mathcal{FV}(\sigma) = \bigcup_{X\in\mathcal{D}om(\sigma)} \mathcal{FV}(\sigma(X))$.

Lemma 3. *If the composition of two LSO-substitutions is idempotent, then it is also an LSO-substitution. (Composition preserves linearity).*
Given two terms t and u, there are finite many LSO-substitutions σ satisfying $t =_{\beta\eta} \sigma(u)$ and $\mathcal{D}om(\sigma) \subseteq \mathcal{FV}(u)$.[2]

[2] Notice that this is not true for non-linear substitutions: there are infinitely many substitutions $\sigma = [F \mapsto \lambda x\,.\,a, X \mapsto t]$ satisfying $\sigma(F(X)) = a$.

Second part of this lemma suggests us that LSO-substitutions are specially adequate for basing on it a definition of second-order rewriting systems.

3 A Linear Second-Order Unification Procedure

In this section we describe a sound and complete procedure for the LSO-unification problem. This procedure is non-terminating in general, but remind that decidability of LSO-unification and context unification are open problems. In following sections we will use modified versions of this procedure to prove decidability of the LSO-unification problem in some restricted cases. Thus, those modified versions are terminating, although they are complete only for some subset of problems.

In the description of the procedure we use a compact notation based on lists of indexes and indexed lists of indexes. We denote lists of indexes by capital letters P, Q, R,...For any list of indexes $P = \{p_1, \ldots, p_n\}$, the expression $a(\overline{b_P})$ denotes $a(b_{p_1}, \ldots, b_{p_n})$, and for any P-indexed list of indexes $Q_P = \{Q_{p_1}, \ldots, Q_{p_n}\} = \{\{q_1^1, \ldots, q_1^{m_1}\}, \ldots, \{q_n^1, \ldots, q_n^{m_n}\}\}$ the expression $a(\overline{b_P(\overline{c_{Q_P}})})$ denotes $a(b_{p_1}(c_{q_1^1} \ldots c_{q_1^{m_1}}), \ldots, b_{p_n}(c_{q_n^1} \ldots c_{q_n^{m_n}}))$. As usual, small letters like p denotes correlative lists of indexes $[1..p]$, so $a(\overline{b_p})$ denotes $a(b_1, \ldots, b_p)$.

We also use the notation on transformations introduced by Gallier and Snyder [2] for describing unification processes. Any state of the process is represented by a pair $\langle S, \sigma\rangle$ where $S = \{t_1 \stackrel{?}{=} u_1, \ldots, t_n \stackrel{?}{=} u_n\}$ is the set of unification problems still to be solved and σ is the substitution computed until that moment, i.e. the substitution leading from the initial problem to the actual one. The initial state is $\langle S_0, Id\rangle$. The procedure is described by means of transformation rules on states $\langle S, \sigma\rangle \Rightarrow \langle S', \sigma'\rangle$. If the initial state can be transformed into a normal form where the unification problem is empty $\langle S_0, Id\rangle \Rightarrow^* \langle \emptyset, \sigma\rangle$ then σ is a solution –minimal unifier– of the original unification problem S_0.

We suppose that any term of the initial state is in $\beta\eta$-normal form, and that after applying any transformation rule the new unification problem and the new substitution are also $\beta\eta$-normalized. Therefore, we can suppose that any pair $t \stackrel{?}{=} u \in S$ has the form $\lambda\overline{x_N}\,.\,a(\overline{t_P}) \stackrel{?}{=} \lambda\overline{x_N}\,.\,b(\overline{u_Q})$ because, if t and u have the same type, then they have the same number of more external λ-bindings. We give the same name to these bound variables using α-conversion.

Definition 4. All *problem transformation rules* have the form:

$$\langle S \cup \{t \stackrel{?}{=} u\}, \sigma\rangle \Rightarrow \langle \rho(S \cup R), \rho\circ\sigma\rangle$$

where, for each rule, the transformation $t \stackrel{?}{=} u \Rightarrow R$ and the LSO-substitution ρ are defined as follows.

1. *Rigid-rigid rule (or Simplification rule).* If a is a constant, or a bound variable then

$$\lambda\overline{x_N}\,.\,a(\overline{t_P}) \stackrel{?}{=} \lambda\overline{x_N}\,.\,a(\overline{u_P}) \;\Rightarrow\; \bigcup_{i\in P}\{\lambda\overline{x_N}\,.\,t_i \stackrel{?}{=} \lambda\overline{x_N}\,.\,u_i\}$$
$$\rho = Id$$

2. *Imitation rule.* If a is a constant[3] and F is a free variable, and $\{R_i\}_{i\in P}$ is a

[3] Notice that if a is a bound variable and $\lambda\overline{x_N}\,.\,a(\overline{t_P})$ is a LSO term, then $P = \emptyset$ and this situation is captured by the projection rule.

P-indexed family of disjoint lists of indexes satisfying[4] $\bigcup_{i\in P} R_i = Q$, then

$$\lambda\overline{x_N}\,.\,a(\overline{t_P}) \stackrel{?}{=} \lambda\overline{x_N}\,.\,F(\overline{u_Q}) \;\Rightarrow\; \bigcup_{i\in P}\{\lambda\overline{x_N}\,.\,t_i \stackrel{?}{=} \lambda\overline{x_N}\,.\,F_i'(\overline{u_{R_i}})\}$$
$$\rho = [F \mapsto \lambda\overline{y_Q}\,.\,a(\overline{F_P'(\overline{y_{R_P}})})]$$

where $\{F_j'\}_{j\in Q}$ are fresh free variables of the appropriate type that can be inferred from the context.

3. *Projection rule.* If a is a constant or a bound variable and F is a free variable, and $a(\overline{t_p})$ and u have the same type, then

$$\lambda\overline{x_N}\,.\,a(\overline{t_p}) \stackrel{?}{=} \lambda\overline{x_N}\,.\,F(u) \;\Rightarrow\; \{\lambda\overline{x_N}\,.\,a(\overline{t_p}) \stackrel{?}{=} \lambda\overline{x_N}\,.\,u\}$$
$$\rho = [F \mapsto \lambda y\,.\,y]$$

4. *Flexible-flexible rule with equal heads (or Simplification rule).* If F is a free variable, then

$$\lambda\overline{x_N}\,.\,F(\overline{t_P}) \stackrel{?}{=} \lambda\overline{x_N}\,.\,F(\overline{u_P}) \;\Rightarrow\; \bigcup_{i\in P}\{\lambda\overline{x_N}\,.\,t_i \stackrel{?}{=} \lambda\overline{x_N}\,.\,u_i\}$$
$$\rho = Id$$

5. *Flexible-flexible rule with distinct-heads (or Distinct-heads rule).* If F and G are free distinct variables, $P' \subseteq P$ and $Q' \subseteq Q$ are two lists of indexes, and $\{R_j\}_{j\in Q'}$ is a Q'-indexed and $\{S_i\}_{i\in P'}$ a P'-indexed family of disjoint lists of indexes satisfying R_j and P' are disjoint, S_i and Q' are also disjoint, $\left(\bigcup_{j\in Q'} R_j\right) \cup P' = P$ and $\left(\bigcup_{i\in P'} S_i\right) \cup Q' = Q$, then

$$\lambda\overline{x_N}\,.\,F(\overline{t_P}) \stackrel{?}{=} \lambda\overline{x_N}\,.\,G(\overline{u_Q}) \;\Rightarrow\; \bigcup_{j\in Q'}\{\lambda\overline{x_N}\,.\,F_j'(\overline{t_{R_j}}) \stackrel{?}{=} \lambda\overline{x_N}\,.\,u_j\} \,\cup \bigcup_{i\in P'}\{\lambda\overline{x_N}\,.\,t_i \stackrel{?}{=} \lambda\overline{x_N}\,.\,G_i'(\overline{u_{S_i}})\}$$
$$\rho = [F \mapsto \lambda\overline{y_P}\,.\,H'(\overline{F_{Q'}'(\overline{y_{R_{Q'}}})}, \overline{y_{P'}})][G \mapsto \lambda\overline{z_Q}\,.\,H'(\overline{z_{Q'}}, \overline{G_{P'}'(\overline{z_{S_{P'}}})})]$$

where H', $\{G_i'\}_{i\in P'}$ and $\{F_j'\}_{j\in Q'}$ are fresh free variables of the appropriate types. Notice that if $R_j = \emptyset$ then F_j' is a first-order typed variable (resp. for S_i and G_i').

Compared with the general second-order unification procedure [7], we avoid the use of the prolific *elimination* and *iteration* rules, which always compromise the termination of their procedure. It does not mean that our procedure terminates, but it avoids many redundant states. Moreover, in contrast to Jensen and Pietrzykowski's procedure, our procedure only computes minimal unifiers.

To ensure that the final substitution is linear, we only instantiate free variables by linear terms. This means that when we apply imitation rule like $[F \mapsto \lambda\overline{y_Q}\,.\,a(\overline{F_P'(\overline{y_{R_P}})})]$, we have to make sure that the Q arguments of F are distributed among the F_P' new variables. This imposes the restrictions $\{R_i\}_{i\in Q}$ are disjoint lists of indexes and $\bigcup_{i\in P} R_i = Q$. Notice that this condition ensures that $\lambda\overline{y_Q}\,.\,a(\overline{F_P'(\overline{y_{R_P}})})$ is a linear term.

---

[4] Union and comparison of lists of indexes is computed without considering their order.

4 Soundness and Completeness

In this section we schematize the proofs for soundness and completeness of our procedure.

Theorem 5. Soundness. *For any second-order unification problem S_0, if there exists a derivation $\langle S_0, Id\rangle \Rightarrow^* \langle \emptyset, \sigma\rangle$, then σ is a minimal linear second-order unifier of S_0.*

Simplification steps preserve the set of minimum unifiers of an unification problem. Imitation, projection and distinct-heads steps may be considered as the composition of an instantiation and a simplification step, where the substitution instantiates a free variable by a linear term. For instance, the imitation rule may be decomposed as follows.

$$\begin{array}{lll} \lambda\overline{x_N}\,.\,a(\overline{t_P}) \stackrel{?}{=} \lambda\overline{x_N}\,.\,F(\overline{u_Q}) \Rightarrow & \lambda\overline{x_N}\,.\,a(\overline{t_P}) \stackrel{?}{=} \lambda\overline{x_N}\,.\,a(\overline{F'_P(\overline{u_{R_P}})}) & \text{Instantiation} \\ \Rightarrow & \bigcup_{i\in P}\{t_i \stackrel{?}{=} F'_i(\overline{u_{R_i}})\} & \text{Simplification} \end{array}$$

Now, taking into account that composition of linear substitutions is also a linear substitution (see lemma 3, taking into account that we only introduce fresh variables, which ensures idempotence), it is not difficult to prove that the final substitution is really a unifier.

Theorem 6. Completeness. *If σ is a minimum linear second-order unifier of the second-order unification problem S_0, then there exists a transformation sequence $\langle S_0, Id\rangle \Rightarrow^* \langle \emptyset, \sigma\rangle$.*

We can prove easily that whenever exists a minimum unifier σ of a unification problem S_0, we can generate a sequence of transformations:

$$\langle S_0, Id\rangle \Rightarrow \langle S_1, \sigma_1\rangle \Rightarrow \cdots \Rightarrow \langle S_n, \sigma_n\rangle \Rightarrow \cdots$$

satisfying $\sigma_n \preceq \sigma$ for any $n \geq 0$. There are two possibilities, either this sequence is infinite or its last state is $\langle \emptyset, \sigma\rangle$.

Now, we can prove that no such infinite sequences exist. In first-order we can define the *size of a substitution* as $size(\sigma) = \sum_{X\in Dom(\sigma)} \sigma(X)$, where the size of a term is the number of applications it contains. Then, we can prove that each new instantiation increases this size, i.e. if $\sigma \preceq \rho$ then $size(\sigma) \leq size(\rho)$. This is not true in second-order because we can instantiate a second-order variable by a function which disregards its parameters[5]. This is not true in linear second-order unification either, due to the projection rule. Fortunately, in our case we can avoid this problem defining the size of a substitution w.r.t. another substitution.

Definition 7. The *size of a term* t w.r.t. a substitution ρ is defined as follows

$$size(\lambda\overline{x_P}\,.\,a(\overline{t_Q}), \rho) = \sum_{q\in Q} size(t_q, \rho) + \begin{cases} 0 & \text{if } a \text{ is a free variable and } \rho(a) = \lambda x\,.\,x \\ \#Q & \text{otherwise} \end{cases}$$

[5] In this case we could define the size of a term as the number of applications contained in its $\beta\eta$-normal form.

where $\#Q$ is the cardinality of Q, and the *size of a LSO-substitutions* is defined as follows

$$size(\sigma,\rho) \stackrel{def}{=} \sum_{X \in Dom(\sigma)} size(\sigma(X),\rho)$$

Lemma 8. *For any LSO-term t and LSO-substitutions σ, ρ and τ we have*

$$size(\,t\,,\,\tau\circ\rho\,) \leq size(\,\rho(t)\,,\,\tau\,)$$
$$size(\,\sigma\,,\,\tau\circ\rho\,) \leq size(\,\rho\circ\sigma\,,\,\tau\,)$$

Although projection steps do not increase the size of the unifier computed till that moment, they decrease the free arity of the problem, defined as $arity(S) = \sum_{X\in\mathcal{FV}(S)} arity(X)$ where as usual the arity of a variable X is the maximal number of parameters it admits.[6]

Finally, we can define the size of a state $\langle S_n, \sigma_n\rangle$, of our particular sequence of transformations, w.r.t. the unifier σ as a triplet where first and second component are integers and the third component is a multiset of integers:

$$size(\langle S_n,\sigma_n\rangle) = \min_{\{\tau \mid \sigma=\tau\circ\sigma_n\}} \Big\langle arity(S_n), size(\sigma,Id) - size(\sigma_n,\tau), \bigcup_{t\stackrel{?}{=}u\in S_n}\{size(t,\tau), size(u,\tau)\}\Big\rangle$$

Now we have to prove that if $\langle S_n,\sigma_n\rangle \Rightarrow \langle S_{n+1},\sigma_{n+1}\rangle$ then $size(\langle S_n,\sigma_n\rangle) > size(\langle S_{n+1},\sigma_{n+1}\rangle)$, where $>$ is a lexicographic ordering, and third components of the triplet are compared using the usual multiset ordering. We may check that any projection step strictly reduces the free arity of the problem, whereas any other transformation does not change it. For imitation steps and flexible-flexible steps the result depends on the size of the variable (or variables) being instantiated before and after applying the transformation step. If it does not increase, then the size of the substitution remains unchanged but the size of the problem decreases. If it increases, although the size of the problem increases, the size of the substitution also increases (the difference $size(\sigma,Id) - size(\sigma_n,\tau_n)$ decreases). For simplification steps, $\sigma_n = \sigma_{n+1}$, the substitution does not change but the size of the problem decreases (maybe its free arity, too).

Notice that this result proves the completeness of the unification procedure, but not its termination and, therefore, not the decidability of the unification problem. The function *size* could be used to prove the termination of the procedure if we would be able to fix an upper bound $size(\sigma,Id) \leq MAX$ for the size of one of the minimum unifier of a unification problem, if it has any.

5 A Termination Result

In the following we will prove that our procedure always finishes for a very useful case: if no free variable occurs more than twice in an unification problem. This fact is related with the termination of the *naive* string unification procedure when variables occurs at most twice [18].

Theorem 9. Termination. *If no free variable occurs more than twice in a linear second-order unification problem, then this unification problem is decidable.*

[6] If $X : \tau_1 \to \ldots \to \tau_n \to \tau$ and τ is a first-order type, then $arity(X) = n$.

To prove this theorem we define the following *size* function, where we suppose that any term is normalized previously to compute its size.

$$size(\lambda x_1 \dots x_n \,.\, a(t_1, \dots, t_p)) = p + \sum_{i=1}^{p} size(t_i)$$
$$size(\{t_1 \stackrel{?}{=} u_1, \dots, t_n \stackrel{?}{=} u_n\}) = \sum_{i=1}^{n} size(u_i) + size(t_i)$$

We prove now that if $\langle S, \sigma\rangle \Rightarrow \langle S', \rho\circ\sigma\rangle$ and any free variable appears at most twice in S then $size(S') \leq size(S)$ and any free variable also appears at most twice in S'. There are five cases. Here we only show the case of flexible-flexible steps with distinct-heads.

$$\lambda\overline{x_N}\,.\,F(\overline{t_P}) \stackrel{?}{=} \lambda\overline{x_N}\,.\,G(\overline{u_Q}) \;\Rightarrow\; \bigcup_{j\in Q'} \{\lambda\overline{x_N}\,.\,F'_j(\overline{t_{R_j}}) \stackrel{?}{=} \lambda\overline{x_N}\,.\,u_j\} \cup \bigcup_{i\in P'} \{\lambda\overline{x_N}\,.\,t_i \stackrel{?}{=} \lambda\overline{x_N}\,.\,G'_i(\overline{u_{S_i}})\}$$
$$\rho = [F \mapsto \lambda\overline{y_P}\,.\,H'(\overline{F'_{Q'}(\overline{y_{R_{Q'}}})}, \overline{y_{P'}})][G \mapsto \lambda\overline{z_Q}\,.\,H'(\overline{z_{Q'}}, \overline{G'_{P'}(\overline{z_{S_{P'}}})})]$$

The size of the problem decreases in $\#P + \#Q - \sum_{i\in P'} \#S_i - \sum_{j\in Q'} \#R_j = \#P' + \#Q'$ and is increased in $\#Q'$ for any instantiation of F and in $\#P'$ for any instantiation of G. Therefore, in the worst case, the size of the problem remains equal. It is also easy to see that in the worst case we introduce two occurrences of each one of the fresh variables H', $\{F'_i\}$ and $\{G'_j\}$.

Finally, taking into account that for any finite signature and given size there are finitely many unification problems, it easy to see that it is enough to control loops to ensure the termination of the procedure described in the previous sections.

6 Extension of Comon's Decidability Result

To extend Comon's condition [1] to linear second-order unification we have to consider non-unary free variables and λ-bindings. The later makes necessary to introduce λ-equivalent terms.

Definition 10. Given two LSO-terms $\lambda x_1, \dots, x_n \,.\, t$ and $\lambda y_1, \dots, y_m \,.\, u$, we say that they are *$\lambda$-equivalent*, noted $\lambda x_1, \dots, x_n \,.\, t =_\lambda \lambda y_1, \dots, y_m \,.\, u$, if $\lambda x_1, \dots, x_n \,.\, t|_{\beta\eta} =_\alpha \lambda z_1, \dots, z_{n-m}, y_1, \dots, y_m \,.\, u|_{\beta\eta}$, where we suppose that $n \geq m$ and $\{z_1, \dots, z_n\} \not\subseteq \mathcal{FV}(u)$.

Given a normalized unification problem S, we say that it satisfies the *extended Comon's condition* if, for any pair of occurrences of a free variable F, they are in two subterms $F(t_1, \dots, t_n)$ and $F(u_1, \dots, u_n)$ satisfying $\lambda\overline{x_N}\,.\,F(t_1, \dots, t_n) =_\lambda \lambda\overline{y_M}\,.\,F(u_1, \dots, u_n)$, where $\overline{x_N}$ and $\overline{y_M}$ are respectively the sequence of λ-bindings above these subterms.

Notice that λ-equivalence is an extension of α-conversion between $\beta\eta$-normal terms. We can prove that Comon's condition is also enough to ensures decidability in the more general linear second-order unification setting.

Theorem 11. Termination II. *Any linear second-order unification problem satisfying the extended Comon's condition is decidable and finitary.*

To ensure the termination of our unification procedure we have to apply a kind of problem normalization before any transformation. This is equivalent to working with *generalized equations* like it is done in A-unification [18]. We deal with sequences of equalities $t_1 \stackrel{?}{=} \cdots \stackrel{?}{=} t_n$ and we concatenate any pair of sequence sharing two λ-equivalent terms. Thus, apart from the normalization procedure described in section 2, we will apply the following *concatenation rule*:

$$\{t_1 \stackrel{?}{=} \cdots \stackrel{?}{=} t_n \,,\, u_1 \stackrel{?}{=} \cdots \stackrel{?}{=} u_m\} \cup S \Rightarrow \{t_1 \stackrel{?}{=} \cdots t_n \stackrel{?}{=} \lambda \overline{x_N} \,.\, u_2 \stackrel{?}{=} \cdots \stackrel{?}{=} \lambda \overline{x_N} \,.\, u_m\} \cup S$$

whenever $t_1 =_\alpha \lambda \overline{x_N} \,.\, u_1$, i.e. whenever $t_1 =_\lambda u_1$.

This normalization procedure and Comon's condition ensures that no free variable F occurs in the outermost head of more than one term, although F may occur below the head of other terms.

Definition 12. Given a unification problem S, let $\approx_S$ be the reflexive-transitive closure of the relation defined by: if $t =_\lambda u$ or $t \stackrel{?}{=} u \in S$ then $t \approx_S u$, for any pair of terms t and u. Consider the finite set of $\approx_S$-equivalence classes of terms containing a term of S or a subterms of one of them.

Let $\succ_S$ be the relation, on this set of classes of terms, defined by the transitive closure of the strict subterm relation: $[\lambda \overline{x_N} \,.\, a(\overline{t_P})] \succ_S [\lambda \overline{x_N} \,.\, t_i]$ for any $i \in P$ and any term $\lambda \overline{x_N} \,.\, a(\overline{t_P})$ of S.

Since there are finitely many classes of terms, $\succ_S$ is either cycling or well-founded. Definitions of $\approx_S$ and $\succ_S$ are invariants for concatenation of generalized equations (normalization of unification problems), moreover any two terms belonging to the same generalized equation are $\approx$-equivalent. Finally, if σ is a unifier of S and $t \approx_S u$ then $\sigma(t)$ and $\sigma(u)$ have the same size (number of applications), and, if $t \succ_S u$ then the size of $\sigma(t)$ is greater or equal to the size of $\sigma(u)$. This fact allows us to prove the following lemma, which characterizes two possible situations we have to consider.

Lemma 13. *For any unification problem S, either a) the relation $\succ_S$ is irreflexive and therefore well-founded, or b) any unifier σ of S satisfies $\sigma(F) = \lambda x \,.\, x$ for some free variable F.*

In case b) of the lemma the only chance to get a solution is applying —after maybe some simplification steps— the projection rule to a free variable involved in a $\succ$ cycle, i.e. if we have $[\lambda \overline{x_N} \,.\, F(t)] \succ_S [\lambda \overline{x_N} \,.\, t] \succ_S \cdots \succ_S [\lambda \overline{x_N} \,.\, F(t)]$, then any unifier σ of S, if there is any[7], satisfies $\sigma(F) = \lambda x \,.\, x$. As we know, projection rule strictly decreases the free arity of the problem, whereas any other transformation rule preserves it. This allows us to define a well-founded lexicographic ordering on unification problems where first component is free arity.

In case a) if S satisfies Comon's condition and $\succ_S$ is not cycling, we can prove that —after applying some simplification steps— there exists a free variable occurring in the head of a term and no occurring elsewhere. We will try to find an instantiation for this variable. Suppose we decide to apply imitation rule, and such variable is F. This imitation rule may be extended to deal with generalized

[7] Some unification problems, like $\{\lambda x \,.\, F(x) \stackrel{?}{=} \lambda x \,.\, a(G(x)), \lambda y \,.\, G(y) \stackrel{?}{=} \lambda y \,.\, b(F(y))\}$, defining a cycling $\succ_S$ relation, have no solutions, even if we try instantiate F or G by $\lambda x \,.\, x$.

equations as follows.

$$\lambda\overline{x_N}\,.\,a(\overline{t_P}) \stackrel{?}{=} \lambda\overline{x_N}\,.\,F(\overline{u_Q}) \stackrel{?}{=} v_1 \stackrel{?}{=} \ldots \stackrel{?}{=} v_r$$
$$\Downarrow$$
$$\lambda\overline{x_N}\,.\,a(\overline{t_P}) \stackrel{?}{=} v_1 \stackrel{?}{=} \ldots \stackrel{?}{=} v_r \;\cup\; \bigcup_{i\in P}\left\{\lambda\overline{x_N}\,.\,t_i \stackrel{?}{=} \lambda\overline{x_N}\,.\,F'_i(\overline{u_{R_i}})\right\}$$

Most important thing is noticing that no instantiation is necessary on such transformation step because F occurs only once. After normalizing the new problem, new equations $\lambda\overline{x_N}\,.\,t_i \stackrel{?}{=} \lambda\overline{x_N}\,.\,F'_i(\overline{u_{R_i}})$ may be appended to other generalized equations, however this is not a problem because $\succ_S$ is invariant for such process. Moreover, although we have modified the unification problem, the (finite) set of $\approx$-equivalence classes of terms does not change (or it has decreassed if $v_1 \stackrel{?}{=} \cdots v_r$ is empty). We have introduced two different kinds of new terms: $\lambda\overline{x_N}\,.\,t_i$ and $\lambda\overline{x_N}\,.\,F'_i(\overline{u_{R_i}})$, but both of them belong to already taken into account classes of equivalences. Furthermore, subterms of these new terms are also subterms of other old terms. However, the relation $\succ_S$ has changed, for any transformation $S \Rightarrow S'$ we have $\succ_S \subseteq \succ_{S'}$. (Notice that now $[\lambda\overline{x_N}\,.\,t_i] = [\lambda\overline{x_N}\,.\,F'_i(\overline{u_{R_i}})] \succ_{S'} [\lambda\overline{x_N}\,.\,u_{R_i}]$).

Summing up, term $\lambda\overline{x_N}\,.\,F(\overline{u_Q})$ has been replaced (from a generalized equation) by several $\succ_S$-strictly smaller terms (introduced in other generalized equations), and $\succ_S$ has been replaced by a bigger relation $\succ_{S'}$ over the same set of classes of terms. Something similar applies to the distinct-heads rule. This fact and the reduction of free arity due to projection rule may be used to define a well-founded ordering on unification problems, and conclude that linear second-order unification under Comon's restriction is finitary.

7 Decidability Result for Stratified Terms

Schmidt-Schauß [17] describes another class of decidable context unification problems, called ***stratified second-order unification***. Hence, a stratified second-order term is a second-order typed term where the ***string*** or sequence of second-order variables we find going from the root of the term to an occurrence of a second-order variable is always the same, for any occurrence of this variable. We can represent these stratification of second-order variables as a set of trees (i.e. as a ***forest***). This is an example of stratified term and its corresponding forest:

$$f(F(H(b))\,,\,G(a)\,,\,F(g(H(b), I(a))))$$

The restriction on the ***string*** of each variable is extended to all the occurrences of such variable in a unification problem. This introduces a new problem, because such restriction neither is stable for instantiations nor for simplifications. For instance, term $F(G(a))$ becomes non-stratified after applying substitution $[F \mapsto \lambda x\,.\,G(x)]$, and the stratified unification problem $\left\{F(G(a)) \stackrel{?}{=} F(H(a)), F(G(a)) \stackrel{?}{=} f(a)\right\}$ is transformed into the non-stratified unification problem $\left\{G(a) \stackrel{?}{=} H(a), F(G(a)) \stackrel{?}{=} f(a)\right\}$ after simplification. The second problem suggests us to generalize the definition of stratified problem. Moreover, we have also to generalize it to consider non-unary free variables.

Definition 14. Given a set of variables $\mathcal{V}$, a ***stratified forest*** is a set of trees W

where, for any n-ary variable $F \in \mathcal{V}$, we have n distinct nodes $F^1, \ldots, F^n$ such that, either all them are roots of some tree, or all them are sons of the same father.

A $\beta\eta$-normal term t is a ***stratified term*** w.r.t. (a position $p = [\,]$ of) a stratified forest W if for any free variable F of t we have:

(i) if the corresponding nodes $F^1, \ldots, F^n$ are roots of trees of W, then no free occurrence of F is below any other free variable occurrence of t,

(ii) if the corresponding nodes $F^1, \ldots, F^n$ are sons of another node G^i of W, then any free occurrence of F is in the ith argument of an occurrence of G and there is no other free variable occurrence between these occurrences of F and G.

We define a ***position p of a forest W***, denoted by $W|_p$, recursively as follows.

(i) $\{t_1, \ldots, t_n\}|_{[\,]} \stackrel{def}{=} \{t_1, \ldots, t_n\}$

(ii) $\{t_1, \ldots, t_n\}|_{[p_1, \ldots, p_m]} \stackrel{def}{=} \{u_1, \ldots, u_p\}|_{[p_2, \ldots, p_m]}$ where $p_1 \in [1..n]$ and $u_1, \ldots, u_p$ is the list of subtrees of t_{p_1}.

(Notice that, in order to define positions in a forest, we have to suppose a certain ordering on trees and subtrees).

A $\beta\eta$-normal term t is a ***stratified term*** w.r.t. a position p of a stratified forest W, if t is a stratified term w.r.t. the forest $W|_p$.

Given a unification problem S, we say it is a ***stratified unification problem*** if there exists a forest W such that for any $t \stackrel{?}{=} u \in S$, terms t and u are both stratified w.r.t. the same position p of W. For any stratified problem S there exists a unique minimum —the one which has less nodes— forest W_S, called the ***associated*** forest of S.

Theorem 15. Termination III. *It is decidable whether a stratified unification problem has a solution or not. Moreover, we can find the complete set of minimum unifiers, although the unification problem may be infinitary.*

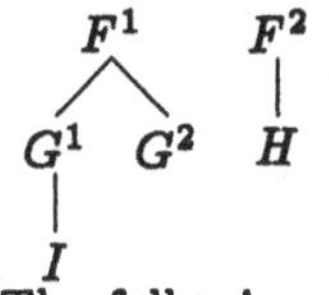

On the left there is an example of stratified forest of $\mathcal{V} = \{F, G, H, I\}$, where F and G are binary variables and H and I are unary variables.

The following are examples of stratified terms w.r.t. (the position $p = [\,]$ of) this stratified forest.

$$F(f(G(a,b),\, G(I(a),b))\,,\; H(a)) \qquad\qquad F(a, H(b))$$

The following are examples of stratified terms

$$G(I(a), b) \qquad\qquad f(H(a)\,,\, g(H(b))) \qquad\qquad g(I(a))$$

w.r.t. positions [1], [2] and [1, 1] respectively, of the same forest. The unification problem $\{G(I(a), b) \stackrel{?}{=} g(I(a))\}$ is not stratified because, although both terms are stratified, they are stratified w.r.t. two different positions.

Notice that any term without free variables is a stratified term w.r.t. any position of any stratified forest. However, such terms may be suppressed from any unification problem using a second-order matching algorithm.

Since for any n-ary variable F there are only n nodes $F^1, \ldots, F^n$ in the stratified forest and all them are sons of the same father or roots, we can not have a stratified term with an free occurrence of F below any other free occurrence of the same variable F.

We will give now some results which will allow us to prove termination of a modified version of our unification procedure when we deal with stratified unification problems.

Lemma 16. *Any substitution applied by the unification procedure transforms a stratified unification problem S w.r.t. a forest W_S, into another stratified unification problem S' w.r.t. a new forest $W_{S'}$, such that $W_{S'}$ has less or as many nodes as W_S.*

Let us see how imitation rule transforms these stratified forests. We take $P = [1..p]$ and $Q = [1..q]$ for simplicity. Given a family of disjoint lists of indexes $\{R_i\}_{i\in[1..p]}$ satisfying $\bigcup_{i\in[1..p]} R_i = [1..q]$. The substitution applied by this rule is written as follows.

$$\rho = \left[F \mapsto \lambda\overline{y_q}\,.\,a\big(G_1(y_{r_1^1},\ldots,y_{r_{n_1}^1}),\ldots,G_p(y_{r_1^p},\ldots,y_{r_{n_p}^p})\big)\right]$$

where $R_i \stackrel{def}{=} \{r_1^i,\ldots,r_{n_i}^i\}$ and $\{G_j\}_{j\in[1..p]}$ are fresh free variables. Nodes corresponding to F have to be substituted by nodes corresponding to the G_i, in the new forest, as it is shown in figure 1. In the same figure we show also how projection rule and distinct-heads rule transform stratified forests.

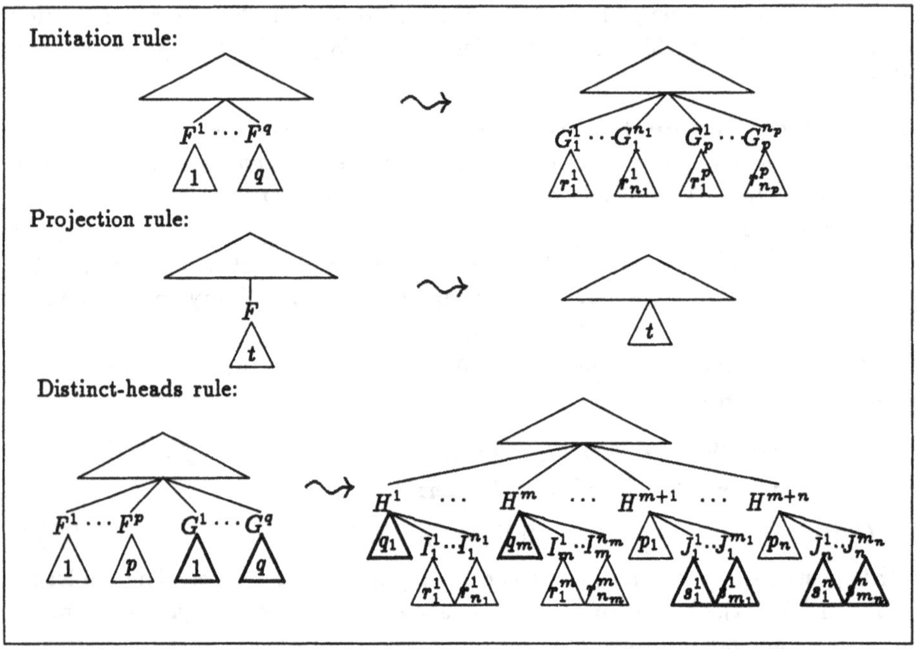

Fig. 1. Forest transformation obtained for each one of the transformation rules.

Notice that not all new G_i appear in the new forest, only the second-order typed ones, i.e. those which satisfy $R_i \neq \emptyset$.

The restriction on the family of indexes R_i ensures that $\sum_{i=1}^{p} n_i = q$ and $\bigcup_{i\in[1..p]} R_i = \{r_1^1 \dots r_{n_1}^1, \dots r_1^p \dots r_{n_p}^p\}$ is a permutation of $[1..q]$, therefore the number of nodes, even the shape of the tree, do not change. Nodes $F^1, \dots, F^q$ have been replaced by nodes G_i^j, and subtrees below them have been permuted and reallocated below new nodes.

Notice that when a subtree of W is reallocated in W' then, except in the case of projection rule, it either goes to a deeper position or remains in the same forest level. This allows to prove the following lemma.

Lemma 17. *If S is a stratified unification problem w.r.t. a position p of W, then $\rho(S)$ is a stratified unification problem w.r.t. a position p' of W' such that either*

(i) $p = p'$, *or*

(ii) *p' is shorter than p, if ρ is the substitution corresponding to a projection step,*

(iii) *p and p' have the same length, if ρ corresponds to an imitation step,*

(iv) *p' is longer or has the same length than p, if ρ corresponds to a distinct-heads step.*

This lemma suggests us to define a notion of depth level of a stratified term.

Definition 18. Term t is said to be a *n-level stratified term* w.r.t. a forest W, noted $depth(t, W) = n$, if it is a stratified term w.r.t. a position p of W and $\texttt{length}(p) = n$.

We associate a multiset of integers to each stratified unification problem S w.r.t. a forest W, defined as follows

$$depth(S, W) = \{Nod - depth(t, W) \mid t \stackrel{?}{=} u \in S \wedge u \stackrel{?}{=} t \in S\}$$

where Nod is the number of nodes of W (i.e. the maximum depth W can reach).

After showing how imitation, projection and distinct-heads rules transform a stratified forest, let us analyze what happens with simplification rules.

Lemma 19. *If $\lambda\overline{x_N} \,.\, a(\overline{t_P}) \stackrel{?}{=} \lambda\overline{x_N} \,.\, a(\overline{u_P})$ are both stratified term w.r.t. a position p of a forest W, then so they are $\lambda\overline{x_N} \,.\, t_i \stackrel{?}{=} \lambda\overline{x_N} \,.\, u_i$, for any $i \in P$.*

If $\lambda\overline{x_N} \,.\, F(\overline{t_P}) \stackrel{?}{=} \lambda\overline{x_N} \,.\, F(\overline{u_P})$ are both stratified term w.r.t. a position p of a forest W, then $\lambda\overline{x_N} \,.\, t_i \stackrel{?}{=} \lambda\overline{x_N} \,.\, u_i$ are both stratified terms w.r.t. a position p' of W, where $\texttt{length}(p') = \texttt{length}(p) + 1$, for any $i \in P$.

If we consider each problem transformation as an instantiation followed by a simplification, then this two lemmas allow us to define an ordering on unification problems taking into account the following facts.

(i) Each projection step strictly decreases the size (number of nodes) of the associated stratified forest of a problem, whereas the rest of rules preserve this size.

(ii) Each flexible-flexible step with equal heads or distinct-heads strictly decrease the depth level of any unification problem S, whereas the rest of rules also decrease or preserve this depth level.

(iii) Each rigid-rigid step strictly decreases the size of a unification problem.

We can conclude that any non-terminating transformation sequence of a stratified unification problem contains infinitely many imitation steps. We can go a bit farther and state the following theorem.

Theorem 20. *Any infinite sequence of transformations of stratified unification problems contains an infinite subsequence of imitation steps of the form:*

$$\lambda\overline{x_N}\,.\,a(\overline{t_p}) \stackrel{?}{=} \lambda\overline{x_N}\,.\,F(\overline{u_q}) \;\Rightarrow\; \big\{\lambda\overline{x_N}\,.\,t_i \stackrel{?}{=} \lambda\overline{x_N}\,.\,F'_i(u_1,\ldots,u_q)\big\}\cup \bigcup_{j\in P\wedge j\neq i}\{\lambda\overline{x_N}\,.\,t_j \stackrel{?}{=} \lambda\overline{x_N}\,.\,F_j\}$$

$$\rho = \big[F \mapsto \lambda\overline{y_Q}\,.\,a\big(F'_1,\cdots,F'_{i-1},F'_i(y_1,\ldots,y_q),F'_{i+1},\cdots,F'_p\big)\big]$$

for some $i \in [1..p]$ such that F occurs free in t_i, and no other free variable occurs between the root of t_i and this occurrence of F.

Once we have characterized the only type of infinite transformation sequences we can have, we substitute them by a single transformation rule without losing completeness property of the procedure. This rule will be the only source of infinitary solutions of this class of problems. Notice that all pairs involved in such infinite sequences must be treated together, so this new rule is a bit complex and we have no room here to describe it in detail. We will do that in the case of A-unification, using the parallelism existing between A-unification and linear second-order unification.

We have, in general, a set of unification pairs

$$\big\{F\cdot\alpha_1 \stackrel{?}{=} \beta_1\cdot F\cdot\delta_1\;,\cdots,\;F\cdot\alpha_n \stackrel{?}{=} \beta_n\cdot F\cdot\delta_n\big\}$$

where greek letters represent sequences of symbols and F does not occur in them. Moreover, β_i does not contain any variable occurrence. There are two kinds of solution for F.

If there exists a decomposition of $\beta_i = \gamma_i\cdot\eta_i$ and there exists an exponent n_i such that $(\beta_i)^{n_i}\cdot\gamma_i = \omega_1$ for any $i \in [1..n]$ then substitution $[F \mapsto \omega_1]$ transforms the previous problem into

$$\big\{\alpha_1 \stackrel{?}{=} \eta_1\cdot\gamma_1\cdot\delta_1\;,\cdots,\;\alpha_n \stackrel{?}{=} \eta_n\cdot\gamma_n\cdot\delta_n\big\}$$

If additionally there exists another exponent m_i such that $(\beta_i)^{m_i} = \omega_2$ for any $i \in [1..n]$ then $[F \mapsto (\omega_2)^p\cdot\omega_1]$ transforms the original problem into the same new one, for any value of p. Therefore, this second kind of solutions is infinitary because the value of p is not fixed.

Finally, it can be proved that the existence of such decompositions and exponents is decidable, even in the more complex case of linear second-order unification.

8 Conclusions

In this paper we have extended decidability results of Comon [1] and Schmidt-Schauß [17] for context unification to a proper extension of this unification problem, that we have called *linear second-order unification*, where n-ary free variables and λ-bindings are allowed. We have also described a complete unification procedure for this problem on which we have based all our decidability proofs. These proofs are completely independent from those given by Comon and Schmidt-Schauß.

This class of unification problems has good chances to become the basis of a notion of second-order rewriting. Then it would be interesting to find termination orderings and a critical pairs lemma for them. Decidability of general linear second-order unification problems, like decidability of general context unification problems, still remain as open questions.

References

1. H. Comon. Completion of rewrite systems with membership constraints, part I: Deduction rules and part II: Constraint solving. Technical report, CNRS and LRI, Université de Paris Sud, 1993. (To appear in J. of Symbolic Computation).
2. J. H. Gallier and W. Snyder. Designing unification procedures using transformations: A survey. *Bulletin of the EATCS*, 40:273–326, 1990.
3. W. D. Goldfarb. The undecidability of the second-order unification problem. *Theoretical Computer Science*, 13:225–230, 1981.
4. W. E. Gould. *A Matching Procedure for ω-Order Logic.* PhD thesis, Princeton Univ., 1966.
5. G. Huet. The undecidability of unification in third-order logic. *Information and Control*, 22(3):257–267, 1973.
6. G. Huet. A unification algorithm for typed λ-calculus. *Theoretical Computer Science*, 1:27–57, 1975.
7. D. C. Jensen and T. Pietrzykowski. Mechanizing ω-order type theory through unification. *Theoretical Computer Science*, 3:123–171, 1976.
8. J. Levy and J. Agustí. Bi-rewriting, a term rewriting technique for monotonic order relations. In *4th Int. Conf. on Rewriting Techniques and Applications, RTA'93*, volume 690 of *LNCS*, pages 17–31, Montreal, Canada, 1993.
9. J. Levy and J. Agustí. Bi-rewriting systems. *J. of Symbolic Computation*, 1995. (To be published).
10. C. Loría-Sáenz. *A Theoretical Framework for Reasoning about Program Construction based on Extensions of Rewrite Systems.* PhD thesis, Univ. Kaiserslautern, 1993.
11. C. L. Lucchesi. The undecidability of the unification problem for third-order languages. Technical Report CSRR 2059, Dept. of Applied Analysis and Computer Science, Univ. of Waterloo, 1972.
12. O. Lysne and J. Piris. A termination ordering for higher-order rewrite systems. In *6th Int. Conf on Rewriting Techniques and Applications, RTA'95*, volume 914 of *LNCS*, Kaiserslautern, Germany, 1995.
13. D. Miller. A logic programming language with lambda-abstraction, function variables, and simple unification. *J. of Logic and Computation*, 1:497–536, 1991.
14. T. Nipkow. Functional unification of higher-order patterns. In *8th IEEE Symp. on Logic in Computer Science, LICS'93*, pages 64–74, Montreal, Canada, 1993.
15. T. Pietrzykowski. A complete mechanization of second-order logic. *J. of the ACM*, 20(2):333–364, 1973.
16. C. Prehofer. *Solving Higher-Order Equations: From Logic to Programming.* PhD thesis, Technische Universität München, 1995.
17. M. Schmidt-Schauß. Unification of stratified second-order terms. Technical Report 12/94, Johan Wolfgang-Goethe-Universität, Frankfurt, Germany, 1995.
18. K. U. Schulz. Makanin's algorithm, two improvements and a generalization. Technical Report CIS-Bericht-91-39, Centrum für Informations und Sprachverarbeitung, Universität München, 1991.

Unification of Higher-Order Patterns in a Simply Typed Lambda-Calculus with Finite Products and Terminal Type

Roland Fettig and Bernd Löchner

Universität Kaiserslautern, Fachbereich Informatik, Postfach 3049,
D-67653 Kaiserslautern, Germany

{fettig,loechner}@informatik.uni-kl.de

Abstract. We develop a higher-order unification algorithm for a restricted class of simply typed lambda terms with function space and product type constructors. It is based on an inference system manipulating so called higher-order product-patterns which is proven to be sound and complete. Allowing tuple constructors in lambda binders provides elegant notations. We show that our algorithm terminates on each input and produces a most general unifier if one exists. The approach also extends smoothly to a calculus with terminal type.

1 Introduction

Functional programming languages based on typed lambda calculus like *ML* or *Haskell* are usually equipped with type constructors for cartesian products besides the function space constructor. This offers the possibility of modelling and processing complex data structures in a strictly typed framework where type checking can avoid many programming errors. Moreover, the tupling of values is a very successful strategy for improving the efficiency of recursive functions due to the availability of all intermediate results needed by the computation.

On the other hand, higher-order rewriting covers a large part of typed functional languages and demonstrates its computational power in the context of equational reasoning on functional programs. Typical applications are partial evaluation and program transformation. This kind of reasoning requires the solution of complex higher-order unification problems, which is demonstrated by a case study on the transformation of a program modifying a state monad [Joh94]. However, reasonable unification algorithms for calculi containing product types are not yet available. It turns out that one has to put a lot of effort into the solution of problems introduced by the presence of projection functions.

Example 1. Consider the following set of equations: $\{\pi_1^2(x) =^? \pi_1^2(s),\ \pi_2^2(x) =^? \pi_2^2(t)\}$, where x is a variable of product type and s, t are ground terms. Neither $\theta_s = \{x \leftarrow s\}$ nor $\theta_t = \{x \leftarrow t\}$ unifies both equations. Nevertheless, the unification problem has the (unique) solution $\theta = \{x \leftarrow \langle \pi_1^2(s), \pi_2^2(t)\rangle\}$.

In this paper we propose an inference system for higher-order unification of simply typed lambda terms with function space and product type constructors. It is based on a calculus with extended lambda abstractions. In general, higher-order unification is undecidable [Gol81], even if product types are abandoned. We therefore describe a decidable subsystem by generalizing the concept of higher-order patterns – introduced by Miller [Mil91] and reformulated by Nipkow [Nip91] – to so called ***higher-order product-patterns.*** For this class of terms a sound and complete unification algorithm is presented. Moreover, we show that our algorithm terminates on each input and produces a most general unifier if one exists. Finally, we outline an extension to integrate the so called terminal type.

2 Types, Terms and Substitutions

Since we want to distinguish between objects being tuples and objects being functions it is necessary to describe what kind of types we are dealing with. Additionally, we have to lay down the way objects of certain types are created.

2.1 Type constructors

Besides the usual function space constructor we introduce a type constructor $\times_n$ for each $n \geq 2$ describing finite products of arity n. Because the arity of a finite product can always be inferred from the context, we omit the subscript of $\times$.

Definition 1 (Types). Let $\mathcal{B}$ be a denumerable set of base types. The set of *types* $\mathcal{T}(\mathcal{B})$ generated by function space ($\rightarrow$) and finite product ($\times$) type constructors is defined by the following grammar. Here B ranges over base types.

$$T \;=\; B \mid T \rightarrow T \mid T \times \cdots \times T$$

Note that several isomorphisms can be described in $\mathcal{T}(\mathcal{B})$ (c.f. [DC95]). But, even if e.g. the types $A \rightarrow (B \times C)$ and $(A \rightarrow B) \times (A \rightarrow C)$ are isomorphic, we do not identify them, nor any others.

2.2 Term constructors and Typing rules

Abstraction in lambda calculus binds variables in λ-expressions. Product types lead to a more general way of abstraction, namely binding of tuples of variables.

Definition 2 (Abstraction Patterns). Let $\mathcal{V}$ be a denumerable set of variables. The set of *abstraction patterns* $\mathcal{P}(\mathcal{V})$ is defined to be the set of all linear terms generated by the following grammar. Here V ranges over variables.

$$P \;=\; V \mid \langle P, \ldots, P\rangle$$

Note that abstraction patterns necessarily have to be linear in order to permit unconstrained β-reduction. For example, the term $((\lambda\langle x, x\rangle.t)\, s)$ would only be reducible if s were equivalent to $\langle \hat{s}, \hat{s}\rangle$.

Definition 3 (Terms). Let $\mathcal{V}$ be a denumerable set of variables and $\mathcal{F}$ be a denumerable set of constants. The set of *untyped terms* $\mathit{Term}(\mathcal{F}, \mathcal{V})$ is defined by the following grammar. Here V ranges over Variables, F ranges over constants, and P ranges over abstraction patterns.

$$T \;=\; V \mid F \mid \lambda P.T \mid (T\, T) \mid \langle T, \ldots, T\rangle \mid \pi_i^n(T)$$

$$\frac{sig(a) = \tau}{\Gamma \vdash a : \tau}\ const$$

$$\frac{}{\Gamma, x : \tau \vdash x : \tau}\ var \qquad \frac{\Gamma, p_1 : \tau_1, \ldots, p_n : \tau_n \vdash t : \tau}{\Gamma, \langle p_1, \ldots, p_n \rangle : \tau_1 \times \cdots \times \tau_n \vdash t : \tau}\ \times pattern$$

$$\frac{\Gamma \vdash t : \tau_1 \times \cdots \times \tau_n}{\Gamma \vdash \pi_i^n(t) : \tau_i}\ \times elim \qquad \frac{\Gamma \vdash t_1 : \tau_1 \quad \cdots \quad \Gamma \vdash t_n : \tau_n}{\Gamma \vdash \langle t_1, \ldots, t_n \rangle : \tau_1 \times \cdots \times \tau_n}\ \times intro$$

$$\frac{\Gamma \vdash s : \tau \to \hat{\tau} \quad \Gamma \vdash t : \tau}{\Gamma \vdash (s\, t) : \hat{\tau}}\ \to elim \qquad \frac{\Gamma, p : \tau \vdash t : \hat{\tau}}{\Gamma \vdash \lambda p.t : \tau \to \hat{\tau}}\ \to intro$$

The notation $\Gamma, p : \tau$ is used as an abbreviation for $\Gamma \cup \{p : \tau\}$. All inference rules are supposed to respect linearity of abstraction patterns and environments.

Fig. 1. Typing rules

A sequence of terms is denoted by $\overline{t_m}$ where m is the number of terms in such a sequence. Sequences of variables are denoted by $\overline{x_m}$ and sequences of abstraction patterns are denoted by $\overleftrightarrow{u_m}$. We also use the notation $f(\overline{t_m})$ as an abbreviation for $(\ldots(f\, t_1)\ldots t_m)$ and the notation $\lambda\overleftrightarrow{u_k}.\,t$ as an abbreviation for $\lambda u_1.\ \ldots\ \lambda u_k.\,t$. The set of variables of an abstraction pattern p is denoted by $Var(p)$. Occurrences of variables in a term are distinguished as being free or bound (by a surrounding lambda abstraction). Hence, the set of free (resp. bound) variables of a term t is denoted by $FVar(t)$ (resp. $BVar(t)$). These notions also apply to sequences and sets of terms.

Definition 4 (Signature and Typing). A *signature sig* is a mapping from the set of constants $\mathcal{F}$ to the set of types $\mathcal{T}(\mathcal{B})$. A set Γ of statements of the form $p : \tau$ where p is an abstraction pattern and τ is a type is called an *environment* if it is linear, i. e. each variable x appears at most once in Γ.
A statement of the form $\Gamma \vdash t : \tau$ where Γ is an environment, t is a term, τ is a type is called a *typing judgement* if it is generated by the typing rules in Fig. 1.
If $\Gamma \vdash t : \tau$ is a typing judgement then τ is called the *type of t under Γ*.
If there is a type τ of t under Γ then t is called *typable under Γ*.

The linearity of Γ guarantees that each variable x typable under Γ has a unique type τ_x. Therefore, terms typable under Γ have unique types determined by Γ (assuming that abstraction patterns in lambda expressions are decorated with their types). Moreover, it is well known that typability is decidable. In the remaining parts of the paper we assume that all terms introduced are typable under a fixed environment Γ. Accordingly, the type of each term is fixed by Γ.

2.3 Typed Substitutions

A substitution in a typed lambda calculus framework has to be typed, i. e. a term substituted for a variable has to have the same type as the variable.

Definition 5 (Substitution). Let Γ be an environment. A mapping θ from $\mathcal{V}$ to $Term(\mathcal{F}, \mathcal{V})$ is called a Γ-substitution if $\Gamma \vdash \theta(x) : \tau$ for each $x : \tau \in \Gamma$.

Substitutions are lifted to terms by replacing all free variables by its substitutes and renaming bound variables in order to avoid accidental capturing. Substitutions are applied to sequences and sets of terms in the same way. We will use some standard notions for handling substitutions summarized below.

Composition of substitutions is usual function composition. The domain $Dom(\theta)$ is the set of variables x, s.t. $\theta(x) \neq x$. The image $Im(\theta)$ is the set of terms $\theta(x)$, s.t. $\theta(x) \neq x$. $\mathcal{I}(\theta) = FVar(Im(\theta))$ is the set of free variables in the image of θ. If $Dom(\theta_1) \cap Dom(\theta_2) = \varnothing$ then their union $\theta_1 \cup \theta_2$ is defined to be a substitution which applies both parts in parallel.

The restriction of a substitution θ to a set of variables V is a substitution denoted by $\theta|_V$ and defined as $\theta|_V(x) = \theta(x)$ for each $x \in Dom(\theta|_V) = Dom(\theta) \cap V$. For comparing substitutions we use a subsumption ordering which can be parameterized by any equivalence relation $=_\omega$ on terms which is stable w.r.t. substitutions. Thus, $\theta \geq_\omega \sigma$ holds if there is a substitution ρ s.t. $\theta(t) =_\omega (\rho \circ \sigma)(t)$ for each typable term t. The concept of subsumption ordering is further generalized by restricting the domains of the substitutions compared, i.e. $\theta \geq_\omega \sigma\,[V]$ holds if $\theta|_V \geq_\omega \sigma|_V$.

A substitution θ is called ω-idempotent w.r.t. a stable congruence relation $=_\omega$ if $\theta \circ \theta =_\omega \theta$. It is called ω-normalized w.r.t. a normalizing rewrite relation $\rightarrow_\omega$ if $\theta(x)$ is in ω-normal form for each $x \in Dom(\theta)$.

3 Equational Theory

Lambda calculus comes equipped with two congruence relations called β- and η-conversions. Introducing these relations as well as their counterparts for terms of product type and analyzing their properties is the purpose of this section.

Note that all conversions of our calculus will be applicable to any (typable) term of appropriate structure, like in ordinary lambda calculus. For β-conversion the existence of a matching substitution has to be established. Besides providing linear abstraction patterns only, this is guaranteed by allowing *sp*-equivalence in the condition for elementary β-reduction instead of requiring syntactic identity.

Definition 6 (congruence relations). For $\omega \in \{\alpha, \beta, \eta, \lambda, \pi, sp, \lambda\times\}$ let $=_\omega$ be the smallest congruence relation on typable terms containing the elementary relation $\rightarrow^\epsilon_\omega$ defined as follows.

α: $\lambda p.t \rightarrow^\epsilon_\alpha \lambda q.\theta(t)$ if $Dom(\theta) \subseteq Var(p) \wedge \theta(p) = q \wedge \mathcal{I}(\theta) \cap FVar(t) = \varnothing$

β: $((\lambda p.t)\, s) \rightarrow^\epsilon_\beta \theta(t)$ if $Dom(\theta) \subseteq Var(p) \wedge \theta(p) =_{sp} s$

η: $\lambda p.(t\, p) \rightarrow^\epsilon_\eta t$ if $Var(p) \cap FVar(t) = \varnothing$

π: $\pi^n_i(\langle t_1, \ldots, t_i, \ldots, t_n\rangle) \rightarrow^\epsilon_\pi t_i$ $\qquad$ λ: $\rightarrow^\epsilon_\lambda = \rightarrow^\epsilon_\alpha \cup \rightarrow^\epsilon_\beta \cup \rightarrow^\epsilon_\eta$

sp: $\langle \pi^n_1(t), \ldots, \pi^n_n(t)\rangle \rightarrow^\epsilon_{sp} t$ $\qquad$ $\lambda\times$: $\rightarrow^\epsilon_{\lambda\times} = \rightarrow^\epsilon_\lambda \cup \rightarrow^\epsilon_\pi \cup \rightarrow^\epsilon_{sp}$

All elementary relations $\rightarrow^\epsilon_\omega$ are decidable. While $\rightarrow^\epsilon_\alpha$ requires syntactic (first order) matching of abstraction patterns, which is trivial, $\rightarrow^\epsilon_\beta$ requires matching an abstraction pattern against an arbitrary term modulo *sp*-equivalence. Since abstraction patterns are defined to be π_i^n-free, finitely many *sp*-expansions can transform this matching problem into a syntactic one, the decidability of which is trivial again.

Example 2. Let x be of type $A \times B$. Then $\lambda x.\pi_1^2(x) \rightarrow_\alpha^\epsilon \lambda\langle y, z\rangle.\pi_1^2(\langle y, z\rangle) =_\pi \lambda\langle y, z\rangle.y$. Moreover, $((\lambda\langle y, z\rangle.y)\, s) \rightarrow_\beta^\epsilon \pi_1^2(s)$ for any term s of type $A \times B$.

The usual $\alpha\beta\eta$-conversions of simply typed lambda calculus without product types are contained in $=_\lambda$ as special cases. Compatibility with substitutions carries over to the calculus with product types: All relations of Def. 3 have the property of being stable w. r. t. substitutions. This is very important for the solution of unification problems modulo a congruence relation since terms can be restricted to be appropriate representatives of their congruence classes. The question is, what do appropriate representatives for higher-order unification modulo $=_{\lambda\times}$ look like. For higher-order unification in the simply typed lambda calculus without product types those representatives usually are the 'long $\beta\eta$-normal forms' introduced by Huet [Hue75]. We generalize this concept here in order to obtain 'long $\lambda\times$-normal forms'.

Definition 7 (α-conversion). Let $\geq_\alpha$ be the smallest quasi ordering on typable terms containing the relation $\rightarrow_\alpha^\epsilon$ and closed under context embedding.
The partial ordering induced by $\geq_\alpha$ is defined as $\quad \rightarrow_\alpha \;=\; \geq_\alpha \setminus {}_\alpha\!\leq$.
The equivalence relation induced by $\geq_\alpha$ is defined as $\quad \approx_\alpha \;=\; \geq_\alpha \setminus \rightarrow_\alpha$.

The variable renaming part of α-conversion is now denoted by $\approx_\alpha$ whereas $\rightarrow_\alpha$ additionally introduces structural information into abstraction patterns. There are $\rightarrow_\alpha$-irreducible terms because the set of abstraction patterns of the same type is finite (up to variable renaming). Moreover, it is easy to prove that $\rightarrow_\alpha$ is strongly normalizing and confluent modulo $\approx_\alpha$. The corresponding α-normal form of a term t is denoted by $t{\downarrow_\alpha}$.

There are several ways of handling the extensional conversions. An overview of their advantages and weaknesses can be found in [JG95]. Here we introduce contractions as well as restricted expansions.

Definition 8 (extensional reductions). The extensional rewrite relations $\rightarrow_\eta$, $\twoheadrightarrow_\eta$, $\rightarrow_{sp}$, and $\twoheadrightarrow_{sp}$ on typable terms are defined as follows.

$t \twoheadrightarrow_\eta^\epsilon \lambda p.(t\, p) \quad$ if $\quad \lambda p.(t\, p) \rightarrow_\eta^\epsilon t$ and $t \neq \lambda q.\hat{t}$
The *η-contraction* $\rightarrow_\eta$ is the smallest relation containing $\rightarrow_\eta^\epsilon$ which is closed under context embedding. The *restricted η-expansion* $\twoheadrightarrow_\eta$ is the smallest relation containing $\twoheadrightarrow_\eta^\epsilon$ which is closed under context embedding except for applications, i. e. $(t\, s) \not\twoheadrightarrow_\eta ((\lambda p.(t\, p))\, s)$.

$t \twoheadrightarrow_{sp}^\epsilon \langle\pi_1^n(t), \ldots, \pi_n^n(t)\rangle \quad$ if $\quad \langle\pi_1^n(t), \ldots, \pi_n^n(t)\rangle \rightarrow_{sp}^\epsilon t$ and $t \neq \langle t_1, \ldots, t_n\rangle$
The *sp-contraction* $\rightarrow_{sp}$ is the smallest relation containing $\rightarrow_{sp}^\epsilon$ which is closed under context embedding. The *restricted sp-expansion* $\twoheadrightarrow_{sp}$ is the smallest relation containing $\twoheadrightarrow_{sp}^\epsilon$ which is closed under context embedding except for projections, i. e. $\pi_i^n(t) \not\twoheadrightarrow_{sp} \pi_i^n(\langle\pi_1^n(t), \ldots, \pi_n^n(t)\rangle)$.

Note that both $\twoheadrightarrow_\eta$ and $\twoheadrightarrow_{sp}$ are strongly normalizing due to the restrictions imposed but, that only $\twoheadrightarrow_{sp}$ is confluent. However, each diverging situation of the form $\lambda p.(t\,p)\ {}_\eta\!\twoheadleftarrow t \twoheadrightarrow_\eta \lambda q.(t\,q)$ can be closed using $\geq_\alpha$. Because p and q are both linear abstraction patterns of the same type, they are unifiable. Therefore we know that $\lambda p.(t\,p) \geq_\alpha \lambda o.(t\,o)\ {}_\alpha\!\leq \lambda q.(t\,q)$ where o is some abstraction pattern more specific than p and q.

Definition 9 (computational reductions). The computational rewrite relations $\rightarrow_\beta$ and $\rightarrow_\pi$ on typable terms are defined as the smallest extensions of their corresponding elementary relations which are closed under context embedding. Finally, $\twoheadrightarrow_\lambda$ and $\twoheadrightarrow_{\lambda\times}$ are defined as follows.

$$\twoheadrightarrow_\lambda\ =\ \rightarrow_\alpha \cup \rightarrow_\beta \cup \twoheadrightarrow_\eta \qquad\qquad \twoheadrightarrow_{\lambda\times}\ =\ \twoheadrightarrow_\lambda \cup \rightarrow_\pi \cup \twoheadrightarrow_{sp}$$

Combinations of several rewrite relations other than $\rightarrow_\lambda$ and $\rightarrow_{\lambda\times}$ are denoted by a sequence of their corresponding subscripts, e. g. $\rightarrow_{\eta\,sp} = \rightarrow_\eta \cup \rightarrow_{sp}$. The reflexive, transitive (and symmetric, resp.) closure of a rewrite relation $\rightarrow_\omega$ is denoted by $\overset{*}{\rightarrow}_\omega$ ($\overset{*}{\leftrightarrow}_\omega$, resp.).

Lemma 10. $\quad =_{\lambda\times}\ =\ \overset{*}{\twoheadleftarrow\!\!\twoheadrightarrow}_{\lambda\times}$

Proof. $\overset{*}{\twoheadleftarrow\!\!\twoheadrightarrow}_{\lambda\times}\ \subseteq\ =_{\lambda\times}$ is trivial. $=_{\lambda\times}\ \subseteq\ \overset{*}{\twoheadleftarrow\!\!\twoheadrightarrow}_{\lambda\times}$ is shown by simulating the missing $=_\eta$- and $=_{sp}$-steps by appropriate $\overset{*}{\twoheadleftarrow\!\!\twoheadrightarrow}_{\alpha\beta}$- and $\overset{*}{\twoheadleftarrow\!\!\twoheadrightarrow}_\pi$-steps.

Note that the proof of Lem. 10 also establishes stability of $\overset{*}{\twoheadrightarrow}_{\lambda\times}$ w. r. t. context embedding and substitutions despite the fact that $\twoheadrightarrow_{\lambda\times}$ lacks both properties.

Lemma 11 (termination and confluence).
The rewrite relation $\twoheadrightarrow_{\lambda\times}$ is confluent modulo $\approx_\alpha$ and strongly normalizing.

Proof. Confluence is proved along the lines of Kesner given in [Kes94] for a similar calculus. The only difference besides not dealing with fixpoint types is in our definition of η- and α-conversion. The additional divergences produced by $\twoheadrightarrow_\eta$ can be closed by $\rightarrow_\alpha$ as discussed above. In order to prove strong normalization we use an argument of reduction. It is well known that the restriction of $\twoheadrightarrow_{\lambda\times}$ to terms which only abstract over variables is strongly normalizing, see e. g. [DCK93, Aka93, JG95]. Suppose that there were an infinite chain in $\twoheadrightarrow_{\lambda\times}$. Then, using $=_{\alpha\pi}$, it is easy to construct a similar infinite chain consisting of terms which do not contain any product-pattern. This contradicts the strong normalization of the restricted relation and we are done.

The unique (up to α-equivalence) $\lambda\times$-normal form of a term t is denoted by $t\updownarrow_{\lambda\times}$ and is called *long $\lambda\times$-normal form* of t, as usual.

Theorem 12. *It is decidable whether two terms are $\lambda\times$-equivalent.*

Proof. By Lemmas 10, 11 and decidability of $\approx_\alpha$.

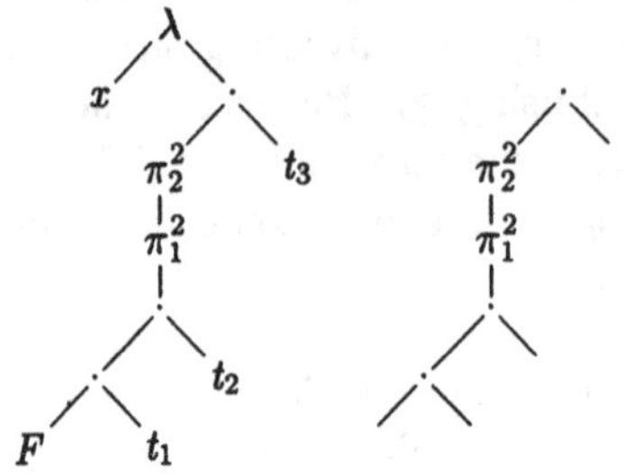

$t : \tau \rightarrow \hat{\tau}$

$t = \lambda x.(\pi_2^2(\pi_1^2((F\, t_1)\, t_2))\, t_3)$

$\quad = \lambda x.\mathfrak{B}(F)(\overline{t_3})$

with $\mathfrak{B} = [1, (2,2), 0, (1,2), 2]$

and $F : \tau_1 \rightarrow \tau_2 \rightarrow ((\tau' \times (\tau_3 \rightarrow \hat{\tau})) \times \tau'')$

Fig. 2. The backbone of a term

4 Unification

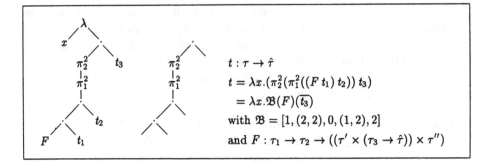

We assume the reader to be familiar with some basic concepts of higher-order unification, see e. g. [SG89]. Please remember that if S is in solved form, the induced substitution σ_S is a most general unifier of S.

Since the seminal work of Huet [Hue75], one differentiates between flex and rigid terms. A substitution may alter the whole term structure of a flex term but only the arguments of a rigid term. In our extended calculus, these notions have to be generalized. We therefore introduce the concept of a *backbone* of a term, which is illustrated by an example in Fig. 2.

Definition 13. The *backbone* of a term $\lambda\overleftrightarrow{x_k}.(\pi_{i_j}^{n_j}(\cdots(\pi_{i_1}^{n_1}(a(\overline{t_{m_0}}))(\overline{t_{m_1}}))\cdots))(\overline{t_{m_j}})$ denotes the sequence of applications and projections and may be described by a sequence $[m_j, (i_j, n_j), \ldots, m_1, (i_1, n_1), m_0]$ of naturals to count the number of successive applications and pairs of naturals to identify a specific π-symbol, respectively. We introduce a shorthand notation $\lambda\overleftrightarrow{x_k}.\mathfrak{B}(a)(\overline{t_{m_0}}, \overline{t_{m_1}}, \ldots, \overline{t_{m_j}})$ where $\mathfrak{B}$ is a meta-variable representing the backbone.
A term $\lambda\overleftrightarrow{x_k}.\mathfrak{B}(a)(\overline{t_m})$ is called an *xflex term* if its *head* a is a free variable, otherwise it is called an *xrigid term*. The terms $\overline{t_m}$ are the *arguments* of a.

Note that these concepts truly generalize the ones used by Huet. A flex/rigid term is an xflex/xrigid term not containing any π-symbol in its backbone.[1]

4.1 Introducing Higher-Order Patterns

It is well known that the unification problem for the simply typed lambda calculus is undecidable in general [Gol81]. But by analyzing a restricted form of β-reduction, Miller [Mil91] discovered a class of terms, so called higher-order patterns, which have an 'easy', i. e. decidable and unitary, unification problem.

[1] Note that Duggan introduces in [Dug93] the concept of a 'locator' which somehow serves the same purpose than our backbone. However, his locators are concrete syntax, whereas backbones are metasymbols describing the structure of terms.

The essential property of higher-order patterns is that substituting free variables can only result in β_0-normalizable terms. This relation is very restrictive, since it only consists of steps of the form $((\lambda x.t)\, x) \rightarrow_{\beta_0} t$ (modulo implicit α-conversions). Hence, the implicit reduction steps following a substitution can not alter the term introduced by the substitution. Nipkow reformulated the approach in the context of higher-order rewriting [Nip91].

We introduce an adequate normal form to get a nice generalization of this concept. Note that $\rightarrow_{\eta\, sp}$ is confluent and strongly normalizing [Pot81]. This normal form permits an elegant definition of a higher-order product-pattern.

Definition 14. The *pattern normal form* $t{\downarrow}_P$ of a term t is the term which results from $t\updownarrow_{\lambda\times}$ by replacing the arguments of free variables with their $\rightarrow_{\eta\, sp}$ normal forms.

Definition 15. A *higher-order product-pattern* is a term t, where in $t{\downarrow}_P$ the arguments of free variables are restricted to be abstraction patterns of bound variables and in each xflex sub-term $\mathfrak{B}(F)(\overleftrightarrow{u_n})$ the sequence of abstraction patterns $\overleftrightarrow{u_n}$ is linear.

Example 3. Product-patterns[2] are e.g. $\lambda\langle x, y\rangle.F\langle y, x\rangle$, $((\lambda x.f\langle g\, x, (\lambda y.y)\, x\rangle)\, Z)$, or $t = \lambda u.((\pi_2^2\pi_1^2((F\, \pi_1^2\pi_2^2 u)\, \pi_1^2 u))\;\; \pi_2^2\pi_2^2 u)$, since its pattern normal form is $t{\downarrow}_P = \lambda\langle x, \langle y, z\rangle\rangle.((\pi_2^2\pi_1^2((F\, y)\, x))\, z) = \lambda\langle x, \langle y, z\rangle\rangle.\mathfrak{B}(F)(y, x, z)$. Non-patterns are e.g. $\lambda x.F(G(x))$ or $s = \lambda x.((F\, x)\, \pi_1^2(x))$, since $s{\downarrow}_P = \lambda\langle y, z\rangle.((F\, \langle y, z\rangle)\, y)$.

Please note that higher-order product-patterns are closed under $=_{\lambda\times}$ and pattern-substitutions. In the sequel we will only consider higher-order product-patterns which are implicitly converted to their pattern normal form. Furthermore, substitutions are supposed to be $\lambda\times$-idempotent and ${\downarrow}_P$-normalized.

4.2 Unification by Transformation

A very successful approach to describe unification methods is the use of inferences, which transform systems of equations into equivalent solved forms.

In contrast to [SG89] we explicitly distinguish the solved part S in the inferences of $\mathcal{PU}$, which are given in Fig. 3. This eases termination considerations. We write $(E, S) \vdash_{\mathcal{PU}} (E', S')$ for the transformation of E and S to E' and S' by use of an inference of system $\mathcal{PU}$.

There are two important invariants we have to mention: First, $\approx_\alpha$-conversions and ${\downarrow}_P$ normalizations are performed implicitly. Second, since substitutions may not alter the type of a term, both terms of an equation must have identical types. This ensures an appropriate typing of the newly introduced variables H.

One may distinguish two groups of inferences: The first four resemble first-order unification. The latter four handle free higher-order variables by some approximation technique. This will influence the structure of our proofs. The inferences of each group behave similarly.

[2] Uppercase letters denote free variables.

Delete:

$$\frac{\{s =^? s\} \cup E, S}{E, S}$$

Decompose:

$$\frac{\{\lambda\overleftrightarrow{x_k}.\mathfrak{B}(a)(\overline{s_n}) =^? \lambda\overleftrightarrow{x_k}.\mathfrak{B}(a)(\overline{t_n})\} \cup E, S}{\{\overline{\lambda\overleftrightarrow{x_k}.s_n =^? \lambda\overleftrightarrow{x_k}.t_n}\} \cup E, S}$$

if $a \in \mathcal{F} \cup Var(\overleftrightarrow{x_k})$.

Product-Decompose:

$$\frac{\{\lambda\overleftrightarrow{x_k}.\langle\overline{s_n}\rangle =^? \lambda\overleftrightarrow{x_k}.\langle\overline{t_n}\rangle\} \cup E, S}{\{\overline{\lambda\overleftrightarrow{x_k}.s_n =^? \lambda\overleftrightarrow{x_k}.t_n}\} \cup E, S}$$

Eliminate:

$$\frac{\{\lambda\overleftrightarrow{x_k}.F(\overleftrightarrow{x_k}) =^? t\} \cup E, S}{\sigma(E), \sigma(S) \cup \sigma}$$

if $F \in \mathcal{V} - Var(\overleftrightarrow{x_k})$, $F \notin FVar(t)$, and $\sigma = \{F \leftarrow t\}$.

flex-xrigid:

$$\frac{\{\lambda\overleftrightarrow{x_k}.F(\overleftrightarrow{u_n}) =^? \lambda\overleftrightarrow{x_k}.\mathfrak{B}(a)(\overline{t_m})\} \cup E, S}{\{F =^? \lambda\overleftrightarrow{u_n}.\mathfrak{B}(a)(\overline{H_m(\overleftrightarrow{u_n})})\} \cup \{\lambda\overleftrightarrow{x_k}.F(\overleftrightarrow{u_n}) =^? \lambda\overleftrightarrow{x_k}.\mathfrak{B}(a)(\overline{t_m})\} \cup E, S}$$

if $F \in \mathcal{V} - Var(\overleftrightarrow{x_k})$, $a \in \mathcal{F} \cup Var(\overleftrightarrow{u_n})$, $F \notin FVar(\lambda\overleftrightarrow{x_k}.\mathfrak{B}(a)(\overline{t_m}))$, and $\overline{H_m}$ new.

flex-flex-eq:

$$\frac{\{\lambda\overleftrightarrow{x_k}.F(\overleftrightarrow{u_n}) =^? \lambda\overleftrightarrow{x_k}.F(\overleftrightarrow{v_n})\} \cup E, S}{\{F =^? \lambda\overleftrightarrow{u_n}.H(\overline{z_r})\} \cup \{\lambda\overleftrightarrow{x_k}.F(\overleftrightarrow{u_n}) =^? \lambda\overleftrightarrow{x_k}.F(\overleftrightarrow{v_n})\} \cup E, S}$$

if $F \in \mathcal{V} - Var(\overleftrightarrow{x_k})$, $\{\overline{z_r}\} = \{z \mid z \in Var(\overleftrightarrow{u_n}), \overleftrightarrow{u_n}|_p = z = \overleftrightarrow{v_n}|_p\}$, and H new.

flex-flex-neq:

$$\frac{\{\lambda\overleftrightarrow{x_k}.F(\overleftrightarrow{u_n}) =^? \lambda\overleftrightarrow{x_k}.G(\overleftrightarrow{v_m})\} \cup E, S}{\{F =^? \lambda\overleftrightarrow{u_n}.H(\overline{z_r}), G =^? \lambda\overleftrightarrow{v_m}.H(\overline{z_r})\} \cup \{\lambda\overleftrightarrow{x_k}.F(\overleftrightarrow{u_n}) =^? \lambda\overleftrightarrow{x_k}.G(\overleftrightarrow{v_m})\} \cup E, S}$$

if $F, G \in \mathcal{V} - Var(\overleftrightarrow{x_k})$, $F \neq G$, $\{\overline{z_r}\} = Var(\overleftrightarrow{u_n}) \cap Var(\overleftrightarrow{v_m})$, and H new.

xflex-any:

$$\frac{\{\lambda\overleftrightarrow{x_k}.\mathfrak{B}(\pi_i^r(F(\overleftrightarrow{u_n})))(\overleftrightarrow{v_m}) =^? \lambda\overleftrightarrow{x_k}.t\} \cup E, S}{\{F =^? \lambda\overleftrightarrow{u_n}.\langle\overline{H_r(\overleftrightarrow{u_n})}\rangle\} \cup \{\lambda\overleftrightarrow{x_k}.\mathfrak{B}(\pi_i^r(F(\overleftrightarrow{u_n})))(\overleftrightarrow{v_m}) =^? \lambda\overleftrightarrow{x_k}.t\} \cup E, S}$$

if $F \in \mathcal{V} - Var(\overleftrightarrow{x_k})$ and $\overline{H_r}$ new.

Fig. 3. Unification for Higher-Order Product-Patterns

4.3 Soundness and Completeness of $\mathcal{PU}$

The next two lemmas are of rather technical nature. Their proofs are omitted due to lack of space.

Lemma 16. *Let θ be an arbitrary substitution, $t = \lambda\overleftrightarrow{x_k}.\mathfrak{B}(a)(\overline{t_m})$ an xrigid term and $s = \lambda\overleftrightarrow{x_k}.\langle\overline{s_m}\rangle$ a product term. Then*
(a) $\theta(\lambda\overleftrightarrow{x_k}.t_i)\Downarrow_P = \lambda\overleftrightarrow{x_k}.t'_i$ for all $i \in \{1, \ldots, m\}$ and $\theta(t)\Downarrow_P = \lambda\overleftrightarrow{x_k}.\mathfrak{B}(a)(\overline{t'_m})$
(b) $\theta(\lambda\overleftrightarrow{x_k}.s_i)\Downarrow_P = \lambda\overleftrightarrow{x_k}.s'_i$ for all $i \in \{1, \ldots, m\}$ and $\theta(s)\Downarrow_P = \lambda\overleftrightarrow{x_k}.\langle\overline{s'_m}\rangle$.

Lemma 17. *(a) Let* $\theta \in \mathcal{U}(\{\lambda\overleftrightarrow{x_k}.F(\overleftrightarrow{u_n}) =^? \lambda\overleftrightarrow{x_k}.F(\overleftrightarrow{v_n})\})$ *and* $\{\overline{z_r}\} = \{z \mid z \in Var(\overleftrightarrow{u_n}), \overleftrightarrow{u_n}|_p = z = \overleftrightarrow{v_n}|_p\}$*. Then* $\theta(\lambda\overleftrightarrow{x_k}.F(\overleftrightarrow{u_n})) \xrightarrow{*}_{\beta_0} \lambda\overleftrightarrow{x_k}.t \;{}_{\beta_0}\!\xleftarrow{*} \theta(\lambda\overleftrightarrow{x_k}.F(\overleftrightarrow{v_n}))$ *and* $BVar(\lambda\overleftrightarrow{x_k}.t) \cap Var(\overleftrightarrow{x_k}) \subseteq \{\overline{z_r}\}$*.*
(b) Let $\theta \in \mathcal{U}(\{\lambda\overleftrightarrow{x_k}.F(\overleftrightarrow{u_n}) =^? \lambda\overleftrightarrow{x_k}.G(\overleftrightarrow{v_m})\})$ *and* $\{\overline{z_r}\} = Var(\overleftrightarrow{u_n}) \cap Var(\overleftrightarrow{v_m})$*. Then* $\theta(\lambda\overleftrightarrow{x_k}.F(\overleftrightarrow{u_n})) \xrightarrow{*}_{\beta_0} \lambda\overleftrightarrow{x_k}.t \;{}_{\beta_0}\!\xleftarrow{*} \theta(\lambda\overleftrightarrow{x_k}.G(\overleftrightarrow{v_m}))$ *and* $BVar(\lambda\overleftrightarrow{x_k}.t) \cap Var(\overleftrightarrow{x_k}) \subseteq \{\overline{z_r}\}$*.*

Now we are able to show that the set of unifiers essentially remains unchanged when performing an inference step.

Lemma 18. *Let* $(E, S) \vdash_{\mathcal{PU}} (E', S')$ *with one of the inferences* Delete, Decompose, Product-Decompose, *or* Eliminate. *Then* $\mathcal{U}(E \cup S) = \mathcal{U}(E' \cup S')$*.*

Proof. Delete is trivial. For Decompose and Product-Decompose, this is a corollary of Lem. 16. The proof for Eliminate is analogous to the proof found in [SG89].

Lemma 19. *Let* $(E, S) \vdash_{\mathcal{PU}} (E', S')$ *with one of the inferences* flex-xrigid, flex-flex-eq, flex-flex-neq, *or* xflex-any. *Then* $\mathcal{U}(E' \cup S') \subseteq \mathcal{U}(E \cup S)$ *and for each* $\theta \in \mathcal{U}(E \cup S)$ *exists a uniquely determined* θ_0 *such that* $(\theta \cup \theta_0) \in \mathcal{U}(E' \cup S')$*, and* $Dom(\theta_0)$ *consists of the newly introduced variables.*

Proof. For the first part consider $E' \supset E$ and $S' = S$. For the second part, we may assume with no loss of generality that the newly introduced variables are neither in the domain nor in the image of θ. We get the definition of θ_0 by an analysis of θ. In the case flex-xrigid, θ unifies $\lambda\overleftrightarrow{x_k}.F(\overleftrightarrow{u_n}) =^? \lambda\overleftrightarrow{x_k}.\mathfrak{B}(a)(\overline{t_m})$. Thus by Lem. 16(a), $\theta(\lambda\overleftrightarrow{x_k}.F(\overleftrightarrow{u_n})) \xrightarrow{*}_{\beta_0} \lambda\overleftrightarrow{x_k}.\mathfrak{B}(a)(\overline{r_m}) \;{}_{\lambda\times}\!\xleftarrow{*} \theta(\lambda\overleftrightarrow{x_k}.\mathfrak{B}(a)(\overline{t_m}))$, since we only consider product-patterns and θ is normalized and therefore $\theta(F) \approx_\alpha \lambda\overleftrightarrow{u_n}.\mathfrak{B}(a)(\overline{r_m})$. To unify the newly introduced equation, θ_0 has to be $\theta_0 = \{\overline{H_m \leftarrow \lambda\overleftrightarrow{u_n}.r_m}\}$. This is a sound extension of θ, since it uses the same binder and thus no free variable gets bound or vice versa. We get $\theta_0(\lambda\overleftrightarrow{u_n}.\mathfrak{B}(a)(\overline{H_m(\overleftrightarrow{u_n})})) = \lambda\overleftrightarrow{u_n}.\mathfrak{B}(a)(\overline{(\lambda\overleftrightarrow{u_n}.r_m)(\overleftrightarrow{u_n})}) \xrightarrow{*}_{\beta_0} \theta(F)$. The other equations in $E \cup S$ are already unified by θ, so they will be by $\theta \cup \theta_0$. For the other cases, analogous argumentations apply, using Lem. 17(a), Lem. 17(b), and Lem. 16(b) respectively. Please note that for the argumentation the use of $\rightarrow_{\beta_0}$ was essential.

By a simple inductive argument, we get the following

Corollary 20. *Let* $(E, S) \vdash_{\mathcal{PU}} \dots \vdash_{\mathcal{PU}} (E', S')$*. Then* $\mathcal{U}(E' \cup S') \subseteq \mathcal{U}(E \cup S)$ *and for each* $\theta \in \mathcal{U}(E \cup S)$ *exists a uniquely determined* θ_0 *such that* $(\theta \cup \theta_0) \in \mathcal{U}(E' \cup S')$*, and* $Dom(\theta_0)$ *consists of the newly introduced variables.*

Now, we are able to state the central results of this section:

Theorem 21 (Soundness). *Let* $(E, \varnothing) \vdash^*_{\mathcal{PU}} (\varnothing, S)$*. Then* $\sigma_S|_{FVar(E)} \in \mathcal{U}(E)$*.*

Proof. By Cor. 20, we have that $\sigma_S \in \mathcal{U}(E)$. But then, even the restricted substitution is a unifier, as only the free variables of E are affected.

Theorem 22 (Completeness). *Let* $\theta \in \mathcal{U}(E)$*. Then, there exists a finite derivation* $(E, \varnothing) \vdash_{\mathcal{PU}} \dots \vdash_{\mathcal{PU}} (\varnothing, S)$ *and* $\theta \gtrsim_{\lambda\times} \sigma_S[FVar(E)]$*.*

Proof. The proof for the existence of a finite derivation leading to $(\emptyset, S)$ whenever $\mathcal{U}(E) \neq \emptyset$ will be given in the next section in a constructive manner. Then, by Cor. 20 there exists a θ_0 such that $(\theta \cup \theta_0) \in \mathcal{U}(S)$. Since S is in solved form, $(\theta \cup \theta_0) \gtrsim_{\lambda\times} \sigma_S$. But then $\theta \gtrsim_{\lambda\times} \sigma_S[Dom(\theta)]$ and furthermore $\theta \gtrsim_{\lambda\times} \sigma_S[FVar(E)]$.

Since in the above theorem the derivation is independent of the substitution θ, we get the important corollary:

Corollary 23 (Existence of mgu). *Let* $(E, \emptyset) \vdash^*_{\mathcal{PU}} (\emptyset, S)$. *Then* $\sigma_S\big|_{FVar(E)}$ *is a most general unifier of* E.

4.4 Adding Control

To ensure termination of the unification process we have to introduce some control on the application of the different inferences. One obvious reason for this is the formulation of the latter four inferences, which add some new equations. Also, to some equations different inferences may be applicable, e. g. Eliminate and flex-flex-neq. A third problem arises when the subproblems generated by flex-xrigid are not solved before the rest of the problem, which was already noted by Nipkow [Nip93]. His example was $\{F =^? c(G), G =^? c(F)\}$.

Therefore, we formulate an algorithm $\mathcal{A}$, the control strategy of which is sufficient to guarantee termination as we will show in the sequel.

Definition 24 Algorithm $\mathcal{A}$. Algorithm $\mathcal{A}$ is based on the inferences of system $\mathcal{PU}$. It organizes the set E as a *stack*. To each equation on top of that stack Delete and Eliminate are applied with priority. Then, only one of the other inferences may be applicable. If no inference is applicable $\mathcal{A}$ returns FAIL, otherwise it proceeds until E is empty. Then the solved part S is returned.

In the sequel, we will denote by $(E, S) \vdash_{\mathcal{A}} (E', S')$ inference steps according to that strategy. Considered as relations, $\vdash_{\mathcal{A}} \subset \vdash_{\mathcal{PU}}$.

That there is in fact no unifier, if no inference is applicable at some point, is shown by the following lemma:

Lemma 25. *Let* $(E, S) \vdash_{\mathcal{PU}} \dots \vdash_{\mathcal{PU}} (\{s =^? t\} \cup E', S')$, *and to* $s =^? t$ *no inference is applicable. Then* $\mathcal{U}(E \cup S) = \emptyset$.

Proof. Since there is no inference applicable to $s =^? t$, one of the following cases must hold (which we get by inverting the conditions of the inferences).

- Both s and t are xrigid terms with different heads or different backbones.
- Failure of occur check (Eliminate or flex-xrigid)
- t is an xrigid term with head a which is a bound variable but does not occur in the arguments of the flex term s.

In each case, s and t are not unifiable and the result is established by Cor. 20.

To show that $\mathcal{A}$ will only generate finite derivations, we use some notions of complexity of equations, which is decreased by $\mathcal{A}$ w.r.t. a well-founded ordering.

Definition 26. The following sets describe the occurrences of backbones in terms (distinguished by their heads):

$B(t) = \{\mathfrak{B}(a) \mid t|_p = \mathfrak{B}(a)(\overline{t_m}) : \tau, \tau \in \mathcal{B}\}$

$B_f(t) = \{\mathfrak{B}(a) \mid \mathfrak{B}(a) \in B(t), a \in FVar(t)\}$ $\qquad B_r(t) = B(t) - B_f(t)$

The multiset versions of these sets are denoted by $B^m(t)$, $B_f^m(t)$, and $B_r^m(t)$ respectively. To count the occurences of π-symbols in xflex backbones, we define:

$\mathrm{dp}_\pi(E) = \left|\bigcup_{t \in E} B_f(t)\right|_\pi$

whereby $|M|_\pi$ denotes the number of π-symbols occuring in M.

The *size* $|t|$ of a term t is inductively defined as $|a| = 1$ for $a \in \mathcal{F} \cup \mathcal{V}$ and

$|\lambda p.t| = |t| \qquad |\langle\overline{t_m}\rangle| = 1 + |t_1| + \ldots + |t_m|$

$|s\ t| = |s| + |t| \qquad |\pi_i^n(t)| = 1 + |t|$

We call a substitution θ *size increasing*, if $|(\theta(t))\Downarrow_P| > |t\downarrow_P|$ for some term t. The *complexity* $\mathbf{C}(E)$ of a finite system of equations E is defined as the triple $(\mathrm{dp}_\pi(E), |FVar(E)|, |E|)$, where $\mathrm{dp}_\pi(E)$ is defined as above, $|FVar(E)|$ denotes the number of distinct free variables of E, and $|E|$ is the size of E, i.e. the sum of the sizes of its terms. These triples are compared by $\succ$, the lexicographical combination on triples of the standard ordering $>$ on the naturals.

The first four inferences do directly decrease the complexity:

Lemma 27. *Let* $(E, S) \vdash_{\mathcal{PU}} (E', S')$ *with inferences* Delete, Decompose, Product-Decompose, *or* Eliminate. *Then* $\mathbf{C}(E) \succ \mathbf{C}(E')$.

Proof. Delete may decrease $\mathrm{dp}_\pi(\cdot)$ or $|FVar(\cdot)|$, but surely decreases $|\cdot|$. Decompose and Product-Decompose do not alter $\mathrm{dp}_\pi(\cdot)$ or $|FVar(\cdot)|$, but decrease $|\cdot|$ by at least 2. Eliminate clearly decreases $|FVar(\cdot)|$ by 1, and may decrease but never increases $\mathrm{dp}_\pi(\cdot)$ even if xflex terms are substituted. This is due to the use of the *set* of *backbones*, which is different from the set of xflex terms. Thus, the possible duplicating effect of the substitution followed by implicit reductions, which may lead to different argument structures, is harmless.

Since the other inferences clearly increase the complexity by introducing new equations, we have to consider sequences of inferences determined by the control strategy of algorithm $\mathcal{A}$.

Lemma 28. *Let* $(E, S) \vdash_{\mathcal{PU}} (E', S')$ *with inferences* flex-xrigid, flex-flex-eq, flex-flex-neq, *or* xflex-any. *Then* $(E', S') \vdash_{\mathcal{A}}^{*} (E'', S'')$ *such that* $\mathbf{C}(E) \succ \mathbf{C}(E'')$.

Proof. After applying flex-flex-eq, the next step is Eliminate followed by Delete, because the considered equation is unified by the introduced approximation. In this sequence $\mathrm{dp}_\pi(\cdot)$ remains unchanged, $|FVar(\cdot)|$ is constant (F is replaced by H), and as the substitution is not size increasing, the Delete-step decreases $|\cdot|$. The inference flex-flex-neq is followed by two Eliminate-steps and a Delete, since the original equation is unified. As above, $\mathrm{dp}_\pi(\cdot)$ remains unchanged, but

Inference	$\mathrm{dp}_\pi(E)$	$\lvert FVar(E)\rvert$	$\lvert E\rvert$
Delete	$\geq$	$\geq$	$>$
Decompose	$=$	$=$	$>$
Product-Decompose	$=$	$=$	$>$
Eliminate	$\geq$	$>$	$*$

Sequ. of Inf.	$\mathrm{dp}_\pi(E)$	$\lvert FVar(E)\rvert$	$\lvert E\rvert$
flex-flex-eq'	$=$	$=$	$>$
flex-flex-neq'	$=$	$>$	$*$
xflex-any'	$>$	$*$	$*$
flex-xrigid'	$>$	$*$	$*$
	$=$	$>$	$*$

Fig. 4. Decreasing the complexity ($*$ means "don't care")

$|FVar(\cdot)|$ is decreased, since the two variables F and G are replaced by the new H. In the case of xflex-any, the implicitely performed π-reductions during the following Eliminate will decrease $\mathrm{dp}_\pi(\cdot)$.

The case flex-xrigid is more complicated. Let $E = \{s =^? t\} \cup E_0$ with $s = \lambda\overleftrightarrow{x_k}.F(\overleftrightarrow{u_n})$ and $t = \lambda\overleftrightarrow{x_k}.\mathfrak{B}(a)(\overline{t_m})$. After performing flex-xrigid and Eliminate, a Decompose takes place. Then we have the following situation:

$$(\{\lambda\overleftrightarrow{x_k}.H_1(\overleftrightarrow{u_n}) =^? \lambda\overleftrightarrow{x_k}.t_1, \ldots, \lambda\overleftrightarrow{x_k}.H_m(\overleftrightarrow{u_n}) =^? \lambda\overleftrightarrow{x_k}.t_m\} \cup \sigma_0(E_0), \hat{S})$$

Assuming the system is unifiable, i. e. algorithm $\mathcal{A}$ does not stop with FAIL, the inferences performed by $\mathcal{A}$ for the i-th subproblem are equivalent to

$$(\{\lambda\overleftrightarrow{x_k}.H_i(\overleftrightarrow{u_n}) =^? \sigma_{S_{i-1}}(\cdots(\sigma_{S_1}(\lambda\overleftrightarrow{x_k}.t_i))\cdots)\}, \varnothing) \vdash_{\mathcal{A}}^{*} (\varnothing, S_i)$$

which eventually leads to the situation $E'' := \sigma(E_0)$ with $\sigma = \sigma_{S_m} \circ \cdots \circ \sigma_{S_1} \circ \sigma_0$.

Before we analyze $\mathbf{C}(E'')$ we have to assure that the subproblems really have finite derivations. Since all the other inferences decrease the complexity, the only chance to get non-termination is the use of flex-xrigid itself. Here, $B_r^m(t)$ comes into play, which in this situation describes the chances to apply flex-xrigid in the derivation. We have $B_r^m(t) \supset B_r^m(\lambda\overleftrightarrow{x_k}.t_j)$ for each $j \in \{1, \ldots, m\}$ and a careful analysis of the substitutions σ_{S_i} reveals, that they do not change $B_r^m(\lambda\overleftrightarrow{x_k}.t_j)$.

It remains to compare $\mathbf{C}(E)$ with $\mathbf{C}(E'')$. We have to distinguish two cases: If $\mathrm{dp}_\pi(t) > 0$ at least one xflex-any-inference will be performed, because t gets fully decomposed. This decreases $\mathrm{dp}_\pi(E)$ and we are done. If, however, $\mathrm{dp}_\pi(t) = 0$ σ does not change $\mathrm{dp}_\pi(\cdot)$. But then $|\mathcal{I}(\sigma|_{FVar(t)})| = |FVar(t)|$ and furthermore $\mathcal{I}(\sigma|_F) = \mathcal{I}(\sigma|_{FVar(t)})$. Therefore $|\mathcal{I}(\sigma|_{FVar(E)})| = |FVar(s = t)| - 1$ which establishes $|FVar(\{s = t\} \cup E_0)| > |FVar(E'')|$.

A summarized version of the above argumentation is shown in Fig. 4. The primed versions denote the sequences which lead to E'' in Lem. 28.

Now, $\succ$ is well-founded and therefore $\mathcal{A}$ will only generate finite derivations to return either FAIL when no unifier exists or a solved form S. This establishes the missing part of the proof of Thm. 22 and leads to the following

Theorem 29. *The unification problem for higher-order product-patterns is decidable. In the positive case, a most general unifier can be computed.*

5 Extension: Integrating the Terminal Type

Adding the terminal[3] type $\mathbf{T}$ is motivated by the close relationship between lambda-calculus and category theory. This type represents the terminal object (hence its name) in *cartesian closed categories* and consists of just one element, denoted by $*$, which may be seen as the nullary tuple. The following extensional axiom describes this property:

$$top: \qquad t =_{top} * \qquad \text{if } t : \mathbf{T}$$

In contrast to the other extensional axioms, this equation may only be oriented from left to right. As is well known [DC95], there are no problems with terms in $\lambda\times$-long form [Aka93, JG95], but $\rightarrow_{top}$ destroys confluence with $\rightarrow_{\eta\, sp}$ [LS86]. This is important to our approach, since we require $\eta\, sp$-short forms for the arguments of free variables.

To overcome these obstacles, we adopt the approach of [DC95, Chap. 2.3] to our pattern calculus. First, for all types $\tau \in Iso(\mathbf{T})$, i. e. the types which are isomorphic to $\mathbf{T}$ such as $\hat{\tau} \rightarrow \mathbf{T}$ or $\mathbf{T} \times \mathbf{T}$, we introduce a generic representative $*_\tau$. The relation *top* has to be stated in a general version:

$$gentop: \qquad t \rightarrow_{top} *_\tau \qquad \text{if } t : \tau,\ t \neq *_\tau, \text{ and } \tau \in Iso(\mathbf{T})$$

Then, we extend Def. 2 to allow the (multiple) occurrence of some $*_\tau$ in abstraction patterns and adjoin $\rightarrow_{top}$ to $\rightarrow_\alpha$. This resolves the confluence problem between $\rightarrow_\eta$ and $\rightarrow_{top}$.

To get full confluence, we have to extend $\rightarrow_{sp}$ to tuples with some components with a type $\tau_i \in Iso(\mathbf{T})$ and at least one with $\tau_j \notin Iso(\mathbf{T})$.

$$sp_{top}: \qquad \langle \ldots *_{\tau_i} \ldots \pi_j^n(t) \ldots \rangle \rightarrow_{sp} t$$

This re-establishes the uniqueness of the pattern normal form.

Since we have a simply typed framework, the occurrences of $*_\tau$ are covered by Delete resp. by the definitions of the sets $\{\overline{z_\tau}\}$ in flex-flex-eq and flex-flex-neq. This means that neither the inference system nor the proofs have to be changed by this extension besides the definition of the pattern normal form and that $|*_\tau| = 1$. Especially, the proofs of Sect. 4.3 and Sect. 4.4 literally remain the same.

6 Conclusion and Future Work

Our approach is characterized by a successful combination of several generalizations of known concepts. Binding of variables is generalized to the binding of abstraction patterns. Flex/rigid terms are generalized to xflex/xrigid terms due to the introduction of the concept of a backbone. Higher-order patterns are generalized to higher-order product-patterns by allowing abstraction patterns as arguments of xflex terms. The combination of these concepts supports the generalization of β_0-reduction to a calculus with integrated products. The availability of this highly restricted kind of β-reduction permits the formulation of elegant inference rules.

[3] This is the *unit* type in functional programming languages such as *Haskell* or *ML*.

The elegance of our system becomes evident when comparing it to the work of Duggan [Dug93]. He deals with a richer type language than we do. However, when restricted to product and function space types his approach still needs a much more complicated framework than ours. The complications mostly arise from the translation of the usual lambda calculus in his locator calculus. Due to the conceptual clearness of the inference system $\mathcal{PU}$ and since it specializes to that presented by Nipkow [Nip91] when terms without product types are unified we think that our approach is more natural than that of Duggan's. Moreover, as outlined in section 5 the integration of the terminal type is possible by extending the definitions of abstraction patterns and $\downarrow_P$ only which demonstrates the modularity of our approach. Therefore, we are confident that we will soon present an extension to second order polymorphic types.

References

[Aka93] Y. Akama. On Mints' reductions for ccc-Calculus. In *Typed Lambda Calculi and Applications*, volume 664 of *LNCS*, pages 1–12, 1993.

[DC95] R. Di Cosmo. *Isomorphisms of Types*. Birkhäuser, 1995.

[DCK93] R. Di Cosmo and D. Kesner. A confluent reduction for the extensional typed λ-calculus with pairs, sums, recursion, and terminal object. In A. Lingas et al., editors, *ICALP*, volume 697 of *LNCS*, pages 645–656, 1993.

[Dug93] D. Duggan. Unification with Extended Patterns. Technical Report CS-93-37, University of Waterloo, 1993. To appear in *Theoretical Computer Science*.

[Gol81] W. D. Goldfarb. The undecidability of the second-order unification problem. *Theoretical Computer Science*, 13:225–230, 1981.

[Hue75] G. P. Huet. A Unification Algorithm for Typed λ-Calculus. *Theoretical Computer Science*, 1:27–57, 1975.

[JG95] C. B. Jay and N. Ghani. The virtues of eta-expansion. *J. Functional Programming*, 5(2):135–154, April 1995.

[Joh94] T. Johnsson. Fold-unfold transformations on state monadic interpreters. In K. Hammond et al., editors, *Functional programming, Glasgow*, Workshops in Computing. Springer-Verlag, 1994.

[Kes94] D. Kesner. Reasoning about Layered, Wildcard and Product Patterns. In G. Levi and M. Rodríguez-Artalejo, editors, *Algebraic and Logic Programming*, volume 850 of *LNCS*, pages 253–268, 1994.

[LS86] J. Lambek and P. J. Scott. *Introduction to higher order categorical logic*. Cambridge University Press, 1986.

[Mil91] D. Miller. A Logic Programming Language with Lambda-Abstraction, Function Variables, and Simple Unification. *J. Logic Comp.*, 1(4):497–536, 1991.

[Nip91] T. Nipkow. Higher-order critical pairs. In *Proc. sixth annual IEEE Symposium on Logic in Computer Science*, pages 342–349, 1991.

[Nip93] T. Nipkow. Functional unification of higher-order patterns. In *Proc. eighth annual IEEE Symposium on Logic in Computer Science*, pages 64–74, 1993.

[Pot81] G. Pottinger. The Church Rosser Theorem for the Typed lambda-calculus with Surjective Pairing. *Notre Dame J. of Formal Logic*, 22(3):264–268, 1981.

[SG89] W. Snyder and J. Gallier. Higher-Order Unification Revisited: Complete Sets of Transformations. *Journal of Symbolic Computation*, 8:101–140, 1989.

Decidable Approximations of Term Rewriting Systems

Florent Jacquemard

Laboratoire de Recherche en Informatique. CNRS URA 410
Univ. Paris-Sud, Bât. 490
91405 Orsay cedex. France
phone: +33 (1) 69 41 66 35 e-mail: jacquema@lri.fr

Abstract. A linear term rewriting system $\mathcal{R}$ is *growing* when, for every rule $l \rightarrow r \in \mathcal{R}$, each variable which is shared by l and r occurs at depth one in l. We show that the set of ground terms having a normal form w.r.t. a growing rewrite system is recognized by a finite tree automaton. This implies in particular that reachability and sequentiality of growing rewrite systems are decidable. Moreover, the word problem is decidable for related equational theories. We prove that our conditions are actually necessary: relaxing them yields undecidability of reachability.
Concerning sequentiality, the result may be restated in terms of approximations of term rewriting systems. An approximation of a system $\mathcal{R}$ is a renaming of the variables in the right hand sides which yields a growing rewrite system. This gives the decidability of a new sufficient condition for sequentiality of left-linear rewrite systems, which encompasses known decidable properties such as strong, NV and NVNF sequentiality.

1 Introduction

Most properties of term rewriting systems are undecidable. For instance, this is the case of termination (Huet and Lankford [12]), (Dauchet [3] for the case of one rule rewrite system), confluence (Huet [10]), word problem (Post [20]), reachability and sequentiality (Huet and Lévy [14]). Hence much efforts have been devoted to give sufficient conditions under which these properties are decidable. For example, for ground rewrite systems all these properties are decidable (Dauchet et al [5]). When the systems are just right ground and left-linear, the reachability (Oyamaguchi [17]) and the termination (Dershowitz [6]) are still decidable.

Our result can be understood in two ways:

1. to give a class of rewrite systems for which sets of normalizable ground terms are recognizable and reachability and other properties are decidable,
2. to give a general decidable approximation of rewrite systems.

Indeed, instead of restricting the class of term rewriting systems under consideration, one may see the problem as finding decidable approximations of the reduction relation. This approach may be interesting e.g. when studying sequential reduction strategies. The sequentiality is a property which has been introduced by Huet and Lévy [14]. They characterize left-linear rewrite systems for which there exists a normalizing reduction strategy. Sequentiality is undecidable for (general) left-linear rewrite systems. Thus, if we want to apply Huet and Lévy's reduction strategy, we are left to check sufficient conditions, namely properties stronger than sequentiality which are decidable. For instance, Huet and Lévy [14] show the decidability of strong sequentiality in the case of orthogonal term rewriting systems, and Sadfi [21] and Comon [1] generalized this result to left linear systems. This corresponds to the sequentiality of an approximation of the rewrite system in which all right hand sides are replaced by fresh variables. The interesting point is that roughly, a rewrite system is sequential as soon as its approximation is sequential, which allows to use the normalizing strategy of [14] for rewrite systems whose approximation is sequential – yet decidable.

In this paper, we give a class of rewrite systems for which both reachability and sequentiality are decidable. This corresponds also to a finer approximation than forgetting about the right hand sides. There were a lot of works in this direction. For example, Nagaya, Sakai and Toyama [16] show that the renaming of variables in the right hand sides with fresh variables yields a finer – yet decidable – approximation. They call NVNF-sequential an orthogonal and left-linear rewrite system for which this approximation is sequential. Actually, NVNF-sequentiality is an extension of Oyamaguchi [19] NV-sequentiality. Dauchet and Tison [4] showed that the first order theory of left-linear and right-ground and rewrite systems is decidable. Decidability of NV-sequentiality (resp. NVNF-sequentiality), even without the orthogonality assumption, is a direct consequence of this result, as noticed by Comon [1]. More generally, Comon shows that the sequentiality is decidable for a class of linear rewrite system whenever for each system $\mathcal{R}$ of the class, the set of ground terms which have a normal form w.r.t. $\mathcal{R}$ is recognizable by a finite tree automaton. He proves this result by showing that if the above hypothesis holds, then sequentiality may be expressed in Rabin's weak second order monadic theory of the tree. As a consequence, sequentiality is decidable for shallow linear rewrite systems [1] – in which all the variables occur at depth at most 1. Following this idea, we give a more general result here: if in any rule $l \to r$ of a linear rewrite system $\mathcal{R}$, each variable occurring in both l and r occurs at depth 1 in l, then the sequentiality of $\mathcal{R}$ is decidable, as well as the reachability. A rewrite system satisfying these properties is called *growing*. We achieve this result, proving first that the set of normalizable ground terms for a growing rewrite system is recognized by a finite tree automaton. Growing rewrite systems provide a better approximation of rewrite systems, hence of sequentiality: there are indeed rewrite systems whose such approximations are sequential and not the rougher ones.

The paper is organized as follows: the basics concerning term rewriting systems and tree automata are recalled respectively in Sect. 2 and 3. We give our recognizability result in Sect. 4. In Sect. 5 we derive that reachability is decidable for growing rewrite systems and give similar results for the word problem in section 6. In Sect. 7, we show that these results also apply to sequentiality, defining a new decidable criterium for sequentiality. Moreover, we present a comparison between different notions of sequentiality in the literature, redefined in terms of approximations. At last, we remark in Sect. 8 that these results cannot be generalized: we give undecidability results for systems in which the growing condition is relaxed.

2 Term Rewriting

We assume that the reader is familiar with notions of terms and term rewriting system. We recall some basic definitions. Missing ones can be found in the survey of Dershowitz and Jouannaud [7].

Terms. $\mathcal{F}$ is a finite ranked alphabet of function symbols. The set of (ground) terms with function symbols in $\mathcal{F}$ is written $\mathcal{T}(\mathcal{F})$. The *arity* of a function symbol $f \in \mathcal{F}$ is noted $ar(f)$. $\mathcal{T}(\mathcal{F}, \mathcal{X})$ is the set of terms built over $\mathcal{F}$ and a set of variable symbols $\mathcal{X}$. $\mathcal{V}ar(t)$ is the set of variables occurring in t. A term $t \in \mathcal{T}(\mathcal{F}, \mathcal{X})$ is called *linear* if every variable $x \in \mathcal{V}ar(t)$ occurs at most once in t.

A term $t \in \mathcal{T}(\mathcal{F}, \mathcal{X})$ may be viewed as a labeled tree $t = f(t_1 \ldots t_n)$ where $n = ar(f)$ and the subtrees $t_1 \ldots t_n$ are terms of $\mathcal{T}(\mathcal{F}, \mathcal{X})$. We may also see $t \in \mathcal{T}(\mathcal{F}, \mathcal{X})$ as a mapping from the set of strings $\{1 \ldots k\}^*$ into $\mathcal{F} \cup \mathcal{X}$, where $k = Max\{ar(f) \mid f \in \mathcal{F}\}$. If ε is the empty string and $p \cdot p'$ is the concatenation of strings p and p', we define this mapping recursively by $t(\varepsilon) = f$ and for each $1 \leq i \leq k$, and each $p \in \{1 \ldots k\}^*$, $t(i \cdot p) = t_i(p)$. $\mathcal{P}os(t)$ is the domain of the mapping t and is called the set of *positions* of t.

The *subterm* of $t \in \mathcal{T}(\mathcal{F}, \mathcal{X})$ at position $p \in \mathcal{P}os(t)$ is $t|_p$ and $t[t']_u$ is the term in $\mathcal{T}(\mathcal{F}, \mathcal{X})$ obtained by *replacement* of the subterm $t|_p$ at position $p \in \mathcal{P}os(t)$ by $t' \in \mathcal{T}(\mathcal{F}, X)$. We may also use the notation $t[t']_p$ to indicate that $t|_p = t'$.

A substitution is a mapping from $\mathcal{X}$ to $\mathcal{T}(\mathcal{F}, X)$. As usual, we do not distinguish between a substitution and its homomorphism extension in the free algebra $\mathcal{T}(\mathcal{F}, X)$. A bijective substitution from $\mathcal{X}$ to $\mathcal{X}$ is called a *variable renaming*. The postfix notation $t\sigma$ is used for the application of a substitution σ to a term t. A term $t\sigma$ is called an *instance* of t.

Rewrite Systems. A *Rewrite system* over $\mathcal{F}$ is a finite set of *rules* which are ordered pairs of terms $(l, r) \in \mathcal{T}(\mathcal{F}, \mathcal{X})^2$, commonly written $l \to r$. The term l (resp. r) is called the left (resp. right) member of the rule $l \to r$. When all the terms l and r in $\mathcal{R}$ are ground, resp. linear, $\mathcal{R}$ is a *ground rewrite system*, resp. *linear rewrite system*. Moreover, if all the left hand sides l (resp. right hand sides r) of $\mathcal{R}$ are ground or linear, then $\mathcal{R}$ is called a *left-ground*[1], *left-linear* (resp. *right-ground*, *right-linear*) rewrite system.

A term $t \in \mathcal{T}(\mathcal{F}, \mathcal{X})$ rewrites to t' by the system $\mathcal{R}$ iff there exists a rule $l \to r$ in $\mathcal{R}$, a position $p \in \mathcal{P}os(t)$ and a substitution σ such that $l\sigma = t|_p$ and $t' = t[r\sigma]_p$. The subterm $t|_p$ is called a *redex*. In that case, we write $t \xrightarrow[\mathcal{R}]{} t'$. We

[1] Never occurs

also say that t is *reducible* by $\mathcal{R}$. A term is said to be a *normal form* of $\mathcal{R}$ if it is not reducible by $\mathcal{R}$. A term t is *normalizable* w.r.t. a rewrite system $\mathcal{R}$ iff there exists a normal form n of $\mathcal{R}$ such that $t \xrightarrow[\mathcal{R}]{*} n$, where the binary relation $\xrightarrow[\mathcal{R}]{*}$ is the reflexive and transitive closure of $\xrightarrow[\mathcal{R}]{}$. A rewrite system $\mathcal{R}$ is non-ambiguous if there is no rule $l \to r \in \mathcal{R}$ with $\exists l'\ l \xrightarrow[\mathcal{R}\setminus\{l\to r\}]{} l'$

3 Tree Automata

Tree automata could also be called *term automata*. Following the custom, we use the former terminology, though it is in the use to talk about *terms* in rewriting theory. Moreover, though we didn't mention it in the previous section, the terms we consider are always finite, i.e. of finite domain. Thus we will also use *finite* tree automata.

Definition 1. A bottom-up finite tree automaton is a t-uple $(\mathcal{F}, Q, Q_f, \Delta)$ where $\mathcal{F}$ is a finite ranked alphabet, Q is a finite set of states and $Q_f \subseteq Q$, Δ is a ground rewriting system over $\mathcal{F} \cup Q$ whose rules have the form $f(q_1 \dots q_n) \to q$ where $f \in \mathcal{F}$, the arity of f is n and $q_1 \dots q_n, q \in Q$.

The term $t \in \mathcal{T}(\mathcal{F})$ is *accepted* - recognized - by the automaton $(\mathcal{F}, Q, Q_f, \Delta)$ iff there exists $q \in Q_f$ such that $t \xrightarrow[\Delta]{*} q$ [2]. The language $L(\mathcal{A})$ of an automaton $\mathcal{A}$ is the set of ground terms in $\mathcal{T}(\mathcal{F})$ accepted by $\mathcal{A}$.

Let us recall some basic properties of finite tree automata – see the reference book of Gécseg and Steinby [9] for more details.

Proposition 2. *The class of languages of ground terms recognized by a finite tree automaton is closed under Boolean operations.*

This means, for every automata $\mathcal{A}_1$ and $\mathcal{A}_2$, there are automata accepting respectively the languages $L(\mathcal{A}_1) \cup L(\mathcal{A}_2)$, $L(\mathcal{A}_1) \cap L(\mathcal{A}_2)$ and $\mathcal{T}(\mathcal{F}) \setminus L(\mathcal{A}_1)$.

Proposition 3. *Emptiness is decidable for finite tree automata.*

In other words, there is an algorithm which decides for any automaton $\mathcal{A}$ whether $L(\mathcal{A}) = \emptyset$ or not.

4 Recognizability of Sets of Normalizable Ground Terms

Now, we are ready to state our main result, concerning recognizability of set of ground normalizable terms.

Definition 4. A *growing* rewrite system is a linear rewrite system over an alphabet $\mathcal{F}$ such that for every rule $l \to r \in \mathcal{R}$ and every pair of positions $u \in \mathcal{P}os(l)$, $v \in \mathcal{P}os(r)$ such that $l(u) = r(v) \in \mathcal{X}$ we have $|u| \leq 1$.

[2] We may write also write $\xrightarrow[\mathcal{A}]{}$ for the relation $\xrightarrow[\Delta]{}$.

Theorem 5. *Let $\mathcal{R}$ be a growing rewrite system. Then the set of ground terms which are normalizable w.r.t. $\mathcal{R}$ is recognizable by a tree automaton.*

To prove the theorem, we have to construct a tree automaton from the given rewrite system $\mathcal{R}$. For this purpose, the two following lemmas will be helpful.

Lemma 6. *For each linear term $t \in \mathcal{T}(\mathcal{F}, \mathcal{X})$, there exists an automaton $\mathcal{A}_t$ which recognizes the ground instances of t.*

Lemma 7. *There exists an automaton $\mathcal{A}_{NF}$ which recognizes the set of ground terms which are in normal form w.r.t. $\mathcal{R}$.*

Such constructions have been exposed by Gallier and Book [8].
Let $\mathcal{L} = \bigcup_{f(l_1 \ldots l_n) \to r \in \mathcal{R}} \{l_1 \ldots l_n\}$ and let $\mathcal{A}_0$ be the following sum of automata:

$$\mathcal{A}_0 = (\mathcal{F}, Q, Q_0, \Delta_0) := \biguplus_{l \in \mathcal{L}} \mathcal{A}_l \uplus \mathcal{A}_{NF}$$

where the (disjoint) sum of two automata with the same alphabet is the automaton whose set of states, set of final states and set of rules are the union of corresponding sets of the two automata, provided that they are all disjoint.

Then, we complete Δ_0 using the following two inferences rules. Each application of 1 or 2 transforms Δ_k ($k \geq 0$) into Δ_{k+1}.

$$\frac{f(l_1 \ldots l_n) \to g(r_1 \ldots r_m) \in \mathcal{R} \quad g(q_1 \ldots q_m) \to q \in \Delta_k}{f(q'_1 \ldots q'_n) \to q \in \Delta_{k+1}} \tag{1}$$

with the conditions:

1. For all $1 \leq i \leq n$, if l_i is a variable then q'_i is any state of Q, otherwise q'_i is a final state of $\mathcal{A}_{l_i}$.
2. For all $1 \leq j \leq m$ there exists a substitution $\theta : \mathcal{X} \to Q$ such that $r_j\theta \xrightarrow[\Delta_k]{*} q_j$ and for each $l_i \in \mathcal{X}$ occurring in $g(r_1 \ldots r_m)$ $(1 \leq i \leq n)$, we have $l_i\theta = q'_i$.

$$\frac{f(l_1 \ldots l_n) \to x \in \mathcal{R}_w \quad q \in \Delta_k}{f(q'_1 \ldots q'_n) \to q \in \Delta_{k+1}} \tag{2}$$

with the conditions:

1. x is a variable
2. For all $1 \leq i \leq n$, if $l_i = x$ then $q'_i = q$
   if l_i is a variable different from x then q'_i is any state of Q
   otherwise q'_i is a final state of $\mathcal{A}_{l_i}$

The number of states of $\mathcal{A}_0$ ($|Q|$) is finite and no new state is added in 1 or 2. So the process stops with a set Δ when there is no new rule to add.

The desired automaton is

$$\mathcal{A} := (\mathcal{F}, Q, Q_{NF}, \Delta)$$

where Q_{NF} is the set of final states of $\mathcal{A}_{NF}$. Now, we show the two inclusions in the next two lemmas. Let $\mathcal{A}_k$ be the automaton $(\mathcal{F}, Q, Q_{NF}, \Delta_k)$.

Lemma 8. *For each k, $L(\mathcal{A}_k) \subseteq \{t \in \mathcal{T}(\mathcal{F}) \mid t$ is normalizable w.r.t. $\mathcal{R}\}$.*

Proof. (sketch) First, we show by induction on k that
(fact1) for every k, for every ground term $t \in \mathcal{T}(\mathcal{F})$ and for every final state q_l of some automaton $\mathcal{A}_l$ ($l \in \mathcal{L}$) if $t \xrightarrow[\mathcal{A}_k]{*} q_l$ then $t \xrightarrow[\mathcal{R}]{*} l\sigma$ where $l\sigma$ is a ground instance of l.

1. For $k = 1$, by construction of $\mathcal{A}_1$ as a disjoint sum of automata, if $t \xrightarrow[\mathcal{A}_1]{*} q_l$, a final state of an $\mathcal{A}_l$ ($l \in \mathcal{L}$), then t is a ground instance of l.
2. Assume this is true for k and that $t \xrightarrow[\Delta_{k+1}]{*} q_l$, a final state of an $\mathcal{A}_l$ ($l \in \mathcal{L}$). We use an induction on the number n of reduction steps using the rule $\Delta_{k+1} \setminus \Delta_k$ in the above reduction sequence.
   (a) If $n = 0$, we can directly use the induction hypothesis concerning $\mathcal{A}_k$.
   (b) If $n > 0$, we consider the first application of the rule $\Delta_{k+1} \setminus \Delta_k$ in the reduction sequence. Let $f(q'_1 \ldots q'_n) \to q$ be this rule and assume it had been added to $\mathcal{A}_k$ by inference 1 with the hypothesis $f(l_1 \ldots l_n) \to g(r_1 \ldots r_m) \in \mathcal{R}$ and $g(q_1 \ldots q_m) \to q \in \Delta_k$. Then the proof can be summarized in the following diagram:

$$
\begin{array}{ccccccc}
t = t[f(t_1 \ldots t_n)]_p & & & & & & \\
\Big\downarrow {\scriptstyle * \, \mathcal{R}} & & & & & & \\
t[f(l_1 \ldots l_n)\sigma]_p & \xrightarrow[\mathcal{A}_k]{*} & t'[f(q'_1 \ldots q'_n)]_p & \xrightarrow[\mathcal{A}_{k+1} \setminus \mathcal{A}_k]{} & t'[q]_p & \xrightarrow[\mathcal{A}_{k+1}]{*} & q_l \\
\Big\downarrow {\scriptstyle \mathcal{R}} & & & & \Big\uparrow {\scriptstyle \mathcal{A}_k} & & \\
t[g(r_1 \ldots r_m)\sigma]_p & \xrightarrow[\mathcal{A}_k]{*} & t'[g(r_1 \ldots r_m)\theta]_p & \xrightarrow[\mathcal{A}_k]{*} & t'[g(q_1 \ldots q_m)]_p & &
\end{array}
$$

   For the reduction $t \xrightarrow[\mathcal{R}]{*} t[f(l_1 \ldots l_n)\sigma]_p$, condition 1 of inference 1 says that if $l_i \notin \mathcal{X}$, q'_i is a final state of $\mathcal{A}_{l_i}$ and by induction hypothesis, $t_i \xrightarrow[\mathcal{A}_k]{*} q'_i$ implies $t_i \xrightarrow[\mathcal{R}]{*} l_i\sigma$.
   The substitution θ is defined in condition 2. We have $r_i\sigma \xrightarrow[\mathcal{A}_k]{*} r_i\theta$ for each $1 \leq i \leq m$ because $l_j \in \mathcal{V}ar(r_i)$ implies $l_j\theta = q'_j$ (condition 2) and $l_j\sigma \xrightarrow[\mathcal{A}_k]{*} q'_j$. On the other hand, $\mathcal{V}ar(r_i) \cap \mathcal{V}ar(f(l_1 \ldots l_n)) \subseteq \{l_1 \ldots l_n\}$, because $\mathcal{R}$ is growing. Condition 2 also implies $r_i\theta \xrightarrow[\mathcal{A}_k]{*} q_i$. By induction hypothesis on the number of applications of $\Delta_{k+1} \setminus \Delta_k$, $t[g(r_1 \ldots r_m)\sigma]_p$ reduces to some ground instance of l, thus so does t. The proof would have been almost the same if the rule $\Delta_{k+1} \setminus \Delta_k$ had been deduced using the inference 2.

Now, we prove the lemma 8 by induction on k using **fact 1**.

1. The case $k = 1$ is obvious because $L(\mathcal{A}_1) = L(\mathcal{A}_{NF})$ by construction.
2. For $k+1$, assume $t \xrightarrow[\mathcal{A}_{k+1}]{*} q_f$ where q_f is a final state of $\mathcal{A}_{k+1}$. We use the same induction as in the proof of **fact 1**. The diagram for the step (case of inference 1) is now:

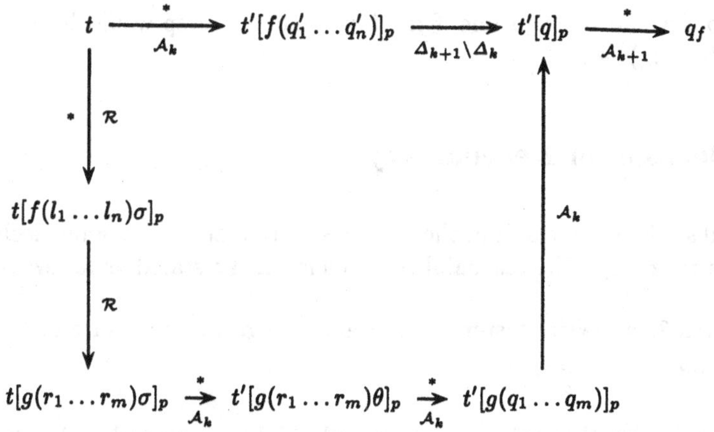

The reduction $* \downarrow_{\mathcal{R}}$ follows from **fact 1**. The other reductions are deduced as in the proof of **fact 1**. By induction hypothesis – on the number of applications of $\Delta_{k+1} \setminus \Delta_k$, $t[g(r_1 \dots r_n)\sigma]_p$ reduces to a normal form w.r.t. $\mathcal{R}$, thus so does t. □

Lemma 9. $L(\mathcal{A}) \supseteq \{t \in \mathcal{T}(\mathcal{F}) \mid t$ *is normalizable w.r.t.* $\mathcal{R}\}$

Proof. Assume that $t \xrightarrow[\mathcal{R}]{*} n$ for some normal form n w.r.t. $\mathcal{R}$. We show by induction on the length n of this reduction sequence that $t \in L(\mathcal{A})$.

1. If $n = 0$, $t \in L(\mathcal{A})$ because $L(\mathcal{A}_{NF}) \subseteq L(\mathcal{A})$.
2. If $n > 0$, assume that the first reduction step uses the rule $f(l_1 \dots l_n) \rightarrow g(r_1 \dots r_m) \in \mathcal{R}$ with substitution σ, that $r_i\sigma \xrightarrow[\mathcal{A}]{*} q_i$ and that $g(q_1 \dots q_m) \rightarrow q \in \Delta$.

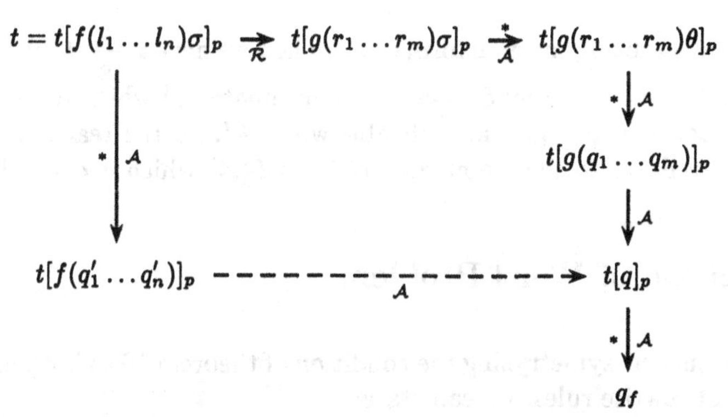

The reduction $t[g(r_1 \dots r_m)\sigma]_p \xrightarrow[\mathcal{A}]{*} q_f$ follows from the induction hypothesis (q_f is a final state of $\mathcal{A}$). The substitution θ is deduced from this reduction by $\mathcal{A}$ and has the right form for condition 2. For each l_i which is a variable ($1 \leq i \leq n$), the corresponding state q'_i is defined by θ and then q'_i fulfills the condition 1. Thus, the inference rule 1 has been applied during the construction of Δ and the transition $t[f(q'_1 \dots q'_n)]_p \xrightarrow[\mathcal{A}]{} t[q]_p$ is possible. The proof would be the same if the first reduction step would have used a rule $f(l_1 \dots l_n) \to x$. □

5 Decision of Reachability

We will see how the result of the previous section applies to some decision problems in rewriting. The reachability problem can be stated as follows:

> Given $\mathcal{R}$ a rewrite system over $\mathcal{F}$ and two ground terms t and t' in $\mathcal{T}(\mathcal{F})$, do we have $t \xrightarrow[\mathcal{R}]{*} t'$?

It is well known that this problem is undecidable in general. It has been shown decidable for ground rewrite systems by Togachi and Noguchi [22], for left-linear and right-ground rewrite systems by Dauchet et al. [5] and Oyamaguchi [17] and for right-ground rewrite systems by Oyamaguchi [18]. Now, applying Theorem 5, we have:

Theorem 10. *Reachability is decidable for growing rewrite systems.*

Note that this result extends (strictly) former results for left-linear systems.

Proof. (sketch) Let $\mathcal{R}$ be a rewrite system as in the theorem, over an alphabet $\mathcal{F}$ and $t, t' \in \mathcal{T}(\mathcal{F})$. Let $\mathcal{F}' := \mathcal{F} \uplus \{c, d\}$ and $\mathcal{R}'$ be the following system over $\mathcal{F}'$:

$$\mathcal{R}' := \mathcal{R} \cup t' \to d \cup \bigcup_{f \in \mathcal{F}} f(x_1 \dots x_n) \to c \cup \{c \to c\} .$$

Note that d is the only normal form of $\mathcal{R}'$. Then we have $t \xrightarrow[\mathcal{R}]{*} t'$ iff t is normalizable w.r.t. $\mathcal{R}'$. By Theorem 5, there is an automaton $\mathcal{A}$ which recognizes the set of ground terms which are normalizable w.r.t. $\mathcal{R}'$. So the reachability problem for $\mathcal{R}$, t, t' reduces to the membership of t to $L(\mathcal{A})$ which is decidable. □

6 Decision of Word Problem

As a consequence, symetryzing the condition of theorem 10 to both left and right members of rewrite rules, we can state:

Corollary 11. *The word problem*[3] *is decidable for linear rewrite systems $\mathcal{R}$ such that for each rule $l \to r \in \mathcal{R}$ and each pair of positions $u \in \mathcal{P}os(l)$, $v \in \mathcal{P}os(r)$ such that $l(u) = r(v) = x \in \mathcal{X}$ we have $|u|, |v| \leq 1$.*

Proof. If $\mathcal{R} = \{l_1 \to r_1 \ldots l_n \to t_n\}$ is as in the statements of Corollary 11, then $\{l_1 \to r_1, r_1 \to l_1 \ldots l_n \to r_n, r_n \to l_n\}$ is a growing system, thus it has a decidable reachability problem, by Theorem 10. □

This is a slight generalization for linear systems of the decidability proof of the word problem by Comon, Haberstrau and Jouannaud [2] for shallow systems.

The section 8 shows that Theorem 10 and Corollary 11 cannot be easily generalized.

7 Sequentiality

The property of sequentiality for left-linear rewrite systems was introduced by Huet and Lévy [14]. The main property of a sequential rewrite system is that there exists an effective call-by-need normalizing strategy.

7.1 Definition

Our purpose is less to study theoretical and practical implications of sequentiality than to give decidability results. Moreover, the decidability proof refers to a coding of Comon [1]. For all these reasons, we will go quickly with the definitions concerning sequentiality. For a more complete presentation of sequentiality, the reader is referred to Huet and Levy [14] and Klop and Middeldorp [15].

Informally, a rewrite system is sequential if any normalizable term contains a redex which is necessarily contracted in a reduction to a normal form. In the literature, these redexes are called *index*. In order to define formally the notion of necessity, we classically use ***partially evaluated terms*** also called *Ω-terms*. An Ω-term is a term on the signature $\mathcal{F}$ augmented by a new constant Ω. The Ω's represent subterms which have not been evaluated so far. A position p in an Ω-term t such that $t(p) = \Omega$ is an index if it needs to be evaluated (replaced) in order to get a normal form. The formal notion of "more evaluated" is given by the relation $\sqsubseteq$ on Ω-terms and defined by: $\Omega \sqsubseteq t$ for every Ω-term t and if $t_i \sqsubseteq u_i$ for each $1 \leq i \leq n$ then $f(t_1 \ldots t_n) \sqsubseteq f(u_1 \ldots u_n)$. An index of an Ω-term t for a rewrite system $\mathcal{R}$ is a position $p \in \mathcal{P}os(t)$ such that $t(p) = \Omega$ and for each Ω-term $u \sqsupseteq t$ which reduces by $\mathcal{R}$ to a normal form in $\mathcal{T}(\mathcal{F})$, we have $u(p) \neq \Omega$. Then, a left-linear rewrite system $\mathcal{R}$ is sequential if for each Ω-term t which cannot be reduced by $\mathcal{R}$ into a normal form in $\mathcal{T}(\mathcal{F})$ but such that there exists $u \sqsupseteq t$ with $u \xrightarrow[\mathcal{R}]{*} n \in \mathcal{T}(\mathcal{F})$ (n is in normal form), then t has an index.

[3] The word problem for a rewrite system $\{l_1 \to r_1 \ldots l_n \to t_n\}$ over $\mathcal{F}$, and two terms $t, t' \in \mathcal{T}(\mathcal{F})$ is the reachability problem for $\{l_1 \to r_1, r_1 \to l_1 \ldots l_n \to r_n, r_n \to l_n\}$, t and t'.

Example 1. Let $\mathcal{R}$ be the left-linear rewriting system defining the parallel or $\vee$: $\mathcal{R} = \vee(\top, x_1) \to \top, \ \vee(x_2, \top) \to \top$. Consider the partially evaluated term $t = \vee(\Omega, \Omega)$, which is in normal form w.r.t. $\mathcal{R}$. We have $t \sqsubseteq \vee(\top, \Omega) \xrightarrow[\mathcal{R}]{} \top$ where the constant $\top$ is a normal form of $\mathcal{R}$. By the above reduction, the position 2 is not an index. This is neither the case of the position 1, because $t \sqsubseteq \vee(\Omega, \top) \xrightarrow[\mathcal{R}]{} \top$. Thus, $\mathcal{R}$ is not sequential.

In the general case, sequentiality is undecidable [14]. The reachability – see Sect. 5 – indeed reduces to the sequentiality decision, and this problem is known to be undecidable even for linear rewrite systems. Thus we are left to check sufficient conditions, namely properties stronger than sequentiality which are decidable. When a non-ambiguous left-linear rewrite system fulfills such a property, the normalizing strategy is still applicable. Toyama investigates in [23] some case of ambiguous left-linear systems for which the index reduction strategy is normalizing. We will give some conditions of the literature in term of *approximations.*

7.2 Approximations of Rewrite System

An approximation of a rewrite system is a rougher system, in the sense that the associated binary relation on terms is rougher.

Definition 12. An approximation of a rewrite system $\mathcal{R}$ is another system $\mathcal{R}'$ such that $\xrightarrow[\mathcal{R}]{} \subseteq \xrightarrow[\mathcal{R}']{}$.

Example 2. $\{f(x_1, x_2) \to h(x_1', x_2'),\ f(x_3, 0) \to x_3'\}$ and $\{f(x_1, x_2) \to x_1'$, $f(x_3, 0) \to x_3\}$ are approximations of $\{f(x_1, x_2) \to h(g(x_1), x_1),\ f(x_3, 0) \to x_3\}$.

In the following, an approximation is understood as a mapping τ which associates to each rewrite system $\mathcal{R}$ one of its approximations $\tau(\mathcal{R})$ in the sense of definition 12. If an approximation τ is such that for every $\mathcal{R}$, $\tau(\mathcal{R})$ is right-linear, as in the case presented in example 2, then we say that τ is a *right-linear approximation.*

The idea is to find a right-linear approximation τ such that given a left-linear rewrite system $\mathcal{R}$, it is decidable whether $\tau(\mathcal{R})$ is sequential. In this case, we may say for short that sequentiality for τ is decidable. The fact that these conditions really imply sequentiality is given by the following lemma:

Lemma 13. *For any right-linear approximation τ and any left-linear system $\mathcal{R}$, if $\tau(\mathcal{R})$ is sequential, then so is $\mathcal{R}$.*

7.3 Decidable Approximations and Sequentiality

Historically, the first approximation which has been considered consists in replacing the right hand sides of the rules by distincts fresh variables. The sequentiality for such an approximation is Huet and Lévy's *strong sequentiality* [13]. These two authors showed the decidability of strong sequentiality for left-linear and non-overlapping (any rule cannot reduce another) systems in [14]. Sadfi [21] and Comon [1] have shown the decidability in the possibly overlapping and left-linear case.

Nagaya et al. introduced in [16] NVNF-sequentiality which is sequentiality of a finer approximation for left-linear and non overlapping systems and extends NV-sequentiality of Oyamaguchi [19]. This consists in renaming all variables of all right members of rules by pairwise distincts fresh variables.

Example 3. If $\mathcal{R}$ is $\{f(x_1, f(x_2, x_3)) \to f(g(x_1, x_2), x_3), f(x_4, 0) \to x_4\}$ its NVNF approximation is $\{f(x_1, f(x_2, x_3)) \to f(g(x_1', x_2'), x_3'), f(x_4, 0) \to x_4'\}$.

Comon [1] proved this result for left-linear systems.

At last, Comon [1] also proved that sequentiality is decidable for shallow linear rewrite systems, this is for systems whose all left and right hand sides of rules are a variable or have all their variables occurring at depth 1. This result could be generalized to show that the sequentiality for a *shallow approximation* (shallow sequentiality for short) is decidable, where shallow approximating a rewrite system consists in renaming by fresh variables in right members all the sharing variables except those which are at depth less or equal than 1 in both left members and right members.

7.4 Growing Sequentiality

We consider here *growing approximation* generalizing former approximations:

Definition 14 Growing Approximation. The growing approximation of a left-linear rewrite system $\{l_1 \to r_1 \dots l_n \to r_n\}$ is a growing rewrite system $\{l_1 \to r_1' \dots l_n \to r_n'\}$ where r_i' $(1 \le i \le n)$ is obtained by renaming the variables of r_i which do not match the conditions of growing systems.

Example 4. Let us go back to the system of example 3. Its growing approximation is $\{f(x_1, f(x_2, x_3)) \to f(g(x_1, x_2'), x_3'),\ f(x_4, 0) \to x_4\}$.

Growing-sequentiality refers to sequentiality for the growing approximation. To prove the decidability of growing-sequentiality for left-linear systems, we use the following fundamental theorem of Comon [1], which we give a reformulation with the notations of our paper.

Theorem 15 Comon [1]. *Consider a right-linear approximation τ. If for any left-linear rewrite system $\mathcal{R}$, the set of ground terms normalizable w.r.t. $\tau(\mathcal{R})$ is recognizable by a tree automaton, then the sequentiality for τ is decidable.*

To prove this theorem, Comon used Rabin's correspondence between tree automata and the decidable weak second order monadic theory of the finite k-ary tree WSkS. More precisely, he shows that sequentiality may be expressed in a WSkS formula with an additional unary predicate satisfied by grounds terms normalizable w.r.t. $\tau(\mathcal{R})$. This has been used by Comon [1] to show the decidability results mentioned in Sect. 7.3.

Theorem 16. *The growing-sequentiality of any left-linear rewrite system is decidable.*

Proof. From Theorems 15 and 5.

7.5 A gap between growing sequentiality and the previous notions of sequentiality

To conclude this section and for those who are familiar with sequentiality, we give two examples illustrating the *strict* hierarchy between the approximations we have presented above. They are variation on Gustave example [11].

Proposition 17. *The two rewrite systems of examples 5 and 6 below are respectively shallow-sequential and non NVNF-sequential and on the other hand growing-sequential and non shallow-sequential.*

The hierarchy is depicted in Fig. 1. In this figure, all the non-dashed sets of term rewrite systems are recursive. For a comparison between NV-sequentiality and NVNF-sequentiality, see [16].

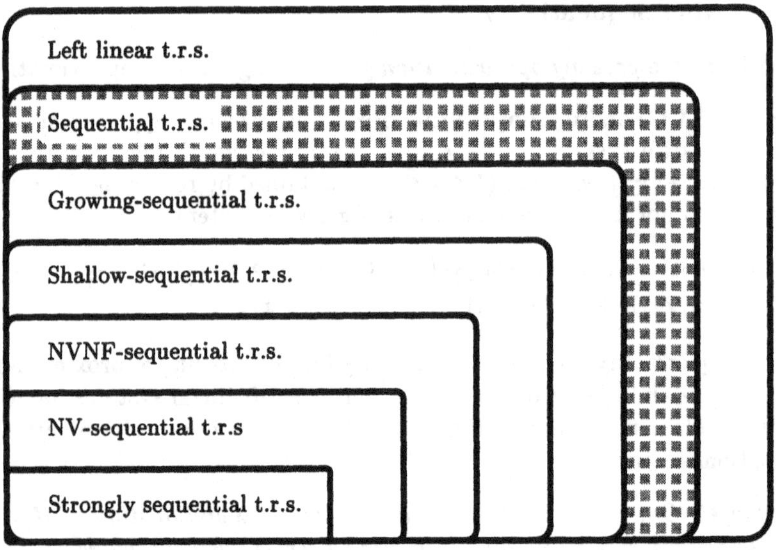

Fig. 1. A hierarchy between different sets of sequential rewrite systems

Example 5. Let $\mathcal{R} = \{f(x_1, a, b) \to f(a, x_1, a),\ f(b, x_2, a) \to f(a, a, x_2),$ $f(a, b, x_3) \to f(x_3, a, a)\}$ (f is ternary, a, b are constants). Its approximation for NVNF-sequentiality of Nagaya et al. [16] is $\mathcal{R}' = \{f(x_1, a, b) \to f(a, x'_1, a),$

$f(b, x_2, a) \to f(a, a, x'_2)$, $f(a, b, x_3) \to f(x'_3, a, a)\}$ though its approximation for shallow sequentiality is $\mathcal{R}$ itself. The Ω-term $t := f(\Omega, \Omega, \Omega)$ has no index w.r.t. $\mathcal{R}'$ and is a normal form of $\mathcal{R}'$. Thus $\mathcal{R}'$ is not sequential, $\mathcal{R}$ is not NVNF-sequential. It can be shown that $\mathcal{R}$ is sequential, thus $\mathcal{R}$ is shallow-sequential. To prove this, we may use a result from Huet and Lévy [13] saying that if a left-linear *non-ambiguous* rewrite system $\mathcal{R}$ is such that for each Ω-term t in normal form w.r.t. $\mathcal{R}$ which contains an occurrence of Ω and such that there exists $u \sqsupseteq t$ with $u \xrightarrow[\mathcal{R}]{*} n \in \mathcal{T}(\mathcal{F})$ (n is in normal form), then t has an index[4].

Example 6. Let $\mathcal{R} = \{f(x_1, a, b) \to f(a, f(a, x_1, a), a)$, $f(b, x_2, a) \to f(a, a, f(a, a, x_2))$, $f(a, b, x_3) \to f(f(x_3, a, a), a, a)\}$ Its approximation for shallow-sequentiality is $\mathcal{R}' = \{f(x_1, a, b) \to f(a, f(a, x'_1, a), a)$, $f(b, x_2, a) \to f(a, a, f(a, a, x'_2))$, $f(a, b, x_3) \to f(f(x'_3, a, a), a, a)\}$ though its growing approximation is $\mathcal{R}$ itself. As in example 5, we can show that $\mathcal{R}'$ is not sequential ($\mathcal{R}$ is not shallow-sequential) and that $\mathcal{R}$ is growing-sequential.

8 Undecidability Results

To conclude, we show that a further weakening of the conditions of Theorems 10, 16 and Corollary 11 yields in undecidability.

8.1 Non-Linear Case

If we relax the linearity condition in Theorem 10, then reachability becomes undecidable.

Theorem 18. *Reachability is undecidable for rewrite systems $\mathcal{R}$ such that for each rule $l \to r \in \mathcal{R}$ and each pair of positions $u \in \mathcal{P}os(l)$, $v \in \mathcal{P}os(r)$ with $l(u) = r(v) \in \mathcal{X}$ we have $|u| \leq 1$.*

Proof. (sketch) We describe a reduction of an intance of the (undecidable) Post Correspondence Problem (PCP). Let A be an alphabet and $u_1 \ldots u_n, v_1 \ldots v_n \in A^*$ an instance of PCP. The problem is to find a finite sequence $i_1 \ldots i_m$ of integers smaller than n – which may contain repetitions – such that $u_{i_1} u_{i_2} \cdots u_{i_m} = v_{i_1} v_{i_2} \cdots v_{i_m}$. We let $\mathcal{F} := A \uplus \{f, 0, c, b\}$ where the symbols of A are unary, f is binary and 0, c and b are constants. We note $u_i(x)$ $(1 \leq i \leq n)$ for the term $u_{i,1}(u_{i,2}(\ldots(u_{i,k}(x))\ldots))$, if $u_{i,1} \ldots u_{i,k} \in A$ and $u_i = u_{i,1} \ldots u_{i,k}$.

$$\mathcal{R} = \bigcup_{1=1}^{n} c \to f(u_i(0), v_i(0)) \cup \bigcup_{1=1}^{n} f(x_1, x_2) \to f(u_i(x_1), v_i(x_2)) \cup f(x, x) \to b \ .$$

Then the PCP has a solution iff $c \xrightarrow[\mathcal{R}]{*} b$. □

The Corollary 11 neither holds without the linearity condition. Oyamaguchi showed indeed in [18] that the word problem is undecidable for right-ground term rewriting systems, which constitutes a particular case of Corollary 11 without linearity.

[4] This result does not hold for ambiguous left-linear systems

8.2 Linear Case with a Weaker Restriction

If, in Theorem 10, we keep the linearity condition but we weaken the restriction about variables sharing, this also results in undecidability.

Theorem 19. *Reachability is undecidable for linear rewrite systems $\mathcal{R}$ such that for each rule $l \to r \in \mathcal{R}$ we have either for each pair of positions $u \in \mathcal{P}os(l)$, $v \in \mathcal{P}os(r)$ such that $l(u) = r(v) \in \mathcal{X}$, $|u| \leq 1$ or for each pair $u \in \mathcal{P}os(l)$, $v \in \mathcal{P}os(r)$ such that $l(u) = r(v) \in \mathcal{X}$, $|v| \leq 1$.*

Proof. (sketch) Once again we reduce an instance $A, u_1, \ldots, u_n, v_1, \ldots, v_n \in A^*$ of PCP to a reachability problem for a system $\mathcal{R}$ as in statement of Theorem 19. Let $\mathcal{F} = A \uplus \{f, g, 0, c\}$ with arities where the symbols of A are unary, f and g are binary and 0 and c are constants.

$$\mathcal{R} = \biguplus_{i=1}^{n} c \to f(u_i(0), v_i(0)) \cup \biguplus_{i=1}^{n} f(x_1, x_2) \to f(u_i(x_1), v_i(x_2))$$
$$\cup f(x_1, x_2) \to g(x_1, x_2) \cup \biguplus_{a \in A} g(a(x_1), a(x_2)) \to g(x_1, x_2) \ .$$

Then the above PCP has a solution iff $c \xrightarrow[\mathcal{R}]{*} g(0, 0)$. □

Because of the reduction of reachability to sequentiality in [13], sequentiality is also undecidable for the kind of linear rewrite systems of Theorem 19.

Acknowledgments

I am very grateful to Hubert Comon for his helpful suggestions and remarks as well as for his careful reading of a first version of this paper, and also to the referees for their useful comments.

References

1. H. Comon. Sequentiality, second-order monadic logic and tree automata. In *Tenth Annual IEEE Symposium on Logic in Computer Science*, San Diego, CA, June 1995. IEEE Comp. Soc. Press.
2. H. Comon, M. Haberstrau, and J.-P. Jouannaud. Decidable properties of shallow equational theories. In *Proceedings of the Seventh Annual IEEE Symposium on Logic in Computer Science.* IEEE Comp. Soc. Press, 1992.
3. M. Dauchet. Simulation of a turing machine by a left-linear rewrite rule. In *Proc. 3rd Rewriting Techniques and Applications, Chapel Hill, LNCS 355*, 1989.
4. M. Dauchet and S. Tison. The theory of ground rewrite systems is decidable. In *Proc. 5th IEEE Symp. Logic in Computer Science, Philadelphia*, 1990.
5. M. Dauchet, S. Tison, T. Heuillard, and P. Lescanne. Decidability of the confluence of ground term rewriting systems. Technical Report IT-102, LIFL, Université de Lille, May 1987. Actes de logic in Computer Science Second Annual Conference New-York Juin 87.

6. N. Dershowitz. Termination of linear rewriting systems. In *Proceedings of the Eihgth Int. Colloquium on Automata, Languages and Programming*, pages 448–458, Acre, Israel, 1981.
7. N. Dershowitz and J.-P. Jouannaud. Rewrite systems. In J. van Leeuwen, editor, *Handbook of Theoretical Computer Science*, volume B, pages 243–309. North-Holland, 1990.
8. J. Gallier and R. Book. Reductions in tree replacement systems. *Theorical Computer Science*, 37:123–150, 1985.
9. M. Gécseg and M. Steinby. *Tree Automata.* Akademia Kiadó, Budapest, 1984.
10. G. Huet. Confluent reductions: abstract properties and applications to term rewriting systems. *J. ACM*, 27(4):797–821, Oct. 1980.
11. G. Huet. Formal structures for computation and deduction. In: Working material for the International Summer School on Logic of Programming and Calculi of Discrete Design, Marktoberdorf, May 1986.
12. G. Huet and D. S. Lankford. On the uniform halting problem for term rewriting systems. Research Report 283, INRIA, Mar. 1978.
13. G. Huet and J.-J. Lévy. Computations in orthogonal term rewriting systems. In G. Plotkin and J.-L. Lassez, editors, *Computational Logic: essays in Honour of Alan Robinson.* MIT Press, 1990.
14. G. Huet and J.-J. Lévy. Call by need computations in non-ambiguous linear term rewriting systems. In J.-L. Lassez and G. Plotkin, editors, *Computational Logic: Essays in Honor of Alan Robinson.* MIT Press, 1991.
15. J. W. Klop and A. Middeldorp. Sequentiality in orthogonal term rewriting systems. *Journal of Symbolic Computation*, 12:161–195, 1991.
16. T. Nagaya, M. Sakai, and Y. Toyama. NVNF-sequentiality of left-linear term rewriting systems. In *Proc. Japanese Workhop on Term Rewriting*, Kyoto, July 1995.
17. M. Oyamaguchi. The reachability problem for quasi-ground term rewriting systems. *J. Inf. Process.*, pages 232–236, 1986.
18. M. Oyamaguchi. On the word problem for right-ground term rewriting systems. *Trans. IEICE Japan*, E73:718–723, 1990.
19. M. Oyamaguchi. NV-sequentiality: a decidable condition for call-by-need computations in term rewriting systems. *SIAM J. Comput.*, 22(1):114–135, 1993.
20. E. L. Post. Recursive unsolvability of a problem of Thue. *Journal of Symbolic Logic*, 13:1–11, 1947.
21. W. Sadfi. *Contribution à l'étude de la séquentialité forte des définitions de fonctions par règles.* Thèse de doctorat, Université Paris-Sud, Orsay, France, Dec. 1993.
22. A. Togashi and S. Noguchi. Some decision problems and their time complexity for term rewriting systems. *Trans. IECE Japan*, J66(D):1177–1184, 1983.
23. Y. Toyama. Strong sequentiality of left linear overlapping term rewriting systems. In *Proc. 7th IEEE Symp. on Logic in Computer Science*, Santa Cruz, CA, 1992.

Semantics and Strong Sequentiality of Priority Term Rewriting Systems

Masahiko Sakai and Yoshihito Toyama

Japan Advanced Institute of Science and Technology, Hokuriku
Tatsunokuchi, Ishikawa 923-12, Japan
{sakai, toyama}@jaist.ac.jp

Abstract. This paper gives an operational semantics of priority term rewriting systems (PRS) by using conditional systems, whose reduction is decidable and stable under substitution. We also define the class of strong sequential PRSs and show that this class is decidable. Moreover, we show that the index rewriting of strong sequential PRSs gives a normalizing strategy.

1 Introduction

Baeten, Bergstra and Klop[BBKW89] proposed the formalism of priority term rewriting systems (PRSs) to capture the theoretical basis of order dependency in rules. A PRS differs from an ordinary TRS in that whenever a rule matches a given redex, it can only be chosen if none of the rules with higher priority can match the (internally rewritten) term, where a reduction step is internal if it proceeds entirely within the arguments of the leftmost symbol of the term. For example, the factorial function can be defined as follows:

$$\mathcal{R} = \left\{ \Big\downarrow \begin{array}{l} fac(0) \to 1 \\ fac(x) \to x * fac(x-1). \end{array} \right.$$

Here, the down arrow sign indicates that the top rule has higher priority than the bottom rule. If the argument of fac is 0 then the first rule is applicable. However, if it is somehow known that the argument can never be reduced to 0, then the priority of the rules makes it possible to choose the second rule without actually reducing the argument. Hence, the second rule can be applied on $fac(1+1)$ but not on $fac(1-1)$.

On the other hand, most functional languages admit priorities in rules and evaluation methods such as the functional strategy[PvE93, TSvEP93], an implementation method for lazy evaluation[Hen80, Jon87], possess the ability to handle priorities implicitly. However, it is hard to use PRSs as a theoretical computation model for analyzing the functional strategy. The main reason is that the PRSs in [BBKW89, Moh89] have limitations, for example "bounded", to ensure well-defined operational semantics.

This paper develops a new semantics for PRSs. This new semantics is natural as a model of actual computation systems such as the functional strategy. The key idea is translating PRSs to conditional term rewriting systems (CTRSs) with direct approximants in conditions. Our operational semantics of PRSs are then defined as that of the corresponding CTRSs. This technique allows us to discuss behaviors of PRSs both theoretically and in practice. By using our framework of PRSs, we discuss a normalizing strategy of PRSs and provide a class of PRSs with a decidable normalizing strategy.

2 Term Rewriting Systems

We mainly follow the notation of [Klo92] and assume readers are familiar with abstract reduction systems and conditional term rewriting systems (TRS)[Hue80, Klo92, DJ90].

A reduction system is a structure $A = \langle D, \rightarrow \rangle$ for some set D and binary relation $\rightarrow$ on D called a reduction relation. A reduction is a finite sequence $x_0 \rightarrow x_1 \rightarrow \cdots \rightarrow x_n$ $(n \geq 0)$ or an infinite sequence $x_0 \rightarrow x_1 \rightarrow \cdots$ of reduction steps. The identity of elements $x, y \in D$ is denoted by $x \equiv y$. $\xrightarrow{+}$ is the transitive closure of $\rightarrow$, $\xrightarrow{*}$ is the reflexive and transitive closure of $\rightarrow$, and $=$ is the equivalence relation generated by $\rightarrow$. $\xrightarrow{k}$ denotes a reduction of k steps. If there are no element y such that $x \rightarrow y$, then we say x is a normal form (w.r.t. $\rightarrow$); let $NF_{\rightarrow}$ be the set of normal forms. If y is a normal form such that $x \xrightarrow{*} y$ then we say y is a normal form of x (w.r.t. $\rightarrow$). If there is a normal form of x, we say x has a normal form.

We say a reduction system $A = \langle D, \rightarrow \rangle$ is terminating, if and only if there are no infinite reduction. A is confluent, if and only if $x \xrightarrow{*} y \wedge x \xrightarrow{*} z$ imply $\exists w \in D[y \xrightarrow{*} w \wedge z \xrightarrow{*} w]$ for any $x, y, z \in D$.

Let $A = \langle D, \rightarrow \rangle$ and $\rightarrow_s$ be a sub-relation of $\xrightarrow{+}$. If $NF_{\rightarrow_s} = NF_{\rightarrow}$, we say that $\rightarrow_s$ is a reduction strategy for $\rightarrow$. A reduction strategy $\rightarrow_s$ is normalizing, if and only if there exists no infinite sequence $x \equiv x_0 \rightarrow_s x_1 \rightarrow_s \cdots$ for any x having a normal form w.r.t. $\rightarrow$.

Let $\Sigma = V \cup F$ be a signature, where F and V are a set of function symbols with arity and a set of variables, respectively. T_Σ(or simply T) denotes the set of terms well constructed by symbols in Σ. $|t|$ denotes the size of a term t. Letting $\Box$ be an extra constant, a term $C \in T_{\Sigma \cup \{\Box\}}$ is called a context denoted by $C[\ ,\ldots,\ ]$. For a $C[\ ,\ldots,\ ]$ which contains n $\Box$'s and for $t_1, \ldots, t_n \in T_\Sigma$, $C[t_1, \ldots, t_n]$ denotes the obtained term by replacing $\Box$'s with $t_1, \ldots, t_n$ from left to right order. A context that possesses exactly one $\Box$ is denoted by $C[\ ]$.

Let σ be a substitution. We denote the application of σ to term t by $t\sigma$. $\subseteq$ indicates a subterm relation. If a term t has some symbol e, we write $e \in t$. The list $t_1, \ldots, t_n$ of terms for some $n \geq 0$ is often abbreviated by $\mathbf{t}$.

A conditional term rewriting system (CTRS) R is a finite set of conditional rewrite rules, each of which is $l \rightarrow r\ if\ P(\mathbf{x})$, where l and r are terms and $P(\mathbf{x})$ is a (decidable) condition such that $x_i \in l$ for each i. A conditional rewrite rule must satisfy two requirements: (a) l is not a variable, (b) variables in r must appear in l. A term $l\sigma$ is called a redex if $P(x_1\sigma, \ldots, x_n\sigma)$ holds.

We say that the term t reduces to s by rule $l \rightarrow r\ if\ P(\mathbf{x})$, if and only if there exist a substitution σ and context $C[\ ]$ such that $t \equiv C[l\sigma]$, $s \equiv C[r\sigma]$, and

$l\sigma$ is a redex. We write $t \rightarrow_R s$ when t reduces to s. Sometimes we write $t \xrightarrow{\Delta}_R s$ to describe redex $\Delta \equiv l\sigma$ explicitly.

A CTRS is called left-linear, if every variable of l occurs only once for every rule $l \rightarrow r\ if\ P(\mathbf{x})$. We say that rules $l \rightarrow r\ if\ P(\mathbf{x})$ and $l' \rightarrow r'\ if\ P'(\mathbf{x})$ are overlapping, if there exist a term $s \subseteq l'$ ($s \notin V$) and substitutions σ and σ' such that $l\sigma \equiv s\sigma'$(except the trivial case, i.e., the rules are the same and $l \equiv s$). There is root overlap if $s \equiv l'$. A CTRS has overlap if it has overlapping rules. A CTRS has root overlap if the only root overlapping rules are overlapping.

A rewrite rule is a rule $l \rightarrow r\ if\ P(\mathbf{x})$ whose condition $P(\mathbf{x})$ alway holds(i.e. $P(\mathbf{x}) \equiv true$), and we abbreviate rewrite rules as $l \rightarrow r$. A term rewriting system(TRS) is a CTRS that has only rewrite rules.

3 Priority Term Rewriting Systems and their Operational Semantics

The definition of P-rewriting was given by Baeten et.al.[BBKW89] as a reduction of PRSs. Since P-rewriting is not always decidable, they introduced the notion of "bounded". As bounded is too strong a restriction, Mohan[Moh89] introduced the notion of I-rewrite, which is a decidable definition of reduction. However, since I-rewrite includes the notion of inner most reduction strategy, it cannot be used as a normalizing strategy.

In this section, we give an operational semantics of PRSs that is decidable and is independent from the notion of strategy.

Definition 1 (PRS). A priority term rewriting system(PRS) $\mathcal{R}$ is a pair $\langle R_0, \sqsupset \rangle$ of an underlying TRS R_0 and an acyclic relation $\sqsupset$ on R_0.

Example 1. The "parallel or" is described in PRS as follows:

$$POR = \left\{ \begin{array}{|l} or(tt, x) \rightarrow tt \\ or(x, tt) \rightarrow tt \\ or(x, y) \rightarrow ff. \end{array} \right. \downarrow$$

Before we define a semantics of PRS, we need the notion of an approximation of PRS by ignoring priorities and right-hand sides.

Letting Ω be an extra constant, we represent prefixes of terms by Ω-terms in $T_{\Sigma \cup \{\Omega\}}$ (also denoted by T_Ω simply). t_Ω denotes the Ω-term obtained from a term t by replacing each variable with Ω. The prefix ordering $\succeq$ on T_Ω is defined as follows [HL79, Klo92, KM91]: (i) $t \succeq \Omega$, (ii) $t \succeq t$, (iii) $f(t_1, \ldots, t_n) \succeq f(s_1, \ldots, s_n)$ if $t_i \succeq s_i$ for $i = 1, \ldots, n$.

t and s are compatible, written by $t \uparrow s$, if $u \succeq t$ and $u \succeq s$ for some u; otherwise they are incompatible, denoted by $t \# s$. $s \sqcup t$ denotes a minimal Ω-term u such that $u \succeq s$ and $u \succeq t$ if it exists. We say an Ω-term t and a set S of Ω-term are incompatible, denoted by $t \# S$, if t and s are incompatible for any $s \in S$.

Definition 2 (ω-systems). Let R_0 be a TRS. The ω-system of R_0 is a CTRS $R_\omega = \{f(\mathbf{x}) \to \Omega \ if\ f(\mathbf{x}) \uparrow f(\mathbf{l})_\Omega \mid f(\mathbf{l}) \to r \in R_0\}$. The reduction relation $\to_{R_\omega}$ on T_Ω is called ω-reduction and often abbreviated as $\to_\omega$.

Example 2. ω-system of POR in example 1 is

$$POR_\omega = \begin{cases} or(x,y) \to \Omega \ if\ or(x,y) \uparrow or(tt,\Omega) \\ or(x,y) \to \Omega \ if\ or(x,y) \uparrow or(\Omega,tt) \\ or(x,y) \to \Omega \ if\ or(x,y) \uparrow or(\Omega,\Omega) \end{cases}$$

$f(or(a,tt)) \to_\omega f(\Omega)$ by the second or the last rule.

Lemma 3 [Klo92]. *ω-reduction is confluent and terminating.*

The direct approximant $\omega(t)$ of an Ω-term t is the normal form of t w.r.t. ω-reduction. $\overline{\omega}(f(t_1,\ldots,t_n))$ denotes $f(\omega(t_1),\ldots,\omega(t_n))$.

Definition 4. The set $Hlhs(e)$ of left-hand-side skeletons of rules each of which has higher priority than a rule e is defined by

$$Hlhs(e) = \{l_\Omega \mid l \to r \in R_0,\ l \to r \sqsupset e\}$$

Now we can define an operational semantics of PRSs.

Definition 5 (a semantics of PRS). Let $\mathcal{R} = \langle R_0, \sqsupset\rangle$.

(a) $Sem_\omega(\mathcal{R}) = \{l \to r \ if\ \overline{\omega}(l_\Omega)\#Hlhs(l \to r) \mid l \to r \in R_0\}$.
(b) The reduction relation $\to_\mathcal{R}$ is defined as $\to_{Sem_\omega(\mathcal{R})}$.

Example 3. For POR defined in example 1,

$$Sem_\omega(POR) = \begin{cases} or(tt,y) \to tt \ if\ \overline{\omega}(or(tt,y_\Omega))\#\{\} \\ or(x,tt) \to tt \ if\ \overline{\omega}(or(x_\Omega,tt))\#\{or(tt,\Omega)\} \\ or(x,y) \to ff \ if\ \overline{\omega}(or(x_\Omega,y_\Omega))\#\{or(tt,\Omega), or(\Omega,tt)\} \end{cases}$$

(i) $or(ff,tt) \to_{POR} tt$ by using the second rule. But, the last rule cannot be applied to $or(ff,tt)$. (ii) $or(x,tt)$ is a normal form. (iii) $or(ff,ff) \to_{POR} ff$ by using the last rule. On the other hand, $or(x,y)$ is a normal form. (iv) $or(or(ff,ff),tt) \to_{POR} or(ff,tt) \to_{POR} tt$ by using the last rule and the second rule. But $or(or(ff,ff),tt)$ cannot directly be reduced to tt.

Remark. (i) According to definition of t_Ω, x_Ω and y_Ω in $Sem_\omega(POR)$ seem to be Ω. However this is not the case as the variables x and y are bounded in the rules. Hence, the replacements of x_Ω and y_Ω should take place after they are substituted.

(ii) $Sem_\omega(\mathcal{R})$ does not have limitations like "bounded" in [BBKW89] or "ground" in [Moh89] for $\mathcal{R}$. Thus, $Sem_\omega(\mathcal{R})$ can give well-defined semantics to larger class of PRSs.

(iii) Rewrite relations of our semantics are included in those of the original semantics in [BBKW89]. However, both semantics have the same ground normal forms.

Proposition 6. *Let $\mathcal{R} = \langle R_0, \sqsupset \rangle$ be a PRS. $\rightarrow_{\mathcal{R}}$ is stable under substitution, i.e., $s \rightarrow_{\mathcal{R}} t$ implies $s\sigma \rightarrow_{\mathcal{R}} t\sigma$ for any substitution σ.*

Proof. Let $s \equiv C[l\theta] \rightarrow_{\mathcal{R}} C[r\theta] \equiv t$ for some context $C[\ ]$, substitution θ and $l \rightarrow r\ if\ \overline{\omega}(l_\Omega)\#S \in Sem_\omega(\mathcal{R})$. Then, we have $\overline{\omega}((l\theta)_\Omega)\#S$. Since $l_\Omega \preceq (l\theta)_\Omega \preceq (l\theta\sigma)_\Omega$, we can show $\overline{\omega}((l\theta)_\Omega) \preceq \overline{\omega}((l\theta\sigma)_\Omega)$ by the definition of $\overline{\omega}$. It follows $\overline{\omega}((l\theta\sigma)_\Omega)\#S$, which concludes $(C\sigma)[l\theta\sigma] \rightarrow_{\mathcal{R}} (C\sigma)[r\theta\sigma]$. □

Example 4. Consider the following PRS:

$$\mathcal{R} = \left\{ \begin{array}{l} \left\downarrow \begin{array}{l} f(a) \rightarrow b \\ f(x) \rightarrow c \end{array} \right. \\ \ \ d \rightarrow h(d) \end{array} \right.$$

The conditional TRS giving semantics of above $\mathcal{R}$ is

$$Sem_\omega(\mathcal{R}) = \left\{ \begin{array}{l} f(a) \rightarrow b\ if\ \overline{\omega}(f(a))\#\{\} \\ f(x) \rightarrow c\ if\ \overline{\omega}(f(x_\Omega))\#\{f(a)\} \\ d \rightarrow h(d)\ if\ \overline{\omega}(d)\#\{\} \end{array} \right.$$

We have $f(g(y)) \rightarrow_{\mathcal{R}} c$. Thus, $f(g(d)) \rightarrow_{\mathcal{R}} c$ by proposition 6.

Remark. P-rewriting[BBKW89] is not stable under substitution. Mohan[Moh89] modified P-rewriting by restricting the application of rules without highest priority to only ground term, so that P-rewriting has stability. However, this restriction is not natural. For example, consider the PRS in example 4. It is natural that $f(g(y))$ can be reduced to c, since g of $g(y)$ is not changed even if y is substituted for any term. $f(g(y))$ cannot be reduced to c by modified P-rewriting, but it can be reduced in our definition.

Definition 7 (orthogonality).

(a) We say that $\mathcal{R}$ has complete priority, if $r \sqsupset r'$ or $r' \sqsupset r$ for any root overlapping rules r and r' in R_0.
(b) $\mathcal{R}$ is orthogonal, if it has complete priority, R_0 is left-linear and R_0 possibly has root overlap.

A orthogonal PRS $\mathcal{R}$ may have root overlapping rules in R_0, but two different rules cannot apply to the same redex because of priority between the rules. From this 'non-overlapping property' and the stability under substitution indicated in the above proposition, PRS $\mathcal{R}$ works like orthogonal (i.e., left-linear and non-overlapping) TRSs. Thus, the confluent property of orthogonal PRSs can be easily proven in the same way as for orthogonal TRSs, by tracing the classical proof in [Hue80].

Theorem 8. *A orthogonal PRS is confluent.*

4 Strong Sequentiality of PRSs

The fundamental concept of strong sequentiality for orthogonal TRSs was introduced by Huet and Lévy[HL79]. In this section, we first explain the basic notions related to strong sequentiality, according to [HL79], for orthogonal PRSs. We next describe a useful decision procedure that determines the index of a given Ω-term with respect to $R_?$.

Definition 9 (arbitrary-systems). Let $\mathcal{R}$ be a PRS. The arbitrary-system of $\mathcal{R}$ is a CTRS $R_? = \{l \to q \; if \; P \mid q \in T, l \to r \; if \; P \in Sem_\omega(\mathcal{R})\}$. The reduction relation $\to_{R_?}$ is called an arbitrary reduction, which is abbreviated as $\to_?$.

Definition 10 (strongly sequential PRS). Displayed occurrence Ω in term $C[\Omega]$ is an index (denoted by $C[\Omega_I]$), if the following condition holds for any t and context $C'[\;]$ s.t. $C'[\;] \succeq C[\;]$: If $C'[t]$ has an Ω-free normal form w.r.t. ?-reduction then $t \not\equiv \Omega$. $C[\Omega_{NI}]$ denotes that the occurrence Ω in $C[\Omega]$ is not an index. A orthogonal PRS $\mathcal{R}$ is strongly sequential if every Ω-term t with Ω that is in normal forms w.r.t. $\to_{\mathcal{R}}$ has an index.

For analyzing the decidability of strong sequentiality of orthogonal TRSs, Klop and Middeldorp[KM91] proposed a useful procedure that determines whether a given Ω occurrence in a term t is an index, by using Ω-reduction and the test symbol $\bullet$. We now develop a similar procedure that determines index with respect to $R_?$. The most difficult problem in constructing Ω-reduction for PRSs is how to handle the test symbol $\bullet$. Although $\bullet$ is introduced for preventing reductions, $\bullet$ has an opposite effect in conditions of rules. Hence, wrong application of rewriting rule occurs if we handle $\bullet$ as a mere constant symbol as in [KM91]. To overcome this difficulty, we exchange $\bullet$ and Ω in a term t when we compute normal forms w.r.t. ω-reduction for deciding applicability of rules.

Definition 11 (Ω-systems). Let $\mathcal{R}$ be a PRS. Let $\bullet$ be a new constant. $\bar{t}$ denotes the Ω-term obtained from an Ω-term t by exchanging $\bullet$ and Ω. The Ω-system of $\mathcal{R}$ is a CTRS

$$R_\Omega = \{f(\mathbf{x}) \to \Omega \; if \; f(\mathbf{x}) \uparrow f(\mathbf{l})_\Omega \; \wedge \overline{\omega}((\overline{f(\mathbf{x}) \sqcup f(\mathbf{l})_\Omega})_\Omega) \# Hlhs(f(\mathbf{l}) \to r) \\ \mid f(\mathbf{l}) \to r \in R_0\}.$$

The reduction relation $\to_{R_\Omega}$ on T_Ω is called Ω-reduction and often abbreviated as $\to_\Omega$.

Example 5. For POR defined in example 1,

$$POR_\Omega = \begin{cases} or(x,y) \to \Omega \; if \; or(x,y) \uparrow or(tt,\Omega) \\ \qquad \wedge \overline{\omega}((\overline{or(x,y) \sqcup or(tt,\Omega)})_\Omega) \# \{\} \\ or(x,y) \to \Omega \; if \; or(x,y) \uparrow or(\Omega,tt) \\ \qquad \wedge \overline{\omega}((\overline{or(x,y) \sqcup or(\Omega,tt)})_\Omega) \# \{or(tt,\Omega)\} \\ or(x,y) \to \Omega \; if \; or(x,y) \uparrow or(\Omega,\Omega) \\ \qquad \wedge \overline{\omega}((\overline{or(x,y) \sqcup or(\Omega,\Omega)})_\Omega) \# \{or(tt,\Omega), or(\Omega,tt)\} \end{cases}$$

Proposition 12. *Let s, t and u be Ω-terms.*

(a) If u is $\bullet$-free, $s \preceq t$ and $\omega((\bar{t})_\Omega)\#u$, then $\omega((\bar{s})_\Omega)\#u$.
(b) If s is $\bullet$-free and $s \preceq t$, then $s \preceq \bar{t}$.

We can show the following lemma similarly to the proof of lemma 3.

Lemma 13. *Ω-reduction is confluent and terminating.*

Definition 14. The approximant $\Omega(t)$ of an Ω-term t is the normal form of t w.r.t. Ω-reduction.

Lemma 15. *Let s and t be Ω-terms.*

(a) $s \preceq t$ and $t \to_\Omega \Omega$ imply $s \equiv \Omega$ or $s \to_\Omega \Omega$.
(b) $s \preceq t$ and $t \xrightarrow{*}_\Omega u$ imply $s \xrightarrow{*}_\Omega v$ for some $v \preceq u$.
(c) $s \preceq t$ implies $\Omega(s) \preceq \Omega(t)$.

Lemma 16. *Let q be a $\bullet$-free Ω-term. If $p \xrightarrow{*}_\Omega q$, then $\overline{p'} \xrightarrow{*}_? \bar{q}$ for some Ω-free term $p' \succeq p$.*

Proof. Prove by induction on k in $p \xrightarrow{k}_\Omega q$. In case of $k = 0$, the lemma holds by taking $p' \equiv p$. Next, we consider $p \to_\Omega q_1 \xrightarrow{*}_\Omega q$. By induction hypothesis, there exists an Ω-free term $q_2 \succeq q_1$ such that $\overline{q_2} \xrightarrow{*}_? \bar{q}$. Since $p \equiv C[f(\mathbf{v})] \to_\Omega C[\Omega] \equiv q_1$ for some $C[\,]$, f and $\mathbf{v}$, there exist a context $C'[\,] \succeq C[\,]$ and an Ω-free term q_3 such that $q_2 \equiv C'[q_3]$.

On the other hand, since $f(\mathbf{v}) \to_\Omega \Omega$, we have $f(\mathbf{v}) \uparrow f(\mathbf{t})_\Omega$ and $\overline{\omega}((\overline{f(\mathbf{v}) \sqcup f(\mathbf{t})_\Omega})_\Omega)\#P$ for some rule in R_Ω:

$$f(\mathbf{x}) \to \Omega \ \mathit{if}\ f(\mathbf{x}) \uparrow f(\mathbf{t})_\Omega \ \wedge \overline{\omega}((\overline{f(\mathbf{x}) \sqcup f(\mathbf{t})_\Omega})_\Omega)\#P.$$

Letting $f(\mathbf{r}) \equiv f(\mathbf{v}) \sqcup f(\mathbf{t})_\Omega$, it follows from $f(\mathbf{r}) \succeq f(\mathbf{t})_\Omega$ and proposition 12(b) that $\overline{f(\mathbf{r})} \succeq f(\mathbf{t})_\Omega$. Hence, we have $\overline{f(\mathbf{r})} \to_? \overline{q_3}$ by applying a rule $f(\mathbf{t}) \to \overline{q_3}\ \mathit{if}\ \overline{\omega}(f(\mathbf{t})_\Omega)\#P$ in $R_?$, because of $\overline{\omega}((\overline{f(\mathbf{r})})_\Omega)\#P$. Therefore, we can take $p' \equiv C'[f(\mathbf{r})]$, which leads $\overline{p'} \equiv \overline{C'}[\overline{f(\mathbf{r})}] \to_? \overline{C'}[\overline{q_3}] \equiv \overline{q_2} \xrightarrow{*}_? \bar{q}$. □

Lemma 17.

(a) $\overline{\Delta} \to_\Omega \Omega$.
(b) If Δ is $\bullet$-free, $\Delta \to_\Omega \Omega$
(c) $p \to_? q$ implies $\exists q' \preceq \bar{q}, \bar{p} \to_\Omega q'$.
(d) $p \xrightarrow{*}_? q$ implies $\exists q' \preceq \bar{q}, \bar{p} \xrightarrow{*}_\Omega q'$.

Proof. (a) We can assume $\Delta \equiv f(\mathbf{r}) \succeq f(\mathbf{t})_\Omega$ and $\overline{\omega}(f(\mathbf{r})_\Omega)\#P$ for some rule $f(\mathbf{t}) \to q_1\ \mathit{if}\ \overline{\omega}(f(\mathbf{t})_\Omega)\#P$ in $Sem_\omega(\mathcal{R})$. Since $f(\mathbf{r}) \succeq f(\mathbf{t})_\Omega$ and $f(\mathbf{t})_\Omega$ is $\bullet$-free, we have $\overline{f(\mathbf{r})} \succeq f(\mathbf{t})_\Omega$ by proposition 12(b). Hence, $\overline{f(\mathbf{r})} \equiv \overline{\overline{f(\mathbf{r})} \sqcup f(\mathbf{t})_\Omega}$. Since $\overline{\omega}(f(\mathbf{r})_\Omega)\#P$, we have $\overline{\omega}(f(\mathbf{r})_\Omega) \equiv \overline{\omega}((\overline{\overline{f(\mathbf{r})}})_\Omega) \equiv \overline{\omega}((\overline{\overline{f(\mathbf{r})} \sqcup f(\mathbf{t})_\Omega})_\Omega)\#P$. Therefore, $\overline{f(\mathbf{r})} \to_\Omega \Omega$ by a rule in R_Ω:

$$f(\mathbf{x}) \to \Omega \ \mathit{if}\ f(\mathbf{x}) \uparrow f(\mathbf{t})_\Omega \ \wedge \overline{\omega}((\overline{f(\mathbf{x}) \sqcup f(t)_\Omega})_\Omega)\#P.$$

(b) We can show it similarly to (a). Since $f(\mathbf{r})$ is $\bullet$-free and $f(\mathbf{r}) \equiv f(\mathbf{r}) \sqcup f(\mathbf{t})_\Omega$, we have $f(\mathbf{r}) \preceq f(\mathbf{r}) \sqcup f(\mathbf{t})_\Omega \equiv \overline{(f(\mathbf{r}) \sqcup f(\mathbf{t})_\Omega)}_\Omega$ by proposition 12(b). Hence, we have $\overline{\omega}(f(\mathbf{r}))\#P$ imply $\overline{\omega}((f(\mathbf{r}) \sqcup f(\mathbf{t})_\Omega)_\Omega)\#P$ by the definitions of $\overline{\omega}$ and $\#$.

(c) We can assume $p \equiv C[\Delta] \to_? C[q_1] \equiv q$ for some $C[\,]$ and q_1. From (a), we have $\overline{p} \equiv \overline{C}[\overline{\Delta}] \to_\Omega \overline{C}[\Omega] \preceq \overline{C}[\overline{q_1}] \equiv \overline{q}$ that concludes the lemma by taking $q' \equiv \overline{C}[\Omega]$.

(d) We prove by induction on k in $p \xrightarrow{k}_? q$. In case of $k = 0$, the lemma holds by taking $q' \equiv \overline{p}$. Next, we consider $p \to_? q_1 \xrightarrow{*}_? q$. We have $\exists q_2 \preceq \overline{q}, \overline{q_1} \xrightarrow{*}_\Omega q_2$. We also have $\exists q_1', q_1' \preceq \overline{q_1}, \overline{p} \to_\Omega q_1'$ by (c). Hence, there exists q' such that $q' \preceq q_2, q_1' \xrightarrow{*}_\Omega q'$ by lemma 15(b). Therefore, we can get $q' \preceq q_2 \preceq \overline{q}$. □

Lemma 18. *Let $C[\,]$ be $\bullet$-free context. The followings are equivalent.*

(a) $C[\Omega_I]$.
(b) $\Omega(C[\bullet]) \not\equiv \Omega(C[\Omega])$.
(c) $\bullet \in \Omega(C[\bullet])$.

Proof. **(a)⇒(b)** Assuming $\Omega(C[\bullet]) \equiv \Omega(C[\Omega])$, we have $C[\bullet] \xrightarrow{*}_\Omega \Omega(C[\Omega])$. Letting $t \equiv \Omega(C[\Omega])$, t is $\bullet$-free Ω-term in normal forms w.r.t. Ω-reduction. By lemma 16, there is an Ω-free context $C'[\,]$ such that $C'[\,] \succeq C[\,]$ and $\overline{C'[\bullet]} \equiv \overline{C'}[\Omega] \xrightarrow{*}_? \overline{t}$. If $\overline{t}$ is a normal form w.r.t. ?-reduction, we can conclude that $C[\Omega_I]$ does not hold, since $\overline{C'}[\,] \succeq C[\,]$ by proposition 12 and $\overline{t}$ is Ω-free. Next we must show $\overline{t}$ is a normal form w.r.t. ?-reduction. If we assume $\overline{t} \to_? u$ for some u, there exists $u' \preceq \overline{u}$ such that $\overline{\overline{t}} \equiv t \to_\Omega u'$ by lemma 17(c), which contradicts the fact that t is the normal form w.r.t. Ω-reduction.

(b)⇒(c) If we assume $\bullet \notin \Omega(C[\bullet])$, we have $\Omega(C[\bullet]) \preceq C[\Omega]$. Since $\Omega(\Omega(t)) \equiv \Omega(t)$ for any t, we have $\Omega(C[\bullet]) \preceq \Omega(C[\Omega])$. On the other hand, it follows from $C[\Omega] \preceq C[\bullet]$ by lemma 15(c) that $\Omega(C[\Omega]) \preceq \Omega(C[\bullet])$. Therefore, we have $\Omega(C[\bullet]) \equiv \Omega(C[\Omega])$.

(c)⇒(a) If we assume that $C[\Omega_I]$ does not hold, we have $C'[\Omega] \xrightarrow{*}_? n$ for some $C'[\,] \succeq C[\,]$ and Ω-free term n in normal forms w.r.t ?-reduction. Then we have $\overline{C'[\Omega]} \xrightarrow{*}_\Omega n'$ for some $n' \preceq \overline{n}$ by Lemma 17(d). Moreover, $\overline{C'}[\,] \succeq C[\,]$ by proposition 12(b). Hence, it follows by lemma 15(b) that $C[\bullet] \xrightarrow{*}_\Omega n'' \xrightarrow{*}_\Omega \Omega(n'')$ for some $n'' \preceq n'$. Since $\Omega(n'')$ is $\bullet$-free from the fact that $\overline{n}$ is $\bullet$-free and $\overline{n} \succeq n' \succeq n'' \succeq \Omega(n'')$, we get that $\Omega(\bullet)$ is also $\bullet$-free, contradicting to $\bullet \in \Omega(C[\bullet])$. □

Example 6. Consider *POR* defined in example 1.

- $or(\Omega_I, \Omega_{NI})$ because $or(\bullet, \Omega)$ is normal form w.r.t. Ω-reduction and $or(\Omega, \bullet) \xrightarrow{*}_\Omega \Omega$.
- $or(ff, \Omega_I)$ because $or(ff, \bullet)$ is normal form w.r.t. Ω-reduction.

From lemma 18, we can write $C[\Delta_I]$ for some redex Δ instead of $C[\Omega_I]$. $t \xrightarrow{\Delta}_\mathcal{R} s$ is an index reduction if Δ is an index of t. We write $t \to_I s$ if there exists an index reduction $t \xrightarrow{\Delta}_\mathcal{R} s$.

5 The normalizability of index reduction

We will now show the normalizing property of index reduction for orthogonal PRSs by using the balanced weak Church-Rosser property proposed in [Toy92]. We first explain the basic notions and properties related to the balanced weakly Church-Rosser property according to [Toy92].

$\rightarrow$ is balanced weakly Church-Rosser(BWCR), if for any term t,s and s', $t \rightarrow s \ \wedge \ t \rightarrow s'$ imply $\exists w, \exists k \geq 0, s \xrightarrow{k} w \ \wedge \ s' \xrightarrow{k} w$.

We write $s \leftarrow\!\!\twoheadrightarrow t$ if there exists a connection $s \xrightarrow{m_1} \cdot \xleftarrow{n_1} \cdot \xrightarrow{m_2} \cdot \xleftarrow{n_2} \cdots \xrightarrow{m_p} \cdot \xleftarrow{n_p} t$ such that $\Sigma m_i > \Sigma n_i$. We also write $t \twoheadleftarrow\!\!\rightarrow s$ instead of $s \leftarrow\!\!\twoheadrightarrow t$

Lemma 19 [Toy92]. *Let $\rightarrow_s$ be a reduction strategy for $\rightarrow$ such that*

(a) $\rightarrow_s$ is balanced weakly Church-Rosser,
(b) If $s \rightarrow t$ then $s =_s t$ or $s \leftarrow\!\!\twoheadrightarrow_s \cdot \leftrightarrow \cdot \twoheadleftarrow\!\!\rightarrow_s t$.

Then $\rightarrow_s$ is a normalizing strategy.

Now let's show that $\rightarrow_I$ on orthogonal PRS is a normalizing strategy.

Lemma 20. *Let $C[\Delta_I, \Delta']$. Then $C[\Delta_I, t]$ for any t.*

Lemma 21. *Let $\mathcal{R}$ be orthogonal. Let $\Delta \equiv C[\Delta']$ and $\Delta \not\equiv \Delta'$. Then, $C[t]$ is a redex for any t.*

Proof. Since Δ is a redex, we have $l_\Omega \preceq \Delta$ and $\overline{\omega}(\Delta_\Omega)\#P$ for some rule $l \rightarrow r$ *if* $\overline{\omega}(l_\Omega)\#P$ in $Sem_\omega(\mathcal{R})$. Since $\omega(\Delta') \equiv \Omega$ and Δ and Δ' are not overlapping, we can show $l_\Omega \preceq C[t]$ and $\overline{\omega}(C[\Delta']_\Omega) \preceq \overline{\omega}(C[t]_\Omega)$ from left-linearity. Hence $C[t]$ is a redex. □

The parallel reduction $t \twoheadrightarrow\!\!\!\!\!\!+\ s$ is defined with $t \equiv C[\Delta_1, \ldots, \Delta_n] \xrightarrow{\Delta_1} \cdots \xrightarrow{\Delta_n} s \equiv C[s_1, \ldots, s_n]$ $(n \geq 0)$.

Lemma 22. *Let $\mathcal{R}$ be orthogonal and strong sequential. If $t \twoheadrightarrow\!\!\!\!\!\!+\ s$ then $t =_I s$ or $t \leftarrow\!\!\twoheadrightarrow_I \cdot \twoheadrightarrow\!\!\!\!\!\!+ \ \cdot \twoheadleftarrow\!\!\rightarrow_I s$.*

Proof. Let $t \overset{\Delta_1 \cdots \Delta_n}{\twoheadrightarrow\!\!\!\!\!\!+} s$ $(n \geq 0)$. Prove by induction on n. If $n = 0$, then we have $t =_I s$ trivially. Next we consider $n > 0$:

- In case that one of Δ_i, say Δ_1 is an index, we have $t \xrightarrow{\Delta_1}_I t' \overset{\Delta_2 \cdots \Delta_n}{\twoheadrightarrow\!\!\!\!\!\!+} s$. By induction hypothesis, we can show the lemma.
- Consider the case that none of Δ_i is an index. From strong sequentiality, there exists an index Δ in t. From orthogonality, Δ is not overlapping to any Δ_i. If Δ is disjoint from any Δ_i, we obtain the lemma by lemma 20. In case that Δ_i appear in Δ for some i, we can assume $\Delta \equiv C[\Delta_1, \Delta_2] \overset{\Delta_1, \Delta_2}{\twoheadrightarrow\!\!\!\!\!\!+} C[t_1, t_2]$ without loss of generality. From lemma 21, $\Delta' \equiv C[t_1, t_2]$ is a redex. We can show $t \xrightarrow{\Delta}_I \cdot \twoheadrightarrow\!\!\!\!\!\!+ \ \cdot \xleftarrow{\Delta'}_I s$ by using lemma 20.

□

Lemma 23. *Let $\mathcal{R}$ be a orthogonal PRS. Let $t \xrightarrow{\Delta}_I s$ and $t \xrightarrow{\Delta'}_I s'$. Then, we have $s \rightarrow_I u$ and $s' \rightarrow_I u$ for some term u.*

Proof. From orthogonality, $\Delta \not\equiv \Delta'$. Hence, the redex Δ and Δ' are disjoint from definition of index. Thus, the lemma holds trivially by lemma 20. □

Theorem 24. *Let $\mathcal{R}$ be orthogonal and strongly sequential. Then index reduction $\rightarrow_I$ is a normalizing strategy.*

Proof. Since $\rightarrow_I$ is a reduction strategy of $\rightarrow$, it is also a reduction strategy of $\twoheadrightarrow\!\!\!\!\!\!+\!\!+$. Taking $\rightarrow_I$ and $\twoheadrightarrow\!\!\!\!\!\!+\!\!+$ as $\rightarrow_s$ and $\rightarrow$, the premises of lemma 19 are satisfied by lemma 23 and lemma 22. Hence, we have $\rightarrow_I$ is a normalizing strategy for $\twoheadrightarrow\!\!\!\!\!\!+\!\!+$. Since $\xrightarrow{*}=\xrightarrow{*}\!\!\!\!\!\!+\!\!+$, the theorem follows. □

6 Decidability

In this section, we show strong sequentiality of orthogonal PRS is decidable according to Comon's method[Com95]. This method depends on two results relating to weak second-order monadic logic(WSkS)[Rab77, Tho90]. One is that WSkS is decidable. The other is that a set of finite trees is definable in WSkS if and only if it is recognized by a finite tree automaton. By using these results, Comon showed decidability of several kind of sequentialities.

Proposition 25 [Com95]. *If a predicate P is definable in a tree automaton, the sequentiality of P is decidable.*

According to proposition 25, if we have a finite tree automaton that accepts terms having Ω-free normal form w.r.t. ?-reduction, we can prove the decidability of sequentiality of PRS.

Definition 26. A finite tree automaton is $A = \langle \mathcal{F}, Q, Q_f, T\rangle$, where $\mathcal{F}$ is a finite set of symbols with arity, Q is a finite set of states, Q_f is a subset of Q called final states, and T is a set of transition rules.

A transition rule is the one of the forms:

- $f(q_1, \ldots, q_n) \rightarrow q$ with $f \in \mathcal{F}$, $q_1, \ldots, q_n, q \in Q$,
- $q \rightarrow q'$ with $q, q' \in Q$.

Reduction relation $\rightarrow_A$ is naturally defined on $T(\mathcal{F} \cup Q) \times T(\mathcal{F} \cup Q)$. A tree automaton accepts $t \in T(\mathcal{F})$, if and only if there is a reduction $t \xrightarrow{+}_A q \in Q_f$.

We can assume that every variable contained in object terms is only x, since rewrite rules are linear. Thus, in the following we fix $\mathcal{F} = F \cup \{x, \Omega\}$.

First, we define a finite set MR of terms that are used as states maintaining information for matching and compatibility check.

$$\begin{aligned} MR_0 &= \{t \mid t \subset l_\Omega, l \to r \in R_0\} \\ MR_{n+1} &= MR_n \cup \{t \mid t \preceq (s \sqcup s'),\ s, s' \in MR_n \text{ s.t. } s \uparrow s'\}, \end{aligned}$$

Let $MR_\Omega = \bigcup_{i \geq 0} MR_i$. Let $\bot$ be a fresh constant. Then, MR is the set of terms each of which is obtained from $t \in MR_\Omega$ by replacing arbitrary number of Ω occurrences in t with $\bot$. $MR_\bot$ is the set of Ω-free terms in MR. $t \preceq_\bot s$ displays that s can be obtained from t by replacing occurrences of $\bot$ in t with (possibly different) terms.

Lemma 27. *Let s be maximal in MR w.r.t. $\preceq_\bot$ such that $s \preceq_\bot t$. Then s is unique.*

First we construct a tree automaton A^ω that characterize ω-reduction.

Definition 28. Tree automaton A^ω is $\langle \mathcal{F}, Q^\omega, Q^\omega, \mathcal{T}^\omega \rangle$, where $Q^\omega = \{\langle t \rangle \mid t \in MR\}$, and $\mathcal{T}^\omega$ is the following transition rules:

(a) $\Omega \to \langle \Omega \rangle$.
(b) $x \to \langle \Omega \rangle$.
(c) $f(\langle t_1 \rangle, \ldots, \langle t_n \rangle) \to \langle \Omega \rangle$, if $f(t_1, \ldots, t_n) \uparrow l_\Omega$ for some $l \to r \in R_0$.
(d) $f(\langle t_1 \rangle, \ldots, \langle t_n \rangle) \to \langle t \rangle$, if $f(t_1, \ldots, t_n) \# l_\Omega$ for any $l \to r \in R_0$, and t is maximal in MR w.r.t. $\preceq_\bot$ such that $t \preceq_\bot f(t_1, \ldots, t_n)$.

Note that A^ω is deterministic by lemma 27. To show properties on A^ω, we need several definitions and lemmas.

Lemma 29. *Let s be maximal in $MR_\bot$ w.r.t. $\preceq_\bot$ such that $s \preceq_\bot t$. Then $\forall u \in MR_\Omega[u \preceq s \iff u \preceq t]$.*

Lemma 30. *Let s be maximal in MR w.r.t. $\preceq_\bot$ such that $s \preceq_\bot f(p_1, \cdots, p_n)$, and let every p_i be maximal in MR w.r.t. $\preceq_\bot$ such that $p_i \preceq_\bot t_i$. Then s is maximal in MR w.r.t. $\preceq_\bot$ such that $s \preceq_\bot f(t_1, \cdots, t_n)$.*

Lemma 31. *Let $t \in T(\mathcal{F})$ and $t \xrightarrow{+}_{A^\omega} \langle s \rangle$. Then, s is maximal in MR w.r.t. $\preceq_\bot$ such that $s \preceq_\bot \omega(t_\Omega)$ and $\forall u \in MR_\Omega[u \uparrow s \iff u \uparrow \omega(t_\Omega)]$.*

We next define a tree automaton A^{NF} that accepts Ω-free normal forms w.r.t. ?-reduction. Since each rule in $R_?$ has a condition, the states in A^{NF} must keep extra information associated to ω-reduction. Hence, we design each state as a triple $\langle s, r, q \rangle$ associated to a term t, where s and r keep the structures of u and $\omega(u_\Omega)$, respectively. q shows whether t is an Ω-free normal form or not.

Definition 32. Tree automaton A^{NF} is $\langle \mathcal{F}, Q^{NF}, Q^{NF}_f, \mathcal{T}^{NF} \rangle$, where $Q^{NF} = \{\langle s, r, q \rangle \mid s \in MR_\bot, r \in MR, q \in \{tt, ff\}\}$, $Q^{NF}_f = \{\langle s, r, tt \rangle \in Q^{NF}\}$, and $\mathcal{T}^{NF}$ is the following transition rules;

(a) $\Omega \to \langle \bot, \Omega, ff \rangle$.
(b) $x \to \langle \bot, \Omega, tt \rangle$.
(c) $f(\langle s_1, r_1, q_1 \rangle, \ldots, \langle s_n, r_n, q_n \rangle) \to \langle s, r, q \rangle$, if all of the following conditions hold:
  i. s is maximal in $MR_\bot$ w.r.t. $\preceq_\bot$ such that $s \preceq_\bot f(s_1, \ldots, s_n)$,
  ii. $f(\langle r_1 \rangle, \ldots, \langle r_n \rangle) \to \langle r \rangle \in T^\omega$;
  iii. $q \equiv tt$, if $q_i \equiv tt$ for any i and $\neg(l_\Omega \preceq f(s_1, \ldots, s_n) \wedge f(r_1, \ldots, r_n)\#P)$ for any rule $l \to r\ if\ \overline{\omega}(l_\Omega)\#P$ in $Sem_\omega(\mathcal{R})$. Otherwise, $q \equiv ff$.

Note that A^{NF} is deterministic by lemma 27.

Lemma 33. *Let $t \in T(\mathcal{F})$ and $t \xrightarrow{+}_{A^{NF}} \langle s, r, q \rangle$. Then,*

(i) s is maximal in $MR_\bot$ w.r.t. $\preceq_\bot$ such that $s \preceq_\bot t$,
(ii) $t \xrightarrow{+}_{A^\omega} \langle r \rangle$,
(iii) t is a Ω-free normal form, iff $q \equiv tt$.

Proof. From the construction of A^{NF}, (ii) is trivial. Prove by induction on $|t|$.

Consider the case $|t| = 1$. If t is Ω then $t \xrightarrow{+}_{A^{NF}} \langle \bot, \Omega, ff \rangle$ by (a). If t is x then $t \xrightarrow{+}_{A^{NF}} \langle \bot, \Omega, tt \rangle$ by (b). If $t \equiv c \not\equiv \Omega$ then $t \xrightarrow{+}_{A^{NF}} \langle s, r, q \rangle$ by (c), which satisfies the lemma.

Consider the case $|t| > 1$. Let $t \equiv f(\mathbf{t})$. We have $f(\mathbf{t}) \xrightarrow{+}_{A^{NF}} f(\langle s_1, r_1, q_1 \rangle, \ldots, \langle s_n, r_n, q_n \rangle) \to_{A^{NF}} \langle s, r, q \rangle$, where s, r and q satisfy the conditions in rule (c). Then, (i) follows from induction hypothesis by lemma 30. Next, consider (iii).

Case 1. t_i is in Ω-free normal forms for any i. From induction hypothesis, we have $q_i \equiv tt$ for any i.

- If t is not in Ω-free normal forms, there exists some rule $l \to r\ if\ \overline{\omega}(l_\Omega)\#P$ such that $l_\Omega \preceq t$ and $\overline{\omega}(t_\Omega)\#P$. From induction hypothesis and lemma 29, we can show $l_\Omega \preceq f(\mathbf{s})$. Moreover, it follows from lemma 31 that $f(\mathbf{r})\#P$. Hence, we have $q \equiv tt$ from the definition of (c).
- If t is in Ω-free normal forms. We can show that $\neg(l_\Omega \preceq f(\mathbf{s}) \wedge f(\mathbf{r})\#P)$ for any rule $l \to r\ if\ \overline{\omega}(l_\Omega)\#P$. Hence, $q \equiv ff$.

Case 2. t_i is not in Ω-free normal forms for some i. From induction hypothesis, we have $q_i \equiv ff$. Hence, $q \equiv ff$ from the definition of (c). □

Corollary 34. *Let $f(t_1, \cdots, t_n) \in T(\mathcal{F})$ and $f(t_1, \cdots, t_n) \xrightarrow{+}_{A^{NF}} f(\langle s_1, r_1, q_1 \rangle, \cdots, \langle s_n, r_n, q_n \rangle)$. Then for any rule $l \to r\ if\ \overline{\omega}(l_\Omega)\#P$, $l_\Omega \preceq f(t_1, \cdots, t_n)$ and $\overline{\omega}(f(t_1, \cdots, t_n)_\Omega)\#P$ iff $l_\Omega \preceq f(s_1, \cdots, s_n)$ and $f(r_1, \cdots, r_n)\#P$.*

Proof. Straightforward from lemmas 29, 31 and 33. □

Now, we construct a tree automaton $A^?$ that recognizes terms having Ω-free normal form w.r.t. ?-reduction. We start some preliminary properties of $R_?$.

A position (denoted by $\alpha, \beta, \cdots$) in a term can be viewed as a finite sequence of natural numbers, pointing out a path from the root of this tree [Hue80]. For two positions α and β we write $\alpha \leq \beta$ if there exists some position γ such that $\alpha \cdot \gamma = \beta$. $\alpha < \beta$ if $\alpha \leq \beta$ and $\alpha \neq \beta$. We write $t \xrightarrow{\alpha}_R s$ if $t \xrightarrow{\Delta}_R s$ and Δ is the redex at position α in t.

Lemma 35. *Let $t \xrightarrow{\alpha}_? \cdot \xrightarrow{\beta}_? s$ and $\alpha \leq \beta$. Then $t \xrightarrow{\alpha}_? s$.*

We define a tree automaton $A^?$ that recognizes terms having Ω-free normal form w.r.t. ?-reduction as follows.

Definition 36. Tree automaton $A^?$ is $\langle \mathcal{F}, Q^?, Q^?_f, \mathcal{T}^? \rangle$, where $Q^? = Q^{NF}$, $Q^?_f = Q^{NF}_f$. $\mathcal{T}^?$ is a set both of transition rules in $\mathcal{T}^{NF}$ and the following rules:

(d) $f(\langle s_1, r_1, q_1 \rangle, \ldots, \langle s_n, r_n, q_n \rangle) \rightarrow \langle s, r, q \rangle$, if all of the following conditions hold:
  i. $l_\Omega \preceq f(s_1, \ldots, s_n)$ and $f(r_1, \ldots, r_n) \# P$ for some rule $l \rightarrow r$ *if* $\overline{\omega}(l_\Omega) \# P$ in $Sem_\omega(\mathcal{R})$.
  ii. $u \xrightarrow{+}_{A^{NF}} \langle s, r, q \rangle$ for some term u.

Remark that $A^?$ is obviously non-deterministic because of the condition ii. in (d), and non-deterministic selection between (c) and (d).

Lemma 37. *Let $t \in T(\mathcal{F})$ and $t \xrightarrow{+}_{A^?} \langle s, r, tt \rangle$. Then there exists some Ω-free normal form t' such that $t \xrightarrow{*}_? t'$.*

Proof. By induction on the number of transitions by rule (d) occurring in $t \xrightarrow{+}_{A^?} \langle s, r, tt \rangle$, we prove the claim.

Base Step: Since no transition by rule (d) occurs in $t \xrightarrow{+}_{A^?} \langle s, r, tt \rangle$, we have $t \xrightarrow{+}_{A^{NF}} \langle s, r, tt \rangle$. Thus, t is Ω-free normal form by lemma 33. Take $t' \equiv t$.

Induction Step: Without loss of generality, we can write $t \equiv C[f(\mathbf{t})] \xrightarrow{+}_{A^?} C[f(\langle s_1, r_1, q_1 \rangle, \ldots, \langle s_n, r_n, q_n \rangle)] \rightarrow_{A^?} C[\langle s', r', q' \rangle] \xrightarrow{*}_{A^?} \langle s, r, tt \rangle$, where the first transition by rule (d) is $C[f(\langle s_1, r_1, q_1 \rangle, \ldots, \langle s_n, r_n, q_n \rangle)] \rightarrow_{A^?} C[\langle s', r', q' \rangle]$. Then, we have $l_\Omega \preceq f(\mathbf{s})$ and $f(\mathbf{r}) \# P$ for some $l \rightarrow r$ *if* $\overline{\omega}(l_\Omega) \# P$, and $u \xrightarrow{+}_{A^{NF}} \langle s', r', q' \rangle$ for some u. Hence, the number of transitons by rule (d) in $C[u] \xrightarrow{+}_{A^?} C[\langle s', r', q' \rangle] \xrightarrow{*}_{A^?} \langle s, r, tt \rangle$ is less than that in $t \xrightarrow{+}_{A^?} \langle s, r, tt \rangle$. From induction hypothesis, it follows that $C[u] \xrightarrow{*}_? t'$ for some Ω-free normal form t'. Since $f(\mathbf{t}) \xrightarrow{+}_{A^{NF}} f(\langle s_1, r_1, q_1 \rangle, \ldots, \langle s_n, r_n, q_n \rangle)$, $l_\Omega \preceq f(\mathbf{s})$, and $f(\mathbf{r}) \# P$, we have $l_\Omega \preceq f(\mathbf{t})$ and $\overline{\omega}(f(\mathbf{t})_\Omega) \# P$ by corollary 34. Thus, $C[f(\mathbf{t})] \rightarrow_? C[u]$. Therefore, $t \equiv C[f(\mathbf{t})] \rightarrow_? C[u] \xrightarrow{*}_? t'$. □

Lemma 38. *Let $t, t' \in T(\mathcal{F})$ and $t \xrightarrow{*}_? t'$. Then there exist some s, r, q such that $t \xrightarrow{+}_{A^?} \langle s, r, q \rangle$ and $t' \xrightarrow{+}_{A^{NF}} \langle s, r, q \rangle$.*

Proof. By lemma 35, we can suppose that $t \xrightarrow{*}_? t'$ is an innermost reduction. By induction on $|t|$ we prove the claim.

Base Step($|t| = 1$): If $t \equiv t'$, then the claim holds as $t \equiv t' \xrightarrow{+}_{A^{NF}} \langle s, r, q \rangle$. Let $t \equiv c \not\equiv t'$. Then there exists some rule $c \to r \ if \ c\#P$. Hence, by applying transition rule (d) to c we have $c \to_{A^?} \langle s, r, q \rangle$ where $t' \xrightarrow{+}_{A^{NF}} \langle s, r, q \rangle$.

Induction Step:

Case 1. Let $t \equiv f(t_1, \cdots, t_n) \xrightarrow{*}_? t' \equiv f(t'_1, \cdots, t'_n)$ where $t_i \xrightarrow{*}_? t'_i$ for all i. Then, from induction hypothesis we have $t_i \xrightarrow{+}_{A^?} \langle s_i, r_i, q_i \rangle$ and $t'_i \xrightarrow{+}_{A^{NF}} \langle s_i, r_i, q_i \rangle$ for some s_i, r_i, q_i. Let $f(\langle s_1, r_1, q_1 \rangle, \ldots, \langle s_n, r_n, q_n \rangle) \to_{A^{NF}} \langle s, r, q \rangle$. Then, we have $t \equiv f(t_1, \cdots, t_n) \xrightarrow{+}_{A^?} f(\langle s_1, r_1, q_1 \rangle, \ldots, \langle s_n, r_n, q_n \rangle) \to_{A^{NF}} \langle s, r, q \rangle$ and $t' \equiv f(t'_1, \cdots, t'_n) \xrightarrow{+}_{A^{NF}} \langle s, r, q \rangle$.

Case 2. Let $t \equiv f(t_1, \cdots, t_n) \xrightarrow{*}_? f(u_1, \cdots, u_n) \xrightarrow{\epsilon}_? t'$ (ϵ denotes the root position) where $t_i \xrightarrow{*}_? u_i$ for all i. Then, from induction hypothesis we have $t_i \xrightarrow{+}_{A^?} \langle s_i, r_i, q_i \rangle$ and $u_i \xrightarrow{+}_{A^{NF}} \langle s_i, r_i, q_i \rangle$ for some s_i, r_i, q_i. Since $f(u_1, \cdots, u_n) \xrightarrow{\epsilon}_? t'$, there exists some rule $l \to r \ if \ \overline{\omega}(l_\Omega)\#P$ such that $l_\Omega \preceq f(u_1, \cdots, u_n)$ and $\overline{\omega}(f(u_1, \cdots, u_n)_\Omega)\#P$. Then by corollary 34 we have $l_\Omega \preceq f(s_1, \cdots, s_n)$ and $f(r_1, \cdots, r_n)\#P$. Hence, by applying transition rule (d) it holds that $f(t_1, \cdots, t_n) \xrightarrow{+}_{A^?} f(\langle s_1, r_1, q_1 \rangle, \ldots, \langle s_n, r_n, q_n \rangle) \to_{A^?} \langle s, r, q \rangle$ where $t' \xrightarrow{+}_{A^{NF}} \langle s, r, q \rangle$. □

Corollary 39. *Let $t, t' \in T(\mathcal{F})$ and $t \xrightarrow{*}_? t'$. If t' is in Ω-free normal forms, then there exist some s, r such that $t \xrightarrow{+}_{A^?} \langle s, r, tt \rangle$.*

Proof. Straightforward from lemma 38. □

Theorem 40. *The strong sequentiality of PRS is decidable.*

Proof. It follows from lemma 37, corollary 39, and proposition 25. □

Acknowledgment

This work is partially supported by Grants from Ministry of Education, Science and Culture of Japan, #07680350 and #07680347, and from the OKAWA Institute of Information and Telecommunication, 95-09.

References

[BBKW89] J. C. M. Baeten, J. A. Bergstra, J. W. Klop, and W. P. Weijland. Term rewriting systems with rule priorities. *Theoretical Computer Science*, 67:283–301, 1989.

[Com95] H. Comon. Sequentiality, second order monadic logic and tree automata. In *Logic in Computer Science*, pages 508–517, 1995.

[DJ90] N. Dershouwitz and J.-P. Jouannaud. Rewrite Systems. In J. van Leeuwen, editor, *Handbook of Theoretical Computer Science*, volume B, pages 243–320. North-Holland, 1990.

[Hen80] P. Henderson. *Functional Programming*. Prentice Hall International, 1980.

[HL79] G. Huet and J.-J. Lévy. Call by need computations in non-ambiguous linear term rewriting systems. Technical Report 359, INRIA, 1979.

[Hue80] G. Huet. Confluent Reductions: Abstract Properties and Applications to Term Rewriting Systems. *Journal of Association for Computing Machinery*, 27(4):797–21, October 1980.

[Jon87] S. L. P. Jones. *The Implementation of Functional Programming Languages*. Prentice Hall International, 1987.

[Klo92] J. W. Klop. Term rewriting systems. In S. Abramsky, D. Gabbay, and T. Maibaum, editors, *Handbook of Logic in Computer Science*, volume I. Oxford University Press, 1992.

[KM91] J. W. Klop and A. Middeldorp. Sequentiality in orthogonal term rewritng systems. *J. Symbolic Computation*, 12:161–195, 1991.

[Moh89] C. K. Mohan. Priority rewriting: Semantics, confluence, and conditionals. In *LNCS*, volume 355, pages 278–291. Springer-Verlag, 1989.

[PvE93] R. Plasmeijer and M. van Eekelen. *Functional Programming and Parallel Graph Rewriting*. Addison-wesley, 1993.

[Rab77] M. Rabin. Decidable theories. In J. Barwise, editor, *Handbook of Mathematical Logic*, pages 595–629. North-Holland, 1977.

[Tho90] W. Thomas. Automata on infinite objects. In J. van Leeuwen, editor, *Handbook of Theoretical Computer Science*, pages 134–191. Elsevier, 1990.

[Toy92] Y. Toyama. Strong sequentiality of left-linear overlapping term rewriting systems. In *Proc. of the 7'th annual IEEE Symposium on Login in Computer Science*, pages 274–284, 1992.

[TSvEP93] Y. Toyama, S. Smetsers, M. van Eekelen, and R. Plasmeijer. The Functional Strategy and Transitive Term Rewriting Systems. In Ronan Sleep, Rinus Plasmeijer, and Marko van Eelkelen, editors, *Term Graph Rewriting: Theory and Practice*, pages 61–75. John Wiley & Sons Ltd, 1993.

Higher-Order Families

Vincent van Oostrom*

Institut für Informatik, Technische Universität München
80290 München, Germany

Abstract. A redex *family* is a set of redexes which are 'created in the same way'. Families specify which redexes should be *shared* in any so-called *optimal* implementation of a rewriting system. We formalise the notion of family for orthogonal higher-order term rewriting systems (OHRSs). In order to comfort our formalisation of the intuitive concept of family, we actually provide three conceptually different formalisations, via *labelling*, *extraction* and *zigzag* and show them to be equivalent. This generalises the results known from literature and gives a firm theoretical basis for the optimal implementation of OHRSs.

1 Introduction

In general, a computation of a result is optimal if its cost is minimal among all computations of the result. Taking rewrite steps as computational units the cost of a rewrite sequence is simply its length. Given a rewrite system the question then is: does an effective optimal strategy exist for it?

In the case of lambda calculus, a discouraging result was obtained in [BBKV76]: there does not exist a recursive optimal strategy. However, the observation made in [Lév78] was that it is possible to define an optimal strategy if one takes contraction of *families* of redexes as cost unit. Here the notion of family stands intuitively for a 'set of redexes which are created in the same way'.

Lévy provided three conceptually distinct formalisations (via *labelling*, *extraction* and *zigzag*) of the notion of family in the lambda calculus ([Lév78]), which he subsequently proved to be equivalent, thereby comforting the formalisation. Those results were later generalised to the class of *Interaction Systems* (ISs [AL94]). This generalisation required quite some effort and even failed in the case of zigzag.

We formalise all three characterisations of family for the class of orthogonal higher-order rewriting systems (OHRSs [Nip93]). In view of the above, this is a little surprising since the class of OHRSs properly contains the class of ISs. However, already in [AL94, Exa. 10] it was observed that the problems where due to the coarseness of higher-order rewrite steps and they provided an example showing that splitting a rewrite step into simpler moves might be a solution. Our work can be viewed as following up on that observation, employing the

* Work partially performed at NTT BRL, Atsugi, Japan and VU, Amsterdam, The Netherlands, and supported by a HCM grant. `http://www.cs.vu.nl/~oostrom`.

decomposition of HRSs into a rule component and a substitution (simply typed λ-calculus) component as in [Oos94, Raa96]. More specifically, as we see it the problems reported in [AL94] are due to the fact that in a single HRS step symbols (redexes) can be first created and then multiplied.[2] In our decomposition of a HRS step, the rule component takes care of the destruction and creation of function symbols and the substitution component takes care of the multiplication of parts of the term, thereby avoiding the problems. In the rest of the paper, we use the following example to illustrate our methods.

Example 1 Running. 1. Consider the OHRS:

$$\begin{aligned} f &\rightarrow_f \cdots \\ g(x.X(x)) &\rightarrow_\delta X(f) \end{aligned}$$

It yields a rewrite step $\sigma: g(x.h(x,x)) \rightarrow_\delta h(f,f)$ in which f is first created and then duplicated in the same step, hence intuitively the two occurrences of f in the final term belong to the same family. This becomes visible in its decomposition:

$$\tilde{\sigma}: g(x.h(x,x)) \rightharpoonup (X.X(f))(x.h(x,x)) \twoheadrightarrow_\beta h(f,f)$$

First the *partial HRS step* (see Definition 2) creates f, after which it is duplicated in the subsequent β-reduction.

2. Consider the OHRS:

$$\begin{aligned} f &\rightarrow_f \cdots \\ g(X) &\rightarrow_\epsilon f \\ \mu(x.X(x)) &\rightarrow_\mu X(\mu(x.X(x))) \end{aligned}$$

and the rewrite sequences

$$\tau: M = \mu(x.g(x)) \rightarrow_\mu g(\mu(x.g(x))) \rightarrow_\epsilon g(\mu(x.f)) = N$$

$$\upsilon: M = \mu(x.g(x)) \rightarrow_\epsilon \mu(x.f) = O$$

Intuitively, the two occurences of the redex f in the final terms of these sequences are in the same family. This becomes visible in their decompositions

$$\tilde{\tau}: M \rightharpoonup_\mu (X.X(\mu(x.X(x))))(x.g(x)) \twoheadrightarrow_\beta g(\mu(x.g(x))) \rightharpoonup_\epsilon g(\mu(x.(X.f)(x))) \twoheadrightarrow_\beta N$$

and

$$\tilde{\upsilon}: M \rightharpoonup_\epsilon \mu(x.(X.f)(x)) \twoheadrightarrow_\beta O$$

In both cases only g is 'responsible for creating' f.

[2] This cannot happen in either (first-order) TRSs or lambda calculus.

3. To disable trivial solutions to the formalisation of the family relation, we will also consider the following non-example. Consider the rule:

$$f \to_f f$$

the redex f in the initial term of the step is intuitively not in the same family as the redex f in its final term, since their 'creation histories' differ.

To show equivalence of the three approaches to the family relation, we work directly with the decomposition as in the example such that destruction and creation are caused by partial HRS steps and multiplication is caused by β-steps.

Familiarity with abstract and term rewriting ([Klo, DJ]), the lambda calculus ([Bar84, HS86]), higher-order term rewriting ([Nip91, HMMN94, DHMM96]) is assumed. Moreover, some familiarity with the study of optimality for those classes of rewriting systems ([Mar92, Lév78, AL94]) will be helpful. Except for the ones introduced here all notations can be found in these (standard) references. Since quite some (technical) ground needs to be covered, we have no hope to present proofs. Hence we will be satisfied with giving proofsketches and hopefully clarifying examples, details will be presented in the full version.

2 Higher-Order Rewriting Systems

Higher-order rewriting is rewriting modulo simply typed λ-calculus. The following account is based on [Oos94, Raa96].

Definition 1. 1. We first define the objects of a higher-order term rewriting system. *(Simple) types* are built from a set of *base* types (e.g. booleans, naturals) using the *function* type constructor $\to$. *Preterms* are objects M such that $M{:}\,A$ for some type A can be inferred from
(var) $x^A{:}\,A$ for variables x,
(app) $M{:}\,A \to B,\ N{:}\,A \Longrightarrow M(N){:}\,B$.[3]
(abs) $M{:}\,B \Longrightarrow x^A.M^4{:}\,A \to B$.
Higher-order *terms* are obtained from the preterms by quotienting by the theory consisting of α, β and η (that is, $\lambda\eta$ in [Bar84]). To make terms concrete we use their $\beta\overline{\eta}$-normal forms as representatives (unique up to α-conversion, see e.g. [Aka93]) of the equivalence classes. Among the (typed) variables a set $\mathcal{A}$ of *function symbols* is distinguished. They will be used as constants, i.e. bound externally in the the sequel.
2. Next, rewrite rules are defined. A *(pattern) rewrite rule* $\aleph$ is a pair $l \to r$ of closed (note that function symbols are considered bound already, as per the previous item) terms of the same type A, where the *left-hand side* l is a pattern. Here a *pattern* ([Mil91]) is a term of the form $\mathbf{X}.M$,[5] such that

[3] To stress the functional nature of function symbols we use functional notation $f(M_1,\ldots,M_m)$ instead of applicative notation $f(M_1)\ldots(M_m)$ in case $m \geqslant 1$.
[4] We omit the usual λ in abstractions.
[5] We employ boldface to denote sequences, i.e. $\mathbf{X}$ is a sequence of variables.

(a) M is a term of basetype of the form $f(M_1, \ldots, M_m)$,
(b) each X_k among $\mathbf{X}$ in M has only (representatives of) pairwise distinct variables not among $\mathbf{X}$ as arguments.

For such a pattern (rule), $\mathbf{X}$ is called the *binder*, the variables (not) in it (*bound*) *free* variables, and an occurrence $X(\mathbf{M})$ in l (so $\mathbf{M}$ is a vector of representatives of bound variables) is called a *binding hole*. A *higher-order pattern rewriting systems* (HRS) is a pair $(\mathcal{A},\mathcal{R})$ consisting of an alphabet $\mathcal{A}$ and a set $\mathcal{R}$ of rewrite rules.

3. Finally, the rewrite relation can be defined. Let $M =^{\text{def}} C\boxed{l_1,\ldots,l_m}$, $N =^{\text{def}} C\boxed{r_1,\ldots,r_m}$ be preterms, where $\aleph_1 =^{\text{def}} l_1 \to r_1, \ldots, \aleph_m =^{\text{def}} l_m \to r_m$ are rewrite rules, and C is an m-ary *precontext*, i.e. a preterm containing variables $\Box_1, \ldots, \Box_m$. Then we say that N can be obtained from M by *contracting* the *(complete) development redex* $C\boxed{\aleph_1,\ldots,\aleph_m}$. This will be denoted by $M \multimap_{C\boxed{\aleph_1,\ldots,\aleph_m}} N$. We use u, v, w to denote redexes, and identify them with their induced steps whenever convenient. This is extended to (the unique representatives of) terms by defining a *development step* $M \multimap N$ if there exist preterms M' and N' in the same $\beta\overline{\eta}$-equivalence classes as M and N, respectively, such that $M' \multimap N'$. The abstract rewriting system (ARS) associated to the HRS $\mathcal{H}$ is the relation on terms obtained by requiring the precontext employed in a development step to be a unary *context*, i.e. a term containing exactly one occurrence of $\Box$. The so-obtained relation $\to_{\mathcal{H}}$ (or simply $\to$) is called the *rewrite step* relation.

We often omit the binder of a HRS rule and write $l \to r$ instead of $\mathbf{X}.l \to \mathbf{X}.r$. We notationally distinguish free and bound variables by using capitals (X, Y) for the former and small letters (x, y) for the latter.

A redex family consists of a set of redexes in a preterm which are created 'in the same way'. The contraction of a family of redexes is the simultaneous contraction of all the redexes in the family. This simultaneous contraction makes sense if contracting a redex is a *local* action and if the redexes in a family are *far enough apart*, such that they operate on disjoint parts of the structure. On top of *orthogonality* ([Nip93, Oos94, Raa96]), i.e. left-linearity and non-ambiguity of the rules, familiar from the first-order case ([HL, Klo]), this requires the following *fully extendedness* condition (cf. [HP]) on HRSs.

> Every free variable in the left-hand side of a rule has all bound variables in which scope it is, as arguments.

Such systems are well-behaved in the sense that they are confluent ([Nip93, Oos94, Raa96]) and they possess a nice nice theory of permutation equivalence (see below). For that reason: *we only consider fully-extended orthogonal HRSs (OHRSs).*

From standard facts for λ-calculus it follows that each rewrite step can be written as an *expansion* $M \twoheadleftarrow_\beta C\boxed{l}$, followed by a *replacement* $C\boxed{l} \to_{C\boxed{l\to r}} C\boxed{r}$, and a *reduction* $C\boxed{r} \twoheadrightarrow_\beta N$. The replacement is said to *destroy* l and to *create* r. In the normalisation phase *multiplication* of parts of C can occur.

Example 2. Consider the term rewriting rule $f(X,Y) \to g(Y,Y)$. The step $f(h,i) \to g(i,i)$ using this rule ***destroys*** f, ***creates*** g, ***erases*** h and ***duplicates*** i. This becomes visible when we employ the decomposition mentioned above: $f(h,i) \twoheadleftarrow_\beta (X.Y.f(X,Y))(h,i) \to (X.Y.g(Y,Y))(h,i) \twoheadrightarrow_\beta g(i,i)$. Destruction of f and creation of g take part in the middle step, replacing the left-hand side of the rule by the right-hand side, and erasure of h and duplication of i are performed by the trailing β-reduction.

The initial β-expansions are 'precisely there' to make the subsequent replacement possible. Due to the pattern restriction this can be enforced in general, suggesting to combine the initial β-expansion and the subsequent replacement (but no β-reduction!) into a *partial* HRS step, denoted by $\rightharpoonup$.

Example 3 Partial HRS step. The rewrite step in the previous example can be decomposed as a partial HRS step followed by a β-reduction:

$$f(h,i) \rightharpoonup (X.Y.g(Y,Y))(h,i) \twoheadrightarrow_\beta g(i,i)$$

To clarify what we mean by 'precisely there' above, consider a step

$$(X.Y.f(X,Y))(h,i) \to (X.Y.g(Y,Y))(h,i)$$

This is not a partial HRS step since its initial β-expansion (empty) does 'too little', i.e. it was not used to create (match) the $X.Y.$-part of the HRS rule application. Initial β-expansions should also not do 'too much' in a partial HRS step. A sequence

$$f \twoheadleftarrow_\beta (x.x)(f) \to (x.x)(\ldots)$$

for a HRS rule $f \to \ldots$ is not a partial HRS step, since the initial β-expansion was useless for performing the step. Both $f \to \ldots$ and $(x.x)(f) \to (x.x)(\ldots)$ are partial HRS steps for this rule.

Wlog we may η-normalise the bound holes in left-hand sides of rules (i.e. bound holes then look like $X(\mathbf{x})$ for bound variables $\mathbf{x}$ instead of their $\beta\overline{\eta}$-normal form).

Definition 2 Partial HRS step. Let M, N be preterms. A *partial* (HRS) step $M \rightharpoonup_{C\boxed{l \to r}} N$ is obtained from a sequence $M \twoheadleftarrow_\sigma C\boxed{l} \to_{C\boxed{l \to r}} C\boxed{r} = N$, where σ^{-1} is a maximal standard β-rewrite sequence in which in each step a descendant of a symbol (abstraction or application) in l is destroyed (with the usual descendant relation for λ-calculi, see Figure 1).

The length of the β-expansion in a partial step used to split off the left-hand side from its surroundings is completely fixed by the shape of the left-hand side; actually it's the number of (free and bound) variables occurring in its bounding holes. Furthermore, although the left-hand side of the applied rule is not (necessarily) in $\overline{\eta}$-normal form, both the context $C\Box$ and the right-hand side r are, yielding that partial steps preserve $\overline{\eta}$-normal forms.

3 Optimality

In literature ([Lév78, AL94]), a family relation is an equivalence relation on pairs consisting of a rewrite sequence, and a redex in the final term of the sequence. We deviate from this in two ways. The first and main deviation will be that for the first component we do not consider HRS rewrite sequences, but work on their decomposition as rewrite sequences consisting of partial and β-steps. The second modification is that the second component can be any part of a preterm not just a redex.

Definition 3 Family Relation. A *locked* sequence is a structure $\sigma \lhd \partial$, where the *history* $\sigma: M \twoheadrightarrow N$ is a rewrite sequence (on preterms) and the *lock* ∂ is a *part* of N, meaning that ∂ is a pair consisting of a position ϕ and a linear fully-extended pattern O, such that $N = C[O^{\theta}]_{\phi}$ for some precontext C and substitution θ. The sequence is said to be *locked on to* O *(at* ϕ*)*. When clear from the context, we often omit explicit mention of ϕ and confuse a lock with its pattern. A *family* relation $\simeq$ is an equivalence relation on coinitial rewrite sequences locked on to the same lock. (i.e. their patterns are identical).

The definition of optimality is parametrised over the notion of family.

Definition 4 Family Rewrite. A *family* rewrite is a development rewrite sequence in which in each step a non-empty *family* of redexes is contracted. A family rewrite σ to normal form is *optimal* if its length is minimal, i.e. $|\sigma| \leqslant |\tau|$ for all family rewrites τ starting and ending in the same preterms as σ. A rewrite strategy is optimal if it constructs optimal family rewrites.

4 Forth

The purpose of *labelling* is to keep track of the creation history of a term through time (rewriting), in the term itself. This is done by equiping the elements of a term with a label to record their history. Applying a rewrite step then consists of replacing a part together with its history by a new part whose history should record the old one and additionaly how it has been created. Parts having the same history are declared to be in the same *forward* family.

In first-order TRSs and the lambda calculus this idea is still pretty easy to implement (see e.g. [Mar92, Lév78]), but the situation becomes quickly more complicated for higher-order systems (cf. [Klo80, AL94]).

Our approach is to first conceive of labellings for HRS rules and simply typed λ-calculus separately and then to combine them. The idea for labelling HRS rules is that the created elements get as label the labels of the destroyed elements together with the (name of the applied) rule, and a sequence number (distinct for distinct elements of the right-hand side). Moreover, the edges connected to splitt-off parts get a number indicating where they were connected to the left-hand side. For the λ-calculus the labelling introduced in [Lév78] is employed.

Example 4 (See Example 1). In order to improve readability. we forget about the labelling of the simply typed λ-calculus and since at most one function symbol is created by the rules in the examples, we forget about the sequence number in the labels as well. Initially, distinct (occurrences of) function symbols have distinct labels (the labelling is *initial*).

1. Labelling $\tilde{\sigma}$ yields

$$g^a(x.h^b(x,x)) \rightharpoonup_\delta (X.X(f^{(a,\delta)}))(x.h^b(x,x)) \twoheadrightarrow_\beta h^b(f^{(a,\delta)}, f^{(a,\delta)})$$

and we see that both occurrences of f have label (a,δ) so are in the same forward family.

2. Labelling the first step of the (decomposition) of τ yields

$$\mu^a(x.g^b(x)) \rightharpoonup_\mu (X.X(\mu^{(a,\mu)}(x.X(x))))(x.g^b(x)) \twoheadrightarrow_\beta g^b(\mu^{(a,\mu)}(x.g^b(x)))$$

and the second step becomes

$$g^b(\mu^{(a,\mu)}(x.g^b(x))) \rightharpoonup_\epsilon g^b(\mu^{(a,\mu)}(x.(X.f^{(b,\epsilon)})(x))) \twoheadrightarrow_\beta g^b(\mu^{(a,\mu)}(x.f^{(b,\epsilon)}))$$

3. Labelling $\tilde{v}$ gives

$$\mu^a(x.g^b(x)) \rightharpoonup_\epsilon \mu^a(x.(X.f^{(b,\epsilon)})(x)) \twoheadrightarrow_\beta \mu^a(x.f^{(b,\epsilon)})$$

Both occurrences of the symbol f in the final terms of the labellings of $\tilde{\tau}$ and $\tilde{v}$ have the label (b,ϵ), so they are in the same forward family.

4. Labelling ϕ yields $f^a \rightharpoonup_f f^{(a,f)}$ and clearly the occurrences of f in the initial and final term have distinct labels (a and (a,f)).

Definition 5 Labelled HRS. 1. Let $(a, b \in)\ \mathcal{L}$ be a set of labels. The following grammar defines the set of λ-*labels*.

$$\alpha ::= a \mid \alpha\,;\alpha$$

where ; denotes string composition. The labelled λ-calculus λ^ℓ is obtained from the unlabelled λ-calculus by labelling elements (nodes and edges)[6] of the (Bourbaki) graph representation. This graph representation is relatively standard by now (see e.g. [AL94]), hence we refrain from presenting the (tedious) formal definition and show a picture instead (Figure 1).

2. Steps in a labelled HRS are either
   (a) labelled β-steps as defined above, or
   (b) labelled partial steps. Elements of the set $\mathcal{L}$ of *rule-labels* are defined by the grammar:

$$a ::= \langle \alpha, l \to r, m\rangle \mid m$$

where m ranges over natural numbers. For the construction of the labelled partial step, first perform the labelled β-expansion as defined

[6] Labelling edges could be avoided by introducing a unary function symbol e to represent each edge as a function symbol and working modulo $e(X) = X$.

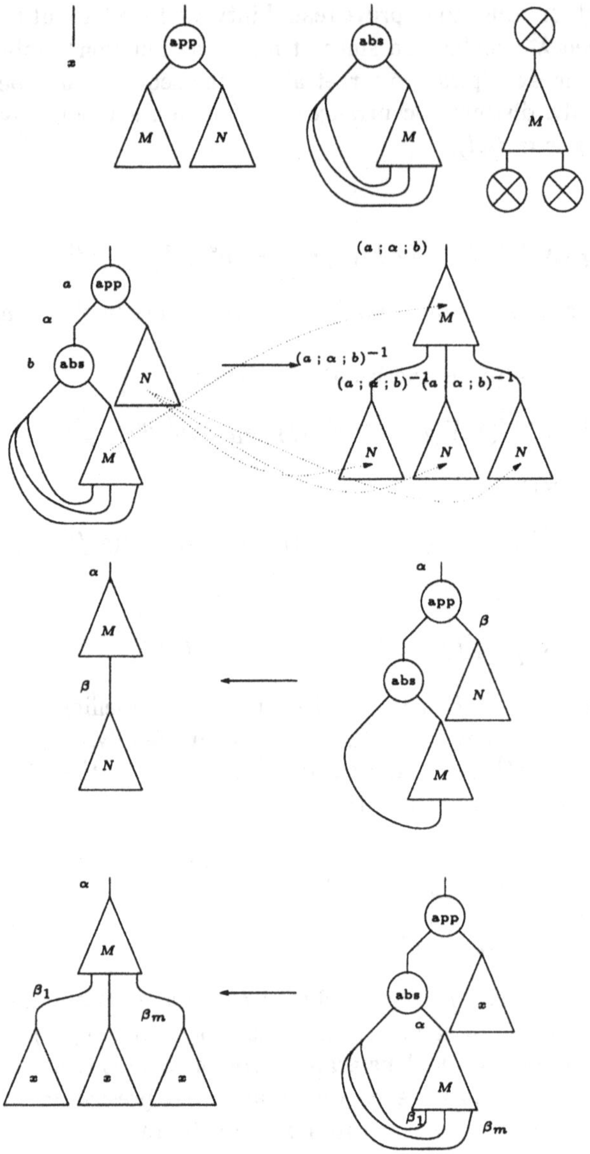

Fig. 1. (Labelled) Bourbaki-representation

The top row presents the graphical representation of λ-terms where the root and the free variables are connected to 'terminator' nodes. The next row shows a labelled β-reduction step, where $\cdot^{-1}$ denotes string inverse. while the last two rows show the β-expansion steps needed. The first way is needed for splitting off argument parts (N) from the redex part (M) in a partial step. The second way of labelled β-expansion is needed to split bindings (of x) between redex parts and argument parts.

above (this only depends on the left-hand side). Then perform the (unlabelled) HRS replacement step and after that label all created (either by the β-expansion or by the replacement) elements by $\langle \alpha, l \to r, m \rangle$, where α is an enumeration (fixed by l) of the labels in the left-hand side, and m is a sequence number in an enumeration of the elements (fixed by r and the β-expansion). Finally, the edges connecting the created symbols to its surroundings are provided with a sequence number (establishing the interface).

We will use I, J to denote labelling functions. The labelled preterm obtained by labelling the preterm M using I is denoted by M^I. There is a tight correspondence between an OHRS and its labelled version.

Proposition 6. *Consider an OHRS and its labelled version.*

1. *Let M^I be a labelling of M. Every partial step (β-step) $M \to N$ can be lifted in a canonical way to a labelled step (β-step) $M^I \to N^J$ for some labelling J of N.*
2. *A labelled partial step (β-step) $M^I \to N^J$ projects in a canonical way onto a partial step (β-step) $M \to N$.*

Proof. 1. Cf. [Lév78] for β-steps and observe that the contruction is deterministic for partial steps.
2. Forgetting labels yields the result. □

Definition 7 Initial Labelling. In an *initial* labelling of a preterm all elements of the labelled preterm have distinct atomic (not composed of other) labels.

By the proposition, labellings of terms can be uniquely extended to labellings of rewrite sequences via the labelling of their initial term. In particular, initially labelling the initial term of a (locked) rewrite sequence yields a unique (locked) labelled rewrite sequence, called its *initial* labelling. The labelling of a part ∂ of a term, is called the *degree* of that part.

Definition 8 Forward Family. Let $\sigma \lhd \partial$, $\tau \lhd \partial$ be two locked rewrite sequences. They are in the same *forward family*, $\sigma \lhd \partial \simeq_f \tau \lhd \partial$, if their initial labellings are locked onto the same labelled part, yielding an equivalence relation.

5 Back

A characterisation of families which is at first sight unrelated to the one via labelling works via the so-called extraction procedure. Rewrite sequences are first sorted in an outside-in order after which exactly those steps which contribute to the redex in the final term are extracted from the rewrite sequence. The former procedure is known as *standardisation* and the latter as *extraction.* Locked rewrite sequences which extract into the same sequence after standardisation are declared to be in the same *backward* family.

Example 5 (See Example 1). The rewrite sequences in this example are already in outside-in order.

1. Cosider $\tilde{\sigma}$ to be locked on to either occurence of f in its final term. One observes that only the initial partial step contributes to the creation of f in either case, hence this sequence extracts in both cases into

$$\ddot{\sigma}: g(x.h(x,x)) \rightharpoonup_{\delta} (X.X(f))(x.h(x,x))$$

   locked on to the (unique) occurrence of f in the final term, showing that both f-redexes belonged to the same backward family. Note that the resulting rewrite sequence is not a HRS rewrite sequence, since the final term is not in β-normal form; it is only a partial step.
2. The first HRS step in $\tilde{\tau}$ does not contribute to f at all, so it can be 'thrown away', resulting in $\tilde{v}$ and we can already conclude from this (and the fact that the extraction procedure gives a unique result) that the occurrences of f in the final terms of $\tilde{\tau}$ and $\tilde{v}$ are in the same backward family.
3. As in the first item, $\tilde{v}$ extracts to a partial step $\ddot{v}$ since the final erasing β-step does not contribute to f at all,

$$\ddot{v}: \mu(x.g(x)) \rightharpoonup_{\epsilon} \mu(x.(X.f)(x))$$

4. Both the redex (empty sequence) f and the sequence $f \rightharpoonup_f f$ are in extraction normal form, so the redex f in the initial term of the step is not in the same backward family as f in its final term.

If HRS steps are considered (not decomposed ones), then in the first item it is not directly possible to relate the two redexes to each other as was noted in [AL94, Exa. 7] (note that in order to be related both the extracted histories *and* the extracted locks must be identical), due to the fact that σ is a 'create and duplicate' HRS step. To solve this problem in [AL94] the lambda calculus extraction procedure was enhanced with a *shift* operation, which in this example would shift the history of the right occurrence of f towards that of the left occurrence, showing they're in the same backward family.

5.1 Standardisation

Adopting development steps as basic steps induces a *permutation equivalence* relation on sequences consisting of single steps in much the same way as true concurrency induces interleaving concurrency.

Definition 9 Permutation. An *elementary diagram* (ED) is a pair (σ,τ), where both *sides* $\sigma = u\,;\sigma'$ and $\tau = v\,;\tau'$ are complete developments of $\{u,v\}$. If $u = v$ the diagram is *trivial.* The *permutation* relation $\equiv^1$ between rewrite sequences is defined by $v\,;\sigma\,;\phi \equiv^1 v\,;\tau\,;\phi$ if (σ,τ) is an ED. *Permutation equivalence* $\equiv$ is defined as the equivalence closure of $\equiv^1$.

Permutations only change the order in which, but not how structures are created and this motivates defining backward families to be invariant with respect to permutation equivalence. Then, in order for the family relation to be effective the permutation equivalence relation has to be effective. One way of achieving this is to give an effective procedure for constructing unique representatives of $\equiv$-equivalence classes. *Standardisation* sorts the steps first into an outside-in order and then into a left-to-right order. The resulting sorted sequence is called *standard.*

Definition 10 Standardisation. 1. Rewrite steps (either β- or partial steps) are related via the positions of their constituent elements. In particular $u \leq v$ for steps u, v if there is a position affected by u which is a prefix of a position affected by v. Derived relations are its inverse $\geq$, the *outside* relation $< =^{\text{def}} \leq - \geq$ and its inverse $>$, the *inside* relation. Steps which are related by neither $\leq$ nor $\geq$ are *parallel* denoted by $|$, and steps which are related by both of them have *overlap* denoted by $\#$. The left-side of an ED is related to the right-side via the relationship between their initial steps and this is naturally extended to permutations. The relation $||$ on rewrite-sequences is defined as the transitive-reflexive closure of the parallel relation.

2. Let $\Rrightarrow =^{\text{def}} || \,;\, > \,;\, ||$, where ; denotes (sequential) composition, be the *standardisation* relation (cf. [GLM92]) on rewrite sequences. A rewrite sequence is said to be *standard* if it is in $\Rrightarrow$-normal form. Standardisation of a locked sequence is standardisation of its history, leaving the lock untouched.

The permutation relation $\equiv^1$ is partitioned into $<$, $>$, $||$, and $\#$. Note that since partial steps and β-steps do not have overlap with each other or themselves by orthogonality, $\#$ is the identity on these steps.

Remark. It can happen that a HRS rewrite sequences is standard in the traditional sense, but its decomposition is not standard. On the other hand, from each standardisation obtained by standardising the decomposition of a HRS sequence one can obtain a HRS sequence which is standard in the usual sense by projecting to β-normal form after each partial step.

Just like comparison-based sorting procedures work by removing 'inversions', standardisation procedures work by removing 'anti-standard' pairs, where a sequence contains an *anti-standard* pair if sometime a redex is contracted and later a redex outside it to which it didn't contribute is (cf. [Klo80, Def. I.10.2.1]). Termination of removal of anti-standard pairs was proven in [Klo80, Sec. II.6] for orthogonal combinatory reduction systems.[7] We've extended his method to OHRSs (at the same time correcting the error reported in [Mel96, Sec. 6.2.2]). This highly technical method can be avoided by observing that any standardisation method suffices for our purposes, e.g. the (non-deterministic) algorithm **STD** in [GLM92] corresponding to selection sort will do.[8]

[7] This is much more difficult than showing termination of removal of inversions for lists.

[8] The reader might enjoy studying standardisation analogues of other sorting procedures such as insertion sort.

Theorem 11 Standardisation. *1. $\Rrightarrow$ is strongly normalising and confluent modulo* $||$.
2. $\equiv = \Rrightarrow^! ; || ; {}^!\Lleftarrow$.

Proof. 1. By extending (and correcting) the method in [Klo80, Sec. I.10].
2. Easily from the first item. □

The parallel relation $|$ on positions can be partitioned into $\langle|$ and $|\rangle$, where $u \langle| v$ if u is to the left of v. Formally, $\langle| =^{\text{def}} <_{lex} \cap |$ and $|\rangle =^{\text{def}} | \cap >_{lex}$ where $>_{lex}$ is the usual lexicographical ordering on positions. It is easy to see and show that the induced relation $|\rangle$ on rewrite sequences is strongly normalising and confluent, which means that uniqueness up to $||$ is sharpened into uniqueness proper by $|\rangle$-normalising standard rewrite sequences.

5.2 Extraction

Working with decomposed steps allows for an in our opinion much simpler definition of extraction than the one in [AL94] using an algorithm for the shift operation mentioned above.

Definition 12 Extraction. The extraction relation $\rhd$ is the minimal relation on standard locked sequences, such that

1. it's compatible ([Bar84]), i.e. closed under λ-calculus contexts and substitutions,
2. Let $\sigma: M \twoheadrightarrow N$ be a rewrite sequence, $u: N \to_\phi O$ be a step $\tau\lhd\partial: P \twoheadrightarrow Q$ be a locked sequence.
   (a) If u is either a β-step, or a partial step, $N \to_\psi O$ such that $O|_\psi = P$ and $\phi \mid \psi$ then $\sigma ; u ;_\psi \tau\lhd\partial \ \rhd \sigma ;_\psi \tau\lhd\partial$, where the composition 'at position ψ' is defined in the obvious way.
   (b) If u is a partial step, $N \twoheadleftarrow_\beta C[l(\mathbf{M}')] \to C[r(\mathbf{M}')] = O$ and $M'_m = \mathrm{x}.P$, then $\sigma ; u ;_m \tau\lhd\partial \ \rhd \sigma ;_m \tau\lhd\partial$, where τ is confined to the mth argument of the left-hand side l and the right-hand side r respectively.
   (c) If u is a β-step $N = C[(x.P)(M')] \to_\beta C[P^{[x \mapsto M']}] = O$, then $\sigma ; u ; C[\tau\lhd\partial^{[x\mapsto M']}] \ \rhd \sigma ; C[(x.\tau\lhd\partial)(M')]$.
   (d) If u is a β-step $N = C[(x.M')(P)] \to_\beta C[M'^{[x\mapsto P]}] = O$ then $\sigma ; u ; C[M'^{[x_m \mapsto \tau\lhd\partial]}] \ \rhd \sigma ; C[(x_m.M')(\tau\lhd\partial)]$, where the locked sequence is confined to only the mth-copy of P in both sequences.

A sequence in extraction normal form is said to be *extracted.*

Extraction is clearly effective so combined with effectivity of standardisation this yields effectivity of the backward family relation to be defined next.

Definition 13 Backward Family. Define $\succeq_{bw} =^{\text{def}} \Rrightarrow^! ; |\rangle^! ; \rhd^!$. The *backward-family* relation is defined as $\simeq_b =^{\text{def}} \succeq_{bw} ; {}_{bw}\preceq$.

Theorem 14 Extraction. *1.* $\rhd$ *preserves standardness.*

2. $\rhd$ *is strongly normalising and confluent.*
3. $\simeq_b$ *is an equivalence relation.*

Proof. 1. The only thing which could happen is that the first step in τ is 'outside' the last step in σ, and the latter did not contribute to the former. The statement is proven by cases over the definition of extraction.
2. Strong normalisation is trivial, so it remains to show confluence, or equivalently, uniqueness of normal forms. If some locked sequence extracts to two distinct sequences, there must be a first step in the original sequence which *contributes* (see Definition 17) to one, but not to the other extracted sequence. Then Proposition 18 yields that their labellings differ, but this cannot be since labelling is preserved under extraction and both originate from the same (labelled) locked sequence.
3. Easy from confluence and termination (modulo $||$ for $\Rrightarrow$) of $\Rrightarrow$, $|\rangle$, and $\rhd$. □

6 Back and Forth

The zigzag approach defines redex-occurrences to be in the same *back-and-forth* family if they can be related to each other via the equivalence closure of the *copy* relation (modulo *permutation equivalence*). Here, a redex v in the final term of a rewrite sequence $\sigma\,;\tau$ is said to be a copy of a redex u in the final term of σ, if it is a descendant of v along τ.

Example 6 (See Example 1). For the rewrite sequences we consider in this example we don't need permutation equivalence.

1. Extending the partial step $\ddot{\sigma}$ ending in $(X.X(f))(x.h(x,x))$ by two β-steps yields the rewrite sequence $\tilde{\sigma}$ ending in $h(f,f)$, and this shows both occurrences of f in that term are copies of the redex f in the final term of $\ddot{\sigma}$. From this it follows that the occurrences are in the same back-and-forth family.
2. The rewrite sequence $\tilde{\tau}$ can be extended with the partial step $\check{\tau}$: $g(\mu(x.f)) \rightharpoonup_{\epsilon} (X.f)(\mu(x.f))$ and the innermost f-redex in its final term is clearly a descendant of the redex f in its starting term N.
3. The rewrite sequence $\tilde{\upsilon}$ can be extended with the rewrite sequence $\check{\upsilon}$: $\mu(x.f) \rightharpoonup_{\mu} (X.X(\mu(x.X(x))))(x.f) \twoheadrightarrow_{\beta} (x.f)(\mu(x.f))$ and also here the innermost f-redex in the final term is a descendant of the redex f in the starting term O. Since $\check{\tau}$ and $\check{\upsilon}$ end in the same term, we conclude from this and the previous item that the f redexes in N and O are in the same back-and-forth family.
4. The rule $f \rightarrow_f f$ does not do any copying (only destruction and creation), and it follows directly from the definition of back-and-forth families that the initial and final terms of $f \rightarrow_f f$ cannot be related to each other; they're not in the same back-and-forth family.

If HRS steps are considered (not decomposed ones), it is not possible to find a suitable zigzag in the third item as was noted in [AL94, Exa. 10], due to the fact that completing the $\check{\tau}$ and $\check{\upsilon}$ rewrite sequences to (decompositions of) HRS steps (by β-normalising their final terms to f) leads to HRS steps which 'create and erase', in particular the innermost f witnessing the equivalence is erased.

Definition 15 Zigzag. 1. Let $M \to_\phi N$ be either a partial step or a β-step. A part ∂ of N is said to be a *copy* of the same part in M, if
   (a) no position of ∂ is inside ϕ and then it's a copy of itself in M,
   (b) ∂ is inside an argument of the partial step at ϕ. This means that it uniquely stems from a part of (an instance of) the corresponding bound hole in M,
   (c) ∂ is completely inside the (substitution instance of) the body of the β-step at ϕ. This means that it descends from a unique part in the body of the step in M.
   (d) ∂ is completely inside an occurrence of the argument of the β-step at ϕ. This means that it descends from a unique part in the argument of the step in M.
2. The *back-and-forth* family relation $\simeq_{bf}$ is defined as the equivalence closure of the copy and the permutation relations.

7 Back = Forth = Back and Forth

Our main results show that it is not a coincidence that for the examples the three distinct family relations coincide. This requires quite some technicalities but is in principle an adaptation of the techniques in the appendices of [AL94].

The easy part is to show that if two locked sequences extract into the same sequence, labelling them yields identically labelled locks.

Proposition 16. *Labelling is preserved by* $\Rrightarrow$, $|\rangle$, *and* $\rhd$.

Proof. For the first two, this follows from the fact that labelling an ED yields a labelled ED. Preservation of $\rhd$ is a consequence of Proposition 18. □

We define two *contribution* relations, one via labelling and one via extraction and show them to coincide.

Definition 17 Contribution. Let $u\,;\sigma\lhd\partial$ be a locked standard sequence.

1. The step u is said to *forwardly contribute* to ∂ if its degree is a *sublabel* (in the obvious way) of the degree of the lock in the initial labelling.
2. The step u is said to *backwardly contribute* to ∂ if the sequence extracts into $u\,;\sigma'\lhd\partial$ for some σ'.

Proposition 18. *Forward contribution is backward contribution.*

Proof. See [AL94, Pro. 6]. □

Theorem 19. *Forward families are the same as backward families.*

Proof. This is [AL94, Thm. 6]. One half is easy and follows directly from Proposition 16. The other half is difficult. One proves by induction that if two locked sequences do not extract to the same sequence, their locks are differently labelled after inital labelling. This follows essentially the proof in op. cit. relying on the crucial notion of *connection*. □

Definition 20 Connection. *Connectivity* of labels is defined as follows.

1. One can decompose every edge label into labels which are not concatenated labels. Each of these labels is *connected* to its neighbour(s) and the ones next to a node are also connected to that node.
2. An 'interfacenumber' m next to the composed label $\langle \alpha, l \rightarrow r, n \rangle$ is connected (via a jump) to the corresponding element in the labelled left-hand side determined by the composed label.
3. Connection is closed under making it part of a composed label, (i.e. if a left-hand side is put into a label in a partial step, connectivity inside that label is the same as it was for the left-hand side).
4. An element inside a composed label is connected to that same element of its identical neighbour.

Since the definitions of extraction and zigzag make use of similar concepts, it's no surprise that, like for λ-calculus, they can easily be proven to be equal.

Proposition 21. *Backward families are the same as back-and-forth families.*

8 Further Research

Once a solid notion of family is established, the next question is whether it is possible to effectively implement an evaluator for OHRSs in which redexes in the same family are actually represented by the same structure, and which only ever contracts redexes which will contribute to the final result of the computation. We hope to achieve this goal for the class of *strongly sequential* ([HL]) OHRSs.

Acknowledgements I thank Zurab Khasidashvili, Tobias Nipkow, Christian Prehofer and Femke van Raamsdonk for feedback.

References

[AGM92] S. Abramsky, Dov M. Gabbay, and T. S. E. Maibaum, editors. *Handbook of Logic in Computer Science*, volume 2, Background: Computational Structures. Oxford University Press, New York, 1992.

[Aka93] Yohji Akama. On Mints' reduction for ccc-calculus. In TLCA'93, LNCS 664, pp. 1–12, 1993.

[AL94] Andrea Asperti and Cosimo Laneve. Interaction systems I: The theory of optimal reductions. *Mathematical Structures in Computer Science*, 4:457–504, 1994.

[Bar84] H. P. Barendregt. *The Lambda Calculus, Its Syntax and Semantics*, volume 103 of *Studies in Logic and the Foundations of Mathematics*. North-Holland, revised edition, 1984.

[BBKV76] H. P. Barendregt, J. Bergstra, J. W. Klop, and H. Volken. Degrees, reductions and representability in the λ-calculus. Report 22, Rijksuniversiteit Utrecht, February 1976. The Blue Preprint.

[DHMM96] G. Dowek, J. Heering, K. Meinke, and B. Möller, editors. *Proceedings of the Second International Workshop on Higher-Order Algebra, Logic, and Term Rewriting, (HOA '95)*, volume 1074 of *LNCS*. Springer-Verlag, 1996.

[DJ] Nachum Dershowitz and Jean-Pierre Jouannaud. Rewrite systems. In [Lee90, Ch. 6].

[GLM92] Georges Gonthier, Jean-Jacques Lévy, and Paul-André Melliès. An abstract standardisation theorem. In LICS 7, pp. 72–81, 1992.

[HL] Gérard Huet and Jean-Jacques Lévy. Computations in orthogonal rewriting systems. In [LP91].

[HMMN94] J. Heering, K. Meinke, B. Möller, and T. Nipkow, editors. *Higher-Order Algebra, Logic, and Term Rewriting, First International Workshop, HOA '93*, volume 816 of *LNCS*. Springer-Verlag, 1994.

[HP] Michael Hanus and Christian Prehofer. Higher-order narrowing with definitional trees. In these proceedings.

[HS86] J. Roger Hindley and Jonathan P. Seldin. *Introduction to Combinators and λ-Calculus*, volume 1 of *London Mathematical Society Students Texts*. Cambridge University Press, 1986.

[Klo] J. W. Klop. Term rewriting systems. In [AGM92, pp. 1–116].

[Klo80] J. W. Klop. *Combinatory Reduction Systems*. PhD thesis, Rijksuniversiteit Utrecht, June 1980. Mathematical Centre Tracts 127.

[Lee90] Jan van Leeuwen, editor. *Handbook of Theoretical Computer Science*, volume B : Formal Models and Semantics. Elsevier Science Publishers B.V., Amsterdam, 1990.

[Lév78] Jean-Jacques Lévy. *Réductions correctes et optimales dans le λ-calcul.* Thèse de doctorat d'etat, Université Paris VII, 1978.

[LP91] Jean-Louis Lassez and Gordon Plotkin, editors. *Computational Logic: Essays in Honor of Alan Robinson.* The MIT Press, Cambridge, Massachusetts, 1991.

[Mar92] Luc Maranget. *La stratégie paresseuse.* Thèse de doctorat, Université Paris VII, 6 juilliet 1992.

[Mel96] Paul-André Melliès. *Description Abstraite des Systèmes de Réécriture.* Thèse de doctorat, Université Paris VII, 1996. To appear.

[Mil91] Dale Miller. A logic programming language with lambda-abstraction, function variables, and simple unification. In ELP'89, LNAI 475, 1991.

[Nip91] Tobias Nipkow. Higher-order critical pairs. In LICS 6, pp. 342–349, 1991.

[Nip93] Tobias Nipkow. Orthogonal higher-order rewrite systems are confluent. In TLCA'93, LNCS 664, pp. 306–317, 1993.

[Oos94] Vincent van Oostrom. *Confluence for Abstract and Higher-Order Rewriting.* PhD thesis, Vrije Universiteit, Amsterdam, March 1994.

[Raa96] Femke van Raamsdonk. *Confluence and Normalisation for Higher-Order Rewriting.* PhD thesis, Vrije Universiteit, Amsterdam, May 1996.

A New Proof Manager and Graphic Interface for the Larch Prover

Frédéric Voisin

C.N.R.S. U.R.A. 410 and Université de Paris-Sud,
L.R.I., Bât. 490, F-91405 Orsay Cedex, France

Abstract. We present PLP, a proof management system and graphic interface for the "Larch Prover" (LP). The system provides additional support for interactive use of LP, by letting the user control the order in which goals are proved. We offer improved ways to investigate, compare and communicate proofs by allowing independent attempts at proving a goal, a better access to the information associated with goals and an additional script mechanism. All the features are accessible through a graphic system that makes the proof structure accessible to the user.

1 Introduction

The "proof-debugger" LP is part of the Larch project. It has been designed to help reasoning about algebraic specifications written in the Larch specification language by making it easier to prove properties of such specifications [2]. LP has also been applied to other domains such as the proof of circuits, of software components or of distributed algorithms [1, 3]. Here we focus on proof management since our system does not add any new logical mechanism to the ones already present in LP. We shall only recall that LP supports multi-sorted first-order formulas and offers various proof mechanisms, usually applied on user's request. The main operational mechanism is term rewriting with additional commands on top of it. Proof commands in LP are split in two groups: the "forward-inference" commands, used to enrich the current logical system without modifying the goal to be proved (like in critical-pairing or quantifier elimination), and the "backward-inference" commands, used to decompose the proof of a goal into the proofs of several subgoals (as in proof by cases or by induction), usually with some hypotheses. Therefore each subgoal is proved in a independent logical system formed by the initial axiomatization and the hypotheses corresponding to the various proof commands at the origin of a particular subgoal. The original formulas and rewrite systems can be altered as part of the proof process: orientation of equations into rewrite rules, inter-normalization of rewrite systems.

2 What's new with plp

The preliminary objectives and design of our system are described in [4]. Our system enriches LP with additional support for the interactive work on proofs and provides better mechanisms to investigate and compare proofs. LP is guided by the "design, code, debug" approach and offers very efficient commands for running large proofs written as scripts, but we also need more interactive support for helping in completing unfinished proofs or in correcting failed ones. Part of the problem is that it is not easy to write a script from scratch and to guess the exact form of the subgoals to prove, or the associated rewrite systems, after a few proof commands. Moreover, for a given subgoal, one can sometimes think of several ways to prove it and we want to be able to compare them, their subgoals or the contexts in which they are proved, without having to discard one strategy for trying another one. Also, with LP, a subgoal is discarded once proved, and its logical system is no longer accessible to the user. When the user is blocked in the proof of some subgoal, there is no possibility of switching to another subgoal, for instance for gaining some experience on another subgoal, or to understand why the proof of some subgoal succeeds while the proof of another do not. This hinders the comparison of similar proofs and this is where our system can help !

User control on the order of proof steps: LP does not provide the user with the control over the order in which the subgoals are proved: Each subgoal must be proved as soon as it is introduced, and the relative order of the subgoals originating from a given command is imposed by the system. We use the same default ordering, but at any moment the user of PLP can switch to another subgoal without first completing the current goal. New conjecture can be introduced by the user, that rely on conjectures that have not yet been completed. Therefore a user can prove the subgoals in the order that is the most natural for he/her, skip parts of a long proof when wanting to focus on a subpart of it, or state a sequence of conjectures whose proofs are deferred to separate files. The system automatically records which goals are unproved and proposes a new goal when the current task is completed.

Multiple attempts at proving subgoals: We allow independent attempts at proving subgoals, using different proof strategies. Variants can be started, cancelled, left uncompleted and later resumed, and the user can switch back and forth among them. A variant at a node is logically compatible with any variant at a node in an independent subtree: The validity depends only on the formulas in the subgoals. All subgoals have a "current" variant, with respect to which commands are interpreted. Switching between variants is done only on user request to minimize the risk of confusion for the user.

Variants are also useful to "replay" part of a proof either to try to simplify it or to have a closer look at its execution. This may be more convenient than retrieving the corresponding part in the log file produced by LP.

Better access to proof information: With PLP, proved subgoals are not discarded automatically and it is possible to re-enter them to inspect their logical systems or to perform some computation (like normalization). This gives an easier way to compare the proofs of independent subgoals. Part of the information is recorded within the interface part and is accessible by mouse clicking without interaction with the proof engine (that can be working on a different subgoal).

This includes the basic information about subgoals: logical status, the formula as initially stated and its current form after processing by the proof engine, current hypothesis etc. The rest of the information for a subgoal, even proved, can be retrieved by selecting that subgoal as the current focus for LP. This gives access to additional information, like the associated rewrite system, that would be too large to record within the interface part. Being able to run a whole proof and later browse through it, while picking up local information easily, provides valuable help when trying to understand someone else's proof.

Graphical presentation of proofs: We provide an explicit view of the tree that is the natural representation of a proof, with a proof command connecting a goal to the list of its subgoals. The selection of goals is done by mouse clicking or by name. The tree structure is used for representing backward-inference commands, the only ones that introduce subgoals. Forward-inference commands, which are not undoable in LP and which do not introduce subgoals, are displayed with a square box whose opening lists all the forward-inference commands issued for the subgoal. Different displays for completed and uncompleted subgoals make clear where unfinished parts are. Pointing at a node provides information about it (logical status, associated hypothesis, etc) while selecting it as the current focus for LP allows to (re-)enter the associated logical context and make it ready to accept new commands.

Variants can also be displayed in separate windows. This helps the comparison between different attempts at proving a goal. No proof action can be issued from the windows associated with variants, to prevent confusion about the node at which a proof action will take place. A variant must be selected as the current variant at a goal before one can issue a command for it. A "stack" display of commands for subgoals with variants makes explicit the presence of variants.

The tree structures can be dumped in Postscript format for later printing or inclusion into documents, in a form more readable than textual scripts.

New script mechanism: An additional script mechanism complements the one that exists in LP which provides an on-line recording of all user's actions, even the ones that have no impact on the proof (displays, cancelled actions, errors, etc). The new mechanism traverses the proof tree structure and lists only the commands that are necessary to rebuild the tree structure (or a selected part of it), cleared of all superfluous commands.

3 Conclusion

The new prototype system runs on SUN workstations. It is based on a customized release of LP, built in collaboration with Steve Garland from MIT. The proof engine is in CLU, the proof-manager part is in C and uses Tcl/Tk for the graphic manipulation. This prototype can be viewed as a first step towards a "proof editor" that would take advantage of the explicit proof structure to provide additional facilities. Among them we can mention dynamic annotation of scripts, scratch-pad facilities for performing computations at subgoals, a "replay" mechanism for reusing a proof at some subgoal for another subgoal, or the

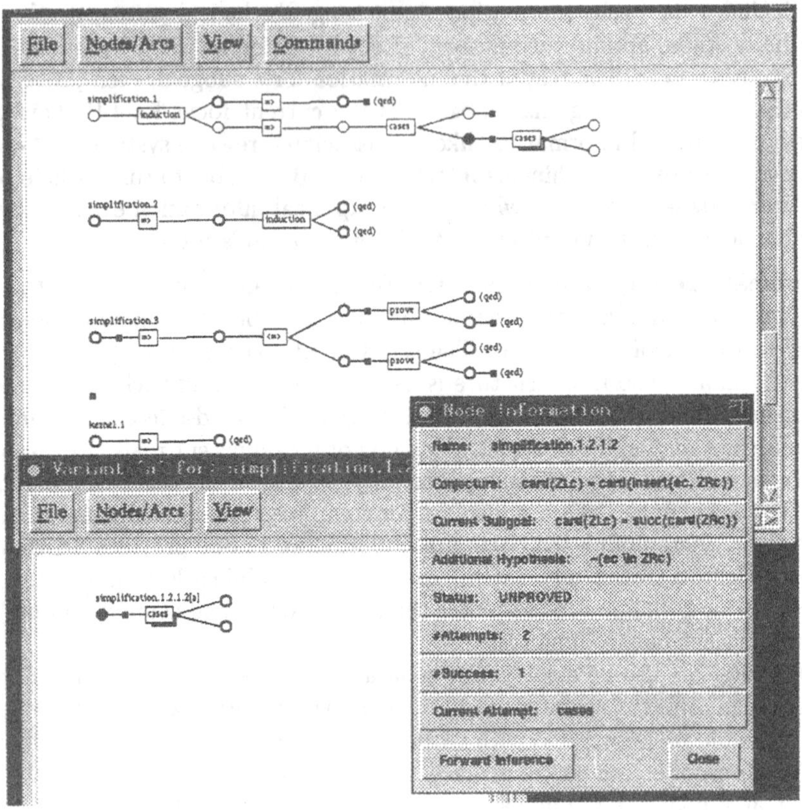

Fig. 1. A snapshot of the system

dynamic reshaping of proofs like when moving lemmas higher in a proof tree to make them sharable by several subgoals.

References

1. S. Garland and J. Guttag. A Guide to LP, The Larch Prover. Technical Report 82, DEC-SRC, 1991.
2. J. V. Guttag and J. J. Horning. *Larch: Languages and Tools for Formal Specification.* Springer-Verlag, 1993.
3. U. Martin and J. M. Wing (Eds). *First International Workshop on Larch, Dedham, 1992.* Workshop in Computing, Springer Verlag, 1992.
4. F. Voisin. A new front-end for the larch prover. In *First International Workshop on Larch, Dedham, 1992*, pages 282–296. Springer Verlag, 1992.

ReDuX 1.5: New Facets of Rewriting

Reinhard Bündgen and Carsten Sinz and Jochen Walter

Wilhelm-Schickard-Institut, Universität Tübingen
Sand 13, D-72076 Tübingen
⟨{buendgen,sinz,walterj}@informatik.uni-tuebingen.de⟩

The ReDuX system is a term rewriting laboratory that allows the user to experiment with completion procedures. It features Knuth-Bendix completion with critical pair criteria, Peterson-Stickel completion for commutative and/or associative-commutative theories, inductive completion procedures based on positional ground reducibility tests, tools to analyze the set of irreducible ground terms, an unfailing completion procedure based on ordered rewriting and a random term generator. ReDuX has been first presented in [Bün93] where the state of version 1.2 is reported. This system description will be restricted to extensions and modification since then.

The New Syntax

The most conspicuous modification of the ReDuX system concerns the new syntax of its input language for equational specifications and terms. An example of a ReDuX specification is given in Figure 1. ReDuX specifications describe

```
%% comment
DATATYPE LIST;
SORT        LIST, NAT;
CONST       0: NAT;                              []: LIST;
OPERATOR    cons: LIST, LIST -> LIST;            ': NAT  -> LIST;
            +: NAT, NAT      -> NAT;             s: NAT  -> NAT;
            <: NAT, NAT      -> LIST;            |: LIST -> NAT;
NOTATION    cons: LISP;                          s: FUNCTION;
            <: ROUNDFIX >;                       |: ROUNDFIX |;
%% default +: INFIX,                             ': PREFIX
ASSOC       +: RIGHT;                            PREC  ' < +;
VAR         A, B, C: NAT;                        L, M, N: LIST;
AXIOM       [1] |[]| == 0;                       [3] |(cons L M)| ==  s(|M|);
            [2] |'A| == s(0);                    [4] <A,B> == (cons 'A 'B);
%% ...
END
```

Fig. 1. A ReDuX specification

a many sorted signature, and a set of implicitly all-quantified equations. For notational convenience operators may be declared as prefix-, postfix-, infix- or roundfix operators, or they can be used with function, or Lisp notation. Declarations of precedences and associativities help avoiding superfluous parenthesis. Thus `|(cons 'A+B+C L)|` is a correct input w.r.t. the specification of Figure 1. Declaring a binary operator to be commutative (COM), or associative and commutative (AC) has semantical implications on the treatment of equality tests, matches and unifications. Terms with AC-operators may be written in flattened form. The new syntax also allows to mix terms with external objects as explained below.

Completion Strategies

The Peterson-Stickel completion procedure for completion modulo AC and/or COM has been extended to allow experimenting with different completion strategies. The base procedure is the same as in version 1.2. Yet several options are added controlling the computation of redundancy criteria for critical pairs, and the strategy for selecting the next pair to be oriented.

If a term ordering has been selected completion can be run either automatically or manually. In the latter case, equations can be oriented by the user, and critical pairs can be computed selectively using the fertilization feature.

The following redundancy criteria for critical pairs may be selected: The user may choose between standard critical pair computation and the computation of generalized critical pairs [Bün94]. The subconnectedness criterion for collapsed rules[1] [Küc86] can be switched on or off as well as a subsumption test for critical pairs.

The critical pair selection strategy may be influenced by giving priority to the input equations and/or the collapsed rules. Finally the selection is strongly influenced by choosing whether the critical pairs in the critical pair queue shall or shall not be kept always completely normalized.

It is hard to give a general statement saying which strategy (combination of completion options) is the best one. Experience indicates that it is worthwhile to compute generalized critical pairs, and to keep all critical pairs normalized. Note that the combination of both critical pair subsumption and the subconnectedness criterion is not fair.

Random Term Generation

The ReDuX random term generator *trd* is a program that computes pseudo random terms for a given input specification. The variables declared in the specification determine the variables that may occur in the random terms.

The method to compute the random terms is based on a bijective mapping between the set of terms and the natural numbers such that a "small" term is associated with a smaller number than a "bigger" term. Two choices of "smaller" are implemented in *trd*: (1) $t_1 \prec t_2$ if t_1 has less positions than t_2, and (2) $t_1 \prec t_2$ if t_2 is deeper than t_1. Thus the generation of a random term with at most n positions (or maximal depth d) is mapped to computing a random number using

[1] rules whose left-hand sides are reducible

the SAC-2 function IRAND.

Trd can (1) enumerate terms (w. r. t. size or depth), (2) compute k random terms of maximal size n (or depth d) and (3) compute statistics on computation times and the distributions of sizes and depths for a sequence of random terms. The output may be directed to the console or to a file. The output of the statistics is in gnuplot format. Due to the flexible syntax of ReDuX specifications the random terms generated by *trd* may also be used by other systems. In particular, by using Lisp notation for terms test data for Lisp programs may be produced.

External Objects

ReDuX 1.5 allows incorporating external objects into terms. External domains are declared as *external sorts*, that are determined by a set of operations on external objects. In particular, the names of input and output procedures must be provided to read and write terms containing external objects. In order to perform more complicated operations, like matches or unifications on terms containing external objects, also the names of equality tests and a total ordering must be assigned to the external sort. External objects are imported into a term by a special coercion operator. This coercion operator can be declared like other unary operators. It serves as a delimiter for the input routine reading an external object and internally encapsulates an object together with its methods in the sense of object oriented programming.

Ground terms can be computed to external objects. Therefore each operator may be assigned a function name denoting its external interpretation functions. Yet the combination of rewriting and computations is still in an experimental stage. See [Bün95b, Bün95a] for theoretical background and [BL96] for an alternative approach based on evaluation domains.

Example 1. Adding the declarations

```
EXTERNAL    SAC2INT: XREAD=IREAD, XWRITE=IWRITE, XEQ=EQUAL, XLT=ICOMP;
COERCION    ": SAC2INT -> NAT;              NOTATION    ": ROUNDFIX ";
PROPERTY    0: XINT=ALDESZERO;              +: XINT=ISUM;
```

to those of Figure 1 allows to import SAC-2 integers into the sort NAT. The constant 0 and the operator + can be interpreted as the SAC-2 constant 0 and function ISUM (integer sum) respectively such that the term "222" + 0 + "5" can be computed to, "227". □

By default, all ALDES/SAC-2 algorithms [CL90] are available to support external objects but additional functions can easily be added to the system.

Miscellaneous

Since Version 1.2 a term ordering based on polynomial interpretations [BCL87] and an unfailing completion procedure using ordered rewriting [BDP89] have been added to ReDuX. In addition the power of the inductive completion procedure has been improved.

ReDuX comes with documentation and tools to support both programmers and users. Among others there are manual pages for all ReDuX programs and tools. An interesting new tool is *blif2rdx* that automatically converts a gate level hardware description in BLIF format [BLI92] to ReDuX specifications that can be used for hardware verification [BKL96].

ReDuX on the Internet

ReDuX may be used for free provided it is used for non-commercial purposes. It is available from *ftp.informatik.uni-tuebingen.de* in *wsi/ca/software/ReDuX*. A further source of information is available on WWW:
URL http://www-ca.informatik.uni-tuebingen.de/~buendgen/redux.html.

References

[BCL87] Ahlem Ben Cherifa and Pierre Lescanne. Termination of rewriting systems by polynomial interpretations and its implementation. *Science of Computer Programming*, 9:137–159, 1987.

[BDP89] Leo Bachmair, Nachum Dershowitz, and David A. Plaisted. Completion without failure. In H. Aït-Kaci and M. Nivat, editors, *Resolution of Equations in Algebraic Structures*, volume 2 of *Rewriting Techniques*, chapter 1. Academic Press, 1989.

[BKL96] Reinhard Bündgen, Wolfgang Küchlin, and Werner Lauterbach. Verification of the Sparrow processor. In *IEEE Symposium and Workshop on Engineering of Computer-Based Systems*. IEEE Press, 1996.

[BL96] Reinhard Bündgen and Werner Lauterbach. Experiments with partial evaluation domains for rewrite specifications. In *11th Workshop on Abstract Data Types*, 1996. (Proc. WADT'95, Oslo, N, September 1995, to appear).

[BLI92] University of California, Berkeley, CA. *Berkeley Logic Interchange Format (BLIF)*, July 1992.

[Bün93] Reinhard Bündgen. Reduce the redex → ReDuX. In Claude Kirchner, editor, *Rewriting Techniques and Applications (LNCS 690)*. Springer-Verlag, 1993.

[Bün94] Reinhard Bündgen. On pots, pans and pudding or how to discover generalized critical pairs. In Alan Bundy, editor, *12th International Conference on Automated Deduction, (LNCS 814)*. Springer-Verlag, 1994.

[Bün95a] Reinhard Bündgen. Combining computer algebra and rule based reasoning. In *Integrating Symbolic Mathematical Computation and Artificial Intelligence.* Springer-Verlag, 1995.

[Bün95b] Reinhard Bündgen. Preserving confluence for rewrite systems with built-in operations. In Nachum Dershowitz and Naomi Lindenstrauss, editors, *Conditional and Typed Rewriting Systems (LNCS 968)*. Springer-Verlag, 1995.

[CL90] George E. Collins and Rüdiger G. K. Loos. Specification and index of SAC-2 algorithms. Technical Report 90–4, Wilhelm-Schickard-Institut für Informatik, Tübingen, 1990.

[Küc86] Wolfgang Küchlin. A generalized Knuth-Bendix algorithm. Technical Report 86-01, Mathematics, Swiss Federal Institute of Technology (ETH), CH-8092 Zürich, Switzerland, January 1986.

C*i*ME: Complet*i*on Modulo $E^\star$

Evelyne Contejean and Claude Marché

LRI, CNRS URA 410
Bât. 490, Université Paris-Sud, Centre d'Orsay
91405 Orsay Cedex, France
Email: {contejea,marche}@lri.fr

1 Background

Completion is an algorithm for building convergent rewrite systems from a given equational axiomatization. The story began in 1970 with the well-known Knuth-Bendix completion algorithm [8]. Unfortunately, this algorithm was not able to deal with simple axioms like commutativity ($x + y = y + x$) because such equations cannot be oriented into a terminating rewrite system. This problem have been solved by the so-called AC-completion algorithm of Lankford and Ballantyne [9] and Peterson and Stickel [14], which is able to deal with any permutative axioms, the most popular being associativity and commutativity.

In 1986, Jouannaud and Kirchner [6] introduced a general T-completion algorithm which was able to deal with any theory T provided that T-congruence classes are finite, and in 1989, Bachmair and Dershowitz extended it to the case of any T such that the subterm relation modulo T is terminating. Because of these restrictions, these algorithms are not able to deal with the most interesting cases, AC plus unit ($x+0 = x$ denoted ACU) being the main one. The particular case of ACU has been investigated first in 1989 by Peterson, Baird and Wilkerson [1]: they used constrained rewriting to avoid the non-termination problem; and an ACU-completion algorithm has been described then by Jouannaud and Marché in 1990 [7].

Independently from this story, in the domain of computer algebra, an algorithm for computing Gröbner bases of polynomial ideals has been found by Buchberger in 1965 [3] and much later than that, in 1981, Loos and Buchberger [11, 4] remarked that this algorithm and the previous completion algorithms behave in a very similar way. The problem of unifying these two algorithms into a common general one arised.

In 1993, using the ideas introduced for ACU-completion, Marché described a new completion algorithm based on a variant of rewriting modulo T: *normalized rewriting* [12, 13], where terms have to be normalized with respect to a convergent rewrite system S equivalent to T. Of course, this assumes the existence of such an S, but this appears to be true for the examples we were interested in: AC plus unit, AC plus idempotence ($x + x = x$), nilpotence ($x + x = 0$), Abelian group theory, commutative ring theory, Boolean ring theory, finite fields theory.

* This research was supported in part by the EWG CCL, the HCM Network CONSOLE, and the "GDR de programmation du CNRS".

The system C*i*ME presented in this article is an implementation of the normalized completion algorithm.

2 Main features

The two main features of the program come from the features of the normalized completion method: one has to declare a theory T among the ones proposed by C*i*ME (see next section the list of available theories), rewriting will be done by T-normalization, and deductions will use efficiently some knowledge about T (see [12, 13] for details).

Second, one may also declare a theory E with which the unification will be made. E contains by default at least AC(f) (and also C(f)) for each AC (resp. C) operator f declared, and has to be included in T. This choice must be made cleverly in order to, first, avoid as much as possible AC because of its complexity (prefer ACU unification for example), and second to avoid infinitary or undecidable unification (avoid distributivity for example).

See next section for the list of supported theories E.

3 How to use the program

The sources of the program are available by ftp[2] or by the Web[3]. C*i*ME is written in CAML-light, a ML family language developed at INRIA Rocquencourt [10], together with some parts written in C (AC-matching[4]).

There is no interactive top level, the program consists only in a stand-alone executable, which has to be run with a specification file as a parameter, possibly with some options.

The specification file is a sequence of declarations of various kinds. It allows first to declare operator names together with their arity, and possibly declare them as commutative or AC. One may declare the theory T modulo which the T-normalized completion will be run (empty by default, hence completion will behave as AC completion). Currently, the supported theories are A (associativity), AU (A plus unit), ACU, ACI (AC plus idempotence), ACUI, ACUN (ACU plus nilpotence), G (group theory), AG (Abelian group theory), CR (commutative ring theory), FP (finite fields theory) and BR (Boolean ring theory). Additionally, one may also declare the theory E modulo which the unification will be done, which have to be a subset of T. Currently are supported ACU, AG and BR.

The other declarations are standard: the set of equational axioms to be completed, the completion ordering, and finally a set of problems to be solved (proving identities, normalizing a term, unifying two terms).

---

[2] `ftp://lri.lri.fr/LRI/soft/cime/cime.tar.Z`

[3] `http://lri.lri.fr/~marche/cime.html`

[4] We thank Steven Eker at INRIA Lorraine for making available its very efficient AC-matching algorithm [5]

4 One representative example

Many examples can be found in the directory **examples** of distribution. Let us show one representative example: the theory of a ring homomorphism. Given two commutative rings with operators $(+, 0, -, \times, 1)$ and $(\oplus, O, \ominus, \otimes, I)$ respectively, the theory of an homomorphism h is given by $h(x+y) = h(x) \oplus h(y)$ and $h(x \times y) = h(x) \otimes h(y)$. Thus, one may try to complete this set by giving the following specification file to C*i*ME:

```
operators
  +,.,plus,times : AC
  0,1,zero,one   : constant
  -,minus,H      : unary
  x,y,z,t,u      : variable
theory
  CR(+,0,-,.,1)  CR(plus,zero,minus,times,one)
axioms
  H(x+y) = H(x) plus H(y);
  H(x.y) = H(x) times H(y);
order
  rpo( H>1>.>->+>0, H>one>times>minus>plus>zero  )
```

Completion takes 0.76 seconds, computing 24 critical pairs, to obtain a convergent rewrite system of 5 rules:

$$h(0) \to O \qquad h(-(x)) \to \ominus(h(x)) \qquad h(x) \otimes h(1) \to h(x)$$
$$h(x+y) \to h(x) \oplus h(y) \qquad h(x \times y) \to h(x) \otimes h(y)$$

Completion is made efficient by use of *symmetrization* [12, 13], that is from the equation $h(x) \oplus h(0) = h(x)$, the rule $h(0) \to O$ is generated directly without any call to unification; and similarly, from $h(x) \oplus h(-(x)) = O$, $h(-(x)) \to \ominus(h(x))$ is directly generated. Completion can be made even more efficient by using a better unification algorithm [2]: one simply has to add the declaration

```
unification theory
  AG(+,0,-) ACU(.,1) AG(plus,zero,minus) ACU(times,one)
```

to the specification file, and then completion takes 0.33 seconds, computing 11 critical pairs.

Notice that standard AC-completion takes on this example 8.58 seconds and computes 471 critical pairs.

(Computation times are obtained on a PC Pentium 90, running Linux 1.2.13, C*i*ME being compiled with the Caml Special Light optimizing compiler)

5 Future work

C*i*ME is the base for a future term rewriting laboratory developed by the "DEMONS" team at LRI, directed by Hubert Comon. We planned to developed the following points: termination orderings, unification, extension of the normalized rewriting technique to Horn clauses and to constrained rewriting, constraint solving.

References

1. T. Baird, G. Peterson, and R. Wilkerson. Complete sets of reductions modulo Associativity, Commutativity and Identity. In *Proc. 3rd Rewriting Techniques and Applications, Chapel Hill, LNCS 355*, pages 29–44. Springer-Verlag, Apr. 1989.
2. A. Boudet, E. Contejean, and C. Marché. AC-complete unification and its application to theorem proving. In H. Ganzinger, editor, *7th International Conference on Rewriting Techniques and Applications*, Lecture Notes in Computer Science, Rutgers University, NJ, USA, July 1996. Springer-Verlag. To appear.
3. B. Buchberger. *An Algorithm for Finding a Basis for the Residue Class Ring of a Zero-Dimensional Ideal.* PhD thesis, University of Innsbruck, Austria, 1965. (in German).
4. B. Buchberger and R. Loos. Algebraic simplification. In *Computer Algebra, Symbolic and Algebraic Computation. Computing Supplementum 4.* Springer-Verlag, 1982.
5. S. Eker. Improving the efficiency of AC matching and unification. Rapport de DEA, INRIA Lorraine, 1993.
6. J.-P. Jouannaud and H. Kirchner. Completion of a set of rules modulo a set of equations. *SIAM J. Comput.*, 15(4):1155–1194, 1986.
7. J.-P. Jouannaud and C. Marché. Termination and completion modulo associativity, commutativity and identity. *Theoretical Comput. Sci.*, 104:29–51, 1992.
8. D. E. Knuth and P. B. Bendix. Simple word problems in universal algebras. In J. Leech, editor, *Computational Problems in Abstract Algebra*, pages 263–297. Pergamon Press, 1970.
9. D. S. Lankford and A. M. Ballantyne. Decision procedures for simple equational theories with permutative axioms: Complete sets of permutative reductions. Research Report Memo ATP-37, Department of Mathematics and Computer Science, University of Texas, Austin, Texas, USA, Aug. 1977.
10. X. Leroy and M. Mauny. *The Caml Light system, release 0.5.* INRIA, Rocquencourt, 1992.
11. R. Loos. Term reduction systems and algebraic algorithms. In *Proceedings of the Fifth GI Workshop on Artificial Intelligence*, pages 214–234, Bad Honnef, West Germany, 1981. Available as *Informatik Fachberichte*, Vol. 47.
12. C. Marché. Normalised rewriting and normalised completion. In *Proceedings of the Ninth Annual IEEE Symposium on Logic in Computer Science*, pages 394–403, Paris, France, July 1994. IEEE Comp. Soc. Press.
13. C. Marché. Normalized rewriting: an alternative to rewriting modulo a set of equations. *Journal of Symbolic Computation*, 1996. to appear.
14. G. E. Peterson and M. E. Stickel. Complete sets of reductions for some equational theories. *J. ACM*, 28(2):233–264, Apr. 1981.

Distributed Larch Prover (DLP): An Experiment in Parallelizing a Rewrite-Rule Based Prover

Mark T. Vandevoorde[1] and Deepak Kapur[2]

[1] Lab. for Computer Science, Massachusetts Institute of Technology, Cambridge, MA 02139, +1 617 253-3538, mtv@lcs.mit.edu

[2] Dept. of Computer Science, State University of New York, Albany, NY 12222. kapur@cs.albany.edu

Abstract. The *Distributed Larch Prover*, DLP, is a distributed and parallel version of LP, an interactive prover. DLP helps users find proofs by creating and managing many proof attempts that run in parallel. Parallel attempts may work independently on different subgoals of an inference method, and they may compete by using different inference methods to prove the same goal. DLP runs on a network of workstations.

1 Introduction

The *Distributed Larch Prover*, DLP, is an experiment in parallelizing LP, the *Larch Prover*. LP is an interactive, rewrite-rule based reasoning system for proving formulas in first-order, multi-sorted logic by first-order reasoning and induction [4]. DLP runs on a network of workstations.

DLP uses a novel approach for exploiting parallelism. The user of DLP is encouraged to launch many parallel attempts to prove conjectures. Some attempts compete by using different inference methods, such as proof-by-cases and proof-by-induction, to try to prove the same goal. Other attempts work independently on different subgoals. The basic idea is to find a proof more quickly by exploiting coarse-grain parallelism and by trying more inference methods in parallel [5].

In contrast, the conventional approach for adding parallelism to a prover is to exploit parallelism in the implementation while leaving the user interface unchanged. For example, a rewrite-based prover can exploit parallel algorithms for matching, normalization, and completion, for instance, by generating critical pairs among rewrite rules in parallel, or by running completion using different strategies as in DISCOUNT [1]. Resolutions-based provers such as Peers [2] and ROO parallelize closure computation by distributing work among processors for performing resolution steps among different subsets of clauses in parallel. Model-elimination and model-generation theorem provers exploit parallelism in searching independent parts of the or-search tree and for generating different models, respectively. Each of these provers aims to improve performance while presenting a familiar, sequential interface to the user.[3]

[3] In [3], a survey of parallel theorem provers as of 1992 is included.

2 Adding Parallelism to LP

LP was developed at MIT by Steve Garland and John Guttag to reason about designs for circuits, concurrent algorithms, hardware, and software [4]. LP is an interactive prover whose design is based on the assumption that most attempts to prove interesting conjectures fail initially because of errors or omissions in the formalization. Consequently, LP does not support aggressive heuristics for automatically finding proofs. Instead, the user is given considerable control in guiding the proof finding process, and LP provides useful feedback when a proof attempt is unsuccessful.

The theorem proving approach in LP is based on term rewriting techniques. The main automated inference step in LP is *normalization* of a goal by terminating rewrite rules. LP provides additional mechanisms for establishing conjectures using both forward and backward inference. Two key forward inference methods are *critical pair* computation among rewrite rules and *instantiating* free variables in a formula. Among backward inference methods, *proof-by-cases* and *proof-by-induction* are frequently used in proofs. LP never applies these forward and backward inference methods automatically because one would need heuristics to decide when and how to apply them. Instead, when normalization fails to prove a goal, the user can explicitly invoke an inference method.

The main contribution of DLP is that it lets users try many different combinations of forward and backward inference methods automatically and in parallel. DLP provides a default heuristic for selecting and applying the inference methods; this heuristic can be controlled by the user. Furthermore, in keeping with LP's design philosophy, the user can examine any unsuccessful proof attempt to get feedback as to why the attempt didn't succeed.

Voisin has an interface to LP that also supports multiple proof attempts, but these attempts are created manually and do not exploit parallelism [10].

2.1 Speculate and Find-instantiations: New Commands in DLP

The most important new commands in DLP are `spec` (short for `speculate`) and `find` (short for `find-instantiations`). The `spec` command executes a proof strategy for recursively spawning proof attempts automatically. Proof strategies are somewhat like tactics in HOL. The default strategy is to create competing attempts for each possible proof by induction, for proof of implication (if the top-level conjecture is an implication), for one proof by cases (the case is chosen heuristically from the boolean subterms of the conjecture), and for proof by contradiction (if there is nothing in the conjecture to perform any case analysis). By default, `spec` interleaves a `find` command with the generation of subgoals. `spec` is programmable and it provides hooks for the user to change the strategy.

The `find` command is used to derive new facts from subgoal hypotheses. Ground facts typically generated from case analysis and induction hypotheses are matched against other facts (typically axioms and lemmas) to generate simplified instantiations of the axioms and lemmas. This command can be viewed as an efficient subset of the critical pair method in LP to generate instantiations.

2.2 Changes to the User Interface

LP's user interface presents the user with a stack of proof obligations; the user can work only on the obligation at the top of the stack. When a backward inference method is used, proof obligations for the subgoals are pushed onto the stack.

To support parallel proof attempts, DLP presents the users with an and/or-tree of goals and proof attempts. Each goal is an or-node with one or more proof attempt nodes as children. At any leaf node, the user can issue commands to perform inference methods. The amount of or-parallelism as well as the proof strategy realized by an and/or-tree can be programmed by the user using `spec`.

DLP uses Emacs as a front-end for communicating with the user. One Emacs window displays a textual version of the and/or tree. Another Emacs window displays the full input and output associated with each goal and proof attempt. DLP has many facilities for navigating through the and/or tree, for selectively hiding portions of the and/or-tree, broadcasting and multicasting commands to a selected subset of leaf nodes, etc. [9, 5].

2.3 Implementation

DLP runs on a network of uniprocessor workstations. It is implemented as n worker UNIX processes—one per workstation—plus a coordinator process and an Emacs process. The coordinator is a scheduler that tells the workers what tasks they should execute. The coordinator also performs load balancing by telling a worker to migrate a task to another worker. All communication between processes follows the message-passing paradigm rather than the shared-memory paradigm. More details are given in [9].

3 Experiments with DLP

DLP has been successfully tried on a variety of problems, including examples from Larch and LP libraries of specifications and proofs as well as problems never tried before on LP, *e.g.*, subproblems arising from experiments with Robbins' algebra conjecture [11], McCarthy's mutilated checker board problem [7], and first-order problems including SAM's Lemma, Bledsoe's Intermediate Value Theorem, and a problem involving equalities in clauses suggested by Ganzinger. Below we provide some highlights of our experience in using DLP; more details about proofs of these problems are given in [5].

We asked John Guttag, an LP developer, to try DLP. Guttag decided to try to prove properties about double-ended queues, a problem similar to one he had tried some years ago using LP and for which, he remembered, many proofs required considerable effort using LP. Guttag believed he was able to prove the properties faster using DLP than he would have using LP [6].

Using DLP, we found a simpler and shorter proof of one of the main conjectures in verifying the correctness of a pipeline processor in [8]. This came as a pleasant surprise to one of the coauthors of [8] since they had spent considerable effort in manually trying to find short proofs.

LP is not designed to automatically prove first-order formulas, as it does not support any complete inference strategy for first-order theorem proving. We did not expect DLP to perform well on problems whose proofs did not require induction. To our pleasant surprise, we found that a combination of proof by cases and `find` commands was quite useful in solving many nontrivial and challenging problems with relative ease. E.g., though unfamiliar with Bledsoe's Intermediate Value Theorem and Ganzinger's Equality Problem [5], the first author was able to prove each of these problems in about an hour with DLP.

We have identified useful proof strategies that can be invoked at the top level of DLP to automatically solve many problems; see [5] for details. DLP complements LP's philosophy, by assisting not only in the initial stages of design where the emphasis is on finding bugs and correcting them in specifications and conjectures, but also at a later stage, when the focus is on quickly establishing properties with minimal user guidance and intervention.

Acknowledgments

We thank Steve Garland and John Guttag for their many suggestions and encouragement for developing DLP. This work was done during Kapur's sabbatical at MIT Lab. for Computer Science, and was partially supported by the National Science Foundation Grants no. CCR-9303394 and CCR-9504248, and by the Advanced Research Projects Agency under contracts N00014-92-J-1795 and N00014-94-1-0985.

References

1. Avenhaus, J., and Denzinger, D., "Distributed equational theorem proving," Proc. *5th Conf. on Rewriting Techniques and Applications,* LNCS 690 (ed. Kirchner), Montreal, 62-76, 1993.
2. Bonacina, M. P., and McCune, W., "Distributed theorem proving by *Peers,*" Proc. *12th Intl. Conf. on Automated Deduction (CADE-12),* LNAI 814 (ed. Bundy), Nancy, France, 1994, 841-845.
3. Fronhoefer, B., and Wrightson, G. (eds). *Parallelization in Inference Systems.* Proc. of Intl. Workshop, Germany, Dec. 1990, Springer LNAI 590, 1992.
4. Garland, S., and Guttag, J., "An overview of LP," Proc. *3rd Conf. on Rewriting Techniques and Applications,* LNCS 355 (ed. Dershowitz), 1989, 137-151.
5. Kapur, D. and Vandevoorde, M.T., "DLP: A paradigm for parallel interactive theorem proving," http://larch-www.lcs.mit.edu:8001/~mtv/pitp96.ps.
6. J. Guttag. Personal communication. September 1995.
7. McCarthy, J., "The mutilated checkerboard in set theory," in *The QED II Workshop* report (ed. R. Matuszewski), L/1/95, Warsaw University, Oct. 1995, http://www.mcs.anl.gov/qed/index.html.
8. Saxe, J., Guttag, J., Horning, J., and Garland, S., "Using transformations and verification in circuit design," *Formal Methods in System Design,* 1993, 181-209.
9. Vandevoorde, M.T., and Kapur, D., *Parallel user interfaces for parallel applications,* http://larch-www.lcs.mit.edu:8001/~mtv/hpdc96.ps.
10. Voisin, F., "A New Proof Manager and Graphic Interface for the Larch Prover," *7th Conf. on Rewriting Techniques and Applications,* 1996.
11. Winker, S., "Robbins algebra: conditions that make a near-boolean algebra boolean," *J. of Automated Reasoning,* 6, 4, 1990, 465-489.

EPIC: An Equational Language – Abstract Machine and Supporting Tools –

H.R.Walters* and J.F.Th.Kamperman ({pum,jasper}@cwi.nl)

CWI, P.O. Box 94079, 1090 GB Amsterdam

1 Introduction

Equational programming is the use of (confluent) term rewriting systems as an implementation language with don't care non-determinism, against a formal background of algebraic specification with term rewriting as a concrete model.

EPIC is an equational programming language primarily developed as a 'formal system language'. That is, it is strongly based on equational specification and term rewriting, but its operational semantics are too specific for a specification language.

EPIC has two main applications:

- It can be used as a target language, where other specification languages are given an implementation by translating them to EPIC. EPIC is a suitable target for many languages based on pattern matching, tree- (dag-) replacement and term rewriting since it provides precisely the needed primitives, without superfluous detail.
  Historically, EPIC has evolved in the context of the algebraic specification language ASF+SDF [2];
- EPIC can be used as a 'systems programming language' in which to write executable specifications. For example, EPIC's compiler, and several other tools for EPIC, have been implemented in EPIC itself.
  It must be said from the start, however, that EPIC has little to offer as a programming language. Suitability as a programming language is at odds with suitability as a target language.

EPIC's syntax is intentionally abstract: when used as a target language, generating the abstract syntax directly (as a data structure or in a textual representation aimed at machine readability) avoids producing and parsing human readable text. A concrete syntax for the use of EPIC as a system programming language is provided, but doesn't offer many of the features commonly available in programming languages. The EPIC tool set – a collection of software for the support of EPIC, including the compiler and run-time system, – uses a front-end written in, and accepting this concrete syntax, and producing EPIC's abstract syntax.

EPIC's type-system is liberal: it is single-sorted, requiring only the usual restrictions for TRSs (the left-hand side of a rule is not a sole variable, and is

* Partial support received from the Foundation for Computer Science Research in the Netherlands (SION) under project 612-17-418, "Generic Tools for Program Analysis and Optimization".

linear; all functions have a fixed arity; and every variable in the right-hand side of a rule must also occur in the left-hand side of that rule), and one restriction concerning modules (free and external functions may not become defined).

The simplicity of EPIC's type-system makes EPIC a suitable target for many different source languages. Type correctness is established at source level, and need not be checked again; and the translation to EPIC isn't complicated by a complex target structure.

2 EPIC in a nutshell

EPIC features (left-linear) rewrite rules with syntactic specificity ordering [7] (a simplified version of specificity ordering [1]). It supports external data types and separate compilation of modules.

An EPIC module consists of a signature and a set of rules. The signature declares functions, each with an arity (number of arguments). In addition, functions can be declared *external* (i.e., defined in another module, or directly in C), or *free* (i.e., not defined in any module).

Rules are ordered by a syntactic specificity ordering: a more specific rule has higher precedence than a more general rule.

3 EPIC's tool set

The EPIC tool set includes the following tools:

- an EPIC parser and an EPIC (pretty) printer;
- a (primitive) type checker;
- a compiler which translates EPIC to μArm. As can be seen, various features are added to EPIC by separate tools. The compiler combines all of the above;
- a printer for μArm code;
- the μArm interpreter.

In addition several stand-alone tools exist:

- a curryfier, which handles function symbol occurrences with too few arguments. EPIC doesn't provide currying, but this tool adds that facility;
- an ML to EPIC translator, which translates a subset of ML to EPIC.
- a μArm to C translator which compiles μArm code into C functions, one for each function in the original TRS. These functions can be linked, statically, to the interpreter.
- a tool which implements associative matching by a TRS transformation.

EPIC is available via www at `http://www.cwi.nl/epic/`

4 System design philosophy

The development of EPIC and its supporting tools is fueled by our conviction that term rewriting isn't less efficient, intrinsically, than any other implementation mechanism.

Accordingly, all tools relating to EPIC are themselves TRSs written in EPIC; the single exception is the run-time system, which is the abstract rewriting machine μArm discussed in Section 5.

All tools in the EPIC tool set are based on a simple design principle: they consume and produce text. They are usually composed of four parts: a parser, which interprets the input text and builds the term it represents; the essential computation performed by the tool; a (pretty) printer which produces a text given the term resulting from the computation; and a 'top module' which glues the three together. Obviously intermediate printing and parsing is avoided when tools are combined. The graph exchange language GEL [4] can be used to store or pass on, in a very compact form approaching one byte per node, terms, dags and graphs, where sharing should be preserved.

5 A high-performance engine for hybrid term rewriting

μArm is an efficient abstract machine for hybrid term rewriting, which allows for an incremental style of software development and supports the transparent combination of compiled (stable) code with interpreted code still earlier in the software development cycle.

μArm supports external functions and data types, and μArm's dispatcher uses a combination of directly and indirectly threaded code to achieve an efficient, transparent interface between different types of functions.

μArm has efficient memory management, where garbage collection takes up less than 5% of the overall execution time. In addition, μArm uses a space-efficient innermost reduction strategy, whilst allowing for lazy rewriting when this is desired (as described in [6]).

Finally, μArm is parameterized with a small number of C macro's which can be defined either for portable ANSI C, or for a machine specific variant which performs two to three times better. In this manner ports for SUN SPARC, SGI R5000, and Macintosh (680xx) have been defined.

A precursor of μArm is described in [5]; a successor in [7].

6 Future work

We have investigated several fundamental extensions to innermost term rewriting which are deemed desirable for practical application of EPIC.

- EPIC assumes (rightmost) innermost rewriting; in [6] a method is described which makes lazy (outermost) rewriting available by TRS transformation.
- In [9] a model for I/O in term rewriting is presented.
- In [8] a method is described which allows external datatypes to be viewed as if generated over a signature of free constructors, thus making the implementation of data types truly hidden.
- EPIC does not support conditions, since these often lead to unclear, or unsatisfactory formal and operational semantics. Restricted use of conditions, however, can improve readability of programs. Examples are the use of conditions for common sub-expression high-lighting and for case-based reasoning. To this end a tool is provided which defines a meaning of 'conditional EPIC' by way of a translation to EPIC.

7 EPIC's efficiency

EPIC was designed specifically with efficiency in mind, where a balance was struck between compilation speed and execution speed. In lieu of the former, an interpreter is used for the intermediate (abstract machine) level; this interpreter has been optimized and fine-tuned to achieve acceptable execution speeds.

In [3] a compute-bound benchmark comparing implementations of functional languages is reported on in which μArm presented itself as the most efficient interpreted system. Since the benchmark relies heavily on floating point computations, with little control-flow overhead, it favors compiling implementations, which fare better in that benchmark.

The (portable; non machine-specific) μArm interpreter performs 350000 simple reductions per second (of the form $f(s(X)) \rightarrow f(X)$) on a SUN SPARC. On the same platform, the Larch Prover (LP 3.1a) performs 488 reductions per second, on the identical example. This is not mentioned as a comment on LP, but rather to provide a basis for comparison with other platforms.

References

1. J.C.M. Baeten, J.A. Bergstra, J.W. Klop, and W.P. Weijland. Term-rewriting systems with rule priorities. *Theoretical Computer Science*, 67(1):283–301, 1989.
2. J.A. Bergstra, J. Heering, and P. Klint, editors. *Algebraic Specification*. ACM Press Frontier Series. The ACM Press in co-operation with Addison-Wesley, 1989.
3. Pieter H. Hartel, Marc Feeley, et al. Benchmarking implementations of functional languages with "pseudoknot", a float-intensive benchmark. *Journal of Functional Programming*, 1996. Accepted for publication.
4. J.F.Th. Kamperman. GEL, a graph exchange language. Report CS-R9440, Centrum voor Wiskunde en Informatica (CWI), Amsterdam, 1994. Available by *ftp* from ftp.cwi.nl:/pub/gipe as Kam94.ps.Z.
5. J.F.Th. Kamperman and H.R. Walters. ARM – Abstract Rewriting Machine. In H.A. Wijshoff, editor, *Computing Science in the Netherlands*, pages 193–204, 1993.
6. J.F.Th. Kamperman and H.R. Walters. Lazy rewriting and eager machinery. In Jieh Hsiang, editor, *Rewriting Techniques and Applications*, number 914 in Lecture Notes in Computer Science, pages 147–162. Springer-Verlag, 1995.
7. J.F.Th. Kamperman and H.R. Walters. Minimal term rewriting systems. Technical Report CS-R9573, CWI, december 1995. Available as http://www.cwi.nl/epic/articles/CS-R9573.ps.Z. To appear in the proceedings of the 11th Workshop on Abstract Data Types, published by Springer-Verlag.
8. H.R. Walters. *On Equal Terms, Implementing Algebraic Specifications*. PhD thesis, University of Amsterdam, 1991. Available by *ftp* from ftp.cwi.nl:/pub/gipe/reports as Wal91.ps.Z.
9. H.R. Walters and J.F.Th. Kamperman. A model for I/O in equational languages with don't care non-determinism. Technical Report CS-R9572, CWI, december 1995. Available as http://www.cwi.nl/epic/articles/CS-R9572.ps.Z. To appear in the proceedings of the 11th Workshop on Abstract Data Types, published by Springer-Verlag.

SPIKE-AC: A System for Proofs by Induction in Associative-Commutative Theories

Narjes Berregeb[§] Adel Bouhoula[§‡] Michaël Rusinowitch[§]

[§] INRIA Lorraine & CRIN
Campus Scientifique, 615, rue du Jardin Botanique - B.P. 101
54602 Villers-lès-Nancy Cedex, France
E-mail:{berregeb, bouhoula, rusi}@loria.fr

[‡] Computer Science Laboratory, SRI International
333 Ravenswood Avenue, Menlo Park, California 94025, USA
E-mail: bouhoula@csl.sri.com

1 Introduction

Automated verification problems often involve Associative-Commutative (AC) operators. But, these operators are hard to handle since they cause combinational explosion. Many provers simply consider AC axioms as additional properties kept in a library, adding a burden to the proof search control. Term rewriting modulo AC is a basic approach to remedy this problem. Based on it, we have developed techniques to treat properly AC operators, that have been integrated in SPIKE, an automatic theorem prover in theories expressed by conditional equations [4]. The system SPIKE-AC obtained, written in Caml Light, have demonstrated that induction proofs become more natural and require less interaction. In contrast with other inductive completion methods [6, 9, 11] needing AC unification to compute critical pairs, our method does not need AC unification which is doubly exponential [10]; only AC matching is required. An other advantage is that our system refutes all false conjectures, under reasonable assumptions on the given theories. Experiments have shown that in presence of AC operators, less input from the user is needed, comparing with related systems such as LP [8], NQTHM [5] and PVS [12].

2 An overview of the proof mechanism

Given a set of conditional equations R, SPIKE-AC starts by orienting R using an *apo* order [2] which is a well-founded and AC-compatible ordering. Then, solely based on the rules of R, it computes the *induction positions of functions* and a *test set*. Note that this computation is done only once, before the proof process, and independently from the conjecture to prove.

We have developed a new algorithm for computing the *induction positions of functions* [3], that allows to determine the *induction variables* of a conjecture, on which induction will eventually be applied. This algorithm is based on the idea that a variable is inductive if it may trigger a rewriting step after it is instanciated.

A *test set* is a finite set of terms, which enables to detect when a term possesses an irreducible ground instance. Such set allows SPIKE-AC to refute a false conjecture by construction of a counterexample. We have implemented an algorithm for the restricted case where the rewrite system is left-linear and sufficiently complete, and the relations between constructors are equational (constructors can be AC). This algorithm takes into account the shape of rules more closely than with Bündgen's method [6]; this is a crucial point for efficiency in proof search.

Our procedure is defined by a set of transition rules which are applied to pairs (E, H), where E is the list of conjectures and H is the list of inductive hypotheses. To prove a conjecture c, SPIKE-AC applies the *generation* rule which instantiates the induction variables of c by elements from the test set. Then, each sub-goal is simplified and added to E, and c is added as a new induction hypothesis to H. In a second step, SPIKE-AC applies the *simplification* rule to simplify conjectures by axioms, other induction hypotheses or other conjectures (which permits to simulate simultaneous induction), and deletes trivial or subsumed conjectures. Every cycle generates new sub-goals that are processed in the same way as the initial conjectures. The simplification process uses elaborated techniques of rewriting modulo AC: inductive contextual rewriting, inductive case rewriting [3]. To perform AC matching, the system uses an algorithm written in C based on [7].

3 Computer experiments and discussion

3.1 Iterated additions multiplier

It is a sequential circuit with a structural loop (see figure 1). The circuit computes the product of two integers X and Y, by adding Y X times. Its outputs are a boolean *DONE* and an integer OUT. If *DONE* equals *True*, then the result of the multiplication equals OUT. The specification we have given to SPIKE-AC is the one proposed by [13], for proving the circuit correctness with NQTHM. It uses a tail-recursive model. The circuit function which performs the multiplication is *mult*. Its arguments are two integers x and y, *DONE*, OUT and an internal register. The correctness theorem is: $mult(x, True, 0, 0, y) = x * y$. To prove it with SPIKE-AC, we specify that $+$ and $*$ are AC, and introduce only the lemma:

$$mult(s(x), False, out, s(s(x)), s(z)) = out + mult(s(x), True, 0, 0, s(z)).$$

It means that the product of two (non null) integers equals to the sum of *out* (which is the accumulating parameter of the result) and the rest of the product of these integers with *out* set to 0. The proof of the lemma is automatic. The same problem was proved with the $NQTHM$ system, but it needs a generalisation [13]. A proof was also done with LP [1] using the invariant technique, but then it requires many interactions.

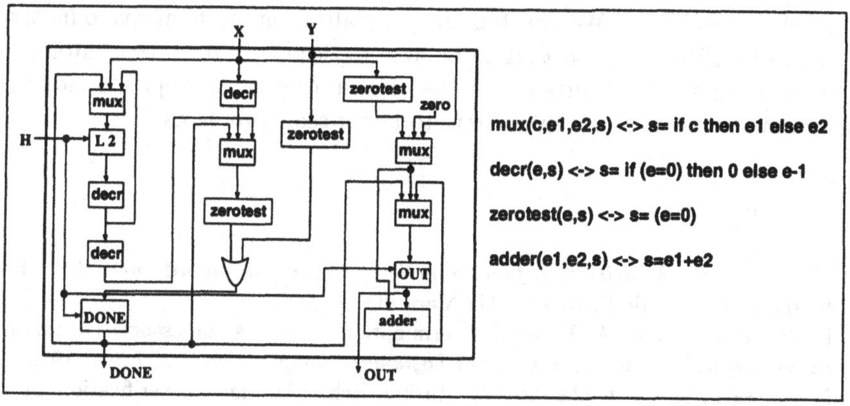

Fig. 1. Iterated additions multiplier

3.2 Binomial theorem

Let $\mathcal{A}$ be a commutative ring, we want to show that for each element x of $\mathcal{A}$, and for each natural n:

$$(x+1)^n = \binom{n}{0} + \binom{n}{1} * x + \ldots + \binom{n}{n} * x^n.$$

We define a function *pointsum* adds up two lists element-wise to obtain a third one. We use this to define the list of binomial coefficients $bin(n)$, that is:

$$\left[\binom{n}{0}, \cdots, \binom{n}{r}, \cdots, \binom{n}{n}\right]$$

using the recursive definition from Pascal's triangle. Finally the function $seq(x)$ turns a list of natural numbers $[a_0, a_1, \cdots, a_n]$ into the polynomial $a_0 + a_1 * x + \cdots + a_n * x^n$. Thus the binomial theorem, for any element x of any commutative ring and for any natural number n, is: $power(n, s(x)) = seq(x, bin(n))$. The proof with SPIKE-AC requires the lemma:

$$seq(x, pointsum(z_1, z_2)) = seq(x, z_1) + seq(x, z_2)$$

The proof of this lemma requires only the distributivity lemma $(x * (y + z) = (x*y)+(x*z))$. To prove the main theorem with LP, we need three lemmas in addition to the associativity and commutativity properties of $+$ and $*$. Using these arithmetic properties too, with the distributivity of $*$ on $+$ and cancellativity $(a + b = a + c \Rightarrow b = c)$, a proof can be derived with NQTHM.

4 Conclusion

SPIKE-AC has been successfully tested on interesting problems. The proofs obtained required less interaction w.r.t explicit induction based systems, such as

NQTHM, LP and PVS. We are studying generalization mechanisms to incorporate them in SPIKE-AC, so that to be able to decrease interaction. Moreover, we are developing new heuristics for the computation of appropriate induction schemes, and plan to apply the system to larger scale problems.

References

1. M. Allemand. *Modélisation fonctionnelle et Preuve de circuits avec LP.* PhD thesis, Université de Provence (Aix-Marseille I), 1995.
2. L. Bachmair and D. A. Plaisted. Termination orderings for associative-commutative rewriting systems. *Journal of Logic and Computation*, 1:329–349, 1985.
3. N. Berregeb, A. Bouhoula, and M. Rusinowitch. Automated verification by induction with associative-commutative operators. To appear in *Proceedings of the International Conference on Computer Aided Verification*, 1996.
4. A. Bouhoula and M. Rusinowitch. Implicit induction in conditional theories. *Journal of Automated Reasoning*, 14(2):189–235, 1995.
5. R. S. Boyer and J. S. Moore. *A computational Logic Handbook.* 1988.
6. R. Bündgen, W. Küchlin. Computing ground reducibility and inductively complete positions. In N. Dershowitz, editor, *Rewriting Techniques and Applications, LNCS* 355, pages 59–75, 1989.
7. Steven Eker. Improving the efficiency of AC matching and unification. Research report 2104, INRIA, Inria Lorraine & Crin, November 1993.
8. S. J. Garland and J. V. Guttag. An overview of LP, the Larch Prover. In N. Dershowitz, editor, *Rewriting Techniques and Applications, LNCS 355*, pages 137-151, 1989.
9. J.-P. Jouannaud and E. Kounalis. Automatic proofs by induction in theories without constructors. *Information and Computation*, 82:1–33, 1989.
10. D. Kapur and P. Narendran. Double-exponential complexity of computing a complete set of AC-unifiers. In *IEEE Symposium on Logic in Computer Science*, 1992.
11. P. Lescanne. Orme, an implementation of completion procedures as sets of transitions rules. In M. Stickel, editor, *International Conference on Automated Deduction*, pages 661–662, 1990.
12. S. Owre, J.M. Rushby, and N. Shankar. A prototype verification system. In D. Kapur, editor, *International Conference on Automated Deduction, LNAI 607*, pages 748–752, 1992.
13. L. Pierre. The formal proof of sequential circuits described in CASCADE using the Boyer-Moore theorem prover. In L. Claesen, editor, *Formal VLSI Correctness Verification*, 1990.

On gaining efficiency in completion–based theorem proving

Thomas Hillenbrand Arnim Buch Roland Fettig

Universität Kaiserslautern, FB Informatik, 67653 Kaiserslautern, Germany
email: {hillen,buch,fettig}@informatik.uni-kl.de

Abstract. Gaining efficiency in completion–based theorem proving requires improvements on three levels: fast inference step execution, careful aggregation into an inference machine, and sophisticated control strategies, all that combined with space saving representation of derived facts. We introduce the new WALDMEISTER prover which shows an increase in overall system performance of more than one order of magnitude as compared with standard techniques.

1 Introduction

In [KB70], Knuth and Bendix introduced the completion algorithm which tries to derive a set of convergent rules from given equations. With the extension to unfailing completion in [HR87], it has turned out to be a valuable means for proving theorems in equational theories. As today's completion–based provers often fail in solving hard problems, substantial improvements are in demand.

Looking closer at typical system structures, we find a three level hierarchy: the level of inference steps, such as simplifying or orienting an equation, then the inference machine aggregating the inference steps into an algorithm, and, at the top, the selection strategy guiding the search for promising derivations.

In this paper we give an overview of the requirements to be met for designing an efficient prover and show the concepts we believe to fit them best. By skillful design of appropriate algorithms and data structures, furthermore by careful, statistically affirmed aggregation of the inference components into an inference machine we have gained a considerable increase in overall system performance. Our detailed analysis of this subject can be found in [BH96]. Finally, we demonstrate the power of our new prover WALDMEISTER by solving hard problems.

2 Fishing for efficiency

Supporting selection strategies is the most important requirement any inference machine has to meet, for they determine the order in which critical pairs (*cps* for short) are processed. It is generally accepted that useful information for the top–level control can be extracted from the terms of the cps. For that reason, every superposition of a new rule or equation (selected but unorientable cp) with itself and with all other rules and equations is built, analyzed and then (unless trivial) added to the set of cps. Hence, the system state is a triple of sets: rules and equations for reducing, and partially simplified cps waiting for selection.

2.1 Speeding up the inference machine

Normalizing cps. We distinguish three different phases in the life–cycle of a cp: generation, storage, and selection. The inference system allows normalization of cps at any time. We have compared many strategies to tackle cps in the different phases, ranging from "lazy" ones to those reducing each pair whenever possible: In most cases, it is sufficient to normalize newly generated cps with rules only, ditto periodically the stored cps, and with "full power" after selection.

Applying rules and equations. Normalization requires a certain term traversal strategy. Although every prover has its own favorite one, sometimes other strategies are needed to manage certain proof tasks. WALDMEISTER offers many different variants like leftmost–outermost, –innermost, or top–down.

Combining rules and equations. As reduction attempts with equations invoke the reduction ordering, which is very costly and most often fails, we prefer to apply equations only to terms that have already been normalized w.r.t rules.

Interreduction. To eliminate redundancies, the set of rules and equations should always be kept minimal with respect to the actual rewrite relation. Otherwise, every neglected simplification of a rule or equation yields manifold superfluous work on cps.

Parameterization. Leaving the inference step aggregation open to the user as far as possible, WALDMEISTER offers a set of relevant parameters. Measurements have ascertained a default setting, but adjusting the system to difficult proof tasks is encouraged.

2.2 Speeding up the inference steps

Tackling the bottle–neck. Running the KB–completion procedure, most of the time is spent in rewriting. Consequently, fast matching operations between a query term and a term set are the pre–condition for substantial improvements.

Indexing techniques are one promising solution of this problem. Their use in automated theorem proving dates back to the early 70'ies. For an overview see [Gra95]. To index the left–hand sides of the rewrite rules, we employ perfect discrimination trees (cf. [McC92]) in a new, refined variant. Every edge of such a tree is marked with a function symbol or a normalized variable. Each path from the root to a leaf carries the corresponding term on the edges. Following McCune, we combine this data structure with a linear term representation as in [Chr89], but singly linked only. Using these flatterms with free–list based memory management allows us to dispose terms in constant time.

The refinement we propose consists in shrinking all branches leading to a single leaf node. In the average, this saves about 40% of all tree nodes. When retrieving, there are much less backtracking points, and the index switches to term–to–term operations as soon as a given query has only one candidate in the current subtree. Table 1 compares our system with a variant that makes exactly the same inferences but stores rules and equations in a top symbol hashed list. The R+E column gives the number of generated rules and equations. All runs were executed on a Sun SPARCstation 20/712 with Solaris 2.4.

Example	Crit. Pairs	R+E	Match Queries	Reductions	T(Ind.)	T(No Ind.)
sims2 [Sim91]	15,999	338	1,597,397	57,964	8.84s	24.74s
Luka10 [Tar56]	53,782	267	836,016	85,477	5.86s	49.51s
Lusk5 [LO85]	190,904	337	9,030,295	345,999	73.82s	617.88s
Lusk6 [LO85]	93,587	521	5,178,169	291,538	80.10s	256.84s
mv2 [LW92]	404,977	484	8,515,560	756,992	164.24s	1797.78s
mv4 [LW92]	943,607	851	23,784,439	1,956,268	685.72s	6285.74s

Table 1. Using Indices

In his PhD thesis [Gra95], Graf gave an overview of indexing techniques. He compared the run–times of implementations taken from his ACID–toolbox on average term sets and concluded that "the average retrieval performance in substitution trees is faster than the average retrieval time of any other technique." Nevertheless, for the employment in rewriting we think that our data structure is more appropriate. First, only perfect discrimination trees allow retrieval of subterms of indexed terms, which is useful both for the generation of cps and for interreduction. Second, tree traversal is many times less costly, for descending from a father node to a son is based on a single symbol comparison, whereas the use of substitution trees requires consideration of a list of variable substitutes, which themselves are lists of symbols. We have compared our refined perfect discrimination tree indexing with the routines from the ACID–toolbox: It is faster than the included perfect discrimination and substitution trees.

2.3 Lean management

The storage of critical pairs, ordered by some weighting function, has to meet two major requirements: first, to support arbitrary insertion and smallest entry retrieval; operations characterizing priority queues. Second, to minimize memory consumption, as this set causes most of the system's memory consumption.

We identified three ways to attack the latter problem: the size of the cps themselves, the additional management overhead, and the number of superfluous cps in the set ("orphans", as their parents have been discarded). Deleting an orphan not before it has become the minimal entry saves reorganization and management overhead but wastes lots of memory. We realized this strategy with a regular heap. The wish to remove an orphan immediately after the deletion of one of its parents led us to an extended pairing heap. However, the memory savings have been outweighed by the structure's overhead as the term pair representation has shrunk (see below). A recently developed two–level data structure, a heap of heaps, behaves between lazy and immediate "orphan murder": Critical pairs generated by a new rule or equation are stored together with the generating parent and thus can be removed without additional overhead. Measurements show that this way between 60% and 90% of all orphans are removed.

Flatterms are necessary for fast rewriting, but they cause high memory consumption when cps are stored in such a manner. For that reason, we developed a string-like term representation which cuts down the size of term pairs to some 10%. This even speeds up runs, for it takes less time to allocate term pairs at once and no longer symbolwise. Since stringterms still grow with the size of the terms, we came upon a representation that stores minimal information to recompute the cps. Topped by the heap of heaps, this results in a very space–efficient realization of the cp set and needs only few additional time.

3 WALDMEISTER at Work

As a useful theorem prover should allow to solve many problems with its default strategy, we have statistically approved a parameter setting. Using a simple *add–weight* heuristic, WALDMEISTER solved two problems claimed as "never proved in a single run unaided" in [LW92]. The success of our system stems from its inference speed, economical stringterm representation, and intermediate reduction of the cp set. Have a look at table 2, and note the high system throughput.

Problem	Crit.Pairs	R+E	Max. Size of CP set	Process Size	Time (Sec.)	Per Second: Crit.Pairs	Reductions	Match Queries
gt6	1,421,317	1,006	856,545	94 MB	968.4	1,467.7	2,344.5	81,740.3
ra4	923,508	1,549	811,044	88 MB	3,759.5	245.7	756.4	59,459.0

Table 2. Cracking hard nuts

Our experience shows that a high performance theorem prover can succeed on hard problems using a general purpose strategy only. The comparison with the established DISCOUNT system ([AD93]) in its sequential version justifies the effort spent on realizing the above mentioned techniques in the new prover: WALDMEISTER outperforms DISCOUNT by more than one order of magnitude.

References

[AD93] J. Avenhaus and J. Denzinger. Distributing equational theorem proving. In *Proc. 5th RTA*, vol. 690 of *LNCS*, 1993.

[BH96] A. Buch and Th. Hillenbrand. Waldmeister: Development of a high performance completion–based theorem prover. SEKI–Report 96–01, Universität Kaiserslautern, 1996.

[Chr89] J. Christian. Fast Knuth–Bendix completion: A summary. In *Proc. 3rd RTA*, vol. 355 of *LNCS*, 1989.

[Gra95] P. Graf. *Term Indexing*, vol. 1053 of *LNAI*. Springer Verlag, 1995.

[HR87] J. Hsiang and M. Rusinowitch. On word problems in equational theories. In *Proc. 14th ICALP*, vol. 267 of *LNCS*, 1987.

[KB70] D.E. Knuth and P.B. Bendix. Simple word problems in universal algebra. *Computational Problems in Abstract Algebra*, 1970.

[LO85] E. Lusk and R.A. Overbeek. Reasoning about equality. *JAR*, 2, 1985.

[LW92] E. Lusk and L. Wos. Benchmark problems in which equality plays the major role. In *Proc. 11th CADE*, vol. 607 of *LNCS*, 1992.

[McC92] W. McCune. Experiments with discrimination-tree indexing and path indexing for term retrieval. *JAR, 8(3)*, 1992.

[Sim91] C.C. Sims. The Knuth–Bendix procedure for strings as a substitute for coset enumeration. *JSR*, 12, 1991.

[Tar56] A. Tarski. *Logic, Semantics, Metamathematics.* Oxford Univ. Press, 1956.

Index

Lecture Notes in Computer Science

For information about Vols. 1–1026

please contact your bookseller or Springer-Verlag

Vol. 1027: F.J. Brandenburg (Ed.), Graph Drawing. Proceedings, 1995. XII, 526 pages. 1996.

Vol. 1028: N.R. Adam, Y. Yesha (Eds.), Electronic Commerce. X, 155 pages. 1996.

Vol. 1029: E. Dawson, J. Golić (Eds.), Cryptography: Policy and Algorithms. Proceedings, 1995. XI, 327 pages. 1996.

Vol. 1030: F. Pichler, R. Moreno-Díaz, R. Albrecht (Eds.), Computer Aided Systems Theory - EUROCAST '95. Proceedings, 1995. XII, 539 pages. 1996.

Vol.1031: M. Toussaint (Ed.), Ada in Europe. Proceedings, 1995. XI, 455 pages. 1996.

Vol. 1032: P. Godefroid, Partial-Order Methods for the Verification of Concurrent Systems. IV, 143 pages. 1996.

Vol. 1033: C.-H. Huang, P. Sadayappan, U. Banerjee, D. Gelernter, A. Nicolau, D. Padua (Eds.), Languages and Compilers for Parallel Computing. Proceedings, 1995. XIII, 597 pages. 1996.

Vol. 1034: G. Kuper, M. Wallace (Eds.), Constraint Databases and Applications. Proceedings, 1995. VII, 185 pages. 1996.

Vol. 1035: S.Z. Li, D.P. Mital, E.K. Teoh, H. Wang (Eds.), Recent Developments in Computer Vision. Proceedings, 1995. XI, 604 pages. 1996.

Vol. 1036: G. Adorni, M. Zock (Eds.), Trends in Natural Language Generation - An Artificial Intelligence Perspective. Proceedings, 1993. IX, 382 pages. 1996. (Subseries LNAI).

Vol. 1037: M. Wooldridge, J.P. Müller, M. Tambe (Eds.), Intelligent Agents II. Proceedings, 1995. XVI, 437 pages. 1996. (Subseries LNAI).

Vol. 1038: W: Van de Velde, J.W. Perram (Eds.), Agents Breaking Away. Proceedings, 1996. XIV, 232 pages. 1996. (Subseries LNAI).

Vol. 1039: D. Gollmann (Ed.), Fast Software Encryption. Proceedings, 1996. X, 219 pages. 1996.

Vol. 1040: S. Wermter, E. Riloff, G. Scheler (Eds.), Connectionist, Statistical, and Symbolic Approaches to Learning for Natural Language Processing. IX, 468 pages. 1996. (Subseries LNAI).

Vol. 1041: J. Dongarra, K. Madsen, J. Waśniewski (Eds.), Applied Parallel Computing. Proceedings, 1995. XII, 562 pages. 1996.

Vol. 1042: G. Weiß, S. Sen (Eds.), Adaption and Learning in Multi-Agent Systems. Proceedings, 1995. X, 238 pages. 1996. (Subseries LNAI).

Vol. 1043: F. Moller, G. Birtwistle (Eds.), Logics for Concurrency. XI, 266 pages. 1996.

Vol. 1044: B. Plattner (Ed.), Broadband Communications. Proceedings, 1996. XIV, 359 pages. 1996.

Vol. 1045: B. Butscher, E. Moeller, H. Pusch (Eds.), Interactive Distributed Multimedia Systems and Services. Proceedings, 1996. XI, 333 pages. 1996.

Vol. 1046: C. Puech, R. Reischuk (Eds.), STACS 96. Proceedings, 1996. XII, 690 pages. 1996.

Vol. 1047: E. Hajnicz, Time Structures. IX, 244 pages. 1996. (Subseries LNAI).

Vol. 1048: M. Proietti (Ed.), Logic Program Syynthesis and Transformation. Proceedings, 1995. X, 267 pages. 1996.

Vol. 1049: K. Futatsugi, S. Matsuoka (Eds.), Object Technologies for Advanced Software. Proceedings, 1996. X, 309 pages. 1996.

Vol. 1050: R. Dyckhoff, H. Herre, P. Schroeder-Heister (Eds.), Extensions of Logic Programming. Proceedings, 1996. VII, 318 pages. 1996. (Subseries LNAI).

Vol. 1051: M.-C. Gaudel, J. Woodcock (Eds.), FME'96: Industrial Benefit and Advances in Formal Methods. Proceedings, 1996. XII, 704 pages. 1996.

Vol. 1052: D. Hutchison, H. Christiansen, G. Coulson, A. Danthine (Eds.), Teleservices and Multimedia Communications. Proceedings, 1995. XII, 277 pages. 1996.

Vol. 1053: P. Graf, Term Indexing. XVI, 284 pages. 1996. (Subseries LNAI).

Vol. 1054: A. Ferreira, P. Pardalos (Eds.), Solving Combinatorial Optimization Problems in Parallel. VII, 274 pages. 1996.

Vol. 1055: T. Margaria, B. Steffen (Eds.), Tools and Algorithms for the Construction and Analysis of Systems. Proceedings, 1996. XI, 435 pages. 1996.

Vol. 1056: A. Haddadi, Communication and Cooperation in Agent Systems. XIII, 148 pages. 1996. (Subseries LNAI).

Vol. 1057: P. Apers, M. Bouzeghoub, G. Gardarin (Eds.), Advances in Database Technology — EDBT '96. Proceedings, 1996. XII, 636 pages. 1996.

Vol. 1058: H. R. Nielson (Ed.), Programming Languages and Systems – ESOP '96. Proceedings, 1996. X, 405 pages. 1996.

Vol. 1059: H. Kirchner (Ed.), Trees in Algebra and Programming – CAAP '96. Proceedings, 1996. VIII, 331 pages. 1996.

Vol. 1060: T. Gyimóthy (Ed.), Compiler Construction. Proceedings, 1996. X, 355 pages. 1996.

Vol. 1061: P. Ciancarini, C. Hankin (Eds.), Coordination Languages and Models. Proceedings, 1996. XI, 443 pages. 1996.

Vol. 1062: E. Sanchez, M. Tomassini (Eds.), Towards Evolvable Hardware. IX, 265 pages. 1996.

Vol. 1063: J.-M. Alliot, E. Lutton, E. Ronald, M. Schoenauer, D. Snyers (Eds.), Artificial Evolution. Proceedings, 1995. XIII, 396 pages. 1996.

Vol. 1064: B. Buxton, R. Cipolla (Eds.), Computer Vision – ECCV '96. Volume I. Proceedings, 1996. XXI, 725 pages. 1996.

Vol. 1065: B. Buxton, R. Cipolla (Eds.), Computer Vision – ECCV '96. Volume II. Proceedings, 1996. XXI, 723 pages. 1996.

Vol. 1066: R. Alur, T.A. Henzinger, E.D. Sontag (Eds.), Hybrid Systems III. IX, 618 pages. 1996.

Vol. 1067: H. Liddell, A. Colbrook, B. Hertzberger, P. Sloot (Eds.), High-Performance Computing and Networking. Proceedings, 1996. XXV, 1040 pages. 1996.

Vol. 1068: T. Ito, R.H. Halstead, Jr., C. Queinnec (Eds.), Parallel Symbolic Languages and Systems. Proceedings, 1995. X, 363 pages. 1996.

Vol. 1069: J.W. Perram, J.-P. Müller (Eds.), Distributed Software Agents and Applications. Proceedings, 1994. VIII, 219 pages. 1996. (Subseries LNAI).

Vol. 1070: U. Maurer (Ed.), Advances in Cryptology – EUROCRYPT '96. Proceedings, 1996. XII, 417 pages. 1996.

Vol. 1071: P. Miglioli, U. Moscato, D. Mundici, M. Ornaghi (Eds.), Theorem Proving with Analytic Tableaux and Related Methods. Proceedings, 1996. X, 330 pages. 1996. (Subseries LNAI).

Vol. 1072: R. Kasturi, K. Tombre (Eds.), Graphics Recognition. Proceedings, 1995. X, 308 pages. 1996.

Vol. 1073: J. Cuny, H. Ehrig, G. Engels, G. Rozenberg (Eds.), Graph Grammars and Their Application to Computer Science. Proceedings, 1994. X, 565 pages. 1996.

Vol. 1074: G. Dowek, J. Heering, K. Meinke, B. Möller (Eds.), Higher-Order Algebra, Logic, and Term Rewriting. Proceedings, 1995. VII, 287 pages. 1996.

Vol. 1075: D. Hirschberg, G. Myers (Eds.), Combinatorial Pattern Matching. Proceedings, 1996. VIII, 392 pages. 1996.

Vol. 1076: N. Shadbolt, K. O'Hara, G. Schreiber (Eds.), Advances in Knowledge Acquisition. Proceedings, 1996. XII, 371 pages. 1996. (Subseries LNAI).

Vol. 1077: P. Brusilovsky, P. Kommers, N. Streitz (Eds.), Mulimedia, Hypermedia, and Virtual Reality. Proceedings, 1994. IX, 311 pages. 1996.

Vol. 1078: D.A. Lamb (Ed.), Studies of Software Design. Proceedings, 1993. VI, 188 pages. 1996.

Vol. 1079: Z.W. Raś, M. Michalewicz (Eds.), Foundations of Intelligent Systems. Proceedings, 1996. XI, 664 pages. 1996. (Subseries LNAI).

Vol. 1080: P. Constantopoulos, J. Mylopoulos, Y. Vassiliou (Eds.), Advanced Information Systems Engineering. Proceedings, 1996. XI, 582 pages. 1996.

Vol. 1081: G. McCalla (Ed.), Advances in Artificial Intelligence. Proceedings, 1996. XII, 459 pages. 1996. (Subseries LNAI).

Vol. 1082: N.R. Adam, B.K. Bhargava, M. Halem, Y. Yesha (Eds.), Digital Libraries. Proceedings, 1995. Approx. 310 pages. 1996.

Vol. 1083: K. Sparck Jones, J.R. Galliers, Evaluating Natural Language Processing Systems. XV, 228 pages. 1996. (Subseries LNAI).

Vol. 1084: W.H. Cunningham, S.T. McCormick, M. Queyranne (Eds.), Integer Programming and Combinatorial Optimization. Proceedings, 1996. X, 505 pages. 1996.

Vol. 1085: D.M. Gabbay, H.J. Ohlbach (Eds.), Practical Reasoning. Proceedings, 1996. XV, 721 pages. 1996. (Subseries LNAI).

Vol. 1086: C. Frasson, G. Gauthier, A. Lesgold (Eds.), Intelligent Tutoring Systems. Proceedings, 1996. XVII, 688 pages. 1996.

Vol. 1087: C. Zhang, D. Lukose (Eds.), Distributed Artificial Intelliegence. Proceedings, 1995. VIII, 232 pages. 1996. (Subseries LNAI).

Vol. 1088: A. Strohmeier (Ed.), Reliable Software Technologies – Ada-Europe '96. Proceedings, 1996. XI, 513 pages. 1996.

Vol. 1089: G. Ramalingam, Bounded Incremental Computation. XI, 190 pages. 1996.

Vol. 1090: J.-Y. Cai, C.K. Wong (Eds.), Computing and Combinatorics. Proceedings, 1996. X, 421 pages. 1996.

Vol. 1091: J. Billington, W. Reisig (Eds.), Application and Theory of Petri Nets 1996. Proceedings, 1996. VIII, 549 pages. 1996.

Vol. 1092: H. Kleine Büning (Ed.), Computer Science Logic. Proceedings, 1995. VIII, 487 pages. 1996.

Vol. 1093: L. Dorst, M. van Lambalgen, F. Voorbraak (Eds.), Reasoning with Uncertainty in Robotics. Proceedings, 1995. VIII, 387 pages. 1996. (Subseries LNAI).

Vol. 1094: R. Morrison, J. Kennedy (Eds.), Advances in Databases. Proceedings, 1996. XI, 234 pages. 1996.

Vol. 1095: W. McCune, R. Padmanabhan, Automated Deduction in Equational Logic and Cubic Curves. X, 231 pages. 1996. (Subseries LNAI).

Vol. 1096: T. Schäl, Workflow Management Systems for Process Organisations. XII, 200 pages. 1996.

Vol. 1097: R. Karlsson, A. Lingas (Eds.), Algorithm Theory – SWAT '96. Proceedings, 1996. IX, 453 pages. 1996.

Vol. 1098: P. Cointe (Ed.), ECOOP '96 – Object-Oriented Programming. Proceedings, 1996. XI, 502 pages. 1996.

Vol. 1099: F. Meyer auf der Heide, B. Monien (Eds.), Automata, Languages and Programming. Proceedings, 1996. XII, 681 pages. 1996.

Vol. 1101: M. Wirsing, M. Nivat (Eds.), Algebraic Methodology and Software Technology. Proceedings, 1996. XII, 641 pages. 1996.

Vol. 1103: H. Ganzinger (Ed.), Rewriting Techniques and Applications. Proceedings, 1996. XI, 437 pages. 1996.